THE WORLD TRANSFORMED

1945 to the Present

Second Edition

MICHAEL H. HUNT

New York   Oxford
OXFORD UNIVERSITY PRESS

Oxford University Press is a department of the University of Oxford.
It furthers the University's objective of excellence in research,
scholarship, and education by publishing worldwide.

Oxford   New York
Auckland   Cape Town   Dar es Salaam   Hong Kong   Karachi
Kuala Lumpur   Madrid   Melbourne   Mexico City   Nairobi
New Delhi   Shanghai   Taipei   Toronto

With offices in
Argentina   Austria   Brazil   Chile   Czech Republic   France   Greece
Guatemala   Hungary   Italy   Japan   Poland   Portugal   Singapore
South Korea   Switzerland   Thailand   Turkey   Ukraine   Vietnam

For titles covered by Section 112 of the US Higher Education
Opportunity Act, please visit www.oup.com/us/he for the
latest information about pricing and alternate formats.

Published by Oxford University Press
198 Madison Avenue, New York, New York 10016
http://www.oup.com

Oxford is a registered trademark of Oxford University Press

Library of Congress Cataloging-in-Publication Data

Hunt, Michael H.
   The world transformed : 1945 to the present / Michael H. Hunt, The University of
North Carolina at Chapel Hill. -- Second edition.
      pages cm
   Original edition published in 2004.
   Includes bibliographical references and index.
   ISBN 978-0-19-937102-0 (pbk., acid free : alk. paper) 1. History, Modern--1945–1989.
2. History, Modern--1989- I. Title.
   D840.H86 2015
   909.82'5--dc23

                                                                        2015002227

Printing number: 9 8 7 6 5 4 3 2 1

Printed in the United States of America
on acid-free paper

All people are born free

All people are equal before God

All people are innocent until proven guilty

All people are good until some do evil

All people are righteous until
some do the unrighteous

All men of Srebrenica were alive
until some were murdered

All people are innocent until those
who committed crimes are judged

Evil is forever, but not absolute

Good is absolute, but sometimes absent.

—Imam Cekić at the memorial service for the victims
of the Srebrenica massacre, July 11, 2005[1]

---

[1]Quoted in Selma Leydesdorff, *Surviving the Bosnian Genocide: The Women of Srebrenica Speak*, trans. Kay Richardson (Bloomington: Indiana University Press, 2011), p. v.

CONTENTS

SPECIAL FEATURES

List of Maps

List of Graphs and Tables

PREFACE

PREPARING THIS TEXT has been a prolonged and delightful exercise in self-indulgence from which, I hope, others will benefit. I was born a few years before the dropping of the first atomic bomb. I grew up overseas, a witness to Japan's struggle to recover from war and to other countries' search for a way to true independence and a better life. My family and I benefited from amazing economic and technological progress during the postwar years, and marveled at the accumulation of power in our own country. I was too young when the postwar era dawned to predict its trajectory, and few of the pundits at the time got it right. Looking back, I am amazed at how much has changed, often for the better, but also how many difficulties remain. My hope is that readers will come to share my sense of the drama and importance of contemporary history and my faith in the social utility of history as a powerful discipline essential to understanding the place humans have created for themselves.

This retrospective exercise began in earnest in a course surveying the post-1945 world that I have taught along with colleagues at the University of North Carolina at Chapel Hill since the 1980s. That course has proven popular for its historical immediacy and its relevance—as a vehicle for filling in the background on the world that students inherit and the issues that they as part of an informed electorate will have to address. Experience with that course along with growing immersion in the new global history deepened my interest in figuring out what the past half-century has meant. Informal class notes slowly turned into a text after I found no published survey that did justice to my notion of what has transpired in recent decades.

Two challenges faced me. One was to move away from international relations, which framed—and limited—the concerns of most published surveys. The explosion of global history scholarship helped here, as did new literature on a wide variety of discrete topics. Combing through bibliographies and library shelves has left me in awe of the cumulative achievements of scholars around the world, especially in recent decades. The other challenge was to see the developments of the post-1945 era in relation to the dramatic changes over the past dozen years, beginning with the collapse of European and Russian socialism and continuing with the decade of global economic expansion and growing global awareness, and finally the reverberations set off by the events of September 11, 2001, and the 2008 financial crisis. All of us unavoidably see the past through the prism of the present. The historian's task is to strike a balance between a past that does not speak to the world in which the reader lives and one that is robbed of its richness by presentist concerns.

THEMES

The premise on which this text rests is that 1945 is best understood not as a new phase in a long or short twentieth century. It marks rather a major watershed in its own right in the history of the modern world—the beginnings of a distinct, profoundly transformative epoch. The defining features of the world of 1945 would within a half-century fade from view, to be replaced by new ones that few in 1945 would have predicted or could even have imagined. Hence the title that this volume carries: *The World Transformed*. To make this case for fundamental change is hard enough for a single country or region, but it is especially daunting when an entire world is the subject. Peter Stearns has observed perceptively that if history may seem to some like "one damn thing after another," then world history will feel like "an unusual number of damn things."[1] Any broad claim about change on a global scale badly needs discrete interpretive threads that will give order and coherence to the argument. This text has three.

The first theme most likely to occur to readers is the transformation that occurred in interstate relations. The emergence of a sharp and unusually ideological rivalry between the United States and the Soviet Union dominated much of the postwar era. And then this unusual bipolar distribution of international power gave way to an even more unusual condition: an American hegemony with an uncertain future. The U.S. exercise of global influence has encountered difficulties that seem to mount the deeper we get into the twenty-first century.

The second theme is to be found in the distinct trajectory of the post-1945 international economy. A world in shambles as the war drew to a close managed some spectacular wealth creation over the next half-century while also generating adverse effects, including unparalleled environmental stress and widening gaps between the rich and poor. Whether for good or ill, this globe-encircling system of production, finance, and consumption has had a far-reaching social and cultural influence over lives everywhere.

The third theme deals with the striking set of changes in that part of the world that was either colonial or semicolonial in 1945. Following this theme provides insight into the aspirations and conditions of most of the Earth's people as they embarked on what many at the time imagined would be a path-breaking course of liberation and development. Launched into independence with shared high hopes and bound together by a common set of problems and historical experiences, those countries increasingly took divergent paths toward century's end. Some made notable headway toward realizing their early aspirations, while others found themselves mired in poverty and dissension.

ORGANIZATION

In a world of simultaneous, multilevel communication, it should be possible to clearly convey the complex, evolving interrelationships among these three strands in a seamless fashion. But this kind of "virtual reality" presentation is impossible to get on the printed page and equally impossible to absorb. With a bow to these limits, this account opens with an introductory essay that provides crucial background and analysis to help students tackle the post-1945 world. It also introduces the three themes that define the chapters that follow. Those chapters are organized into four parts, each corresponding to a major phase in the unfolding of the postwar period and each opening with a vignette meant to highlight a defining moment in the postwar period. To give the reader a more integrated picture of the past, the connections among the three major themes—great power relations, the international economy, and the Third or developing World—receive constant attention. The new Part Four appearing in this second edition expands considerably on the Conclusion in the first edition. It offers a "where are we now" survey of the past several decades, emphasizing the tension between global trends and regional developments.

While focusing on the three themes from the Introduction to the final chapter, the text's organization is broadly speaking chronological. This approach makes possible a nuanced and essentially historical sense of the major contours and key developments defining the contemporary world. This interpretive strategy easily accommodates to courses organized along either chronological or topical lines. While instructors wanting to proceed in more or less chronological fashion can assign the three parts consecutively, those preferring a more topical approach will find it easy to pick and choose. Part Four provides an appropriate cap whether the course is taught chronologically or topically.

APPROACH

In tracing the evolving postwar world, I have made several carefully considered choices about my approach.

I have first of all emphasized the role of personality. Individuals do have an outsized influence on events, as will become repeatedly evident in cases from Joseph Stalin to Rachel Carson to Angela Merkel. That individuals are also shaped by their times and that individual ambitions can take surprising and sometimes disappointing turns seem to me an especially important point for students to grasp as they develop a sense of their own potential and limits. Peoples around the world have over the past half-century faced complex choices. That they did not all make the same choices and that they could revise those choices in light of experience and altered circumstances are also important points for students to understand as they confront the problems of a still-diverse world very much in flux. Finally, I have been concerned to show the way in which prominent individuals and guiding ideas operate within a social and cultural setting that can be both enabling and restrictive. Popular needs and preferences regarding issues ranging from gender roles to market forces are essential to understanding each of the major sets of transformations discussed here. This emphasis on individuals, both elite and ordinary, makes possible the introduction into the text of enlivening vignettes, anecdotes, and voices. These along with the biographical sketches help to bring history alive for students by humanizing it.

A second major set of choices has shaped my approach to what is referred to here as the Third or developing World. I have opted for in-depth case studies that serve to highlight landmarks and patterns in what for many students is murky terrain. A limited number of carefully selected cases can avoid an overload of information while conveying a sense of the commonalties as well as the variations within the general pattern. These case studies thus serve as an invitation to exercise the skills of historical comparison. Instructors wanting to add their own favorite cases through lectures, supplementary readings, and assignments on the World Wide Web should find here a good basis on which to build.

A third area of concern has been to strike the right balance in the attention given the United States. I have been mindful of the dangers of ethnocentrism—of placing prominently the country with which most readers of this volume identify. Such prominent placement runs the risk of encouraging the notion that the rest of the world is like us or wants to be like us. It may also promote the equally mistaken idea that the United States can reshape the world regardless of the preference of others. On the other hand, a close examination of the post-1945 world reveals American fingerprints everywhere. Not only did the United States maintain a clear edge throughout the Cold War, but U.S. victory resulted in a true political and military hegemony. tightly intertwined with economic and cultural globalization. The way in which Americanization is conventionally used interchangeably with Westernization and modernization testifies to a recognition of strong, pervasive U.S. influence. Finally, the United States has had a pronounced impact throughout the Third World, whether as patron, model, or foe. It is difficult to find the case where there was not some substantial sort of American involvement. That the United States looms large may at first blush seem to flatter the national pride of many students, but they will encounter here an often-unsettling perspective on their country's past.

While I made these choices with the needs of a history survey course primarily in mind, my hope is that this text will provide coverage adaptable to a variety of disciplinary needs. Those teaching in political science, international relations, and international/global studies with a contemporary focus should find this volume helpful in establishing both the broad historical backdrop for current developments and the antecedents for particular issues of the moment. Those in search of supplementary materials are invited to look at the documentary collection, *The World Transformed, 1945 to the Present: A Documentary Reader*. This reader, which serves as a companion to the main text, offers a wealth of primary sources on the pivotal events that shaped the post-1945 world. Its 11 chapters provide a wide-ranging selection of documents—from Joseph Stalin on Soviet ideology to a U.S. Marine's experiences in Vietnam, from Mexican critics of NAFTA to European youth in 2013 confronting austerity. Like the main text, this reader demonstrates the fundamental interdependence among developments in the realm of great power politics, the international economy, and the developing world.

FEATURES

To assist students in their grasp of post-1945 world history and engage them in the process of learning, *The World Transformed* offers the following pedagogic features.

The comprehensive introduction explains the significance of the watershed year 1945 and sets the stage for the material to come with an overview of the main events in the history of international politics, the global economy, and the colonial system both pre- and post-1945. Drawing students into the text, each part introduction opens with a vignette that embodies some of the most significant themes of that part, followed by an overview of the topics to come. Chapter conclusions offer students the opportunity to review the chapter's main themes. Because making sense of recent history can be especially hard for students, the new Part Four on "Integration and Fragmentation" identifies major trends and explores their meaning and implications.

A striking photo program with interpretive captions strengthens students' understanding of history through images from the period under discussion. Plentiful maps, tables, and graphs help students in comprehending world geography and drawing conclusions based on statistics. Throughout the text, brief "spot" chronologies provide a handy review of significant events and prominent organizations and personalities for the period or country under discussion. "Recommended Resources," a section at the back of this volume, offers for each chapter guidance on accessible scholarship in a variety of forms, from general works to films and websites. For leads on the rich range of primary sources that can illuminate the post-1945 world, consult this volume's companion documentary reader, the general collections listed in the Recommended Resources for the Introduction, and the notes for this volume.

Now more than ever I realize that any textbook, and especially one with a global focus, has to be selective. It has to emphasize some points and neglect or even omit others—not randomly or arbitrarily but guided by some interpretive framework. As a historian who has grappled with synthesis has sensibly pointed out, "A textbook is not an encyclopaedia, and can hardly be judged in terms of how exhaustive it is, but should be evaluated from the point of view of its structural coherency, and its ability to stimulate the reader's interest."[2] Here is the test—accessibility, breadth, and coherence—that I want this survey to pass. My hope is that in making my choices about which parts of the past to capture and how to treat them I have created a balanced, focused account. If I have succeeded, instructors will find this text easy to supplement at some points and fruitful to challenge at others. Even more important, students will gain a better understanding of how their world came into being and what sorts of challenges they face as citizens and moral agents.

CHANGES IN THE SECOND EDITION

This second edition updates and refines what has proven a survey of the post-1945 world with lasting classroom appeal. The basic approach of the first edition remains. Coverage of developments over the past seven decades gives roughly equal attention to all regions and time periods while providing sustained treatment of crucial themes that transcend place and time. But this approach has needed updating. In the decade since first publication, new issues have pushed to the fore, old issues have assumed a new guise, and considerable new scholarship has appeared.

The most important specific revisions are as follows:

▪ A new Part Four replaces and considerably extends the old Conclusion. Beginning with a sketch of the 9/11 attack in New York, this new material provides a fresh survey of the past several decades, emphasizing the tension between global trends and regional developments.

▪ Chapter 10 in the new Part Four explores the various ramifications of globalization that became dramatically apparent in the 1990s (what drives it, what consequences it has had, and what kinds of responses it has evoked).

▪ Chapter 11 in the new Part Four puts the stress on regional developments and thus stands in counterpoint to Chapter 10. The treatment here of the Americas, the Middle East, Asia, and Europe/Russia is set in the context of pressures generated by globalization.

▪ The narrative for the Introduction and Chapters 1 to 9 has been thoroughly revised so that it is tighter and in line with current scholarship.

▪ The illustrative material (photos, posters, cartoons, tables, and graphs) for Chapters 1 to 9 has been carefully reviewed and significantly revised.

▪ Recommended resources have been updated to reflect the large body of new scholarly literature and now include more websites and films.

These changes will, I hope, help this well-received text to continue to play a role in putting in historical perspective the world students now live in.

ACKNOWLEDGMENTS

I could not have explored the highways and byways that this volume travels and then prepared my trip report without the help of many people. This volume, like its companion documentary reader, began as a Bedford/St. Martin's product. I remain indebted to Katherine Kurzman, Bridget Leahy, Patricia Rossi, and above all my expert and discerning development editor Louise Townsend. For helping to make a reality of this second edition, I'm grateful to Charles Cavaliere, who has provided excellent guidance and support, and to the rest of the Oxford University Press team, including notably George Chakvetadze (maps), Lynn Luecken (manuscript preparation), Cailen Swain (permissions and photo research), Christian Holdener (production oversight, and Wendy Walker (copy editing). Thanks to all for a fine job!

I benefited greatly from the discerning comments of the readers solicited by Bedford/St. Martin's and by Oxford University Press for this new edition. For guidance on the first edition published by Bedford, I am grateful to Michael Adas (Rutgers University), Brian Bonhomme (Youngstown State University), Charles Bright (University of Michigan), Jürgen Buchenau (University of North Carolina at Charlotte), Susan Carruthers (University of Wales, UK), Andrew F. Clark (University of North Carolina at Wilmington), Kenneth Curtis (California State University at Long Beach), Gary Darden (Rutgers University), Carole Fink (Ohio State University), Jeff Hornibrook (State University of New York at Plattsburgh), Caroline Kennedy-Pipe (Durham University, UK), Paul Gordon Lauren (University of Montana), Steven I. Levine (University of Montana), Michelle Mannering (Butler University), Melvin E. Page (East Tennessee State University), George Schuyler (University of Central Arkansas), Gerald Surh (North Carolina State University), Alexander Sydorenko (Arkansas State University), David S. Trask (Guilford Technical Community College), and Marilyn Young (New York University). Since moving this text to Oxford, I have benefited from commissioned reviews by Chad Bryant (University of North Carolina at Chapel Hill), John Cox (University of North Carolina at Charlotte), W. Taylor Fain (University of North Carolina at Wilmington), Larry Grubbs (Georgia State University), Chris Laney (Berkshire Community College), Michael Marmé (Fordham University, Lincoln Center Campus), Don Ostrowski (Harvard University), Aaron Retish (Wayne State University), and Jeff R. Schutts (Douglas College, Canada). Michael Adas and Heather Streets-Salter were good enough to read the entire manuscript and give it their benediction.

A small army of folks have helped in other way. Those who worked with me as graduate students and stayed in touch as they progressed in their own professional careers have over the years sharpened and broadened my thinking on what to include and how to present it. I owe special thanks in this regard to Peter Coogan, Christopher Endy, Shuhua Fan, Anthony Fins, John Hepp, Matthew Jacobs, Bethany Keenan, Alan McPherson, Jongnam Na, Howard Odell, Max Owre, Jenifer Parks, Leah Potter, Nathaniel Smith, Odd Arne Westad, and Bill Wisser. Colleagues in the UNC Department of History and elsewhere were unfailingly responsive to my requests for guidance on their areas of expertise: Judith Bennett, Alessandro Brogi, Chad Bryant, John Chasteen, Peter Coclanis, W. Miles Fletcher, Yukiko Koshiro, Lisa Lindsay, Debin Ma, Louis Pérez, Donald Raleigh, Anne Richards, Sarah Shields, Jeffrey Wasserstrom, Wyatt Wells, and Yafeng Xia. I owe special thanks to old friends for excellent critical feedback on the draft of this second edition: Steve Levine, Michaela Hoenicke Moore, and Don Reid. Don put me in touch with Elizabeth Gramento, who offered helpful feedback. He also took the new concluding chapters for a trial run in a fall 2014 course. The Reynolds Fund, the Institute for Arts and Humanities, and the Department of History—all at UNC—gave me the gift of time to work on this project in its initial phase. Paula Hunt has kept me grounded, listened patiently, and emphatically perked up when matters relating to Italy, peace, and social justice came into view. Once more I have a chance to express my deep gratitude to her. To all my sincere thanks!

More errors than I would like to contemplate doubtless remain despite all those who have tried to set me straight. Those flaws have to be set against my name.

Introduction
THE 1945 WATERSHED

AN ATTENTIVE READER of a good daily newspaper in August 1945, just as World War II reached its end, would have encountered a world damaged and disrupted. Beginning in 1937 in Asia and in 1939 in Europe, warfare had spread over broad stretches of the globe. The fighting, together with genocide and privation, brought death to over 60 million people (about two thirds of them civilians) and left countless others wounded or displaced. China and Russia alone lost some 40 million. Nothing captured better the awful destructive power of the war than one of its final images: a mushroom cloud rising above Hiroshima, Japan. In an instant that city had become rubble, joining the many others not only in Japan but also China, the Soviet Union, and continental Europe that were reduced no less completely by more conventional bombing or ground combat. Debris—once homes, schools, and churches—spread out in great vistas. This orgy of destruction mocked the achievements of the old European-dominated international order, humbling once-powerful states, tearing apart societies, arresting international trade and finance, and leaving distant colonies in ferment. Much of the world was in ruins.

But our reader would also have glimpsed the first signs of a world rebuilding animated by hopes for a new era of peace and prosperity. Newspapers had already reported the defeat of Germany's aggressive and genocidal regime and the launching of a fresh international initiative, the United Nations, to bring the world community together in a new spirit of collective security and commitment to human welfare. Even before the Japanese surrender, reporters noted that the U.S. economy, the largest in the world and the only major one undamaged by the war, was beginning to shift production back to civilian goods. This transition was cheering news, especially for people overseas who needed help in the arduous task of reconstruction after years of economic depression and military conflict. To judge from the press, the colonial world might have seemed stable, but a careful reader would have noticed reports of Indian and Vietnamese calls for independence and might

1

A Cameo of the Postwar Forces in Play

In this photo published in the *New York Times* on August 8, 1945, British soldiers on routine patrol in lower Burma represent the authority of a colonial order already tottering and soon to pass from the scene. No country would undergo a more dramatic fall from imperial eminence than Britain. The soldiers were in turn cultural worlds away from the peasant in the foreground plowing his rice field. He had been born into and grown up within an intimate set of village relations that defined status, obligations, and rights. But global economic forces had altered those relations, creating a highly competitive market for rice. Producers for that market, such as the man pictured here, would have had foremost in their concerns the likely price at harvest time, while questions of independence from Britain then preoccupying the Burmese political elite would have seemed relatively remote. (© Imperial War Museums [SE 4340]. Photo by Sgt. A. Stubbs)

have guessed self-determination was becoming a burning question among peoples under foreign control.

Our attentive newspaper reader, whether in Shanghai, Chicago, Rome, or Accra, would not have found this text's premise surprising—that the year 1945 was a watershed date. It marked a distinct shift in contemporary global history, the ending of one era and the beginning of another. But our reader could not have begun to guess how the changes already in motion in August 1945 would play out. The economic power and missionary sense of the United States would propel it to a position of dominance, first evident in the contest with the Soviet Union and then accentuated after the Soviet rival faltered and finally collapsed. Individual states within the global economy recovered, but more significantly the most pro- ductive of them—all on the U.S. side of the Cold War line—embraced variations on the market model (where supply and demand theoretically determined price) and set off on a relentless integration that by degrees encompassed the entire world. While total economic output soared, so too did the number of people with a claim on that output and the level of environmental stress, with increasingly ser- ious global as well as local effects. Finally, the challenge to the colonial system proved irresistible. As it rapidly gained momentum and support, decolonization sparked international crises and spawned heady if ultimately disappointed hopes for a new, more equitable global order. These pronounced and interacting postwar trends would combine to produce broad and fundamental transformations over the latter half of the twentieth century. Our 1945 newspaper reader, however per- ceptive and farsighted, could not have imagined how these trends would combine to produce by the twenty-first century a world barely recognizable in its main features.

INTERNATIONAL POLITICS RECONFIGURED

The most obvious break in 1945 occurred in the realm of international politics. A system that had long consisted of multiple powers with shifting ties gave way after World War II to a stark, bipolar rivalry between the world's two most power- ful states, the Soviet Union and the United States.

This shift is best appreciated against the backdrop of international struggle centering on the major powers of Europe. The British and the French embarked on a rivalry in the late seventeenth and eighteenth centuries. Their long and costly contest drew in other, lesser powers such as Spain, Holland, Austria, and Russia, but it also reached well outside of Europe. London and Paris each sought control of land and resources in the Americas and maritime Asia and began building rival colonial empires. This accelerating pattern of imperialism into which virtually all the European powers would be drawn began to bind the globe into a single inte- grated economy. The French Revolution of 1789 and the ambitions of Napoleon I ignited the last round in this long Anglo-French contest. In 1815 Great Britain emerged as the victor and established its dominance among the major powers, which included France, Austria, and Russia. By the late nineteenth century Germany and Italy had joined the great-power club, soon followed by the United States and Japan.

But mounting tensions among the powers would strain and finally destroy this multipolar state system. A popular Japanese song from the 1880s captured the anxiety inherent in this loose, competitive arrangement of states:

There is a Law of Nations, it is true,
but when the moment comes, remember,
the Strong eat up the Weak.[1]

A newly united Germany sought dominance on the European continent and began a naval buildup that threatened British supremacy on the high seas. Alarmed by the German threat, Britain and France put aside their rivalry and joined with Russia to form an alliance known as the Triple Entente. Germany's reaction was to consolidate political and military ties with Austria-Hungary and the Ottoman Empire to create the Central Powers. The stage was set for conflict when in 1914 a minor crisis in the Balkans spun out of control. The resulting war, which would drag on for over four years, was the first blow to European power. The incredible carnage of 1914–1918 was finally brought to an end by exhaustion and by U.S. intervention in 1917 on the side of the Entente. Although the Entente triumphed, the war's blind destruction left 10 million dead and European societies shaken.

Wilson and Lenin as Rival Visionaries

By 1917 two distinct visions had taken shape that were to have an enormous global impact. One issued from U.S. President Woodrow Wilson, while the other came from Vladimir Lenin, the leader of the revolution that year in the Russian empire (soon renamed the Soviet Union). Each in its own way pronounced bankrupt the prewar European-dominated international system with its costly military rivalry, its repression of popular sentiment, and its imposition of colonial control on non-European peoples. Both leaders called for nothing less than a basic overhaul of the international regime. Each was in his own way championing a program of sweeping liberation that would become part of the official creed of his country. Each associated his cause with the future welfare of humankind. And thus each at a fundamental ideological level challenged not just the European-dominated international system but also the legitimacy of states organized around outmoded political, economic, and social principles. But fatefully, whatever the similarities, these were mutually incompatible, indeed directly antagonistic outlooks.

President Wilson took his country into the deadlocked European war in 1917, calling for "a world made safe for democracy." His 14-point peace program was built on a fundamental American commitment, as old as the nation itself, to "show mankind the way to liberty." Wilson sought nothing less than to promote free trade, halt the arms race, banish secret diplomacy with its alliances and terrible carnage, pull down empires, and promote self-determination throughout Europe. Out of the popular unrest after World War I, he hoped to see emerge moderate, democratic, constitutional regimes in Germany, Russia, and the nations newly liberated from the Austro-Hungarian empire. At the heart of Wilson's program was an organization of democratic states, a League of Nations committed to peace and security and determined to bring an end to the tyranny and aggression that lay at the roots of the world war. His program spoke, as he put it, to the "universal unrest" of all peoples seeking justice and had the support "of forward looking men and women everywhere, of every modern nation, of every enlightened community." His principles were in short "the principles of mankind."[2]

Wilson's belief—one that would become the pivot of much subsequent U.S. foreign policy—was that the internal composition of countries bore a critical relationship both to the rights and well-being of their citizens and to harmony within the international community. To the degree that democracy prevailed, peace and prosperity would also prevail both within countries and internationally. Where autocracies, dictatorships, militarism, and imperialism held sway, the free flow of goods and ideas would give way to political repression and international conflict.

As leader of the revolutionary Bolshevik party, Lenin championed a no less fundamental reshaping of the global system. His views built on the writings of Karl Marx and Friedrich Engels, above all their *Communist Manifesto* of 1848, and on their premise that material conditions, specifically the prevailing economic system, shaped who people are and what they think. Marx put the matter succinctly: "The mode of production in material life determines the general character of the social, political, and spiritual processes of life. It is not the consciousness of men that determine their existence, but, on the contrary, their social existence determines their consciousness."[3] Engels put this essential idea more concretely: "Mankind must first of all eat, drink, have shelter and clothing, before it can pursue politics, science, art, religion, etc."[4] In this conception of society and history, changing systems of economic production drove and defined human development. New systems gave rise to new social classes at odds with the established ones. The most recent of those systems to arise was capitalism (an industrial economy commanded by a bourgeois or middle class). Capitalism had eclipsed feudalism (an agricultural economy with peasant producers at the bottom of a social hierarchy). But capitalism would in time fall to the working class (an exploited proletariat) that was growing within its industrial centers. The Communist Party would lead the transition to worker domination. As the guide of the new revolutionary class, the party had first to overthrow capitalism and then establish in its place socialism. representing a higher stage of economic development and human freedom.

Lenin made his own contribution to this ideology by elaborating on how the transition from capitalism to socialism was to occur. His *Imperialism*, published in 1916, identified the three fundamental flaws within global capitalism that spelled its imminent doom. First was the contradiction within advanced capitalist economies. Sharpening exploitation of the working class had saved those economies from a crisis of overproduction for a time. But as overproduction increased, capitalists looked abroad for cheap raw materials and new markets for sale of goods. The result was an economically driven imperialism. As the advanced capitalist countries became ever more dependent on overseas markets, they had to ensure their own prosperity by securing control, either informal or formal, over them. The second contradiction was among the major capitalist countries as they increasingly collided over control of world markets. This rivalry had (in Lenin's view) precipitated World War I. He was confident that other wars would follow, each further weakening the major powers. The third contradiction pitted the advanced capitalist states against the greater part of the world's population living in colonial and dependent countries. As the imperialists sought to exploit weaker peoples, they would not only arouse nationalist resentments but also spawn an industrial working class on the economic periphery. As capitalism developed and these three contradictions sharpened, revolutionary outbreaks would eventually begin among the working class in advanced capitalist countries and then radiate out to the rest of the world.

Lenin imagined his Bolshevik revolution of 1917 as the first break in the capitalist chain of control then encircling the globe. That revolution would serve as an inspiration and model for others. Above all, it demonstrated what Lenin had earlier argued—the capacity of a tightly knit, dedicated, ideologically united revolutionary party to accelerate the victory of socialism. The prime task of this "Leninist" or vanguard party was to instill in the working class (or proletariat) a deeper sense of its identity and historical mission to bring capitalism down. Once victorious, the party would run the new workers' state, control the means of production in the name of the workers, and end economic exploitation. Increasing material abundance would eventually pave the way for the transition from socialism to communism and the final withering away of the state itself.

But after World War I and throughout the 1920s, neither Washington nor Moscow seemed about to remake the world. The former Entente powers, together with Japan, devoted themselves to combating the Bolsheviks, who found their only friend in an equally ostracized Germany. The U.S. government shared the aversion of its wartime allies to Bolshevism, but Americans were also in a cautious mood. National leaders and the public turned against Wilson's democratic crusade. In 1919–1920 the Senate rejected membership in the League of Nations, and the postwar Republican presidents resisted entanglement in the politics of an unreformed Old World.

World War II and the Onset of the Cold War

During the 1930s resurgent nationalism destabilized the postwar settlement and doomed Europe to its second major conflict in barely two decades. Germany's Adolf Hitler promoted an ideology of national revenge and racial purification, while Benito Mussolini in Italy and a military-dominated Japan were gripped by dreams of empire. Those three powers joined in a coalition known as the Axis. By bringing Germany together with its two foes from World War I, the Axis provided an illustration of the continuing fluidity of the alliance system. By 1939 Britain and France had aligned against the Axis. Joseph Stalin, Lenin's successor as head of the Soviet Union, stood aside after overtures to London and Paris had failed, while the American president, Franklin Roosevelt, showed increasing sympathy for the anti-Axis cause.

The Second World War, like the first, centered on Europe, but it proved more global and more destructive as the belligerents mobilized ever more formidable resources

FROM WORLD WAR I TO WORLD WAR II

1914	World War I breaks out between the Entente and the Central Powers
1917	President Wilson intervenes on the side of the Entente; Bolsheviks led by Lenin take power in Russia
1918	World War I ends with Entente victory
1919–20	Wilson presses 14-point peace plan on Entente partners; the U.S. Senate rejects participation in the League of Nations
1931	Japan invades China's northeast provinces (Manchuria)
1937	Japan and China go to war
1939	Germany and the Soviet Union sign nonaggression pact; German invasion of Poland plunges Europe into war
1940	German invasion of France
1941	Germany invades the Soviet Union; Japanese attack on Pearl Harbor brings the United States formally into World War II

and technology against their foes. In 1939, after secretly agreeing with Stalin to divide Poland in a nonaggression pact, Hitler invaded that country (thus snuffing out a state resurrected only 20 years earlier). The next year German forces rolled over France. In 1941 Germany directed a surprise attack against the Soviet Union, pushing Stalin to the side of the emerging Anglo-American alliance. In East Asia Japan's imperial ambitions had collided with rising Chinese nationalist sentiment, most overtly beginning in 1931 when Japan seized China's northeast provinces (known in the West as Manchuria). A formal state of war came in 1937. The Japanese attack on Pearl Harbor in December 1941 turned the European and Asian battle zones into a single global conflict. The United States at once declared war on Japan. Hitler, already fighting the Americans in the Atlantic, quickly closed the circle of hostilities by declaring war on the United States. The country that had sought to avoid the fighting now stood against the Axis in both Europe and the Pacific.

The main players in World War II reflected the decline of European predominance on the international stage. Japan, the Soviet Union (a Eurasian power), and the United States (a Pacific as well as an Atlantic power) were all to have prominent roles, and the latter two carried the burden of the conflict on the ultimately victorious Allied side. Soviet and American might, already evident in wartime, was to bring an end to the era of multipolarity and give rise to a new bipolar world. No longer could the old contenders for advantage within the European sphere— Britain, France, Germany, and Italy—keep up with the two new global giants. These Old World powers had spent down their wealth and exhausted their will. That other relative newcomer, Japan, lay in ruins.

This postwar bipolar system spawned a Cold War that locked the United States and the Soviet Union in an intense, far-reaching rivalry spanning four decades. Like the two world wars earlier in the century, this contest began in Europe, with the war-weary region split by what was then called an "iron curtain" into U.S. and Soviet areas of influence. The contest then gradually spread, igniting distant, proxy wars and ultimately leaving no people or point of the globe untouched. However, the rivals would avoid the trauma of a direct clash of arms (hence the designation "Cold War"). The development of nuclear weapons perhaps above all helped set limits by making the prospect of such a clash especially fearsome. Although on the whole cautiously managed, this superpower rivalry would prove enormously costly. By one estimate Americans alone would pay out $12 trillion before the contest came to a definitive close.

The Cold War proved overall strikingly fluid. Already by the 1950s the antagonistic outlook that had taken hold in Washington and Moscow had begun to soften. The divisions between the blocs would become increasingly difficult to delineate in the 1960s as superpower clients grew restive and superpower leaders began talking to each other. Flux increasingly characterized the latter stages of the Cold War. It came to a sudden and surprising end in 1989 with the rapid collapse of socialist regimes in eastern Europe, followed two years later by the demise of the Soviet Union itself. While this outcome represented the victory of ideals championed by the United States, the extent of the victory remained in doubt. The relationship between the United States and its two old rivals, Russia and China, was plagued by uncertainty, and Americans had to face knotty questions about what role they could or should play in an international system that they alone now dominated militarily.

The Reach of Nationalism

The era of interstate rivalry spanning the nineteenth and early twentieth century and culminating in the Cold War had a basic animating faith: nationalism. Wonderfully malleable, this ideology had at its core a belief in a shared sense of identity among a group of people that entitled them to statehood and obliged them to sacrifice, even die for their common cause. It made its first appearance during the American and French revolutions as a claim to emancipation from oppressive rule made by those who wished no longer to be subjects but rather citizens determining their own destiny. By the end of the nineteenth century, this nationalist faith had a firm grip in all the great powers, reshaping established states such as Britain and France and giving rise to new ones, notably Italy (1861) and Germany (1871).

The nationalist notions that had taken such deep root on both sides of the Atlantic had come to constitute a state ideology. Agents of the state played a pivotal role in planting in the imagination of many a loyalty to a single overarching political community grounded in a common language, ethnicity, and history. These agents included the primary school teacher charged with mass education, the drill sergeant conducting compulsory military training, the postal clerk presiding over a dense communications network, and the bureaucrat fitting all citizens to the same requirements. Thanks to their efforts, nationalist refrains could be found at every turn—in religious sermons, popular songs, political speeches, public rituals, and schoolbooks. The resulting popular loyalty had broad and powerful implications. It facilitated the state's claim over the lives and economic resources of its citizens, helped integrate large populations in the midst of rapid and often disruptive industrial and social change, and fueled enthusiasm for military strength and overseas empire. This role of the state as agent and benefactor of nationalism was critical. Without a state, nationalism was merely a struggling and frustrated political or even intellectual movement. Once the state existed, nationalists had the power to impose cultural uniformity, craft sustaining historical myths, silence dissenters, and reach for greatness.

Euro-American nationalisms fed off each other as they sought to prove their superiority, whether measured by industrial output, naval power, or colonial holdings. The resulting rivalries easily led nationalists into superheated discussions drawing damning distinctions between good and evil people, superior and inferior cultures. The examples are legion—the longstanding British contempt for the French, the German envy of the British, and the Russian fear of the Germans. This collective sense of a dangerous difference among peoples, infused with a strong moral dimension, gave nationalism a frightening intensity. It fed the ambitions and fears sustaining the rival alliances that pitched Europe into a frenzy of killing between 1914 and 1918. It also could turn collections of other humans into a virus, a plague, an infection, and even vermin. They thus deserved to be destroyed or at least removed, subordinated, or quarantined. Hitler's genocidal campaign against Jews and others deemed "outsiders" was but the most extreme example of a commonplace nationalist tendency toward murderous intolerance.

Far from discrediting nationalism, World War I accentuated its appeal. Nationalist ambitions guided those who negotiated the peace terms ending the war just as nationalist movements set about destroying the empires of Austria-Hungary and the Ottomans on the way to creating new Polish, Serbian, Czech, Bulgarian, and other states. In Germany and Italy, insecurity and resentment combined with economic turmoil to feed a bitter nationalism that made possible the dictators Hitler and Mussolini. By the interwar years, nationalism had transcended its North Atlantic origins to become a near-universal ideology. In Japan a state-sponsored faith that had been in the making since the late nineteenth century flared in the face of what appeared to be Anglo-American cultural contempt and strategic encirclement. Within the colonial world, nationalism's message of liberation had already won an enthusiastic following. The vigorous political activity in such places as Egypt, Ghana, India, China, and Vietnam signaled a major upheaval in the making.

It is a tribute to the power of nationalist ideas that a second world conflict far more destructive than the first ended with nationalism a more powerful and pervasive force than ever. A sharp sense of national mission drove the United States after 1945 to stand up to the communist challenge. At the same time, national pride survived in that bastion of internationalism, the Soviet Union, in both popular and elite thinking and in both its Russian core and its peripheral lands. Western Europeans still clung to the old nation-state even as they began to explore supranational integration, while the Japanese, shorn of territorial empire, went to work with determination and pride on a new economic empire. Elsewhere nationalism would intensify anticolonial feelings, speed the rapid triumph of liberation movements, and inspire some of the major revolutions of the postwar era, including China's and Cuba's.

Even today, nationalism remains one of the world's most potent belief systems, with a grip on peoples in widely scattered places and diverse circumstances. It remains a prominent force among the well-established states such as China, Russia, and the United States just as it is still a preoccupation of the stateless, such as the Chechens in Russia, the Basques of Spain, and the Palestinians in Israel's occupied territories. Even in a time of transnational forces unleashed by globalization, there is good reason to think that nationalism will remain a major source of group identity, state legitimacy, ethnic discontent and oppression, and international contention.

A GLOBAL ECONOMY IN TRANSITION

Along with the emergence of a new constellation of international power, 1945 also brought significant changes in the international economy. The architects of the post-1945 economic system followed a back-to-the-future strategy. They rejected the practices that had prevailed during the interwar period and instead took as their model the achievements of a great wave of economic globalization spanning the late nineteenth and early twentieth centuries. This redirection of economic activity gave rise to the second phase of modern globalization, with enormous implications for countries great and small all around the world over the following half-century.

The victors of World War II were quick to focus their energy and resources on economic reconstruction even as they split into two competing blocs. The bloc led by the Soviet Union included the parts of eastern Europe occupied by the Red Army during its advance against Germany. China would link up with the Soviet bloc in 1949 following the triumph of Communist forces. This bloc was united by the belief that the global system of capitalism was a spent force. In contrast to the economic exploitation and social disruption associated with capitalism, socialists called for an egalitarian system in which the working class was properly rewarded and honored for its labor. Instead of an erratic market economy dominated by a wealthy minority, the socialist economy would be centrally and rationally planned and serve the interest of all. Socialism promised not only fairer but also more efficient economic development, minimizing waste and avoiding the sharp ups and downs that characterized the capitalist system.

The market-oriented bloc of states had a far larger output and ultimately more staying power. Even before World War II had ended, the American government, in cooperation with the British, turned to the rescue of a damaged world economy. They operated from the conviction that the free exchange of goods would make for a more prosperous world. Each country would specialize, engaging in the kind of economic activity in which it was best suited by natural resources or skills. The free flow of goods on a global scale presupposed free domestic markets and would promote (so its advocates claimed) international interdependence and understanding and ultimately eliminate the curse of war. The experience of the nineteenth century inspired these hopes. International trade had grown, bringing greater prosperity and a long era of relative peace among the great powers.

The First Phase of Globalization, 1870s–1914

The economic system that the Americans and British meant to rescue was the product of several hundred years of industrialization and commercialization. Trade and finance during the closing decades of the nineteenth century and the beginning of the twentieth had demonstrated considerable vitality and yielded impressive benefits within the North Atlantic area. So strong was its appeal that it served in the thinking of economic reformers as the template for post-World War II initiatives.

The steadily accumulating economic momentum in the middle of the nineteenth century had caught the attention of two perceptive observers, best known as the fathers of communism. Writing in 1848, Karl Marx and Friedrich Engels foresaw the imminent rise of global capitalism. In strikingly prophetic terms, they described a world market that would soon shape production and consumption virtually everywhere. Driving the change would be new industries "whose products are consumed, not only at home, but in every quarter of the globe. In place of the old wants, satisfied by the productions of the country, we find new wants, requiring for their satisfaction the products of distant lands and climes. In place of the old local and national seclusion and self-sufficiency, we have intercourse in every direction, universal inter-dependence of nations."[5]

The process that made this vision of an integrating global economy a reality had begun in Britain, spread across western Europe and to the United States, and then drew in Japan and Russia. In each case, overseas trade expanded as a byproduct of burgeoning industry. First in Britain from the middle of the eighteenth century and then in the later industrializers in the course of the nineteenth century, the steam engine made possible dramatically higher levels of production, a rising surplus available for export, and the low-cost transport essential to distribute factory-made goods to consumers at home and abroad. Manufactured goods as well as raw materials moved in greater volume, first within Europe but increasingly on a broader world stage. The value of international trade registered a 15-fold jump between the mid-nineteenth century and 1910, and it represented a rapidly increasing if still small proportion of production around the world. International investments also rose sharply. The acceptance of gold as the standard of international value facilitated both trade and investment.

As new centers of industrial and agricultural production sprang up, migrants looking for better jobs moved by the millions. Nearly 50 million Europeans left their homeland between the 1840s and the onset of World War I. Most headed toward the Americas—Argentina, Brazil, Canada, and above all the United States (the destination for two thirds of those transplants). A massive movement of people from China into Southeast Asia was occurring simultaneously and in the process transforming not just the ethnic makeup but also the economy of colonies within the region. Overall, the sheer number of those traveling, often long distances, in search of better economic opportunity at the turn of the century was unprecedented.

This dynamic, increasingly international economy bore three important features. First, it was sustained by a system of finance that underwrote overseas trade and supplied investment needs in both newly industrializing countries (such as the United States) and colonies rich in raw materials (such as French Indochina, with its rubber plantations, and Belgian Congo, with its mines). London was the chief financial center until loans made by U.S. bankers during World War I established New York as a serious rival. The second feature was the appearance of the first multinational corporations in manufacturing and marketing and in the extraction of raw materials. These multinationals, so called because they had headquarters in one country but operated in many, would come to dominate global markets. Finally, new technology played a critical role in creating a truly global pattern of trade and finance by the turn of the century. The steam engine driving trains and ships and the opening of interoceanic canals made transport cheap and rapid, while the telegraph and underwater cable greatly accelerated communications. These technological innovations were critical to the unfolding of this first wave of global economic integration.

The new trend toward globalization had demonstrated along with its vitality a propensity toward troubling downswings, for example during the 1890s. Excess production forced factories to close, swelling the ranks of the unemployed and generating social and political tensions. The global economy was also vulnerable to disruption by international conflict. World War I marked the beginning of the end of the first phase of globalization. It was followed at once by a drop in production and by protectionist measures such as tariffs on imports that raised barriers to foreign trade in major markets. The financial crash of 1929 on New York City's Wall Street sent economies around the world into the most serious downward spiral of the twentieth century. By 1931 financial markets were in crisis. Britain abandoned the gold standard. Germany and Austria imposed controls over exchange of their currencies. They and others were acting to insulate their economies from the outside pressures dragging them down. The resulting Great Depression hit the industrial states first. In Europe industrial production dropped by one third, and in Germany alone it fell by 40 percent. This slump in turn caused foreign trade to further fall off, thereby making the depression global. Already by 1933 international trade overall was down by one third. Some countries, such as Japan, where exports had fallen by half, were especially hard hit. The economic pain felt by national communities opened the door to strong leaders in Europe, Japan, and even the United States championing state intervention and shared sacrifice. This authoritarian trend arising from economic hard times facilitated the march to war in East Asia and Europe between 1937 and 1945—and to still more punishment to economies already damaged by prolonged depression.

Globalization Reborn, 1945 to the Present

As World War II drew to a close, U.S. and British leaders set about repairing the shattered international economy. Their handiwork would bear striking similarities to the earlier phase of globalization. As earlier, the system of finance had its prominent centers: New York and London and in time Tokyo and Bonn. Multinational corporations would continue to dominate the production and international distribution of goods and services even if they bore new names such as Disney, Sony, and Volkswagen. Finally, technology now as then figured critically in driving and defining the new phase of global economic activity, with ever more powerful and efficient engines, the telephone, commercial aircraft, satellite, computer, and Internet only the most prominent products of an era of innovation.

The efforts of the Americans and the British would prove over the long haul an enormous success. The new framework for trade and finance brought unrivaled prosperity to Americans, and it soon restored prosperity to western Europe and Japan. It made deep inroads in countries on the margins of the international economy. Even newly independent states with a socialist bias had to confront the fact that the global market economy was the most promising outlet for their exports and the best source for technology and capital. Peasants from the interior of Central America to western Africa watched as crops grown for sale overseas increasingly dominated the land. The accompanying disruption was in some cases new, but in most cases it was an extension of a process that had begun in the nineteenth century or even earlier.

This global market-oriented system of production and investment not only had a wide and deep impact but also began as early as the 1950s to set a standard against which citizens as well as leaders in the bastions of socialism came to measure the performance of their own system. By the early 1980s China was succumbing to the temptations of the market; eastern Europe, Russia, and other successor states to the Soviet Union would soon follow. By the 1990s the competitive, market-oriented rules and organizations put in place in the mid-1940s had become the basis for a genuinely global system. Socialism was on the defensive; free-market principles seemed well on their way to becoming de facto the world's governing economic faith.

This increasingly international economy exercised extraordinary power over ordinary lives. In developed economies, it surrounded consumers with a wondrous array of goods, many of foreign origin. At the same time it placed workers there in keen competition with others around the world and made education and a productive workplace the key to making a good living. The international economy left business managers as well as investors vulnerable to rapid, unforeseeable developments in distant markets. In poorer countries, the impact of outside economic forces could be benign, providing opportunities for attracting new industry that could no longer operate competitively in developed economies and for gaining access to rich markets for agricultural and basic manufactured goods. But the international market economy could also be harsh, driving peasants from the land as the wealthy consolidated land holdings to implement more efficient farming methods. The now-redundant labor emptied out of villages, tearing the fabric of community, while filling cities with the poor desperate for work. Foreign markets, once alive with promise, could suddenly close, and foreign capital, once the engine of local development, could flee. The effects on small economies could be instantaneous and disastrous.

Finally, the international economy confronted citizens with a broad range of new challenges that were inexorably and profoundly altering their lives. The social dynamism promoted by the market set gender roles in question, pitted a newly assertive individualism against the good of the group, and gave rise to far-reaching migrations that affected not only those who went abroad looking for opportunity but also the societies where they came to settle. It was becoming impossible to escape the international flow of information and entertainment with its powerful cultural impact. And the same economic forces that carried manufactured goods, immigrant laborers, and popular culture also carried diseases such as HIV/AIDS rapidly over long distances and sustained far-reaching networks of terrorism that gave the few a remarkable power to frighten the many. Perhaps even more ominous for the long term, the international economy by its very productivity created serious threats to the natural environment that in turn imperiled plants, animals, and human health and welfare, even perhaps the survival of the human species.

Yet even as the global economy fixed its grip on the lives of people everywhere, the way that economy functioned within one country or another remained to a surprising degree culturally conditioned. National economies from Indonesia to Iceland and from Kazakhstan to Nigeria continued to reflect widely varying but firmly held preferences on fundamental issues. These issues can be expressed in the following questions: How important is individualism and individual opportunity? Should group solidarity or social stability take precedence? How large a gap between the richest and poorest in a society is permissible? Are economic rights inextricably tied to political rights, and if so, how broadly defined should economic rights be? Finally and perhaps most important of all, how large a role in the economy should the state play, and precisely what should that role be? Answers have varied significantly from one market economy to another, suggesting the importance of being alert to what might be called "economic culture." In the increasingly integrated post-1945 global system of production and consumption, a diversity of beliefs and practices survived, even flourished.

TABLE I.1 Key Economic Terms

Despite its importance, the international economy is not well or easily understood by the public. Part of the reason is that economic phenomena can be complex to the point of obscurity. The British writer H. G. Wells lamented that economics "hangs like a gathering fog in a valley, a fog which begins nowhere and goes nowhere." His countryman George Bernard Shaw ridiculed its practitioners for their irrelevance: "If all the economists in the world were laid end to end, they still wouldn't reach a conclusion." It is true that economics cannot be reduced to simple generalizations, but mastering the following basic terms (to appear repeatedly in the chapters to follow) is an important first step toward functional economic literacy.

gross national product (GNP) and **gross domestic product (GDP):** Closely related measures of overall economic activity and economic growth. Both GNP and GDP represent the value of all goods and services produced by a country in a given year. GNP includes income earned abroad by citizens of that country and excludes income earned by foreigners from domestic production. GDP includes only the output that occurs within a country. The practical difference between the two terms is usually negligible. By contrast, the significance of small differences in the rate of growth, whether expressed in terms of GNP or GDP, is huge. For example, at 1 percent it takes 70 years for living standards to double, while at 2 percent they double every 35 years.

per capita GDP: Derived by dividing GDP by the total population of a country or a region. The result is an average, indicating what portion of the total output each person would claim if it were equally shared. It thus serves as a rough general measurement of standard of living without giving any sense of how equally the income is divided.

inflation: A gauge of a currency's declining purchasing power. Inflation is usually the result of a scarcity of goods or of government printing money too freely. Either way a market imbalance develops that raises the prices of goods while diminishing the purchasing power of money. High levels of inflation are associated with wartime or political upheaval.

constant dollar: A recalculation of value that takes account of the effects of inflation, which over time diminishes what a dollar or other currency can actually purchase. Constant dollars thus allow more realistic comparisons between GNP, GDP, or per capita income statistics over different periods because the dollars at each point represent the same purchasing power.

infrastructure: Those public investments essential to economic activity, including roads, airports, telecommunications, electrical power, and health and educational programs. Usually the more developed a country's infrastructure, the more favorable its prospects for economic growth.

laissez faire: A French phrase meaning literally "let (people) do as they wish" but taken in economics to stand for the doctrine formulated in the eighteenth century that markets worked best when freed from government interference. The doctrine inspired support in the nineteenth and twentieth centuries for expanding free trade and the sphere of individual choice.

protectionism: a policy of shielding producers of goods and services in one country from competition by those in other countries. Devices for limiting or cutting off access to the home market include a charge on imports (a tariff) and regulatory measures difficult for foreign producers to meet. Critics argue that the benefits of protectionism to a few local producers are offset by losses to the much larger number of local consumers, who must pay more or receive less than in a free-trade system in which each country specializes in what it can produce most efficiently.

THE COLONIAL SYSTEM ON THE BRINK

Before 1945 much of the world—roughly half the surface of the globe and some 70 percent of its population—had fallen under direct colonial administration or informal great-power control. The process of subjugation occurred in two successive waves as Europeans effectively laid claim to mastery over other lands and peoples. The first expansionist thrust came between the sixteenth and eighteenth centuries with the main targets the Americas, the Indian subcontinent, and parts of the Pacific. The second imperial impulse, as we have seen, came in the late nineteenth century (coincident with state nationalism and economic globalization). The major European powers, joined by Japan and the United States, established new colonies in Africa, the Middle East, Southeast Asia, and the Pacific. Britain was the clear frontrunner in the colonial race. By the early part of the twentieth century it exercised authority over roughly two thirds of all colonized peoples. China resisted outright colonization but fell under the sway of multiple states, while Central America and parts of the Caribbean came under informal U.S. dominion.

This subjugation of vast and distant territories and the maintenance of control there depended on the imperial powers' possession of superior technology. The application of science to the concerns of everyday life made possible material wealth and military might previously unimaginable. This technology took a striking variety of forms—potent weapons of war, rapid transportation and communications, and improved public health that helped European troops, administrators, and settlers withstand otherwise deadly tropical diseases. The intruders' technical skills often impressed non-European peoples with their own inferiority and prompted some to seek cooperation with these outsiders.

The process of subjugation was also driven, as Marx and Engels argued, by the needs of thriving industrial economies for a secure supply of foodstuffs and raw materials such as rubber, minerals, and timber as well as an outlet for manufactured goods. The growing stake created by trade and investment often led to a decision to secure direct political control. By firmly tying foreign lands to the home market, producers in one country could be certain of meeting their own needs and, if necessary, denying the needs of international rivals. The great China market, for example, fixated Europeans and Americans at the turn of the century. And so began an international tussle over dividing that weakened empire into spheres of influence. Colonial administrations had the additional benefit of ensuring that valued raw materials along with the labor needed to work mines and fields could be had at extremely low cost. One of the most extreme examples was the Belgian Congo, the personal possession of Belgium's king, which became a vast graveyard of those worked to death to ensure a steady supply of low-cost minerals. But conditions in the cotton fields of British Uganda and the rubber plantations in French Indochina were only marginally better.

Finally, nationalism played a major role in this subjugation. Expansionist Europeans, soon followed by Americans and Japanese, argued that national standing depended on conquest. The richer and larger the prizes a country could claim,

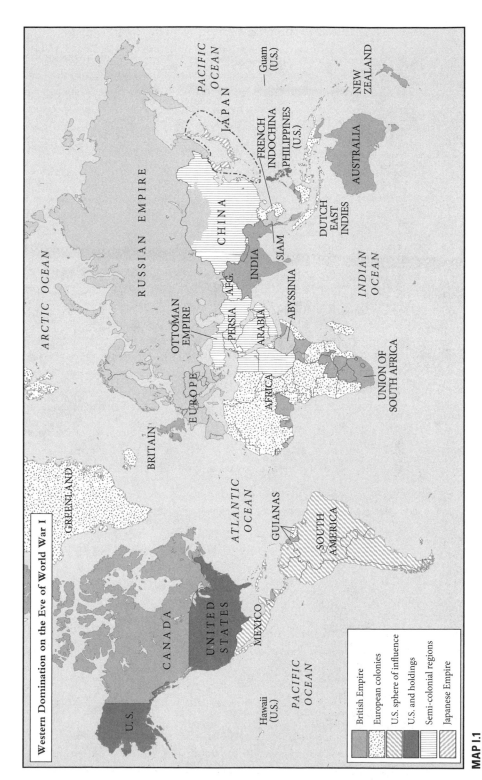

Western Domination on the Eve of World War I

PACIFIC OCEAN

— Guam (U.S.)

NEW ZEALAND

JAPAN

FRENCH INDOCHINA

PHILIPPINES (U.S.)

AUSTRALIA

RUSSIAN EMPIRE

CHINA

SIAM

DUTCH EAST INDIES

ARCTIC OCEAN

AFG.

INDIA

OTTOMAN EMPIRE

PERSIA

ABYSSINIA

INDIAN OCEAN

EUROPE

ARABIA

BRITAIN

AFRICA

UNION OF SOUTH AFRICA

GREENLAND

ATLANTIC OCEAN

GUIANAS

SOUTH AMERICA

CANADA

UNITED STATES

MEXICO

PACIFIC OCEAN

U.S.

Hawaii (U.S.)

British Empire
European colonies
U.S. sphere of influence
U.S. and holdings
Semi-colonial regions
Japanese Empire

MAP I.1
Western Domination on the Eve of World War I

the higher its international prestige. Nationalism inspired popular support critical to financing and manning imperial armies and administrations. But it also sharpened rivalries among nations at the end of the nineteenth century as each raced to win territory abroad.

Whatever the commonalities in the pressures behind empire, the form of control exercised by outsiders varied considerably from place to place and even at one place over time. With administrative personnel and armed forces almost always stretched thin, informal empire had much in its favor. Empire builders, whether in a gunboat offshore, in a consular office, or in a lightly staffed administration, would then have to exercise control indirectly, relying on local elites to do their bidding, usually at a price. British domination in central China and over Egypt fits this pattern. Territorially, colonies might take the form of a string of commercial outposts along valued trade routes or of extensive plantations dependent on work by imported slaves or impressed natives. Portuguese control in Brazil, for example, began as a mercantile colony but evolved into a plantation society. The numbers of settlers from the metropolis in some cases rose dramatically as pressures, whether political, demographic, or economic, encouraged migration. The Japanese colonial project in the northeastern part of China is a case shaped by domestic pressures. A sufficiently large influx of outsiders determined to make a new home overseas could give rise to a settler colony in which a substantial minority rode roughshod over the majority native population. Dutch settlement in southernmost Africa and French settlement in Algeria fit this pattern. The form each colony took had implications for the course of decolonization. The more informal the rule and the smaller the settler stake, the easier the path to independence. The larger the number of settlers and the greater their economic and political dominance over indigenous peoples, the more likely that prolonged racial and ethnic conflict would occur.

Vulnerabilities of Empire

The impressive structure of imperial control was not to last. By 1945, within roughly half a century of its apogee, it teetered on the brink of collapse. Almost at once after World War II the march from formal subordination to formal independence began, and the pace accelerated in the 1960s. By the early 1970s, colonies were increasingly rare. New states swelled the ranks of the United Nations. By 1970 it had grown to 127 members, up from the 51 charter members in 1945, and more were waiting in the wings. What accounts for this rapid collapse of empire?

One explanation is to be found in the conflicts of the first half of the twentieth century that demoralized and weakened Europe. As the imperial powers battered each other with ever more destructive weapons of war, they sapped the sources of their strength, confidence, and prestige critical to maintaining control of distant colonies. In any case, the losers had to surrender their overseas possessions. After World War I Germany's colonies in sub-Saharan Africa and the Pacific went as spoils to the victors. The Ottoman empire fell, opening an opportunity for the French and British to extend their control into such places in the Middle East as

Iraq and Syria. World War II completed the colonial shakeup. Japan's war machine drove the Europeans and Americans from East and Southeast Asia, discrediting foreign mastery in Asia. And then following their defeat, Italy and Japan forfeited their imperial holdings. While victorious British, French, Dutch, and American forces reclaimed old possessions throughout Southeast Asia, including Malaya, Indochina, the East Indies, and the Philippines, the commitment to empire was fading. European elites sought with varying degrees of intensity to continue their civilizing mission, "liberating the primitive societies from the great calamities which are ravaging them and which are called: disease, ignorance, superstition, tyranny."[6] But to no avail. The imperial collapse quickly began, accelerating as the American and Soviet rivals joined in dismissing European colonies as outmoded and obstacles to assembling their own stable of Cold War clients.

The other explanation for this rapid imperial collapse is to be found in the capacity of subjugated peoples to turn the ideological weapons of the West to their own ends. In country after country, an educated, politically engaged minority, usually from relatively privileged backgrounds, mixed indigenous values with imported ideas. The resulting amalgam provided the vision that gave energy and direction to the independence struggles and then to the programs of domestic renovation that dominated the first decades after independence. Facing an organized popular opposition, the vastly outnumbered colonial administrators and troops could no longer enforce their will.

Nationalism was the most significant of the imports that would help subvert the colonial order. As in Europe, the United States, and Japan, so too in the countries they dominated, nationalists worked to create a body of unifying myths and values that would overcome internal divisions and lay the groundwork for ending foreign control. New nation builders in places as far-flung as Guatemala, Algeria, and Ghana turned to the methods that European nationalists had developed to build mass support—print and other communications technologies, education, and promotion of an official language.

The other Western ideology with a strong appeal to anticolonial leaders was Marxism-Leninism. For leaders and intellectuals from Cuba to Cambodia, it proved appealing as a tool for explaining why their societies were divided and poor. It seemed also to offer an explanation for foreign domination at the same time that it promised liberation from a morally corrupt and economically declining capitalism. Finally, it made an attractive case for the effectiveness of a loyal, determined, and ideologically united party in fighting for liberation and creating a new, better society. The achievements of the Communist Party in the Soviet Union seemed to strengthen the case for Marxism as a guide to revolution and development.

Already by 1945, the ideological tide was flowing strongly against the colonial status quo. The winning side in two world wars had set the stage by promoting the principle of self-determination trumpeted by Woodrow Wilson and Vladimir Lenin in the immediate aftermath of World War I. In 1919 representatives of restive colonial peoples had pressed the victors of the First World War to honor that principle. That same year Lenin's new Bolshevik regime in Moscow organized the Communist International (Comintern) on the premise that the Western ideology of Marxism would find eager converts in the colonial world. Soviet emissaries were soon reaching out to restive peoples eager to throw off foreign control, encouraging the organization of local Communist parties, and providing support in the form of money, advisers, and schooling. Moscow thus demonstrated in the 1920s and 1930s that it alone among the world powers was genuinely committed to the principle of liberation. World War II, a conflict that the United States and Britain claimed to be about freedom, saw them line up behind self-determination as a general principle. By the mid-twentieth century Western colonial control had become suspect on the basis of its own ideologies of nationalism and Marxism. Unable to match the nationalist and revolutionary energies of subjugated people, colonial powers such as France and Britain had only their superior wealth and technology to maintain an increasingly fragile grip. The devastation of World War II took away that advantage. The imperial game for them was all but over.

The Appearance of the "Third World"

"Third World" was the term that came to be widely applied to newly emerging countries. In the nineteenth and early twentieth centuries arrogant European colonizers would have described those lands as "uncivilized" or "barbaric." The term "Third World," first used in France in 1952 and then adopted in the United States, was a less offensive way to refer to peoples who had to be located within a world already divided two ways by the Cold War. The United States and its allies in western Europe and Japan became the "First World." The socialist bloc (essentially the USSR and its eastern European satellites) was the "Second World," leaving the rest as the "Third World." More recently, the term of choice has become "the developing world" or even the "South" (to distinguish areas generally below the Equator still marked by poverty from the more affluent and economically developed countries that are for the most part in the "North").

The difficulties in finding a blanket term for the regions engaged in struggles for independence and development are insurmountable if the line of division is

MAP I.2　　　　　　　　　　　　　　　　　　　　　　　　　　　　　　　➤
How to Carve Up the Post-1945 World?
This map delineates two answers that found widespread acceptance. The lighter line traces what during the Cold War became the critical distinction between the first and second worlds of capitalism and communism, leaving the rest the "Third World." The heavy line indicates an alternative geography that came into vogue in the latter part of the twentieth century. Here the developed north is set against the underdeveloped south. The three countries marked with dots (Yugoslavia, South Africa, and Turkey) have resisted easy classification under either the Cold War notion of three worlds or its north–south alternative. China also fits awkwardly into this schema. During most of the Cold War it identified itself with Third World, although it allied with the Soviet Union for a decade and remained under Communist control through the Cold War and beyond. (Based on Lewis and Wigen, *Myth of Continents*, 5)

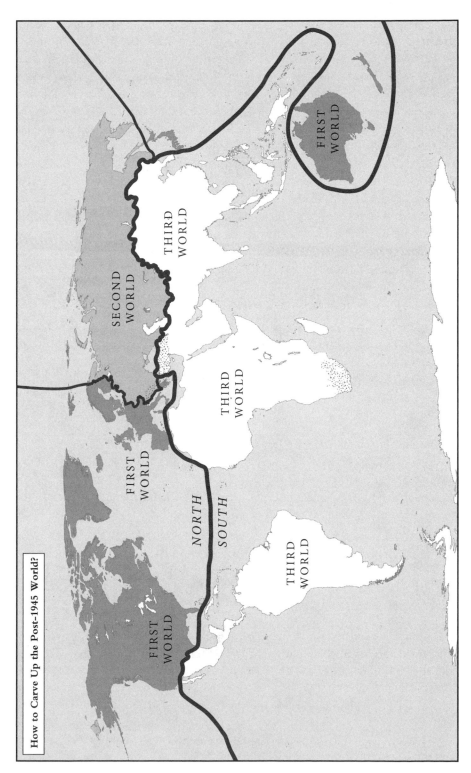

How to Carve Up the Post-1945 World?

FIRST WORLD

THIRD WORLD

SECOND WORLD

THIRD WORLD

FIRST WORLD

NORTH

SOUTH

THIRD WORLD

FIRST WORLD

thought of as simple and all-encompassing. The decolonization that followed World War II hid within it enormous variation from region to region and even within regions. Some countries, such as Vietnam and Iran, gravitated toward strong state authority, and others, such as India, the Philippines, and Guatemala, resisted that course. Some, such as Egypt, began with a relatively homogenous ethnic and linguistic population, while others, such as Algeria and South Africa, were fragmented or even sharply, violently divided. Some, such as China, had experienced the turmoil of civil war and revolution; others, such as India and Ghana, enjoyed a relatively peaceful transition to independence. Is there anything that Chinese, Guatemalans, Egyptians, and South Africans who find their way into this survey had in common that might make any blanket term useful?

Even if every one of the newly independent states has a unique story of dramatic changes to tell, they do share some important features. For the first three decades of the postwar era, the term "Third World" has some value, although it has to be used not in terms of Cold War alignments but of a set of features that created a sense of community among countries around the world and gave rise to shared hope and identity. It included countries such as China, Cuba, and Vietnam that were at least for a time aligned with the Soviet Union but not dominated by it. As we will see, increasingly toward century's end countries in the Third World set off on divergent developmental trajectories, rendering less and less relevant the preoccupations they had formerly shared. From the 1970s onward, the terms "developed" and "developing" are more appropriate. They reflect the growing preoccupation with measuring relative levels of economic productivity and prosperity around the world on a scale ranging from the richest to middle income to the poorest countries.

The first of the features that gave reality to the Third World during the early postwar decades was the experience of foreign domination by Europeans and to a lesser degree Americans and Japanese. All members of the Third World ultimately took up the struggle to end foreign dominance and win independence. Early in the twentieth century advocates of independence—a minority with foreign education and a sense of the broader world—began to make their appearance. After World War II in country after country, they turned with special urgency to the task of overthrowing foreign masters wounded or vanquished in two world wars. By the 1960s formal colonial control had become an anachronism, although the memory of the struggle was still fresh and the wounds were still sensitive.

The second feature that gave reality to the Third World was the need to make choices about post-independence political and economic development in light of what foreigners, usually Europeans, had wrought. In colonies such as Ghana, Algeria, and the Philippines, they had imposed political systems and introduced their political values. They created state boundaries in some cases (notably in sub-Saharan Africa) and often played favorites, offering education and political advancement to some groups at the expense of others. They reshaped economies by linking them to outside markets and promoting foreign investment. Even countries such as China and Cuba not under direct colonial control felt the far-reaching cultural as well as economic effects of these outside initiatives. Time and again those attempting to get out from under foreign domination had to face the question of which of these legacies was worth keeping and which should be discarded. In grappling with that question they encountered another: How were strong indigenous values, institutions, and practices to be reconciled with these foreign legacies, some of which were attractively "modern"? These related questions were in part practical. No one could, for example, ignore the efficacy of Western military arms and organization. But there was also a large psychological dimension to these questions involving nothing less than identity and pride after a time of confusion and humiliation. Different Third World peoples came to different answers, but everyone had to wrestle with the same broad set of questions.

The struggle for independence and the subsequent search for an appropriate development path unfolded against the backdrop of the Cold War. U.S.–Soviet rivalry brought unwanted pressures and even blatant intervention but also the prospect of generous aid and invaluable protection. All in the Third World had to deal with the superpowers as best they could. This shared preoccupation by weaker countries led to the emergence of the self-styled nonaligned movement in the 1950s. Beginning with the first meeting in Bandung, Indonesia, in 1955, newly independent states pressed for an end to colonialism, attacked racism, opposed great-power intervention, and resisted pressure from the Cold War rivals to commit to one side or the other. Participants in the movement, led by India, Egypt, and Yugoslavia, called for an international order in which political self-determination and economic development took precedence over the Cold War military and ideological rivalry.

A final feature that the Third World had in common during the early postwar decades was a heavily peasant population, typically 70 to 80 percent right after the war. That the specific conditions governing peasant life differed from country to country should not obscure qualities of social and political life that were widely shared. To begin with, the life of most rural dwellers was hard. Most peasants lived with uncertainty on the economic margin and under conditions of poverty attended by such woes as high infant mortality, low educational levels, poor health, and short lifespans. The caloric intake of any single villager from year to year or even season to season could vary enormously depending on what rainfall, disease, or warfare did to crop yields. The risks were especially acute for those dependent on growing their own food (subsistence farmers), whose condition a British economic historian described as "like that of a man permanently up to his neck in water, so that even a ripple might drown him."[7] Bad years could bring widespread hunger and even death.

Isolated and stalked by adversity, peasants had long depended on social solidarity expressed through local traditions, rites, and myths and often organized around kinship. Although weakening in the nineteenth and early twentieth centuries, shared community values still served to govern *and* constrain peasant behavior. They sanctioned maintenance of communal land and sharing of food in hard times.

Solidarity also meant placing the interest of the group over the interest of individuals or particular families. Those who prospered but did not share were criticized and even excluded from community life. Fellow villagers who became plantation overseers or went to work in the city might well encounter suspicion from those who stayed at home. This sense of solidarity often created an attachment to the status quo puzzling to outsiders. Giving up tried-and-true methods of farming might disrupt production or village harmony. A new seed strain, for example, might promise greater yield or disease resistance. But the peasant had to wonder whether it was suited to local growing conditions and to worry that buyers might steer clear of unfamiliar, untested produce. Why take a risk that might create the ripple that drowns families or entire villages barely clinging to survival?

The forces of globalization effected a kind of quiet revolution in rural life, weakening solidarity and disrupting society. This process in most places began well before 1945. As the rising capitalist powers began to create a global market, their economies penetrated ever deeper into remote rural communities. Those who were not caught up by the time of the first wave of globalization in the late nineteenth and early twentieth centuries were engulfed by the second, post-1945 wave. The timing varied considerably. Some regions, such as China's Yangzi Valley, had peasants producing for distant markets well before European trade intruded, while regions of Guatemala were still largely isolated into the 1960s. Whatever the precise timing, peasant production everywhere increasingly was not for local consumption but for cash sales and for shipment to distant markets. As the well-to-do consolidated control of land, trade, and finance, they fundamentally redefined social relations within villages. When a food crisis developed, landlords were no longer obliged to supply food, waive rents, or mobilize community resources. No longer would they have to display their generosity by sponsoring lavish celebrations and giving generously to local shrines, temples, and schools. Ambitious, profit-maximizing landlords worked to break down peasant landholdings and turn former owners or tenants into low-cost seasonal laborers. Colonial officials hastened this rural transformation by demanding tax payments in cash rather than in goods. Unless peasants began producing crops for the market, where they could make cash sales, they could not pay their taxes and thus risked losing their most prized possession, their land. The bonds of solidarity long critical to survival within rural communities further eroded as the young and able-bodied left to look for work in the cities or on new agricultural frontiers, leaving behind women, children, and old people.

Some peasants reacted to rising market forces in an entrepreneurial spirit. They wanted to escape subsistence agriculture and to reap the rewards for producing more and better in response to the market with its changing levels of supply and demand. The industrious and the innovative could get ahead. But those who followed the entrepreneurial path also found themselves subject to the vagaries of distant markets. For example, overproduction of rice in Southeast Asia could mean ruin for peasants in China growing rice for that same, now glutted international market. Whether world commodity prices were high or low, taxes had to be paid; the family fed until the next harvest; and certain necessities purchased, such as cloth and tools. Moneylenders would supply the funds to get peasants through hard times but at rates that were exorbitant (sometimes 8 to 10 percent per *month*). Once in debt peasants often could not extricate themselves. Some might become virtually hired hands working their own, now heavily mortgaged property. Others would have to sell land and livestock to cover their debt.

Peasants passing through this economic and social transformation engaged in a kind of politics peculiar to rural conditions. Whatever the resentments they felt, peasants were notably reluctant to risk a confrontation. An Ethiopian proverb urged dissembling even by those with grievances: "When the great lord passes, the wise peasant bows deeply and silently farts."[8] But sufficiently provoked, peasant communities would resort to a range of public, collective, sometimes even desperate actions to protect their way of life, keep their land, and ensure the survival of their families. Angry peasants might begin by trying to shame powerful locals guilty of seizing public lands or cheating tenants. If songs, stories, dances, or plays mocking them had no effect, then peasants might become bolder, for example withholding their labor from abusive landlords by feigning illness, committing arson, or spoiling crops. In extreme situations, peasants might attack tax, rent, or debt collectors, resort to banditry, or even stage an armed uprising (as with the Huks in the Philippines or more recently with the Mayans in Mexico's Chiapas region). These desperate measures usually failed. Linguistic, ethnic, and regional differences prevented peasants in one area from forming alliances with other peasants. Insurgent forces lacked arms, discipline, and experienced leadership. They risked starvation if military or political activities disrupted food production. For all these reasons, government- and landlord-controlled forces easily crushed rebellious peasants, often in the process massacring whole families and seizing their lands. The exceptions to this generalization can be found in modern-day China, Vietnam, the Philippines, and Guatemala. In these cases (to be discussed in the upcoming chapters), reformers or revolutionaries from outside the village convinced the locals to support programs that would improve their security and livelihood. These programs had to knit local discontents into a broad, organized, sustainable movement, and to target abuses that peasants deeply resented. Thus these programs attacked exploitative landlords and moneylenders, merchants who sought to establish monopolies and fix prices, and corrupt colonial officials who took more in taxes and bribes than they returned in benefits such as health care, education, or roads to market.

While the experience of foreign domination, the challenge of liberation and development, and the conditions of a large peasantry buffeted by powerful outside forces created marked commonalities among a group of countries called the "Third World," that sense of sharing a similar fate did not endure. It reached its peak in the 1960s and thereafter began to fade. The era of domination meant less to a younger generation who knew it only secondhand. Socialism as a developmental model lost its luster. Elites, once the advocates of radical change, turned more cautious and experimented with increasingly diverse practices attended by widely varying success.

Finally, rural conditions underwent a major alteration. The consolidation of land into larger, more efficient holdings meant fewer opportunities for work even as the rural population increased thanks to better medical care. With increased migration to the cities, urban populations exploded and village life atrophied. This process was as familiar to Egyptian, Iranian, and Indian villages as it was to rural Mexico, Nicaragua, and Brazil. This exodus reduced the peasantry as a portion of the total population through the last half of the twentieth century as industry and service work began to catch up with and in some cases overtake the agricultural sector. By the late 1990s the downward trend had played out in countries once part of the "Third World" in strikingly different degrees. In countries such as China, Guatemala, and Ghana those making their living from the soil were still half or more, while in the Philippines, Cuba, Iran, and Egypt agriculture accounted for only 25 to 40 percent of the workforce (still high compared with no more than 5 percent in Germany, Japan, and the United States at century's end). Even those left behind were transformed as they became more tied to city ways through better roads, radios, television, higher literacy, and contact with those who had migrated. Thus as the proportion of peasants shrank, so too did their distinctive isolation and wariness fade.

By the late twentieth century, so diverse had become its members that the term Third World had outlived its usefulness. But whatever we choose to call these countries, be it "developing nations" or "the South," the importance of understanding the greater part of humankind cannot be understated. Africa's population is one and a half times as large as Europe's. The peoples of Asia combined are 10 times more numerous than those in North America. China alone is almost five times more populous than the United States. Among these large populations have occurred some of the most horrific events of the post-1945 era that outsiders find difficult to understand. China's leader Mao Zedong sought to improve rural conditions by bringing industry to the countryside in the late 1950s, and as a result millions upon millions died from starvation and disease. Peasants in sub-Saharan Africa have in recent decades come face to face with the scourges, often cruelly combined, of deteriorating land conditions, soaring birth rates, explosive ethnic antagonisms, and HIV/AIDS sweeping through households and villages. Precisely because we know so little still about so many, we have much to gain by stretching our imagination and exercising our empathy.

CONCLUSION

The themes sketched here unfold in greater detail in the pages that follow. The story of the post-1945 world begins with the rise of a dangerously competitive Cold War order. Between 1945 and 1953 the Soviet Union and the United States embarked on a struggle that both overshadowed international economic reform and implicated the Third World. (This is the subject of Part One.) Between 1953 and 1968 that Cold War order gained a modicum of stability. On the one side, stability facilitated economic revival in the developed world, but on the other side it faced unexpected challenges—from rising discontents within the decolonizing world but also even more surprisingly from a new generation of youth raised under conditions of peace and affluence. (These developments are treated in Part Two.)

From the 1970s through the 1980s, the Cold War order eroded. Superpower rivalry imposed heavy costs on its Soviet and American protagonists. At the same time an increasingly intrusive international economy exerted competitive constraints on the behavior of all countries. Nowhere did that economy have a greater impact than on the Third World, creating striking differences among countries once marked by strong commonalities. (Part Three covers these events.) A new post-Cold War international regime emerged in the course of the 1990s. It was defined by the interplay between strong globalizing forces (both economic and cultural) on the one side and, on the other, strong states as well as vital local cultures seeking to brake or bend globalization to their own needs. (These trends and what they portend are treated in Part Four.)

In moving through these phases, the reader should gain some sense of the world as our imagined newspaper reader knew it in 1945 and experience the surprises, hardships, fear, joy, and disappointments associated with the decades that followed. Along the way the reader should gain a better grasp of the origins of the world we inhabit and of the other cultures that share that world with us. This kind of historical knowledge is not, for better or worse, free of controversy. As a French philosopher once said, "Whoso writes the history of his own time must expect to be attacked for everything he has said, and for everything he has not said."[9] The risks are more than offset by the gains. A sense of the past is essential to acting as responsible moral agents and as citizens well enough informed to understand, debate, and decide critical issues. By exposing us to the diversity of cultures around the world, that knowledge also sharpens our sense of self, both as individuals and as members of national and transnational communities. Finally, the past teaches what is durable and difficult to change and helps us distinguish between problems beyond our control and those where the application of our energy and imagination might make a difference. In all these ways history of this or any era remains a critical part of the equipment of an educated person.

Part One
HOPES AND FEARS CONTEND, 1945–1953

SHORTLY AFTER EIGHT in the morning of August 6, 1945, Mr. Katsutani finished his breakfast and was about to light a cigarette. He suddenly saw, he later recalled, "a white flash" followed by "a tremendous blast," and then "a big black cloud" filled the sky. What he had seen was a nuclear device dropped by a U.S. Air Force bomber, the *Enola Gay*. This single bomb had detonated about 2,000 feet above the ground. One of the bomber crew described the city of Hiroshima below turning into "a big mess of flame and dust." Another saw "a pot of bubbling tar." The co-pilot noted in his log simply, "My God!"[1]

The ensuing impressions cut deep into the memory of the survivors of Hiroshima as they began searching that day through the ruins for relatives. On his way into town, Katsutani recalled averting his gaze from the bomb victims. The features of their heads—eyes, noses, mouths, ears—had all been burned away. "They were all so badly injured. I could not bear to look into their faces. They smelled like burning hair." He remembered all the victims begging for water and children crying for their mothers. The scene was "a living hell." Fujie Ryōso strapped her infant on her back and went looking for her husband, who had that morning set off to work in the city. For seven days she picked through piles of charred bodies pulled from the river, from incinerated streetcars, and from collapsed, burnt buildings. Empty-handed, the 35-year-old Ryōso finally returned to her farm and children, clinging to the hope that somehow her husband had survived. She admitted in a 1981 interview that she still waited: "If I hear a noise outside in the middle of the night, my heart starts pounding, thinking that he's come back." With personal trauma and family loss went new political attitudes. Ryōso drummed into the heads of her grandchildren the constant message: "War is really cruel; it's really cruel. Never make war!" Ikuko Wakasa, a five-year-old on August 6, confessed six years later that she still trembled to recall that fateful day in Hiroshima. Any reference to war, even in movie newsreels, made her shudder.[2]

Hiroshima Flattened, 1945
The young photographer, Shigeo Hayashi, arrived in Hiroshima two months after the bombing as part of an investigation team sent by the Ministry of Education. The photo taken from atop a still-standing building captures the scale of the destruction in the city center. Note the small figures of people on the road. (Photo by Shigeo Hayashi. Created by Ari Beser)

The terrifying impact on the ground that day would cast a dark cloud over the balance of the century. In 1942 President Franklin Roosevelt had set in motion the large-scale, top-secret effort known as the Manhattan Project to develop a nuclear weapon, the first of which was successfully tested in July 1945. Three weeks later the second bomb, known as "Little Boy," exploded with the strength of 13,500 tons of TNT on Hiroshima. Some 100,000 residents died at once, and several tens of thousands more would perish later as a result of blast, fire, and radiation, bringing the total to 130,000 to 150,000. This devastation in Hiroshima set off a chain of events that would bring World War II in the Pacific to a rapid conclusion. On August 8 the Soviet Union declared war against Japan. The next day the U.S. Air Force, following the established plan to use the remaining bomb ("Fat Man") as soon as operationally possible, instantly flattened the city of Nagasaki and killed a total of 60,000 to 80,000 people. On August 14, Japan offered to surrender. As the Japanese emperor delicately put it in a radio announcement to his subjects hearing his voice for the first time ever, "The war situation has developed not necessarily to Japan's advantage." On September 2 surrender ceremonies in Tokyo Bay brought the war in the Pacific to an official end.[3]

The American scientists who had turned theoretical notations into searing heat and crushing, deafening blast began to realize the ominous implications of their handiwork. The preeminent physicist Albert Einstein offered the memorable lament: "The unleashed power of the atom has changed everything save our modes of thinking, and thus we drift toward unparalleled catastrophe." Robert J. Oppenheimer, the director of the Los Alamos center where the first bombs were made, had at the first test in July 1945 watched a ball of light burst and swell in the desert dawn.

Oppenheimer later recalled that the foreboding line from one of the Hindu classics had jumped into his mind: "Now I have become death, the destroyer of worlds." These men's comments were prophetic: They understood that atomic bombs could now inflict destruction greater than conventional firebombing of Dresden in Germany or Japan's capital, Tokyo. They also understood that in time nuclear weapons would have the capacity to literally destroy worlds.[4]

The broad reaction within the United States to the nuclear dawn was at first euphoric. The *New York Times* reported the Hiroshima blast with banner headlines, stressing the extraordinary power of this new American weapon. Publicly President Harry Truman warned Japan of a "rain of ruin" while also welcoming "a new era in man's understanding of nature's forces," thus linking this triumph of science to promising peacetime uses. When Japan surrendered, he shared the joy of the troops gathering for the invasion of Japan. They would not have to endure an attack that would have cost many lives. Public opinion polls in the United States indicated a widespread view of nuclear weapons as a godsend. Two weeks after Hiroshima, 85 percent approved dropping the bomb. The "good" atom quickly entered U.S. popular culture in a lighthearted way through songs and popular new phrases such as "anatomic bomb" applied to a starlet a few weeks after Hiroshima. What the public and leading policymakers had not yet grasped was that the scientists in Germany and Japan, no less than in the Soviet Union and Britain, had already grasped the destructive potential of the atom but had not produced a bomb for sheer want of resources and commitment. In the postwar years that situation would change and the "good" atom would cease to be an American monopoly.[5]

For those in 1945 peering into the immediate future, the bomb posed acutely the nagging question of how states would use their power. Would they apply their imagination and resources to rebuilding a world battered by economic collapse and the second major war of the twentieth century? Or would they stumble amidst the ruins blinded by fear and enmity until the next cycle of bloodshed and destruction? All over the world those first postwar years witnessed a battle between hope and fear.

Nowhere was it more tempting to imagine better times ahead than in an emerging Third World in the grip of independence fever. Allied propaganda, most notably the Atlantic Charter proclaimed by Roosevelt and Churchill in 1941, had depicted World War II as a battle for freedom, and so Third World proponents of a new postwar order gladly saw it. Thus encouraged, they entertained dreams of rapidly realizing national liberation and social justice. Many were ready to turn their backs on the world of political anarchy, material deprivation, foreign domination, and battlefield carnage that they had grown up in. They wanted badly to believe that colonialism was over and that something better was within reach of their peoples. The leader of the Chinese Communist movement, Mao Zedong, concluded that Soviet–American cooperation signified nothing less than "the opening of a new stage in the history of the world"—one conducive to peace and reform in

China. Ho Chi Minh as the leader of a struggling anticolonial movement in Vietnam quoted from the American Declaration of Independence in August 1945 while proclaiming an end to French colonial control. That independence fever also gripped India, where a weakened Britain struggled to maintain control, as well as the Philippines, which the United States had already declared a readiness to free. In the General Assembly of the newly organized United Nations, the head of the Indian delegation, Vijaya Lakshmi Pandit, rose in December 1946 to protest religious and racial discrimination in the name of "millions of voiceless people" in Asia and Africa. "It is only on the foundation of justice that we can create a new world order," she cautioned.[6]

Popular hopes for peace and reconstruction also took shape within the societies of the major belligerents after an exhausting war. Throughout Europe voices called for focusing national attention and resources on social and political betterment after the upheaval and destruction that had blighted the earlier decades of the twentieth century and turned Europe from the showcase of civilization into an exhibit for human folly. Surely two world wars in 30 years was enough. In 1942 British historian E. H. Carr noticed especially among the younger generation a revulsion against "a bad and mad world" and a conviction that "almost everything in it needs to be uprooted and replanted." In the Soviet Union the population longed for a respite from the society-wide mobilization campaigns that their leaders had imposed on them, first to collectivize agriculture and build up the economy and then to repulse the German invaders. One Soviet veteran recalled how as the war approached its end, soldiers dwelt on the promise of postwar life: "We pictured things in rainbow colors." Although spared the direct effects of fighting on their own soil, Americans, too, longed to put the pinch of depression and the sacrifice of war behind them. In 1943 the poet Archibald MacLeish looked out from his wartime office in Washington and thought that he saw forming not only in his own country but around the world a determination to turn the sacrifice of war into "something admirable, something of human worth and human significance."[7]

But an undercurrent of fear was already building as the war came to an end. Nuclear weapons at once injected a dangerous new dynamic into the U.S.–Soviet relationship. They would figure as a major impetus for the Cold War and one of its defining features. Adding to the fear was a dark Cold War vision of moral struggle that promised more sacrifice and danger—looming tests on the battlefield, a race for nuclear advantage, and the specter of internal subversion. Hardly had the war ended than those fears took form in Washington and Moscow. They would soon begin to shape U.S. and Soviet foreign policy and spill over into their respective societies. With the U.S. and Soviet leaders (Harry Truman and Joseph Stalin) as the presiding presences, the Cold War began to etch a line across the globe.

As hopes gave way to fears, Cold War concerns increasingly informed superpower plans for the war-wounded countries of Europe and Asia. In Japan and western Europe it was the United States that prevailed in collaboration with conservative elites operating through center-right parties, while in eastern Europe, the Soviets exerted strong control, making genuine self-determination as problematic as in any traditional sphere of great-power influence. With superpower political influence also went the promotion of a way of life: "Coca-colonization" on one side of the Cold War divide and socialist education on the other.

The miasma of Cold War fears gradually engulfed the Third World, throwing a major obstacle in the way of impatient liberators and destroying their sanguine expectations for the postwar period. Washington listened anxiously to the rising call for decolonization and reacted with outright hostility where decolonization threatened to unleash radical programs at odds with the American political and economic model or with U.S. Cold War interests. Stalin, for whom suspicion was second nature, was only marginally more receptive to Third World voices. Here as in general he was cautious in dealing with states and situations that he could not control. And he was in any case eager not to provoke the United States or waste scarce resources on distant and dubious causes. The superpowers thus in combination made the inherently difficult path toward national independence and domestic renovation more arduous, prolonged, and dangerous.

For witnesses to the immediate postwar years, whatever their vantage point on the surface of the globe, every step forward seemed matched in these turbulent times by a step back. Hopes for peace barely survived rising Cold War tensions and even a limited war in Korea. Hopes for prosperity struggled through a time of economic adjustment and reconstruction with little sense of the long-term benefit that the global system of trade and investment then beginning to take shape might yield. Science and technology, which could deliver higher living standards, showed their potential for destruction in the American Manhattan Project and its Soviet counterpart. Finally, dreams of independence among those under foreign domination quickly ran up against the tenacity of colonial powers, the intrusion of the Cold War rivals, and often deeply divergent views about the future within countries charting a fresh course. While in retrospect we can see that the first years after 1945 marked the beginning of a new era, it was far less clear to people at the time. Did these events that buffeted their lives add up to something better or worse for them and their children?

1

THE COLD WAR: TOWARD SOVIET–AMERICAN CONFRONTATION

THE UNITED STATES and the Soviet Union emerged from World War II the dominant powers. They looked out on a devastated world. Except for the United States, all the major participants in the war were economically wounded. American leaders could see the potential for chaos that might in turn invite communist subversion or invasion. Just as plausibly, Soviet leaders had good reason to suspect that the United States might exploit its unrivaled economic power to extend its influence. Guided by their competing political and economic views, those two powers not surprisingly collided over postwar arrangements, above all for Europe.

That collision produced the Cold War. Wartime cooperation turned into a decades-long rivalry in part because of the simple bipolar division of international power created by World War II and the ideological antagonisms taking shape as early as World War I (both noted in the introduction). The personalities of Soviet and American leaders in the mid-1940s and the sudden intrusion of the nuclear issue into the Soviet–American relationship also played an important part in generating tension. Taken together, these ingredients proved a potent combination. Soon each side began to mobilize against the other, with effects that would reverberate throughout both societies and increasingly around the world. But the Soviet Union and the United States avoided a direct military contest. Both preferred to do their fighting through proxies, avoid the risks of nuclear war, but otherwise pursue their rivalry in every imaginable way. "Cold War" was a fitting name.

ORIGINS OF THE RIVALRY

Controversy has long surrounded the opening phase of the Cold War. The debate began during the late 1940s, revived in the 1960s with the publication of official U.S. documents, and picked up again in the 1990s following the opening of Soviet records. The controversy has consistently turned on the question of responsibility for initiating the struggle. Do we conclude that both Americans and Soviets over-reacted and exaggerated the threat from the other side? Or do we place primary blame on one side—or not place blame at all? These questions remain worthy of debate. Arriving at convincing answers requires first a basic understanding of the specific steps that carried the two powers to their historic confrontation. We then need to see that series of steps from the distinct perspectives of the American leaders, Franklin D. Roosevelt and Harry Truman, and their Soviet counterpart, Joseph Stalin.

From Cooperation to Conflict

The Soviet–American rivalry began with the two powers' involvement in World War II. Germany launched a surprise attack against the Soviet Union in June 1941. That attack pushed leaders in Washington and Moscow from wariness of each other toward alliance against a common foe. The Japanese attack on Pearl Harbor the following December completed the process of alliance formation by bringing the United States fully into the global war. President Franklin Roosevelt was eager to keep Russians fighting while the American war machine got into high gear. He drew an embattled Soviet Union into a coalition that already included Britain and China. In early 1943 Soviet forces turned back the German invaders and began their drive to Germany's capital, Berlin, and in the middle of the next year American and British forces landed in France to open a second front against Germany. The Allies had thus only begun their march on Germany, whereas Soviet forces were already occupying eastern Europe. The Soviet military advance would give Stalin a distinct advantage in negotiating the postwar settlement. At the same time Roosevelt was asking for Soviet participation in what was expected to be the last bloody phase of the war against Japan.

By 1945 the Soviet–American alliance had passed its high point of cooperation and entered a time of strain. The first notable signs of tension appeared in February at Yalta (a Crimean resort on the Black Sea) where Stalin hosted Roosevelt and British Prime Minister Winston Churchill. While Stalin reassured Roosevelt with the promise that Soviet forces would intervene in the war against Japan soon after the defeat of Germany, the leaders otherwise sparred over the postwar settlement in Europe. The most divisive issue was the political future of Poland.

Germany's surrender in May and the obvious weakening of Japan intensified the pressure to reach agreement on peace terms. To that end the Big Three of the alliance (the Soviet Union, the United States, and Britain) met in July 1945 at Potsdam on the outskirts of devastated Berlin. This was the occasion for the first and only meeting between Stalin and Roosevelt's successor, Harry S. Truman. A month later the final act of the global war played out in a rush with the dropping of the two U.S. atomic bombs on Japan, the entry of Soviet forces into the Pacific War, and Japan's surrender. Despite the welcome peace, terms of the postwar set-tlement remained a sensitive issue among the former allies. Through 1946 Moscow and Washington managed to maintain a publicly civil stance, but privately the acid of suspicion on both sides was corroding the relationship. Soviet troops that had entered China's northeast provinces (Manchuria) and northern Iran during the war were becoming a particular source of irritation in Washington. Even more worrisome was Moscow's tightening grip on Poland, Czechoslovakia, Hungary, Romania, and Bulgaria. Thanks to the presence of the Soviet army and Moscow's support, Communist parties in those countries began imposing themselves despite their minority status. The future of an occupied Germany remained unsettled, with the lines of division hardening between the Soviet-controlled zone and the rest where the Americans, British, and French were in control.

The end of the road on the way to the Cold War came in 1947 as American and Soviet leaders publicly proclaimed the world divided into two antagonistic blocs. Americans took the lead. In March in a speech to Congress, Truman proposed a program of assistance to Greece and Turkey. This speech announced what would become known as the Truman Doctrine, a commitment by the United States to take a stand against the perceived global threat posed by communism to free peoples everywhere. A few months later Truman's secretary of state, George Marshall, announced a fresh initiative—an ambitious program that became known as the Marshall Plan to help rebuild and stabilize European economies and preempt any popular turn toward communist programs.

FROM WORLD WAR TO COLD WAR

1945	February	Roosevelt, Stalin, and Churchill meet at Yalta
	April	Roosevelt's death puts Truman in the White House
	May	Germany surrenders
	July 16	First U.S. A-bomb tested while Truman and Stalin spar over the future of eastern Europe at the Potsdam conference
	August 6	A-bomb dropped on Hiroshima
	August 8	Soviet Union declares war on Japan
	August 9	A-bomb dropped on Nagasaki
	August 14	Japan offers to surrender
1946	Spring	U.S.–Soviet tensions develop over Soviet troops in northeast China and Iran and over Communist party control in eastern Europe
1947	March	Truman uses proposal for aid to Greece and Turkey to declare Truman Doctrine
	June	Marshall Plan proposed for European economic recovery
	September	Stalin sees collapse of cooperation with the United States and organizes Cominform as first step toward tightening grip on eastern Europe

Stalin was close behind in endorsing the view of a fundamentally divided world. He responded with alarm to the Marshall Plan and called for a meeting of Europe's major Communist parties for September to create a coordinating body, the Communist Information Bureau (Cominform). The Soviet delegates set the tone at that meeting with their call to European Communists and "progressive forces" around the world to rally against an expansionist United States.

These two emergent rivals both claimed superpower status, but they did not in fact stand on an equal footing. The United States enjoyed a number of important advantages over the Soviet Union. Americans had suffered relatively little from World War II. There had been no fighting on their soil, and American casualties came to only 300,000, while the Soviet Union would lose over 6 million soldiers and some 20 million civilians at the hands of the German army as it marched deep into Soviet territory. Moreover, the United States enjoyed the advantage of an economy that had more than doubled in the value of gross national product (GNP; see "Key Economic Terms" on p. 15) in the course of the war, while the Soviet economy had suffered serious destruction. Finally, the United States came out of the war with a marked military advantage. Washington commanded the only major navy and air force and held a monopoly on nuclear weapons. Although the Soviets had the largest ground force (11.3 million men), peace brought a steep and rapid demobilization.

U.S. Policy in Transition

U.S. foreign policy underwent a major transformation in 1945 and 1946. Roosevelt and then Truman were responsible for managing that policy, especially the sensitive relationship with the Soviet Union. They had contrasting backgrounds and personalities and thus not surprisingly saw international developments and shaped U.S. policy along somewhat different lines. In making any comparison, however, it is important to keep in mind the differing contexts in which they operated. Roosevelt was president at the height of wartime cooperation among the Allies, while Truman took charge in the midst of the rocky transition to peace.

Roosevelt, a New York patrician, had enjoyed the best private schooling, including a Harvard education. He had taken as his political model none other than his own cousin, Theodore Roosevelt, a two-term president and larger-than-life public figure early in the twentieth century. During World War I, while serving as an assistant secretary of navy, FDR had warmly embraced President Woodrow Wilson's dream of the United States playing a larger role in ordering the world, and he stayed true to that dream while running unsuccessfully in 1920 as the Democratic Party's vice-presidential nominee. Despite crippling polio, he stayed in politics and in 1932 tried for the presidency—and won.

Once in office, Roosevelt focused on the deep economic depression gripping the country and sought to stay clear of international entanglements. Like many Americans, he believed that participation in World War I had been a serious mistake. Pushing Wilson's plans for international reform had come to seem a bad idea.

But by 1937 the Wilsonian in Roosevelt revived as he watched the rise of two international outlaws, Japan in Asia and Germany in Europe. He cautiously led the country toward greater support for China, Britain, and the Soviet Union in their respective contests with Japan and Germany. Even before the Japanese attack on Pearl Harbor pushed the United States fully into World War II, he publicly tied the Allied cause to the distinctly Wilsonian aims of creating a new international order. The Atlantic Charter, proclaimed by Churchill and Roosevelt in August 1941, enshrined the goals of this new order. The postwar world was to be governed by the principles of self-determination and support for democracy, collective security through what was to become the United Nations, and the freedom to trade and travel the high seas. Once in the war, Roosevelt made clear that he would settle for nothing less than the unconditional surrender of Germany and Japan, clearing the way for thoroughgoing internal reforms of both countries so that they could be made into respectable members of international society.

The United Nations was the most prominent symbol of this return to Wilson's program. The League of Nations had been the centerpiece of his plans for a peaceful, democratic world. But the Senate and seemingly the electorate in the 1920 presidential vote had rejected the League along with Wilson's overall peace plan. With the onset of a new world war, Roosevelt resolved to make a second attempt at creating a league. When the 51 nations fighting the Axis met in San Francisco in spring 1945 to form the new international organization, they divided it into two bodies. A security council was to consist of the big-five states of the time (the United States, the Soviet Union, France, Britain, and China), together with a rotating group of other states. Each of the big five was to have veto power over UN action. The General Assembly was to contain all member states. It would make its decisions by majority vote, and those decisions would be nonbinding. Unlike Wilson, Roosevelt won overwhelming Senate support for U.S. membership in this new league, and as a sign of his country's commitment arranged to place the UN headquarters in the United States.

Privately, however, FDR's thinking about the immediate postwar period revealed him a wary Wilsonian. In a letter in 1943 he claimed to see ahead "a trial or transition period after the fighting stops—we might call it even a period of trial and error." He favored setting aside difficult international issues for two to four years while "shell shocked" societies around the world recovered. To keep the peace during this transitional period, Roosevelt wanted Russia, China, Britain, and the United States to work together—in effect to "act as sheriffs for the maintenance of order." These "four policemen" would control Japan and Germany, preside over the UN, and generally maintain the peace. Rigid, universal principles should not get in the way of reconciling the divergent interests among the Allies. This goal of maintaining a working relationship among the Allies meant in concrete terms accepting, for the time being at least, Moscow's ambitions along the Soviet periphery as well as the continued existence of the British empire. Self-determination might have to wait.[1]

Churchill, Roosevelt, and Stalin at Yalta, February 1945
Although this is a posed, formal photo, it highlights the vigor of the British and Soviet leaders in contrast to the American president: His face is sagging, his eyes are dark and hollow, his jaw is slack, and his hands are drooping. These signs of declining health foreshadow the president's death only a few months later and would subsequently raise questions in the mind of Roosevelt's critics about his effectiveness in dealing with Stalin at this pivotal moment as the war in Europe drew to a close. (Franklin D. Roosevelt Presidential Library & Museum)

At Yalta, his last major meeting with Stalin, Roosevelt hewed to this middle way. He conceded the Soviet Union's special interests along its border (reflecting his view that great powers had to respect the influence that each wielded within its own region). At the same time he pushed Stalin to respect self-determination in Poland and neighboring countries occupied by the Red Army. He realized, however, that the implementation of self-determination would have to be gradual, and that continued goodwill and cooperation among the powers (each secure in its interests) was the best way to create a better world. More immediately, he saw that cooperation as a way to keep the coalition together through the final phase of World War II and into the period of peacemaking.

In April 1945, with the German Third Reich in ruins and Japan under constant aerial bombardment, Roosevelt died at age 63 at his vacation retreat at Warm Springs, Georgia. His death put Vice President Harry S. Truman, just two years FDR's junior, in the White House. Truman could with justification call himself a "man of the people." He was raised in Independence, Missouri, a town whose pace and mores epitomized middle America. His family was of modest means, and he had little formal education. After fighting in France during World War I and then struggling in business after the war, Truman gave politics a try. He joined the Missouri Democratic political machine. He began his training in his new line of work at the state level and in 1934 advanced to the U.S. Senate. In 1944 FDR plucked

Truman from relative obscurity to play the role of the bland vice-presidential candidate needed on the Democratic ticket.

On the afternoon of April 12, 1945, Vice President Truman was called to the White House. Tight-jawed, he arrived to hear the newly widowed Eleanor Roosevelt say, "Harry, the president is dead." After a hastily called meeting with the Roosevelt cabinet, Truman was sworn in. Through that terrible day, it dawned on the new president how difficult his situation was. The next day he asked some reporters to pray for him. Roosevelt's death had left him feeling "like the moon, the stars, and all the planets had fallen on me."[2]

Truman was ill prepared to bear the daunting responsibility for the last phase of the war and for the peacemaking challenge. He was dogged by self-doubt. How could he possibly fill the shoes of a great man and beloved leader? Truman was unversed in international affairs and the making of foreign policy, and he had seen Roosevelt only eight times in his last year. Truman had to act with arguably less insight into Roosevelt's wartime strategy and commitments than anyone else in the upper levels of the administration.

With little time for preparation, a president in need of guidance fell back on his own general views. At the core of those views was a fairly stark, pugnaciously held Wilsonian faith. Truman believed deeply in the principle of self-determination and the duty of the United States to lead a community of free peoples. He looked back with pride on his country's sacrifice in World War I. While others had developed second thoughts about Wilson's crusade, Truman had held rock steady. He welcomed participation in World War II as an opportunity for the country to redeem the earlier lost chance to play a constructive role in world affairs. Truman's view of what U.S. foreign policy should be was also informed by his reading of history as an ongoing contest between civilization and barbarism waged by a succession of major powers. The United States had in his day emerged as the foremost of the civilized countries, and now had to fulfill its duty to prevent aggression and discipline wrongdoers.

Truman also depended on advisers inherited from the Roosevelt administration. They offered him contradictory guidance, beginning with the sensitive issue of Soviet influence in Poland. On one side was a set of political conservatives and anti-Soviet diplomats previously ignored by FDR. They argued for taking a firm line. Specifically, they contended that Poland was a test case of Soviet intentions toward the postwar world and of the American commitment to self-determination. Some even warned the new president that he faced a "barbarian invasion of Europe." On the other side was a group that had worked closely with Roosevelt throughout the war. They questioned the wisdom of taking a hardline stance on Poland, a country right on the Soviet border. Secretary of War Henry L. Stimson wondered whether "the Russians perhaps were being more realistic than we were in regard to their own security." He and others argued that a diplomacy of compromise was essential to keeping the Soviets involved in the final phase of the war against Japan and to sustaining good relations with Stalin into the postwar period.[3]

From the start the new president tilted sharply to the side of the hardliners. They offered clear-cut advice that was consistent with Truman's general outlook as well as his desire to show himself, despite his inexperience, a tough, decisive policymaker. He assured them of his intention "to be firm with the Russians and make no concessions from American principles or traditions" to win them over.[4] A marked shift in the tone of high-level discussions on Soviet policy became strikingly evident in the first meetings that Truman held in late April. While the hardliners were to stay on as his chief advisers, some former FDR intimates began to leave, exhausted by long service or dismayed by the new, increasingly belligerent tone.

Policy toward the Soviet Union did not shift abruptly but rather vacillated through the balance of 1945. Truman was not yet certain in his get-tough views and in any case was unready to translate those views into an unambiguous policy of confrontation. He still needed Soviet support in imposing unconditional surrender on Japan, and the public wanted peace and demobilization, not a renewal of international tensions. In talks with the Soviets in London and Moscow late in the year, Truman's new secretary of state, James F. Byrnes, expressed Washington's profound resentment over the Soviet breach of the principle of self-determination in eastern Europe but finally agreed to recognize the Soviet-backed governments there. Meanwhile, the Pentagon demobilized the armed forces. Standing forces would fall from 12.1 million in 1945 to 1.6 million in 1947, while the military budget would drop between those years from $81 billion to $13 billion. At the same time the Pentagon set up military bases around the world to ensure that no enemy would be able to strike suddenly across the Atlantic or Pacific in the way that Japan had. Despite calls to seek an international agreement on nuclear arms, Truman was not about to compromise his monopoly of a weapon that had helped bring Japan to its knees and that gave the United States a distinct edge over the Soviet Union. In the fall of 1945 he rejected Secretary of War Stimson's proposal to consult with the Soviets on nuclear issues in order to establish an atmosphere of trust. The next year the Truman administration as well as the Soviets offered plans to forestall a nuclear arms race, but neither was serious about finding common ground.

In the course of 1946 Truman ended his vacillation over which road to take. In January the angry president privately denounced what he now saw clearly as Stalin's designs on Iran, Turkey, and the Dardanelles (the narrow passage that provided Soviet ships an outlet from the Black Sea to the Mediterranean) just as he had gone after the Baltic states of Latvia, Estonia, and Lithuania in 1940 and Poland after the war. "Unless Russia is faced with an iron fist and strong language[,] another war is in the making. Only one language do they understand— 'How many divisions have you?'" He resolved not to recognize Soviet-dominated Romania and Bulgaria. He would defend Iran and China's northeast provinces against Soviet troops that had entered during the war and had stayed beyond the

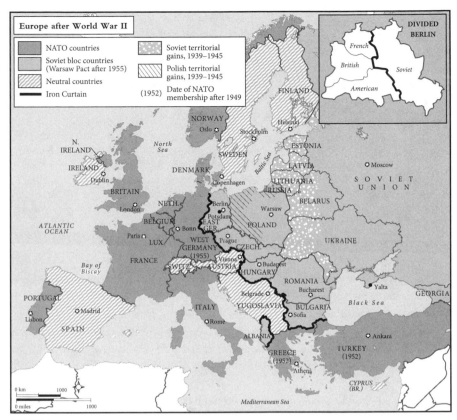

MAP 1.1
Europe after World War II

deadline for their withdrawal. He would assert control over Japan and the entire Pacific and make sure that China and South Korea had strong central governments able to resist communism. He concluded, "I'm tired babying the Soviets."[5]

Truman's private fears over aggressive Soviet intentions were soon confirmed by the analysis by Soviet expert George Kennan serving in the Moscow embassy. Responding to a speech delivered by Stalin in February 1946 generally perceived in the United States as a declaration of hostility, Kennan offered an interpretation of Soviet policy that was at once embraced in official circles. The Kremlin suffered from a "neurotic view of world affairs," rooted in the "traditional and instinctive Russian sense of insecurity." It was further distorted by a Marxist ideology that "is seemingly inaccessible to considerations of reality in its basic reactions." The result was "a political force committed fanatically to the belief that with US there can be no permanent *modus vivendi*, that it is desirable and necessary that the internal harmony of our society be disrupted, our traditional way of life be destroyed, the international authority of our state be broken, if Soviet power is to be secure."[6]

Harry Truman Fishing off the Florida Coast, 1946
Truman escaped the pressures of policy and politics in Washington for the relaxing routine of fishing and poker with his aides. (U.S. Navy, Courtesy of Harry S. Truman Library)

But, he stressed, Soviet leaders were cautious and sensitive to the logic of force. If the United States and its allies stood firm in the face of attempted Soviet expansion, then it would be possible to hold the line and in the long term force internal changes in the Soviet system. This formulation by Kennan evolved into a policy known as "containment." It stipulated that Soviet pressure at any point would be met by U.S. counterforce. Containment became the master doctrine for U.S. Cold War policy.

Truman's bottled-up concerns over the Soviet threat began bubbling over. In June, he fulminated in his diary, "Get plenty of Atomic Bombs on hand—drop one on Stalin, put the United Nations to work and eventually set up a free world." Finally, Soviet pressure on Turkey and apparent Soviet sponsorship of a leftist insurgency in Greece pushed Truman to make his views public. The Truman Doctrine proclaimed in March 1947 effectively declared that the United States was embarked on a Cold War. More important than the call for aid to Greece and Turkey was the president's stark picture of a world divided between two ways of life—one defined by the path toward freedom and the other toward totalitarian control. The United States would now take as its fundamental policy "to support free peoples who are resisting attempted subjugation by armed minorities or by outside pressures." In the monumental struggle now looming, free countries and peoples around the world looked to the United States. "If we falter in our leadership," Truman warned, "we may endanger the peace of the world—and we shall surely endanger the welfare of this Nation."[7]

Some within the administration worried that the speech made an open-ended commitment at a time of budgetary stringency, while public critics doubted the inherent wisdom of the president's sweeping statement on the defense of freedom. But Truman stuck to his promise to defend threatened countries everywhere, even on the periphery of American global interests and even where for the moment American forces could not reach without leaving Europe vulnerable. The

announcement a few months later of the Marshall Plan to rebuild the European economies revealed his determination to make good on this commitment beginning with
the region judged the highest priority in the emerging rivalry with the Soviets.

Stalin's Pursuit of Territory and Security

Joseph Stalin dominated the Soviet scene to a degree unequaled in the United States
by Truman or even Roosevelt. Stalin was born in the Russian empire's southern
province of Georgia in 1879. He began studying for the priesthood but was
thrown out of seminary for revolutionary activity and (some accounts say) laziness.
After the 1917 Bolshevik revolution he climbed to prominence in the new ruling
Communist Party thanks to his administrative skills and adroit political maneuvering. As party general secretary, he demonstrated patience, avoided controversy,
and built up a following of supporters.

Following Lenin's death in 1924, Stalin made himself the dominant figure in
the party. By 1929 he had fully consolidated his control and proceeded to make
the party-state serve as an extension of his will and vision for almost a quarter-
century. Within this highly centralized political system lower-level committees
formed the mass base of the party pyramid (about 4 percent of the population in
the Stalin years). Near the top was a central committee elected by what were supposed to be regular party congresses. The top 10 or so central committee members
stood at the apex of the pyramid. As members of the Politburo (short for Political
Bureau), their task was to guide the party and direct the operations of the state.
In practice they took their cues from Stalin.

Stalin brought to his era of unchallenged control a variety of striking personality traits. He was provincial in his outlook and thus markedly at odds with the
cosmopolitan group that had surrounded Lenin and taken a leading role in the
founding of the Soviet state. Stalin was neither intellectually cultivated nor well
traveled. He proved a domineering leader who insisted on making the final decision on a wide range of issues. Comrades turned into servile courtiers full of praise
for the "genius leader," or they fell victim to his mistrust.

What Stalin's successors would come to call a dangerous cult of personality reflected not just his drive to dominance but also a terrible suspicion of others.
Paranoia drove him to fix blame for errors that he regarded as serious whether in
family matters or party and national affairs. Almost invariably the blame came to
rest on one person or class of people even if the likelihood of their responsibility
was highly improbable. He rejected explanations that involved abstract forces,
bad luck, or a complex combination of events. He wanted a clear villain to hold accountable. For example, when the Germans captured his son during World War II,
he inexplicably blamed the son's wife and had her arrested. Once he had found a
scapegoat, he was an implacable avenger impervious to appeals from the "guilty"
party, relatives and friends, and respected colleagues. In the world Stalin controlled,
one serious mistake could prove disastrous for an individual, a family, or a whole
class of people. This paranoia, sometimes manipulated by Stalin's underlings to

their own advantage, injected fear and mistrust into elite Soviet political and intellectual circles and spelled misery, even death, for millions whom he judged a threat to him or his program.

In the late 1940s, just as Cold War tensions sharpened, an increasingly frail Stalin grew more suspicious, finding enemies all around him. First it was the Communist Party organization in Leningrad. He had it purged in 1949 and had six of its leaders executed. Lesser purges followed in Moscow, Estonia, and Georgia. He became obsessed with the idea that Soviet Jews, abetted by British and American intelligence, were plotting against him. His suspicions finally settled in November 1952 on the doctors, predominantly Jewish, assigned to the Kremlin. Under torture, they admitted to conspiring to kill the leadership. Stalin showed the confessions to his colleagues and lamented, "You are like blind kittens; what will happen without me? The country will perish because you don't know how to recognize enemies." As the circle of suspicion narrowed, Stalin wondered aloud whether close colleagues were also working for Western intelligence agencies. Those at Stalin's side well knew that a personal misstep or a rival's slander might plant the seeds of deadly suspicion in their master's mind. They were thus "temporary people," as future Soviet leader Nikita Khrushchev chillingly put it. "As long as he trusted us to a certain degree, we were allowed to go on living and working. But the moment he stopped trusting you, Stalin would start to scrutinize you until the cup of his distrust overflowed. Then it would be your turn to follow those who were no longer among the living."[8]

Stalin's handling of his relationship with the United States was to some degree conditioned by his personality. But arguably more important was his fixation from the late 1930s onward with a surprisingly traditional set of territorial aims. Acting like a latter-day czar, he focused relentlessly on restoring the land once attached to the Russian empire stretching across Eurasia. He also gave priority (as had the czars) to promoting influence in areas along the Russian periphery, especially in eastern Europe but also in East Asia. Where the old empire had been dominant, Stalin wanted to be dominant. Where territory and privileges had been lost, Stalin wanted them back. In his devotion to these goals, Stalin played the diplomat— shrewd, hard bargaining, cautious, and opportunistic. His achievements in this regard were formidable, evident in gains all along the Soviet border.

Stalin might talk the language of Lenin and even see the world through the prism of Marxist-Leninist concepts, but he had long since abandoned early Bolshevik hopes for world revolution. As he saw it, a strong and secure Soviet Union was the best guarantee of socialism's ultimate global victory. Already in the interwar period he had put the Soviet Union first. In keeping with the priority he gave security along the Soviet border, Stalin treated the international communist movement as an instrument of Soviet foreign policy and, where necessary, sacrificed Communist movements in other lands to advance Soviet goals.

In contrast to a consistent policy on border areas, Stalin's policy toward the United States moved by zigs and zags toward Cold War enmity. In large measure this was the result of his understanding of what made capitalist powers such as the United States tick. Stalin's own training as a disciple of Marx and Lenin led him in two rather distinct directions. The official orthodoxy pushed him toward suspicion of their intentions, reinforcing a tendency that also derived from Stalin's paranoia and historical sense of Russian vulnerability. But he also believed that capitalist states, however malign their intentions, were ultimately not formidable threats. Like other Marxists, he was confident that their maturing capitalist economies faced crises that would sooner or later precipitate an internal collapse or a debilitating war among them over markets. Whichever course it took, capitalism was a doomed system that daily grew weaker while the Soviet Union grew stronger. Out of the debris of capitalist collapse, socialist states would arise to cooperate with the Soviet Union in constructing a new world order. Time was on the Soviet side.

Initially Stalin had good reason for suspicion of the United States. Shortly after the Bolshevik revolution, U.S. as well as British, French, and Japanese forces had intervened militarily against it. In the 1930s they had refused to cooperate with the Soviet Union against Adolf Hitler. Stalin then shifted to appeasement of Hitler and sought to extract the best bargain possible. Their 1939 nonaggression pact laid the basis for Soviet control over parts of Poland. The surprise German attack in June 1941 betrayed Stalin's calculations. Badly shaken, a dejected Soviet leader moaned, "Lenin left us a state and we have turned it to shit."[9] The only bright spot was that the disaster would move Washington to align with Moscow against their new common enemy.

Stalin entered the alliance from a position of weakness. Overrun by German forces, he desperately needed supplies and the prompt opening of a second European front that would draw away German divisions. FDR was forthcoming with the supplies, but repeated delays in launching Anglo-American military operations on the European continent left Stalin fuming. In November 1942 American and British troops finally went into action in North Africa and moved into Italy in 1943; however, the overdue cross-channel invasion of France did not take place until June 1944. In the meantime, the Soviet Union bore the brunt of the struggle against Germany.

Stalin complained about British and American military passivity but otherwise put the best face on the situation. In November 1943 he pronounced his alliance with the two major capitalist powers in good shape despite (as he phrased it) their "different ideologies and social systems."[10] At the same time, he associated himself with the broad Anglo-American war aims such as national self-determination. That same year he formally disbanded the Comintern, set up in 1919 to promote world revolution, as a goodwill gesture to his capitalist allies.

By 1944 Stalin's military position had gone from weak to strong. Soviet forces were advancing on Germany. When the Allies met at Yalta early in 1945, Stalin agreed to enter the Pacific War within three months after the end of the European war. In return he secured his claim to territory lost to Japan in 1905 and during World War I (the Kuril Islands and the southern half of Sakhalin) and to the former

Russian sphere of influence in China's northeast region. Exactly three months after Germany's surrender in May 1945, Stalin made good on his promise to join the fight against Japan. The Soviet declaration of war together with the American atomic bombing quickly forced Japan's capitulation. The end of the war found the Soviet Union the dominant power across Eurasia.

Two interrelated concerns regarding the shape of the postwar settlement were already preoccupying Stalin by late 1944. One was the prospect for maintaining the Soviet–American partnership on a mutually advantageous basis. The Marxist theoretician in Stalin told him that the postwar American economy would need markets to absorb its excess production and surplus capital. Stalin could help Roosevelt hold economic crisis at bay and at the same time speed Soviet reconstruction by opening his country to American goods and capital. Cooperation would gain time for him to rebuild and consolidate his wartime gains while securing international acceptance of the Red Army's recovery of territory from Japan and Russia's dominance in eastern Europe. In practical terms this last consideration was probably the most important in Stalin's dealings with the United States.

Stalin's most immediate concern was the future of Poland. That country had served as an invasion route into Russia three times—by Napoleon in 1812, by Germany in 1914, and by Germany again in 1941. Each time the invaders had penetrated deeply into Russian territory and left behind appalling destruction. Stalin had already tried to bar this strategic Polish door to Russia when in 1939 he agreed with Hitler on a partition—but had gotten an invasion anyway. Once the Red Army had turned the Germans back, Stalin seized his second chance to solve this strategic problem. He agreed with his alliance partners on restoring an independent Poland, but he also wanted that new Poland to be pro-Soviet and to hand over to him land in the east in exchange for German land in the west. When the conservative Polish government in exile in London rejected a deal, Stalin turned to the Polish Communist Party. That weak and divided party needed the Red Army to gain and maintain power and thus was ready to subordinate itself on the territorial issue as on other matters.

Stalin's unilateral decision to deal with the Communist-controlled Polish provisional government based in Lublin did not sit well with his British and American partners. At the Yalta conference Stalin defended his action on the grounds of immediate wartime necessity and long-term Soviet security interests. The advancing Red Army, he explained, required a friendly administration in its rear area, and the Soviet Union needed to be sure that Poland did not serve again as Germany's invasion route. FDR conceded the legitimacy of Stalin's concerns while at the same time pressing for an Allied agreement on self-determination that would give the London Poles a role in a reorganized, broad-based government. Churchill was even more emphatic in defense of London's Poles. The Yalta conference closed with a declaration on liberated Europe pledging respect for democratic forms and providing a diplomatic mechanism for constituting a generally acceptable Polish government. The declaration made no reference to Soviet security interests, but Stalin would not (as it turned out) let go of what his army had won for him. He spelled out this basic principle several months later: "Whoever occupies a territory also imposes on it his own social system. Everyone imposes his own system as far as his army can reach."[11]

Once Harry Truman took over the White House, Stalin faced additional challenges and slights from the Americans. Immediately after victory in Europe and despite the Soviet commitment to join in the war against Japan, the Truman administration made an abrupt and awkwardly executed decision to cut off aid to the Soviets and followed a policy toward eastern Europe that made no allowance for Soviet interests. The ill omens continued. Truman surrounded the U.S. atomic bomb project with secrecy (just as Roosevelt had), and at Potsdam he informed Stalin of the first successful test in only the most terse and casual terms. Then, despite the Soviet Union's intervention in the Pacific War, Stalin found himself effectively excluded from a real role in the postwar occupation of Japan. Finally, by early 1946 Washington was beginning to apply pressure to get Soviet troops out of China and Iran.

Truman's off-handed announcement of the first U.S. nuclear test set off alarm bells even though Stalin had reacted with feigned indifference. He was already aware of a top-secret U.S. nuclear weapons program thanks to his intelligence services, and indeed had in fall 1942 initiated a parallel Soviet program at the urging of Soviet scientists and in late 1944 put Beria in charge to move work along. The bombing of Hiroshima prompted Stalin to observe that it "has shaken the world. The balance has been destroyed."[12] The Soviet bomb project pushed urgently ahead, assisted by technical details about the U.S. bomb secured through espionage.

Stalin's reaction to the ominous developments in U.S. policy was otherwise surprisingly restrained. He maintained a rough-edged working relationship with the Truman administration, seeking an understanding that would ratify Soviet territorial gains and win acceptance of Soviet standing as a leading power in the postwar world. Although irritated by U.S. policy, he couched his comments to both Hopkins and Truman in the language of hardheaded bargaining and accommodation of mutual interests.

Following Japan's surrender, a fatigued Stalin (now in his mid-sixties) took a long vacation on the Black Sea. He could take satisfaction from the way heavy Soviet sacrifices in the war had paid off in major gains along the Soviet periphery. He had in 1940 seized the Baltic states of Estonia, Latvia, and Lithuania. He had extended the Soviet border westward at the expense of Finland, Poland, Czechoslovakia, Hungary, and Romania. Thanks to the Red Army, he controlled part of Germany and Austria and exercised a strong political influence throughout eastern Europe. He had regained Russian privileges in China's northeastern provinces, recovered influence in Korea lost a half-century earlier, and redeemed territory lost to Japan. These were by any standard impressive achievements. Having repaired the breaches suffered by the Russian empire, Stalin was determined to hold his advanced positions.

Stalin expressed, at least in public, a hopeful view about the prospects for cooperation. In the February 1946 speech that George Kennan and other American policymakers had found so alarming, Stalin focused not on international dangers but on the tasks of rebuilding at home. He balanced a vaguely worded injunction to raise production over the next two decades—so that "our homeland will be guaranteed against all possible accidents"—with a reference linking the United States and Britain to the Soviet Union as "freedom-loving" states. The next month the Soviet leader decried warmongering by British leader Winston Churchill, while in September insisting that cooperation was still possible between countries with different ideologies.[13]

To calm U.S. policymakers increasingly agitated by evidence of Soviet expansion, Stalin also staged a series of retreats. He pulled his forces out of northeastern China, Iran, and several points in Scandinavia, and dropped demands for changing the rules for passage of ships through the Dardanelles. Military spending continued to fall from its wartime high, while the steep demobilization of his wartime force continued apace.

But in the course of 1947 Stalin's hopes for avoiding estrangement gradually evaporated. In March Truman laid down his doctrine drawing an ideological line around the world, and a few months later endorsed the Marshall Plan. Stalin's reaction was somewhat mixed. For example, an insurgency in Greece launched in late 1944 and led by the Greek Communist Party proved an inconvenience to Stalin's management of relations with his old capitalist allies, so he pressed Yugoslavia, Albania, and Bulgaria to terminate their support for the insurgents. Moreover, he did not immediately reject the Marshall Plan and even went so far as to send a delegation to explore its details. But after deciding that the United States was trying to use its economic power to tighten its grip on Europe, he withdrew his delegation and took his European clients with him.

The Marshall Plan finally moved Stalin to accept the idea of a Cold War dividing line between the two rival blocs, and he began to take a tougher stance on his side. As we have seen, to counter rising U.S. influence in Europe, in September he pulled nine European Communist parties more tightly under his control through the new coordinating body, the Cominform. He wanted to make sure that the large and influential parties in France and Italy were on a short leash. Addresses by Politburo members Andrei Zhdanov and Molotov delivered at the inauguration of the Cominform emphasized the American drive toward world domination. According to this new and more pessimistic public Soviet reading of the international situation, the United States was seeking a far-reaching solution to its economic problems. The Americans wanted nothing less than control of the industrially advanced areas of western Europe along with Japan, penetration of the colonial world, and creation of a ring of bases around the Soviet Union. The world was now sharply divided, Zhdanov and Molotov contended, into two ideological camps, one "imperialist and anti-democratic" and the other "anti-imperialist and democratic."[14]

THE CONFLICT GOES GLOBAL

When in the course of 1947 U.S. and Soviet leaders declared the Cold War begun, they set in motion developments with consequences they could not control or foresee. The overriding concern in both Washington and Moscow was maximizing their influence in Europe. But at the same time they began to look far beyond Europe with an eye to recruiting allies and winning friends. Examining the early globalization of the Cold War helps explain the origins of "limited wars," the small-scale conflicts into which both the rivals became drawn but during which they avoided a direct collision and with it the risks of a nuclear crisis. These limited wars played out at scattered points distant around the globe—first in Korea and later in Vietnam, the Middle East, sub-Saharan Africa, and Afghanistan. More broadly, Cold War rivalry led to a costly arms race with nuclear weapons and missile technology the main areas of competition. The combined effects of widening competition, rising fears, and growing costs would shake people's lives not just in the Soviet Union and the United States but at virtually every point around the world for decades to come.

Drawing the Line in Europe

By 1950 the Cold War had deeply and intractably divided Europe. Suspicions spawned by disputes at the end of World War II soon gave rise to what Churchill would call in 1946 an "iron curtain" falling across Europe. Once leaders on both sides gave private fears public voice in the course of 1947, the process accelerated, and by 1950 Truman and Stalin had completed cutting Europe in two (Map 1.1).

The Truman administration's effort began in earnest in 1948 when Marshall Plan assistance started reaching western European economies and helped undermine local Communist parties. The two senior Communist parties in western Europe at the end of World War II had grown rapidly—the French party to one million members and the Italian party to two million—thanks to their prominent role in wartime resistance against the Germans and the appeal of their postwar programs of popular welfare. By 1950 Marshall Plan and other forms of U.S. aid had risen to $10 billion and had contributed to the beginnings of economic recovery. U.S. political pressure had encouraged Christian Democratic parties occupying a center-right position on the political spectrum to consolidate their hold on power. They would remain the predominant political presence throughout most of western Europe during the Cold War. (The European perspective on these developments is covered in Chapter 2.) The final step in the process of strategic consolidation came in 1949 with the formation of the North Atlantic Treaty Organization (NATO), committing the United States to the defense of western Europe. The charter members of NATO were Britain, France, Italy, Belgium, the Netherlands, Denmark, Norway, Portugal, and Luxembourg as well as the United States, Canada, and Iceland. Greece and Turkey joined in 1952, followed by West Germany in 1955.

Stalin pursued a roughly parallel strategy on his side of the line. As the Red Army had swept through eastern Europe, Moscow-aligned Communist parties had followed close behind. One by one they took power, in Poland, Hungary, East Germany, Romania, Bulgaria, and Albania. By 1948 Stalin had good reason to further tighten Soviet control: The military balance was not favorable. American estimates at the time made the Soviets seem more formidable than they were. In fact, the U.S. armed forces together with the British were roughly equal to the Soviets in numbers alone, and they had in addition an atomic monopoly and an unrivaled strategic bombing capability.[15]

Stalin lacked the economic resources available to the United States to win and shore up European clients. So dire were Soviet straits that Stalin pillaged rather than provisioned eastern Europe. A ditty popular in Soviet-occupied Germany remarked ironically on the Soviet dragnet for valuables:

Welcome, liberators!
You take from us eggs, meat, and butter, cattle and feed
And also watches, rings, and other things
You liberate us from everything, from cars and machines.
You take along with you train cars and rail installations.
From all this rubbish—you liberated us![16]

Even with the loot from eastern Europe, the Soviet Union did not emerge from its own terrible war-induced food shortage until the late 1940s. So in the new, tougher mood of 1948, Stalin's only option was straightforward repression to snuff out the last sparks of independence in his zone of control. Czechoslovakia, which had retained both its traditionally strong economic ties westward and its democracy, was made to submit. Stalin would not allow the Czechs to participate in the Marshall Plan, and the Communist coup completed the process of assimilation into the Soviet bloc. By the end of 1948 Poland had become a one-party state. To ensure that his satellites remained responsive to Soviet direction, Stalin assigned each of his colleagues in the Politburo a country to supervise. To coordinate trade and investment, he imposed a regional economic mechanism (COMECOM, short for the Council for Mutual Economic Assistance) in 1949. But he would leave to his successors the task of creating a military alliance (the Warsaw Pact) as a counter to NATO.

At one point, in Josip Tito's Yugoslavia, Stalin's crackdown backfired. Unlike the leaders of other socialist regimes in eastern Europe, Tito had fought his own way to power during World War II and insisted on national independence within the Soviet-led bloc. Tensions developed in early 1948 as a result of Tito pursuing an independent regional policy in defiance of Stalin's wishes. Along with Bulgaria and Albania, Tito had offered support to the Greek Communist insurgents even though Stalin wanted the Greek struggle closed down. Tito favored close ties with Albania, and he sought to deal directly with neighboring Bulgaria rather than go through Moscow. This dogged independence angered Stalin. He is supposed to have growled,

"I will shake my little finger—and there will be no more Tito."[17] But the Soviet leader lacked the tools available to him elsewhere in the region to enforce his will—an occupying Red Army and a significant body of loyalists within the local Communist Party. Unwilling to risk an invasion for fear it might trigger a broader war, Stalin's only recourse was to expel Yugoslavia from the Cominform in June 1948 and impose an economic embargo.

Germany, which had been divided at the end of the war into U.S., British, French, and Soviet zones, was the last point of division to be resolved between the superpowers. Negotiations among the occupiers on terms for uniting Germany had dragged on inconclusively as Cold War frictions intensified. Frustrated British, American, and French authorities finally took steps to integrate their western zones of occupation economically and politically and to back a distinct West German government located in Bonn and tied to the rest of western Europe. Stalin responded in June 1948 by imposing a blockade on Berlin, which itself had been divided into separate occupation zones among the four powers. By sealing off Berlin he hoped not just to oust his former allies from that divided city but also to create a rift among the western powers that would derail their unification plans. When an American airlift nullified his blockade, Stalin abandoned crude pressure in May 1949 in favor of a return to negotiations. As the United States moved toward the creation of NATO and sponsored West German membership, he countered with his own proposal for a united but demilitarized Germany, but to no avail. He would have to settle for an East German state (the German Democratic Republic) under his sway. Like Europe as a whole, Germany was now split. As Germany's old capital and leading city, Berlin remained divided, a flashpoint of Cold War tensions and playground for spies.

The Nuclear Arms Race Accelerates

These mounting tensions over Europe had broad consequences. One was a sharp boost to Soviet and American military spending. Stalin seems to have made the first move to raise arms expenditures either in 1948 or shortly thereafter. Military spending quickly became a heavy burden on a Soviet economy that was smaller than the American and in any case still struggling to recover from wartime destruction. By 1950, according to one recent estimate, a quarter of Soviet national income was going to military and police forces and the bureaucracies in charge of aviation, shipbuilding, and atomic weapons. For the United States the critical date was 1950. In April an alarmist and influential Truman administration policy review known as National Security Council Study 68 (NSC-68) called for tripling the defense budget. The call was prompted by the 1949 Soviet atomic bomb test (breaking the U.S. nuclear monopoly) and the victory of Communist forces in China. NSC-68 warned, "The assault on free institutions is world-wide now, and in the context of the present polarization of power a defeat of free institutions anywhere is a defeat everywhere." Truman at once endorsed the study's dire findings and after the outbreak of war in Korea in June its recommendation for dramatically increased spending on global containment.[18]

The other consequence of the European standoff was to accelerate nuclear weapons research and production. With arms control dead and the Cold War very much alive, nuclear weapons assumed an important place in the U.S. arsenal. Totaling no more than 13 in 1947, the number of warheads had grown to 50 by 1948.[19] Without the funds to build up a conventional force that could stop the Soviets in western Europe, the Mediterranean, the Middle East, or northeastern Asia, the U.S. military planners developed plans for an atomic air offensive designed to "kill a nation" by destroying its industries and urban centers. Some skeptics in the military predicted that a campaign of atomic bombing would destroy only about a third of Soviet industrial capacity while arousing popular patriotism in Russia. American conventional forces would still face the difficult task of recovering the territory of western Europe, which the Red Army would have easily seized during the opening months of any war. Despite these inadequacies of a nuclear strategy, there were no military alternatives that would work within the budget limits Truman had imposed. And so in the spring of 1949 Truman formally accepted atomic bombs as the principal weapon against the Soviets.

These American strategic calculations suffered a major blow in 1949 when the Soviet Union tested its first nuclear device. Responding to Stalin's mandate, Soviet scientists had worked furiously in their own isolated research centers, determined to show that their country's science was up to world-class standards and to safeguard their country's security. One recalled, "The feeling of defenselessness increased particularly after Hiroshima and Nagasaki. For all who realized the realities of the new atomic era, the creation of our own atomic weapons, the restoration of equilibrium became a categorical imperative." When a 20-kiloton nuclear device exploded on the steppes of Kazakhstan at six in the morning of August 29, 1949, one project scientist described what was becoming a familiar scene on the planet's surface: "The fireball, rising and revolving, turned orange, red. Then dark streaks appeared. Streams of dust, fragments of brick and board were drawn in after it, as into a funnel." After a time the shock wave "reached us like the roar of an avalanche." The Soviet team had produced the bomb in four years of all-out effort, about the same time taken by the Manhattan Project.[20]

The successful Soviet test surprised U.S. policymakers, alarmed the public, and pushed the president to order more atomic bombs to cover a longer list of Soviet targets. Some American scientists argued for developing a new, far more powerful weapon, the hydrogen bomb, even as others warned that it would prove so powerful that it could become an instrument of genocide. The public and most political leaders favored forging ahead on the new weapon. In January 1950 Truman approved the H-bomb project after only seven minutes of discussion with his advisers and without having read their recommendations. He had once more shown that he was tough and decisive.

In November 1952 the U.S. H-bomb proved itself, producing an explosion over 700 times more powerful than the Hiroshima blast. The following August the Soviets tested their own H-bomb. Each side would continue to reach for ever more destructive, accurate, and costly strategic weapons systems. In the decades ahead the Soviet and American arsenals would not only grow rapidly in numbers of nuclear warheads but also improve dramatically in sophistication. The technological imperative to develop, manufacture, and deploy whatever new devices scientists dangled before policymakers would continue to govern. Its logic was irresistible to Soviet no less than American leaders: New technology might provide an edge over the enemy, and if one side hesitated, then the other might acquire the new weapon first, thus gaining a significant, perhaps decisive advantage. This nuclear arms race not only raised the risk of devastation for both sides but also exacerbated mounting tensions between the superpowers anxiously eyeing each other across a divided Europe.

Opening a Front in the Third World

Despite the tensions generated by the nuclear buildup and deepening Soviet and American suspicions of each other, the superpowers settled into an acceptance of the political division of Europe. Neither was prepared to go to war to improve its position there. Thus increasingly each side looked elsewhere for opportunities to press its advantage and weaken its rival. Most of the contested sites were strategically peripheral to both powers, yet neither was prepared to duck a challenge or accept losses that might create the impression that the tide of history was running the other way.

The U.S. concern with the periphery was already apparent as World War II came to an end. While the U.S. military built a global system of bases, it also controlled Japan, which increasingly figured as a strong point in the effort to contain the Soviet Union along its Asian borders. (Chapter 2 contains an account of Japan's occupation and recovery.) The list of U.S. commitments along the periphery lengthened considerably through the late 1940s and the 1950s as Washington moved to shore up the long containment line stretching around the Soviet Union and China and to forestall a communist leap over that line into Latin America, the Middle East, or Africa.

U.S. policymakers engaged in the battle against communism worried deeply about the Third World, especially when the currents of change ran strong—toward ending foreign control, promoting democracy and social justice at home, and reducing great-power domination of the international system. Washington reacted in a time-honored and distinctly paternalistic way to the prospect that apparently "immature" Third World peoples would mishandle their affairs, creating not only instability but also an irresistible opportunity for Soviet intrigue. George Kennan, the intellectual father of containment, reported after touring Latin America in 1950 that he was unable to imagine "a more unhappy and hopeless background for the conduct of human life" than he found in those "confused and unhappy societies." The American ambassador to Egypt surveyed the Middle East in 1954 and concluded that the United States "must to a certain extent adopt the attitude of an intelligent parent faced with a 'problem child'." To get the child to accept guidance, he warned, would require parental "circumspection and finesse." To counter communist penetration in the contested Third World, policymakers sought to find nationalists and democrats with whom they could work to block Soviet influence. But when effective centrists could not be found, Washington did not hesitate to make allies of military and other authoritarian regimes. Right-wing strongmen proved effective anticommunists.[21]

In pursuing its interests in the Third World, Washington worked with three basic tools. It could offer military and economic aid (to total $175 billion between the inception of the Cold War and the late 1970s). At particularly imperiled points Washington could also raise the ante by concluding defense agreements. One wit described Washington's frenzy of treaty signing during the early Cold War as "pactomania." Where the lure of American aid or the promise of U.S. military backing was not enough to keep Third World countries in the free-world camp, Washington resorted to a third option: CIA-sponsored covert operations. The most notable of these were directed against regimes that resisted taking sides in the Cold War (for example, the Iranian government, overthrown in 1953) and against leftist governments tilting toward the Soviet side (for example, the Guatemala government, toppled in 1954, or Fidel Castro's Cuba, made a target in 1960). (All three of these cases are treated in Chapter 6.)

The Soviet Union also looked to the Third World, although cautiously as long as Stalin lived. He wanted to avoid provoking the United States into a costly military collision. Better to concentrate on building up socialism at home and let the contradictions mounting within the capitalist camp intensify. Moreover, he distrusted Communist leaders such as Mao Zedong in China and Ho Chi Minh in Vietnam who had won power on their own and whose nationalist impulses made them less responsive to Soviet direction. Reflecting his doubts, he did not include these and other non-European Communist parties in the Cominform.

Even so, Stalin did make some important contributions of his own to a globalized Cold War in the volatile East Asian region. Although he had consistently doubted the capacity of the Chinese Communists to win power, he did begin funneling small amounts of aid to them after they launched a major military campaign from their stronghold in China's northeastern provinces in 1946. The victory of the

MAP 1.2 ➤

"Pactomania": U.S. Cold War Alliances around the World, 1947–1959

NATO, concluded in 1949, was the most important but only one part of a far-flung U.S. system of alliances that served to encircle the Soviet bloc. These military agreements began by covering Latin America (Inter-America treaty of 1947) even before the conclusion of NATO. The western Pacific took center stage during the early 1950s (separate treaties with Japan in 1951, Australia and New Zealand in 1951, South Korea in 1953, and Taiwan in 1954). In 1954 Southeast Asia became part of the alliance network (Southeast Asia Treaty Organization, or SEATO). Finally, in 1959 the Middle East fell into place (Central Treaty Organization, or CENTO). With these alliances went the grant of bases for U.S. forces and the dispatch of new equipment and advisory groups to train host-country forces and coordinate planning.

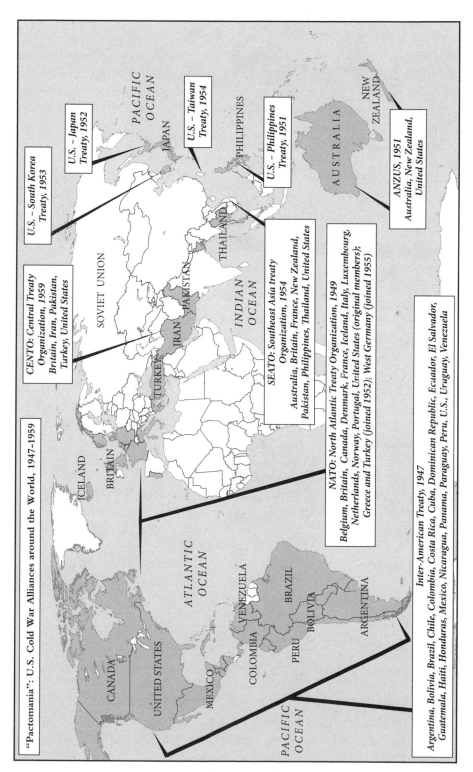

"Pactomania": U.S. Cold War Alliances around the World, 1947–1959

CENTO: Central Treaty Organization, 1959
Britain, Iran, Pakistan, Turkey, United States

U.S. – South Korea Treaty, 1953

U.S. – Japan Treaty, 1952

U.S. – Taiwan Treaty, 1954

U.S. – Philippines Treaty, 1951

ANZUS, 1951
Australia, New Zealand, United States

SEATO: Southeast Asia treaty Organization, 1954
Australia, Britain, France, New Zealand, Pakistan, Philippines, Thailand, United States

NATO: North Atlantic Treaty Organization, 1949
Belgium, Britain, Canada, Denmark, France, Iceland, Italy, Luxembourg, Netherlands, Norway, Portugal, United States (original members); Greece and Turkey (joined 1952); West Germany (joined 1955)

Inter-American Treaty, 1947
Argentina, Bolivia, Brazil, Chile, Colombia, Costa Rica, Cuba, Dominican Republic, Ecuador, El Salvador, Guatemala, Haiti, Honduras, Mexico, Nicaragua, Panama, Paraguay, Peru, U.S., Uruguay, Venezuela

Chinese Communists in 1949 and their establishment that same year of a People's Republic of China prompted Stalin to send more advisers and aid. In early 1950 Stalin received Mao in Moscow, where they concluded an alliance. At the same time Stalin granted diplomatic recognition to Ho Chi Minh's revolutionary movement (the Viet Minh) fighting the French in Vietnam, and he urged the Chinese to provide the Vietnamese with assistance. (See Chapter 3 for a fuller account of the first stages of the revolution in China and Vietnam.) In a divided Korea, Stalin exercised the most influence of anywhere in East Asia—but ironically managed there to lose control of events.

The crisis that would hit Korea in 1950 made it the scene of the first of the Cold War's limited wars. That crisis was rooted in events of 1945. Having liberated the country from Japanese colonial control going back to 1910, the representatives of the Soviet Union and the United States agreed on a temporary division along the 38th Parallel, with Soviet troops in control north of that line and U.S. forces to the south. For nationalist Korean leaders, the defeat of Japan meant something quite different—not foreign military occupation but the prospect of full and immediate independence. One of those nationalists was Syngman Rhee. He had been educated by Christian missionaries in Korea, and later as a nationalist in exile he had looked to the United States as Korea's patron. In 1945 a 70-year-old Rhee finally came home behind the arriving U.S. military. Rhee's political nemesis, Kim Il Sung, came from the other end of the Korean nationalist spectrum. As a relatively junior member of the Korean Communist Party, he had commanded guerrillas across the Korean border in China and then served during World War II in the Soviet army. He was only 33 years old when he returned home with Soviet forces.

The provisional dividing line gradually hardened between 1945 and 1948 thanks to growing international tensions between the two dominant powers on the peninsula. Kim consolidated his authority in the north with the backing of the Soviet occupation authorities. Preoccupied with national unity, he sought Stalin's support for a military initiative against the South. Stalin was not at first interested in a confrontation. He cautioned Kim, "The Americans will never agree to be thrown out of there and because of that, to lose their reputation as a great power. The Soviet people would not understand the necessity of a war in Korea, which is a remote place outside the sphere of the [Soviet Union's] vital interests."[22] On the other side, Rhee took control, abetted by the American military governor who feared losing the South to Moscow. Like Kim, Rhee was keen on reunification by force if necessary. But like Stalin Truman was cool to his client's military schemes.

The situation changed dramatically in the course of 1950. Stalin made a fateful shift in January, about the same time as he allied with Mao and offered diplomatic backing to Ho. The previously skeptical Soviet leader agreed to back an invasion, persuaded by Kim's argument that North Korean forces could quickly seize the South without provoking the United States into sending in its own troops. The American-created regime looked weak, and the Truman administration had indicated publicly

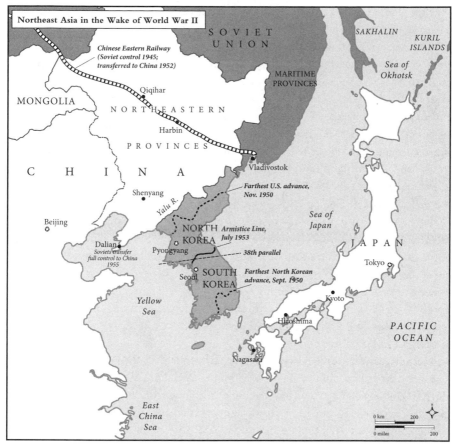

MAP 1.3
Northeast Asia in the Wake of World War II

that it lacked the forces to make a firm commitment to defend this strategically marginal area. Kim and Stalin interpreted Washington's express reluctance to take a strong stand on Korea's defense as a green light.

The stage was now set for the first major superpower crisis in the Third World. With the guarded blessings of Stalin as well as Mao, and reinforced by Soviet arms and Korean forces that had fought with the Chinese Communists, Kim attacked in late June, driving deep into South Korea. Truman took the attack as a classic case of aggression that spoke directly to the historical lessons his generation had just painfully learned. He recalled "how each time that the democracies failed to act it had encouraged the aggressors to keep going ahead. Communism was acting in Korea just as Hitler, Mussolini, and the Japanese had acted." Truman and his advisers were also influenced by growing alarm over the first Soviet atomic test and the loss of China to Communist forces. An aroused president blustered, "By God[,] I'm going to let them have it."[23]

Now galvanized, Truman ordered U.S. forces deployed from Japan to Korea to resist the invasion. He told his advisors to make preparations for an atomic strike on the Soviet Union in case it were to enter the conflict. He expanded the CIA's overseas operations. And he set about raising the military budget (as recommended in April by NSC-68)—from $15.5 billion in August to $42 billion by December. By the end of 1951 annual military spending had reached almost $70 billion. Truman did not seek a congressional declaration of war, calling the commitment in Korea a "police action." He did, however, move quickly to secure UN backing thanks to a Soviet decision to boycott Security Council meetings and thus not exercise its veto. The UN command would be led and financed by Washington.

The June surprises by Kim and then by Truman were followed by a Chinese surprise in the fall. Beijing watched anxiously as the UN commander, U.S. General Douglas MacArthur, reversed the tide of battle late in the summer and began a march northward to unify Korea by force. With their Korean adventure turning into a disaster, Stalin and Kim now appealed to Mao to bail them out. After some hesitation, Mao resolved to stop the Americans, who were rapidly advancing toward the Yalu River and Chinese territory. The sudden appearance of Chinese forces once more reversed the fortunes of war, driving stunned UN forces southward. An equally stunned Truman spoke publicly of using atomic weapons, and he declared a national state of emergency.

Once begun, the Korean War was not easily ended, even though by spring 1951 the battle lines had stabilized not far from the 38th Parallel. Peace talks, begun in July 1951, bogged down, and Truman faced public discontent with this stalemated war and Republican attacks on his no-win strategy. Frustrated, he repeatedly entertained proposals for expanding the scope of the war or bringing nuclear weapons into play. But caution prevailed, and finally in mid-1953 an armistice brought the fighting to a halt. The war had in the meantime devastated the Korean peninsula and killed some four million Koreans (combatants and civilians from both sides) along with some 380,000 Chinese soldiers. Korea would remain divided, each side deeply hostile toward the other. The autocratic Rhee would survive in power until 1960. Kim outlasted him, retaining power until his death in 1994.

The Korean War is sometimes seen as a watershed in the development of the Cold War. An alternative, more compelling view is that the conflict served to accelerate trends already gaining impetus. In general, lines already hardening in 1948 and 1949 grew harder. Suspicions of the enemy mounting since 1945 and fears of traitors within reached phobic proportions in the Soviet Union, the United States, and China. Beijing and Moscow grew closer. Washington for its part decided to expand its commitments in Asia (notably the Philippines and Vietnam) and other parts of the Third World and to further toughen its policy toward China. The outbreak of war in turn convinced U.S. leaders to elevate even higher Japan's geopolitical importance, to intensify support for the French struggle in Vietnam, and to give even more attention to rearmament in Europe.

THE SUPERPOWER RIVALRY INTENSIFIES AND SPREADS

1948	On the Soviet side: Stalin tightens grip on eastern Europe, beginning with coup in Czechoslovakia, and cuts off West Berlin to halt the formation of a West German state; Tito–Stalin split drives Yugoslavia from the Soviet orbit
	On the U.S. side: Congress approves Marshall Plan; North Atlantic Treaty Organization (NATO) formed
1949	Soviet Union imposes Council for Mutual Economic Assistance on European clients, ends Berlin blockade, and tests its first A-bomb; Communists win in China
1950	Stalin and Mao conclude alliance; NSC-68 calls for tripling U.S. military budget; Korean War begins; United States and then China intervene in Korean conflict
1952	United States tests first hydrogen bombs (followed by the Soviet Union less than a year later)

SUPERPOWER SOCIETIES IN AN UNQUIET TIME

Wars have a major impact on the societies that fight them. The Cold War was no exception. From the start Soviet and American leaders asked fresh sacrifices of their citizens in the name of national security and international prestige. Those sacrifices can be measured in material terms—investments made on defense and foreign aid that could have gone to the civilian sector. But they can also be measured in terms of the ideological chill both countries experienced. The boundaries of political tolerance narrowed as embattled officials settled into a knee-jerk defense of the domestic status quo while keeping vigilant watch for enemies within.

Domestic mobilization meant different things for the Soviet Union and the United States. For the Soviets, the Cold War hindered recovery from wartime destruction as military spending in the late 1940s took more and more out of an economy never geared to civilian production and considerably smaller than that of the United States. The Cold War also crushed hopes entertained by many that the postwar period would bring a political and cultural thaw. Americans entered the postwar period with similar hopes for an end to tensions, and the Cold War brought instead for them too a renewal of military preparations and repression in the face of a global threat so powerful that it seemed to have even subverted elements of American society. For U.S. citizens, however, the sacrifices associated with the Cold War were softened by the vitality of the American economy. Its quick conversion back to civilian production and rapid growth made possible alongside an ambitious military program the abundant output on which revived consumer expectations depended. Americans, unlike Soviet citizens, could have both "guns and butter"—sustain a major military effort while also enjoying domestic abundance. (See Chapters 2 and 5 for treatment of the good times that the postwar years would bring for an increasing number of American consumers.)

Soviet Society Under Stress

Postwar Soviet society was in large measure a prewar creation that bore the stamp of its principal architect, Joseph Stalin. While Vladimir Lenin made the Bolshevik revolution and consolidated it before his death in 1924, it was Stalin who gave the Soviet domestic system its shape in the 1930s. "Stalinism" is the label applied after Stalin's lifetime to describe what Stalin and his lieutenants created as they went about "building socialism."

The collapse of socialism in the Soviet Union as well as in its European satellites between 1989 and 1991 makes it tempting to dismiss Stalinism as a bankrupt experiment run by immoral men fully deserving the harsh verdict commonly laid on them abroad and even in their own countries. But this sweeping condemnation obscures two important historical points. First, Stalin should be seen in the context of a recurrent modernizing impulse in Russian history. Like his predecessors, he followed a pattern of forced, often brutal, state-guided modernization, first evident with Tsar Peter the Great in the 1680s and reappearing in the nineteenth and early twentieth centuries as the imperial government emancipated the serfs and spurred industrialization. The goal was to bring the country to the front ranks of the great Western powers by creating an advanced military, acquiring cutting-edge technology, achieving high levels of literacy, and developing a base of heavy industry and efficient communications and transport systems. Second, Communist leaders were moved by the conviction that a new, highly centralized system could transform Russia into a superpower as well as create a better life for many under Soviet sway.

When the Bolsheviks took power in 1917, Russia's social and economic circumstances were closer to the Third World than a modern great power. This depressing condition, plus the determination to change it, makes it easier to understand the mixture of hope, envy, hatred, and fear that drove Stalinism. Its proponents entertained a utopian vision of an essentially peasant Russian society overcoming its humiliating backwardness and catching up with the West. They would catapult their country into a new age of enlightenment and development. In this leap they imagined that the forces of history and the sympathy of most ordinary peoples around the world would be on their side. Arrayed against them were powerful capitalists eager to frustrate Soviet ambitions and destroy the Soviet experiment. Faced by the capitalist powers' campaign of encirclement, the Soviet Union had a simple choice—as Stalin is supposed to have observed in 1931, either catch up in industrial capacity in 10 years or be crushed by enemies. At home the regime imagined another menace, resistance from the remnants of the old order. These included nationalist groups hostile to central control, class enemies in hiding, spies, intellectuals promoting reactionary ideas, peasants wedded to their land, and ideologically tainted party members.

Stalin pursued his ambitious program through a powerful, party-controlled state apparatus. It was totalitarian in its aspirations though not in actuality. The system was supposed to be able to shape every facet of Soviet life. A large central-ized bureaucracy was indispensable to running an all-encompassing command economy in which the state owned farms and factories, staffed leading adminis-trative positions, and elaborately planned production of most if not all goods and services. Putting the state in charge and having one coherent vision seemed the only way to make the most of limited resources. In December 1929 the senior party planner articulated the widely shared vision of a great united economic effort: "We need to organise a social and political mechanism with which 150 million people will act, guided by a single plan, a single concept, a single will, a single effort to accomplish what is laid down by the plan."[24] Maintaining popular enthusiasm and imposing popular sacrifice accordingly represented a critical state function. That state was also to have the task of social engineering, expunging objectionable traces of the old society and nurturing socialist values throughout a vast and varied pop-ulation. Directing the arts, the media, and science along approved lines thus became a central concern of the Soviet state. Finally, the state had to keep the Bolshevik experiment safe by repressing internal class enemies. Although in Marxist theory the socialist era was ultimately to bring the withering away of the state, in point of fact the opposite tendency was evident during Stalin's time and after.

The Stalinist program left an enduring mark in four critical areas of Soviet life. First of all it dramatically expanded the industrial sector. Stalin pressed between 1928 and 1939 (through two five-year economic plans) for the rapid buildup of Soviet industry and succeeded in making his country a major industrial power. Second, he drove the peasantry into collectivized agriculture. The Communists were determined to end private land holdings and bring agricultural production under state control and at the same time transform the rural sector from back-ward, small-scale farming into an efficient, modern, large-scale enterprise. This factory system in the countryside was in effect to remake the peasantry into a rural proletariat, while at the same make it possible for Soviet economic planners to extract from agriculture the resources essential to building industry. When Stalin launched agricultural collectivization in 1929–1930 and some of the 100 million targeted peasants resisted, he struck back in brutal fashion, especially against prosperous peasants (*kulaks*) whom he regarded as a dangerous capitalist influence in the countryside. Millions were expropriated and deported. The disruption that attended collectivization resulted in food shortages in 1932–1933 that created urban hardship and rural starvation. But Stalin had his way: By the end of the 1930s the collective system covered most of the countryside.

In both the industrial and agricultural spheres what in theory looked efficient and rational proved in practice not so. Central bureaucrats exercised imperfect control over a vast landmass. Their plans imposed high costs not just in lives but also in terms of industrial pollution, social disruption, and popular alienation. And planners themselves were hostage to the vagaries of the top leadership: Today's plan might be arbitrarily modified by tomorrow's order. Below them were a sullen peasantry and a lethargic industrial workforce, both ingenious at finding ways to frustrate the stream of directives calling for ever-higher output.

The third major feature of Stalin's program was a strong domestic security force, a succession of agencies best known by their initials (GPU, OGPU, NKVD, and finally KGB). Their target was broadly defined to include any anti-Soviet ideas or actions. The security apparatus made arrests without legal restraints and either executed class enemies or dispatched them to brutal labor camps, where many died. At the local level the process of purging often got out of control of the central authorities as ambitious subordinates denounced their superiors or vengeful rivals evened old scores. The "liquidation of the kulaks" was the first broad-scale "cleansing" operation. Through the 1930s Stalin's suspicions fell on other suspected counter-revolutionaries—in the party, in the army, and among intellectuals. Stalin's purges reached their peak between 1936 and 1938 and included among the victims party leaders Sergei Kirov (assassinated in 1934) and Nikolai Bukharin (put on trial and executed in 1938). One recent estimate puts those dispatched to one of an extensive complex of labor camps (*gulags*) at some point during the Stalin years (1929–1953) somewhere around 18 million. Another six million were sentenced to special exile. To these chilling figures must be added those executed for political crimes—probably approaching a million.[25]

The final feature of the Stalinist system to note is the emergence of an entrenched, privileged class. This group, known as the *nomenklatura*, consisted of those members of the Communist Party appointed to posts at the top of the party and state bureaucracy as well as the military. The *nomenklatura* enjoyed special access to housing, education, medical care, food, and other consumer goods. They used their power over economic resources to benefit clients and family and also to block reforms that might imperil their position.

In its last years Stalin's rule was conservative socially as well as politically. After the upheaval of the war, many in the Soviet Union longed for an end to heroic exertion and personal sacrifice. But the postwar period brought hardly any relaxation of tensions and certainly no alteration of the system. The new five-year plan, prepared in fall 1945 and announced by Stalin in February 1946, continued the emphasis on heavy industry. Soon the rising military budget would claim a substantial chunk of the economic output. The hunger for consumer goods would have to wait.

The domestic security forces remained vigilant. They packed returning prisoners of war off to labor camps on suspicion of collaboration with the Germans, while "pacifying" the westernmost part of the Soviet Union (especially recently annexed parts of Ukraine), where anti-Soviet groups had formed during the war and remained a threat into 1948. By 1950 labor camps contained 2.8 million prisoners there for all types of "crimes." Stalin insisted on ideological conformity not just in politics but also in literature, science, and the social sciences, with himself the ultimate arbiter. The ideological vise tightened as the Cold War took shape and as official campaigns took aim at elements within Soviet society supposedly infected by decadent Anglo-American values.

Most people in the Soviet Union experienced the first few years of peace as a time nearly as trying as war. In cities through which the German army had swept, many homes and factories had been reduced to rubble and public facilities destroyed. With housing in short supply, some lived in dugouts or in the open air through the bitter winter cold. Basic goods such as food, clothes, and shoes were all desperately scarce. Soldiers returning home were shocked by the conditions so unlike those they had dreamed about. Some two million invalid veterans received only limited care. The streets were filled with beggars and with vagabond youth orphaned or otherwise cut loose from family. Crime became rampant, with bands robbing and killing with seeming impunity.

The low point came during 1946–1947 when drought combined with the lingering effects of wartime disruptions to produce the lowest harvest in a century. The ensuing famine caused some two million deaths from malnutrition between 1946 and 1948. Loud complaints could be heard on the street about food aid rumored to be going to France as well as to eastern Europe. One citizen angrily observed, "We feed the bourgeois while we ourselves starve."[26] As hunger worsened, the discontented looked to Stalin to save them. As the good ruler, he could not wish his people ill; therefore, the popular plight must be the fault of corrupt and incompetent lower-level officials who were conspiring to keep him in the dark.

Russia in Ruins, 1943
These Stalingraders return after the epic battle that had destroyed their city. This is one of many scenes of destruction that awaited civilians and soldiers at war's end. The fighting had engulfed territory where nearly half of the Soviet population had lived. (Sovfoto/UIG via Getty Images)

Recovery finally came in 1948. By then industrial production had regained prewar levels, the demobilization of the armed forces had been completed, and the wartime rationing system had ended. Even so, conditions of housing and food remained difficult. Occasional rumors of war with the West would ignite panic buying. Discontent festered within groups who had been poorly treated during the war, including minorities deported from their homelands and workers assigned to distant factories. Perhaps most ominous for the long term was the discontent among pockets of urban youth who had been swept up in the war. In informal discussions they focused on the gap between party propaganda and the reality of peacetime hunger and other kinds of deprivation and questioned whether the party had turned into an exploitative state capitalism.

A powerful, pervasive Stalin cult steered such subversive musings away from the leader. The Communist Party's central bureaucracy promoted and monitored the cult, while the popular media dutifully celebrated Stalin as a poor man from a backwater region who had proven himself a friend of Lenin and a hero during the revolution and civil war. Following Lenin's death, he had assumed the role of the fearless, all-knowing leader who had industrialized the country, looked after the welfare of its hardworking, ordinary people, beaten back the German invader, and won international respect. The cult made Stalin into a demi-god in the eyes of many, even those whose families had felt the sting of loss from war or purges. The news of Stalin's death on March 6, 1953, would plunge the Soviet Union into shock and mourning. The outpouring of grief revealed how deeply the cult had taken hold. "What will become of us now," people asked as crowds pressed forward to pay respects to the embalmed body lying in state covered with flowers and honors.[27] In the press of tearful mourners, some were literally crushed to death.

Of all those experiencing hardship and discontent in the postwar period, the rural majority—some 100 million people, representing 60 percent of the population in 1945—led the way. Country folk lived in poor backwaters, frightened by change and waiting for higher-ups to resolve the problems of their hopelessly inefficient agriculture. The collectives, the product of Stalin's drive to remake the countryside, were as unpopular as ever after the war. Meanwhile, Moscow continued to make demands on the collectives so heavy that rural people were virtually working for the state without pay. Resentment focused on the heads of the collectives who had to meet assigned quotas and who sometimes ran the collective like private fiefdoms. One demoralized peasant woman complained in mid-1946, "We work on the collective farm as we used to work for the landlords in the days of serfdom. They drive us to work, and they neither feed nor pay us."[28] Villagers responded as they had in the past by investing more time on their small private plots and trying to expand private holdings at the expense of the collective.

Compounding the quiet crisis in the countryside was a sharp decline in numbers of able-bodied males available for agricultural work, resulting from wartime levies and casualties and flight from rural hardship by those with education and initiative. And the decline continued under the lure of better living conditions in the cities. With only one man left in the villages after the war for every three women, women were left to bear the brunt of care for children, the infirm, and the elderly as well as meet state-imposed production quotas and wring a subsistence from their own private plots. The famine of 1946–1947 added to their burden by draining foodstuffs to feed the cities. One woman appealed from the countryside, "Our children are living like animals—constantly angry and hungry."[29]

Discontent and alienation also persisted among the industrial workforce. In theory, the working class was the group in whose name the Bolshevik Party functioned. But in practice, Stalin's effort in the 1930s to harness the workforce to his ambitious industrialization plans had strained the relationship. Managers sharply limited the autonomy that workers had carved out for themselves in previous decades on the factory floors of Russia's nascent industries. In expressing their resentments workers used their capacity to "speak Bolshevik," normally a sign of political allegiance, to turn the political rhetoric of their bosses back on them. Workers regarded managers and specialists above them as a new exploiting class who lived a markedly better life thanks to the toil of the common man. They complained of incompetence, speculation, and privilege of these higher-ups and responded by "liberating" collective goods under their control for sale or personal use. They resented the boring meetings with their empty slogans. "A lot of chatter and little business. I go to the meetings, but the waste of time makes me angry," fumed one worker.[30]

Whatever their discontents, workers generally fared better than peasants. Material conditions were superior in urban areas and the shortage of labor gave workers the option of leaving for a better post elsewhere. A manager who lost workers would have a hard time meeting quotas assigned by the economic authorities above him. In the resulting accommodation, management would avoid punishing such forms of worker indiscipline as drunkenness and absenteeism and tended to tolerate low productivity. This pact built lasting distortions into the system of production. Defective products and inefficient use of labor, raw materials, and fuel would permanently plague Soviet industry.

The educated were the smallest but also the most closely monitored part of the population. In a society that Stalin thought should run like a machine, writers, painters, teachers, and scientists had a critical long-term influence as (in his words) "engineers of human souls." Their work would create the new socialist man. Some intellectuals gladly embraced the role, for example, by publicly celebrating Stalin as an all-knowing and inspiring leader. He was everywhere watching and evaluating the work his people did. As one popular poet expressed it: "You work badly—his brow lowers/But when good, he smiles in his moustache."[31]

But to an impressive degree, intellectuals and artists proved stubbornly independent and outspoken even as Stalin cowed workers and peasants into submission. After the frightening repression of the 1930s, the war brought more tolerant times in which patriotic unity displaced class suspicion. Many loyal intellectuals, from scientists to philosophers to economists to artists, hoped for liberalization in the postwar period. A more open, creative atmosphere would allow the country to deal with past mistakes, especially persistent problems in the economic sphere. The rigidly conservative atmosphere in Stalin's last years would, however, disappoint them, while the campaign from 1947 onward against "worshipping foreign cultures" and "kowtowing before the West" would intimidate scientists, philosophers, and others with professional links to the outside world.

Composer Dmitri Shostakovich nicely illustrates the perseverance of the intellectual class in the face of official pressure and blasted hopes for a humane revolutionary path. He had gotten into trouble in 1937 for music that Stalin and the cultural commissars thought too "complex" and "dark." At the same time, a purge in Leningrad was proceeding at full tilt against friends and colleagues, while his patron in Moscow (a senior army general) had just been executed on espionage charges. Shostakovich still found a way in his next composition—his famous brooding Fifth Symphony—to communicate what he and his audience of Leningraders felt but could not openly say: their grief for relatives and friends lost in the purges, the fear for their own lives, the resentment at the pompous, domineering leader who controlled their destiny, and the failure of a revolutionary ideal. By the third, slow movement of the symphony many in the audience were in tears. The standing ovation at the end lasted over 40 minutes, longer than the musical performance. Shostakovich got away with this piece of surreptitious resistance and survived to

THE STALIN ERA

1924	Lenin's death
1929	Stalin consolidates grip on power, presses industrialization, and collectivizes agriculture
1935–39	Stalin purges party, military, and intellectual elites
1939	Soviet Union signs nonaggression pact with Germany, dividing Poland between them
1941	Germany launches surprise attack on the Soviet Union, providing basis for alliance with United States and Britain
1943	Battle of Stalingrad marks the turning point of war against Germany
1945	Red Army marches into eastern Germany
1946	Stalin's reconstruction plan emphasizes heavy industry
1946–47	Massive famine in war-torn areas results in two million deaths
1947	Cominform organized to strengthen Soviet control over European Communist parties; Stalin begins crackdown in eastern Europe
1948	Soviet economy regains prewar levels
1953	Stalin's death

become one of the stars in the Soviet cultural firmament. Before his death in 1975, he was finally able to talk openly about how much his music stood as "tombstones" to those lost to political oppression: "Too many of our people died and were buried in places unknown to anyone, not even their relatives. It happened to many of my friends." He added, "I think constantly of those people, and in almost every major work I try to remind others of them."[32]

Stalin's domestic program left a mixed legacy. Its most notable achievement is tied to the two five-year plans (1929–1939) that built industry, promoted urbanization, and created a better-educated society. This rapid, state-directed economic and social development transformed a "backward," peasant society into a modern one in which many enjoyed a better, longer life and greater geographical and social mobility. That economic transformation had also made possible Soviet successes in international affairs after 1939: the defeat of the German invaders, the extension of control into eastern Europe, the sponsorship of junior partners in Asia (China, North Korea, and Vietnam), and the rise to the status of a superpower rival to the United States. Stalin's critics, on the other hand, recoiled from the terrible cost in lives and wondered whether the achievements of those years required such human sacrifice. How to create a humane socialism, one that brought modernization in a less ruthless fashion, would be the central problem to confront Stalin's successors, Nikita Khrushchev (see Chapter 4) and Mikhail Gorbachev (see Chapter 7).

The U.S. Anticommunist Consensus

While the Cold War reinforced Stalin's repressive instincts and the priority he had long given to heavy industry and the military over civilian needs, in the United States rising international tensions led most notably to fears of radicals and subversives not seen since the last "Red scare" in the immediate aftermath of World War I. This growing alarm over "penetration" by an alien ideology promoted by the Soviet Union had a pervasive impact on domestic society and political culture, and it created the basis for a potent anticommunist consensus at home critical to waging the Cold War abroad. But the effects of anticommunism were buffered by a popular preoccupation with enjoying the fruits of postwar prosperity (treated in Chapter 2). Anticommunism thus had in some ways to compete with consumerism and in other ways to accommodate to it.

This preoccupation with communist subversion is usually associated with the figure of Joseph McCarthy. This small-town Wisconsin lawyer had served in the Pacific during World War II and won a Senate seat as a Republican in 1946. He jumped into the public spotlight in February 1950 with his charges of communist subversion and Democratic Party betrayal. His main target was a State Department "thoroughly infested with Communists" and "the bright young men [there] who are born with a silver spoon in their mouths." He called for a clean sweep of "the whole sorry mess of twisted, warped thinkers" who had reduced the United States to its current "position of impotence."[33] In pursuit of "Communists and queers" in high places, he conducted Senate hearings with raw energy and a gift for the sensational. McCarthy quickly overreached himself. Fellow senators launched an investigation of his methods and in December 1954 voted to censure him. By the time of his death in 1957 the discredited McCarthy had come to epitomize an hysterical fear of communist subversion and a disposition to root out communists and communist sympathizers by means of inquisitorial congressional investigations and public accusations and innuendoes.

In fact, the pressures for ideological conformity unleashed by the Cold War were bigger than this one man. Fear of communism had deep roots. During the late nineteenth century, radicals in the labor movement, in immigrant communities, and elsewhere had stirred fears of socialism and anarchism undermining American institutions and values. The Bolshevik revolution precipitated another eruption of fear at the end of World War I. With communist contagion seemingly spreading into Europe and threatening to infect the United States, the Wilson administration and local governments were gripped by a "Red scare." They launched programs to eliminate "dangerous" dissenters, and universities dismissed faculty with "radical" views. The American Left revived during the Depression and the wartime alliance with the Soviet Union. But already by the late 1930s a backlash was building. Congressional investigators began looking for subversives, and the FBI under its long-time leader, J. Edgar Hoover, targeted U.S. citizens and foreign residents thought to be in the service of the Soviet Union.

Conservatives suspicious of the Soviets and mistrustful of Roosevelt's judgment began to raise their voices as World War II drew to a close. The march of communism across Europe, along with revolutionary stirrings around the world, deepened their sense of alarm. The internal security issue had become especially attractive to Republicans after their party's frustrating loss in the 1948 presidential election. They charged "twenty years of treason" under the Democrats. The welfare and regulatory policies developed by the Roosevelt administration to fight the Depression seemed to them akin to communist ideas promoted by Moscow, and leftist inroads, they argued, had created conditions conducive to subversion now so threatening in the context of the Cold War struggle. These charges became a galvanizing issue for a wide range of organizations, including the American Legion, the Catholic Church, and conservatives within the American Federation of Labor.

The crucial development that gave resources and legitimacy and thus great impetus to the postwar anti-Red drive was the support of the federal government. Hoover wanted action, and he enjoyed support from his nominal boss, Truman's attorney general, who warned that communists were everywhere—"in factories, offices, butcher shops, on street corners, in private business, and each carries in himself the germs of death for society." Truman finally swung over in 1947. In late March, he put into effect a loyalty program targeting communists and sympathizers within the federal government. Hoover underlined the importance of Truman's security measures by warning of the vulnerability, especially of labor and liberals, to the "virus of communism," which was a "disease that spreads like an epidemic and like an epidemic a quarantine is necessary to keep it from infecting the Nation."[34]

Truman was motivated in part by domestic political calculations. The Republicans had taken control of Congress in 1946. The 1948 presidential election found him facing opposition from former vice president Henry Wallace, who was running as a third-party candidate decrying the growing anticommunist hysteria and enjoying the support of the U.S. Communist Party as well as left-leaning Democrats. By taking a strong anticommunist stance, Truman could blunt the inroads of his Republican challenger, Thomas Dewey, while discrediting Wallace. His surprise election in 1948 seemed to vindicate that strategy.

But genuine alarm over foreign crises and spy revelations also moved the president as it did others. Dramatic communist gains in 1949 and 1950—the first Soviet A-bomb test, the resounding defeat of the U.S.-backed government in China, and the North Korean invasion—left many Americans shaken. A string of highly publicized spy cases further added to the atmosphere of anxiety. State Department official Alger Hiss, pursued for espionage by ambitious Republican Representative Richard Nixon, was convicted in early 1950 of the lesser charge of perjury. At the same time British authorities arrested Karl Fuchs, who had worked on the Manhattan Project, for helping Moscow acquire atomic secrets. He in turn pointed to Julius and Ethel Rosenberg as atomic spies. They were convicted in March 1951 and executed. The presiding judge handed down a death sentence as a warning to "traitors in our midst."[35]

Between 1947 and 1950—in parallel with the international struggle against the Soviet Union—federal efforts to deal with disloyal Americans turned into a crusade. In Congress, the Senate Internal Security Subcommittee and the House Un-American Activities Committee gained new prominence and legitimacy and paved the way for McCarthy's own Permanent Subcommittee on Investigations of the Committee on Governmental Operations. Within the executive branch, Truman and his successor, Dwight Eisenhower, made it easier to fire government employees under suspicion. The accused could not confront their accusers and had no right to know the source of the information on which charges were based. Security measures became a prime concern of such federal agencies as the Post Office, the Internal Revenue Service, the Immigration and Naturalization Service, and the National Security Agency, each of which used its power to identify and intimidate those with tainted pasts or "un-American" views. State and local bureaucracies and officeholders in turn took their cue from federal actions. Anticommunism was becoming a prominent part of the fabric of American society.

At the center of the anticommunist bull's eye was the U.S. Communist Party, with its 40,000 to 50,000 members. It had channeled the bulk of its energy into the union cause, civil rights, and peace rallies in the face of what it charged was an increasingly expansionist U.S. foreign policy. As if these positions did not give its enemies enough ammunition, the party also operated in a secretive fashion with no real internal democracy and with covert links to the Soviet Union. The Red hunters got the party leaders arrested in July 1948 for conspiring to overthrow the U.S. government. In 1951 the Supreme Court upheld their conviction by a 6–2 vote.

By then the party was well on its way to collapse. Legal battles exhausted its treasury and its leadership while media attacks and administrative harassment beat down the rank and file.

The political chill produced by this anticommunist campaign proved far-reaching. Businesses fired employees suspected of radical sympathies. Hollywood blacklisted those who did not cooperate with congressional investigators. Left-wing unions fell under suspicion and either capitulated or collapsed, while universities expelled suspected communists from their faculties. African American leaders were split. Those such as the writer W. E. B. Du Bois and the singer and actor Paul Robeson were opposed to letting anticommunism override their commitment to civil rights at home and self-determination for Africa, while others, such as Walter White of the old-line National Association for the Advancement of Colored People (NAACP), reasoned that embracing the Cold War crusade would help blacks gain freedom and that, in any case, defiance would cost civil rights popular support. Dissent became dangerous in the press, and when academics or journalists appealed their right to freedom of speech, the courts generally sidestepped the issue, giving "national security" precedence over constitutionally protected civil liberties. An accusation of communist beliefs and associations was enough to shatter lives. The accused faced the overwhelming costs of defending themselves, they lost their jobs and were entered on blacklists, their privacy was destroyed, and their good names were impugned without means of redress.

The figures on those affected can only be approximated. The government internal security probes between 1947 and 1956 prompted some 12,000 to resign rather than engage in a costly fight without access to the evidence against them. Some 2,700 fought and then suffered formal dismissal. Jobs lost outside government—for example, in corporations, foundations, and schools—are hard to estimate with any accuracy. Many were caught in the net of guilt by association when organizations to which they had belonged appeared on the attorney general's list of 197 subversive organizations.

Some examples give a sense of the broad impact. Despite his accomplishments on the atomic bomb project, Robert Oppenheimer had his security clearance revoked in 1954 on the basis of prewar left-wing political associations and his decision to protect a friend who had approached him in 1943 on behalf of the Soviet Union. Owen Lattimore, an accomplished and outspoken authority on China at Johns Hopkins University, fell afoul of Republican investigators determined to cast him as the "architect" of a U.S. policy designed to help the Communists to victory in China. A perjury conviction in 1952 quickly fell apart, but Lattimore's professional reputation was so damaged that he moved to Britain. A postal clerk faced charges in 1954 that included having communist literature and art in his home. He explained that the literature was from a college course and that the art included Picasso and Renoir. He sought without avail to see the sources on which the charges were based. The Civil Service Commission ended a year of appeals by making the dismissal definitive.

Learning about the Red Menace, 1947
This cover from a 1947 comic circulated in U.S. Catholic schools conveys a sense of the hysteria generated by the Cold War. It highlights in particular the threat of violence the Red menace posed to African Americans, women, and the religious. (Catechetical Guild)

The effects of this anticommunist fervor were long-lasting. It convinced many Americans that their country could not deal with the global communist monolith except by eradicating the enemy within. The anticommunist campaign pushed the center of American political and intellectual life noticeably to the right, leaving the high ground to anticommunist liberals and even more anticommunist conservatives. Foreign policy specialists in the State Department and academe, above all those charged with helping to "lose China," were intimidated into silence at a time when such eminently debatable Cold War issues as intervention in Vietnam were beginning to take shape. On domestic issues as well, anticommunism was a handy stick to silence critics and hold back change. For example, campaigns to unionize factories and to dismantle the system of racial segregation in the South met charges that those involved were communists or communist dupes and either way un-American.

Just as policymaking was a man's domain, the battle against communism at home was couched in terms of manliness and vigor. A strong, vigilant America could resist communism's insidious inroads, McCarthy and others argued, only if the vulnerable points—the overeducated, the effeminate, the gay community, and foreign-born citizens who pretended loyalty the better to betray—were properly monitored. A tabloid reported in 1950 that "more than ninety twisted twerps in trousers had been swished out of the state department" but that "at least 6,000 homosexuals [were still] on the government payroll." In the State Department itself George Kennan, influential Soviet analyst, worried that American society was becoming soft and passive as social disintegration left individuals adrift. He welcomed the Soviet challenge; it gave Americans a chance at "pulling themselves together and accepting the responsibilities of moral and political leadership that history plainly intended them to bear." Out of this image of the Cold War struggle came a long-lasting language of toughness that took competition with the Soviets as the yardstick of the nation's and its leaders' virility. The language was as likely to appear in presidential addresses as in such popular media as *Reader's Digest*.[36]

This campaign to restore masculine values in public life had broad implications for gender roles in society. From the mid-1910s to the mid-1940s, the United States had gone through two wartime economic mobilizations, a bout of liberating prosperity, and a dislocating depression. The cumulative effect was to unsettle established notions of the proper place of men and women in ordinary life. Worried by the mounting threat to the stable, male-dominated nuclear family, social conservatives pounced on Cold War fears to press their case. Social stability at home no less than national security abroad, they argued, depended on men and women assuming their "traditional" roles. While strong men took responsibility outside the home and the homeland, women were supposed to turn their energies to domestic affairs. Working women were guilty of evading their obligations and as a result they betrayed their men, confused their children, and ultimately weakened their nation in its time of testing. Strong men and subservient women were as important in family health as muscular political leadership was to national survival.

This look at McCarthyism suggests comparisons with the ideological straitjacket that Stalin fastened on his country. As there, so too in the United States, the courts, the legislature, and the executive at all levels imposed a more restrictive social and political atmosphere. In the United States, as in the Soviet Union, the easiest way to discredit challengers to the status quo was to link them somehow to the foreign enemy and thus make them appear unpatriotic, even dangerously subversive. McCarthyism reminds us of the unpleasant paradox that attended the American side of the Cold War struggle. Americans went crusading in foreign lands in the name of freedom even as those freedoms significantly narrowed at home. That those who fell victim to McCarthyism lost their jobs and reputations and not their lives and that their numbers were far fewer than those exiled to Soviet labor camps or executed serves to qualify, not invalidate, the comparison and to extenuate, not excuse, the betrayal of fundamental American political values.[37]

CONCLUSION

The first years of the Cold War proved a dark moment for many people around the world, but especially for those in the United States and the Soviet Union. Cold War fears and dangers had rapidly displaced the hopes for peace and prosperity for a combination of reasons. The completeness of the Allied triumph during World War II was paradoxically part of the problem. It placed the fate of the postwar world to a large extent in the hands of the two leading Allied powers with strongly divergent worldviews. Their differences spawned mistrust as well as misunderstanding as they sought to deal with a wide range of complex issues amidst the confusion and desperation of a world just torn by war. Sharply accentuating the potential for conflict were marked differences in the styles and outlooks of the two leaders who happened to be at the helm between 1945 and 1953. Truman was inexperienced, impatient, and insecure—not the best combination of traits for resolving the complicated issues thrust upon him following Roosevelt's death. Stalin, on the other hand, brought to his postwar tasks personal paranoia and skill at dissembling and maneuvering honed in Soviet domestic and foreign policy over decades. These qualities combined to make his approach both cautious and opaque. Of all the circumstances leading to the rise of the Cold War, the personalities of leaders may be both the most important but also the most easily overlooked. The postwar period was bound to be contentious, but these personal differences helped turn differences into a deep and disruptive rivalry that would last for decades.

The mounting Soviet–American tensions of the early postwar period might have risen higher, leading to another world war with destruction on a magnitude previously unimagined. But in early 1953 (just months apart), Truman and Stalin disappeared from the center of power, marking the end of the worst of the Cold War peril and the first glimmers of a thaw. The efforts by their successors to limit the rivalry bore fruit in the 1950s and 1960s. Promoting this trend were the increasingly apparent costs of waging the Cold War, growing popular discontent on both sides, and above all the ever-clearer realization of nuclear war's suicidal potential. Nikita Khrushchev and Dwight Eisenhower would begin what would prove a long, meandering path toward accommodation and ultimately the end of the Cold War some 40 years after its start (see Chapter 4).

2

THE INTERNATIONAL ECONOMY: OUT OF THE RUINS

AT THE END of World War II the United States stood as the premier economic power. It accounted for half of all manufacturing around the world and held two thirds of the world's gold reserves. U.S. dominance was enhanced by the wartime destruction that had spared none of the other economic powers. American goods, capital, and leadership were the main source of hope for recovery in other lands. With its vast scale married to considerable military, political, and cultural clout, the United States entered the postwar era at the peak of its power. It had the capacity to give a significant boost to a market-oriented system of trade and finance. Quick to use that capacity, the United States had an incredible impact as a global economic reformer, as a rescuer of stricken western Europe and Japan, and as a fount of goods and dreams for foreign no less than American consumers.

In knitting together an international economy devastated by depression and war, the United States by necessity had to work with others, especially in the developed world where the Cold War stakes were proving highest and where the potential for a rapid recovery of production and living standards was greatest. Although drained by two world wars, the British government collaborated closely with Washington on international economic reforms. In western Europe, Catholic politicians determined to block Communist electoral advances looked to the United States for relief supplies and capital critical to meeting popular demands for food, fuel, and housing. In a Japan exhausted by war and devastated by bombing, a new generation of leaders emerged who, like their European counterparts, were anticommunist, bent on reconstruction, and dependent on the United States for assistance. The popular dreams for a better life in both Europe and Japan, to which democratic politicians had to be attuned, took on a strong U.S. flavor. Even before World War II, U.S. cultural imports had planted in the minds of the working and middle classes images of a lifestyle of comfort and pleasure. The postwar presence of American soldiers, films, and advertising only intensified the taste for a level of consumption made possible only by an economy of abundance. Americanization, the code word for this pervasive U.S. economic and cultural influence, was for many a welcome social reality but for cultural elites a source of alarm.

ANGLO-AMERICAN REMEDIES FOR AN AILING SYSTEM

The revival of a battered international economic system was a project undertaken jointly by leaders in Washington and London during wartime and the early postwar years. Both knew that the United States would dominate the postwar scene. London and the British pound, both formerly central to trade and investment, had lost their pivotal, commanding role as a result of the damage that two wars had done to the British economy. No longer the premier international power, Britain could hope to maintain a modicum of influence only in league with the ascendant United States. Now, both parties recognized, was the time to write new rules and create new institutions that would promote international trade and investment. Through this collaboration, the Americans and British would set their stamp on the international system and lay the foundation for the renewal of globalization.

They took as an article of faith that a restored global economy held the best hope for bringing a better life for their own as well as other people. The late nineteenth- and early twentieth-century record offered ample argument for the gains that would flow from the free movement of goods and capital. The more recent interwar past also offered a powerful warning of how excessive state interference in the market, including protecting home markets from foreign producers and restricting currency exchange, could not only plunge the world into depression but also derange the entire system. Perhaps above all, traders and investors needed the promise of a stable international environment for the profitable and predictable conduct of their business. But restoration of beneficial market forces—at the very least the removal of trade barriers and the implementation of a mechanism to facilitate the international flow of capital—would not happen automatically. Paradoxically, the achievement of these free market goals would take state initiative, regulation, even intervention.

Keynesian Economics and a Design for Prosperity

A mischievous bit of verse scribbled by a British participant in talks with the Americans on postwar economic arrangements claimed, "It's true *they* have the money bags/But *we* have all the brains."[1] John Maynard Keynes was the British brains.

Born in 1883 into modest circumstances, Keynes was raised and educated in Cambridge, England. Within the insulated, clubby atmosphere of that town's university, he developed economic ideas that proved stunningly original, even revolutionary. In London Keynes led another life. He lived within the iconoclastic Bloomsbury circle devoted to the arts, good food, and stimulating conversation, while also serving as an influential adviser to the British government. In his spare time he made a personal fortune trading on the currency and stock markets. Although a homosexual, he courted and married the beautiful Russian ballerina Lydia Lopokova in the early 1920s in what would prove a lasting and mutually supportive match. He was loyal to his friends and colleagues, yet was the master of the cutting remark and the rude putdown. He was at once a social and political conservative and an unorthodox thinker, religious agnostic, and proponent of popular welfare. In 1946, shortly before his death, he was honored by elevation to the House of Lords.

Keynes once observed, as though anticipating his own influential place in post-war history: "The ideas of economists and political philosophers, both when they are right and when they are wrong, are more powerful than is commonly understood."[2] Keynes's idea that would gain wide political acceptance was that the free market internationally as well as domestically would perform better if subject to constant state oversight and periodic intervention. He laid the foundation for this point by demonstrating in his interwar writings the exaggerated faith that economists since the eighteenth century had put in the impersonal operations of the market. As Keynes came to see it, the doctrine of noninterference (known as *laissez-faire*; see "Key Economic Terms," p. 15) failed to take account of the ways supply and demand could fall out of sync and inflict serious damage. The widespread deprivation brought on by the Great Depression cast serious doubt on the old market faith and led Keynes and his colleagues to conclude that markets left to themselves could not be counted on to produce optimal economic efficiency and growth.

Having concluded that the hidden hand of the market did not always work, Keynes called for intervention by the state at those moments when the economy threatened to plunge or languish. To smooth out the economic cycles, Keynes proposed a greater role for government than either British or American practice sanctioned before the 1930s. His idea was counter-cyclical spending. That meant to get a stalled economy going, the government would increase its outlays, for example on infrastructure (see "Key Economic Terms," p. 15) or social welfare, and thereby restore investor and consumer confidence. If the economy was reaching the peak of its capacity, the government's role was to lower spending or raise taxes, thus cooling the economy while also using the budget surplus to pay down debt incurred by earlier stimulus programs. Keynes's advocacy of government intervention did not make him a socialist. Committed to the capitalist system, he did not want a planned economy, nor did he favor states taking from firms the fundamental decisions about what and how much to produce.

Taken in broader terms, Keynes pointed toward a new age of capitalism in which the state would play a prominent social welfare role. From quite early on he was moved by the belief that the survival of democracy depended on attending to the needs of its citizens. If democracy did not function humanely as well as efficiently, the consequences could be fearsome, as Keynes himself had seen in his own life-time in Hitler's Germany and Stalin's Soviet Union. The veneer of respectability

Keynes gave to a larger state role in economic affairs ran up against a general bias among Americans in favor of the free operation of the market subject to only the most minimal state intervention. On the other hand, on the European continent Keynes reinforced a propensity across a broad spectrum of political opinion to look to the state to tend to the common good. Interwar governments in Germany and Italy had intervened deeply to promote prosperity and development, and while Mussolini and Hitler were discredited, their economic policies retained popularity. On the postwar Left, socialists committed to a democratic way advocated extensive state intervention, and they found a measure of agreement with Christian Democratic parties guided by a strong Catholic tradition of social justice.

Seen in this postwar context, Keynes stood for a middle way between Soviet state planners and conservative Americans suspicious of centralized power, especially when it intruded in the market. In 1926 he wrote of the mix of values that informed his hybrid views. Economic efficiency and individual liberty were important but not by themselves sufficient. Social justice, which he associated with "an unselfish and enthusiastic spirit, which loves the ordinary man," was an indispensable part of the mix.[3] Keynes had no illusions about the brutality of the Soviet system of state planning and consistently rejected it as a negation of all the values that he cherished. The ultimate goal as Keynes saw it was to save the capitalist system and with it much of the free market by according a regulatory role to a conservatively and humanely activist state.

During World War II Keynes made his main contribution to the support of that middle way by leading the British delegation in talks with the Americans on the shape of the postwar international economy. He could not have found a better partner than the Roosevelt administration. Americans, usually fundamentalist in their devotion to the free market and rugged individualism, had been shaken by the Great Depression and also impressed by how state intervention could alleviate suffering. The president and his influential secretary of the treasury, Henry Morgenthau, shared Keynes's belief that an inherently good free market had to be combined with state intervention to avert another economic disaster.

Keynes was perhaps even more important in the long term for the way his justification of state intervention drew the lines of the single most important economic debate of the last half of the twentieth century. The proposition Keynes articulated would divide economists in an ongoing battle over a fundamental question: Did the dangers posed by an activist state exceed any good that it might do? The role of the state would also increasingly divide Americans inclined to favor individual opportunity and corporate freedom of action from western Europeans and Japanese, who took Keynes's ideas on the role of the state as common sense, the only debatable point being not *whether* but *how* the state would intervene in the economy. The European path led to the "welfare state" as the guarantor of individual and group interests against the workings of an impersonal market, while the Japanese embraced "guided capitalism" with an eye to making the economy competitive and the people prosperous. These divergent views of state–market relations would increasingly become a source of contention among the leading economic powers. (See Chapters 5 and 8.)

The Bretton Woods Agreement

Keynes joined his American counterpart, the Treasury Department's Harry Dexter White, at Bretton Woods, New Hampshire, in July 1944. The United States had called the conference to hammer out the basis for the postwar economic system. Forty-four countries sent representatives. The Soviet Union did not attend. The British and the Americans were fully in charge, represented by Keynes and White, who took the lead in designing the institutional framework in which the postwar economy would function and evolve. When twenty-eight nations signed the Bretton Woods agreement in late 1945, they were approving the handiwork of Keynes and White.

Their major achievement was to lay down a new system for capital flow that took the place of the gold standard, abandoned at the outset of the Depression. The U.S. dollar became the pivotal currency. With its value set at $35 for an ounce of gold, the dollar became the basis for establishing the value of all other currencies. The United States agreed to exchange dollars presented by foreign governments for gold at the fixed rate. Those governments for their part agreed to keep their currencies in a stable relationship to the dollar. Free and predictable, this currency exchange system promised to facilitate trade.

To ensure stability and facilitate international economic activity, Bretton Woods established two long-lived institutions. The International Monetary Fund (IMF), created with a reserve of $8.8 billion, provided a mechanism for preserving currency convertibility and avoiding government-imposed exchange controls. It was to lend funds to ensure that trading countries would be able in the short term to pay for their imports and sustain their economic development. The other major Bretton Woods institution was the World Bank, initially called the International Bank for Reconstruction and Development to reflect its first mission of promoting the recovery of war-ravaged economies. Launched with a fund of $9.1 billion, the bank first focused primarily on Europe but then in the 1950s shifted to addressing the needs of newly independent countries.

Far from constituting a bold return to the pre-1931 open, liberal international financial order, the Bretton Woods blueprint explicitly gave states control over capital flows. Keynes and White agreed that speculative capital movements had created turmoil and threatened states' control of their economies critical to serving popular welfare. It was the responsibility of elected leaders, not distant bankers, to select the policies that best served their country. State control of capital movements made it possible to adjust interest rates to attract needed capital. Moreover, state control would prevent the wealthy from evading welfare legislation by shifting capital abroad. Finally, state control was good for trade, which was easily disrupted by speculative capital movements. Stable exchange rates would mean a more predictable commercial environment. In the Keynes–White plan the state role was to be exercised at two levels. All states retained the right to control capital moving across their borders, and the leading economic powers had an additional say through such international institutions as the IMF and World Bank. Representatives from the major economies dominated the governing boards of those institutions and wrote the marching orders. As the source of much of the funding for both institutions, the United States commanded the largest bloc of votes.

In both the United States and Britain a coalition of government, industrial, and labor leaders supported the Bretton Woods reforms against the preferences of private bankers and the heads of state-run central banks for a restoration of the open, unregulated international financial system that prevailed during the earlier era of globalization. The New York financial community, eager to secure its international dominance, had opposed the drift toward what it saw as a "welfare state" under the New Deal, and now saw the IMF as an extension of that trend to the global economy. Those enthusiastic free marketers wanted the western European countries to remove restrictions on currency exchange. Let the international market decide the value of each nation's currency, they argued. This approach threatened upheaval for countries already grappling with enormous problems of postwar recovery. One obstacle was that investors worried by the heavy clouds hanging over Europe would move their money from their own countries with their desperate capital needs to the United States, where the returns were good and the investment was secure. A second problem was serious trade deficits. Europeans had little to export but were heavily dependent on imports to rebuild the economy and restart production. How were they to pay off the resulting deficits? Capital flight from Europe thus spelled more economic pain and the risk of dangerous social strains.

To the disappointment of strict free market advocates, the Truman administration finally supported restrictions on capital flight, while arranging U.S. grants to the western Europeans to close trade deficits and boost reconstruction. These decisions, taken in the course of 1946 and 1947, provided the basis for a new consensus within the United States behind the Bretton Woods arrangements. Cold War fears of instability were beginning to trump the free market principles favored by New York bankers and conservative Republicans.

Free market principles also suffered a setback in negotiations over postwar trade. The Roosevelt administration had launched those talks guided by a strong faith in the virtues of international free trade. If each country specialized by producing and exporting what it was best at doing, international exchange would keep prices low and quality high, to everyone's benefit. For example, a country that produced expensive agricultural goods but also made cheap, well-made cars would shift out of the former the better to focus its resources on the latter, the product that was most competitive on the international market. As tariff and other protectionist barriers fell, so the argument went, international trade would gain a fresh stimulus and bring prosperity to all. The lessons that American leaders drew from the recent past reinforced their belief that long-term political stability depended on an open, stable system of international trade. According to this common wisdom, the crash of 1929 had been brought on by shortsighted protectionism (see "Key Economic Terms," p. 15). Once the crash had occurred, a difficult situation was made worse as each country turned inward, trying to solve its economic crisis independently and rejecting the cooperation that was the surest road to an international recovery. The result, according to this reading of the recent past, was social and political unrest in Germany, Italy, and Japan; the rise of Hitler, Mussolini, and the Tokyo militarists; and ultimately aggressive policies that brought on World War II. Secretary of State Cordell Hull, the staunchest of the free traders in the Roosevelt administration, articulated the core principles of his faith when he observed that "unhampered trade dovetailed with peace; high tariffs, trade barriers, and unfair economic competition with war."[4]

The Bretton Woods conference anticipated the free movement of goods in the postwar economy, but when Washington got down to the details of the free trade regime, it ran into trouble. Ambitious provisions for rapidly dismantling trade barriers provoked Britain and its imperial partners such as Australia and South Africa determined to protect their close, exclusive trade relationship. Within the United States, wool producers, independent oil firms, dairy farmers, and others vulnerable to foreign competition had steadfast supporters among Republicans in Congress and were sure to defeat any agreement with teeth.

By 1950 the Truman administration abandoned any plans for a major makeover of the trade system; an alternative, more modest mechanism for promoting free trade had taken shape. The General Agreement on Tariffs and Trade (GATT), concluded in Geneva in 1947, proved the sleeper amidst the ambitious designs and major negotiations of the period. Originally part of an overall U.S. free trade initiative, GATT provided an informal method for negotiating multilateral arrangements for tariff reductions. Without a permanent secretariat, however, GATT seemed of limited importance, and to get the agreement approved, the United States had to open its market to its trading partners and in short order effect sharp cuts on U.S. tariffs on foreign imports. By making one-sided concessions, U.S. officials hoped to enshrine the principle of ever-freer trade in international discussions and at the same time give access to the large and prosperous U.S. market for producers in countries who were allied to the United States in the Cold War struggle and whose growing prosperity would create a rising demand for American goods. Promoting postwar recovery in Japan and western Europe thus made both political and economic sense.

However, modest its early achievements, GATT would prove over the decades an important vehicle for gradually but dramatically lowering trade barriers all around the world. GATT would also come to serve as an important forum where its members could define and adjudicate the rules for their increasingly complex and interdependent trade relationships. By the 1960s GATT had established itself alongside the IMF and the World Bank as a major pillar for the international economy.

THE U.S. RESCUE OPERATION

In the immediate postwar years Japan and the states of western Europe began a remarkable economic recovery. As they did so, they fundamentally rethought their national goals. After years of devoting their economic resources to external expansion and military rivalry, those states now experienced a major paradigm shift. Their leaders took internal economic development as their chief concern, and they made rising per capita income the chief measure of success . If there was any international rivalry in this new era, it was for them over who had the highest popular standard of living, and the results were adjudicated not on the battlefield or in diplomatic confrontations but by citizen-consumers in regular national elections. Leaders who did not deliver did not stay in office.

The United States played an important role in both speeding economic recovery and encouraging the new national goals. It was a source of scarce hard currency and food. It exported industrial goods essential to restarting production. It unilaterally opened its home market to imports from struggling European and Japanese producers. U.S. leaders acted from a mixture of motives: a humanitarian impulse to help former allies, a missionary desire to convert former enemies, the Cold War imperative to preempt Soviet influence, and a selfish conviction that U.S. prosperity depended on economic revival elsewhere. A world floundering in misery was likely to be neither democratic nor immune to communist appeals. The impact of the American role was perhaps most pronounced in Japan, where U.S. occupation authorities exercised direct control for the first seven postwar years. In Europe, American control was direct only in its quarter of occupied Germany. Elsewhere on the continent the United States dealt with sovereign states, but their desperate economic straits left them vulnerable to American pressure even if they did not have to take American orders.

In assessing this U.S. impact, it is important to keep in mind the considerable assets that survived the war in both western Europe and Japan. The workforce was educated and experienced. A sophisticated management was ready to take charge of what remained of productive capacity. State authorities quickly turned their hand to recovery. Above all, participants in the reconstruction effort were familiar with the organizational forms and practices that had worked for them in the past and could be tailored to new conditions. These indigenous endowments were critical to postwar recovery, and without them U.S. recovery efforts would likely have stumbled, perhaps even failed.

Occupation and Recovery in Japan

Japan, which was to emerge as one of the leading economic powers of the late twentieth century, boasts two economic success stories. The first one spanned the first third of the twentieth century. By 1900 Japan was emerging as a prominent participant in the first phase of globalization. With its labor-intensive industries such as textiles and its merchant marine developing rapidly, the country prospered through World War I and the 1920s. The Great Depression dealt Japan a major blow as other countries closed off their markets. In a desperate bid to secure raw materials and markets, Japan sought late in the 1930s to extend its political and military control across a broad sweep of East Asia. This imperial enterprise provoked resistance not only in the region but also from the British and Americans, resulting in war and another major blow to Japan's economy. The second miracle would not begin until the 1950s (see Chapter 5). But the period of economic reconstruction immediately after the war prepared the way.

Rebuilding was a massive challenge. Bombing had done extensive damage to housing stocks and production facilities. Factories still intact had to be converted back to civilian production. Eighty percent of the merchant fleet critical to supplying the resource-poor collection of islands that the Japanese called home lay on the ocean floor. Twenty billion dollars in overseas investments were gone. Inflation (see "Key Economic Terms," p. 15) persisted from wartime to the postwar period. The future was further clouded by the threat of having to pay massive reparations claimed by neighboring countries devastated by Japan's war machine.

Japanese society was no less devastated. Nearly three million people had died. The survivors lived at near-subsistence level. Per capita income was only half of what it had been in the mid-1930s before Japan had embarked on its disastrous experiment in expansion overseas. Some 6.5 million soldiers, sailors, and civilians overseas at war's end began to trickle back empty handed to a land that offered little opportunity or hope. One soldier returning home in May 1946 reported grimly what he found: "My house was burned, my wife and children missing. What little money I had quickly was consumed by the high prices, and I was a pitiful figure. Not a single person gave me a kind word. Rather, they cast hostile glances my way. Tormented and without work, I became possessed by a devil."[5] Women left without support turned to prostitution, while orphans scavenged for food and shelter. Families sold off their possessions in a desperate race between a dwindling stock of goods and rising food prices. Starvation became shockingly commonplace. Only black marketeers seemed to flourish amidst the privation and despondency.

By April 1952, when the U.S. occupation came to an end, Japan was back on its feet. Production was rising. Per capita income had nearly regained prewar levels, and inflation would soon be mastered. That the Japanese were able to overcome a dire situation was partially the result of the policies of the American-dominated military occupation headed by General Douglas MacArthur, but even more important were the assets that Japan carried over from war to peace. The imperial bureaucracy had survived the war and continued to operate with American toleration, even encouragement. This respected and experienced elite, the pick of the university trained, had a strong faith in government economic planning and social direction as the best path to restore Japan's standing in the world. The economic institutions, from major corporations to the dominant business associations, were also tested and commanded respect. Finally, the productivity and discipline of the workforce were at an all-time high. Technical schools as well as company training had improved skills of workers even as their numbers increased dramatically from 1930 onward. While companies took the first steps toward treating workers as part of the family, the government had initiated welfare measures, including the beginnings of medical insurance and pension plans, and celebrated loyalty to the firm and sacrifice for the country. Firms could also turn to a cadre of scientists and engineers active in wartime research and ready to exploit advances in such areas as electronics and petrochemicals.

The initial impetus for this economic turnaround came from basic reforms launched during the first several years of the occupation. Some were projects that career bureaucrats had conceived earlier, and now with the ultranationalist and military elites gone, they had a freer hand to press ahead. For example, on the critical matter of land reform, wartime government agencies had made an important start by intervening directly into food production and distribution. This step cut the ties between the exploitative landlord class and their tenants, reducing rural poverty and discontent.

Other reforms issued from the headquarters of the American proconsul. MacArthur took up his duties at the end of a long and distinguished military career. The latter stages had seen him lead Allied forces fighting across the southwest Pacific. MacArthur ran the occupation through several thousand American military and civilian officials, who in turn supervised a revived Japanese bureaucracy. The Truman administration left him considerable latitude to follow his own design. He was virtually unchallengeable until the added duties of commanding United Nations forces in Korea embroiled him in difficulty with the Truman administration and precipitated his recall and retirement in April 1951 in a blaze of glory. The occupation by then had only a year to go.

From the start MacArthur was confident that he understood "the oriental mind" and acted on a missionary determination to turn a militaristic Japan toward modern civilization. Compared to Anglo-Saxons, the Japanese were (as he put it only after leaving Japan) "like a boy of twelve."[6] The task of the occupation was to help that youth become a responsible adult. MacArthur's dignity and his idealistic commitment to creating a new Japan cleansed of its discredited past won him popularity in a country taught by wartime propaganda to expect the worst from the "American-English demons." He began with the goal of demilitarizing Japan, making it into what he called the "Switzerland of Asia." Japan's new constitution, drafted by the Americans, renounced war as an instrument of national policy. Japan could maintain only a limited self-defense force that was forbidden to operate beyond Japanese waters.

MacArthur also proceeded with a series of steps toward democratization that cumulatively had a major impact on the economy. One of his most consequential decisions was to push farther on the land reform already begun by the bureaucracy. He took hold of an agricultural system in which nearly half of all land had

General Douglas MacArthur with Emperor Hirohito, September 27, 1945 To make clear the new order of things, MacArthur had the emperor, some 20 years the junior but still regarded as divine, come to his offices for the first meeting rather than going to the imperial palace for an audience. MacArthur's dress and demeanor seem calculatedly casual in contrast to the emperor's formality. Taking this photo, published in all major Japanese newspapers, was prologue to a 40-minute conversation through interpreters, the first of 11 meetings, all conducted in the U.S. headquarters. This odd couple enjoyed a mutually beneficial relationship. MacArthur shielded the emperor from the international clamor to charge him along with the other Japanese leaders with war crimes and allowed him to stay on the throne to serve as a unifying symbol and a stabilizing force at a time of national stress and reorientation. To have a role in the new era of democratization, the emperor had to accept a diminished role as a constitutional monarch. (U.S. Army photographer Lt. Gaetano Faillace)

been tenanted. By the time he was finished with redistribution, only 10 percent of the land was worked by nonowners. As a result of this dramatic increase in independent farmers, the countryside became both more politically stable and economically productive. Labor, already given the bureaucratic green light, found the Americans also supportive of the right to organize and bargain collectively for better working conditions and pay, while employers with dangerous or unsanitary working conditions were called to account. Finally, in a distinctly American move without support among Japan's bureaucrats, the occupation turned to breaking up the large, family-controlled business conglomerates known as *zaibatsu* that had dominated the economy. One of these conglomerates might have had hundreds of thousands of employees (in one case almost two million at home and abroad) and controlled hundreds of companies. American reformers implicated these conglomerates in the earlier policy of aggression, and argued that democracy and free markets in Japan required their destruction. As an influential American economic mission asserted after surveying Japan just after the war, "Unless the Zaibatsu are broken up, the Japanese have little prospect of ever being able to govern themselves as free men."[7]

The Cold War provided an additional impetus to recovery. As U.S.–Soviet tensions mounted, occupation policy underwent in 1947–1948 what is known as the

"reverse course." Washington had begun the occupation with political and economic reform uppermost in mind, but it increasingly saw Japan as an important
anticommunist bastion in Asia. The American occupiers, now working closely with
conservative Prime Minister Yoshida Shigeru, took steps to control the political
Left and to blunt labor activism. At the same time growing U.S. commitments
overseas were making it difficult for Washington to continue to bear the costs of
occupying and rehabilitating Japan. Under pressure to speed economic recovery,
the occupation took a more kindly view of industrial concentration. Large Japanese corporations began to form "enterprise groups" (keiretsu) in which members
with diverse lines of production (for example, chemicals, automobiles, iron and
steel, and electrical machinery) joined in a long-term partnership anchored by a
major bank. One major keiretsu brought the Mitsubishi Bank, the Mitsubishi Corporation, Mitsubishi Heavy Industries, and Mitsubishi Motors into close affili-
ation. Like much else in postwar Japan, the leading enterprise groups (Mitsui and
Sumitomo along with Mitsubishi) were based on relationships going back to wartime and earlier.

The outbreak of war in neighboring Korea capped the process of recovery.
Japan served as a staging area for U.S. forces fighting on the nearby peninsula.
Earnings from a broad range of wartime goods and services provided the first
hints of postwar prosperity. In 1952 with Korea still in conflict, Washington and
Tokyo concluded a treaty that brought the occupation to an end and that carried
important economic as well as political consequences. It placed Japan under the
U.S. defense umbrella, allowing Tokyo to keep its military budget low and concentrate its resources on the civilian economy. U.S. bases located on Japanese
soil not only gave substance to this defense commitment but also served as an
important source of economic stimulation. The treaty minimized reparations
due to neighbors victimized during wartime, thus calming Japanese business
interests worried about the loss of already scarce resources available to restart
production.

By the latter stages of the occupation the rough outlines of a unique Japanese
economic model were beginning to form. Joseph Dodge, a U.S. banker sent to advise
on the Japanese economy in 1948, came to a predictable if mistaken conclusion:
"The fundamental problem of the Japanese nation can be expressed in the simple
terms of too many people, too little land and too few natural resources." A skeptical official in the Finance Ministry quickly replied that the same point could be
made about Manhattan![8] One Japanese solution to ensure prosperity for those
crowded islands called for government planning, but both U.S. officials and Prime
Minister Yoshida were staunchly opposed. The alternative that prevailed was a
coordinated public–private approach that brought government direction and resources to bear on economic development but that left business to make the best
market decisions within this benign environment. From this collaboration would
emerge a kind of guided capitalism.

In the first modest exercise of its leadership the Yoshida government focused in 1947 on the revival of the coal and steel industries. It used loans, price subsidies, tariffs to hold back imports, and allocation of scarce resources to stimulate recovery. The government would move on in the early 1950s to "rationalize" key industrial sectors—encouraging investment in modern new facilities that would reduce production costs. It began with steel and coal once more and then moved on to electrical power and shipbuilding, among others. Here too it used incentives, including special tax treatment, interest subsidies, loans, and "administrative guidelines." This flexible approach would make the "Switzerland of Asia" also its Manhattan.

Recovery in Western Europe

Like Japan, the European economies were in a desperate condition. A civilian population that had largely escaped destruction during World War I had felt the full force of bombing and battles during World War II. This time half the deaths had been noncombatants (some 18 million), and facilities for production, transport, and communication had suffered heavy damage. Much of what industry remained had yet to be converted back to civilian use and to find suppliers and markets within new postwar boundaries. Whole cities lay in ruins. Defeated Germany and Italy had suffered especially heavy losses as a result of bombing and invasion. For example, more than half of the housing stock in Germany was depleted. The prospects for recovery looked grim. Everywhere coal for heating and power for production were alarmingly scarce, and neither of the main sources, Britain or Germany, could meet the demand. Food supplies were equally precarious. Livestock was gone, and fertilizer was nowhere to be found. Dollars to pay for imports, even of such essentials as food and coal, were in desperately short supply. The winter of 1946–1947 proved the harshest in memory. Soon rising Soviet–American tensions would further dampen hope.

In contrast to Japan just after the war, general social breakdown in western Europe seemed a real possibility. Demobilized soldiers were coming home to societies in shambles. The refugee problem assumed massive proportions as 30 million people fled before the Red Army, were displaced by redrawn frontiers in eastern Europe, or were freed from prisoner of war, forced labor, or concentration camps. These "displaced" were, an American journalist noted at the end of 1945, "desperate and homeless . . . milling east and west, north and south, across the continent." Disrupted transport systems and a shortage of food and shelter left many in dire straits and uncertain where to turn. A Jewish academic who had survived both the Holocaust and the fire-bombing of Dresden found himself in a world in which the word *unimaginable* had lost its meaning: "This nightmare of destruction, dust, the Americans' speeding vehicles, of lack of everything and, above all, of absolute uncertainty, unreliability, vagueness—this terrible jelly, both literally and metaphorically, of debris, rubble, and dust." Workers angry over continuing hardships that neither governments nor business leaders could solve went on strike, while street demonstrations drew the cold and hungry.[9]

Food shortages had already become serious during the war. Young hostesses in France assigned to escort American liberators to cultural sites recalled viewing these young soldiers with ready access to food "with their eyes in their stomachs. Each soldier, however ugly, was worth his weight in chocolate, protein, glucose, and like Pavlov's dogs, each girl began to salivate at the sight of a uniform." To everyone's dismay, conditions did not rapidly improve with the end of the war in May 1945 but rather further deteriorated. Even as late as the summer of 1946 a hundred million Europeans were down to 1,500 calories or less per day—the level at which health suffers and work becomes difficult if not impossible. Another 40 million were just a shade above this dangerous level. A German politician recalled some 40 years later how those hard times had taught him "what hunger really meant and how it feels, how it looks when the last slice of bread is shared amongst five members of the family."[10]

The Truman administration was slow to grasp the full magnitude of the European crisis. It had supported humanitarian aid administered by the United Nations as a stopgap measure, but Washington insisted on closing that program down at

Rebuilding amidst the Rubble of War, Berlin, 1946

The grim determination evident in this photo was critical to family survival and physical reconstruction at a time when men were scarce. One authoritative account has captured the dire conditions these "women of the rubble" faced. "In a period of utterly inadequate rations, tremendous shortages of housing, fuel, and the most basic of consumer items, women worked the black market, stood in endless food lines, trekked to the countryside to barter away their last belongings, made bread out of acorns and soap out of ash, stole coal from trains and wood from off-limits forests, and mended their families' threadbare clothes when even needles were a scarce commodity on the black market."[11] In Germany, images like this one became a popular symbol. It highlighted the suffering the war had brought ordinary Germans (here significantly women) and turned attention away from the destruction aggressive Germans (men) had inflicted on others. The image thus conveyed the comforting notion that the country was closing the books on the Hitler era. Now hard work, photos such as this one suggested, would usher in a new era of prosperity and peace. Despite praise for their sacrifices and labor during these hard years, German women did not win expanded postwar occupational opportunities. (Deutsches Historisches Museum, Berlin) the end of 1946 because some benefits were going to countries under Soviet sway. Finally in 1947, with the Marshall Plan, the Truman administration embraced a more ambitious effort to replace destroyed industry and restart production. By then, growing concern with the Soviet threat had made Washington more receptive to calls for helping western Europe and especially heavily damaged Germany. In theory the Marshall Plan had allowed for aid to the Soviet Union and the Soviet-aligned states of eastern Europe, but Washington's task was greatly simplified when Stalin pulled his delegation out of preliminary consultations in mid-1947 and took his clients with him. Washington proceeded to work out a recovery plan with the western European states and then made available grants that would total some $12 billion through 1952 (about half of the total U.S. aid to Europe since the end of the war). Of the major western European states, Britain received the most Marshall Plan aid ($3.2 billion) and West Germany the least ($1.4 billion). To ensure that this altruism benefited the U.S. economy, Congress stipulated that roughly 70 percent of the funds be spent on American-made goods.

U.S. assistance had a significant impact economically, although by the time it began to arrive in 1948 conditions were already improving. That year the average level of real earnings of western European workers had already exceeded the level for 1938 by 20 percent. Agricultural production and industrial output were rising, transport problems were easing, and spending by firms as well as ordinary people on goods and services began to increase for the first time, even if housing and food remained in short supply. Thanks to the Marshall Plan, conditions continued to improve. By 1952 industrial and agricultural production had climbed to 35 percent above the prewar point. Western European economies had turned the corner.

More broadly, the Marshall Plan provided an opportunity to promote American economic and political values in an Old World that had seemingly lost its way. American planners on the scene and their superiors in Washington pushed regional economic integration as a first step toward creating a union of states. U.S. officials were also determined to protect the free market from disruption by Communist-led unions and from state schemes to redistribute wealth, certain that such measures would undermine production and sharpen social tensions without solving Europe's economic problems. Finally, American representatives in Europe opposed rapidly increasing consumption. Rather, they favored "productionism" (market-driven economic growth through investment in production), confident that this was the surest way to defuse class tensions and restore prosperity and stability while also promoting exports that would integrate European economies into the global trading system. A Marshall Plan brochure that circulated in Italy in 1949 promised "a higher standard of living for the entire nation" and "maximum employment for workers and farmers" but linked these good things to achieving "greater production."[12]

The substantial U.S. aid program gave Washington less leverage than the planners had expected, however. As one wit has put it, Europe in effect said to the Americans that "we want to be dominated, but on our own terms."[13] U.S. planners had first of all to face rising popular pressure for an immediate improvement in welfare and consumption rather than deferring them in favor of investment and production with the promise of long-term benefits. Governments that did not listen to their citizens clamoring for immediate improvements in food and housing and for jobs risked losing votes. U.S. planners had also to take into account the agenda of centrist conservative politicians at the head of Christian Democratic parties, especially important in France, West Germany, and Italy. These conservatives were favorably disposed to the United States—and ready to play on U.S. fears of communism to extract economic and trade concessions.

Communist parties in the early postwar period were especially large and influential in France and Italy. Both parties had strong labor support and popularity derived from wartime resistance to the Germans. But Washington worried that the ties of those parties to Moscow made them a dangerously subversive force if allowed inside any governing coalitions. Christian Democrats, happy to see their rivals out of favor in Washington, cooperated in the exclusion of Communists from power. In France, for example, in spring 1947 the governing coalition duly dropped its Communist partners. U.S. policy also sought with considerable success to drive a wedge between left-wing and centrist unions, thus in effect destroying the unity of the European labor movement within countries as well as across the continent.

By cultivating conservative European elites and by marginalizing the Left, the Marshall Plan helped pave the way for trans-Atlantic economic cooperation as well as the formation of the North Atlantic Treaty Organization (NATO). Christian Democratic parties would in the bargain secure a prolonged period of dominance in European politics while also defending sovereignty and protecting their own economic preferences in the face of demands for a national remake on American lines. Perhaps more than American leaders at the time realized, Christian Democratic leaders were strikingly traditional in their commitment to preserving state authority and making it serve social stability but also popular welfare. While favorably disposed to a greater degree of regional cooperation, they were not about to give up national power to a united Europe. And while inclined to rely on the market in economic matters, they were not prepared to leave it unchecked and disregard issues of social justice.

For West Germany the Marshall Plan signaled a great turnaround in U.S. policy. Initially the Roosevelt administration was determined to render Germany impotent so that it could not precipitate Europe into war for a third time in the twentieth century. Henry Morgenthau, FDR's influential secretary of the treasury, regarded Germany as militaristic to the core. He was sure that it would inevitably pose a threat to the peace unless the country were dismembered and the people subjected to reeducation. A critical element of Morgenthau's approach was the dismantling of heavy industry, thus removing the potential for remilitarization, and exporting industrial plants as reparations to neighboring countries. FDR shared Morgenthau's hardline perspective. "The German people as a whole must have it driven home to them that the whole nation has engaged in a lawless conspiracy against the decencies of modern civilization."[14]

A leaked version of what Morgenthau ostensibly wanted set off public controversy as well as dissension within the U.S. government. Secretary of State Hull and Secretary of War Henry L. Stimson recalled that the vindictive peace of 1919 following World War I had spurred German desire for revenge and thus planted the seeds for World War II. Hull wanted Germany integrated into a free trade world, the best guarantee in his view of good behavior. Stimson was preoccupied with the challenges of occupation and thus gave priority to ensuring humane treatment, stability, and security in a devastated land. In May 1945, with the Germans now vanquished, President Harry Truman brought the debate over occupation policy to an end. He called for denazification, demilitarization, and a living standard no higher than the lowest elsewhere in Europe, and embraced the idea that democratization would head off any impulse toward renewed aggression. Truman left the details of the new approach to the commanders of the American, Russian, British, and French forces each occupying a zone of Germany along with a section of Berlin (see Map 1.1 on p. 43).

Between 1946 and 1955 the former enemy became an ally with the emergence of a separate West German state closely linked to western Europe politically and economically. With no agreement with the Soviet Union in sight on a common policy toward the four zones of occupation, Washington began in 1946 to chart a separate course in league with the British and French. In June 1948 the territorial pieces of what would become the new West German state came together when the three powers merged their zones and introduced a new currency. This step provoked Stalin late in the month to institute his Berlin blockade in a doomed attempt to avert a permanent division. The blockade hardened American resolve to hold on to western Germany, confirmed anti-Soviet prejudices, and helped consolidate the sense of a new relationship between the United States and western Europe. In May 1949 Stalin ended his blockade of Berlin, followed two weeks later by the emergence of a single West German state (the Federal Republic of Germany, with its capital in Bonn).

In the first postwar elections in West Germany held that year, the Christian Democratic Union won a parliamentary majority. Its leader, the 73-year-old Konrad Adenauer, became chancellor. An opponent of the Hitler regime, he had emerged from prison only to find the Soviets reaching deep into Europe—into Germany itself. Adenauer reacted with repugnance to this alien force embodying "Asian spirit and power."[15] He accepted the painful division of his country with the hope of saving the non-Soviet portion by aligning it with countries to the west. That meant making peace with the old enemy France, seeking economic and military integration within western Europe, and accepting the United States as the ultimate guarantor of German economic recovery and security. These principles would form the basis of his long authoritarian rule. Down to 1963, he would support economic cooperation within the European community and integrate West Germany as a full member into NATO.

The new Adenauer government and its successors shaped economic policy within the framework of the "social market economy." This German model stressed free market competition rather than government management. It gave preference to investment-led and export-oriented growth strategies. It was zealous in pursuit of a balanced budget to avoid a repeat of the soaring inflation that had done such harm to the fledgling German democracy in the 1920s. These features of the German model were congruent with American preferences, but other prominent features were not. The social market approach promoted a paternalistic welfare system with roots in the late nineteenth century. It tolerated, even encouraged, industrial concentration and cooperation among firms. The efficacy of this model would become ever clearer in the postwar decades.

Italy presents a different pattern, highlighting the diversity of the Marshall Plan's impact. Because Italy came out of the war with a postfascist government acceptable to the British and the Americans, it escaped military occupation. But, as in much of the rest of western Europe, the country's dependence on American assistance gave Washington considerable influence over the government in Rome. That influence was reinforced by the covert activities of the Central Intelligence Agency (CIA) and the overt participation of American labor organizations in the shaping of the postwar Italian labor movement. The Truman administration used these resources to force Italy's large Communist Party out of the coalition government in

Italian Election Poster, 1948
This appeal from the Christian Democratic Party implored, "Mothers! Save your children from Bolshevism!" In the background the dark Communist forces march rank upon rank. Their flags carried the Italian Communist Party's hammer and sickle, an ominous reminder of the party's link to the Kremlin.

mid-1947 (at about the same time that the French party suffered its expulsion) and to drive a wedge between Communist and other labor unions. Washington won these victories in close collaboration with an influential center-right Christian Democratic party headed by Alcide de Gasperi.

But collaboration was a two-way street. While loyal to Washington on Cold War issues, Rome maintained considerable autonomy in charting its domestic economic course. It presided over an economy defined by concentrated power and a tangled web of public and private interests shaped during the Mussolini era and even earlier. The Christian Democratic government was allied with a tight-knit business elite based in the Piedmont-Lombard region of northern Italy. That elite controlled the country's major private industry, located in a triangle defined by the cities of Turin, Milan, and Genoa, and articulated its interests through Confindustria, the official association of Italian industry, founded in 1919.

The state itself played a major, direct economic role. The Institute for Industrial Reconstruction (IRI), a huge bank and industrial holding company that had given the interwar Italian government control of a share of economic activity second only to the Soviet Union, remained a major presence on the postwar scene. A socialist adviser to Mussolini, Alberto Beneduce, had created IRI and run it until his death at the end of the war. His son-in-law, Enrico Cuccia (married to Beneduce's wonderfully named daughter Idea Socialista), then took over. A press-shy Sicilian, Cuccia also headed the influential Milan-based Mediobanca. Created at the end of World War II, it would be Italy's only merchant bank until the 1980s. Funded and majority owned by the state, the bank served firms belonging to the northern business elite and acted as a guarantor of stability within the industrial sector by blocking brash interlopers and dubious mergers. The bank exercised its influence through its minority stake in Italy's major corporations such as Fiat (cars), Pirelli (tires), and Olivetti (office machines) and through its power to open or close the funding spigot for these capital-hungry firms.

This tight-knit economic establishment carried forward the distinctly nationalist and modernizing impulse that had governed Italy's development policy since the turn of the century. That policy gave priority to encouraging foreign trade, protecting the home market, and promoting industrial cooperation, with labor and the state as partners with business. The public–private coalition resorted to a wide range of measures to maintain a high rate of investment essential to achieving these basic goals. Those measures included holding down wages, favoring industry over agriculture, and promoting emigration for the remittances it generated. To the dismay of Americans, advocates of the free market had no more influence in the postwar Italian order than they had had earlier.

While 1945 is often referred to as Europe's "year zero," it would be more accurate to think of the years immediately after the war as the real watershed. They witnessed the completion of the process of expulsions, ethnic cleansing, and redrawn borders that remade European states, once distinctly multinational, into considerably more homogeneous entities. Those years allowed Europeans to tame

MENDING THE INTERNATIONAL ECONOMY

1929	Financial crash leads to Great Depression
1930s	Industrial economies resort to inward-looking, protectionist policies
1939–45	World War II devastates production worldwide
1944	Bretton Woods conference makes the dollar the pivotal currency and establishes the International Monetary Fund and the World Bank as oversight institutions for the international economy
1945	The United States accounts for a third of all global production and two thirds of world gold reserves
1947	General Agreement on Tariffs and Trade concluded, beginning a gradual reduction in trade barriers; U.S. occupation policy in Japan reversed in favor of economic recovery; Marshall Plan proposed to revive European economies
1952	U.S. occupation of Japan ends; Japanese and western European economies approach prewar levels

memories of wartime death and cruelty and to put to one side the unsavory record of active collaboration and popular acquiescence to German rule. Punishment of some men who had cooperated politically and some women who had engaged in "horizontal collaboration" with German soldiers helped to draw a line under a past of organized violence and opportunistic behavior. With justice seemingly done, it was possible to sanitize public understanding of the wartime experience, the better to focus on the construction of a new, humane, peaceful, prosperous Europe. Gilbert Murray, the English classicist and League of Nations supporter, had in 1943 articulated what was already then a widespread vision of a more benign path after the carnage of two world wars: "The modern state, even though now for the moment definitely organized to the last button as a killing machine, is far more at home in the work of constructive organization, economic research, social service, care of health, provision against fear and want. The sort of work that we shall have to undertake, amid many dangers and on a gigantic scale, is just the work for which, in contrast to these earlier times, we are splendidly equipped."[16] By the early 1950s signs of economic recovery and the first tentative steps toward economic cooperation between former rivals in constructing that new Europe had given substance to the vision entertained by Murray and many others.

THE AMERICAN ECONOMIC POWERHOUSE

The United States could play the impresario of the postwar system of trade and finance for one simple reason: Its economy was moving to unprecedented levels of output in the late 1940s, unmatched among all the economies of the world.

Without its strength, American leaders would have been nearly impotent in the face of profound postwar challenges, and the American public would likely have been loath to see resources directed overseas. Because of its strength, that economy could not only meet domestic needs but also have a deep impact on other countries. While giving overall structure to the new international economy, American resources and leadership hastened the recovery of western Europe and Japan and offered a vision of a consumer society that many found attractive in the wake of prolonged depression and war. But others, articulating criticisms that would echo into the new century, charged the U.S. economic giant with intimidating its competitors and forcing them to play by its rules. They also contended that U.S. exports threatened local cultures and eroded a younger generation's national identity.

Good Times Return

The economic might that was critical to making the United States a postwar leader with a global reach had built rapidly from the late nineteenth century. By 1914 the United States was the largest and most homogeneous market in the world and had the largest industrial output. For example, already by 1900 American steel output had surpassed that of Britain and Germany combined. Americans by then enjoyed the highest standard of living of any people. And they had the highest level of labor productivity, made possible by sizable capital investments in innovative technology, equipment, and production processes. World War I had further elevated the U.S. position, converting it from a net debtor who had borrowed heavily on European capital markets. It was now banker to the world. The U.S. economy had put on an impressive performance with striking growth between 1870 and 1929. Gross domestic product (GDP) increased nearly eightfold while per capita income rose nearly threefold (see "Key Economic Terms," p. 15). Already the United States stood as the exemplar of what a modern economy could deliver.

As the largest and most vital of the world's economies, the United States had played a prominent role in bringing the long period of growth to a halt. By closing off the home market during the 1920s and refusing to cooperate with Britain and other economic powers once the Great Depression began to hammer global trade and finance, Washington helped create and then prolong the global downswing. Like others around the world, Americans felt the dire effects. In 1933, the grimmest year of the depression, GDP had fallen by over a quarter from its high point in 1929, and at least one out of every four workers was unemployed.

While Europe and Japan suffered destruction during wartime and then in the early postwar years struggled with the essentials of survival, Americans watched their economy begin to improve in what turned into a dramatic resurgence. The turnaround had begun in 1939. In that year GDP recovered to 1929 levels, and by 1944 it had more than doubled, thanks to the stimulus imparted by wartime mobilization.

The first years after the war proved turbulent, although without hardships comparable to what other countries engulfed by war were then going through. GDP dropped by a quarter between 1944 and 1947 as the economy made the transition to peacetime. Some 11 million demobilized men returned to the workforce. Savings accumulated by workers during wartime rationing chased too few goods and unleashed inflation. Industries struggling with converting back to civilian production could not keep up with the heavy consumer demand. Inflation coming on top of wartime restraints on wages left organized labor restive. Strike activity had begun in 1944 and continued to the end of the decade, prompting Republicans in Congress to retaliate by imposing restrictions on labor unions. By 1947 Cold War commitments were adding fresh economic pressures. The Marshall Plan was the first hint of the costs associated with the overseas anticommunist struggle. As we have seen (Chapter 1), Truman tried to hold the military budget down, but after the outbreak of the Korean War he put into effect his advisers' proposal for a tripling of defense spending. This dramatic hike set off a fresh bout of inflation, and Truman declared a state of emergency in December 1950 following the Chinese intervention in Korea.

Social change set in motion by the war created immediate postwar tensions that were harbingers of major upheavals to come. The shortage of wartime labor had drawn women and African Americans into the mainstream economy. Three out of four women in the workforce remained there after the war, although often forced into lower-paying jobs by homecoming veterans. African Americans had migrated out of the South to fill openings in the war industry, and black soldiers returned looking for the freedom at home that their government had asked them to defend abroad. They also wanted economic opportunities to build a better life for their families.

Hanging over these years was the shadow of Keynes. Many economists were convinced that the U.S. economy was approaching maturity, and that as it did so, the prospects for growth would dim and the chances of another major downturn would rise. To avert this outcome and extract from the economy its best performance, the American Keynesians prescribed government intervention to counter any slowdown. The Full Employment Act of 1946 committed the government to act in order to maximize the potential for economic growth and keep that growth steady.

The fear of renewed depression that haunted the first few postwar years dissipated, although the belief in economic management had become an orthodoxy that survived through the boom time ahead. The economy's immediate problem proved if anything the reverse of what economists had anticipated—not an excess of goods but rather insufficient production to meet demand. But then factories completed their transition from wartime to civilian goods, once scarce raw materials became more available, and so production steadily expanded to meet high demand, inflation dropped, and the standard of living climbed impressively. Although Americans made up only 6 percent of the world's population, by the mid-1950s they were producing about a quarter of the global output. American industry was unchallenged in aircraft and aerospace, electrical appliances, chemical synthetics, automobiles, and lightweight metals, and it was developing new technology with a great future. The first photocopy machine appeared on the market in 1947. IBM sold the first computer in 1953. Television, developed from technology that matured in the course of World War II, was proving wildly popular. By 1953 half of all U.S. families owned a set.

The rapid spread of television highlights a broader postwar trend: the capacity of Americans to consume what they produced with such ingenuity and in such abundance. Postwar America witnessed a flowering of consumerism that citizens of all developed countries today take for granted but that at the time was a marvel. Americans led the way in creating a consumer regime, in which much of an individual's daily life as well as the broader culture and economy revolved around the pleasurable acquisition and use of a diverse range of nonessential goods and services. So intense was this engagement in consumption that it helped define personal identity and shape national culture.

The postwar flowering was the culmination of long-term trends. By the end of the nineteenth century rising incomes, especially in cities, a growing population, and the development of industry had created a new society edging toward mass consumption. Providing the critical element in this transformation, U.S. industry took the pioneering steps toward mass-produced goods. High output pushed prices down while at the same time rising family incomes made it possible to cover basic food and housing and still have funds for discretionary spending. The task of the new business of advertising was to make sure that ordinary families spent those funds and thus kept production at a high volume. By the 1920s many Americans were able to purchase new consumer products such as the telephone, radio, phonograph, and automobile and to afford various forms of entertainment such as movies and vacations. These goods and diversions, available to a degree undreamt of a century earlier, were coming to define how substantial numbers of Americans even below the middle class defined the good life.

Although the Great Depression of the 1930s checked the development of consumer culture, and wartime rationing further delayed its return, in the postwar years it revived with a surprising vigor. The return of economic growth intersected with two closely related trends: the rise of the suburbs and a surge in family formation. Marriage and birth rates jumped as soldiers and prosperity returned after the war. Housing sprung up, primarily in the suburbs and mostly owner occupied. Between 1947 and 1953 some nine million Americans relocated to those outlying areas where they could purchase a home, often in low-cost real estate developments. Low down payments and tax deductions for mortgages provided an incentive to buy. Once purchased, homes needed furnishings, and far-flung suburbs made a car essential to get to work and shopping. Mortgage and auto payments came to dominate the family budget. But there was still enough left for weekly diversions as well as an annual vacation. Even a trip to Europe came within reach of ordinary Americans by the early 1950s.

Advertising—from radio jingles to roadside billboards to magazines and newspapers—helped to inspire and shape this outpouring of consumption by celebrating individual choice ("consumer sovereignty") and immediate gratification ("buy now, pay later") and by feeding dreams of ever-greater abundance. Tums appealed to sufferers from indigestion with a catchy jingle: "Night and day, at home or away, always carry TUMS FOR THE TUMMY!" For the busy family, Borden promised the convenience of hot chocolate that "you can make right in the cup!" Listerine asked wives, "Do inhibitions (doubts) threaten married love?"—and offered reassurance in the form of a mouthwash. A lithe, confident skater drew viewers into a fantasy world, "I dreamed I went skating in my maidenform bra."[17] The advent of television provided a potent new means of reaching the whole family, even children with their growing allowances. Catchy jingles heard often enough—such as "double your pleasure, double your fun" (touting Doublemint chewing gum)—could now enter into an entire generation's collective memory.

Focused on the good life at home, Americans responded coolly when asked to foot the Cold War bill. In the late 1940s Truman needed to raise taxes to cover his multiplying overseas commitments, but Congress, reflecting popular sentiment, was resistant. Truman's war in Korea prompted the same popular impatience as taxes and inflation rose and veterans got the call to return to service. Consumers were proving reluctant crusaders. They wanted instead to relax in the warm glow of prosperity and enjoy the abundance of goods that were beginning to cascade from the American economic cornucopia.

Disney and the U.S. Economic Edge

American corporations looking for business abroad had powerful advantages in the early postwar period. Some of the advantages were temporary. Wartime destruction had badly hurt overseas competitors, and the U.S. government used its dominant position to open foreign markets for U.S. companies. But other advantages, more fundamentally economic and long-lasting, had to do with the fact that American goods came out of the world's most advanced economy, geared to mass production for a mass market. They carried costs lower than their foreign competitors in part because of their efficient mode of production but also because the home market—the largest in the world, with the highest per capita income—helped reduce the cost of each item in the overall production run. U.S. firms could have a large sales volume, produce on a standardized, assembly-line basis, and thus keep output high and the company growing. Finally, to win and keep buyers, the masters of the new science of advertising exploited market research and insights on the psychology of the consumer. This impressive combination of market scale and technological and advertising skill helped U.S. firms such as IBM in office machines, Kodak in film stock, Du Pont in chemicals, and Boeing in aircraft hold a competitive advantage in postwar international markets.

The American entertainment and communications industry was among the most visible and vigorous part of the export drive, and U.S. filmmakers were its leaders. Already in the interwar period four major producers—Paramount, Fox, Loew's (later MGM), and Warner Brothers—had established their international dominance, building on a strong, centralized domestic base. They had worked out cartel arrangements among themselves to limit competition. They also enjoyed the backing of the government. Tariffs protected them from foreign competition from 1920 onward, while the U.S. Department of Commerce helped them with overseas marketing and breaching tariff barriers imposed by other countries trying to promote their own film industries. So powerful were the Americans that some European film companies abandoned competition and instead worked out collaborative arrangements.

The Walt Disney enterprise illustrates the international economic edge enjoyed by U.S. business generally and by the burgeoning entertainment industry sector in particular. Although by comparison with the big studios an entrepreneurial upstart, Disney was like them in an ideal position to exploit postwar opportunities to sell abroad, drawing on a tried-and-true formula applied to consistently innovative, entertaining products. Born in 1901 in Chicago, Disney had begun his career as a cartoonist while still in his late teens. In 1928 he created the single most important Disney character, Mickey Mouse. Already in 1929, with five short films out, this star of the Disney stable had inspired a craze, filling theaters and creating fan clubs.

To win and keep a broad audience, Disney lavished attention on packaging a product that gave customers what they wanted—chiefly action and escapist stories. He summed up his unabashedly commercial philosophy in comments to some French cartoonists whose artsy approach left him cold: "Don't go for the *avant garde* stuff. Be commercial. What is art, anyway? It's what people like. So give them what they like. There's nothing wrong with being commercial."[18] Before release of a film, he would gauge audience reaction to a preview screening and identify last-minute improvements. His carefully worked out public relations strategy relied heavily on good marketing, and he carefully protected his brand name with its promise of a quality, standardized product. He wanted no consumer confusion about what Disney productions meant.

Sensitivity to his audience led Disney to keep his changing political values out of his commercial productions. Growing up on a Missouri farm in the first decades of the century, Disney had picked up from his father what he later called a "socialistic" outlook and a sympathy for the ordinary workingman. During the Great Depression, he had supported Roosevelt's New Deal effort, but success as a filmmaker brought out Disney's conservative side. In 1941, with his payroll climbing to 1,100 employees and a state-of-the-art studio under construction, he suddenly found himself facing serious labor unrest. The resulting strike began turning him to the political right. The anticommunist atmosphere in Hollywood during the early Cold War completed the shift. He joined the hunt for subversives in the film industry late in the decade and went on to become a conservative Republican who worried about the threat posed by big unions and big government at home and communists abroad. But those who consumed Disney products had little if any sense of his sharp swing to the Right.

His productions followed widely practiced industrial techniques. Disney projects operated on a tight schedule with work broken into specialized components and under the close supervision of financial specialists. Into this process of mass production for mass consumption, Disney was constantly introducing technological innovations to maintain the novelty of his products and keep one step ahead of the competition. Already in the 1930s he had seen the possibilities of integrating new sound technology to create musical cartoons (in the *Silly Symphony* series culminating in the movie *Fantasia*), the addition of color, and the invention of the multiplane camera (a 14-foot-high mechanical contraption that gave cartoons depth). Other innovations followed after the war, notably big screens (Cinemascope) and stereo sound.

Disney's success in the large and diverse U.S. market made his and other American firms a natural to succeed in foreign markets. The size of the home market alone gave him an advantage. Domestic earnings on most films were so great that they alone would recoup the production costs, thus making overseas income almost pure and sometimes handsome profit. Overseas sales accounted for almost half of Disney's revenue until the outbreak of World War II disrupted that part of his business. The diversity of the home market also helped by forcing him no less than other producers of consumer goods to design products that would appeal to all customers whatever their particular ethnic, regional, or class preferences. This challenge of finding a common denominator at home gave his creations a distinct advantage abroad. Mickey Mouse with his universally appealing character led the way overseas as he had at home. The secret to the mouse's international appeal was an ambiguous identity. His age, nationality, and income status were anyone's guess. Only his gender was clear, and that only from his name. That Mickey Mouse and other cartoon characters such as Pluto, Goofy, and Donald Duck did little talking helped as well. By letting the picture tell the story, Disney could limit the dialogue and the distraction of subtitles or voice-overs. Nervous authoritarians (depending on their ideological proclivities) tried to make Mickey Mouse into a dangerous revolutionary, a meek proletarian, a warmonger, or an antimilitarist. But audiences that flocked to the theaters in droves in the 38 nations where the cartoon character already had a presence by 1937 expected simply fun and fantasy.

At the end of the war, Disney joined other U.S. export giants in forging ahead. The demand was great, especially from audiences eager to forget the nightmare of depression and war. Disney products quickly regained and then surpassed their former popularity in Europe while making inroads in Asia. Building on past strengths, Disney set about to systematically diversify his business, using the large U.S. market as the proving ground and springboard for products that would sell abroad. He moved first into profitable feature-length films and then television, producing for the home market and then reselling the same material abroad. In Disney's last years he opened the famous theme park, Disneyland, in 1955. Within a decade of Disneyland's opening, an estimated quarter of the U.S. population had come for a visit. Following Disney's death in 1966, the company continued to grow and diversify. Disney World opened in 1971. Eventually a chain of retail stores merchandising Disney-related products, a major television network (ABC), and cable outlets were added to the Disney media empire.

That empire flourished abroad. Many shared the American love affair with Mickey Mouse. Merchandise such as watches, toys, comic books, and clothes bearing the image of the famous, adorable rodent had proven popular overseas already in the late 1920s, and Mickey Mouse paraphernalia remained a best-seller in the postwar period. An imaginary mouse had given birth to a distinctly American, globe-girdling corporate enterprise devoted to the sale of pleasant distractions.

"Coca-Colonization" and the Mass Consumption Model

As Mickey Mouse and the Disney theme parks suggest, patterns of consumption indulged in by Americans exercised an appeal well beyond American shores. This global reach has been dubbed "Coca-colonization" after the soft drink originating in Atlanta in the 1880s. Coca-Cola would become the symbol of an international expansion of American popular culture and American-style consumerism through-out the postwar period. It demonstrated above all how advertising could create broad demand, even for a drink with no nutritional value. Coke, which its president once described as containing "the essence of capitalism," first turned to the export market in the 1920s.[19] By the 1930s the company was operating in 28 countries through franchise arrangements. The parent company provided advertising, quality control, and of course the concentrate with its secret formula. Wherever American troops and later tourists arrived in the 1940s and 1950s, Coke was close behind. Advertising promised that with every sip of the sugary beverage went the spirit of adventure, freedom, glamor, and leisure.

Foreigners gravitated to Coke and other uniquely American products precisely because they were appealing symbols of a way of life ("Americanization"). In Europe, young people were often the first and most fervent in embracing things American and thus claiming a symbolic liberation from their own country's or parents' codes. Consuming Coke represented a vote for a different kind of life vaguely imagined from Hollywood Westerns, knockoffs of American comic books, or the fluid, improvisational nature of American jazz. While American dominance and interference in European affairs could irritate some among the broader public and many among the intellectual elite, Europeans were in general drawn to consumer goods and mass culture and admired the economic abundance and technical virtu-osity that the United States represented. As economies recovered and incomes climbed, Europeans acquired the products that defined the new consumer life-style: kitchen appliances, vacuum cleaners, washers and dryers, radios and televi-sions, cameras and film, cosmetics, detergents, processed and pre-packaged food, and even automobiles.

As a marker of Americanization, however, Coke took second place to Hollywood, whose products were already flooding foreign cinemas in the interwar period. U.S. films proved a strong draw in the European market with its relatively high per capita income and especially in cities among women and workers. They liked fast-paced, escapist stories. They were transfixed by images of fantastic wealth playing on the screen. And they found appealing Hollywood's democratic impulse to parody authority and celebrate personal choice and mobility. Hollywood was also moving into the emerging markets of Latin America and Asia.

After World War II Hollywood exports retained their strong position in foreign markets. Defeated Japan and the U.S. portion of occupied Germany were fully open to Tinseltown products. Italy, which came out of the war with a still-vital film industry and an avid movie-going public, proved an especially rich market. Of the 850 films Italians watched in 1946, 600 were American; only 65 were locally made. In 1948 U.S.-made films claimed 75 percent of what Italians spent on movies, while once-thriving domestic production accounted for only 13 percent of theater revenue. The data for other international markets told the same story of Hollywood strength eclipsing local productions.[20]

Film exports after World War II took up the theme first sounded so forcefully by interwar films—the possibilities of a new lifestyle. Popular films such as *The Wizard of Oz*, *Bambi*, *Zorro's Fighting Legion*, *Gone with the Wind*, and *Drums along the Mohawk* (to take just a sample from the early 1950s) celebrated individualism and freedom. They provided a new definition of glamor and physical beauty quickly adopted by fashion-conscious women. They pictured the abundant lifestyle that Americans had achieved (or at least saw within reach). These packaged dreams, reinforced by the new art of advertising and by Cold War propaganda, helped shape postwar aspirations among ordinary people, especially in western Europe and Japan. Ordinary people could have a home of their own with adequate room for all the family, a kitchen filled with appliances, washing and drying machines to take away domestic drudgery, a car for convenience, and regular vacation trips to new and interesting places. Reinforcing Hollywood's messages were American GIs with their slang and casual ways indifferent to class. U.S. military stores in Europe were themselves amazing advertisements for American comfort and abundance. Out of those stores poured food, liquor, cigarettes, candy, cosmetics, and nylons that became either gifts or sales items on the black market. Even literature assumed new prominence as a window on the world of a rich and romantic country. For example, in occupied Japan during 1949 and 1950, the 1936 novel *Gone with the Wind* topped the bestseller list. Americans had become models even for transcending defeat.

"Americanization" in Europe

In Europe U.S. cultural influence was at a transitional point in the early postwar years. It had gained some ground early in the century, especially in the 1920s, but its scope and impact were still limited. The incomes of most Europeans did not extend beyond food, clothing, and housing. They lacked the means for dis-cretionary spending essential to putting consumer dreams within reach. Vested economic interests proved another obstacle to doing business American style. U.S. companies and their trade groups joined Marshall planners in pressing for new distribution methods that would get goods to consumers in the most direct way at the lowest cost. But small shopkeepers, who had enjoyed political protection throughout Europe, successfully fought back. They were determined to preserve their livelihoods from the threat of department stores and low-price, chain-managed stores that prevailed in the U.S. market. More broadly, the immediate hopes for a single market with a homogeneous taste—again the American model—were frus-trated by the persistence of strong differences between urban and rural Europe, between Europeans of different classes, and between regions even within the same country.

Adding to the resistance to U.S. cultural and economic incursion were outspo-ken elites. They had already developed elaborate critiques of American influence in reaction against inroads earlier in the century. Fascist regimes and Communist parties alike had denounced things American as degenerate and doomed. U.S. in-fluence represented materialism, crude mass culture, and rule by an ignorant public or by corrupt political bosses. Cultural nationalists in Nazi Germany saw U.S. films promoting crass values and bad racial attitudes antithetical to their goal of a noble, purified people. In the Nazi indictment Hollywood was run by Jews, and Mickey Mouse and jazz were condemned as parts of a "negroized" popular culture. In interwar France the Right also led the resistance to American films and other products. They found particularly objectionable the depiction of social freedom that seemed to them to border on anarchy. The French government took action to preserve national identity and social order by, for example, subsidizing the French film industry.

After the war the Left, especially the continent's Communist parties, became vocally anti-American, while intellectuals and politicians affiliated with the Catholic Church sometimes seconded their complaints. The Left bristled over the penetra-tion of American capital and the presumed influence that U.S. corporations and government as a result wielded over European life. That influence was particularly worrisome in the context of the emerging Cold War. Socialists and Communists saw this cultural penetration along with the Marshall Plan and NATO as part of a broad American effort to integrate Europe into a U.S.-dominated bloc. Catholic-inspired commentators and critics shared with the Americans a firm anticommu-nism but still deplored the acquisitive individualism and obsession with market values associated with an encroaching American way.

France was the hotbed of European anti-Americanism through the early post-war years and beyond. Critics made frequent attacks on American influence and what they believed was a spiritually empty and culturally stunted American lifestyle. They argued that American methods of mass production and mass consumption promoted conformism and a fixation with efficiency that would overwhelm France's humanistic values and undermine French conceptions of a balanced economy and traditional ways of production, sales, savings, and spending. American economic, military, and political dominance at the end of the war reinforced those prejudices. How could a declining France operate under the shadow of this superpower and still retain its proud national identity? That Americans were guided by a dangerously rigid anticommunism and were ignorant of the Europe that they pretended to lead only made the situation more upsetting for these critics.

The main source of this French anti-Americanism was the French Communist Party. It was joined by a substantial, influential segment of the intellectual class, including artists such as the painter Pablo Picasso, the existentialist philosophers Jean-Paul Sartre and Albert Camus, and the influential *Le Monde* newspaper, whose editors favored a separate European path and rejected any control by the two superpowers. All these groups perceived that a major American invasion was under way. An essay in *Le Monde* complained, "Chryslers and Buicks speed down our roads; American tractors furrow our fields; Frigidaires keep our food cold; stockings 'made by Du Pont' sheathe the legs of our stylish women."[21]

As during the interwar period, Hollywood films drew fire as dangerous vehicles for spreading American values. The French Left denounced Hollywood's films as capitalist propaganda. These banal, escapist, profit-driven products created a standardized taste for the endless pursuit of consumer goods. If given free rein, Hollywood would make the French what the Americans already had become: slaves to their movie magazines, household appliances, automobiles, or whatever advertisers were pushing. The French Left thus called, just as the Right had earlier, for state intervention to protect national values from this foreign plague. The first government's attempt to restrict American films came in 1946, and this official effort to limit the U.S. "cultural invasion" would continue for decades even as audiences flocked to cinemas showing Hollywood's creations.

The most dramatic moment in the French struggle against American inroads came in the late 1940s with Coke rather than Hollywood the target. Coke had had only one bottler in France before the outbreak of war but planned on generally expanding its European operations in the postwar period. It had made a good start during the war by setting up bottling plants close enough to the front lines to supply U.S. troops. When the postwar expansion got under way, it encountered opposition throughout Europe—but nowhere more vociferously than in France. In 1948 the finance ministry took a stand against Coke on the grounds that its operation would bring no fresh capital to help with French recovery and, worse yet, was likely to drain profits back to the parent company in the United States. Threatened domestic interests—notably producers of wine, fruit juice, mineral water, cider, and beer—lobbied the government for protection while publicly charging that Coke was "a poison." They claimed that like other addictive substances such as drugs and tobacco, it threatened public health. The French Communist Party, standing at

Coca-Cola Embraces the World, 1950
The May 15, 1950, cover of *Time*, the popular U.S. weekly magazine, shows a kindly Coke bottle cap helping a thirsty world to a long, cooling drink. Critics in France and elsewhere saw something less benign in the friendly embrace—a campaign to displace local cultures with "the American way of life." (Time Magazine/PARS)

the forefront of this resistance to "the Coca-Cola invasion," launched a sustained and highly polemical assault. It warned that this "American trust" would leave France poorer and even suggested that its distribution system would double as an espionage network.[22]

Coke's lawyers and lobbyists fought back, while its management got the State Department and the U.S. embassy in Paris to lean on the French government. The U.S. media, which closely followed the attack on this national icon, joined Coke spokesmen in framing the issue in terms of French gratitude for wartime sacrifices and loyalty in the Cold War struggle. The head of the Coke export drive chided the French: "Coca-Cola was not injurious to the health of the Americans who liberated France from the Nazis." A U.S. newspaper editorial invoked the anticommunist preoccupations of the time when it stated confidently, "You can't spread the doctrines of Marx among people who drink Coca-Cola."[23]

The controversy over the soft drink finally abated in the early 1950s. Centrist cabinets tied to NATO and dependent on Marshall Plan support had reluctantly lined up against Coke. They were glad to see the issue go away. So too was the French establishment. Parliamentarians, high civil servants, academics, business managers, and other professionals might be uneasy over the encroachment of an immature, uncivilized American culture but, unlike the Left, they tended to be more sympathetic to American political and economic influence and thus less alarmed by Coke's expansion. Finally, domestic producers were feeling less threatened: Polls suggested that only 17 percent of the population would give Coke even a mild personal endorsement, while 61 percent thoroughly disliked it. This response set the postwar pattern in which France would lag behind all the rest of Europe in per capita consumption of the quintessentially American beverage. It was for the tourists to drink. As one French pundit put it, his countrymen would proudly back national tradition, sticking with wine and rejecting the drinks of the superpowers, whether vodka or Coke.

Were these early critics right to attack Coke and other American exports and more broadly American economic domination? One way to think about this question—one that remains pertinent today—is in counterfactual ("What if?") terms. If there had been no United States to wield its influence in the immediate postwar years, how different would the emerging economic order have looked? The U.S. role was probably indispensable to mending the tears in the system. It joined Britain in quickly putting the international economy on a solid footing. It supplied the funds to restore the western European economies. And it took in hand the reform of the Japanese economy.

It is less clear how to appraise the impact of the American consumer model that spread through the medium of popular culture. Was the United States by dint of its leadership and resources transforming the world in its own image? Some would say that the U.S. model sent the lives and imagination of peoples in the advanced economies off in new directions. It is true that Americans were setting the pace in regard to industrial mass production and mass consumption. These trends in production and consumption were in turn associated with urbanization, rising levels of literacy and technological skills, the shift to a nuclear family, and increasing personal mobility at the expense of community.

But rather than seeing the United States creating these trends in other countries, it might be more revealing to think of the United States both as a leading indicator of where other advanced industrial countries were likely to go and as an example encouraging those trends. Perhaps it would be more accurate to see the United States, western Europe, and Japan all following parallel trajectories, all driven by similar technological and social forces, and all moving toward a modernity that would look largely but not entirely alike. In attacking the United States, critics were perhaps more fundamentally attacking features of modern life that they found homogenizing and dehumanizing without also counting the considerable gains in standards of living that went with new conditions. Were homes without electricity, indoor plumbing, and labor-saving appliances really so wonderfully quaint that they should remain unchanged? Could Mickey Mouse and Coke really transform the outlook of unwary consumers, or did those products answer to new tastes made possible by higher incomes and more discretionary spending? Comfortable intellectual and political elites might have doubts, but for ordinary Europeans the chance for a family to go out for a light entertainment and perhaps a quick snack and then return to comfortable quarters was not optional or debatable; it was becoming a right in the new postwar social order.

CONCLUSION

U.S. economic initiatives had proven extraordinarily successful on a broad front in a short time. It was no small feat to set the international economy on a new foundation, thus making possible a new phase in the process of globalization. Closely related was the U.S. contribution to hastening the recovery of western Europe while at the same time rehabilitating former foes in West Germany and Japan. Thanks in large measure to the vitality of the U.S. economy, American leaders could do all these things despite the high costs of the global war just ended and of the Cold War just beginning.

For all its efforts at reconstruction, the United States would (as Chapter 5 will show) reap rewards: participation in international economic growth spanning the 1950s and 1960s, an enhanced reputation as an effective leader of the anticommunist coalition, and loyal allies in Europe and Japan whose prosperity made them assets rather than liabilities in the Cold War. But success also bred problems (as Chapter 5 will also show). Europe and Japan participated in the American-led international economy without fully accepting American notions of how that economy should work. National cultural values, often with deep roots in the premodern period, would prove surprisingly persistent. They would inform economic behavior even in an age of increasing global exchange and turn seemingly universal economic and social trends in regionally distinct directions that would bedevil and annoy American leaders. Alongside contending views on how the free market should operate arose sharp criticism of flaws in its practical effects. Rapid, heedless growth, however welcome in the short term, imposed environmental costs that were dangerous in the long term. Women in the United States and Europe demanded greater opportunities to participate in and benefit from the new prosperity through enhanced educational and job opportunities and family-friendly government policies. Finally, out of the developing world came a sharp critique of the promise that the new international economy would benefit all and close the gap between rich and poor countries.

3
THE THIRD WORLD: FIRST TREMORS IN ASIA

ASIAN LANDS UNDERWENT a profound transformation after World War II. The region running from Korea, through China, Vietnam, and maritime Southeast Asia (including Indonesia and the Philippines), and then on to Burma and India became the most turbulent part of the Third World from the late 1940s through the 1960s. The reasons that Asia led the way during the early and middle phases of the Cold War are clear: Nowhere was the old colonial order weaker. Elite-led nationalist movements were organizing in these regions even before the Pacific War began. During the war Japanese forces drove Americans and Europeans from much of the region, and in some places the Japanese occupation actively encouraged anticolonial sentiment. Only in India did the British retain control in the face of advancing Japanese forces and restive subjects. The sudden end of the Pacific War in August 1945 and the collapse of Japanese authority created confusion that independence-minded Asian leaders were often able to exploit to their advantage. Subject peoples were no longer prepared to accept foreign direction as the natural order of things.

At the very time that their grip on Asian possessions was weakening, Europeans who had once ruled vast sweeps of the globe faced other problems. At home they staggered under the devastation of World War II, while internationally they had to accept their own eclipse before rising Soviet and American powers intent on harnessing decolonization to their own ends. As we have already seen, U.S. cold warriors worried about instability at peripheral Asian points but feared diverting scarce resources from the critical European front. From the perspective of the Kremlin, Asia offered opportunities to win friends and isolate the United States but also posed dangers, as opportunistic nationalists and impetuous Communists proved hard to control.

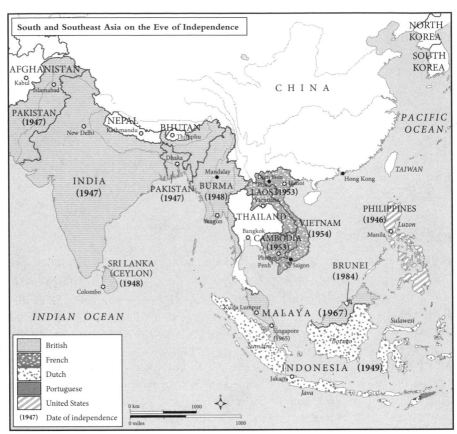

MAP 3.1
South and Southeast Asia on the Eve of Independence

THE APPEAL OF REVOLUTION AND THE STRONG STATE

In parts of Asia, the immediate postwar years were marked by tumult and some-times violence. Korea was liberated by Japan's defeat only to be divided by Soviet and American forces of occupation and then wracked by conflict when the Soviet-backed northern regime attacked the U.S.-supported South in a bid to reunite the country (see Chapter 1). Three years of fighting, drawing in both U.S. and Chinese forces, ended in stalemate. Korea was battered and the political division became permanent. China and Indochina (the French possession out of which the states of Vietnam, Cambodia, and Laos would emerge by 1954) were the scenes of other notable upheavals in the first decade following World War II. The Chinese and Vietnamese revolutions stand in their scope, their ambitions, and their ultimate travails on a par with any of the major revolutions of the twentieth century, in-cluding Russia's. They reshaped the lives of many millions of people, convulsed the region, raised the temperature of the global Cold War, and both inspired and frightened foreign observers.

The Chinese Communist Triumph

China, with its population totaling about half a billion at midcentury, experienced a revolution in several ways. In its narrowest sense it points to the Communist seizure of power in 1949, made possible by the defeat of its Nationalist foes and the ensuing effort by the Communist leader, Mao Zedong, to fundamentally remake China's culture and politics. Taken in its broadest meaning, China's revolution refers to a century-long effort to save a country in decline and to restore its power and prestige. China's loss of sovereignty began in the 1830s with Britain's victory over the Qing dynasty in the Opium War and the conclusion of the first unequal treaties giving foreigners a wide range of special rights and privileges. A long rain of blows followed, including having the capital, Beijing, twice occupied by foreign troops and the empire's vast territory carved up by the major powers into informal spheres of influence.

Already in the late nineteenth century Chinese political leaders were seeking the secret of the wealth and power enjoyed by a dominant West and a newly energized Japan. That search carried those leaders toward an ever more radical agenda. They focused at first on acquiring basic technology, mastering modern weapons, and learning foreign languages. By the turn of the century, impatient reformers were exploring foreign political systems—first constitutional monarchy, then democracy, and finally fascism and socialism—as the cure-all for China's woes. Even after the Chinese Communist Party (CCP) won power, the search continued, with Mao's vision of a permanent revolution at odds with the more technocratic and bureaucratic emphasis on planning favored by some of his colleagues. Finally, in the early 1980s Mao's successors experimented with a free-market economy functioning within an authoritarian political system. (The post-1949 phases of the revolution are covered in Chapters 6 and 8.) "Wealth and power," a phrase coined in the nineteenth century, remained to the end of the twentieth century and beyond a core aspiration of Chinese nationalism and a driving concern of Chinese engaged in this revolutionary makeover of their country.

Mao Zedong's central place in this revolution and the long shadow he cast decades after his death offer another reminder of the important impact strong personalities can have in human affairs. He was the father of one revolution, and his successors would have to carry out a second, market-oriented revolution in order to escape the political and economic constraints that the Mao era had created. Looking through the prism of Mao's life can help us see the stages through which China's revolution unfolded and the concerns that drove it.

Mao grew up in a period marked by the first stirrings of reform and then revolutionary activity among political elites. He was born in 1893 in the interior province of Hunan into a rich peasant family. The young Mao staged his first revolution against his father, whom he regarded as domineering and exploitative. He went away to study in foreign-influenced schools in the capital city of his province, and served briefly in the republican army that toppled the imperial dynasty in 1912. He worked for a time as a librarian in Beijing University and got caught up in the intellectual and political ferment that was gripping educated youth during the late 1910s.

Like other young intellectuals of the time, Mao was outraged by nearly a century of foreign aggression, and he was desperate to save China from the humiliations foreigners had inflicted on a proud people with a glorious history and culture. His earliest years had coincided with the loss of Korea (then a Chinese protectorate) and Taiwan (a frontier territory), the second occupation of Beijing, the repeated payment of indemnities to foreign powers, and the informal Russo-Japanese partition of the northeastern provinces (known to foreigners as Manchuria), so all these events were fresh in mind. Sometime around 1910–1911, Mao (then in his late teens) read a political pamphlet lamenting China's imminent dismemberment. It so impressed him that years later he could still recall its opening line— "Alas, China will be subjugated"—and his own feeling of depression "about the future of my country" and the dawning realization "that it was the duty of all people to help save it."[1]

As a social critic and advocate of reform, Mao sought to understand why China had lost its way. He blamed a feudal society for holding China back. As a young man, he bristled at arranged marriages, lamented neglect of the public good in the name of family and profit, and attacked popular superstition. He wanted a strong Chinese state that could create a modern, united country and secure respect on the international stage. Mao's concerns with social renovation and national salvation came together in 1919. Writing in a magazine that he edited, Mao made the fervid prediction for his country that

> the more profound the oppression, the greater its resistance . . . [O]ne day, the reform of the Chinese people will be more profound than that of any other people, and the society of the Chinese people will be more radiant than that of any other people. . . . We must all exert ourselves! We must all advance with the utmost strength! Our golden age, our age of glory and splendour, lies before us.[2]

True to his faith in China's greatness, he joined other students in 1919 in a nationwide protest (known as the May Fourth Movement) against Japanese inroads in Shandong province and against the warlords and traitors who helped keep China weak. A new generation of intellectuals and their students called for the creation of a new culture that was vigorous, scientific, and democratic. They were measuring China's deficiencies against Western achievements.

These concerns led Mao, like many educated youth of his generation, to take a growing interest in the Bolshevik revolution and Marxist theory. They saw in revolutionary Russia a model applicable to China and an inspiration to a weak and poor country seeking to regain its independence and rid itself of a corrupt and enfeebled ruling class. The Marxist ideology that guided the Bolsheviks appealed strongly to those angry over foreign ("imperialist") domination and exploitation and determined to move China from what they called feudalism to a higher level of development. Marxism in its Russian form (Leninism) offered a tool of analysis and a guide to action. Few Chinese thoroughly understood these imported ideas, but Mao and others were certain that they had found a body of thought and an model of organization that could carry China to salvation and to a new era of national unity, wealth, power, and justice.

The Chinese Communist Party, formally organized in 1921 with only 50 members, was to be the vehicle for bringing this bright future to China. The CCP drew on its members' instinct of patriotism and readiness to sacrifice while providing a Leninist party organization and formal ideology, both critical for collective action. From its start until the 1950s, the party had strong Soviet ties. Its leaders and members alike looked up to Stalin, the peerless Soviet leader, and depended on Moscow for schooling, advice, material aid, and even medical care. A founding member, Mao remained active through its difficult early years. Guided by emissaries from Moscow, the CCP entered into a one-sided alliance with the Nationalist Party and was nearly wiped out when the leader of that party, Chiang Kai-shek, turned on the Communists in 1927. Chiang was bent on bringing central control and order to a country torn by civil war among regional warlords. The Communists threatened his program, while he regarded Soviet support for the CCP as another case of imperialist meddling in China's domestic affairs.

Mao fled to the countryside and began to act on his growing conviction that the secret to revolution in China was to be found not in the urban proletariat but in the peasantry. Mao's convictions on peasant support developed by stages. His own rural roots had introduced him to the harsh realities of rural life. During his early years in the party he had given peasants a prominent place in his reflections on revolutionary strategy, even if party leaders and their Soviet advisers scoffed at the very notion of the party of the proletariat vesting its hopes in the most backward, feudal social element. After he personally conducted studies of rural conditions with an eye to their revolutionary potential, Mao declared in 1927 that peasants "will rise like a fierce wind or tempest, a force so swift and violent that no power, however great, will be able to suppress it."[3] As his views matured, he focused increasingly on the most marginal groups in rural society—the bandits, vagabonds, and paupers—with little to lose from a revolutionary upheaval. Seen through the lens of class conflict, these were the proletarians, and landlords of whatever size became the capitalists.

The application of this class grid on the countryside created problems. A CCP teetering on the brink of collapse in the late 1920s sought safety in a remote rural area (known as the Jiangxi Soviet). The marginal elements it attracted proved incapable of fending off relentless Nationalist military pressure. When the Jiangxi Soviet collapsed in 1934, some 90,000 Communists fled, beginning what came to be known as the "Long March." Only 5,000 with Mao in the lead would reach the new center of party activity in a remote and impoverished area of China's northwest (the region around Yanan). Once more, the peasants to whom Mao looked to keep his revolution alive were largely marginal elements whose prime interest was

MAP 3.2
China and Its Neighbors, 1949
China's boundaries, depicted here, reflect claims advanced by the new Communist government and for the most part realized within its first few years. Mao's regime claimed Taiwan but, much to his frustration, the island remained under the control of the rival Nationalist government.

not waging class warfare but merely surviving in the face of natural disasters, ecological decline, and depredations by outsiders (whether predatory warlords, corrupt Nationalist government officials, or cruel Japanese troops). Further complicating a simple class analysis were conflicts among lineages, clans, and ethnic groups over power and resources at the village level.

Between 1935 and 1949 Mao took control of the CCP and guided it down what would prove a tortuous and dangerous road to victory. By the late 1930s the elements for a successful revolution had come together. Mao had assembled a leadership team with a clear program, an effective party organization, and a skilled guerrilla army. The relocation to Yanan, a sanctuary difficult for Nationalist forces to penetrate, brought Mao's CCP an unprecedented degree of safety. There Mao honed his skills as a political tactician and military strategist. But even this combination of favorable circumstances might not have been enough to bring the CCP victory had not the Japanese invaded China in 1937, further weakening and distracting the Nationalists. The ensuing war against Japan would devastate the eastern portion of the country and kill an estimated 15 million Chinese. Only the Soviet Union had greater losses during World War II. The CCP called almost at once for united national resistance against the invaders and used the ensuing anti-Japanese struggle to expand its area of influence and to attract to its ranks patriotic young people.

The war years engendered in Mao a marked optimism about the postwar situation. Like a broad spectrum of political leaders, he saw China as a semicolonial country in need of liberation and renovation. Allied promises to end the iniquitous old international system that had done such harm to China appealed powerfully to him. He was heartened by the Anglo-American meeting in August 1941 that produced the Atlantic Charter commitment to a new world order and expressions of Anglo-American interest in cooperating with the embattled Soviet Union. America's entry into the war several months later struck him as a guarantee not only of an antifascist victory but also of a lasting international alignment favorable to peace and change within China.

By early 1945 Mao was in even higher spirits. In the benign national and international environment produced by Allied cooperation, he expected that he could force the Nationalists to accept a power-sharing arrangement. The longer-term prospects were in his estimate even brighter. While the United States seemed for the moment economically vital, Mao held to the orthodox Marxist view that ultimately, within a decade perhaps, that country would find itself in the grip of a shattering crisis. The Soviet Union would then come into unchallenged preeminence and press for fundamental change within nations and within the global system. Mao held to this markedly optimistic view well into 1946, but by then the Cold War chill was beginning to reach China. The Nationalists were not interested in power sharing and Washington backed the Nationalists as the best counter to growing Communist influence.

With political reform blocked, Mao fell back on the rural base-area strategy that had earlier proven its worth. He and his colleagues won peasants' support by addressing rural problems such as landlessness and extortionate interest rates. Their efforts had won the party military recruits, a supply of food, intelligence, hiding places, and a stream of sympathizers and ultimately members. Thanks to the resilience of these base areas, Mao had been able to survive before 1945 in the face of far stronger Japanese and Nationalist forces. Now in 1946, with civil war looming, Mao looked to these base areas as the key to ultimate victory. Although initially outnumbered and facing a Nationalist army generously supported by the United States, his forces finally managed to take the offensive thanks primarily to peasant support as well as superior morale and leadership and some assistance from the Soviet Union.

Given the diversity of China's countryside, there was no single peasant perspective on the CCP appeal. One example—Houhua village in northernmost Henan province in north central China—offers a sense of the grim and precarious conditions that many of the rural poor were desperate to escape. Good years provided barely enough to get by, and bad years could be disastrous. A folk saying in the area captured the daily struggle to stay alive:

In Spring the land is white with salt
In Summer floodwaters rush in
In Autumn locusts fill the air
In Winter wind kicks up the sand
In normal years we are cold and hungry
For only half the year is there enough grain.[4]

One of those bad years was 1942. It began with a drought that left the land parched and crops dying. Prayers for rain had no effect. Then swarms of locusts hit, stripping away whatever vegetation was left. With no relief coming from outside, 125 out of Houhua's 800 inhabitants starved to death. Ninety percent of all families had to sell their land and flee to other areas to look for work and food. Nearby markets were soon selling women and female children; even human flesh began appearing for sale. One village resident recalled this "sorrowful period of our history"—how an uncle had had to sell both his daughters for about 20 gallons of grain and how his grandfather had handed over the family's three-room brick house for the same amount. The family's precious acre of farming land had gone too. "It makes me very sad to discuss those times," he confessed.[5]

In Houhua as elsewhere, peasant desperation presented an opportunity for local CCP organizers to win support. A handful of party members in a nearby village began secretly recruiting poor peasants by convincing them that it was possible to organize to resist land grabs and other abuses by rich households. Peasant associations thus took shape, and from the most active and effective participants, the CCP recruited new members. Influence within many villages like Houhua gave the CCP the resources essential to ensuring its survival and making itself a national force.

By 1948 CCP victory was assured; by the end of 1949 most of China was under party control. In October 1949, standing before an enthusiastic crowd filling the square in central Beijing, Mao proudly proclaimed in his high-pitched voice the creation of the People's Republic of China (PRC). China, so long humiliated, had at last stood up. "Our nation will never again be an insulted nation," he had declared a short time earlier. Looking ahead, he defined the ultimate task of the CCP to exploit the potential of the Chinese revolution to "change everything." He promised "before long there will arise a new China with a big population and a great wealth of products, where life will be abundant and culture will flourish."[6]

Mao continued to work alongside other party leaders with whom he had closely collaborated during the Yanan years. Zhou Enlai, a worldly, well-traveled figure from an elite background who had once seemed destined to lead the party, would serve as premier of the PRC as well as Mao's all-too-loyal aide. Liu Shaoqi, who had

The Land Reform Movement in China, Late 1940s
Typically, a party-appointed work team would arrive within a village to initiate land reform. After getting a sense of the local scene, the team would form a peasant association, with poor peasants as the core group. Landlords would then have to face gatherings of the entire village to listen to accusations of exploitation and abuse—a critical moment captured in this photo. Some landlords along with their families were then subjected to deadly beatings. These "struggle sessions" not only discredited the dominant figures and families in the village but also gave the poor a new sense of confidence and control. The final steps, often complicated, consisted of working out the economic status of each family (using both self and group appraisals) and then redistributing goods (household items as well as land) from the privileged to the poor. (Xinhua/Sovfoto)

directed the CCP's work outside the rural base areas, emerged as Mao's successor and, along with the slightly younger Deng Xiaoping, an influential voice in both party and government affairs. These men exercised their power through a political structure modeled on that of the Soviets. The party's Central Committee, nominally elected by periodic national party congresses, served as a rubberstamp wielded by the smaller and more powerful Politburo, which contained its own still more elite Standing Committee entrusted with the supervision of day-to-day policy. Mao stood at the pinnacle of this steep pyramid of power as the chairman of the CCP as well as head of the party's influential military affairs commission. One man surrounded by a handful of personally selected associates operated through a party whose membership totaled only 4.5 million in 1949, less than 1 percent of the total population.

Mao and his comrades had won the struggle for power; what would they now do with that power? They were in agreement on foreign affairs. By 1949 the CCP had already taken sides in the Cold War. The Truman administration had supported the Nationalists to the bitter end of the civil war, and even after their defeat had continued hostile to the Chinese revolution. Responding to Washington's attempt to isolate his country, Mao unceremoniously abrogated the old unequal treaties imposed by the powers on a weak China and began to develop a broad-based relationship with the Soviet Union. He still regarded the United States as strong on the surface but plagued by underlying weaknesses—foremost an economic system with a pronounced tendency to throw itself into crisis and set off social tumult at home and conflicts with allies. "U.S. imperialism is sitting on this volcano," he observed characteristically in 1947.[7] As insurance against possible U.S. military intervention, Mao himself traveled to Moscow to negotiate a defense treaty. In early 1950 he got from Stalin the treaty as well as some economic aid and the help of Soviet advisers.

The leaders of the CCP agreed in broad terms on the next step: regaining territory lost during the last imperial dynasty's waning years. As soon as it came to power, the CCP set in motion military efforts that recovered Tibet and Xinjiang along with part of Mongolia (Inner Mongolia). And in 1959 the Chinese used that military power to put down a revolt in Tibet. When in 1962 India refused to negotiate a border dispute, China's military again acted, this time driving Indian forces back from rugged, sparsely populated territory.

Only in regard to Taiwan was the CCP frustrated. The island had been settled by Chinese and incorporated into the Chinese empire only to be lost to Japan in 1895. China's allies during World War II had endorsed Taiwan's return. By the time of the creation of the PRC, the defeated Nationalists had dug in on the island and soon gained U.S. support, capped by a defense treaty in 1954. Mao denounced this latest example of foreign intervention in China's internal affairs. He pressed China's claim by saber rattling, first in 1954 and then in 1958, on both occasions provoking crises with Washington. But he lacked both the naval force needed for an invasion and the firm Soviet backing critical to going to the brink with the Americans.

Restoring the old imperial borders was not enough. Mao's ultimate foreign policy goal was to raise China into the ranks of the major world powers—as a regional force for revolutionary change, as a model for change in the Third World generally, and as a nuclear power commanding the respect of the other major powers. In its first years the PRC publicly signaled its support for Vietnamese revolutionaries (in 1949), launched a major aid program to help them defeat the French (in 1950), and during the Korean War between 1950 and 1953 (described in Chapter 1) drove back U.S. forces and (as Mao put it) "beat American arrogance."[8] Mao thus asserted China's influence along its border just as strong dynasties had

Mao with His Son, Mao Anying, 1949
This photo captures an exceptional moment. A man fixated on remaking his country seldom had time for his family. The son died a year later while serving with Chinese forces in Korea. (Xinhua/Sovfoto)

earlier. The difference was that Mao determined his allies on the basis of their revolutionary credentials.

On domestic policy China's new leaders were at least initially in rough agreement on the importance of restoring stability and production after over a decade of chaos and destruction. In the countryside, where most Chinese still lived, the CCP focused on bringing some uniformity to agricultural policy. Some places, especially in southern China, where the CCP presence was not well entrenched until the early 1950s, had yet to see even the most rudimentary changes in the land system. Farther to the north, where most base areas were located, moderate reforms were well advanced. They involved redistributing some land from landlords who had actively resisted the CCP, reducing the rent on land, and cutting back on interest paid on loans. As the CCP consolidated rural control, its first step was to apply the moderate program already implemented in parts of the north to all the rest of the country. In the process, more land belonging to landlords and rich peasants went to poor peasants and the landless, while the holdings of middle peasants were generally left alone. This task had been completed by the early 1950s, but Mao's effort to remake life in the countryside had only just begun.

In the modern urban sector the CCP was prepared to work with the capitalist class to speed economic recovery and thus facilitate an eventual transition to socialism. The CCP's initial goal was, as Mao explained in 1949, "to regulate capitalism, not to destroy it."[9] Faced with the awesome enterprise of extending party control from the rural bases into the cities and organizing the new CCP-dominated state, party leaders also hoped to tap the talents of intellectuals. In the cities as in

THE RISE OF A REVOLUTIONARY CHINA

1912	Qing dynasty overthrown; a weak republic emerges, beset by regional warlords
1919	May Fourth Movement marks culmination of a period of intellectual ferment among politicized educated youth
1921	Chinese Communist Party organized
1931	Japanese invade China's Northeast (Manchuria)
1935	Mao emerges as CCP leader during the Long March from Jiangxi to Yanan
1937	Sino-Japanese War begins, with the United States supporting Chiang's Nationalist government
1946–49	Civil war ends in CCP victory over U.S.-backed Nationalists, who take refuge on Taiwan
1949	People's Republic of China created; moderate domestic policy proclaimed
1950	Sino-Soviet alliance concluded; Chinese forces stop American advance in Korea
1959	China puts down revolt in Tibet
1962	Sino-Indian border clashes

the countryside, moderation would, however, soon succumb to an assertive Mao driven by his own, highly personal vision of China's future.

Vietnam's Revolutionary Struggle

The story of the Vietnamese revolution closely parallels that in China and had begun to unfold long before the start of the Cold War (see Chapter 1). This story goes back to the early nineteenth century, when imperial Vietnam confronted French intruders. The French launched their colonial drive guided by a resolve to promote and protect Catholic missionaries, a desire for a base for expanding trade into China, and a hunger for national prestige. In the face of steady French encroachment, the Vietnamese engaged in sporadic and largely ineffectual opposition. The ruling dynasty, which had expelled the Chinese and reunited the country in 1802, could not decide whether to appease or oppose these new invaders. By the 1880s France had imposed direct rule over Cochinchina (the French name for the southernmost part of Vietnam that included the Mekong Delta) and protectorates over Annam (the central region) and Tonkin (the northernmost section, including the densely populated Red River Delta). These three regions, together with the neighboring protectorates of Cambodia and Laos, constituted French Indochina, which was controlled by a single governor general. In securing control the French had exploited their superior technology such as cannons, steamships, and the telegraph, critical in war and in administration, and they won the help of Vietnamese—both elite collaborators and peasant military recruits—so that they could administer the colony and police it at low cost.

By the 1890s the French had crushed armed resistance. Regional peasant armies, ill armed and ill organized, had proven no match for French forces. The morale among the elite that supported the Vietnamese state soon collapsed, and some accepted service in the colonial administration and army, while others continued in the old imperial bureaucracy, now firmly under French supervision. Yet others exploited new opportunities for profit from plantation agriculture and trade opened by French capital. Training in French schools became for this new class the ticket to advancement and the badge of their modernity.

French influence, particularly in the south, accentuated regional differences of lasting importance even today. Cochinchina, a late-settled frontier zone not integrated politically with the rest of Vietnam until early in the nineteenth century, would undergo profound social and economic change. Even before the French conquest, those in the north, the home of Vietnamese civilization, looked down on southerners as crude and culturally backward. Colonialism had had a deep impact on Cochinchina, not least in the spread of plantation agriculture and the pervasive pattern of collaboration. These features accentuated the contempt felt by northerners whose strong sense of patriotism had been forged through two millennia of resistance to Chinese domination. This antipathy, fully reciprocated by southerners, would only increase in the twentieth century.

Ho Chi Minh was the charismatic leader who would set this conquered and divided land on the road to independence and unity. The many aliases that Ho would use during his revolutionary career are revealing of his motives. Named by his family Nguyen Tat Thanh (meaning Nguyen Who Will Be Victorious), he later called himself Nguyen O Phap (Nguyen Who Hates the French) and Nguyen Ai Quoc (Nguyen Who Loves His Country) before picking up in 1945 the name that stuck, Ho Chi Minh (Ho Who Aspires to Enlightenment).

Born in 1890 in the northern Annam region into the local gentry, he had grown up steeped in a rich patriotic tradition. His father was eligible to serve in the imperial bureaucracy but refused because it was under the heel of the French. The province in which Ho came to maturity was noted for its stubborn opposition to foreign rule even after organized resistance had died. Exposed to both Chinese classical and French education, Ho decided in 1911 to study the West at first hand. Once settled in Paris, he had sought support for his country's cause from the victors of World War I with their liberal peace program. Ignored by them, he turned to the French Socialist Party only to discover it was tainted by colonial ambitions. Even the French Communist Party, which Ho helped found, did not extend its professed solicitude for the downtrodden to France's colonial subjects despite the formal position of the Moscow-based Communist International (Comintern). Liberating exploited Western workers was one thing, granting independence to half-civilized Vietnamese altogether another.

In the early 1920s Ho became a Communist. He vividly recalled the ecstatic moment of his conversion. While living in Paris, he had stumbled on a work by Lenin dealing with nationalism in colonial countries. Having figured out the relevance of Leninism to his country's plight, Ho reported, "I wept for joy."[10] He soon moved to Moscow and then served in the 1920s and 1930s as a Comintern operative in China and Thailand. He also helped found the Indochinese Communist Party. Originating in 1925 as a nine-man cell, it was formally organized in Hong Kong in 1930 by uniting rival communist groups. This Communist party would operate like others. The center of decision making was the Politburo, made up of roughly 10 to 15 of the most senior leaders. The general secretary occupied the guiding although not necessarily the determining role in its discussions. Below the Politburo was the Central Committee made up of some 50 to 100 members who, nominally at least, elected the Politburo. Like Mao and his colleagues, Ho and a generation of even younger Vietnamese were drawn to this Leninist party organization. Disciplined and centralized with a mass base and ideological coherence, it gave them a tool to carry forward the formidable task of restoring indigenous political authority against a well-entrenched colonial power.

Only in 1941 did Ho return home. The Japanese occupation of Indochina that year, the first step toward invasion of the rest of Southeast Asia, created an opportunity for patriotic Vietnamese. They could align their anticolonial cause with the gathering Allied coalition preaching self-determination. Ho arrived as the head of the newly created Viet Minh (a shortened version of its full name, the Vietnamese Independence League). The Viet Minh was a united-front organization. Although organized and controlled by the Communist party, it was designed to appeal to Vietnamese from all walks of life—from urban intellectuals to peasants—and unite them in opposition to French control. This particular organizational form allowed the Communists to marshal the popular support that was indispensable for a small, still weak political party, while at the same time soothing any fears about party domination or anxiety about its ultimate goals. The Viet Minh established itself as the only organized, staunchly anti-French and anti-Japanese resistance group, and remained organizationally central to the resistance down to the French defeat in 1954. Ho was already well on his way to capturing the nationalist banner. Other political forces lacked strong organization and a substantial base of popular support, and some were even tainted by collaboration with the French.

When the Japanese surrendered in August 1945, the Viet Minh moved quickly to exploit the opportunity to take power. It had initially operated in the remote, mountainous region in northernmost Vietnam along the Chinese border and then in the last stage of the Pacific War extended its influence and operations into the Red River Delta. In what became known as the August Revolution, Viet Minh forces marched into Hanoi and established an independent Vietnamese state, the Democratic Republic of Vietnam, ruled by a coalition government with Ho as head of state. The Communist party was firmly in control, even though it had at least nominally disbanded that fall. (In 1951 the party was formally revived and renamed the Vietnamese Workers' Party to allow room for the development of separate Cambodian and Laotian Communist parties.)

Realizing its weakness, the new government pursued a moderate policy. It downplayed radical domestic goals to win maximum popular support and reassure French residents as well as the United States. It expressed a willingness to negotiate with France on phased steps toward full independence, and it asked the victorious Allies for support. Its September 1945 declaration of independence quoted from the U.S. Declaration of Independence: "We hold [as] truths that all men are created equal, that they are endowed by their Creator with certain unalienable Rights, among these are Life, Liberty and the pursuit of Happiness." The declaration concluded with an appeal meant as much for foreign as Vietnamese ears: "A people which has so stubbornly opposed the French domination for more than 80 years, a people who, during these last years, so doggedly ranged itself and fought on the Allied side against Fascism, such a people has the right to be free, such a people must be independent."[11]

Moderation, however, proved a fruitless strategy, at least on the international scene. Ho failed in his appeals to the victorious Allies for support on the basis of a presumed common commitment to the principles of liberty and self-determination. Ho had favorably impressed the U.S. intelligence teams operating in northern Vietnam during the war. But President Truman, to whom Ho wrote directly, ignored him. Ho also failed to convince the French to agree to even a gradual withdrawal from Vietnam. French nationals who had made their lives in Indochina understood all too well that their privileged existence depended on their continued political and economic domination. By December 1946 negotiations had collapsed and armed conflict had begun in earnest in what would come to be called the first Indochina War (1946–1954). Ho abandoned Hanoi, returned to the countryside, and resumed his war of resistance. The Viet Minh avoided major military engagements in the first years of the conflict, stressing instead political mobilization of the peasantry and expansion of the party. Membership, no more than 20,000 in 1946, had increased by 1950 to 700,000 (5 percent of the population). The Viet Minh concentrated its efforts in the north, but its activists managed gradually to gain a foothold in roughly half the south.

Ho's forces, aided by advisors, military equipment, and supplies from the new Communist government in China, gradually wore the French down despite rising levels of U.S. assistance to the colonial forces. The war was draining France's national budget, pushing the casualty totals on the French side toward 55,000, and generating popular protests. Ho's colleague in charge of military affairs, Vo Nguyen Giap, dealt the final blow to colonial hopes in early 1954 by encircling and then forcing the surrender of a French garrison at Dien Bien Phu. Certain of victory if only the Vietnamese would stand and fight, the French had underestimated the effectiveness of a popular, well-organized if low-tech resistance force. France and its Cold War allies agreed to sit down with the Communist powers at Geneva and work out some compromise. Under pressure from his Soviet and Chinese patrons,

Discussing the Attack on Dien Bien Phu, November 1953
In this planning session, Ho Chi Minh (center) is flanked by his long-time lieutenants Le Duan, Pham Van Dong, Truong Chinh, and Vo Nguyen Giap (from left to right). (*Ho Chu Tich*, 1970)

ANTICOLONIAL RESISTANCE IN VIETNAM	
1802	Vietnam expels invaders and achieves unity under the Nguyen dynasty
1880s	France completes takeover of Vietnam; resistance subsides
1919	Ho asks World War I victors meeting in Paris to support independence; he then turns to the French Socialists and Communists and finally the Comintern
1930	Indochinese Communist Party established
1941	Japanese troops occupy Indochina; Viet Minh (led by Ho) founded as vehicle for united-front resistance
1945	"August revolution" results in creation of the Democratic Republic of Vietnam headed by Ho
1946	Viet Minh begins armed struggle against France
1954	Viet Minh scores a victory at Dien Bien Phu; Geneva conference divides Vietnam with Ho in control north of 17th Parallel; U.S.-sponsored government takes charge in the South

Ho finally in July 1954 accepted a bargain: temporary partition of his country with the promise of national elections in 1956 to reunify it.

What accounts for the rise of Ho's independence movement and his unexpected success against the French? External factors noted earlier, including a weakened, war-weary France and two superpowers with little or no sympathy for the French effort, are part of the answer. No less important are internal forces, above all the concerns of politically engaged Vietnamese intellectuals arrayed against the French and soon to rally against the United States.

Perhaps the single most powerful idea sustaining the Vietnamese was the patriotic tradition of resistance to foreign intervention. They saw themselves as the descendants of those who had fought and died for independence, first during the epic struggle against Chinese control spanning 2,000 years and then against the French colonizers. Ho and his colleagues in the Communist leadership brought a stubborn determination to the cause of liberation that issued from the carefully cultivated awareness of this long history of patriotic resistance. Their popular appeals could tap a capacity for struggle and sacrifice that antedated the imported Western ideas of nationalism and whose strength Paris and Washington (already resolved by 1950 to block further communist inroads in Indochina) never understood.

A national literature of struggle and sacrifice kept this patriotic spirit alive in those who came to political consciousness in the first half of the twentieth century. They honored those who in the thirteenth century had resisted the Mongol invaders coming down from China and in the nineteenth century had fought the French. An 1864 poem that concluded with a call for sacrifice to expel the French sounded a familiar theme with a powerful appeal: "Life has fame, death too has fame. Act in such a way that your life and your death will be a fragrant ointment to your families and to your country." Even the lullabies sung to nodding children asked them, "What do we love more than our country?" and pointed to the generations past whose labor "is now seen in each foot of river, each inch of mountain, each melon's pith, and each silkworm's innards." Little wonder that many would respond to Ho's call to work with the Communists and by devoting themselves to redeeming their country to take their place in the long line of dedicated and self-sacrificing patriots.[12]

No less important than patriotism in sustaining Vietnamese resistance was Communist success in attracting the peasantry into the resistance. The parallels with the Chinese Communist experience are striking. Like their Chinese counterparts, Vietnamese party organizers searching for a proletarian spearhead for their movement learned early that urban centers were inhospitable, even dangerous. Forced to take refuge in the countryside, where four fifths of their countrymen lived, they had to make a virtue of necessity: winning the support of peasants. They learned that the primary enemy of the rural people was less the humiliating foreign occupation preoccupying the well-educated from privileged backgrounds than the grinding poverty of everyday life. Beginning in the 1940s, the Viet Minh promised peasants a new order and took some practical steps toward its realization, above all by redistributing land and ending exploitatively high interest rates on loans and high rents on land. Ho's forces thus secured their popular influence in northern Vietnam, aided in the final months of World War II by their effectiveness in battling famine.

Interviews with peasants in the Red River Delta testify to the success of the Viet Minh. One Viet Minh activist recalled the importance of famine relief in winning peasant support, which in turn was critical in securing village shelter for the Viet Minh and offering bases for night raids on enemy outposts. A poor and less politically engaged peasant recalled the same process of political mobilization in terms that were perhaps more typical. In 1945, when the Viet Minh showed up for the first time in his village, "I didn't really know what the Vietminh was. Also, I was scared: I was chary of joining them because I couldn't see what good they would do us." By 1947 Viet Minh performance, not propaganda, had brought him around and into a supporting role in the anti-French struggle. "I did my bit by becoming a village security agent, checking people's papers, tracking down poultry thieves, that kind of thing."[13]

The Viet Minh presence in rural areas opened opportunities for women. In Ho Chi Minh's view these "long-haired warriors" had much to contribute to their country's liberation and building an egalitarian society. Organizers entering a village looked first to women along with poor peasants and youth for support. Women carried out tasks that might bring suspicion on men such as visiting relatives in jail, carrying messages, distributing propaganda, and spying for guerrilla units. But they were also trained as combatants and nurses. Nguyen Thi Dinh illustrates the role peasant women assumed in the resistance. Dinh was born in 1920 into a peasant family in a Mekong Delta province known for its revolutionary tradition and the site of repeated anti-French uprisings from the 1860s onward. Vietnam's Communist party had established a presence there during the 1930s. It was then that Dinh, a teenager, had joined the resistance. She had been influenced by her activist brother but also by Confucian and village notions of social justice. A simple hatred for abusive landlords and local bullies had been enough to get her to take her first political risks. "I did not understand anything more than that the Communists loved the poor and opposed the officials in the village." The French figured only secondarily in her pantheon of villains. Dinh became active, passing out publications and leaflets, organizing local women, and carrying messages. She was launched on a political career in which she would lose her activist husband and which landed her in a French labor camp between 1940 and 1943. She participated in the Viet Minh seizure of power in her home province in 1945 and thereafter played a prominent political and military role in the southern resistance, first to the French and then to the Americans.[14]

Revolutionary developments in Vietnam had strikingly paralleled those in China. In both cases foreign subjugation and humiliation during the nineteenth century had set the stage. Political elites found that the imperial political system, a proud past, and a strong cultural identity were not enough to beat back foreign demands and gunboats.

Galled by this abasement, Chinese and Vietnamese nationalist movements began to take shape early in the twentieth century. They aimed at not just eliminating foreign control but also renovating their backward, "feudal" societies, developing their poor, peasant-based economies, and realizing visions of strong, unifying states. These aspirations were most warmly embraced by educated youth. Chinese students were active by the 1910s; their Vietnamese counterparts were in ferment by the following decade. The most radicalized would take the lead in forming revolutionary organizations, the CCP in the 1920s and Vietnam's Communist party soon after. Both sets of young activists were drawn by the appeal of Marxist-Leninist ideas; both would look to the Comintern in Moscow for funding, schooling, literature, and advisors; and both would produce a charismatic leader. Both Mao and Ho played a critical role in expanding the appeal of their parties. Both relied on united-front organizations to mobilize support. Both looked to peasants to sustain guerrilla warfare and thus wear down better-armed foes.

The revolutionary struggle in both cases proved extraordinarily prolonged. The CCP gained political power in 1949, nearly three decades after its founding, and then under Mao's guidance launched a program of radical transformation that convulsed China well into the 1960s. Vietnam's revolution was aimed less at internal transformation than at foreign powers standing in the way of independence and unity. For a quarter-century France was the prime enemy, followed by the United States for another two decades. (The story of these two intimately related revolutions resumes in Chapter 6.)

NEW STATES UNDER CONSERVATIVE ELITES

In contrast to China and Vietnam, where considerable revolutionary momentum developed, new regimes elsewhere in Asia followed a more gradual, less violent path toward more limited objectives, especially where colonial masters proved more accommodating to demands for independence. The United States had already before World War II pledged independence for the Philippines, and in 1946 Washington made good on that promise. A year later the British were on their way out of India. From once-great imperial possessions emerged the new states of Burma (Myanmar), Ceylon (Sri Lanka), and Pakistan as well as India. In 1957 Britain also abandoned Malaya, although not before British forces had put down a Communist insurgency led by ethnic Chinese. In the East Indies the Dutch at first rebuffed calls for independence but finally in 1949 retreated in the face of an internal resistance movement and under U.S. pressure.

Decolonization left already entrenched elites in charge and ruling with the cooperation or acquiescence of their former foreign masters. Under these arrangements, the former colony became formally independent but perpetuated attitudes and practices that had taken root during the period of control. Some scholars call this pattern of continued influence from outside "neocolonialism" and would see it in operation not only in the cases to follow in this chapter but also in sub-Saharan Africa, where the British and French ruled, or even in Central America and the Caribbean, where the United States replaced Spain as the dominant power. Under neocolonialism, foreign influence usually derived from the local elite's identification

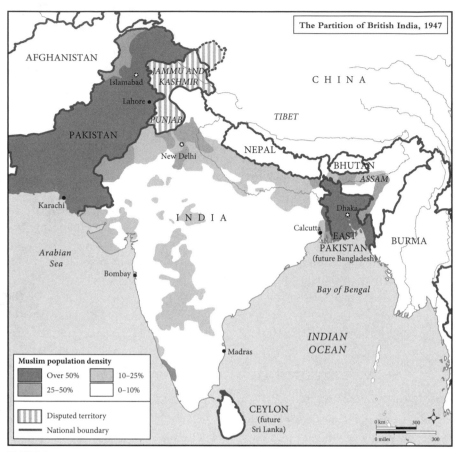

MAP 3.3
The Partition of British India, 1947

with and education under the old regime and was sustained by political and economic clout still in foreign hands, such as corporate operations or control of prestigious schools. These neocolonial regimes were averse to fundamental social change. They did little to mobilize the peasantry, indeed regarded manifestations of peasant discontent as a threat to the postcolonial order. They also harbored reservations about strong, autonomous state power so important to Chinese and Vietnamese revolutionaries.

India's Status Quo Independence

British control over India had its origins in the seventeenth and eighteenth centuries, but not until 1858 did the British Crown and Parliament assume direct rule over two thirds of the subcontinent. The actual exercise of control fell to a British viceroy on the ground, who in turn depended on a British bureaucracy extending down to the district level, a British-led Indian force, and various consultative councils integrating Indian influentials such as landholders and businessmen. The remainder of India remained in the hands of numerous local princes subordinated to the British. The landmass of this major colonial possession was half the size of the United States, with a population that would reach 250 million by 1920. Fewer than 80,000 British officials and troops managed to exercise control over this vast territory and population.[15]

British India was a place of astonishing cultural diversity. It included four distinct language families, each with its own subdivisions, over which was laid English as the language of colonial administration and modern education. Religion added to the complexity. Hinduism was the leading faith, but Islam claimed the adherence of a quarter of the population. Adding to this diversity were sharp regional differences based on ethnicity as well as language. Even after independence many Indians were still more attached to their region than to central authority wielded from the capital, New Delhi. Local movements demanded special standing for one or another of the some 1,500 indigenous tongues spoken in the country, and pressed for political autonomy and even in some cases territorial independence. Finally, at the local level, especially in the countryside, a variety of strong social patterns prevailed that sharply divided Indians into different status groups within a strong caste system. (Caste was a hereditary status that had carried down from precolonial society and ranged from Brahmins at the top to "untouchables," whose "spiritual pollution" placed them at the bottom.) These layers of different identities made central control and political change difficult not only for the British colonial administration but also for the post-independence leaders.

The British colonial regime planted the seeds of its own undoing. While justifying its control as a civilizing influence, in practice it gave priority to more mundane and self-interested goals. Foremost were improvements in transportation, communications, and administration essential to preserving political control and social stability, extracting taxes to help maintain British power around the world, and promoting trade (mainly the import of British manufactured goods in exchange for Indian raw materials). Only a small fraction of the colonial budget went toward such areas critical to human welfare and economic development as education and health. The adverse effects of foreign rule for most Indians could be measured in terms of a per capita income that did not increase in the two centuries preceding independence and a life expectancy that actually fell some 20 percent between 1872 and 1921.[16]

In 1885, less than three decades after London had brought the subcontinent together under the direct rule of the British Crown, indigenous resistance took organized form with the creation of the Indian National Congress. The leaders of this loose political assemblage were English speakers, mostly university-trained professionals and mostly from the higher castes. They took up the ideas of their British educators on nationalism and self-determination—and turned those ideas against their teachers. They charged that a "civilized" country professing to have the best interests of its subjects at heart was in fact draining away India's wealth in the service of its own enterprise and empire and refusing to give its subjects a significant voice in their own affairs.

Mohandas Gandhi would emerge as the commanding figure at the forefront of the independence drive. Born in 1869, he was the son of a minister in one of the semiautonomous princely states that survived under British rule. His devout mother saw to his careful training in the family's Hindu faith. He gained an English education in India and in 1888 (then aged 19) arrived in London to study law. After completing his degree, he returned home for a time. In 1893 he went to work in British-controlled South Africa. Appalled by racial discrimination there, the young lawyer championed the rights of Indian residents.

In 1915, now a well-known and experienced political figure and exponent of nonviolent protest, Gandhi returned to India. He was as personally complex as India was culturally complex. Here was a British-trained lawyer able to deal comfortably with the colonial authorities, an astute political tactician committed out of deep principle to nonviolent methods, and a person of such spirituality and charisma that he would emerge as a venerated holy man widely known as Mahatma (or Great Soul). The holy man had a wry sense of humor. When questioned on wearing his usual loincloth, sandals, and shawl to a tea hosted by the British monarch, he is supposed to have replied that he was fine; "the King had enough on for both of us." Gandhi's simple, engaging style, the directness of his challenge to the fundamental moral claims of British rule, and his mass appeal combined to bore away at British confidence and ultimately determined if not the fact of independence at least the form in which it came.

Gandhi's special contribution to the independence struggle was his philosophy and strategy of nonviolent protest. He had worked out his ideas while leading the civil rights struggle in South Africa and began applying them to India in 1919 when he launched a campaign for self-rule. He relied on such novel tactics as work stoppages, boycotts of British goods, massive demonstrations peacefully defying British authority, and prayers and fasts to advance the nationalist cause. Gandhi himself assumed an increasingly austere lifestyle that commanded respect across

Gandhi with Jawaharlal Nehru, July 1946
By the time of this photo, Nehru was firmly established as Gandhi's heir within the Congress and within the Indian nationalist movement. (AP Photo/ Max Desfor)

a diverse population. He gave up Western clothes in favor of a loincloth and shawl, spun his own fabric, wrote and meditated in a spare cubicle, and refrained from sexual intercourse. By generally cultivating a spiritual outlook, he sought to signal his belief in an Indian way distinct from a degraded, materialistic Western way imposed by the British and to challenge the moral authority of the colonial regime. That regime had, he charged, exploited his country and lured Indians toward a "modern" civilization inferior to their own. He dreamed of an India emerging from the independence struggle that would be the antithesis of the West: just, harmonious, egalitarian, and tolerant. He hoped that these values would transcend the many differences of language, class, caste, region, and religion that divided the subcontinent and would lay the foundations for an enlightened and united country.

This public persona—politically assertive, populist, frail, and profoundly moral—drew a mass following to the Indian National Congress cause for the first time. Repeated rounds of arrests and imprisonment for Gandhi and other Congress leaders failed to still the protest. In 1930 an emboldened Gandhi began pressing for full independence. During World War II he redoubled the pressure, knowing that the British needed peace in India to repel Japanese forces threatening the eastern frontier. In August 1942 the Congress passed a "quit India resolution," making a bold claim to "India's inalienable right to freedom and independence" and conditioning support for the war on the grant of immediate independence. The party proclaimed that it could no longer accept "an imperialist and authoritarian" rule holding back India's national development.[17] Confronted by this challenge, British authorities were unbending. They rode out the mass protest that followed, but their victory was transient.

World War II fatally weakened an already infirm British grip on the subcontinent. During the interwar period, rising nationalist feeling had forced the colonial regime to admit Indians into administration and to give them a growing role at the provincial and local level. They gained a say in economic affairs, a power quickly used to raise protective tariffs and promote an indigenous steel and textile industry. With the outbreak of war, colonial officials cracked down in the face of Congress demands for a set date for independence. They jailed Gandhi and his associates. The war also brought fresh suffering and sacrifice to ordinary Indians as Britain's global war effort drained food and other goods from India, sparked inflation, and in places caused starvation. By the end of the war, colonial authority faced not just widespread unrest, including the first serious outbreaks of violence, but also more seriously the loss of the last shreds of legitimacy. At least in the eyes of Hindus, the Indian National Congress with Gandhi as its symbolic head had become the unquestioned leader of the nation. As sentiment shifted and independence became more likely, collaborators on whom British rule depended became more reluctant. These trends steadily raised the potential cost of maintaining control by force for a Britain exhausted financially and spiritually by war. The British Labour Party was already on record as favoring independence, and the Americans, now Britain's senior partner on the world stage, worried that a prolonged, violent independence struggle would radicalize the colony to the embarrassment of the free world and to the benefit of international communism. In August 1947 Britain transferred power to British-educated moderates at the head of the Congress.

Gandhi had emerged not only as India's founding father but also as a figure of international reputation and influence. The philosophy of nonviolence as a way of creating and demonstrating unity and determination against a more powerful but morally compromised foe won converts around the world (as subsequent chapters will show). Gandhi's example would lead Kwame Nkrumah to confront the British in Ghana peacefully, and in South Africa nonviolence would become an important part of the antiapartheid struggle. Even in the developed world nonviolent methods would gain adherents—for example, Martin Luther King, Jr. at the head of the civil rights campaign in the United States in the late 1950s and early 1960s and Czechs facing a Soviet invasion in 1968 (see Chapter 4).

But independence also brought Gandhi immediate disappointment. Even as the British laid down an independence timetable, splits appeared between the leaders of the Indian National Congress and the Muslim League, organized in 1906 by Muslims no longer willing to work within the Hindu-dominated Congress. The League's declared purpose was to guarantee protection of India's diverse and scattered Muslim communities from majority Hindu prejudice, which was particularly virulent among an extremist minority committed to a religious definition of Indian national identity. As independence drew nearer and the actual distribution of communal power became a pressing, practical issue, communal violence erupted.

Partition seemed the only solution, and India's first prime minister, Jawaharlal Nehru, reluctantly agreed to the creation of a separate sovereign Muslim state—Pakistan—led by Mohammad Ali Jinnah of the Muslim League. This internal trauma would leave the subcontinent deeply and bitterly divided. On the one side was a Hindu-dominated but formally secular India inheriting the British-trained army, police, and civil service. It struggled to contain persistent currents of Hindu hostility toward Muslims, who even after partition constituted 10 percent of the population and made India one of the largest Muslim countries in the world. On the other side was a new Pakistan openly devoted to Islam and incorporating Muslim-majority areas in two widely separated parts of the subcontinent, the larger in the northwest and another smaller but densely populated piece in the east that in 1971 became the independent state of Bangladesh. The armies of the two new states at once clashed over borders, especially in the Kashmir region, a point of lasting tension.

Partition drowned Gandhi's dream of a united, secular, harmonious, tolerant India in the blood of as many as a million dead and the sorrow of some 14 million refugees. One high-level British official recalled watching appalled as "panic and a lust for revenge stalked the land."[18] In early 1948 Gandhi was assassinated by a Hindu militant intent on punishing the frail old man for trying to stop the violence and hold the subcontinent together.

In the years following his death, the goals that Gandhi had preached would fail in a second, major way. In 1945 he had written of his old dream of a rural-based, egalitarian society resistant to Western materialism. "My ideal village will contain intelligent human beings. They will not live in dirt and darkness as animals. Men and women will be free and able to hold their own against any one in the world. There will be neither plague, nor cholera nor smallpox; no one will be idle, no one will wallow in luxury. Everyone will have to contribute his quota of manual labor."[19] Gandhi singled out for particular censure the severe discrimination suffered by untouchables and women.

The new government made but half-hearted efforts to realize Gandhi's vision of social justice. As early as 1949 it outlawed "untouchable" as a category and thus sought to lift disabling stigma from some 14 percent of the population. But despite this and later attacks on caste-defined bars to educational and occupational opportunity, caste continued to determine social status and its rigidities still shaped fundamental aspects of life from marriage to residence to occupation. The government made important legal changes in the status of women immediately after independence. Those in the city did benefit in matters of education, work, and marriage. But for the vast majority of women—those in the countryside—new rules proved largely empty of meaning. Despite protective legislation, they remained subject to imposed marriage arrangements in late childhood or early adolescence and to the control of husbands as they had been of fathers. While marriage dowry had become illegal, the husband's family continued to insist on it. Divorce or separation was still not socially sanctioned, even though each had become legal. Women were left largely illiterate, restricted in matters of inheritance and property ownership despite legal equality, and consigned to the most menial of jobs. Abused, debased, and exploited, women committed suicide at rates unmatched anywhere else in the world.

Rural poverty persisted despite land reform legislation and a campaign of village development launched in the 1950s. These measures did little to change the shocking facts on the ground. A hundred million peasants—nearly a third of the entire population—were then still landless or homeless or both, and 80 percent of the electorate in the world's largest democracy was illiterate. Poverty and deprivation in the countryside, where four fifths of Indians still lived in the 1960s, contrasted powerfully with the urban world of the educated and the wealthy. In the face of population increases of 10 million a year, the government finally in 1959 endorsed family planning but failed to commit sufficient resources to slow this rapid increase that was especially damaging to rural development. Between 1950 and 1975 the population would grow by nearly a quarter of a billion.

The failure of Gandhi's populist commitment to equality and a better life had several sources. The Congress lacked ideological coherence and discipline and thus proved in power more of an impediment than an instrument of deep-seated reform. Not only was the party a coalition of diverse interests and outlooks, but its leadership was averse to sweeping social programs. The party disproportionately served the better-off, the industrialists, the well-educated party leaders, and their privileged allies at the local level. A business community that had taken shape under British protection and that had financially backed the Congress' push for political independence reinforced resistance to social policies involving redistribution of wealth. The civil service was also conservative in its instincts and application of the law. Influential local interests, well entrenched economically and socially, constituted the Congress' political base, and as such was able to block significant change. The failure of the Congress-dominated national and provincial governments to invest in education, health care, and social welfare helped perpetuate the cycle of chronic ill health, infectious disease, and crippling illiteracy. In the end, this failure doomed much of India's population to some of the worst poverty seen in the Third World. A historian of India has provided a graphic reminder of what the abstract notion of poverty meant in this case: "almost perpetual hunger, a monotonous and unbalanced diet at the best of times, cramped and squalid housing, perhaps one change of meagre clothes, insufficient bedding to prevent deaths from cold in the northern Indian winter, children's absence from school for lack of clothes or books or the need to earn to feed the family, and no money for doctors or medicines."[20]

In a broad sense, India's colonial legacy also played a role in undermining Gandhi's vision of a just, egalitarian society. The top of India's political class hailed from privileged groups that had been trained in the best British schools, socialized in British ways, plugged into "old school" networks of influence, and coopted into the colonial government. They shared with the British upper crust who had ruled India a belief in their right to lead. They also shared a commitment to preserving a strongly hierarchical, secular, class-conscious social system that favored them and their kind.

Jawaharlal Nehru was one of those well-born English speakers. His was a prominent Brahmin family, whose wealth came from his father's practice of English law and whose lifestyle was heavily Westernized. Between 1905 and 1912 the young Nehru lived in England, attending a prestigious private secondary school, going on to college at Cambridge, and finally getting a law degree in London. Along the way he acquired the dress, bearing, and outlook of an English gentleman. Once back home, he found purpose in the independence crusade and discovered in the course of his political organizing a side of his country that he had never seen before: a rural population that was "naked, starving, crushed and utterly miserable."[21] Thanks to a razor-sharp mind, a movie-star attractiveness that was balanced by a quiet reserve, and a deep well of energy, he emerged as Gandhi's chief lieutenant, assumed leadership of the Congress, and took on the job of negotiating with the British the terms of independence. He would go on to serve as India's first prime minister, dominating the government and the national political scene until his death in 1964.

Throughout Nehru talked of ending poverty but never matched his high-sounding words with effective action. His major legacy was instead to lay the basis for a political dynasty. Two years after his death, his daughter Indira Gandhi (not related

INDIA'S PATH TO INDEPENDENCE

1858	British crown begins to assert direct control over territory later to become the independent states of India, Pakistan, and Burma (Myanmar)
1885	Hindu-dominated Indian National Congress organized
1906	Muslim League organized
1919	Gandhi launches nonviolent campaign for Indian self-rule
1942	The Congress led by Gandhi demands immediate independence
1947	Britain grants independence; Indian subcontinent partitioned between India led by Nehru and Pakistan led by Jinnah; partition sets off communal violence and war between India and Pakistan
1948	Gandhi assassinated by a Hindu extremist
1950s	Nehru leads international nonaligned movement, begins series of five-year plans
1962	India–China war over disputed Himalayan territory
1964	Nehru's death; political power passes to his daughter, Indira Gandhi, and later to her son, Rajiv Gandhi

to Mohandas) would take control of the government and remain the presiding political figure for almost 20 tumultuous years. Following her assassination in 1984, her son Rajiv Gandhi assumed leadership of the country and the Congress. After Rajiv was also assassinated in 1991, his widow and a favorite of Indira, the Italian-born Sonia Gandhi, sustained family influence over a Congress party whose prominence carried over into the new century. (See Chapter 11.)

Both the institutions and values of the new Indian state drew heavily on a colonial legacy. The state's backbone was an army and bureaucracy trained under the British. Its economic policy was from the start heavily influenced by the British Labour Party's commitment to a mixed economy with a prominent role for public enterprise and bureaucratic regulation. State investments made through a series of five-year plans, together with generous economic assistance from both sides in the Cold War, made India's major cities look like British centers of heavy industry. Although Hindi was designated the official language, English remained the most widely accepted. The English-trained and English-speaking officials of the new India with their eyes set on industrial development took pride in their country's role as a leader of states refusing to take sides in the Cold War even while taking money from the Cold War rivals. Their neglect of the countryside left India what it had been under their colonial predecessors: a land of stark inequalities. With their social prestige, political influence, and economic advantages at stake, high-status Indians in government as well as outside had no sympathy for meaningful measures to promote equality or alleviate poverty.

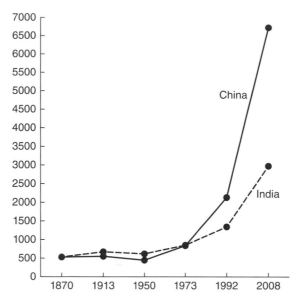

FIGURE 3.1
China Surpasses India in Per Capita GDP, 1870–2008
Data are measured in constant 1990 dollars (defined in "Key
Economic Terms," p. 15). The divergence in performance begins
in the Nehru–Mao years, when China closed the gap, and then
widens under their successors.[22]

New Delhi's modest domestic agenda and even more modest achievements
make a striking contrast with the persistence and vigor with which the Chinese
and Vietnamese states tackled the problems afflicting their societies. Economically, for example, India fell behind China. The two countries' per capita income had
been roughly on a par from the early nineteenth century to 1950. But India's development strategy would leave its per capita income lagging significantly behind
(Fig. 3.1), reflecting both a low economic growth rate and neglect of population
control, whereas the Chinese began to effectively address the population problem
in the 1970s and accelerate the rate of economic growth. In contrast to China's
revolution-minded Communists, India's conservative socialists moved cautiously
if at all to address gaps between rich and poor, raise literacy and longevity, and
better the lives of women. Gandhi's and Nehru's dreams of development had led to
outcomes that in comparison to Mao's did not serve the interests of ordinary
people well. On the other hand, an activist state in China could make mistakes
with terrible consequences (as we will see in Chapter 6). The verdict on the Indian
model, with its more modest programs and smaller risks, thus remains mixed.

The Collaborative Impulse in the Philippines

In the islands making up the Philippine archipelago, the colonial experience bore
parallels with that of India. The Spanish had consolidated their control earlier

than the British: in the latter half of the sixteenth century. But as in India by the nineteenth century, subjects increasingly integrated into international commerce and exposed to notions of nationalism were becoming restive. By the mid-1890s Spain faced armed resistance led by urban, Western-educated Filipinos from a new middle class restive under the restrictions of Spanish rule. This incipient revolution took a sudden and surprising turn when American forces arrived in 1898 during the Spanish–American War. Although the cause of the war was Spain's control of Cuba, the Philippines became the main territorial prize claimed by the victorious Americans.

Filipinos responded to the new colonial master with more armed resistance beginning in 1899. Not to be thwarted, the McKinley administration committed as many as 70,000 troops to pacify the islands. Those troops encountered a stealthy foe who operated with civilian support over familiar home terrain. The war led not only to atrocities by frustrated U.S. forces but also to a stunning loss of life. The number of Filipinos killed in action came to at least 20,000. More striking, war-related famine and disease during the period of resistance first to Spain and then the United States around the turn of the century produced among the general population approximately three quarters of a million deaths (out of a population of about 7.5 million in 1900). In other words, about a tenth of the archipelago's population perished.

The brutality of pacification, combined with charges that Americans were betraying their own ideals, resulted in a basic redirection of the American colonial project. U.S. proconsuls in the Philippines struck a compromise with the Filipinos elite, men of education and good social standing. Those inclined toward collaboration were themselves unhappy with the costs and doubtful about the long-term viability of resistance. This elite's part of the bargain was to help bring the fighting to a close and then cooperate in uplifting a people left ignorant by Spanish misrule and made superstitious by an entrenched Catholic Church. In exchange for their immediate acceptance of American rule, well-to-do, landed Filipino leaders got a promise of ultimate independence for their country, an increasing role for themselves in governance, and the promise of orderly social and economic modernization. In 1916 the United States made formal its pledge of independence, and in 1935 the islands gained self-governing status in preparation for an early end of American control. These arrangements laid the foundation for an enduring neocolonial relationship between the Philippines and the United States.

During these pre-independence years the U.S. colonial administration compiled a mixed record. Public health improved significantly. Education became more widely available and together with a better transportation and communication system helped diminish regional identities in favor of a stronger sense of national unity. Although formally democratic, the country was run by prominent regional families. Their control of land and wealth gave them great power and prestige locally and provided the basis for competing for a share of national power in the capital, Manila, and with that power fresh opportunities for wealth and status.

The Filipino model was also marked by economic stagnation and one of the world's widest gaps between the privileged and the poor. A peculiarly Filipino model of economic and political development had taken hold. Taxes favored the wealthy. Landlords resisted land redistribution programs. Desperate tenants were becoming politically active, and some among the urban educated exposed to social injustice were turning to radical politics.

Independence, long on the agenda, was delayed by the outbreak of war between the United States and Japan and the ensuing Japanese occupation of the islands in early 1942. Many leading political figures opted for collaboration with this latest set of foreign intruders, while guerrilla resistance sprang up in the countryside with popular support. The war years thus fed social tensions that would carry over into the postwar period. Finally, in 1946 the islands received their formal independence, but little changed. Alarmed by the advance of international communism, cold warriors in Washington kept U.S. military bases on the islands and preserved close ties with the old elite. The elite too saw advantage in resuming collaboration with the Americans. This arrangement almost immediately encountered a revolutionary challenge. It erupted suddenly in the late 1940s and then subsided in the early 1950s, following along the way a pattern that departed significantly from the Chinese and Vietnamese cases treated above.

The challenge arose from peasant discontent that had become pronounced in the interwar period. The deterioration of patron–client ties had left peasants without economic security. Landlords with whom peasants had once enjoyed a mutually supportive relationship increasingly embraced commercialized agriculture and "rationalized" their use of peasant labor so as to eliminate traditional but costly welfare practices. Where landlords might once have guaranteed tenants access to land and provided help in hard times, new-style landlords attuned to market forces viewed these kinds of welfare accommodations as unprofitable and thus unsuitable to a modern, rational economy. Landlords, explained one tenant reflecting on what he saw as the breakdown of the moral order, "no longer upheld their end of the relationship between the tenant and his landlord. They were being unfair to the peasants. It was unjust. Besides that, we had no protection any more, and not enough to eat."[23]

Threatened by increasingly high rates of landlessness and tenant debt, peasants began in the 1920s resorting to sporadic, isolated acts of collective protest. The Socialist Party responded to this rising rural discontent by helping to organize peasant unions. The Philippine Communist Party, established in 1930, had also by the end of the decade come around to endorsing calls for rural reform, although peasants were mystified why Communist speakers "went on . . . about how good things were in Russia. It wasn't relevant to our problems. It was also dangerous. The police could have thought we were a bunch of communists and arrested us."[24]

The Japanese occupation of the Philippines in 1941 set the stage for the creation of the People's Anti-Japanese Army, popularly known as the Huks. In March 1942 prominent Socialists and Communists met to organize a united-front, peasant-based force led by Luis Taruc, a leading Socialist. The son of a tenant farmer, he understood the discontents of his peasant followers and sympathizers. Under this charismatic leader, the lightly armed but locally supported Huk forces resisted the invaders and punished Filipinos, many of them landlords, who collaborated with the Japanese. But unlike the CCP and the Viet Minh, Huk leaders failed to build a disciplined organization that would sustain their struggle over the long haul.

At the end of the war the Huks disbanded even as calls for improvements in rural conditions persisted. As earlier, peasants demanded an assured subsistence. As one tenant explained, "We wanted the landlords or the government to guarantee us enough to eat and a roof over our heads." Local security forces sponsored by landlords quickly countered with repression. With the countryside in turmoil and wartime gains evaporating, armed Huk units began springing back to life in the latter part of 1946. One peasant recalled with pride his support for the Huks at this time. He and other peasants had shown that "we weren't slaves" of the landlords and the government: "We didn't lie down like whimpering dogs when they started to whip us. We stood up to them and fought for what was rightfully ours." The Huks reestablished themselves in their old stronghold in central Luzon and began expanding into the southern part of the island. The government responded with an "iron fist" strategy of dealing with restive rural areas. The brutality of army and irregular forces—arresting, torturing, raping, and looting peasants in contested areas—enhanced the Huks' popularity. By late 1949 Huk units had passed from the defensive to the offensive and were beginning to pose a threat to the government in Manila.[25]

In January 1950 the Huk leadership, now dominated by the Communist Party, decided to gamble on an all-out effort to seize power. That decision was prompted in part by the government's ineffectual response to the Huk challenge and in part by the Communist leaders' conviction that the United States was on the defensive in the Cold War and would not be able to save its Filipino allies. The expectation of an imminent economic crisis in the United States and the Communist triumph in China convinced party leaders that a favorable "revolutionary situation" was taking shape. The outbreak of the Korean War in June confirmed this optimistic reading of the international situation and sustained their determination to make a bold bid for power.

However, the Huk general offensive failed and the Huks suffered a crushing defeat. Once the gravity of the insurgent threat became clear during the first half of 1950, Washington had rushed assistance to its Filipino allies. Communist leaders for their part had lost popular support by making much of American imperialism while neglecting rural grievances and the rudimentary state of their military force. Perhaps the most demoralizing blow was the capture of important Communist leaders in October 1950. The survivors briefly persisted in the militant strategy and then retreated to a defensive approach intended to preserve remaining Huk resources. The resistance rapidly declined. At their peak the Huks had boasted 12,000 to 15,000 combatants and 1.5 to 2.0 million followers, but by the mid-1950s they had disappeared as an organized force even as the rural discontents that had given impetus to the Huks continued to simmer.

In Ramon Magsaysay the United States had found an effective Filipino partner in turning back the revolutionary challenge. Known as "America's boy," he was distinctly a product of the Filipino political establishment. He had married into a landed family. During World War II he had used his command of a U.S.-backed guerrilla unit to build his own patronage network. His close ties to Americans, his political skills, and his military background made him a natural choice for the government to place at the head of the anti-Huk effort. In September 1950, with the Huks threatening, Magsaysay became secretary of defense. He skillfully played on Americans' fears of communism, with the result that Washington provided some $500 million in economic and military assistance between 1951 and 1956, while the CIA promoted his image as an effective leader. With U.S. backing, he transformed the army into a better-disciplined and more effective instrument of rural pacification, while himself promising land reform. These efforts, together with his success at capturing Huk leaders and at sowing dissension within the movement, further blunted the revolutionary thrust.

Following his election to the presidency in 1953, Magsaysay cultivated landed interests, industrialists, the Catholic Church, and influential Chinese and U.S. businessmen, while supporting his own set of clients. Rather than dutifully following the U.S. lead, he backed nationalist demands during the renegotiation of U.S. base rights even while securing generous aid from Washington. In relation to his own people, this man of the establishment had no intention of launching a genuine, sustained challenge to the status quo, especially in the countryside. By the time of his death in an airplane crash in 1957 Magsaysay had confirmed the pattern of a weak state under the sway of a strong elite. It would spell hardship for many ordinary Filipinos as well as poor overall economic performance for the islands in the decades to come.

Seen in comparative perspective, the case of the Philippines provides another contrast with the Chinese and Vietnamese preoccupation with reconstructing state power and exercising it to effect social change. After the ouster of the Spanish in 1898, the Filipino elite composed of prominent provincial families not only lacked a tradition or model of a strong state, but was also compromised by a habit of collaboration with foreign masters on a scale unmatched in either China or Vietnam. After briefly resisting the American takeover, that elite had settled into a collaborative relationship that safeguarded its domestic privileges while promising ultimate political independence. When the Japanese conquered the islands during World War II, that elite again accommodated to foreign rule. Finally, when the Americans returned, the Philippines resumed a dependent, neocolonial relationship with the United States, which continued even after the attainment of formal independence in 1946. Rather than forcefully rejecting external domination, a dependent Filipino leadership developed a kind of submissive nationalism that had from their perspective the considerable virtue of protecting the domestic status quo.

CONCLUSION

The unrest already evident at war's end in Asia—in China, Korea, Vietnam, India, the Philippines, and Indonesia—provided a warning of what was to come in other Third World regions in the decades ahead. But more than that, the dramatic changes in the Asian political landscape defined two different paths that others seeking independence would follow.

One path, charted by India and the Philippines, led those demanding independence toward negotiations and compromise with the imperial power. By affording Western education to a privileged few and then bringing them into colonial institutions, the colonial powers took a major step toward coopting future independence leaders. In these cases, the transfer of control was likely to proceed in a relatively smooth and painless fashion. Critical to this sort of outcome was the colonial power's ability to conclude with the indigenous elite a collaborative bargain that served the interest of both sides. Such a bargain usually set a timetable for independence and offered post-independence support from the former colonial power. Such a bargain spared that power a costly war in defense of formal control and afforded a chance to maintain economic and cultural influence in the new nation.

The other path to independence was marked by extended internal conflict to end the old colonial order or to establish a new state strong enough to reassert sovereignty and impose a new domestic order. Under these circumstances, evident above all in China and Vietnam, the independence struggle radicalized the early challengers to the status quo, entangled local players in Cold War rivalry, and created bitterness and scars deeply dividing peoples within the same country. In these cases insurgent leaders had no commitment to preserving Japanese or French colonial institutions or accommodating powerful countrymen tied to the old order. Moreover, faced with armed repression, these leaders often found themselves seeking shelter in the countryside and support from peasants eager for land. Finally, they often had little trust in the West and thus turned to the Soviet Union as a source of outside support. These radical trends would (as Chapter 6 will show) become more pronounced as independence fever spread across the entire Third World.

Part Two

THE COLD WAR SYSTEM
UNDER STRESS, 1953-1968

IN LATE 1947 Kwame Nkrumah, confident and purposeful, returned to West Africa after 12 years away. In the years since his birth in 1909 he had traveled far. He had grown up in comfortable circumstances in the village of Nkroful on the southwest coast of Britain's Gold Coast colony (renamed Ghana after independence). His people, who belonged to the Akan group, had long been active in coastal commerce. His father was a goldsmith; his mother was a market trader. Nkrumah attended a mission school at a time when such opportunities for colonial subjects were sharply restricted, and then secured a teaching post in 1930 that made him part of a privileged minority. In 1935, following a pattern of other ambitious young Africans, he left to study abroad. During his 10 years in the United States, he took a bachelor's and a theological degree at Lincoln University, a major center for black education located near Philadelphia, and then a master's in education at the University of Pennsylvania. In May 1945, the 36-year-old Nkrumah moved to London, where he continued his studies and served as general secretary of the Pan-African Congress, an alliance of pro-independence groups, before finally heading home.

Paralleling Nkrumah's literal journey was a figurative one, both intellectual and cultural. Growing up on the coast with its foreign trade connections had made him aware of the wider world. Missionary training, followed by his long foreign sojourn, had further expanded his horizons and sharpened his political commitment and personal sense of mission. In the United States he and other African students discussed how to combine the best of what they were learning in the West with their own traditions and then how to use that new, uniquely African synthesis to guide the region's political and social reconstruction during the coming era of independence. He read widely and was especially impressed by W. E. B. Du Bois, a black American intellectual who held that Africans and those of African descent

Kwame Nkrumah on the Eve of Fame, 1947
Nkrumah appears here reunited with his mother immediately on his return home—
a brief respite before plunging into national politics. (From *The Autobiography of
Kwame Nkrumah*, Thomas Nelson and Sons)

scattered across the Atlantic world shared a common culture, a similar experience
of racial oppression, and a need for political unity and cultural pride. Nkrumah
spent summers working in a multiethnic Harlem electric with political discussions
about the liberation of African peoples, whether in Africa itself or scattered by
the slave trade across the Western Hemisphere. Later in London, he continued his
political education among the West African community there, also in the grip of
independence fever.

Arriving home to West Africa, Nkrumah carried in his head three important
convictions. First and most obvious was the need for liberation of Africans from
outside control. In a 1943 talk he had declared: "We must take the torch of liberty
in our own hands . . . We cannot get what we want by asking, pleading and arguing . . . We are in a world of action, not talk . . . We must rise and throw off the
chains." He saw Africans following in the steps of the peoples of India and Vietnam
who were already demanding an end to colonial control. Nkrumah's second article
of faith was West African unity and the region's potential to serve as a base for an

all-Africa liberation movement. As a 1946 resolution that Nkrumah coauthored put it: "The day when West Africa, as one united country, pulls itself from imperialist oppression and exploitation[,] it will pull the rest of Africa with her." Finally, Marxism attracted Nkrumah, with its claims that a new, nonoppressive order was a historical inevitability and indeed within reach of those willing to organize and press forward. He was confident that socialist ideals and methods would occupy a central place in the new African synthesis, and by 1944 he had openly professed a socialist commitment.[1]

Nkrumah's homecoming would mark the end of one journey and the beginning of another. He immediately turned to political causes then uppermost in his mind. Independence came first. He would lead the assault on British colonial control, take the first African colony to statehood, rally sub-Saharan Africa against colonialism, and both preach and practice a new path of development that he called African socialism. He looked to a planned, state-controlled economy devoted to promoting and protecting industry as the surest way to raise the standard of living and education and to end foreign economic control (what he and others in the Third World came to denounce ever more insistently as neocolonialism). But his program failed to bring the promised benefits. Overthrown by his own army in 1966 and driven into exile, Nkrumah still sustained his radical hopes. Writing in 1968, he glimpsed signs of a "world revolution against capitalism, imperialism and neo-colonialism which have enslaved, exploited and oppressed peoples everywhere."[2] At this moment when Third World radicalism reached its crest, he was confident that his beloved causes of pan-African unity and socialism were about to prevail.

Nkrumah was but one of a phalanx of Third World leaders whose hopes for decolonization accelerated in the 1950s and 1960s. Mao Zedong in China and Ho Chi Minh in Vietnam had helped to usher in this new age of liberation even as Nkrumah took his first steps on home soil in 1947. Behind them came leaders such as Jacobo Arbenz in Guatemala, Fidel Castro in Cuba, Mohammad Mosaddeq in Iran, and Gamal Abdel Nasser in Egypt, who were also intent on curbing foreign influence and embarking on ambitious plans for economic and social modernization. Like Nkrumah, many had traveled abroad the better to understand how to remake their own world, and turned to Marxist ideas, drawn by the promise of rapid economic development and strong, centralized political authority. Also like Nkrumah, many saw their individual national projects as part of a larger global transformation. Their dedication to socialism and suspicion of the Western-dominated international market economy, coupled with their desire to avoid Cold War entanglements, gave rise to a Third World identity never so strong as in the 1950s and 1960s.

This ferment within the Third World was but one point of stress weakening the Cold War system and providing the first hints of its ultimate end. No less important in effecting a change in superpower relations was Stalin's death in 1953. It unleashed a reform impulse quickly harnessed by Nikita Khrushchev, who undertook a far-reaching reappraisal of Stalin's brutality and ushered in a less repressive and austere era in Soviet life. Closely connected with these domestic initiatives was the new, less threatening face that Khrushchev gave to Soviet foreign policy and his shift toward improved relations with the United States. A parallel lessening of Cold War ardor and suspicion was at work within a new administration in the United States. Truman's successor, Dwight Eisenhower, inclined toward a less pugnacious and more cost-conscious approach to the superpower struggle. The first achievement of these new, more conciliatory Soviet and American outlooks came quickly: an end to the deadlocked war in Korea in mid-1953.

An overlapping set of pressures pushed both Cold War rivals toward their new position. A growing nuclear arsenal left Moscow and Washington equally frightened by the prospect of war. In addition, the post-Stalin and post-Truman leadership faced the first serious stirrings within their respective Cold War blocs. But the Cold War rivals were hardly ready to turn the page on their bitter and dangerous quarrel. However fearful nuclear weapons were, both sides continued to build more and better weapons, thus feeding the anxieties of the other. Only haltingly did they begin to work together to brake the headlong rush toward disaster. At the same time, the restive Third World proved an expanding area of competition that was even harder to manage. By seeking to win friends and defeat foes among the newly independent states, Soviet and American leaders complicated efforts to limit Cold War costs and risks. At no time would the risks prove greater than during the Cuban Missile Crisis, and nowhere would the costs be higher than in the Vietnam War.

Finally, between 1953 and the years immediately following 1968, the market-driven international economy over which the United States presided enjoyed a golden age—and by its very successes added yet another set of pressures on the Cold War system. About the time of Stalin's death, the war-ravaged western European and Japanese economies regained their prewar levels of production and were poised to join the United States in a prolonged period of strong, steady growth. These revived economies soon challenged U.S. economic supremacy.

This era of prosperity effected subtle but profound changes in popular attitudes that added to the pressure on cold warriors on both sides. The stirrings were especially marked in the United States, where income levels and material consumption increased significantly soon after World War II. The politics of anticommunism had to compete with the politics of growth and an intensifying popular pursuit of a better material life. Calls for sacrifice in the name of Cold War crusading had little appeal as a new generation of Americans, born after World War II and raised in abundance in the 1950s, proved impatient with the social and political orthodoxies that had prevailed at the start of the postwar era. Their discontent would inspire a youth revolt in the 1960s and new attitudes toward race relations, foreign policy, gender roles, and the environment. Boom times in western Europe and Japan promoted these same popular expectations, and there too a new generation spoke out forcefully, constructed barricades, and led demonstrations that would shake capitals throughout the developed world and beyond.

Times were good also in Soviet bloc economies as recovery from war and the growing availability of consumer goods raised living standards dramatically. But this socialist consumer revolution created pressure from below for more goods as well as better food and housing. As elsewhere, young people were the most impatient with what they saw as social and political stagnation. Khrushchev and his colleagues labored to improve ordinary people's lives even if it took damping down the Cold War and providing more cultural freedoms. Thus, in the East bloc as elsewhere, the lure of material abundance and personal comfort increasingly defined national priorities and left many questioning why they should gamble the highest living standards in generations—and the hopes for still more—on a throw of the Cold War dice.

By the late 1960s the strains on the Cold War system were becoming acute, creating new possibilities for the years to come. A surprise offensive in South Vietnam in 1968 by forces backed by Hanoi set in doubt the Cold War calculus behind that distant, now misbegotten war. That same year witnessed a weakening of the U.S. economy so serious that Americans would have to surrender their domination of international trade and finance. Finally, the confidence and fervor that animated Nkrumah and others in the Third World climaxed, only to rapidly collapse. It was becoming clear that the transformation of the Third World was not the work of a historical moment but would take generations. The great achievement of the radicals—the end of colonialism—had by then been completed, and they were beginning to discover that their goal of fundamentally remaking their countries would be hard to realize. Frustrations at home combined with the siren call of integration into the international economy and the potential costs of challenging the United States would take the glow off Third World hopes for domestic revitalization and destroy the myth of a common Third World way. The years between 1953 and 1968 were in short a time of transition. The immediate postwar arrangements were on the defensive but not yet overturned; a new, more globally integrated world had not yet come into view.

4
THE COLD WAR: A TENUOUS ACCOMMODATION

NO SOONER HAD the Cold War begun to spread and to raise fears of a new, unprecedentedly costly world conflict than policymakers on both sides began to search for accommodation. During the 1950s and 1960s, the Cold War developed a dynamic that favored stability and imposed limits on the superpowers.

Looking back, it is possible to identify pressures and fears that began to put a brake on the U.S.–Soviet rivalry. Nuclear weapons helped make American and Soviet policymakers more prudent. The prospect of a nuclear catastrophe began to haunt leaders constantly attended by the "black box" that allowed them to authorize an attack. More subtle but no less important were domestic pressures that Cold War leaders could not easily ignore. The U.S. public feared communism but wanted a good life even more. Elected officials could sway the public to accept costly foreign commitments but only within limits. The men in the Kremlin wrestled with the inescapable fact that their economy was too small to sustain superpower ambitions while also underwriting the better life that Soviet citizens were coming to expect.

Despite these constraints, the two wary international rivals moved only hesitantly toward accommodation. The arms race continued at a fast clip, while events in Cuba and then Vietnam demonstrated that Washington and Moscow could still maneuver themselves into dangerous and costly confrontations. The lack of progress toward ending the Cold War, but more generally the social and ideological rigidities associated with it, provoked increasing impatience, especially in the generation coming of political age in the 1960s. In 1968 that impatience erupted in city streets in the United States and western Europe but also in Poland, Japan, and Mexico. All around the world young people demanded fundamental social and political transformations, challenging leaders from an older generation who seemed stuck in the past.

THE BEGINNINGS OF COEXISTENCE

Premier Nikita Khrushchev and President Dwight Eisenhower began during the 1950s the process of rethinking the dangerous rivalry in which their two countries had become locked. Both men found themselves in a nuclear world of enormous peril and increasing cost as strategic weapons proliferated in number and kind. They found their publics wanting prosperity more than the risks and costs imposed by the Cold War rivalry. And both had to deal with Cold War allies with different priorities. However, neither the Soviet nor the American leader was prepared to fully repudiate the Cold War decisions made by their predecessors or step outside the worldview of their particular political cultures. With one foot still solidly planted in the Cold War, each could only cautiously explore a new relationship.

Khrushchev under Pressure

The strongest impetus to dampen Cold War tensions came from Stalin's successor, Nikita Khrushchev. He was born in 1894 in a Russian village near the border with eastern Ukraine to a family of peasant origin. A schoolteacher with radical views first opened Khrushchev to the possibility of political change. His experience as a young man further politicized him. He had watched revolutionary fever grip his village in 1905, and by age 15 family poverty had forced him to leave school and train as a metalworker attached to mines that were a hotbed of labor radicalism. He attended lectures on political economy and read the Bolshevik newspaper, *Pravda*, and Marx's *The Communist Manifesto*.

Khrushchev's sharpening convictions led him into revolutionary politics. Between 1912 and 1914 he emerged as a labor activist leading strikes. By 1917 he was head of the local metalworkers' union and had joined the Bolshevik party. He fought along with the Bolsheviks during the civil war in Russia following their revolutionary seizure of power. His dedication, energy, and ruthlessness, together with his working-class background, helped him move ahead in the party.

Khrushchev's political style and values reflected his peasant origins. He was not interested in abstruse theoretical debate. He wanted for the Soviet Union precisely what was missing in his own early years: a rapidly developing economy to provide for the popular welfare and a strong, stable political system to create respect and security from the outside world. His politics were generally Stalinist: He was impatient with the moderate economic policy of the 1920s, he welcomed Stalin's shift to state planning in 1929, and he voiced enthusiastic support for Stalin as the "genius-leader." As an administrator, Khrushchev was hands-on and often acted impulsively. His outward appearance as a country bumpkin led many to underestimate his shrewdness and political skills and spared him suspicion during the purges of the 1930s.

In 1938 Khrushchev was put in charge of Ukraine, a region roughly the size of France that he enjoyed considerable latitude in running. During his long stint there, Khrushchev built a political machine and recruited party allies such as

Leonid Brezhnev who were later critical to his rise to supremacy. In late 1949 Stalin called Khrushchev to Moscow to join Stalin's immediate entourage. Following Stalin's death in 1953, Khrushchev at first shared power with colleagues, but by 1955 the 61-year-old was well on his way to consolidating his leadership. He had proved himself, as one party observer noted, "shrewder, more talented, energetic and decisive than the others."[1]

Khrushchev's decade in power was to produce a rush of reforms that became known as de-Stalinization. Most of those reforms Khrushchev and his rivals had begun exploring just after Stalin's death, and even those that Khrushchev had then opposed he would make his own after he had secured his place at the top. The reforms were wide-ranging, touching directly political and cultural life, the economy, and foreign relations. Over each of these areas stood the ghost of Stalin. That Khrushchev was a product of the Stalinist system made the break with the past all the more difficult.

Early in his tenure Khrushchev resolved to confront the ghost of his old master. To alter the Stalinist system required rethinking Stalin's significance to the development of the Soviet Union. The new leadership took the first step by downplaying the Stalin cult. In early 1954 Khrushchev issued instructions for gathering data on Stalin-era repression, and two years later he stunned delegates to the Twentieth Party Congress by delivering an address laying out some of Stalin's crimes and the "conditions of insecurity, fear and even desperation" created by this "sickly suspicious" leader.[2] (The details of this supposedly secret speech traveled through the party like a whirlwind, and a copy of the speech itself quickly reached an amazed West.) In 1961 Khrushchev launched another, even more emphatic assault on Stalinism.

De-Stalinization brought into the open long-nurtured discontents within the party leadership. Khrushchev and his colleagues did not question the superiority of socialism over capitalism, the correctness of Marxism-Leninism as a guide to action, or the need for strong, one-party leadership. They acknowledged Stalin's important contributions to the revolution. But they did recognize that his mistakes had demoralized the party and the public and in turn damaged the party's pursuit of economic development and popular welfare, even while they took care to minimize their own complicity in Stalin's misdeeds. Khrushchev himself had begun to have doubts about Stalin in the 1940s. Watching his boss handle the crisis of war revealed to Khrushchev how out of touch and how distrustful of subordinates Stalin was. Possibly adding to the resentment was Stalin's supposed refusal to stop the execution of Khrushchev's son, a pilot shot down by the Germans and, like all returned Soviet POWs, suspected of treason. Seeing Stalin daily between 1949 and 1953 accentuated Khrushchev's awareness of the faults of the old man and of the system he had built. Perhaps more broadly, Khrushchev realized that a half-century of traumas—the 1905 revolution, the German invasion during World War I, the 1917 revolutions followed by brutal civil war, Stalin's revolution from above, and the second German invasion during World War II—had scarred his people. It was time for a respite from national mobilization, class struggle, and personal anxiety.

De-Stalinization had immediate consequences in the Soviet Union. Within the Communist Party, it gave party members and leaders greater security by curbing the terror apparatus that Stalin had wielded so ruthlessly. It affirmed the importance of collective leadership, so that Khrushchev had to pay at least nominal respect to the opinions of his senior colleagues even as he grew more powerful. Khrushchev's bold attack on at least a part of the Stalinist past had a dramatic psychological impact as news of the event began to circulate ever more widely. Yevgeny Yevtushenko, a young poet often embroiled with the authorities in cultural disputes, remembered "how everybody read Khrushchev's so-called secret speech—in factories, at the Writers Union. Even non-party people like me read it. Many people cried and hung their heads. They were shocked."[3]

Reactions were distinctly mixed. Some party members and many intellectuals and artists who would come to refer to themselves as "Children of the Twentieth Party Congress" welcomed the critical scrutiny of Stalinism and hoped for the beginning of a more humane and open socialism. Some at the grassroots were confused: How could Stalin's associates not have known about his excesses, and why did they not stop his evil deeds? How could such excesses occur in a socialist country, and what was to prevent them from happening again? But the speech also gave rise to disbelief and resentment as Khrushchev's revelations collided with a Stalin cult propagated over two decades. At one university a student march to lay flowers on the local Stalin monument turned into a general protest against the unfair treatment of the "great leader." An angry soldier declared, "Stalin raised me from childhood in his ideas, and I will not reject these ideas now." A party loyalist recalled his distress. Even after finding out about Stalin's most serious flaws, he still found it "very difficult to extinguish in the heart that great love that was so strongly rooted in our whole organism."[4]

One of the most important effects of de-Stalinization was to open Soviet cultural life. Artists and intellectuals enjoyed more room for dissent and debate. An unprecedented degree of openness to Western culture ignited musical fads such as big band jazz, swing, and rock and roll. The foreign cultural influx stimulated the Soviet entertainment industry toward more adventuresome and popular work. Literature, for example, turned from tired political themes and spoke more often to readers' everyday lives and personal fantasies. Young people were especially quick to seize on new cultural trends, buying imported records and sporting clothes then trendy in the West. Nightclubs filled with youthful crowds dancing one of a changing array of imported fads, from the jitterbug and boogie-woogie to the twist. One irritated state security officer watched lively young people in a nightclub in 1956 and grumbled, "All this energy could be invested in building a hydro-electric power station, rather than wasted here on a dance floor."[5] But however much the authorities might disapprove of some aspects of this budding consumer society, they did not question the need for a relaxation of the tensions and hardship that had so long marked Soviet life. Now those who defied the party faced a relatively mild response—a rebuke or even exile, but not execution and punishment of family and friends.

Khrushchev himself was ambivalent about the thaw that his criticism of Stalin had encouraged. He directly intervened in favor of the publication of new and more searching literature such as Alexander Solzhenitsyn's novel, *One Day in the Life of Ivan Denisovich*, and Yevtushenko's poem, "Stalin's Heirs." The latter was printed in the party paper *Pravda* after Khrushchev had moved Stalin's body from its place of honor in Red Square. The poem warned against the power of Stalin's ghost to shape the conduct even of those former colleagues now attacking him. Yevtushenko asked, "How can we remove Stalin from within the heirs of Stalin?" But the rough-hewn and mercurial Khrushchev sometimes did not like what artists did with their new freedom. Jazz, he said, made him feel like he had "gas on the stomach." He detested abstract painting. To someone who worked in that genre, he offered his appraisal with characteristic bluntness: "It's a pity, of course, that your mother's dead, but maybe it's lucky for her that she can't see how her son is spending his time. What master are you serving anyway? . . . You've got to get out or paint differently. As you are, there is no future for you on our soil." Precisely because of these apparent excesses that came with greater freedom, Khrushchev felt the party had to keep a watchful eye on artists and intellectuals.[6]

Presiding over cultural changes proved for the reformer in Khrushchev far less complicated than managing an economic system that was failing to deliver fully on its promise, especially to the Soviet people. Stalin had consistently favored developing defense and heavy industry, sectors that would sustain Soviet security and prestige. Khrushchev, by contrast, wanted to give more attention to light industry and agriculture in order to raise living standards. Khrushchev's "bread-and-butter" view of socialism left him sympathetic to pressure from consumers and convinced him that the ability of the system to respond to that pressure was a test of political legitimacy.[7] How could the Soviet Union, he wondered, maintain popular support and make an impression abroad if it suffered economic shortages?

Khrushchev gave domestic welfare policy priority. In May 1957 he dramatically promised to surpass the United States in per capita production of meat, milk, and butter within three years. In 1959 Khrushchev put into effect a seven-year plan meant to push the Soviet Union past the United States in per capita industrial and agricultural output by 1970 and to lay the basis for a fully communist society (one achieving a Western level of abundance, providing goods to its citizens on the basis of need rather than ability to produce, and in general following collectivist, egalitarian values). In 1960 he announced a decision to increase consumer goods production at the expense of the armed forces, and he cut the workweek from 48 to 42 hours. The next year he promised that a communist society would be on the horizon by 1980. The achievements of the new, consumer-friendly leadership were considerable. The priority given to housing construction reduced the number of those stuck in the old, crowded communal living arrangements. Opportunities for schooling expanded. As a result of the shortened workweek, Soviets enjoyed more time for leisure—for sports, movies, listening to the radio, reading, and visiting with family and friends. Vacations at state-run facilities became more commonplace, and people flocked to concerts, open-air poetry readings, clubs, and restaurants. Most of the material and educational gains went to city dwellers. The countryside lagged behind, but rural folk at least finally received an internal passport that gave them greater freedom to travel within the Soviet Union.

Khrushchev had inherited an economy that strained to provide the resources required of a superpower. He thus faced a constant choice between guns and butter—between spending on the military and foreign aid critical to keeping the Soviet Union in the Cold War competition or diverting funds to meet popular needs. His tilt toward the consumer involved him in a delicate balancing act. In the late 1950s he had bet on improved relations with the United States and cut spending for conventional armed forces by one third. To get the most out of his military budget, he channeled funding to submarines, nuclear weapons, and the development of long-range missile systems. These kinds of advanced weapons would not only ensure Soviet security against U.S. attack but also demonstrate to the world Soviet technological skills. The successful test of an intercontinental ballistic missile (ICBM) and the much-heralded launch of the first Earth satellite (named Sputnik), both in 1957, seemed to vindicate that strategy.

President John F. Kennedy's expansion of the U.S. military budget and the Cuban Missile Crisis of 1962 dealt Khrushchev a blow, however, and demonstrated that gaining rough equality in strategic nuclear weapons would take a major, long-term investment. Khrushchev began shifting funds from the consumer sector back to defense and heavy industry. That shift collided with rising consumer discontent. Some complained, "What has become of consumer goods? We have to stand in line all day. Are we under blockade? The truth is that abroad they have everything, and here at home we have only rubbish."[8] In 1962 the southern Russian city of Novocherkassk became the scene of demonstrations protesting empty shop shelves, and scattered disturbances followed elsewhere. Improved relations with the United States by summer 1963 allowed Khrushchev to go back to advocating a better deal for consumers and to cut defense spending.

While domestic economic pressures encouraged the post-Stalin leadership to consider a fresh approach to the Cold War, perhaps even more important was the fear of nuclear war. In the Soviet Union as in the United States, that fear had first taken hold among scientists. A few of those active in the Soviet bomb project anticipated the danger quite early. Reports of the enormous power of the first U.S. H-bomb test in 1952 alarmed the head of the Soviet nuclear program, Igor Kurchatov, and convinced him that nuclear war would end life on Earth. He gained an ally in Andrei Sakharov, the designer of the first Soviet H-bomb. A 1953 tour of ground zero after a powerful test had shaken Sakharov. He found birds flapping helpless on the ground, their feathers scorched and their eyes burned out. Buildings blown away like a house of cards, brick pulverized, and glass melted all conjured up terrible images of what nuclear war would do. Kurchatov, Sakharov, and others impelled by a sense of responsibility for their creation began a campaign to convince Stalin and his successors of the dangers posed by a growing nuclear arsenal. After a full briefing in 1953 shortly after Stalin's death, Khrushchev recalled being so shaken that "I became convinced that we could never possibly use these weapons." He made fresh disarmament proposals to the United States in 1955, and in his first summit with Eisenhower that year made clear his realization that only a madman could contemplate nuclear war. He was reassured to learn that the Americans shared his understanding of the new nuclear era: "Our enemies probably feared us as much as we feared them."[9]

Khrushchev gave special prominence to the doctrine of "peaceful coexistence" in 1956 when the party elite gathered for the Twentieth Party Congress. He hinted at the way nuclear weapons had fundamentally transformed the nature of international relations. The future held only two choices: "either peaceful coexistence or the most destructive war in history. There is no third way." Arms control and better relations with the United States thus became important Soviet objectives. Embracing them did not mean abandoning hopes for the spread of socialism. In fact, Khrushchev argued that the rapid advance of socialism since the end of World War II and the equally rapid disintegration of the colonial system foreshadowed the triumph of the Soviet camp. Precisely because the conditions were so favorable, he indicated that Communist parties might now gain power through parliamentary means, although he did not rule out revolutionary struggle in countries where elite resistance to change was particularly violent. By making this point Khrushchev was conceding, at least in theory, that Communist parties would follow paths appropriate to their particular national situations. In 1959 he extended his optimistic reading of the international situation by pronouncing "capitalist encirclement" of the Soviet Union at an end. By asserting that the country was secure against its external as well as internal foes, Khrushchev provided the basis for a policy of relaxation both at home and abroad.

Europe was a special target of Khrushchev's policy of peaceful coexistence. He promoted a settlement for Austria that ended its occupation by Soviet and Western forces and made it nonaligned within Cold War Europe. Although he responded to West Germany's joining NATO in 1955 by forming the Warsaw Pact, a Moscow-led military alliance made up of Soviet eastern Europe clients, he also cultivated West German leader Konrad Adenauer in hopes of luring him away from the Americans. Khrushchev continued his peace offensive by proposing an end to both NATO and the Warsaw Pact, a comprehensive security treaty for Europe, and the withdrawal of U.S. troops from the continent. But the Eisenhower administration, still in the grip of Cold War suspicions, feared neutralization of Europe would be but the prologue to Soviet domination.

The other major facet of Khrushchev's foreign policy involved managing his allies. He knew that he was at the head not of a mighty "communist monolith" (as Washington saw it) but of a brittle bloc that was inherently difficult to hold together. Allies and dependents wanted more aid than could be easily extracted from a Soviet economy straining to keep up with consumer demand, and they resented the Soviets' cultural insensitivity and often domineering attitude.

Every bit as much as Stalin, his successors had to monitor developments in eastern Europe carefully. They were just as determined to maintain dutiful socialist regimes. They needed forward bases to counter NATO, to keep "fraternal" parties in line, and if necessary to suppress popular demonstrations of anti-Soviet sentiment. But Stalin's heirs also wanted to handle the region with a lighter touch—to avoid his brutality but also to limit the costs of propping up unpopular clients.

Tito's Yugoslavia posed the most direct test of the proposition advanced by the post-Stalin leadership that socialist regimes could legitimately pursue paths other than the Soviet one. Following his break with Stalin, Tito had denounced the Soviet system as a caricature of socialism. An entrenched bureaucracy held the real power, not the working class, while internationally, the Soviet state functioned as "an imperialist machine which is fighting for spheres of influence and the subjugation of other peoples."[10] Tito looked to the West for trade and aid, and reoriented the Yugoslav economy toward a prospering western Europe. He also took an active role as one of the sponsors of nonalignment, popular among newly independent states wanting to avoid entanglement in the Cold War rivalry. He followed an independent line domestically as well and allowed a degree of intellectual freedom. The guiding economic idea in the industrial sector was self-management, a decentralized economic policy that put control in the hands of workers, not bureaucrats.

Once secure at the top, Khrushchev worked to improve relations with Yugoslavia and the eastern European countries under Soviet sway. His 1956 party congress speeches on Stalin and peaceful coexistence called for respecting national differences among socialist countries. To drive the point home he dissolved the Cominform, created by Stalin in 1947 as an instrument to control Communist parties throughout Europe. While Khrushchev's talk of pluralism and repudiation of Stalin's excesses warmed relations with Tito, it stirred up unrest in eastern Europe, galvanizing reformers and angering hardliners who had climbed to power under Stalin and modeled themselves on his policy of tight control.

The first signs of discontent had appeared even before Khrushchev had consolidated his position. In June 1953, soon after Stalin's death, workers in Berlin had made political as well as economic demands on the Soviet-backed East German Communist Party. Protests quickly spread to other cities. Alarmed over the possible loss of control, Moscow ordered the tanks of its occupying forces into action. Rapid repression saved the day.

Three years later Khrushchev suffered a close call in Poland. A strike began in June 1956 in Poznan, a major industrial center. When the protest spread, the authorities cracked down at the cost of over 50 deaths. In July a worried Soviet leadership decided to restore to power Wladyslaw Gomulka, a former party leader who had fallen afoul of Stalin. With unrest continuing in October, Moscow prepared for intervention in the face of what it feared would be intense Polish resistance. Gomulka finally was able to scotch the invasion plans by promising Moscow to retain one-party control and membership in the Warsaw Pact. The crisis passed.

In Hungary the new light-rein policy suffered its most dramatic failure. In October 1956 news of protest in Poland and Khrushchev's denunciation of Stalin's crimes inspired public demonstrations honoring Hungarians who had fallen victim to Stalinist purges. As in Poland, workers took the lead, demanding "socialism but according to our own special Hungarian conditions, which reflect the interests of the Hungarian working class and the Hungarian nation." The reform party leader, Imre Nagy, heralded the mounting protests as "a great national and democratic movement, embracing and unifying all our people." He announced an end to one-party rule and withdrawal from the Warsaw Pact. With Hungary slipping into "counterrevolution," Khrushchev ordered military action in early November. As Soviet forces closed in, a Hungarian newspaper described over the wire to an impotent West scenes of freedom fighters "jumping up at the tanks, throwing hand-grenades inside and then slamming the drivers' windows. The Hungarian

Stalin Brought to Ground, 1956
Hungarians handed down their judgment on the man who had imposed a system of internal repression and foreign domination on their country. The head from a giant statue lays shattered in a Budapest street in the midst of the revolt against Soviet control in October 1956. (AFP/Getty Images)

people are not afraid of death. It is only a pity that we can't stand for long." The Soviets crushed desperate resistance at the cost of several thousand lives, executed Nagy, and installed a more pliant János Kádár. Khrushchev's intervention made clear that pluralism had limits. Soviet-aligned regimes that failed to contain popular protest or themselves strayed from the socialist faith could expect Soviet military intervention and the installation of a more dutiful set of leaders.[11]

Moscow encountered even greater difficulties in dealing with China. Like the Yugoslavs, the Chinese Communists enjoyed considerable independence because they had come to power without the help of the Red Army. Khrushchev had tried to impress his Chinese allies with generous development support. But his speech on de-Stalinization as well as his policy of peaceful coexistence irritated China's leader, Mao Zedong, while Mao's predictions that China would surpass the Soviet Union in the advance toward communism and his cavalier attitude toward nuclear war alienated Khrushchev. By 1959, less than a decade after the conclusion of the Sino-Soviet alliance, mutual suspicion between these two Communist giants had set in. The Chinese began denouncing Soviet socialism as a sham and challenging Moscow's claim to lead the socialist bloc. In mid-1960 Moscow abruptly ended its aid program and recalled its advisors. By the early 1960s the Sino-Soviet split was deep and the two leading socialist powers were headed toward military confrontation.

Other parties once tightly in the Soviet orbit also began drifting away. The de-Stalinization policy gave a strong impetus to the rise of more independent western European Communist parties in a trend that became known as Eurocommunism. For example, the head of the Italian party, Palmiro Togliatti, argued that Stalin's excesses as well as his achievements building socialism reflected the peculiarities of the Russian context. Recognizing that parties would each follow a national path, he declared, "Even in the Communist movement itself we cannot speak of a single guide."[12] These centrifugal pressures at work on the Communist bloc were accentuated by the outbreak of the Sino-Soviet dispute in 1959–1960. Albania followed China in condemning Soviet "revisionism." Khrushchev retaliated by cutting off aid and encouraging a coup against the Albanian party leader, Enver Hoxha.

Khrushchev is a pivotal figure in Soviet history and the unfolding of the Cold War. Like Stalin, he hoped that in the long run capitalism's decline and the successes of socialism would put the Soviet Union in a position superior to the United States. Yet the crisis of capitalism did not materialize, and inefficiencies in the Soviet economic system persisted. The Soviet economy was not large enough to create the promised "workers' paradise" and at the same time fight the Cold War. Beset by contradictory pressures, Khrushchev recognized that some sort of reduction in tensions with the United States was the best all-around solution. The Soviet Union would become more secure, and economic resources could be shifted to the consumer sector. But were American leaders ready to support a decisive turn away from the costs and dangers of the Cold War?

THE KHRUSHCHEV THAW

1953	Stalin's death; collective leadership established with Khrushchev as party secretary; terror apparatus dismantled as first step toward de-Stalinization; demonstrations in East Germany; Korean War armistice concluded
1955	West Germany joins NATO; Warsaw Pact forms
1956	Khrushchev and Eisenhower recognize nuclear vulnerability; at the Twentieth Party Congress Khrushchev denounces Stalin's excesses and advocates "peaceful coexistence"; protests in Poland and Hungary (the latter crushed by Soviet troops)
1957	Soviet ICBM tested and Sputnik launched
1959–60	Beginning of serious, public Sino-Soviet disagreements
1962	The publication of Alexander Solzhenitsyn's novel, *One Day in the Life of Ivan Denisovich*, marks high point of cultural opening

Crosscurrents in American Policy

The preoccupations and pressures at work within the Soviet system—domestic reform, consumer demand, the nuclear danger, and problems with allies—each had its counterpart on the U.S. side of the Cold War line. Nowhere are the parallels more striking than in the way fear of nuclear war gradually gripped policymakers.

While Harry Truman had come to rely heavily on nuclear weapons, Hiroshima and Nagasaki had schooled him in their terrible potential. He began practicing restraint even before the Soviet Union broke the U.S. monopoly on nuclear weapons in 1949. He asserted civilian control over those weapons and their development and sidestepped military pressure to plan for a nuclear war. The Korean War confirmed his cautious attitude. Although once, in late November 1950, with American troops reeling in the wake of Chinese intervention, Truman did blunder into a public comment about the possible use of nuclear weapons to save the situation, he ultimately embraced the more prudent view. A nuclear campaign would probably have little effect on China's fighting force, might trigger Soviet retaliation, and would deeply agitate American allies in Europe. Just before leaving office in early 1953, Truman offered some chilling reflections on what living with the bomb had taught him. Nuclear war would bring "death and destruction" to civilians and result in nothing less than "the end of civilization."[13] The fears that had settled on Truman would haunt his successors.

The Korean War had helped to elect Truman's successor, Republican Dwight Eisenhower, president in 1952. Casualties inflicted by Chinese forces in Korea and war-induced inflation and shortages at home had eroded public support. By early February 1951, half of poll respondents judged this inconclusive limited war a mistake. Support continued to decline to the considerable detriment of Truman's popularity but also the Democratic Party. Once in the White House, Eisenhower arranged an end to the fighting, and the military swore "never again" to intervene with U.S. troops on the Asian mainland. Throughout his presidency, Eisenhower faced the question of military intervention with considerable caution. On the surface his enunciated policy of "massive retaliation" seemed a blatant denial of nuclear fear. That policy placed nuclear weapons at the center of his military strategy. The U.S. leader claimed that he was ready to meet any Soviet-bloc attempt to break through the containment line with an all-out nuclear attack. He could thus dispense with costly conventional forces and rely on nuclear weapons, which would give him what the administration called "more bang for the buck." He accordingly authorized a steady expansion of warheads (from about 1,000 on entering the White House to about 18,000 on his departure) as well as delivery systems (with bombers soon to be supplemented by ground- and submarine-launched missiles).

But in private Eisenhower was quick to recognize that nuclear weapons were both morally dubious and of limited utility. His first major security study acknowledged an emerging nuclear balance of terror. Three years later the president read a secret government report estimating that even under the most favorable conditions millions of Americans would die in a nuclear war with the Soviets. He sought to brake the expansion of the U.S. arsenal, knowing full well from secret U-2 reconnaissance flights that Khrushchev's boasts of major advances in Soviet nuclear delivery systems were hollow. Eisenhower could not make this reassuring information public, but certain of the U.S. lead, he rejected calls for spending more on arms, even though his stand left him open to Democrats' attacks.

Like Khrushchev, Eisenhower worried that Cold War commitments might make excessive claims on national resources and harm domestic welfare. Above all, the American president feared that a crusade for freedom abroad might mortally wound freedom at home. Initially, he thought about this danger in terms of sapping the vitality of the economic system on which long-term security depended. If heavy defense spending hurt economic productivity, the country would lose its ability to support containment over the long haul. But increasingly Eisenhower spied another danger: a threat to democracy within the United States itself. He worried that the military budget would create concentrations of power beyond popular control. His farewell address of January 1961 warned that an emerging "military-industrial complex" represented just such a dangerous degree.

Eisenhower was also, like Khrushchev, constrained by potent domestic pressures. By the late 1950s the public was feeling the nuclear fears that had first fastened on scientists and then gripped political leaders. Feeding this fear was a growing awareness that radioactive fallout from atomic tests (some 423 by 1962) was a silent killer. Scientists had long known of radiation's damaging effects, but growing exposure in the laboratory and fallout that occasionally spread beyond the main U.S. test sites in Nevada and the Pacific intensified concern over this major public health problem. By 1954 some blamed fallout for birth defects and leukemia and called for halting tests in order to limit harm to humans. Serious civil defense discussions also fed nuclear fear rather than reassuring the public. Washington made plans for dispersing factories and the population to make Soviet targeting more difficult, building bomb shelters, and planning emergency urban evacuations. But in general, Washington's idea of civil defense did not go much beyond education and public drills. Most people were on their own to devise some means of protection. A whole generation dutifully performed duck-and-cover exercises in classrooms and listened to Bert the Turtle's reassuring advice on taking shelter at once after a nuclear flash.

Mainstream culture reflected the feeling of vulnerability. Already by the late 1940s popular fiction had picked up the theme of radiation-induced mutations. Movies followed suit. For example, *Them!* in 1954 projected before audiences giant mutant ants emerging from a New Mexico test site. Comic books developed their own heroes touched by radiation—Superman vulnerable to kryptonite and a scientist turned by radiation exposure into Spider-Man. Comedy routines and ballads (such as "What Have They Done to the Rain?" popularized by Joan Baez) also took up the theme of looming nuclear danger. Nevil Shute, an Australian, hit a chord in the United States with his 1957 novel *On the Beach*, made into a movie in 1959. It painted a bleak picture of a world doomed by fallout from nuclear war. The perilous situation confronting humankind was also the subject of the influential Stanley Kubrick film, *Dr. Strangelove, or: How I Learned to Stop Worrying and Love the Bomb*. Released in 1964, it depicted the arms race as an absurd competition conducted by lunatics and fools on both sides of the superpower divide.

Antinuclear activists began to emerge as more and more of the public grasped the danger posed by atomic weapons. The first protest group, the National Committee for a Sane Nuclear Policy (SANE), took shape in mid-1957, quickly expanding to 25,000 members. In 1961 Dagmar Wilson, a housewife and illustrator for children's books, became impatient with the ineffectual all-male politicking on the issue and called for direct pressure by women. She launched Women Strike for Peace, whose public demonstrations stressed the nuclear threat to children. Antinuclear groups in Britain, West Germany, and Japan—all allies and critical bases for the U.S. military—joined their U.S. counterparts in demanding an immediate end to nuclear testing.

This mounting public concern ran up against deep-seated suspicions, especially among the president and his advisors, about negotiating with the enemy. The still vivid memories of World War II told this generation of leaders that appeasement always invited disaster. They had watched the democracies appease Hitler—an attempt that had not spared them war but seemed rather to encourage the ambitions of the German leader. The broad anticommunist consensus forged in the late 1940s and early 1950s was an additional constraint, coloring political debate and policy discussions within the United States and perpetuating a picture of the Soviet Union as a dangerous and implacable force in the world.

The result was a cautious U.S. response to Khrushchev's peace offensive. At first, headway on arms control was impeded by Eisenhower's insistence on an intrusive, on-the-ground, foolproof inspection system. (The technology for remote monitoring of nuclear tests was not yet adequate.) The president did not trust Moscow to keep any bargain and so attached provisions that were unacceptable to a Kremlin determined to hide its inferior military technology. Eisenhower was also unable to control bureaucratic pressure for a nuclear buildup. He wanted to slow the expansion of the U.S. arsenal, but the Air Force successfully championed a strategy of matching every single additional Soviet weapon with several new American weapons. A breakthrough finally seemed possible when in March 1958 Khrushchev declared a unilateral suspension of nuclear testing and Eisenhower agreed in the fall to make it a joint moratorium. The American president now made a belated attempt to develop a personal relationship with Khrushchev. But any chance for progress collapsed in May 1960 when the Soviets shot down a U-2 spy plane, capturing its pilot. An angry Khrushchev publicly denounced the American leader and walked out of what had seemed a promising summit meeting.

CRISIS POINTS

Khrushchev continued to grope toward improved relations with Eisenhower's successor, John F. Kennedy. But with the Cold War still casting a long shadow, Moscow and Washington made only limited progress in containing their rivalry. Despite the horrible knowledge of what nuclear weapons could do, leaders were not prepared to check the arms race or abandon overseas commitments that might lead to superpower confrontations. Indeed, both sides continued their global contest. As a result, Khrushchev and Kennedy blundered into a nuclear crisis over Cuba, and then President Lyndon Johnson became ensnared in a second U.S. Asian war. This time American forces fought against a Vietnamese foe backed by the Soviet Union as well as China. (The Cuban and Vietnamese dimensions of these superpower collisions are treated in Chapter 6.) Although arms control made a comeback after the Cuban crisis and Johnson conducted his war so as not to provoke Beijing or Moscow, the number of nuclear warheads on both sides continued to soar, further highlighting the firm hold the Cold War still exercised over the thinking and behavior of the superpower rivals.

To the Nuclear Brink over Cuba

The Cuban Missile Crisis of October 1962 transformed abstract talk of nuclear disaster into palpable, gut-wrenching fear. For nearly two weeks annihilation seemed an imminent prospect. But just as Kennedy and Khrushchev had helped maneuver their two countries to the brink of nuclear catastrophe, so too did they work together to avoid that last deadly step.

Kennedy campaigned for the presidency in 1960 charging that the Soviets had gained military superiority. Once in the White House he gained the data that refuted these claims but nonetheless dramatically increased American outlays as though the lag were real. This buildup added to an already impressive arsenal and gave the United States a marked superiority, perhaps even a first-strike capability (meaning possession of weaponry sufficient to destroy so much of an opponent's nuclear force so quickly that it would forestall a serious counterblow). In 1962 the Soviets had some 500 strategic warheads, a paltry number compared with the U.S. force of about 7,200 warheads and hundreds of long-range and submarine-launched missiles as well as a large fleet of long-range bombers.

Despite this nuclear advantage, Kennedy was prey to insecurity. This insecurity was pronounced in the Caribbean, where he faced a revolutionary regime in Cuba. Its leader, Fidel Castro, had overthrown the long-time U.S.-backed military strong-man. Once in power, Castro had steadily moved domestic policy to the left and foreign policy toward the Soviet Union. Kennedy responded by endorsing a covert plan to overthrow Castro but found himself deeply embarrassed when in April 1961 a CIA-orchestrated invasion by Cuban exiles failed dismally at the Bay of Pigs. Khrushchev had confronted the new U.S. president with tough talk at a summit meeting in Vienna in June and then in August had a wall built through Berlin to stop East Germans from fleeing their country. At a minimum 3.4 million had fled since 1950 in what amounted to a costly and humiliating loss of talent. Finally, Khrushchev shook Kennedy by predicting that wars of national liberation would sweep the Third World into the Soviet camp. The Kennedy team felt belea-guered, and vulnerable to Republican critics. Kennedy had at least to demonstrate resolve in his own "backyard." He insisted that the CIA continue its covert opera-tions aimed at Cuba, and in the summer of 1962 the U.S. military staged amphibi-ous exercises in the Caribbean against a nominally fictitious country ruled by the evil "Ortsac" (Castro spelled backwards).

Khrushchev responded to Kennedy's hard line by following a more aggressive nuclear policy. In September 1961 he resumed nuclear testing, culminating in a massive 60-megaton test. He resented U.S. placement of nuclear missiles in Turkey on the border with the Soviet Union—at a time when Washington was warning Moscow not to send any rocketry to points next to the United States. Perhaps most fateful was the Soviet leader's refusal to back away from supporting change and winning friends in the Third World. In contrast to a cautious Stalin, Khrushchev actively cultivated the Third World as an important field of peaceful Cold War com-petition. Early in his tenure, he had begun promoting Soviet influence in former colonial areas, visiting India, Burma, Afghanistan, and Indonesia and offering eco-nomic aid to newly independent countries, even if they insisted on nonalignment in the Cold War. This courtship won him friends in the Middle East (Egypt, Syria, and Iraq), in North Africa (Libya, Ethiopia, and Somalia), and in South Asia (India and Indonesia). Khrushchev's sympathy extended from newly independent non-aligned countries to colonial peoples engaged in what he called "wars of national liberation." The Castro regime under U.S. siege was a test case: The Soviet Union would either have to provide help or lose its standing as the superpower genuinely supportive of new nations. Khrushchev began by sending economic and military assistance and then in spring 1962 decided to dispatch missiles secretly to Cuba to deter any American attack on the island.

Now it was Kennedy's turn for outrage when reconnaissance aircraft discovered the missile installations. He publicly demanded their removal. By late October 1962, the American and Soviet leaders were locked in a dangerous nuclear confrontation. Khrushchev's daring gamble left both sides searching desperately for a way back from the brink of disaster and wondering if this day or minute might be the last for them and their loved ones. Deeply shaken, the antagonists moved to defuse the crisis. After exhausting deliberations with a special advisory group, Kennedy held out a pledge not to invade Cuba and privately promised to remove American missiles from Turkey. In a private letter to Kennedy, the Soviet leader warned that the Cuban issues before them was like a knot that could become tied so tightly "that even he who tied it will not have the strength to untie it, and then it will be necessary to cut that knot, and what that would mean is not for me to explain to you, because you yourself understand perfectly of what terrible forces our countries dispose."[14] While signaling a desire to defuse the crisis, Khrushchev also pushed a belligerent Castro to the sidelines. The crisis ended when the Soviet leader accepted Kennedy's face-saving offer of a no-invasion pledge in exchange for removal of the missiles and had to grit his teeth as Castro denounced the Soviet betrayal.

Khrushchev had previously pressed for arms control talks, and the Cuban Missile Crisis had finally made Kennedy receptive. In a sober address at the American University in June 1963, the president conceded that the two nuclear powers had gotten caught in a costly cycle of competition and appealed to a sense of common

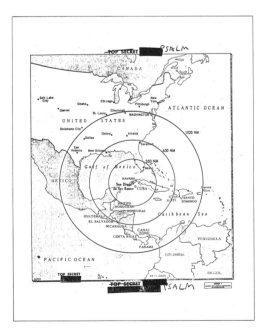

Cuba at the Epicenter of the U.S.–Soviet Nuclear Crisis, 1962

This CIA map, circulated during the first days of the Cuban Missile Crisis in mid-October 1962, was meant to provide a sense of the range of Soviet weapons in Cuba. (Distance is expressed in nautical miles, slightly greater than a conventional mile.) The outer circle defined the farthest reach of medium-range missiles, while the next circle marked the limits of light bombers. "Psalm" was the CIA designation for special handling of intelligence on Cuba. CIA mapmakers added Oxford, Mississippi, after Robert Kennedy, the president's brother and the attorney general, had asked in jest if Soviet missiles could reach that university town, whose desegregation problems were agitating the administration. (CIA) humanity to overcome the distrust and to tame the nuclear danger: "We all inhabit this small planet. We all breathe the same air. We all cherish our children's future. And we are all mortal."[15] Kennedy and Khrushchev now agreed to some small but symbolically important steps. In June 1963 they arranged to install a hotline to facilitate rapid, direct communications between Washington and Moscow in future crises, and in August they signed the first arms control agreement, a ban on tests in the atmosphere.

But they would get no further. In November 1963, just a few months after concluding the test-ban treaty, Kennedy died from an assassin's bullet. Khrushchev's days in office were also numbered. In October 1964 his colleagues, including his protégé, Leonid Brezhnev, ousted him while he was out of Moscow on holiday. They had come to resent his increasingly autocratic leadership style and his rash initiatives at home and abroad. After enduring their extensive critique of his policies, Khrushchev gave up without a fight, remarking, "Well, now I'm retired. Perhaps my most important accomplishment lies in the fact that they removed me from power by a simple vote, an act that would have caused their arrest under Stalin." Perhaps the fairest assessment of his leadership came from the poet Yevgeny Yevtushenko: "Khrushchev was a Stalinist and an anti-Stalinist. He was a rebel against himself."[16]

The problem of arms control was bigger than Khrushchev's flaws or a generally unresponsive U.S. policy. Neither side was prepared or able to break the seemingly relentless spiral of the arms race. Neither Russians nor Americans could control the technological imperative that had already produced the A-bomb and the much more powerful H-bomb as well as a succession of improved delivery systems such as ever better long-range bombers and ICBMs of growing size and accuracy. They would be joined by still more impressive new weaponry, including submarine-launched ballistic missiles and cruise missiles, new warheads, and, finally, new defense systems, notably the antiballistic missile defense. What policymaker could afford to say "no" to weapons development when he well knew that the other side might not hesitate to exploit the fresh technological possibilities constantly opening up before scientists and engineers?

CONFRONTATION OVER CUBA

1961	Failure of Kennedy-approved invasion of Cuba by CIA-backed Cuban exiles at the Bay of Pigs
1962	Kennedy–Khrushchev confrontation over missiles in Cuba between October 16 and 28
1963	Kennedy and Khrushchev sign a treaty limiting nuclear testing; Kennedy assassinated in Dallas
1964	Khrushchev ousted in favor of Brezhnev

The Cuban confrontation in particular convinced Soviet leaders that whatever the difficulties and dangers of acquiring more and better weapons, they would have to plunge ahead if they wished to play the superpower game. In the aftermath of the Cuban crisis, one Russian diplomat supposedly observed: "You Americans will never be able to do this to us again."[17] As a result of this new urgency, Moscow would by 1970 raise its warheads to 2,400, five times what had been available during the Cuban crisis. A serious, sustained effort at arms control would, from the Soviet perspective, have to wait on the achievement of a rough nuclear equality with the Americans.

The Vietnam Quagmire

The deepening American involvement in Vietnam offers a second prime instance of the Cold War continuing to drive policymakers despite their considerable doubts. In mid-1965 President Lyndon Baines Johnson made a decision to commit American combat troops on a major scale to a small, distant country. Within two years half a million Americans would be fighting there and ultimately some 58,000 would die. American taxpayers would have to pay $141 billion in military outlays between 1961 and the end of the war in 1975. The war would in addition create bitter and lasting divisions within American society.

Johnson made his decision against the backdrop of a U.S. commitment to Vietnam going back 15 years—and of a French struggle against a Communist-led resistance going back even farther (see Chapter 3). Washington's general anticommunist resolve first encompassed Vietnam in February 1950 when President Truman formally identified Vietnam and the rest of Indochina as an important front on the containment line. Neither he nor later presidents wanted to see their own forces bogged down in a peripheral area, but neither could they afford to lose Vietnam. Truman threw his support behind the French in their colonial struggle. In May 1950 Washington made the first major grant of aid. As paymaster for French forces, the United States would cover three fourths of the cost during the last years of their war. A long string of presidential decisions followed through the 1950s and early 1960s that repeatedly affirmed the need to block forces in that region allied with Moscow or Beijing. Communism was a threat of global proportions no matter the local manifestation. The Vietnamese were politically "immature" and thus needed U.S. guidance. Revolution in Vietnam could not succeed because communism was an alien ideology that ultimately had to rely on brutal coercion in its bid for power. Finally, U.S. thinking on Vietnam was influenced by the persistent memory of the democracies' appeasement of Hitler. Resort to diplomacy would plant the seeds of future trouble and was certain to result in "falling dominoes," the collapse of nations and communist victory throughout Southeast Asia and even in adjoining regions.

By 1954 French forces were in trouble. Communist troops had surrounded a major French base at Dien Bien Phu and were squeezing it into submission. By then the French electorate had turned against the war. President Eisenhower rejected direct U.S. military intervention to save the situation. Paris accepted a negotiated exit. An international conference in Geneva marked the end of French rule in Vietnam as well as Cambodia and Laos, and it provided for the temporary division of Vietnam at the 17th Parallel. The Communists would take control north of that line, while those associated with the French were to evacuate to the south. All foreign forces were to withdraw from Vietnam. And within two years, so the Geneva agreement stipulated, elections for a government for the entire country were to be held. The Eisenhower administration refused to sign the agreement.

Reluctantly accepting the loss of northern Vietnam, the Eisenhower administration at once went to work on its defenses in the southern part of the country. The British novelist Graham Greene watched the Americans displace the French and anticipated the destruction those innocent newcomers might inflict on Indochina. Innocence, he warned prophetically, "is like a dumb leper who has lost his bell, wandering the world, meaning no harm." Heedless, the Eisenhower administration sent assistance to a new southern regime headed by Ngo Dinh Diem, a staunch anticommunist, a nationalist, and a Catholic, who would rule between 1954 and 1963. Through the late 1950s the U.S. gamble on Diem seemed to pay off: He crushed his opposition (including the Communists) and consolidated his political position. But in the early 1960s Diem faltered. He neglected a resurgent Communist-backed insurgency in the countryside in favor of struggle against urban political foes, above all Buddhists resentful of the government's pro-Catholic policies. The Kennedy administration was reluctant to abandon a beleaguered South Vietnam, but the president was wary of a major U.S. troop commitment: "The troops will march in; the bands will play; the crowds will cheer." But then, he added, "It's like taking a drink. The effect wears off, and you have to take another." Finally, impatience with an increasingly isolated and ineffective Diem led Kennedy to give the nod to a coup by a group of Vietnamese generals. Despite military leadership in Saigon and rising levels of U.S. military and economic aid, the insurgents continued to gain ground. Washington's choices were boiling down to either sending U.S. troops or reaching a negotiated settlement.[18]

President Johnson made the critical Vietnam commitment. Born and raised in rural west Texas, Johnson had launched his political career, serving first in the House of Representatives and then in the Senate, where in the 1950s he emerged as the powerful Democratic majority leader. His bid for the presidency in 1960 fell short, and Johnson reluctantly agreed to become the younger, less experienced John Kennedy's running mate. Kennedy's assassination in November 1963 thrust Johnson into the position of leadership and power that he craved.

Vietnam was sitting on President Johnson's desk from his first day in the White House. He recognized that he had inherited a rapidly deteriorating situation in South Vietnam. He also believed the widely accepted arguments used to justify defending the South: Retreat or appeasement there would imperil lands far beyond as the dominoes toppled. Johnson himself explained to the public, "As long as there are men who hate and destroy, we must have the courage to resist, or we will see it all, all that we have built, all that we hope to build, all of our dreams for freedom—all, *all* will be swept away on the flood of conquest."[19] The Kennedy team of advisers that Johnson had inherited were also committed to winning in Vietnam. None was more influential than Robert McNamara, the secretary of defense who brought to the conduct of the war a tough, can-do attitude.

Inexorably Johnson moved toward intervention. He took a major step in August 1964 following apparent attacks on two U.S. destroyers operating in the Tonkin Gulf off the North Vietnamese coast. Johnson ordered U.S. aircraft to strike nearby enemy bases and then asked Congress for authorization to use U.S. military forces to defend the region. Congress complied with a near-unanimous vote for what has become known as the Tonkin Gulf Resolution. A landslide victory in the November 1964 election gave Johnson command of the powers of the presidency in his own right and put him in a position to apply real pressure on Hanoi. In February he launched fresh bombing raids against North Vietnam in reprisal for attacks on American facilities in the South. He quickly turned the reprisals into a sustained bombing campaign—Operation Rolling Thunder—intended to convince Ho Chi Minh and other leaders in the North to end the southern insurgency or face a barrage of punishing American blows. Hanoi did not flinch, while the war in South Vietnam continued badly for forces commanded by the generals who had ousted Diem only to fall to quarreling among themselves.

Sending in American combat troops was all that was left to avert a collapse of the Saigon government. In March 1965 Johnson ordered 3,500 Marines to patrol around the U.S. air base at Da Nang. He soon gave permission for them to operate offensively. Fresh troops continued to arrive, and by early June 50,000 American soldiers were in Vietnam. In July, following a recommendation from McNamara, Johnson announced a troop buildup that would raise the number of American soldiers in Vietnam to half a million.

Johnson found that the Cold War's second "limited war" was no easier to prosecute than the first one in Korea. The Korean War experience had taught him and other U.S. leaders that China was likely to intervene directly if the United States threatened Hanoi's survival. The Soviet Union might respond by providing more supplies and equipment to raise the cost for U.S. forces. An all-out struggle would weaken U.S. defenses in Europe (the real Cold War prize) and might even trigger a nuclear confrontation. The degree to which Johnson grasped the risks of intervention is evident in a private telephone conversation with McNamara on June 21, 1965, barely a month before the definitive troop commitment. Johnson predicted, "It's going to be difficult for us to very long prosecute effectively a war that far away from home with the [popular] divisions that we have here, particularly the potential divisions." Not only did the president realize that the public was lukewarm on Vietnam, but he also accurately predicted that it was not likely to support him over the long haul. The enemy, on the other hand, was united and resolute: "I don't believe that they [are] ever goin' to quit." He felt his own bureaucracy had failed to

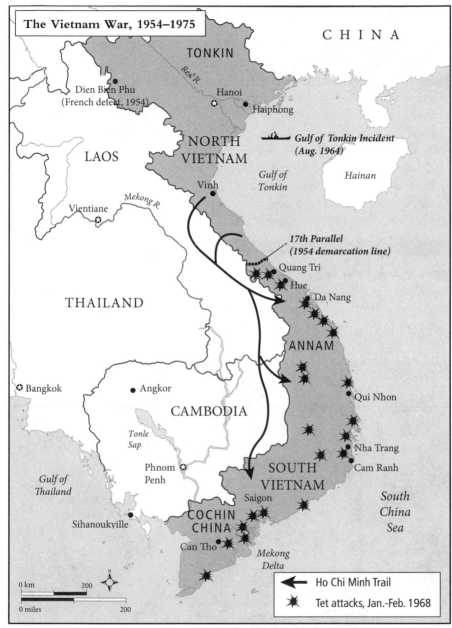

MAP 4.1
The Vietnam War, 1954–1975

come up with a "plan for victory militarily or diplomatically." He thoroughly understood that an American war could turn into a political nightmare. Johnson's advisers reinforced his fears. George Ball in the State Department and other influential insiders warned of a "catastrophe" in the making.[20]

Johnson was trapped within a Cold War framework. His predecessors had made commitments to South Vietnam that had to be honored. He had to preserve American credibility as a world leader. Politically he had to play the tough anticommunist. But as his limited war unfolded, his worst fears were realized. The daily headlines became routine: more troops and more casualties, more bombing of North Vietnam as well as Communist-controlled areas in the South, but no weakening of enemy resistance. China and the Soviet Union lined up behind the North, deterring an American invasion and providing critical support to Hanoi. The war became the target of ever-larger protests and began losing popular support at home. American allies in Europe shunned involvement, and the televised horrors of the war set off a global wave of anti-Americanism.

The Vietnam War was soon threatening Johnson's ambitious Great Society programs. Launched in 1965–1966 with great fanfare and advanced skillfully through Congress by the president, those programs took aim at domestic poverty and racial injustice but also sought to improve education, urban conditions, the environment, and medical care. Opponents seized on soaring war costs to undermine this centerpiece of Johnson's domestic agenda, and even supporters warned that he could not crusade both abroad and at home. Once more the choice between guns and butter confronted the leaders of the superpowers.

LBJ and Secretary of Defense Robert McNamara, February 7, 1968
This photo, taken at a meeting in the wake of the Tet military setback, speaks eloquently to the exhaustion of a president known for his seemingly endless political energy and drive and the disillusion of a close adviser labeled one of the era's "best and brightest." With public opinion steadily turning against the war and the stalemate in Vietnam unbroken, the Johnson administration had only bad choices in front of it. (LBJ Library photo by Yoichi Okamoto)

U.S. ENTANGLEMENT IN INDOCHINA

1950	Truman administration backs French forces fighting for control of Indochina
1954	French defeated at Dien Bien Phu; Geneva conference divides Vietnam; Eisenhower supports creation of an anticommunist state in the south
1961	Kennedy begins increasing U.S. military assistance to South Vietnam
1963	Diem ousted by his generals with Kennedy's tacit approval
1964	Congress passes the Tonkin Gulf Resolution authorizing Johnson to retaliate for acts of aggression in Southeast Asia
1965	Johnson launches U.S. bombing campaign and sends first U.S. combat units
1968	Tet Offensive shocks American public opinion and strengthens protest against the war; Johnson opens peace talks and abandons his reelection bid

The climax of Johnson's ordeal came in early 1968 on the Vietnamese new year, known as Tet. A surprisingly strong enemy offensive shook the Washington establishment, the public, and finally the president himself (Map 4.1). In March 1968 Johnson told the nation that he was limiting the bombing of the North, opening negotiations with Hanoi, and ruling out another term in the White House.

What had gone wrong? Some have seen the Vietnam War as a failure to properly exercise American military power, with much of the blame resting on Lyndon Johnson for fighting the war with one hand tied behind his back. What the critics overlook, but Johnson did not, were the dangers of escalation.

Other critics of the failure to carry the war to a successful conclusion have shifted the blame from Johnson to the "liberal" media, which they argue was biased against resolute action. But in fact the collapse of political will at home was not the product of media betrayal. The policy establishment that decided on intervention in the first place was the first link to snap. By early 1966 key congressional figures had begun to defect, and McNamara was losing faith in the war. The American people were the other weak link. As in Korea earlier, so too in Vietnam, the rising human and economic costs of the war drove more and more of the public to demand an end to the conflict. The Tet Offensive in early 1968 sealed public disaffection while throwing the American political elite into disarray.

Still others have claimed to see in Vietnam above all the American failure to pursue political reform, economic development, and nation-building. This last position may be the most astute in its emphasis on the degree to which American leaders saw the communist threat essentially in military terms and missed the social and political dimensions of the Vietnam conflict. In other words, they failed to understand Vietnam itself, an insight that becomes clearer on examining the Vietnamese perspective (Chapters 3 and 6).

THE QUAKE OF '68

The Vietnam War was only one element in a confluence of developments that would shake American society during the 1960s and early 1970s. Behind opposition to the war, broad and corrosive doubts about the Cold War itself had been developing, which in turn were fed by a rising public taste for the good consumer life. Nowhere were the doubts stronger than among the large youth population, conceived just after World War II and raised in the affluent 1950s. In the swelling ranks of college students, new attitudes challenged old ones with special force. The climax of this broad-based unrest came in 1968, a year in which hopes for change soared and then quickly crashed.

Americans passing through a social and ideological watershed were part of a chain of global upheavals. In the industrially advanced market economies of Europe and Japan and even in some Third World countries, political authority came under sudden youth-led assaults in 1968. The disillusionment, anger, and violence playing out in Chicago also shook Paris, Berlin, Rome, Tokyo, and Mexico City. Upheavals even reached into eastern European, where students joined with restive Communist party leaders in giving vent to dissatisfaction with an ossified socialism and Soviet domination.

The American Epicenter

The U.S. government had demonstrated an impressive capacity to mobilize citizens in the Cold War struggle. But there were limits that first became apparent in resistance to higher military spending during the first years of the Cold War, in a war in Korea that quickly fell from popular favor, and in mounting anxiety over nuclear fallout. In the late 1950s civil rights protesters in the South posed a new challenge to policymakers fixated on foreign problems and comfortable with prevailing domestic race relations. But these signs of popular discontent would seem like twinges compared to the convulsions of the late 1960s, when the Vietnam War emerged as the dominant issue and in turn gave impetus to a striking range of fresh causes, including black power, women's liberation, and environmentalism. Collectively they called into question not just Cold War policy but also the social arrangements carried over from the pre-World War II period.

This challenge to the status quo, sustained over a decade and a half, was to a large degree the work of a passionate minority within a relatively large cohort of 45 million young Americans born between 1942 and 1954. Birthrates had stayed low during the Depression and World War II but then exploded after the war in what is known as the "baby boom." The most vocal, activist youth came not just from a dramatically expanded population of young people but from a rising proportion of that generation that was college-bound (see Fig. 4.1). Most of the

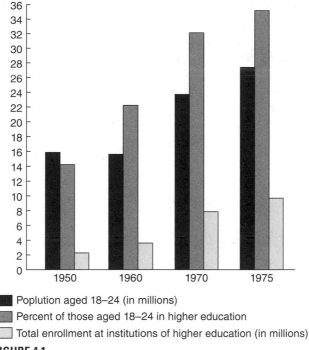

■ Poplution aged 18–24 (in millions)
▓ Percent of those aged 18–24 in higher education
☐ Total enrollment at institutions of higher education (in millions)

FIGURE 4.1
The Baby Boom and the Explosion in Higher Education in the United States, 1950–1975[21]

expansion occurred in public universities. Behind the burgeoning numbers of students was increased federal spending on higher education, increasing enrollment by women and African Americans, and a boom in graduate programs. But above all it was postwar affluence that allowed youth the luxury of continued study, deferring adulthood with its constraining work and family responsibilities.

Compared to a previous, quieter generation, the youth of the 1960s, at least the small but influential politically engaged subset, were less troubled by the communist threat but more anxious about the specter of nuclear war. Having grown up in unprecedented affluence, not Depression-era deprivation, they took for granted the postwar security and abundance that had allowed them to carve out their own cultural niche. It was defined by comic books such as *Mad*, depicting raw violence and expressing bizarre humor, by rock-and-roll record collections and hi-fi sets, and by the freedom that came from owning a car. Sexual freedom would also become a prominent feature of the youth scene once the diaphragm and the birth-control pill became widely available. The ideals that the politically active youth espoused were much like those of their parents: They valued justice, equality, responsibility, decency, and honesty. But unlike their parents, they were impatient to bring social practice into line with those values.

Young African Americans led the charge by drawing attention to the nation's flawed commitment to freedom at home. No one knew better than they the legal disabilities and the social, economic, and political discrimination that betrayed the promise of freedom and opportunity. They came of age just as these disabilities were coming under piecemeal challenge by the legal teams funded by the National Association for the Advancement of Colored People (NAACP) and the Southern Christian Leadership Conference, headed by a young minister, Martin Luther King, Jr. In 1954, in *Brown v. Board of Education*, the Supreme Court had declared that "separate but equal" schooling was "inherently unequal" and thus unconstitutional.[22] A bus boycott in Montgomery, Alabama, sparked the next year by a member of the local NAACP named Rosa Parks, struck another blow against the Southern system of racial segregation known as Jim Crow. King jumped into the fray, thus launching his meteoric rise to national prominence as a civil rights advocate of nonviolent social change inspired by India's Gandhi. At the grassroots, black communities in the South were in ferment, with demands for legislation to protect African American voting rights, access to public accommodations, and implementation of the Supreme Court finding against school segregation.

The emerging civil rights movement finally captured the nation's sustained attention in February 1960 when four black students at North Carolina A&T University demanded service at the "whites-only" lunch counter of a Woolworth's department store in Greensboro. When the store refused, fellow students rallied behind them, defied angry whites, and finally forced the store to close. Other African American college students rapidly took up the civil rights cause across the South and became the backbone for annual summer campaigns for equality dubbed Freedom Summer Projects. Alongside white students rallying to the civil rights cause, they did the grassroots organizing and the public protesting and in the process ran the daily risks of beatings, bombings, and bullets from local and state police and mobs of enraged white supremacists.

From the start these young blacks sought organizational autonomy from their elders. In 1960, following the success of the Greensboro demonstration, they formed the Student Nonviolent Coordinating Committee (SNCC). It embodied their preference for a decentralized operation and for group participation. By 1966 the frustrations of the struggle had radicalized these young activists. They were especially impatient with the compromises favored by established civil rights organizations and with the go-slow attitude of white liberal Democrats in Washington, including Presidents Kennedy and Johnson. To be sure, Johnson had put through the 1964 Civil Rights Act, the 1965 Voting Rights Act, and the measures making up the War on Poverty (an important component of his Great Society program). But it had taken courageous efforts in the South and some 200,000 demonstrators in Washington in August 1963 to achieve these gains. Along the way the presidents had failed to use the federal government's power to protect civil rights organizers, and the FBI was actively hostile. Young black campaigners for civil rights had watched Johnson make a costly commitment in Vietnam while he turned his back on the pressing needs of the poor and disenfranchised in the South and the mounting anger and frustration felt by inner-city black communities outside the South. Defending freedom for foreigners seemed to take priority over winning freedom for American citizens.

SNCC as well as such urban groups as the Black Panthers became radicalized as they lost faith in white resolve to deal with the problems of race in America. The chair of SNCC, Stokely Carmichael, denounced "the betrayal of black dreams by white America." Crowds roared as he proclaimed, "Black Power. It's time we stand up and take over; move on over [Whitey] or we'll move on over you." Demands for separatism came increasingly to the fore. Blacks would have to control their own organizations and agendas and move ahead on their own. Malcolm X, a spellbinding advocate of black nationalism, contended that if the ballot did not work, then it would have to be the bullet. Deepening conflict with whites at home and a war in Vietnam pitting whites against Asians suggested that solidarity among peoples of color should take precedence over national loyalty and service. The Black Panther platform in 1966 flatly stated, "We will not fight and kill other people of color." Even King conceded—belatedly, as far as the young radicals were concerned—the impossible moral problem posed by the Vietnam War. His own government was "the greatest purveyor of violence in the world today."[23]

In declaring that time had run out on accommodation, the black radicals of the late 1960s helped to spur a revival of interest in the bonds uniting oppressed people of color all around the world, an internationalist outlook that had flourished during the 1930s and 1940s. Blacks had fought for freedom in two world wars and Korea and yet still lacked fundamental rights. They conformed to the Cold War orthodoxy but reaped meager political rewards. Setting aside anti-communism as a distraction to the critical task at hand, the radicals advocated a new strategy of demanding fundamental change at home as well as abroad. It was not the grasping hand of Moscow but the dead hand of white colonialism and racism that threatened blacks and created common ground between a decolonizing world in ferment and African Americans. Blacks living outside Africa, like those still there, faced similar problems of outside domination and wounded pride. SNCC, the Black Panthers, and Malcolm X could all argue that the success of revolutions abroad would hasten the revolution in race relations at home.

This growing boldness of black protest galvanized young, well-to-do students. From Harvard, Yale, Princeton, Michigan, Wisconsin, Stanford, and the University of California at Berkeley, students joined the civil rights movement, participating in Southern voter registration drives, Freedom Summer Projects, and protest marches throughout the early 1960s. One volunteer wrote home, "For the first time in my life, I am seeing what it is like to be poor, oppressed, and hated."[24] The civil rights movement was for many a kind of "boot camp" where they learned to challenge authority and came to savor the delights of working within a supportive community of shared values. Soon these students and others would be attacking the large public research universities for their competitive ethos, their impersonal and overbearing bureaucracy, and their restrictions on students' personal and political choices.

The deepening American involvement in Vietnam added to the discontent already loose in the land. Lyndon Johnson's decision in 1965 in favor of massive intervention would spark antiwar activism among a wide array of groups, including the Americans for Democratic Action, the Quaker-run American Friends Service Committee, SANE, and Women Strike for Peace. But the heart of the resistance would from the start be students at elite colleges and universities on the East and West Coast and large Midwestern state institutions such as Michigan and Wisconsin. Most protesters were suburban whites from affluent or solidly middle-class homes, and they tended to be excellent students—the "best and brightest" of a new generation.

The most influential group to speak for young antiwar activists was the Students for a Democratic Society (SDS). Organized in 1960 at the University of Michigan, it operated through loosely coordinated branches on campuses across the country. The SDS set its agenda at a June 1962 meeting in Port Huron, Michigan. There one of its leaders, Tom Hayden, offered a sweeping critique of American democracy. This Port Huron statement expressed the concerns that Americans had withdrawn from public life and in the process weakened democratic institutions. The statement put the blame on a large, impersonal bureaucracy that left workers and students feeling alienated and dissatisfied despite conditions of material abundance. The statement also blamed a foreign policy that had slipped out of popular control and increasingly reflected the interests of those with "economic and military investments in the Cold War status quo." SDS's manifesto gave priority to more participatory democracy, community building, and equality. It assigned students, who were "breaking the crust of apathy," the task of building a coalition for change that included sympathetic faculty, labor and civil rights activists, and community organizers.[25]

The first SDS anti-war protest took the form of a "teach-in" held at the University of Michigan in late March 1965 in response to Johnson's decision on bombing and the dispatch of the first U.S. combat troops. Three thousand students and faculty devoted an entire night to lectures, debates, and discussions. The teach-in model was at once taken up on 35 other campuses. The next month brought the first antiwar demonstrations in Washington, attended by about 20,000 protesters. A second major demonstration followed in mid-October 1965, bringing together some 100,000 protesters in 80 cities and on a wide range of campuses. By year's end the protest against the war in Vietnam, although still relatively limited, had become a self-sustaining movement that would exploit a wide variety of techniques, from teach-ins and marches to letter-writing campaigns, civil disobedience, and draft-card burning.

The rivulet of protest turned into an increasingly turbulent river as public support for the war steadily fell. At the same time demonstrators impatient for results turned to more provocative tactics, including harassing speakers who tried to defend the war, burning flags, and occupying college administration buildings. The climax of this first phase of the antiwar protest came in the first half of 1968 with the "dump Johnson" effort. Unable to change the president's war policy, leading critics decided that they would try to deny him a second term and elect in his stead a candidate committed to peace, Minnesota Senator Eugene McCarthy. Students flocked to his cause and delivered to McCarthy a stunning 42 percent of the vote in the first presidential primary held in New Hampshire in March 1968. This triumph immediately drew a wavering Robert Kennedy, the younger brother and political heir of John Kennedy, into the presidential race and helped force Johnson out.

But having dumped Johnson, the movement watched with dismay as the candidacy of both Kennedy and McCarthy produced a split among antiwar activists. Kennedy's assassination in June made Hubert Humphrey, LBJ's vice president, the odds-on favorite to win the nomination thanks to the backing of the party establishment. Humphrey had publicly defended the war, so "dump the Hump" became the new rallying cry as activists gathered for the Democratic convention in Chicago. Protesters and the police were soon clashing in that city's streets and parks, while a divided Democratic Party imploded within the convention center.

A diverse antiwar movement now fragmented in frustration. Moderates such as those from clergy and established peace groups stressed coalition building and civil protest as the best way to win public support and get American troops out of Vietnam. While the moderates represented the majority of the antiwar movement, radicals with their outrageous views, public posturing, and demands for an immediate end to the war commanded disproportionate media attention. Some identified with the anti-U.S. Vietnamese struggle, and most were sharply critical of the national values and institutions that had created and sustained the war. Groups such as the Weathermen Underground carried out bombings, mostly on campuses but also against some banks and multinational corporations. Some young people gave up on politics altogether and instead cultivated a "hippie" lifestyle consistent with the call from one new-age guru to "tune in, turn on, drop out."[26]

This growing radicalism, turn to violence, and shocking flamboyance alienated the public as much as it fascinated the media. Many Americans were angry over campus chaos and young people's disrespect for authority. That anger melded with resentment at African Americans over five successive summers of urban rioting beginning in New York's Harlem in 1964, continuing in the Watts district of Los Angeles, spreading more widely during the summers of 1966 and 1967, and climaxing in April 1968 when over 100 cities exploded following the assassination of Martin Luther King. Many concluded that Johnson's civil rights and poverty program had helped spawn a disrespect for law and order, especially as civil rights demands began to be heard in Northern cities. Racial tensions were heightened by the emergence of the black power movement. The seeming unraveling of the country helped put Richard Nixon in the White House, a political conservative who seemed ready to continue the war until he obtained an "honorable" peace.

His plans did not take into account the breadth or depth of the opposition to that war. The antiwar movement was thriving on campuses nationwide and attracting many older people as well. Nixon's decision to send American troops across the Vietnamese border into Cambodia to target enemy sanctuaries and supply lines (known as the Ho Chi Minh Trail) ignited demonstrations in May 1970 on hundreds of campuses from coast to coast. When the National Guard fired on students at Kent State University in Ohio on May 4, killing four, campuses across the country exploded. Once more protesters headed for the nation's capital, and Congress voted to revoke the Tonkin Gulf Resolution. April 1971 witnessed the last major demonstrations, including the dramatic scene of 800 disillusioned, angry Vietnam veterans gathering on the steps of the Capitol to throw away their medals and ribbons earned in a war they now repudiated. By then Nixon was well on his way to ending U.S. involvement in the fighting in South Vietnam.

Anti-war activity spanning seven years had put Johnson on the defensive and kept pressure on Nixon. More broadly still, the antiwar and other protest movements of the 1960s popularized social and political values already taking shape in the late 1950s and early 1960s and challenging the rigidities characteristic of Cold War culture. Social critics lamented a democracy that had been commandeered by a "power elite" and a society that left individuals adrift amidst mindless consumption, impersonal corporations, and featureless suburbs. Young writers associated with the "Beat Generation" shocked with their unconventional views on sexuality, drugs, and spiritualism. The bubbling discontent was also evident in popular culture. Films featured young men such as James Dean and Marlon Brando filled with angst. Rebellion in the person of Elvis Presley seized the music scene. A novel that scandalized by its explicit treatment of women's sexuality sold 12 million copies.

Protesters who mounted the barricades in the late 1960s gave impetus to these emergent attitudes that would carry into the following decades: minority rights and pride (gay, brown, black, and native American), multiculturalism, feminism, environmentalism, and neighborhood activism. Each of these major offshoots of movement politics sustained its own criticisms of American life. Feminists scorned rampant patriarchy and institutionalized violence. Advocates of the environment took aim at heedless consumption. Minorities saw hypocrisy in a land ostensibly dedicated to political freedom and human equality. Even among the broader population, the Vietnam years came to represent a major fall from national grace. Although Americans might differ on the precise nature of the fall, they tended to agree that the country's reputation and sense of direction had come into serious question.

Fault Lines around the World

The fissures opening in American society were also appearing in a surprisingly wide range of other countries. Student activism was the common denominator. All over the world, in places that were geographically and culturally disparate, students took to the streets in 1968 to demand social and political change.

The reasons for student prominence bear some resemblance to the case of United States. Postwar birthrates had risen in much of the developed world (with the U.S. boom in the lead), and in most of the developing world those rates were even higher. A new postwar generation of young people grew up amidst steadily improving living standards, and growing numbers were able to enroll in higher education thanks to generous state subsidies. Between 1960 and 1970 those enrolled in western Europe increased from 2 to 4.3 million.[27] Like their American counterparts, these students created a distinct, self-conscious culture with its own slang, music, clothes, and values. They compared the promise of social justice and political democracy championed by their elders with everyday practice in the world around them. The gap between promise and practice disturbed a generation that placed hypocrisy high on its list of sins and whose impulses were strongly individualistic, anti-institutional, and antibureaucratic.

Heightening youth discontent was an international news media that disseminated stories of student insurrections and revolutionary achievements in other countries. Third World radicalism, represented by Mao's audacious young Red Guards taking on an ossified Chinese Communist Party, the courageous Vietnamese battling a formidable U.S. war machine, and Che Guevara championing a spontaneous revolutionary ethos in Latin America (all treated in Chapter 6), and young Americans boldly demonstrating against the racism and imperialism gripping their country became transnational icons. These signs of rising discontent around the globe inspired student activists and others to challenge their own tired leaders and outmoded institutions in the name of popular liberation and popular politics.

Nowhere did student protests form with greater suddenness or break with greater force than in France. In a single week in early May 1968, students in Paris started what snowballed into a massive national upheaval. A minority of students in a branch campus just outside the city set the agitation in motion when they demanded fundamental reform of the university system, denounced by one of their favorite texts as a machine for "mass production of students who are not educated and have been rendered incapable of thinking." Their demands won the support among those attending the University of Paris located in the heart of the city. Police tried to quiet the agitation but succeeded instead in widening its appeal. What had begun as a dispute over university governance turned into a fight for individual emancipation from social and bureaucratic constraints and for greater democracy in what the students derided as a "monarchical republic" headed by President Charles de Gaulle. These themes struck a popular chord, first and most forcefully among other young people who flocked to the scene of the protest.[28]

The climax to a cycle of highly publicized confrontations between police and growing crowds of youth came on May 10–11, the "Night of the Barricades." Protesters sealed off the university quarter to back up their demands for the release of those arrested, a reopening of school, and the withdrawal of the police. The voice of the protest, Daniel Cohn-Bendit, recalls crossing the police lines that night in a last-minute attempt to negotiate an acceptance of the demands and avoid another bloody confrontation. The police recognized him: "I've *never* seen such hatred on

Student Demonstration in Paris, May 1968
One of the protestors, Caroline de Bendern, is waving the revolutionary flag in a setting that was placid compared to the violence to come. Born in England, de Bendern was a model from an aristocratic family who moved in artsy circles. Interviewed in 1997, she praised the idealism of '68 and did not regret her own defiance of her family. Scandalized, they had cut her off. (Photo by Jean-Pierre REY/Gamma-Rapho via Getty Images)

anyone's face. They were also frightened, I think. You could hear the sound of the crowd, the barricades being built up all around." Early in the morning security forces started to clear the area, with such brutality that it stirred public outrage.[29]

The students had created a nationwide crisis that soon would paralyze the economy and shake the political establishment. Young workers, also impatient with the French power structure and union bosses, saw a chance to act. If universities could be democratized, then why not industry? These mavericks demanded reform of authoritarian factory floor practices so that workers would have more of a voice in the workplace. Within a few days as many as nine million workers were on strike and marching with the students.

The crisis created by these young "68ers" (*soixante-huitards*) would evaporate by the end of June almost as fast as it had materialized. Old-line labor leaders were interested in longstanding demands for the redistribution of wealth rather than reform of workplace culture. They helped put the lid back on the bubbling discontent expressed by young hotheads among the rank and file. President de Gaulle also maneuvered to contain the agitation. He called a national referendum and played on popular fears of anarchy to win a major electoral victory. In the face of his challenge the political Left fragmented, while the students, many of whom were below the minimum voting age of 21, turned their backs on conventional political activity.

France's neighbors were also experiencing their own student-led assaults on the postwar system. In West Germany student activism reached its peak at Berlin's Free University between February and fall 1968. Protesters saw signs that fascism was still a vital force in their society. The general hostility that their protests engendered confirmed their pessimistic analysis even as it left them isolated and increasingly demoralized. A frustrated few turned to violence, organizing the terrorist organization the Red Army Faction (popularly known as the Baader-Meinhof gang). In Italy unrest began in the industrial north in 1967 and spread to Rome. It continued sporadically into 1969, when the focal point of protest shifted from the university to industry, especially Fiat automobile plants. As in Germany, the protest movement left behind a terrorist residue, a Red Brigade that targeted prominent politicians and businessmen.

Youthful discontent also erupted in an increasingly prosperous Japan. The country had been experiencing labor and political unrest since the late 1950s, led by the Socialist and Communist opposition to the ruling Liberal Democratic Party. U.S. air attacks against North Vietnam sparked new protests in early 1965. Details of the bombing campaign and the mounting ground war, conveyed daily in newspapers and on television, called to mind Japan's own disastrous invasion of China, brought back memories of Japan's own experience with aerial bombardment, and led to charges that Japan bore responsibility for helping to sustain the savage struggle. The Japanese economy profited richly from the war, while American forces in Vietnam depended on bases in Japan. As one of the protest leaders, Tsurumi Yoshiyuki, argued, "The Vietnam War is not a fire across a distant shore; it is a war that necessarily affects all Japanese in one way or another."[30] The first major demonstration occurred in July 1965, and by 1966 protesters had settled into a pattern of regular activity supplemented by letter-writing campaigns, teach-ins, civil disobedience, and distribution of antiwar leaflets at U.S. bases.

The resulting opposition movement was made up of a wide range of groups, from neo-nationalists to liberals to Socialists and Communists. It was decentralized and largely uncoordinated, indeed at times deeply divided. At its core was the Citizen's Federation for Peace in Vietnam, known for short as Beheiren. That key group's leaders were well educated and worldly. Some spoke English, had lived in the United States, and maintained close contacts with U.S. activists. Although sharply critical of the U.S. war in Vietnam and the U.S. effort to pull Japan into the Cold War, the Beheiren leaders admired what the U.S. occupation had done to bring democracy to Japan. They were also avid consumers of American goods; they could be seen at rallies wearing jeans and drinking Coke.

The outlook of Beheiren activists bore a striking similarity to that of their U.S. and European counterparts. They attacked large, impersonal organizations—big business, big universities, and big government—as threats to individual development and choice. Vietnam revealed, in their eyes, the inhumanity of large, anonymous organizations. Tsurumi, a major Beheiren voice, characterized the movement's goal as "a cultural revolution to create a new type of man determined to act, individually and voluntarily, on behalf of the cause of the antiwar struggle."[31]

While parting with Beheiren over the issue of nonviolent protest, new student groups embraced its emphasis on individualism and spontaneity. Students remarked how after entering college they were "experiencing freedom for the first time."[32] They scoffed at established authority and held out personal authenticity and participatory democracy as the highest goods. As elsewhere around the world, Japanese campuses became hotbeds of political activism as students focused on everything from the promise of the Chinese revolution to university tuition increases. Hippies began to make their appearance, while others patterned themselves after the pure samurai warriors of an earlier era and clashed with the police in over 2,400 incidents in 1969 alone. Campuses also turned into battlegrounds as rival student factions battled each other.

Through 1968 and well into 1969, Japan experienced repeated waves of antiwar and anti-establishment dissent, but then protests died back. Gradually Americans began to withdraw from the Vietnam conflict. With the tide of protest receding, frustrated dissidents, especially angry and radicalized students, reacted in a pattern familiar from other countries: They formed clandestine groups such as the United Red Army to intensify their campaign of violence not only inside Japan but abroad as well.

While protests in the United States, western Europe, and Japan played out against a backdrop of prosperity, the economic and political problems faced by Third World and socialist states in eastern Europe in the mid-1960s helped ignite discontent. In the major cities of such countries as Turkey, Egypt, Ethiopia, Senegal, Brazil, and India, young people took to the streets in opposition to established authority. The most violent and traumatic confrontation played out in Mexico City in 1968. There student protests, intermittent since 1964, turned ugly. Infighting among student groups prompted the police to intervene on campus in late July 1968, but they did so with such brutality that students redirected their energy against the government of the ruling party. By August and early September outraged students, now joined by city residents, were staging massive anti-government demonstrations attended by as many as 400,000 protesters. On September 18 the government tried to break the protest movement by sending the army onto the campus of the country's major public university, the National Autonomous University of Mexico, but instead it set off street clashes and put in question Mexico's ability to host the upcoming Olympic games. On October 2 security forces with machine guns, helicopters, and tanks attacked a rally of some 5,000 students, leaving hundreds dead and thousands wounded or on their way to prison. Eyewitnesses vividly recalled the terror of flying bullets and accumulating blood—"lots of blood underfoot, lots of blood smeared on the walls."[33] The government had reclaimed the streets and silenced the demonstrators, but the massacre would remain an open wound in national politics for decades to come.

On the other side of the Iron Curtain, the quake of '68 took a somewhat different although no less consequential form. Historically eastern Europe had been an economic backwater, and so the demonstrably successful Soviet-socialist planned economy had had appeal after 1945 as a vehicle both for catching up with the economies to the west and for recovering from the extensive damage inflicted by

World War II. Up to the mid-1960s these economies, with their emphasis on heavy industry, seemed in such eastern-bloc countries as Poland, East Germany, and Czechoslovakia to produce modernization and prosperity. Social welfare gains for the bulk of the population were significant as the state provided jobs, housing, and basic health care and education. GDP per capita growth was keeping pace with a prosperous western Europe in what was turning into the best economic run in over a century. But as eastern-bloc economies ran into trouble in the middle and late 1960s, questions about the Soviet-defined postwar order took sharper form. Might giving more scope to the forces of supply and demand yield more abundance than the Soviet model of central planning? The even more dangerous question was whether more democracy and greater national autonomy from the Soviet Union was a possible road to a better life.

Czechoslovakia became the scene of the most dramatic of the explosions of 1968 on the eastern side of the Iron Curtain. Early in the year Alexander Dubček, an established political leader, took the helm of the Czech Communist Party and initiated a reform movement to create "communism with a human face." This effort would come to be known as the Prague Spring for the heady hopes that took hold in that season of renewal in the country's capital. Dubček quickly pressed for economic reforms and advanced supporters into high posts at the expense of hardliners. These changes were wildly popular and in turn created momentum for more reform, including an end to censorship, the creation of new political parties, and an increase in the power of the national legislature. An "Action Program" laid out by the Communist Party in April embraced all of these goals and more. Public discussion became ever more adventuresome, with journalists, intellectuals, and students especially vocal in their demands for opening the political system and bold in their criticism of the Czech Communist Party. A manifesto published in June coolly dismissed that "power organization" as a magnet for "power-hungry egotists, reproachful cowards, and people with bad consciences."[34]

Dubček quickly came under intense Soviet scrutiny and mounting pressure to pull back. He offered assurances to Leonid Brezhnev and other Soviet leaders of his country's adherence to the Warsaw Pact and his determination to preserve the Communist Party's leading role. He also urged his own media to curb their openly anti-Soviet sentiment. As enthusiasm for reform mounted and threatened to escape his party's control, Soviet leaders saw a repeat of events in Hungary 12 years earlier. In early August a half-million Warsaw Pact troops under Soviet command marched into the country in a bloodless coup and arrested Dubček and other reformers. The Soviets faced universal condemnation and peaceful resistance from the Czechs, but by 1969, they were finally able to organize "healthy elements" within the party and begin turning back the reforms. The "Prague Spring" had turned into a "Prague Winter" that would endure for 20 years.

Whereas the challenge to the Czech status quo came from the top, Poland proved truer to the broader European pattern of youth-led agitation. Young intellectuals in the Communist Party youth organization and in Warsaw University began as early as 1965 to criticize economic policy and challenge the party's claim to a monopoly on truth (derided by one writer as the "dictatorship of the dumb").[35] The main target of this discontent was the party leader, Wladyslaw Gomulka. Since returning to power amidst the unrest of 1956, he had maintained Moscow's trust by opposing domestic "revisionism" and supporting the Warsaw Pact as Poland's guarantee against the old German foe. But at the same time he had allowed limited political and economic reforms.

A slowing economy in the late 1960s upset Gomulka's balancing act. His government had had to press workers to raise output and to put in longer hours while reducing food and other subsidies. With popular discontent rising, security forces kept the critics under control until March 1968, when students at Warsaw University dramatically broke the peace, prompted by the reform push in neighboring Czechoslovakia. A student sign read, "Poland is awaiting its own Dubček."[36] Police repression failed to stop the rapid spread of strikes, riots, and demonstrations across the country. At the end of the month the students laid down a long list of demands, including a new youth organization, the end of censorship, economic reforms leading to self-governing enterprises and the introduction of a market mechanism, an independent workers' union, and an independent judiciary.

This time Brezhnev and his colleagues decided to sit tight, convinced that intervention in Poland would only make matters worse in that long-time hotbed of anti-Russian feeling. Gomulka was left to resolve the problem through the arrest of dissidents and a purge within the ranks of the party. By summer the political situation had stabilized, but it was only a reprieve. In August, in the immediate aftermath of the invasion of Czechoslovakia, students organized protests once more, this time decrying Gomulka's involvement in the Warsaw Pact operation. Thereafter antiparty opposition passed to an increasingly restive labor movement that would eventually bring about the collapse of socialism in Poland.

Throughout the developed and the developing world, critics of the status quo led by young people had fallen short of their objectives. The national establishments that they had targeted had survived after an interval of embarrassment. But everywhere the critics had defined agendas for change that would remain prominent in the decades ahead. The old-line Communists and Socialists, who once had offered the only serious political and social alternatives, seemed to a new generation hopelessly doctrinaire and out of touch. Young activists championed instead a new set of values, above all sweeping individualism and broad freedom of personal expression. Stephen Spender, the British poet from the World War II generation, perceptively noted their strange new politics: "They equate revolution with spontaneity, participation, communication, imagination, love, youth."[37] Often denied in the short term, the values of the new generation would over time have almost revolutionary effects on their countries' social life and cultural values.

CONCLUSION

In the course of the 1950s and 1960s the Cold War underwent an extraordinary transformation. Those middle decades of the superpower rivalry had opened with international lines of conflict sharply drawn. Both Moscow and Washington nervously marshaled their allies while lining up their own populations in support of the global struggle. By the late 1960s, however, the Cold War struggle looked strikingly different. The Soviet Union after Stalin's death had mellowed both domestically and internationally, while in the United States the Cold War consensus collapsed in the face of mounting self-doubts over the national commitment to freedom at home as well as abroad.

The forces that had achieved this transformation came from diverse directions. The shared trauma of the Cuban Missile Crisis brought nuclear fear to a critical pitch and gave the Cold War rivals the decisive push into an era of arms control. The long descent into the Vietnam War intensified disarray and disillusionment among Americans, while Soviet leaders could not escape the limits imposed by their modest economy and thus the tension between pursuing the international rivalry with the United States and responding to the material demands of their own people. The discontents of educated youth in developed countries as well as the Third World added to the assault on established habits of thought and behavior.

A once-simple Cold War landscape was further scrambled in the 1960s by changes within the U.S. and Soviet alliances. Western Europeans and Japanese had lost their taste for Cold War tension well before the fever of 1968 reached their shores. Eastern Europe sought greater autonomy from Moscow, while the Chinese moved toward military confrontation with its former ally. Even the repeated repression of eastern Europeans bent on charting their own path seems in retrospect less a Soviet triumph than a harbinger of greater troubles to come. As the region's socialist regimes relied increasingly on their own secret police and ultimately Soviet tanks, they created a profound alienation that would contribute significantly to the socialist collapse of 1989. Although few realized it at the time, the Cold War had taken a decisive turn that anticipated its dramatic conclusion two decades later (treated in Chapter 7).

5
ABUNDANCE AND DISCONTENT
IN THE DEVELOPED WORLD

THE AMERICAN AND British designers of the Bretton Woods agreement and its close cousin, the General Agreement on Tariffs and Trade (or GATT), built well. Through the 1950s and 1960s, the structural reforms implemented at the end of World War II spurred international trade and investment. They helped incorporate western Europe and Japan into the global economy. And they carried at least some of the world's peoples toward unprecedented prosperity. Annual gross domestic product (GDP) growth for the entire globe between 1950 and 1973 was 4.9 percent, while world exports grew at a yearly 7 percent pace. These were rates far faster than anything experienced in any other period of recent history.[1]

The economies of the developed world not only worked more closely and profitably together but also moved along slightly different if parallel paths. The consumer culture already flourishing in the United States became a force in the everyday life of other, increasingly affluent countries. Yet differences in economic culture persisted across the developed world. While everywhere the state played a major role in making this free-market system work to the benefit of its citizens, how precisely it played that role differed significantly from place to place, reflecting the diverse cultural and institutional patterns within the developed world. In Europe states put in place an elaborate welfare system intended to cushion the shocks from the free market and at the same time moved together toward greater integration to make the regional market work more efficiently. In Japan the state played an equally prominent role but less as a direct guarantor of welfare and more as the coordinator of rapid economic growth. Even in the United States, with its professed commitment to limited government, the state's role in the economy was both rising and remarkably multifaceted, ranging from major highway projects to advanced research to new welfare programs.

Despite the impressive economic record laid down in these years, the overall international economic system began to draw fire. Some observers began to worry about the impact of the developed world on the environment. Others fretted over the disadvantaged position of women and the uneven distribution of the gains from growth between developed countries and the developing ones. These worries would persist well into the new century.

AMERICA AT THE APOGEE

The United States was the undisputed leader of the system of trade and investment that encompassed much of the globe in the 1950s and 1960s. Washington supplied aid to economies in distress, while the dollar served as the currency of reference, providing invaluable international monetary stability. U.S. allies on the whole quietly followed the American lead. Cold War fears kept them docile, but so too did the relatively benign role played by Washington, which not only talked about free trade but also opened its valuable domestic market to the products of its allies. What seemed to serve the world also served Americans, who enjoyed an unprecedented domestic prosperity and optimism about their model of abundance.

Triumphant at Home and Abroad

Although many Americans had entered the postwar period worried about a repeat of the Great Depression, the economy quickly made the transition to peacetime and then marched steadily ahead. Between 1945 and 1970 GDP measured in constant dollars more than doubled. The fruits of this sustained growth fell into the laps of Americans in a seemingly endless stream. The tide of economic prosperity would continue to raise the income of most. As a result, a generation that had experienced the deprivation of the 1930s and the rationing of wartime would find themselves better nourished, better housed, better educated, and more productively employed than their parents or grandparents could have ever imagined.

Americans did not participate equally in the good times. For most, income rose sharply. By the end of the 1950s slightly more than half of all families were earning a comfortably middle-class $5,000 or more. The stock market, once a preserve of the wealthy, attracted more and more investors: 6.5 million in 1952, over 20 million in 1965, and almost 32 million in 1970. But at the same time, roughly a quarter of the population lived in poverty. The elderly, female-headed households, rural and central city residents, and nonwhite workers were the groups least likely to share in the good times.

The 1950s version of the American dream has come to be associated with the picture of a split-level house in the suburbs with a station wagon parked in front ready to take the family on vacation. There was considerable truth to this image. Home ownership expanded by 50 percent between 1945 and 1960. By that latter date 60 percent of all families owned their own homes. Almost all of the new homes that met this enormous demand sprang up in the suburbs, which were growing six times faster than cities. By 1960 one quarter of the entire population lived in suburbia. With their incomes rising, Americans went on a spending spree on labor-saving appliances, home entertainment, and automobiles. By 1960 75 percent of families owned washing machines, and the figure for televisions was 87 percent. To keep customers coming, companies quadrupled their outlays on advertising between 1945 and 1960. The success of that effort—or perhaps the enthusiasm of the public for its newfound abundance—is evident in the debt that families piled up. By 1959 almost half of all families had borrowed so heavily that their liquid assets averaged less than $200.

Passenger cars, owned by three quarters of families by 1960, had perhaps the broadest impact of all the postwar consumer goods. The number of cars rose dramatically—from 40 million in 1950 to 102 million in 1970. Cars made the rise of suburbia possible, encouraged the rise of the mall as the prime shopping destination, connected city workplaces to scattered bedroom communities, and planted the seeds of national dependence on imported oil. Cars boosted domestic tourism and encouraged the rise of a new automobile-friendly accommodation, the motel. Cars also facilitated population shifts as one in four Americans moved each year, bidden by the expanded opportunities created by a flourishing economy. States and the federal government responded to the car's popularity by improving and extending the road network. These efforts included the launching in the 1950s of the interstate highway system, a civil defense measure that quickly turned into one of the most popular and costly features of the emergent car culture.

The 1950s and 1960s marked the beginning of the post-industrial, knowledge-based economy that would loom so large by the turn of the twentieth century. In 1940 roughly three million Americans worked in technical and professional occupations; by 1964 that figure had more than doubled. At the same time the number of industrial workers was beginning a decline, so that by 1956 white-collar employees outnumbered blue-collars for the first time. This shift was marked by the growing importance of large corporations, whose billion-dollar budgets included a paycheck for hundreds of thousands. This shift was also marked by the growing importance of an educated workforce. For those providing services, innovations such as the computer were making the generation and control of enormous bodies of data possible. The computer developed rapidly from a costly general-purpose machine in 1944 whose 500 miles of wire made it impossibly bulky. By the early 1950s, it had shrunk enough in size and price to appeal for the first time to businesses. Technological innovation was no less important on the shop floor, where it made possible productivity increases that allowed firms to raise output even while cutting back on their workforce. The rising importance of technology led a steadily growing proportion of Americans to seek higher education. Publicly funded state universities, colleges, and community colleges multiplied beginning in the late 1950s.

Although a bastion of the free market, the United States of the 1950s and 1960s gave government considerable scope in the economy beyond funding infrastructure such as roads, airports, and education. Federal funding spurred science and technology. The first computer was built as part of state-sponsored wartime research that would expand in the context of Cold War competition with the Soviet Union. Pentagon contracts pushed the U.S. economy to the fore in such high-tech areas as electronics and aeronautics, and major research universities such as MIT and Stanford made the most of government largesse, conducting research in a wide range of scientific fields. Already by the mid-1950s the United States was in the midst of a revolution in government spending. By then it had climbed to 17 percent of total gross national product (GNP), up from 1 percent in 1929. And the Johnson administration's Great Society programs would send the figure higher.

The economic advances of the 1950s and 1960s served to confirm Americans' self-conception as a special people destined for great things abroad as well as at home. The country could look forward to growing ever stronger and more prosperous, while realizing the dream of justice and abundance for all. In this context the performance of the American economy assumed nationalist significance in the Cold War contest with the Soviet Union. At the same time the appeal of U.S. popular culture abroad (discussed in Chapter 8) seemed to confirm the universality of the American war.

During the 1960s the American disciples of Keynes were confident that moderate, well-timed government intervention could keep the economy at full employment and thus ensure steady, substantial growth. Spurred by timely government action, the free market could churn out jobs and goods endlessly. This growth would in time promote social justice for the previously marginalized or excluded. Mobilization for World War II had indeed already begun pulling women and African Americans into the urban, industrial sectors. Postwar prosperity would surely complete the job with funds left over to build a Great Society without rural poverty or urban blight while at the same time underwriting the costs of the Cold War.

The United States continued in the 1950s and 1960s to use its considerable clout to shape the patterns of global trade and investment. The free-trade agenda laid down at the end of World War II got a major boost in 1961 when President Kennedy secured congressional approval to bargain for trade cuts under GATT. By the late 1960s tariffs on industrial goods were falling significantly.

The removal of trade barriers was matched by the equally important first steps toward the removal of barriers to the flow of international capital. Bretton Woods had sought to facilitate international trade by making it easy to convert one currency into another and by making the dollar the linchpin of the international currency market. But Bretton Woods had also conceded the right of states to intervene in currency markets in order to protect their recovering economies from outside pressures and reestablish a solid economic foundation for growth. Through the late 1940s and 1950s U.S. leaders had allowed the dollar to flow freely around the world while U.S. allies restricted the movement of capital across their borders. No one wanted private investors and speculators to be able to disrupt economic policy, create social turmoil, and raise the popular appeal of the Communist party. However, with western Europe's and Japan's economies mended by the late 1950s, Washington began calling for an end to restrictions on the international flow of

Nikita Khrushchev and Richard Nixon Engage in the "Kitchen Debate," July 1959
The Soviet leader and the American vice president stand in front of the model kitchen at a U.S. exhibition in Moscow where they sparred over which system, socialist or capitalist, could produce the higher standard of living. This encounter dramatized the growing sense that political legitimacy and the outcome of the Cold War depended as much on generating consumer goods as on finding an effective political and military strategy. To counter Khrushchev's boasts of socialist superiority, Nixon claimed that consumer abundance in the United States made it "closest to the ideal of prosperity for all in a classless society." He gave the statistics: "44 million families in America own 56 million cars, 50 million television sets, 143 million radio sets, and 31 million of those families own their own homes." Khrushchev responded that the Soviet Union would soon surpass the U.S. economy, and in any case the products Nixon touted were just "fancy gadgets," either useless or beyond the reach of ordinary Americans.[2] (AP photo)

capital. Cautiously these allies complied, creating a trend by the 1960s. International finance was embarked on a fundamental shift.

Finally, the United States sought to broaden the scope of international markets to include newly emergent nations. To integrate them into the U.S.-led alliance and trade system, Washington redirected the attention of the IMF and the World Bank from an increasingly prospering western Europe to the Third World. U.S. aid programs also refocused on the Third World beginning in the latter part of the 1950s. Kennedy and Johnson continued the trend with such well-publicized initiatives as the Alliance for Progress in the Western Hemisphere. These aid programs carried the message that markets, not Marx, held the secret to economic development.

Warning Signs of Economic Troubles

Most Americans were convinced that these glory days would last forever, thanks to the magic of the market, prudent government policy, and a long lead in science and technology. But already by the 1960s a variety of threats to U.S. economic supremacy were taking shape, and those threats would combine in the 1970s and 1980s to deal a heavy blow both to the economy and to national self-confidence.

The first signs of trouble began to appear in the 1950s as a result of a growing accumulation of American dollars abroad. Some of that accumulation was the result of Cold War commitments. Maintaining American forces and government representatives overseas involved substantial outlays. In addition, valued military allies needed equipment and advisors, prompting more spending abroad. Generous economic aid directed first to Europe and then to the Third World to secure political stability along the containment line added to the outflow of dollars. Adding to the imbalance was a rising tide of tourism to Europe and the aggressive overseas expansion of American investments and the slipping competitiveness of U.S. goods on international markets. Imports from Japan and western Europe were increasingly attractive to American buyers. The U.S. trade surplus (excess of exports over imports) began to shrink through the 1950s, and eventually (in 1971 for the first time since 1883) Americans imported more than they sold abroad.

With more dollars going out of the country, foreigners held more and more U.S. currency. In the first decade of the postwar period, this overseas accumulation of dollars was welcome because it helped recovering economies. Dollars in foreign hands made possible purchases of U.S. goods critical to rebuilding, helped bolster weak currencies, and raised the standard of living in war-torn lands. Even after foreigners had a less pressing need for dollar reserves, they still gladly held them, so strong was international confidence in the dollar as a secure, liquid asset convertible on demand into gold. During the 1950s that confidence began to erode as total U.S. payments overseas began regularly to exceed those coming in. By 1958 the accumulated foreign holdings of dollars had surpassed U.S. gold reserves, setting in question the U.S. government's commitment made at Bretton Woods to redeem dollars for gold at the rate of $35 an ounce. This doubt that the dollar was "as good as gold" was to deepen through the 1960s as the United States failed to bring its accounts with the outside world into balance, and it foreshadowed an economic crisis that would dethrone the dollar from its special place.

Further eroding the U.S. economic position was a popular addiction to spending on consumer goods. The consequence was falling savings rates that diminished the domestically generated pool of capital and raised the costs for entrepreneurs wanting to make new investments. Moreover, those spending the consumer dollar had a penchant for foreign goods, and the resulting imports further decreased the U.S.

trade surplus. Finally, good consumers resented taxes cutting into their disposable income, but also did not like surrendering their own favorite government programs. The result was the beginning of a long-lasting federal budget deficit, the growing neglect of public investment in infrastructure, and the first inklings of what would turn into persistent inflationary pressure.

The most obvious solution to the mounting U.S. economic problem was the same one Khrushchev had confronted earlier: fewer guns or less butter or some combination of cuts. But cold warriors regarded blocking communist expansion as a top spending priority, while the public valued no less highly the good life that postwar prosperity had brought. Since devoted consumers also voted, their preferences registered clearly in Congress and the White House.

President Eisenhower tried to balance the tension between fighting the Cold War and keeping consumers happy. Once elected, he ended the unpopular and costly war in Korea and also worked to hold down military spending. John Kennedy on the other hand sharply raised military spending on coming into office. A brave Keynesian, he had no fear that increases in the budget would strain the economy and refused to worry about the resulting domestic budget deficit. Lyndon Johnson further fed the budget deficit by pressing ahead with his expensive Great Society programs even as he waged his costly war in Vietnam.

The insistence on both guns and butter had by the end of the decade dealt two serious blows to the U.S. economic position. At home, high levels of government and private spending had combined to ignite inflation. Internationally, the balance-of-payments problem worsened with the annual gap at the $4 billion mark by 1967. In early 1968, Johnson reluctantly took action. "Our fiscal situation is abominable," the president conceded.[3] Although it was an election year, he proposed to Congress a special tax on individuals and corporations. Congress agreed but insisted that the president cut domestic programs. Johnson capped the size of American forces in Vietnam as a way of containing military costs and imposed restrictions on overseas investment. Rather than restoring price stability, these measures precipitated an unexpected combination of stagnant growth and continued inflation (labeled at the time "stagflation"). Here was a malaise that fit neither the Keynesians' experience nor their arsenal of policy tools. They wondered how a low- or no-growth economy with considerable idle productive capacity could generate inflation. Disoriented economists desperately searched for a cure while the electorate began to grumble.

An aggravated balance-of-payments problem now combined with the onset of inflationary fever to further undermine the dollar's standing as the international standard. As the dollar debt abroad rose and inflation reduced the dollar's value, foreigners were less and less willing to hold dollars. Foreign central banks, which kept most of their reserves in dollars, and those engaged in international transactions worried that Americans lacked the reserves to cover the debts they had incurred. Indeed, by the late 1960s the debt had climbed to $40 billion and the gold reserves at Ft. Knox had sunk to $10 billion. Foreign bankers began to sell their holdings, thus bringing closer the day of devaluation.

CLOUDS BUILD OVER THE U.S. ECONOMY

1950	First postwar balance of payments deficit
1958	Short-term financial obligations held abroad exceed U.S. monetary reserves
1959	Foreign governments begin turning in dollars for gold
1968	Fiscal crisis grips Johnson administration; the economy sinks into prolonged period of "stagflation"
1971	First trade deficit since 1883

Charles de Gaulle, the president and self-styled savior of France, happily supplied a good push. He had emerged in the 1960s as the leading critic of U.S. economic leadership—and more broadly of U.S. global influence. His commitment to preserving France's status as a force in the world collided with what he considered a bland mass U.S. consumer culture, a rigid American anticommunism, and the threat corporations and agricultural products posed to French autonomy and welfare. (De Gaulle's preoccupation with finding a special French path was reflected in the complaint of a political loyalist in 1956 that the country was caught between "two colossi, one of which has no heart and the other has no head."[4]) But most significantly for Nixon, de Gaulle saw a chance in to weaken the U.S. position by attacking a dollar rendered vulnerable by Washington's irresponsible fiscal policies. The Americans could not expect the world to endlessly accumulate IOU's while U.S. consumers and cold warriors went their heedless way. In the mid-1960s the French government began presenting millions of dollars in debt for payment in gold, thus sending an unmistakable message that time was running out for the dollars' privileged standing.

Johnson understood that mounting financial difficulties hobbled the U.S. exercise of world economic and political leadership. But he also understood that the postwar boom had helped elevate consumerism in the minds of the electorate into a basic American right. Steps to restore economic health and thus maintain long-term national power collided with the preferences of an electorate that wanted to live well, save little, spend freely on foreign goods, and travel. By 1968 the pressures created by this contradiction were becoming intense.

RECOVERY IN WESTERN EUROPE AND JAPAN

While the 1950s and 1960s saw the gradual erosion of U.S. economic supremacy, western Europe and Japan were the star performers. The demand for new production facilities to replace those destroyed by war or outdated by rapid technological innovation prompted considerable investment and pushed their economies rapidly ahead. Guiding the investments was an experienced managerial class, and working the new machinery was an educated, skilled workforce. Economic vitality restored these old centers of international trade and investment to their former prominence, while their citizens enjoyed an extraordinary run of prosperity.

As the main global economic centers moved into an era of shared prosperity, they still clung to patterns of doing business that reflected values and circumstances peculiar to each. The western Europeans looked to their individual states to create an economy that balanced social justice and efficiency and sought through regional integration to provide enhanced prosperity and an institutionalized guarantee of cooperation among member states once bitter rivals. In Japan the state was no less important in the promotion of prosperity and stability through collaborative arrangements at home and competitiveness in international markets. Looking at two different corporations—Italy's Fiat and Japan's Sony—provides a sense of those distinctions that would persist even as the forces of globalization were gaining headway. For example, unlike the Disney enterprise (see Chapter 2), Sony and Fiat cultivated close ties to state bureaucrats and political leaders to win economic favors, and their handling of labor differed from Disney's as well. Thus strikingly diverse strategies for success existed within the same broad international economic framework.

The Old World's New Course

In the fluid conditions that existed in the wake of World War II, the states of western Europe could have dutifully fallen in behind U.S. economic policy just as they had fallen in behind U.S. Cold War policy. To some extent they did. They availed themselves of the Marshall Plan to stabilize their economies and in the process adopted some American advice and practices. They spared themselves large military budgets by slipping under the U.S. defense umbrella. They took advantage of opportunities within the U.S.-sponsored trade-friendly international regime. They began to agree with Washington's argument that colonial ambitions did not pay. But this perspective should not obscure a critical shift in European political economy that has to be understood in terms not of U.S. influence but of the continent's recent history and political traditions.

In the aftermath of war western Europeans embarked on a fundamental re-thinking of the purposes that the nation-state was to serve. European states had not served popular welfare but instead inflicted widespread loss of life and suffering during two major wars and the Great Depression. Hitler's Germany committed wartime barbarities that demonstrated the potential of the nation-state for inhumanity. Most of the rest of the 26 European countries existing at that time proved ineffectual in protecting their people or even preserving themselves as functioning states. Annexation, partition, occupation, and subordination became the common fate of the French, Dutch, Austrians, Poles, and Czechs, among others. Little wonder that many questioned the legitimacy of the nation-state and longed for some alternative international or regional basis for sovereignty.

But the European state system did not wither away. To the contrary, it enjoyed a post-World War II renaissance thanks to a basic reorientation of purpose. Acquisition of national and colonial territory gave way as the yardstick by which to measure state success, and in its place popular welfare and growth in national income emerged as new goals. Citizens would now judge their states on the basis of their performance in significantly improving the living conditions of all classes. This shift in attitudes was reflected in decisions in cities all across Europe to preserve untouched a patch of wartime destruction as a potent reminder of the dangers of state-driven political and military rivalry.

Under the new dispensation, states thoroughly vindicated themselves and in the process won new legitimacy. Postwar governments guided their economies to their best performance of any time since the emergence of the global economy in the late nineteenth century. After regaining prewar levels of production in the early 1950s, western Europe moved on to enjoy a rapidly rising standard of living within a context of peace and social stability. This was made possible by a GDP growth rate for the major regional economies that ranged over the 1950–1973 period between 4 and 6 percent a year. By 1973 western Europeans had gone a long way toward catching up with U.S. living standards. With these high national growth rates went low unemployment, low inflation, expanding foreign trade, stable exchange rates, and rising public expenditures on welfare, education, and health. Times were extraordinarily good. (See Fig. 5.1.)

For ordinary Europeans, the most welcome feature of these good times was the availability of consumer goods. By the early 1960s western Europe was in the midst of an "auto-frigo" revolution. The rush to purchase automobiles, refrigerators, and other household appliances marked not the birth of a European consumer society

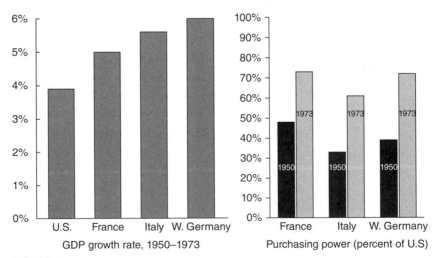

FIGURE 5.1
Good Times Come to Europe, 1950–1973[5]

but its maturation from a start in the interwar period. Now, with more money in their pockets, consumers spent it on comfort and diversion. As in the United States, the emergence of a mass consumer market blurred European social divides. Tastes became more uniform as regional and class distinctions eroded. For example, no frills, self-service shopping, beginning often in small stores before reaching supermarket proportions, gradually spread as price for some shoppers took precedence over service. But western Europe was not becoming an American carbon copy. For example, social diversity persisted to a greater degree, and small family-run businesses survived, beloved by customers expecting expert and fine quality when purchasing clothes, hardware, bread, cheese, or meat. Government protection for small retailers and cooperative arrangements for bulk purchasing helped keep them viable.

Housing conditions in France provide a sense of the dramatic improvements in the lives of ordinary Europeans. In 1954 fewer than three in five French households had running water, only one in four an indoor toilet, and only one in ten a bathroom and central heating. By the mid-1970s, 75 percent of homes had indoor toilets, 70 percent indoor bathrooms, and 60 percent central heat. By then the labor-saving domestic appliances so familiar to American consumers had also made deep inroads. Sixty percent of homes had a washing machine, and almost 90 percent had a refrigerator. By 1990 these amenities were virtually universal. These years of growing consumerism also saw the beginning of the automobile revolution. By 1960 almost a third of all French families owned a car, and the proportion would rise to three quarters by 1990.

At the heart of western Europe's state-sponsored experiment in popular welfare is what one scholar has called the "politics of inclusion."[6] The postwar parliamentary state had to succeed where the prewar state had failed in creating a broad working political consensus. That consensus depended on the state catering to the interests of a wide range of groups but above all labor, agriculture, and the lower and middle classes. John Maynard Keynes was the patron saint of this approach. The activist state in its Keynesian incarnation promised to improve economic efficiency and popular welfare without the brutal impersonality of the free market or the tyranny and inefficiency of Soviet-style socialism. This balance between the efficiency of markets and the commitment to the inclusion of all within a just social order were the two elements that defined the emergent European notion of welfare capitalism.

The consensus on welfare capitalism included western Europe's Socialist and Communist parties, both long-time advocates of working-class interests and champions of social justice. But concern with popular welfare became a staple of the center-right as well, including Europe's Christian Democratic parties and the politically influential Catholic Church. Pope John XXIII issued in 1961 an influential encyclical (formal statement on the faith from the pope to his bishops) that called in effect for capitalism with a human face. This popular pope argued for softening the hard edges of the free market, and condemned the cases in which "the enormous wealth, the unbridled luxury, of the privileged few stands in violent, offensive contrast to the utter poverty of the vast majority." The wealthy had a moral obligation to use property "not only for one's own personal benefit but also for the benefit of others." But John XXIII also argued that the state, too, had an indispensable role to play in promoting social justice and political order.[7] This strong preoccupation with the threats an unchecked capitalism posed to social justice echoed a string of papal pronouncements going back to the nineteenth century on the amorality of market-defined societies. The encyclical was also influenced by his personal experience. He was one of 14 children born to a poor sharecropper family in northern Italy. He had gone on to serve as a priest, first as a chaplain during World War I and later as a diplomat whose missions for the Vatican included working to save Jews from Hitler's death camps.

This emerging postwar consensus manifested itself in welfare initiatives and employment guarantees that expanded steadily along with economic recovery. For example, a relatively poor Italy began extending pension coverage and improving health insurance already in 1950. Western Europe's overall welfare expenditures (including education and housing) increased from 25 percent of GNP in 1950 to about 45 percent in the mid-1970s.[8] These measures did not burden the economy. To the contrary, welfare policies promoted economic growth by playing a counter-cyclical role, injecting into a lagging economy unemployment funds calculated to

Angelo Giuseppe Roncalli after His Election as Pope John XXIII, October 1958
Just installed, the pontiff here greets crowds in St. Peter's Square while a TV camera in the background records the event. Seventy-seven years old, Roncalli was expected because of his age to have a short, uneventful tenure. He instead proved during his papacy, spanning four and a half years, to be an active and inspiring leader who reaffirmed the Church's moral authority even as Europeans turned more secular in their outlook. (AP photo)

stimulate spending and recovery and conversely taking money out of people's pockets in the form of taxes when an economy showed signs of overheating. Welfare policies also helped overall economic performance. Money placed in the hands of the poor went for such essentials as food, clothes, and housing and was especially important in raising domestic demand.

In developing this welfare capitalism, European countries followed their distinct traditions. For example, Britain's Beveridge report, issued during World War II, envisioned the promotion of popular welfare without the state getting involved in micromanaging the economy. Germany was guided by Catholic and patriarchal influences, so its welfare measures focused on the breadwinners and left the welfare of women and children to the male head of the family. Sweden's course was influenced by its tradition of state intervention to promote political centralization and economic rationalization. The government of a fractious Italy used welfare measures to keep the social peace. Between 1969 and 1978 amidst considerable domestic turmoil, it raised pensions, introduced support for the unemployed as well as mothers and children, and set up a national health service.

Of all European workers, farmers were perhaps the most favored under the new dispensation. Their sector, once supreme in the European economy, had suffered a steady drop in terms of the numbers employed and the share of national output that it accounted for. More seriously, agricultural income had for over 100 years lagged behind that of urban workers. The resulting rural discontent had fed the violent, authoritarian politics of the late nineteenth and early twentieth centuries, forcing governments to protect farmers against cheap foodstuffs from abroad and to raise their incomes by administrative controls pushing down production and raising prices. This growing intervention began to create close cooperative relations between the state and agricultural organizations.

After World War II, the number of farmworkers continued to shrink due to labor migration to urban factories and the consolidation of land holdings into more efficient units. Those still engaged in agriculture nevertheless remained a disproportionately powerful interest group that continued to receive state assistance. Protectionist measures such as tariffs and import quotas remained in place. Governments still intervened in the market with price supports, subsidies, and official purchasing at set prices, while providing tax and loan assistance. All these measures helped to prevent rural citizens from falling further behind other groups between 1945 and 1960 and to share in postwar prosperity.

Despite their pursuit of inclusive and generous welfare policies, western European states did not neglect the basic issues of economic development and international competitiveness. Leaders all across the region recognized that popular welfare ultimately depended on economic modernization and accordingly states had a responsibility to promote industry and invest heavily in advanced sectors of the economy. Governments resorted to intrusive and far-reaching measures, including nationalization of strategic businesses as well as guidance of private-sector firms and indirect management of the overall economy. By 1957 public enterprise accounted for 32 percent of total gross fixed investment in Britain and Northern Ireland, between 25 and 27 percent in Austria, France, and Italy, and between 13 and 15 percent in the Netherlands, Norway, and Sweden. Most prominently represented were steel, nuclear engineering, aircraft, and energy production.

Reflecting the growing importance of the state as the prime provider of immediate popular welfare and the sponsor of long-term modernization, total government expenditures as a percentage of GDP had by 1973 dramatically surpassed previous levels. Western European states were not simply surviving; they were burgeoning. (See Fig. 5.2.)

Paradoxically, the very success enjoyed by individual states in western Europe made possible the creation of a new, overarching political, social, and economic framework for the region that would ultimately evolve into the European Community (EC). Governments increasingly recognized that their individual interests were best advanced by cooperating on a widening range of issues and by shifting some

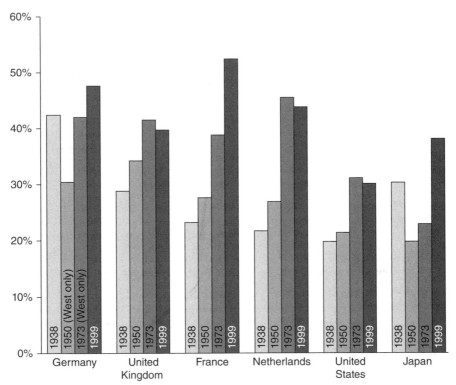

FIGURE 5.2
Government Spending in Western Europe Compared with the United States and Japan, 1938–1999 (as a percentage of GDP)
The regional variations are notable, with the western European states at the high end over the last half-century. No less important, these data show that the modern state has not withered away in the face of increasing globalization and in some cases has actually increased its share of the economic output.[9]

decision-making power to a common entity. As member states developed a symbiotic, mutually supportive relationship, Europeans would find themselves more regulated and better served than ever before.

The direction and pace of these developments were controlled by a new generation of national leaders best represented by Robert Schuman of France, Konrad Adenauer of Germany, and Alcide de Gasperi of Italy. All three were Roman Catholics with deeply democratic impulses and a determination to meet their electorates' cry for a better, more stable life than their states had provided between 1914 and 1945. All agreed that interstate cooperation would facilitate their pursuit of popular welfare.

A western European community took form by gradual stages. The Organization of European Economic Cooperation, created in 1948 to coordinate Marshall Plan programs, sought to clear away some of the obstacles to regional trade. Two years later, the European Payments Union emerged to serve as a clearinghouse for financial claims among member states and provide relief for members having financial problems. In 1952 cooperation took more robust form with the formation of the European Coal and Steel Community. Jean Monnet of France, a leading architect of European unity, had in 1950 proposed a single market for coal and steel resources that would be supervised by a supranational European commission. Once implemented by the major western European economies (France, West Germany, Italy, Belgium, the Netherlands, and Luxembourg), it turned the continent's steel industry into a giant cartel regulating prices and production, and gave governments a mechanism by which they could rationalize production and phase out inefficient plants and mines. This cooperative body demonstrated that states jealous of their autonomy—especially the larger states of Germany, France, Italy, and Britain—were more and more comfortable with the process of coming to terms on specific issues within fixed deadlines. Perhaps most important of all to further progress toward integration, those two long-term rivals, France and Germany, were building mutual trust.

The crowning achievement of this steady trend toward regional cooperation was the EC. Created by a treaty signed in Rome in March 1957 by the six governments already participating in the Coal and Steel Community, it provided for expanded European free trade. Success at dismantling tariffs and other obstacles to trade paved the way for more wide-ranging economic coordination. The Rome treaties also established the basis for closer political cooperation. The key institutions were the Council of Ministers, the European Commission, a European Court, and the European Parliament. To keep members happy, the offices of these institutions did not operate in just one EC capital but were parceled out to Brussels, Belgium, Luxembourg City, and Strasbourg, France. Attempts to carry cooperation further—into the areas of foreign policy and defense organization—foundered over fear of alienating the Americans and over disagreements between the British and French governments.

A collection of discrete considerations drove this trend toward regional integration. Foremost was a shared commitment to promoting intraregional trade as an engine in the economic growth that was so important to political leaders through-out western Europe. Greater unity had the additional appeal of helping to solve the problem of Germany, with its dubious past and rapidly reviving economic power. A Germany thoroughly integrated within the European community was less likely to return to its aggressively nationalist behavior. The desire for international influence also made unity attractive. Only a united Europe could have a meaningful voice on the world stage. As the French minister of foreign affairs, Maurice Faure, put it in July 1957 when he appealed to the French parliament to approve the Rome treaties: "Well, there are not four Great Powers, there are two; America and Russia. There will be a third by the end of the century: China. It depends on you whether there will be a fourth: Europe."[10]

Agriculture did not drive the formation of the EC, but it was so important an element in the fundamental policies of its member states that it had to be incorporated in any regional agreement. A Common Agricultural Policy took shape in the 1960s, and by the end of the decade it was eating up 80 percent of the EC's administrative effort and 70 percent of its budget. This was so despite the fact that member states were among the most industrialized in the world, and agriculture was an ever-dwindling part of their economies. The politics of inclusion that served farmers so well in individual states also got them favored treatment in a united Europe.

Whereas France, Germany, and Italy embraced greater integration, only Britain of the major western European economies hung back. London did not join the Coal and Steel Community, nor did it sign the Treaty of Rome launching the EC. The main source of the British reluctance was the hold a glorious imperial past exercised on policymakers' imagination and the related conviction that Britain was "not just another European country" (as the Labor government's foreign secretary, Ernest Bevin, insisted in mid-1947).[11] Postwar leaders sought to maintain British global power and prestige by cultivating a close relationship with the United States. They also sought to preserve the position of the British pound as a leading international currency, and to that end tried to maintain convertibility with the dollar despite the harm the effort did to British industry and consumers. Finally, the British government tried to hold the diverse parts of its rapidly dissolving empire together in a Commonwealth. Although it was supposed to serve as a framework for close political and economic cooperation, divergences among its members had by the 1960s largely drained the association of its significance.

London's preference for international prestige over closer ties to the continent proved a mistake. Glory imposed costs that Britain could no longer afford. It lacked the capital to invest in its colonies and maintain the troops abroad in defense of its dwindling empire. Manufactured exports, the basis for Britain's reputation as a great trading nation, slid dramatically. One quarter of the world's total in the early postwar period, by 1970 they represented only a tenth. Britain's growth rate and productivity increases lagged behind those of the EC, and Britons enviously watched the rising living standard of their neighbors. Already by the mid-1950s, competitive continental industry was driving British auto exports and other consumer goods from the European market. For example, Germany's Volkswagen ousted Britain's Morris Minor from the low-cost car market. The country's weak economic performance was a source of national pessimism. Economic stagnation was putting consumer dreams beyond reach at the same time that it was undercutting dreams of international influence.

This strong trend toward western European economic integration helped preserve a distinct corporate style that dominated the region. Fiat, a large and powerful Italian conglomerate, reveals the characteristics associated with this postwar European way of doing business. Perhaps the most striking of these characteristics was family ownership. What also distinguished the European corporate culture was the class-consciousness of business leaders, their close ties to the state, and their sometimes contentious relationship with strong, independent labor unions.

Fiat began as an automobile company under Giovanni Agnelli. This astute entrepreneur came from a socially prominent land-owning family with roots in a small village near the northern Italian city of Turin. Convinced of the automobile's promise, he had created Fiat (short for Fabbrica Italiana Automobili Torino) in 1899. Demand during World War I made Fiat the third largest company in Italy and helped it diversify into new areas such as trucks, aircraft engines, and publishing. Agnelli was becoming a rich man.

Already Fiat had developed close ties to politicians in Rome who could assure the Turin-based company preferential treatment and government contracts. Agnelli's embrace of the young political upstart Benito Mussolini in 1914 paid rich dividends from the 1920s into the early 1940s when Mussolini presided over a fascist dictatorship. For example, when the U.S. auto company Ford tried to break into the Italian market by purchasing an Italian car maker, Fiat got Rome to block the deal, thus preserving its dominance in the domestic market. When the war in Europe turned against Mussolini, Agnelli switched sides and welcomed the Allies. American support in the form of Marshall Plan aid helped to rebuild production lines and to make Fiat a rival to Germany's Volkswagen in the race to become the largest European auto producer. Fiat also cultivated close ties to the ruling Christian Democrats, which in turn dealt sympathetically with powerful private business blocs, supported competitive exporters, and tolerated practices that would in the United States have fallen afoul of antitrust or antimonopoly laws.

Agnelli and the other well-born business leaders who ran Italy's major private firms from the economically dominant northern region felt a strong sense of social solidarity. This elite looked with suspicion on firms led by social upstarts. They coordinated their actions with the help of what was long Italy's only commercial bank, the powerful Milan-based Mediobanca, which occupied a commanding place within the Italian economy. Consistent with the strong class-consciousness of his circle, Giovanni Agnelli tended to deal with his workers paternalistically. He avoided layoffs and provided a range of benefits, including medical care, housing, nurseries for working mothers, and retirement homes. But these benefits did not satisfy workers looking for broader rights. Left-wing labor unions began to collide with Agnelli's paternalism during World War I. Labor unrest continued into the 1920s and would erupt once more after World War II.

When Giovanni Agnelli died in December 1945, Fiat remained firmly under family control. His grandson, the 24-year-old Gianni Agnelli, was next in line to run Fiat. Still in a playboy phase, he relied on Vittorio Valletta, a veteran manager, to direct the company. This loyal servitor prepared the company to operate in a more open trading system that favored mass production for mass consumption. As part of moving Fiat in fresh directions, he introduced new technology and imposed greater labor discipline, quadrupling worker output between 1948 and 1955. Finally in the early 1960s Gianni Agnelli had settled down enough to begin taking up the mantle of leadership. Firmly in control by 1966, the new boss quickly accommodated to the prevailing corporate pattern. He worked with the long-ruling Christian Democrats, and this collaboration paid off in direct aid from Rome as well as from the EC headquarters in Brussels. The politicians helped with payments for laid-off workers, covering up to 90 percent of their lost pay. They restricted Japanese auto imports. They purchased struggling Fiat subsidiaries and sold off state-controlled firms to Fiat at below market prices. Agnelli himself took a prominent place in the close-knit Italian corporate establishment, for example serving in the mid-1970s as president of the premier industrial coordinating organization, Confindustria. Among his close associates was the influential Enrico Cuccia, the head of the large state-owned IRI conglomerate as well as Mediobanca.

Agnelli took the company reins just as the Italian economy was entering a difficult period. Inflation was setting in, and the competitiveness of Italian goods was suffering on international markets. In addition, labor was restive. Fiat had hired large numbers of poor southerners to work in its Turin plants but did little to help the city deal with the economic and social stresses created by the newcomers. Fiat compounded local tensions by cracking down on high worker absentee rates and cutting payrolls in order to make the company more competitive. The fall of 1969 brought a climax to a decade of growing labor unrest, now reinforced by student demonstrations. Strikes disrupted production, costs soared, and in the context of mounting political polarization executives faced intimidation and terrorism. Four were killed, and Agnelli himself carried a cyanide capsule against the possibility that terrorists might capture him. Fiat's problems persisted into the 1970s. An economic slowdown combined with high gas prices to hurt car sales, while labor–management relations remained volatile. Finally, to help restore industrial peace, Agnelli lent support to a nationwide scheme to regularly adjust workers' pay to account for inflation. In 1975 the government put this indexed wage arrangement (*scala mobile*, literally moving stairs or escalator) into effect, thus quieting some of labor's discontents. Within its own factories the Fiat management would go on to purge the remaining restive workers.

During the 1980s Fiat enjoyed renewed profitability and growth. By mid-decade it employed 270,000 workers directly and several million indirectly through suppliers, commanded an annual revenue of $30 billion, and accounted for about 5 percent of Italy's total GNP. Auto production, Fiat's core business, controlled 60 percent of the domestic car market. The empire had expanded to include in all 569 subsidiaries and 190 associated companies operating in 50 countries. They covered the business gamut, from banks and insurance groups to aerospace to textiles to publishing to cement and construction.[12]

Their grip on this massive conglomerate made the Agnelli family Italy's uncrowned royal house. With a 40 percent stake, Gianni Agnelli and his close relatives continued to keep a close eye on Fiat's affairs, and worried that a merger in the auto business with such auto giants as Ford or General Motors, prompted by purely competitive concerns, would lose them the jewel in the family corporate crown. The Agnellis were bent on maintaining the tradition of family control even as they began to face the competitive pressures of globalization. The end of an era came in January 2003 with Gianni Agnelli's death. Thousands upon thousands—workers, soccer stars, and government officials among a mass of mourners—paid their respect to the most important figure in Italian public life over the last half-century. Fiat was by then in deep economic trouble but still under family control.

The sort of close ties between Fiat and family were commonplace in postwar Europe. In Britain, France, and Germany, too, families had founded and then as owners run or supervised major, internationally known corporations such as France's Peugeot, Renault, and Michelin. In Germany as late as 1969, 60 of the 150 largest firms were still family-dominated. In Italy almost half of the 100 most dominant businesses between 1950 and 1970 were under family control. This pattern persisted into the 1990s, when over three quarters of Italy's top 150 companies were still family-owned (compared to only one in five in the United States).[13] At odds with the predominant pattern in the United States, business as the family domain has played a critical role in other regions of the world, nowhere more so than in the advanced economic sectors of Japan, with its *keiretsu*, and of South Korea, with its family-owned diversified business groups known as *chaebol*.

EUROPEAN REVIVAL AND CONSOLIDATION

1945	Fiat begins rebuilding with the help of Marshall Plan funds
1952	European Coal and Steel Community marks first major advance toward greater integration
1957	Treaty of Rome lays basis for the European Community with France, West Germany, Italy, Belgium, the Netherlands, and Luxembourg as the founding members
1961	Pope John XXIII calls for a socially just capitalism
1966	Gianni Agnelli assumes full personal control of Fiat

The Second Japanese Miracle

The state, which figured so centrally in the revival and reshaping of European economies, was no less important to Japan's postwar development. The Japanese pattern of government involvement, sometimes described as "guided capitalism," had as its overriding goal the accumulation of national wealth through promoting exports and limiting imports. This approach produced the second Japanese economic miracle, surpassing the first one early in the century.

By the late 1950s Japan had demonstrated that it could grow at a rate that exceeded even the most optimistic expectations. By the 1960s the economy was booming. Its rate of GDP growth was stunning even by comparison with the robust European performance, averaging over 9 percent annually between 1950 and 1973. The torrid pace helped lift the purchasing power of the Japanese people from less than a fifth of the U.S. level in 1950 to two thirds by 1973. Japanese goods were increasingly competitive within the U.S.-guaranteed international free trade regime. Its exports boomed, tripling their share of total world exports between 1955 and 1970. The overseas sales offensive combined with limited foreign sales within Japan swelled foreign exchange reserves from virtually nothing in 1955 to a respectable $18.3 billion in 1972. Already by 1968 Japan's economy was not just the East Asian leader but also the third largest in the world. The loser of the Pacific War had become an economic superpower.[14]

The improvement in the standard of living in less than a generation was extraordinary. The cabinet of Prime Minister Ikeda Hayato committed in 1960 to double the national income. By both expanding the country's wealth and ensuring an equitable division, Liberal Democratic Party leaders hoped to promote mass consumption that would calm the social tension and political conflict that had begun to roil the nation. Workers were unhappy and prone to strike. The Socialist and Communist parties enjoyed strong support. The alliance with the United States was controversial and had just ignited violence in the streets and in the legislature.

The Ikeda plan proved fantastically successful. Japan already had the most equal distribution of income among advanced industrial countries. With prosperity widely shared, Japanese could for the first time in large numbers indulge their taste for consumer goods, mainly appliances and entertainment. By 1970 virtually all urban households had a television, a refrigerator, and a washing machine, and one in five owned a car (rare a decade earlier). Members of this new middle class could buy their own home and send their children to school in ever-larger percentages. High school graduates rose from half of the population in 1955 to 82 percent in 1970. Over the same period the percentage of college graduates more than doubled, reaching almost a quarter of the population by 1970.

Amazingly, Japanese families went on a spending spree while maintaining a savings rate so high that Japanese business did not need to turn to foreign capital to expand. Increasing prosperity seemed to reinforce rather than diminish this high propensity to save. This pattern persisted because the Japanese government, unlike those in western Europe, did not provide rich social security guarantees, so adults had good reason to save, especially to cover their retirement years. Fiscal policy offered tax breaks for savings and no breaks for consumer debt. Finally, consumer credit for major purchases such as homes and cars was not easily available. The byword among Japanese consumers was not "buy now, pay later" but "save now, buy later."

Central to Japan's success was a statist approach to economic development whereby bureaucrats would help firms gain an edge and maintain it by adjusting quickly to constantly changing market conditions overseas. To that end, government agencies encouraged cooperation among firms and exercised wide discretionary power. This "guided capitalism" became orthodoxy during the era of sustained high growth that began in the mid-1950s. In 1955 the government laid down the first of a long string of economic plans, this one geared to 5 percent annual growth. In implementing these plans, the Japanese state orchestrated industrial and export strategies. The Ministry of International Trade and Industry (MITI), created in 1949, worked along with the Ministry of Finance to construct a predictable framework for business growth, to promote efficiency, to ensure cheap capital to encourage investment, and to direct research and development projects toward promising new technologies.

Under this Japanese version of free-market capitalism, the state had at its disposal a striking variety of mechanisms to promote its broad goals. The government might intervene to change the tax system, provide subsidies, or encourage new industries by reclaiming scarce land for factory sites or subsidizing the industrial use of water and electricity. To make sure that firms with the strongest growth prospects secured funding, bureaucrats could ration capital and limit foreign exchange, helping some and denying others. To shelter promising new industry from foreign competition, the state could impose trade restrictions and controls on currency exchange. What the government did not do, in contrast with European practice, was to acquire direct control of important segments of the economy. Nationalization was not in Tokyo's economic toolkit.

Perhaps the most peculiarly Japanese of these government economic tools was "administrative guidance," which involved laying down "guideposts" for business decision-makers. Bureaucrats, usually in MITI, consulted with business leaders on future levels of economic activity within an industry, proposing targets on the basis of their overall knowledge of economic conditions and then persuading businesses to observe them. The business establishment had a strong bias toward cooperation, and in any case every firm knew that to defy the bureaucrats today would surely mean an unfriendly response to tomorrow's request for help with an export license or a low-interest loan. Government agencies stood ready to help should firms following the agreed-upon guidelines run into trouble. For example, in the case of unexpected over-capacity, MITI might step in to indicate how much each firm within an industry should cut back, in what product lines, and to what price levels for the remaining output.

Powerful and efficient career bureaucrats did not dictate to big business. Rather, they engaged in a steady dialogue with the leaders of "enterprise groups" made up of diverse industries linked in long-term relationships (*keiretsu*) permitted by occupation policy after the breakup of large family-controlled business conglomerates known as *zaibatsu* (see Chapter 2). It was up to business to decide how to maneuver on the free market domestically and internationally. Politicians from the Liberal Democratic Party constituted the third element in what some have called the "iron triangle" of the Japanese economy. This conservative, pro-business party first took control of the government in 1955 and would run the country almost continually to the century's end. Its dominance guaranteed political stability and fostered continuity in this winning economic strategy. These three groups operated within a clubby, strongly pro-growth culture ("Japan Incorporated," as some have called it) that made economic success the overriding national goal. Defenders of this tight, closed world argued that it got results and avoided the legal tie-ups and political wrangles common to the much-vaunted U.S. system.

The steel industry provides a good example of how Japan Incorporated worked. Between 1955 and 1974 MITI guided that industry in an orderly fashion from production of 9.4 million tons of crude steel to 117.1 million tons. By that latter date Japan's output was only slightly behind the leaders, the Soviet Union and the United States. At each step of the expansion process, MITI coordinated the plans of the nominally competing Japanese steel firms. In the 1960s it began to stress technological innovation as a response to a developing labor shortage. Faced with an increasingly competitive international market, MITI promoted consolidation of the two biggest firms. In 1970 the merger came to fruition, resulting in the world's largest steel company.

In retrospect, it is clear that the Japanese economy had undergone a fundamental transformation during the 1950s and 1960s, made possible first by supplying U.S. forces fighting in Korea and then by exporting to an open U.S. market. U.S.-bound goods increased from $0.28 billion in 1954 to $1.12 billion in 1960. At the outset the main exports were low-quality, inexpensive products such as toys and textiles. But increasingly production moved into high-technology goods such as cars and electronics that put Japan's manufacturers on the cutting edge of international competition. The introduction of new manufacturing technologies had steadily raised workers' productivity and made export goods attractive to foreign buyers. As industry demonstrated that it could compete internationally, the government began in the early 1960s slowly to open the home market to foreign imports.

These critical economic developments had a profound effect on Japanese society. A country that had been a war machine lavishing its human and material resources on overseas ambitions was becoming an economic engine dedicated to supplying consumers abroad with quality goods and its own people with a richer life. The pieces of the economic juggernaut that would amaze and alarm the world in the 1970s and 1980s had largely fallen into place.

The new direction of the Japanese economy and the energy and imagination of its business leaders in the high-growth export sector are exemplified by Sony, the world-famous consumer electronics firm. Sony's founders brought to their drive to capture foreign markets a long-term vision that stressed a paternalistic relationship to their employees, constantly upgrading technology to enhance competitiveness, and forgoing immediate profits to expand market share. Government backing helped them realize their vision.

The firm had its origins in the months just after the end of the war in the Pacific. The Tokyo Telecommunications Engineering Company had an unpromising name as well as limited startup capital, but the founders had energy and good social connections as well as vision, and they recruited talented engineers. The senior partner, Masaru Ibuka, imagined a business whose employees "could become united with a firm spirit of teamwork and exercise to their hearts' desire their technological capacity." Akio Morita, 13 years Ibuka's junior, was more interested in how to get new technology into customers' hands. His approach, he later explained, was "to lead the public with new products rather than ask them what kind of products they want. The public does not know what is possible, but we do."[15]

The Ibuka–Morita operation got its first big break in the early 1950s with the transistor. Bell Labs, the U.S. inventor of this solid-state electronic processor, imagined it as useful only in hearing aids, while Ibuka thought it might run a small radio. To arrange the $25,000 payment for a license to produce transistors, he had to persuade MITI officials, who doubted both the utility of the transistor and the ability of the small firm to bring a new product successfully to market. Ibuka's engineers proceeded to redesign the transistor, create parts for a small radio, and get it into mass production. Their first pocket transistor radio appeared in 1957. An American firm beat the Japanese to market by a few months but then decided that pocket radios had no future and abandoned the field.

With its first major product doing well, the firm decided it needed a name that would travel internationally. The Latin word *sonus* (sound) appealed, and after some playing with meanings in English and Japanese, "Sony" emerged. It meant nothing but was short and easy to remember and had a transnational look. In January 1958 it became the official name for a company that would become a symbol of the Japanese economic resurgence and a byword internationally for innovative consumer electronics.

Sony's overseas success was in large measure Morita's achievement. He was born in 1921 into a well-to-do, respectable sake-brewing family with roots in a village just outside the industrial city of Nagoya (southwest of Tokyo). The family had been making sake, Japan's national and ceremonial drink, for 300 years. As the first son, Akio (meaning "enlightened") was slated to take over the business. While still attending elementary school, he began sitting in on board meetings. The family atmosphere was distinctly Westernizing. Morita's parents gave him an elevated bed to replace the traditional on-the-floor *tatami*. The family imported a Ford car to take Sunday drives along narrow, bumpy cart roads and purchased a General Electric washing machine and a Westinghouse refrigerator. The father had a taste for foreign movies, including (so the son recalled) *King Kong*. His mother loved European classical music and attended concerts by touring artists. To play her beloved records by the likes of the tenor Enrico Caruso, the family first acquired a crank-powered Victrola and then an electric phonograph. To help the young man toward a broader view of the world, the family sent him on tours of Japan, Korea, and Manchuria. Along with this interest in Western goods and practices went a sense of social obligation, especially toward the welfare of the family village, and a strong sense of family identity and social propriety.

Morita was early on gripped by a keen interest in science. He began to read about electronics, especially sound reproduction and radio, and to make electronic devices. At Osaka Imperial University he studied in its outstanding physics department. During the latter stages of the war with the United States, he went into the navy to do research on heat-guided weapons and night-vision gun sights. He came out of the war sensitive to how far Japan lagged behind the United States technologically. This awareness of Japan's backwardness inspired a determination to catch up that gave Morita's business drive a nationalist impetus. Japan's postwar achievements, to which he would contribute, would be a source of special personal pride.

Already in the 1950s, even before the transistor deal put Sony on a solid foundation, Morita began looking for opportunities abroad. He made his first tour of the United States and Europe in 1953 to size up markets and build business contacts. In convincing affluent foreigners about the quality of Japanese goods, Morita proved an energetic, outgoing, and confident salesman who worked easily

Akio Morita and Masaru Ibuka
Morita (left) and Ibuka were the cofounders of Sony and long-time colleagues whose conflicts were apparently limited to arm-wrestling. (Courtesy of Sony Corporation)

with Americans and Europeans. In 1960 he took charge of the Sony push into the U.S. market.

Within the world of Japan's self-effacing business leaders, Morita was a bit of a maverick. He was sharp-tongued and enjoyed the public spotlight whether promoting Sony's image or speaking out as Japan's business ambassador to the world. Determined to recognize good work at Sony, he introduced a merit element in a salary scheme usually heavily weighted in favor of seniority. Rather than shelter his family, as was the norm, he brought them to New York for a year in the early 1960s to learn American ways. He took up skiing, windsurfing, and skin diving in his sixties. A stroke finally forced him to retire in 1994. His partner Ibuka died in 1997, and Morita two years later.

Under Ibuka and Morita, Sony made its reputation in the United States and overseas more generally with a long string of innovative products. The pocket transistor radio (1957) was followed by a transistor television (1960); the home videotape recorder (1965); Trinitron color television picture tube (1968); Walkman® audiotape player (1979); 3.5-inch floppy disk (1980); compact disk player (1982); and 8-millimeter video camcorder (1985). To achieve this extraordinary run of innovation, Sony put 6 to 10 percent of its sales into research and development. An integral part of product development was careful consideration of likely consumer response, and as a new product approached readiness for the market, Sony would carefully devise an advertising campaign to win buyers. Technology and advertising fueled explosive growth. By 1966 sales were 33 times higher than they had been a decade earlier. Over the following 20 years they would increase another 32 times. In 1991 Sony's sales hit $28 billion and its employees, a mere 20 at the outset in 1946, had climbed to 119,000 for the entire Sony Group.[16] By then Sony's run of innovation in consumer electronics was beginning to run its course. By 2014 the corporation was regularly losing money on that part of its business, much to the detriment of the bottom line.

The business philosophy at Sony reflected broader patterns that made Japan an economic powerhouse. Like the heads of other major firms, Morita thought of the company as a family and instituted measures that promoted loyalty to the firm. He recruited employees right out of college and expected them to stay for life and find satisfaction and support within the company. The task of management, Morita explained, was "to keep challenging each employee to do important work that he will find satisfying and to work within the family."[17] Superiors were supposed to stay in close touch with subordinates and cultivate bonds of loyalty. For example, all employees ate in the same dining room, shared work areas, and wore the same company jacket. Because the wage system rewarded seniority, the longer an employee stayed the higher the pay. Top-level executives were paid only about seven or eight times more than newly hired workers. Unions were organized within companies and promoted cooperation rather than confrontation. With management–labor harmony the watchword, companies functioned as teams and minimized the disruptive antagonisms and worker alienation commonplace in economies where labor and management saw themselves as adversaries. The contrast between Sony, where unions were creatures of the company, and Fiat or Disney, both plagued by labor strife, underlines the differences in national conditions shaping economic behavior.

Like other Japanese business leaders, Morita insisted on following a long-term strategy to gain market share rather than seek short-term profit that would make shareholders happy. To that end Sony sought to keep sales rising steadily, even in economic downturns and even if it meant cutting the profit margin. This strategy also helped to keep trained staff fully employed, avoid layoffs, and thus honor the company's obligations to take care of employees. Japanese firms followed this course with the encouragement of their *keiretsu* partners, who in turn protected the company by working together to prevent hostile takeover bids and to keep foreign interlopers out of their home market. Because business leaders came from within the firms, they tended to give priority to the long-term growth of the firm and welfare of its workers. High levels of corporate spending on research and development helped move Japan to the technological forefront, first in cars and consumer electronics and then in computers, engineering, communications, robotics, and instrumentation. Business happily supported heavy government investment in infrastructure and education that would make the overall economy more competitive and individual firms more productive.

Sony's success and that of other Japanese businesses is hard to imagine without government support. It promoted a broad social consensus in favor of economic growth, hard work, and limited consumption. The government also maintained a protectionist policy that assured Sony a secure domestic market during its early years. Finally, the government not only tolerated but also encouraged the clubby atmosphere among leading corporations. Sony, for example, stockpiled economic and political influentials on its board of directors to ensure the company's strong ties with the major segments of the Japanese establishment. This sort of cooperation, all the partners agreed, was the key to economic stability and success. Morita himself described these arrangements with only slight exaggeration as not so much capitalism as "a socialistic and egalitarian free economic system."[18]

JAPAN BECOMES AN ECONOMIC POWERHOUSE	
1946	Sony created by Ibuka with Morita as junior partner
1955	Government prepares first economic plan; economy begins quarter-century of sustained high growth; Sony produces transistor radio
1960	Prime Minister Ikeda sets sights on income doubling; Sony launches U.S. operations, marking beginning of broad Japanese export drive
1968	Japanese economy enters ranks of top three

VOICES OF DISCONTENT

Just as the Cold War bred its vocal critics (see Chapter 4), so too did a dynamic international economy generate discontents. Although the economic system produced an abundance of goods, it was also producing an abundance of pollutants. Social critics began to speak out on this issue. Within the developed economies, women began to call for fuller consideration in the system of production and consumption and thus to share fully in the new era of abundance, although their goals differed from region to region. Finally, economists dissenting from free-market orthodoxy decried flaws in the international economy that disproportionately favored rich countries. These various critics of the international economy came into their own in the 1950s and 1960s and articulated a set of worries about the environment, the status of women, and the disparities in wealth that would increasingly grip the global community in the decades beyond.

The New Environmentalism

In 1969 the U.S. novelist Kurt Vonnegut looked at the pictures of the planet sent back from space and observed, "Earth is such a pretty blue and pink and white pearl ... It looks *so clean*. You can't see all the hungry, angry earthlings down there—and the smoke and the sewage and trash and sophisticated weaponry."[19] His remarks reflected a deepening concern that more and more people and goods were harming the environment. That concern would in time become international, but it took hold earliest in the United States, where the threat seemed most acute. In part Americans were sensitive because they were the first to confront sprawling suburbs, increasing numbers of autos, and consumer waste that boom times brought. But also stirring the unease was a chemical-dependent agriculture and fallout from nuclear tests on American soil. Once a similar constellation of concerns arose in Europe and Japan, environmentalism would gain momentum there as well.

The new environmentalism had its origins in 1962 when Rachel Carson, a popular nature writer and former government scientist, published *Silent Spring*. This landmark book, perhaps the most consequential published in the United States in the twentieth century, identified the dangerous effects of the pesticide DDT, but Carson's broader message was the threat facing humans as part of the Earth's complex and fragile ecosystem. This unlikely midwife to a new environmental consciousness and activism was born in 1907 just outside Pittsburgh. As a child, Carson was bookish and bright, with a keen interest in nature. At college, she majored in biology, fascinated with the problems it posed. Her professor, a woman herself struggling in a man's world, played the role of mentor and urged Carson to go to graduate school. By the end of college Carson had become a feminist on the basis of seeing the limits imposed on other women. She had seen her mother defer to her father, himself an inept businessman, and had watched her college mentor, like other talented women, run up against closed doors to career opportunities.

Carson took her MA in marine biology at Johns Hopkins University in 1932. But there were no jobs for her in either industry or academe, especially with men given the preference during the Depression as family breadwinners. She was finally able to get a post as a writer for the federal government's Fish and Wildlife Service. It kept her up to date on the latest scientific findings while she made her name as a part-time popular writer adept at rendering those findings in clear, engaging terms. Never married, she particularly needed the income to care for her mother and extended family after her father's death.

Between 1937 and 1955 Carson established financial independence as a popular writer. Her first book, *Under the Sea Wind* (1941), was overshadowed by Pearl Harbor, but her next two books, *The Sea Around Us* (1951) and *The Edge of the Sea* (1955), won wide critical recognition and many readers. Carson conveyed in this string of publications a sense of nature as a good in itself that deserved human wonder. Her prose could be sinuous, as for example in an *Atlantic Monthly* article in 1937 describing how, in a marvelously intricate natural process,

> *the parts of the plan fall into place: the water receiving from earth and air the simple materials, storing them up until the gathering energy of the spring sun wakens the sleeping plants to a burst of dynamic activity, hungry swarms of planktonic animals growing and multiplying upon the abundant plants, and themselves falling prey to the shoals of fish; all, in the end, to be redissolved into their component substances when the inexorable laws of the sea demand it. Individual elements are lost to view, only to reappear again and again in different incarnations in a kind of material immortality. Kindred forces to those which, in some period inconceivably remote, gave birth to that primeval bit of protoplasm tossing on the ancient seas, continue their mighty and incomprehensible work.*[20]

In 1958 Carson began work on her last and most important book. It would make a fresh argument—that nature deserved human protection. She was moved by her alarm over the mounting environmental perils that were filling the news and the scientific literature: radioactive fallout, smog, food additives, and heedless pesticide use. She decided to focus on pesticides, galvanized by scientific studies showing the effects of DDT and other chemicals on wildlife and humans. She decided to treat DDT as a symptom of a broader problem, the absolute faith in science to improve life. DDT, for example, was touted as "the atomic bomb of the insect world."[21] American consumers, industry, and agriculture embraced the quick, cheap chemical fix offered by a widening range of pesticides and herbicides. Carson had another, more personal reason to write about carcinogenic pesticides. She knew that cancer was at work in her body. A radical mastectomy in 1960 failed to stop its progress, and in 1964, just two years after the publication of *Silent Spring*, cancer would kill her.

Silent Spring followed the model of Carson's earlier work. It was scientifically well grounded, beautifully written, and preoccupied with the natural balance. Its specific argument was that limits on pesticides were needed. Once released, they

Rachel Carson
Carson is pictured here at her summer home in Maine around the time she was at work on *Silent Spring.* (© Eric Hartmann/Magnum Photos)

could not be contained but would cycle through the land, water, and air. Carson's call for limits rested in part on her concern for human safety. Pesticides could increase the risks for cancer, sterility, and birth defects. But she also argued that limits made economic sense, saving consumers and businesses from the costs of excessive spraying, protecting the health of employees, and forestalling the development of pesticide-resistant strains. She was not in favor of banning pesticides; she wanted them used more intelligently. Long-term costs needed to be counted against immediate gain and more room left for the operation of nature's own system of insect control.

Carson's specific concerns with pesticides led her to see nature as fragile and technology as dangerous to the survival of humans as well as other species. She argued, "The question is whether any civilization can wage relentless war on life without destroying itself, and without losing the right to be called civilized." She warned: "The 'control of nature' is a phrase conceived in arrogance, born of the Neanderthal age of biology and philosophy, when it was supposed that nature exists for the convenience of man." From "so primitive a science" had come powerful compounds to be used against insects. But "in turning them against the insects [science] has also turned them against the earth." Carson's preoccupation with the threat that humans posed to the world around them established her standing as the herald of a new, anxious environmental outlook.[22]

The chemical industry, farm groups, and the U.S. Department of Agriculture launched a fierce counterattack. They attempted to block publication of *Silent Spring* and later threatened to withhold advertising from publications reviewing it favorably. When that did not work, they launched a public relations campaign to reassure the public and discredit Carson as a "hysterical woman" who lacked solid scientific credentials. Carson survived these attacks. Her dedication to the cause of the environment sustained her personally, while her scientific training and ability to marshal the evidence gave credence to her charges. Science could not conquer nature, she quietly but firmly insisted, but it could destroy it.

While Carson's talents help explain *Silent Spring*'s impact, timing was also important. Carson spoke to an already worried U.S. public. The daily news was full of stories about contaminated milk and cranberries, birds killed by spraying against gypsy moths and mosquitoes, and the health dangers of nuclear fallout. A decade of prosperity had brought suburban sprawl, oil spills, and auto pollution. Technology and economic growth seemed to have run amuck, and government agencies such as the Department of Agriculture were so wedded to growth that they ignored environmental threats. Politicians began taking note of this incipient public environmental consciousness. President Kennedy publicly acknowledged Carson's charges and created a scientific panel to review them. The panel confirmed her findings and urged revising the guidelines for pesticide use.

More broadly, *Silent Spring*, along with the public response that it evoked, needs to be seen as an advance on earlier local and usually episodic responses to environmental problems accumulating over the course of the previous century. In the 1860s in Britain air in major cities fouled by coal burning prompted clean air acts, the first notable environmental measures to become law. There, as well as in Russia, Switzerland, Germany, and the United States in the late nineteenth and early twentieth centuries, nationalists joined the calls for action—to preserve rural life with its intimate connections to the country's past but also wilderness areas as another indispensable part of the national patrimony. Farmers in places as widely separated as Europe and Japan made their voices heard, organizing protests against new industries whose smokestacks spewed pollutants into the air and poisoned the soil for miles around. But in industrial societies, whether under the control of capitalism or socialism, economic growth got the nod over environmental protection. National power took precedence over romantic notions about nature and the warnings about the effects of pollutants. The human cost could be terrible. In London in December 1952 a week of choking air produced by burning coal in homes and factories killed about 4,000 people.

Carson's special contribution to environmentalism was to inaugurate an era of broad-based political and legal activism that built on these earlier localized concerns. In 1960 the major U.S. conservation organizations combined claimed a mere 300,000 members. Ten years later the largest of the environmental groups, the National Wildlife Federation, alone had over half a million members. Burgeoning environmental organizations and public protest reflected deep-seated changes in attitudes and fed off the critical social movements that marked the 1960s, especially among young people. The ferment found expression in new approaches. For example, the Environmental Defense Fund, established in 1967, turned to the courts, using lawsuits and injunctions to champion "environmental rights." The media began popularizing environmental issues. The culmination of all this activity was the first Earth Day (April 22, 1970), when some 20 million Americans showed up to participate in teach-ins on college campuses and in major cities around the country. This celebration of the environment, attended by calls for its protection, would become an annual event observed around the world.

Mushrooming popular concerns quickly registered in Congress, which passed such fresh legislation as the Wilderness Act of 1964 and the Water Quality Control Act of 1965 and created the Environmental Protection Agency in 1969. In 1972, in a development that would have given Carson special satisfaction, Congress finally banned the sale and use of DDT in the United States. That it could still be manufactured in the United States for sale abroad and even brought back into the United States as residue on foreign agricultural products would have roused her ire and indicated just how much farther the environmental cause had to go.

The Feminist Upsurge

If modern environmentalism took shape in the United States, growing discontent among women about their social and economic status was distinctly more international, manifesting itself in the United States, western Europe, and Japan almost simultaneously. In maturing postwar economies marked by growing prosperity, consumerism, and job opportunities, gender relations rapidly emerged in the 1960s as an urgent issue. But the peculiarities of national traditions and social values made for a striking diversity among women from country to country. Not only was there no monolithic Western women's movement, but also Japan provided the first signs that trans-Atlantic societies would not define the terms for activism in the broader world. As we will see in Chapters 6 and 9, women in the Third (or developing) World reinforced this pattern of diversity as they faced their own set of problems and articulated their own needs.

In the United States, women's steadily growing participation in the economy laid the groundwork for the women's movement in the late 1960s. The linkage was nothing new. The push to ensure women the right to vote, finally successful at the national level in 1920, had coincided with the rise of the consumer culture, which gave women new economic clout and public prominence. By 1915 nearly 90 percent of consumer spending was done by women. How could women who exercised such a powerful vote in the marketplace be denied a ballot during elections? The second wave of feminism in the 1960s was also tied to the pressures of an increasingly consumer-oriented economy. It was not only bringing Americans their golden age of material abundance, but it was also attracting increasing numbers of women, no longer just as consumers but also as producers.

Mobilization during World War II had jumpstarted the process of drawing significant numbers of women into the labor force and opening visions of wide occupational opportunities. After Pearl Harbor, millions of women went to work, often in higher-paying jobs previously closed to them. As the war ended, three out of four women wanted to continue working and were already questioning whether their only option was to give up their jobs to the returning soldiers and take their "proper place" within a male-dominated home. Many in fact managed to stay employed, even if they had to step down to lesser jobs at lower pay. By the end of the 1940s women had actually increased their share of the workforce to 32 percent, up from 27 percent at the onset of the decade. The trend continued during the supposedly conservative 1950s. Women flocked into the labor market. Nearly a third of all wives were working by 1960, and 25 percent of middle-class women were employed. By 1970 60 percent of all families with an income over $10,000 had both husband and wife working. Women over 35 who had finished the most intensive of their child-raising duties were especially well represented among the female workforce. The paychecks that women brought home put within family reach home purchases, European vacations, or special after-school activities or even college for their children.

These advances highlighted for more and more working women the discrimination they suffered. They were still segregated into such "gender-appropriate" occupational areas as clerical, retail sales, nursing, and teaching at the elementary level, with few if any chances for advancement. The better-paid professions were largely closed in part because of educational restrictions but also because of hiring and promotion biases. Women seldom received pay comparable to men with similar qualifications and experience performing the same job.

In 1969 Betty Friedan's *The Feminine Mystique*, published the year after *Silent Spring*, articulated the discontent many women felt and marked a no less seismic shift in popular attitudes. While Carson championed respect for nature and protection of the environment, Friedan made the case for American women participating more fully and freely in the workforce and thereby gaining the means to realize their full individual potential.

Friedan had come to confront this issue in the late 1950s. Married with three children and struggling to sustain a freelance writing career, she had helped with a revealing survey of her fellow alumnae from the class of 1942 at Smith College. Respondents who had played a role not just in the home but also in the broader world of work and professional advancement seemed more content with their lives, whereas many of the women who had stayed at home expressed frustration and unhappiness. Friedan's interest in this disparity deepened after talking to current Smith students, who seemed to have absorbed the socially conservative 1950s message that even educated women were not to have ambitions beyond domesticity and community service. A more widely cast set of interviews soon confirmed her suspicion that women were ill served when they had to choose between the stark alternatives of home or work—between the popular notions of becoming either loveless, masculine, incomplete career women or nurturing, protected, and adored wives and mothers. When magazine editors shied away from the story, Friedan resolved to do a book on the "feminine mystique" that she saw constraining postwar women's options.

The energy that Friedan threw into the project, and that would thrust her forward as a leading voice for women in the United States and around the world, derived from the way the Smith survey results confirmed her own experience. A woman of remarkable energy and intelligence, she had been stifled by the expectations of her parents, teachers, and classmates growing up in Peoria, Illinois, in the interwar years. Once enrolled at Smith, Friedan had blossomed. But as graduation approached, social pressures and her own self-doubt ate away at her ambition and ultimately closed off a professional career in her chosen field of psychology. Journalism proved an unwelcoming career path. Why couldn't a woman both have a family and work? Why were men so uneasy with and dominant social values so hostile to working women? Writing the book that would answer these questions was, Friedan later recalled, "mysterious, awesome." The process "took me over. It's as if my whole life, including the mistakes, the pains, the paths not taken, had prepared me for this."[23]

The success of *The Feminine Mystique* proved a surprise. By 1970 the volume had sold some three million copies. It became something of a bible for feminists and a spur to political activism. Friedan went on tour, lecturing widely, appearing on radio and TV talk shows, and building networks of influential professional women determined to fight discrimination. Frustrated by state and federal officials' indifference to job discrimination, Friedan concluded that women needed an advocacy group to make the case for equal rights just as African Americans were doing through the NAACP.

NOW, the National Organization for Women, was formally organized in 1966 at a Washington, DC, meeting of some 30 women from diverse professional backgrounds. Friedan herself helped draft the founding statement laying out the bread-and-butter issues on which she thought most women wanted to focus. The NOW statement called for "true equality for all women" and "full participation in the mainstream of American society." If women were to realize their potential and gain a prominent role in decision making, they would have "to break through the silken curtain of prejudice and discrimination" blocking their way in every area of public life, from government and industry to education and the churches. NOW demanded the removal of all barriers to "equal professional and economic advance."[24]

During the early 1960s, politicians had begun to recognize the frustrations that professional women were feeling and that Friedan was voicing. In 1961 President Kennedy appointed a commission to review the status of women. The commission's 1963 report recommended not just an end to inequities in government jobs but also paid maternity leaves, greater access to education, financial help for women seeking to enter the labor force, and child-care centers. Important legislative victories quickly followed. The Equal Pay Act of 1963 stipulated that women receive the same pay as men for the same work, while the Civil Rights Act of 1964 outlawed workplace discrimination on the basis of sex as well as race. But the federal and state governments were equally resistant to enforcing these protections. It was this very resistance to change that supplied the impetus for the organization of NOW in 1966, two years after the passage of landmark but initially empty civil rights legislation.

The 1960s and 1970s were marked by an upsurge in feminist activism. NOW took the lead, applying political pressure, litigating, and shaping public opinion. Other groups soon followed in what quickly turned into a highly diverse, grassroots movement to redefine the social as well as economic role of women and remove rigid notions of gender relations and identities. For the white, middle-class mainstream that Friedan represented, the women's movement meant primarily equal access to jobs, education, and individual control of reproduction. More radical groups called for a fundamental remake of social attitudes and practices. Radicals were dismayed by the resistance of many to changing gender roles and impatient with the macho, condescending attitude that they had encountered from the men leading the civil rights, antiwar, and student movements during the 1960s. They wanted an end to the objectification of women (for example, outlawing pornography). They wanted space apart from the repressive atmosphere of male-dominated institutions (for example, through women's health collectives, rape-crisis centers, and women's studies programs at the college level). They sought recognition that the concerns and needs of minority women were often distinct. They wanted acceptance for lesbianism and other forms of sexual freedom. And they reached out to Third World women on the basis of presumed common outlooks and interests.

Out of this multifaceted women's movement had come already by the early 1970s a string of major achievements: the repeal of abortion laws, expanded career opportunities backed by legal enforcement, and soul-searching among men about their relationship with women as partners and as coworkers. Young women were the primary beneficiaries of the new dispensation. They began breaking into such male bastions as medicine and the law. By 1980 more than half of women with children under six were employed, and only 15 percent of all families fit the old ideal of a working father and a stay-at-home mother (down dramatically from 70 percent in the 1950s). At the same time divorce rates climbed, and single-parent households, usually headed by women with limited income, rose from 11 percent in 1964 to 23 percent in 1980. And despite advances, women still held a disproportionate share of jobs in the low and dead-end part of the economy and accounted for most of the adults living in poverty.

The burgeoning U.S. women's movement had a western European counterpart whose story diverges in important ways. It unfolded against the backdrop of a war that had inflicted widespread suffering and disrupted family life. The end of the war left European women facing notably greater social disorder. Some had lost husbands, and others found that the men returning from war and prison camps

were strangers. Food was in short supply, and the housing stock reduced by bombing. Established notions of domesticity, epitomized for example in France by the
term "femme au foyer" (woman in the home), placed on women the special responsibility for family care, especially during the difficult early postwar period. With
that challenge surmounted, women encountered a new emphasis on making housework efficient, even scientific, a trend encouraged by experts, classes, and how-
to manuals. The appearance of domestic appliances associated with the emerging
postwar consumer trends had already by the 1950s begun to make housework
easier. Leading the way were refrigerators, vacuum cleaners, and above all semi-
automatic washing machines. So eager were women for mechanical relief from the
drudgery of washing that working-class women who could not afford their own
pooled their funds to purchase one for shared use.

In the context of rising postwar prosperity, European women moved into the
workplace, but on nothing like the scale seen in the United States. The rise in the
proportion of women working outside the home was modest to nil on the continent and closer to U.S. percentages in Britain (Table 5.1). Women in the workplace
ran up against the same barriers of lower pay, restricted opportunity, lack of job
security, and discrimination experienced by their American sisters. Some had
also, like their American counterparts, been galvanized by the macho behavior of
men leading movements for social change.

Feminism in Europe exploded on the scene during the late 1960s and early
1970s in rough parallel with the U.S. movement. European feminists espoused a
diverse range of causes and ideologies. One strain had ties to the American movement for equal rights. It was influenced by *The Second Sex*, published in 1949 by the
pioneer French feminist Simone de Beauvoir, as well as by that American import,
Friedan's *The Feminine Mystique*. Middle-class women read in their translations of
Friedan about suburban U.S. women with a shock of recognition: "I saw them every

TABLE 5.1 Percentage of Women in the First World Workforce, 1950–1980					
	1950	1960	1970	1980	Total Change
United States	37	43	49	59	22
Britain	41	46	51	58	18
West Germany	44	49	48	49	5
France	50	46	48	53	3
Italy	32	37	30	32	0
Japan	58	60	55	52	−6

This chart reveals that the highest increases occurred in the Anglo-American economies and that changes
on the European continent and in Japan were distinctly more modest. Definitions of "work" vary from one
study to another and thus strikingly different data emerge. However, the general variation from country to
country noted here is reflected in all the studies.[25]

day. They were my neighbors."[26] European feminists echoed the demands laid down by NOW in 1966 for greater equality as well as for control of reproductive rights. For example, women in France had not gotten the vote until 1944, and thereafter made slow headway in expanding formal equality from politics to such matters of family law as control of property, contraception, and divorce. Everywhere abortion remained highly controversial. With abortion largely illegal, demands for access to contraceptive devices and medical guidance on birth control intensified through the late 1950s and 1960s. Opponents of the pill responded that legalization would take from men "the proud consciousness of their virility" and make women "no more than objects of sterile voluptuousness."[27] Not until 1967 did the French parliament accommodate women's demands, and even then legalization was qualified. West Germany had adopted such a measure in 1961, but the Italian government did not act until 1971.

However, in broad terms, activist European women stressed alongside equality the importance of transforming society to take account of what they saw as the special concerns and needs of women and the family. This European "social feminism" reflected the conviction that women were not essentially the same as men and that it was a mistake to pursue demands for identical support and opportunities. To the contrary, women had interests to advance that were in critical respects different because women were fundamentally different from men in psychology and in physiology and by extension in the indispensable reproductive role they played as the bearers and nurturers of children. A society cut to the measure of men ill served women and harmed the overall interests of society. This social feminist stress on gender difference rather than simply equality was especially strong in Italy and France.

Social feminism appealed across a broad political spectrum. The Catholic center and right favored women staying at home and, to make it economically possible, supported a family allowance. The Left, on the other hand, took the view that women needed help in managing both work and home and thus embraced such programs as nationally funded day-care facilities, parental leave, shorter workdays, and welfare programs more responsive to the needs of mothers. Going a step further, to ensure that women had a voice in devising and implementing these programs, political parties and labor unions on the Left were strongly committed to getting women into elected and appointed public office. As a result, women's participation in political life in most European countries would far exceed the U.S. level. By the 1990s women in Scandinavia held legislative seats at rates six or seven times that in the United States, while in Austria, Germany, the Netherlands, Italy, and Spain it was anywhere from two to five times higher. From their position of influence within the political process, these activist women worked for programs that supported mothers and children.

If the American feminist movement bore some resemblance to that in Europe, it was largely irrelevant to developments in Japan. Postwar prosperity had seemed to set the stage for women moving into the workforce and then asserting a claim to greater opportunity and state support. As the economy recovered, consumer spending jumped. With household appliances to pay off, perhaps the first small car to buy, the children's college education to cover, and even a small apartment to purchase, Japanese women seemed headed toward new economic and social roles. But in fact changes came slowly and remained limited as Japanese women operated within rules that looked a lot like their own version of the "feminine mystique." The activism that did develop more resembled European social feminism than the individualistic and egalitarian concerns of Friedan and NOW.

Most Japanese understood the role of women in terms of "good wife, wise mother." This gender paradigm had emerged at the end of the nineteenth century and had with variations survived the upheaval of early twentieth-century modernization and the Pacific War. In the postwar era, it enjoyed the backing of politicians in the dominant Liberal Democratic Party, government bureaucrats, and employers. The "good wife, wise mother" ideology held essentially that women had a role in the home that was separate but complementary with the working, public role of men. Accordingly, women followed their own educational track. They usually attended junior colleges rather than the four-year institutions designed for men. There they took courses that prepared them for running the household (including managing the family budget) and raising children. Once out of school, single women might work full-time, but once married (as all women were expected to do) family duties became a full-time job. In the ideal "three-generation household," there were children to bear and raise and a husband to support, but also aging parents or in-laws to care for.

This governing gender ideology demonstrated its power by withstanding two challenges in the 1960s and 1970s. The first of these was a labor shortage that began to appear in the early 1960s, creating a demand for older, married women to return to work. Because they were having fewer children and living far longer, these women responded and became part-timers. They could thus raise family income while still attending to their domestic duties. State policies endorsed this solution, and employers welcomed the infusion of flexible labor into low-paying positions. Because they had no job security, older women could be added to boost production and then laid off during slack time. In contrast to full-time male workers, firing female part-timers did not deprive the family of its main source of income, create social instability, or stir up labor unrest.

The governing gender ideology also demonstrated its power by withstanding the claims of rights-based feminism, which dominated in the United States and was influential in Europe. Feminist organizations sprang to life in Japan as they had elsewhere during the 1960s and early 1970s. Activists most often came out of campus-based groups and the anti-Vietnam War protest, gathered for the first women's liberation conference in 1971, read Friedan's *The Feminine Mystique* (translated in 1971), and followed developments in the United States. But the membership of these organizations remained small, and their initial focus on consciousness-raising had limited public appeal. The sign carried in a 1970 march asking "Mother, is marriage really bliss?"[28] seemed to strike at the family as the bedrock of Japanese society and to commit the heresy of setting the rights of the individual above the needs of the group. By the mid-1970s women's groups had broadened their appeal by shifting attention to the reform of social institutions and government policy so that women would have more choices in schools, in the workplace, and in marriage.

Women remained politically reticent. The constitution drafted and imposed by the American occupiers had included sweeping guarantees of equal rights, including for the first time the right for women to vote. However, interviewed on the subject of voting, women claimed that they cast their ballots not because they prized the right but because it was a new social expectation that they had to live up to. Predictably, few women ran for political office or held positions of authority within the influential state bureaucracy. Where women did protest, they acted not as advocates for their own interests but as defenders of the family and thus more in line with social feminist impulses. They demanded protection of consumers and the environment, and they sharply criticized the nuclear arms race, the presence of U.S. nuclear forces on Japanese soil, and steps toward remilitarization by their own country. Precisely because all these issues had a bearing on the health of their children and the safety of their families, women's organizations raised their voices and took to the streets.

Critics of Unequal Development

While some within the developed world began to fret over the pollution created by an economy of abundance and over constraints placed on women to work and articulate their needs within that economy, critics in the developing world were posing their own challenges to the economic regime. These critics argued that the rules laid down by the United States and Britain at Bretton Woods benefited wealthy countries at the expense of the poor. In particular those rules, they complained, discouraged far-reaching state planning and economic intervention best suited to meeting the urgent development needs of the Third World. Moreover, those rules prescribed a regimen of free foreign trade and free foreign investment calculated to help the developed world while in fact subjecting strategic sectors of Third World economies to foreign control.

These views had their roots in Europe. There countries, notably Germany and Italy during the interwar years, had built tariff walls around their economies. Behind this protective barrier the state had sought to coordinate domestic labor and capital and harness them to national goals. This pattern of development had crossed the Atlantic to Latin American states headed by elites with close cultural and economic ties to Europe, prevailed in key economies during the interwar years, and persisted well into the post-1945 period. This model and the charges its proponents lodged against free trade reverberated powerfully in Third World countries. But the influence of this Latin American development model was to be defuse.

By the time Third World countries began emerging in large numbers from coloni-alism in the 1960s, Latin Americans were reassessing their protectionist policies, while many leaders among the newly independent states in places as diverse as Ghana, Cuba, and Egypt (as we will see in Chapter 6) rejected the relative moder-ation of the Latin American model in favor of state socialism modeled on either the Chinese or Soviet variant.

Already in the late 1940s, the critics of unbalanced development had formu-lated a coherent alternative to the Anglo-American model. Their base was the Eco-nomic Commission for Latin America created by the United Nations in 1948 and located in Santiago, Chile. The head of the Commission and the best known of these early critics was the Argentine economist Raúl Prebisch. He and his able as-sociates came to be known as "structuralists" for their argument that economic inequality and distorted development was built into—indeed, was an inherent, structural feature of—the global system of exchange.

Experience running his country's central bank from the mid-1930s had led Prebisch to question the model of export-led growth. This talented, original thinker came to the conclusion that the participants in the free-trade regime had unequal power. The powerful central economies that manufactured industrial goods, notably Britain and the United States, could control the price of their exports. Moreover, as technology reduced production costs, they could sustain their old prices, thus securing a larger profit margin. Agricultural producers on the per-iphery of the international economy, such as farmers in his native Argentina, were disadvantaged by this system. Competition among them drove down prices for their exports at the same time that industrial imports remained expensive. The growing postwar prominence of the United States was likely, Prebisch pre-dicted, to accentuate this plight of the peripheral economies because the United States had its own highly developed agriculture and had little use for imported agricultural goods.

These unequal terms of trade were deeply damaging, structuralists contended. They drained wealth from struggling Third World countries to already rich and de-veloped economies. Thanks to accumulating capital, the central economies were able to invest in new, more advanced forms of production while maintaining their dominance over their Third World trading partners. Not only did peripheral econo-mies remain poor and technologically laggard, but they also suffered an internal division between an outward-looking export sector and a large, backward, and stagnant subsistence agricultural sector. The latter was burdened by surplus labor that kept wages and overall domestic buying power down. To increase inter-national trade, as the United States and others wanted, would only intensify inter-national economic inequalities and deepen the internal divisions within Third World economies.

To escape these fundamental structural constraints, Prebisch recommended that those economies embark on a program of "import substitution," replacing the industrial imports coming from the advanced economies with homegrown industry. He assigned the state a prominent role as the promoter and protector of domestic industry. The state might impose tariffs on industrial imports to secure infant industries against foreign competition and create the domestic investment and demand for their products that would ensure their steady maturation. The state might also take over pivotal industrial enterprises as well as finance and communications and promote unionization to ensure a fair distribution of the benefits of industrial growth.

Import substitution would in Prebisch's view bring a long list of benefits. It would reduce dependence on high-priced imports and pressure to export low-value agricultural products to pay for those imports. It would raise domestic employment and income and thus create a growing domestic market for continuing industrial development. It would end the stagnation that plagued much of the traditional economy, integrate the national economy, and improve popular welfare. In the long run diversifying economic activity seemed the best way to ensure self-sustaining growth and a degree of insulation from the swings in international markets and from the pressures that major economies were sure to apply to advance their own interests.

Writing in the late 1940s, Prebisch and his colleagues provided the rationale for an approach already well established in practice. The Depression and World War II had in effect imposed an experiment in import substitution on such leading Latin American economies as Argentina, Chile, Brazil, and Mexico (see Map 6.1 on p. 250). The Depression had caused a drastic drop in international demand for their agricultural exports, and with lower foreign earnings went difficulties in paying for industrial imports. The problem continued with the outbreak of World War II. As the economies of the belligerents turned to military production, they sharply curtailed the export of manufactured goods, creating shortages abroad. With international demand for Latin American raw materials high during the war and during the early stage of postwar reconstruction, late industrializers had a favorable environment for experimenting with new development strategies.

The major economies of Latin America responded to these developments in an ad hoc fashion. With finished goods now difficult to buy abroad, established domestic industries expanded and new industries started up. Then in the early 1940s, authoritarian governments in Argentina, Chile, Brazil, and Mexico began intervening to further encourage the growth of the advanced industrial sector. These governments set up tariffs and other protections against foreign competition, invested in infrastructure, and nationalized key industrial sectors (steel in Brazil and Chile and oil in Argentina and Mexico). These initiatives proved successful. Latin American economies began using more of their raw materials at home rather than exporting them. This strategy accelerated the pace of job creation and pushed annual growth rates higher.

With these successes to point to, structuralist thinking had by the 1950s become the new orthodoxy in Latin America and gained a wide following outside the region, in newly independent countries inclined to look to the state as the prime agent of rapid economic development. As early as 1947, during negotiations in Havana over the rules to govern international trade, delegations from Latin America as well as newly independent India sought to define national sovereignty to include such forms of state economic intervention as nationalization of foreign holdings and protection of nascent industries against imports. These mavericks also pressed developed countries to open their markets more fully to the exports from poorer countries.

The Third World countries' call for both greater latitude in development policy and assistance from the developed world would remain a refrain throughout the Cold War. Leaders such as Mosaddeq, Nehru, and Nasser sounded the call in the 1950s. The first meeting of the non-aligned, held in Bandung, Indonesia, in 1955, pushed the issue on to the international agenda. As the number of newly independent states grew rapidly in the 1960s, the UN General Assembly became a forum for pressing their demands. There a concert of developing countries known as the Group of 77 (formed in 1964) was vocal in calling for reform of an international economic system that seemed to serve the interests of foreign corporations and investors and thus to perpetuate the influence of the old colonial powers. They demanded nothing less than an end to this neo-colonialism and an opportunity to chart an autonomous path of economic development.

Not surprisingly, neither Prebisch's views nor more generally the reliance on the state to spur economic growth and industrialization favored by the main Latin American economies and others in the Third World found favor in Washington. U.S. leaders complained that inward-looking economies burdened by state intervention ill served the interests of Third World peoples. President Harry S. Truman reflected the free-market orthodoxy when he assigned private capital the leading role in creating prosperity. If Latin Americans wanted to attract investment from abroad, hold accumulated wealth at home, and maintain stability against leftist or populist agitation, they had to free their economies and respect the rights of private property. American-style capitalism offered a way to a better life.

American academics at Harvard and MIT reinforced this U.S. orthodoxy. These proponents of what would become known as modernization theory argued that the main task for developing countries was to make the transition from "traditional" subsistence economies to ones that were "modern" (meaning technological, capital intensive, and industrial), and that to get there required a free market, supplemented by U.S. economic aid and advice. Together free-market policies and outside assistance would lead developing countries quickly along an economic path that the developed economies had already taken. As one of the leading writers on modernization explained, "What had happened in Europe and North America in the 19th and early 20th centuries was now, more or less, about to happen in Latin America, Asia, and Africa. The progress promised by the [West's] enlightenment . . . now beckoned the Third World newly freed from colonialism and exploitation, and straining against its own parochialisms."[29] The practical goal of modernization U.S.-style was to head off the appeal of communism by promoting material progress and political stability. Notions of proper economic development thus closely dovetailed with the U.S. policy of containment. Modernization theory gave U.S. policymakers good reason to redirect a growing proportion of U.S. development assistance away from a recovering Europe during the late 1950s; soon virtually all of it was going to the Third World.

By the early 1960s structuralism was facing criticism within Latin America as well. Import-substitution programs had faltered over the previous decade. Leading economies had been hurt by a decline in agricultural demand and by the onset of inflation. Latin American economists with a free-market preference went on the attack, arguing that their countries should follow the U.S. advice and rejoin the international economy. Export-import was the best path to prosperity.

Economists with roots in the structuralist school resisted the swing back to free trade. They argued that the structural policies of the 1950s had gotten into trouble not because they were wrong but because the sources of unbalanced development in Latin America were more profound than previously appreciated. Prebisch noticed growing income disparities within Mexico, Brazil, and Argentina, where the wealthy spent their money on imported luxury goods rather than productive investment, while popular demand for domestic products was weak. By 1963 he was calling for internal social reforms (including land and income redistribution to close the wealth gap), controls on non-essential imports, and measures to stimulate demand for domestically produced goods. Prebisch was also worried by the neglect of investment in education needed to train a skilled workforce and by the inefficiencies that had developed within Latin America's protected industries.

An increasingly unsettled, polarized political setting pushed critics of Latin American structural inequalities toward a more radical analysis. Repressive military regimes took power in Brazil in 1964 and in Argentina in 1966. They both sought close ties with the United States. The Cuban revolution, on the other hand, broke with Washington in order to pursue its own independent development path to economic development (see Chapter 6). Agitated policymakers in the Kennedy and Johnson administrations were as supportive of military coups as they were opposed to Cuba's revolution. Reflecting the rising U.S. intolerance of diversity within the hemisphere, the Johnson administration shifted away from Kennedy's reform-oriented Alliance for Progress and in 1965 invaded the Dominican Republic to arrest perceived communist inroads.

Against this backdrop, some critics moved beyond the import-substitution approach in favor of what came to be known as the dependency school. In their view, the problem confronting the Third World was the capacity of advanced economies to create a class of dependent collaborators within peripheral economies. These collaborators helped multinational corporations exploit the labor and resources of their country, and for that assistance were richly rewarded and where necessary protected against any internal threat to their dominant economic position as landlords growing export crops and employing large numbers of low-paid workers in plantation agriculture. Dependency scholars were in effect charging that the landed elites functioned as instruments of the dominant powers in the global economy. Those elites were indifferent to the plight of the people around them and were primarily oriented overseas, where they not only sent their children to school but also invested much of their wealth. By creating and defending inequalities in the social and political life of their countries, these capitalist collaborators sparked popular discontent as well as created rigidities that impeded long-term economic development. Conditions in Central American countries such as Guatemala corresponded closely to this dependency interpretation (see Chapter 6).

The dependency school took direct issue with U.S. economic orthodoxy. In their estimate, North American ideas about modernization were ethnocentric. Not all countries were like the United States, and not all countries would travel the same development path. In fact, notions of modernization in the hands of American academics and policy pundits seemed suspiciously like a rationalization of U.S. dominance within the hemisphere. Latin American and other countries around the world that would not fall into line and allow favorable access to their raw materials and markets faced retaliation. Washington would block investment and aid, impose trade sanctions, and as a last resort overthrow offending regimes by subversion or outright invasion.

By the late 1960s and 1970s dependency ideas were gaining wide currency on the Left in Latin America and abroad, but they never won the official acceptance that structuralism had earlier enjoyed. Although Prebisch had had an affinity for dependency analysis, he never become a convert, and his import-substitution ideas still exercised considerable mainstream appeal. Latin American governments during the 1960s and 1970s combined to various degrees import substitution with international integration financed by foreign investments and facilitated by multinational corporations.

Argentina offers a good example of the divisions over the best development path to follow. Juan Perón, the dominant political figure during the mid-1940s, had at first favored state-sponsored industrialization and had catered to the working class mobilized politically in state-controlled unions. He had nationalized such key sectors as railroads, banks, insurance, and shipping. He had created a state agency to market the country's major exports and to direct domestic investments. But after the economy began slowing in 1952, Perón took a friendlier attitude toward foreign investors. After the military seized power in 1955, it continued the trend toward a more free-market strategy. The trend intensified following a second military coup in 1966 and yet a third in 1976 after an interval of Peronist rule. The military government attacked unions, froze wages, privatized public companies, and courted foreign investors. Popular resentment in turn spawned resistance from the Left, including urban guerrilla movements. Strong in their Catholic faith, the generals and admirals in charge launched an inquisition "against the idolators of totalitarianism." As many as 30,000 of their fellow citizens "disappeared" in the process. Increasingly broad-based political opposition and a debt crisis combined with defeat at the hands of the British in 1982 in a struggle over the Falkland

Islands to finally discredit military rule and open the way to a return to elections and civilian control.[30]

In Chile the retreat from activist state involvement in the economy came later—but it came suddenly, violently, and decisively. The socialist government of Salvador Allende Gossens, elected in 1970, had sought to push through long-stalled social and economic reforms. With divisions within the country deepening and the Nixon administration pressing for a coup, the military seized power in 1973 and brutally repressed the opposition, killing up to 14,000.[31] It quickly repudiated the course of heavy state intervention promoted by Allende and his predecessors, and insisted on a rapid and thorough shift to free markets and integration into the international economy. That shift would define Chile's policy even after the military returned to the barracks in the late 1980s.

In Brazil, import substitution survived despite growing emphasis on international economic integration. The dictator Getúlio Vargas, who had dominated the political scene from the 1930s until his suicide in 1954, had sustained a strategy of heavy state involvement. Successor governments hewed to that popular course while trying to address the long-neglected problem of concentrated landholdings in the rural sector. Resentful landed families resisted those reforms, and in 1964 the military sided with them, seized power, and dramatically altered economic policy. It cut state spending and encouraged an import-export economy. The strategy at first produced rapid growth, but in 1974, under pressure from a flagging global economy, the military made another dramatic shift—back to import substitution, higher government spending, and greater state involvement in the industrial sector. That policy would soon fall victim to a debt crisis similar to the one

CRITICS OF THE POSTWAR ECONOMIC ORDER	
1948	Creation of United Nations Economic Commission for Latin America based in Santiago, Chile; Raúl Prebisch makes it the center of the structuralist approach to development
1949	Simone de Beauvoir publishes *The Second Sex*
1962	Rachel Carson's *Silent Spring* published
1963	Betty Friedan's *The Feminine Mystique* published
1966	National Organization for Women established; Argentine military government shifts away from import substitution, marking a trend within the region toward free-market policies
1970	First Earth Day organized in the United States
1980	Approximately half of all women in the United States, Britain, France, and Germany are in the workforce

that constrained the Argentines. In Brazil as in Argentina, by the early 1980s the military was ready to give up power and leave to civilians the burden of managing an economy now in crisis.

Mexico proved the most consistent practitioner of internal industrialization and protection against foreign goods and capital. This consistency was the product of the governing party's continued iron grip on political power and of the popularity of economic measures that produced a growth rate in the range of 6 to 8 percent from the 1950s to the mid-1970s. During the latter part of this period, a major oil boom contributed significantly to Mexico's success. Industry and the service sector grew dramatically. But as with Argentina and Brazil, financial crisis would grip Mexico in the 1980s. The result was at last a long and at times painful retreat from the protectionism that had helped produce industrialization and prosperity. Mexico embraced a course that would lead to economic integration with its neighbors to the north.

CONCLUSION

The success of the international economy in the 1950s and 1960s had a paradoxical quality for Americans. That period marked the high point of their country's power and influence. Just as the United States led the anticommunist coalition of states that it had formed soon after World War II, so too did it preside over a global economy shaped to its preferences and lavish in its rewards to its citizens. Americans enjoyed a golden age of prosperity during which many came to see the promise of American life more in terms of an ever-rising level of material abundance than the prosecution of the global anticommunist struggle. The nuclear crisis over Cuba and the growing costs and disruption occasioned by the Vietnam War drove home the point that the fundamental American international and domestic preoccupations were not necessarily compatible. Basic economic weaknesses such as low savings rates along with competition from other developed economies began to diminish the relative power of the United States. Washington had increasingly to take into account the views of its once-junior partners across the Atlantic and Pacific. Americans were on the brink of a dispiriting period when both the promise of abundance at home and the proud role of freedom's defender abroad would fall into question.

Western Europeans and Japanese had acquired the power to alter the international landscape because each had crafted in the early postwar period an effective economic strategy suited to their particular political and cultural preferences. Their choices—welfare capitalism in one case and guided capitalism in the other—paid handsome dividends, a period of sustained prosperity and stability without equal in the history of either. Income levels rapidly rising toward that of the United States translated into a flourishing consumer lifestyle. In western Europe, with these economic successes came greater economic integration. The EC would prove a herald of more ambitious plans for regional integration. The Japanese economic miracle ratified another kind of integration, a powerful establishment consisting of corporate leaders, government bureaucrats, and prominent politicians working closely to ensure Japanese international competitiveness and domestic prosperity.

The very prosperity of the 1950s and 1960s encouraged, in some quarters at least, critical reflections on the flaws of the dominant system of production. Critics decried its tendency to privilege men, wealthy countries, and short-term gain over long-term welfare. Critics such as Western feminists asking for a share of the growing economic pie were relatively easy to accommodate, but those such as environmentalists and advocates for the Third World calling for deep-seated, structural changes posed an unsettling and less easily answered challenge. Those questioning a new world of abundance that damaged the environment, made half the population second-class citizens, and distributed its benefits unevenly so that the rich became richer and the poor poorer would continue to speak out, intensifying concerns over flaws in the decades to come over what was to become an increasingly globalized economic system.

6
THIRD WORLD HOPES AT HIGH TIDE

BY THE 1960s the Third World had reached the flood tide of change. Demands for decolonization were overwhelming the old colonial powers. At the same time nominally independent states had begun to assert their right to chart an autonomous course free of foreign interference. Those leading this assault on the old order shared a vision of national liberation and domestic renovation. They saw independence not just as a formal condition easily met once the offending foreigners decamped but rather as one step toward sweeping internal changes. They sought economic autonomy and development. They wanted to replace a national psychology of dependence with one of pride. They aimed to heal social divisions created by long-term foreign influence and to fashion programs with popular appeal. They even looked beyond their borders, where they hoped to join with like-minded states in constituting an international community friendly to a new order of things. In this heady time, it was easy to believe that more and more people around the world would embrace the Marxist critique of capitalism and take the socialist model of development as their own.

This radical impulse played out in four distinct regions. By looking at each in turn we can see how that general impulse varied in its origins and consequences and how it intersected in different ways with the Cold War while setting bounds on the U.S.-sponsored, market-oriented international economy. We begin by returning to the two countries whose revolutions foreshadowed the growing ferment of the 1950s and 1960s. Revolutions in East Asia—in China and in Vietnam—entered a new stage, and by their strength and persistence became as much a source of inspiration to others in the Third World as they were a cause for alarm in Washington. We will then turn to the two regions that began to stir for the first time in the 1950s—the Caribbean and sub-Saharan Africa—and look closely at the cases of Guatemala, Cuba, and Ghana. Finally, we will turn to the Middle East and North Africa, where radicals in Iran, Egypt, and Algeria committed to combating Western influence and renovating indigenous institutions made dramatic advances. Whatever the differences among these cases, all reveal the sharp discontents with the old order long taking shape in the Third World. Calls for patience and moderation went out of season, while bold plans flourished.

REVOLUTIONARY TRAJECTORIES IN EAST ASIA

China and Vietnam had both embarked on a revolutionary path guided by an attachment to centralized political power (see Chapter 3). However, during the 1950s their courses diverged. After taking power in 1949, Mao Zedong's Communists set to work consolidating political control, redefining China's relationship with the superpowers, restoring its hold over border regions, and reviving its economy. With this ambitious program largely completed, Mao began in the mid-1950s to indulge utopian notions of fundamentally transforming Chinese society. As a result, an aging, stubborn leader would plunge China into chaos and precipitate a basic shift in China's development path. Ho Chi Minh was, by contrast, still mired in the struggle to rid Vietnam's "sacred soil" of the foreign presence. No sooner had his forces defeated the French than the Americans stepped in. After trying to limit U.S. involvement through the late 1950s and early 1960s, Vietnamese Communists finally took up the challenge of destroying U.S. resolve just as they had with the French. Radical domestic programs had in the main to take a backseat during this exhausting battle to reunite the country.

The Maoist Experiment in China

In the course of the 1950s the Communist leaders of the People's Republic translated their general vision of building a "new socialist China" into concrete measures. A poor China desperately needed to build on its most advanced sectors—the cities and the more industrialized coastal provinces. To that end the party leaders determined to first tame the bourgeoisie (the better-off and educated living in cities) and then use their talents and their expropriated resources to restore the economy and stimulate growth. Mao had effectively jettisoned the New Democratic program on which the CCP had taken power. He was moreover ready to push hard for a more revolutionary strategy—to maintain the equality, personal sacrifice, and popular mobilization that had marked the party's pre-1949 period of struggle. Mao was haunted by the fear that China's revolutionary spirit would die away and remnants of the old society would reappear. He saw the major danger coming from bureaucrats and technical experts and from the vestiges of the bourgeois class, which seemed to him to have almost magical powers of regeneration. In Mao's view, periodic campaigns against state and party officials and "the intellectuals" (by which Mao meant the educated and politically engaged) were needed to prevent the rise of a new, privileged class. In thus setting his sights on continuously rejuvenating the party's and the people's revolutionary commitment, Mao looked to the rural poor and educated young as his most reliable allies.

Tension at the top developed as Mao increasingly insisted on following his own insights and judgments and began to intervene in daily policymaking, thus betraying the principle of collective decision making. In 1950 Mao overruled his colleagues who questioned the wisdom of confronting a nuclear-armed United States in Korea. Mao again acted on his own in 1952 when he abandoned party plans to stress the multiclass alliance that had helped win the civil war and that the party leadership had deemed important to economic development. This shift removed the bourgeoisie from the revolutionary coalition. In May 1953 Mao wrested from his colleagues the right of ultimate approval of all documents sent out from the party center. About the same time he resolved to push peasants toward fully collectivized agriculture. By 1955–1956 peasants had handed over their private land, tools, and farm animals to shared enterprises that paid them in relation to their labor contribution, measured in work points. Only the land on which their houses stood remained private.

In pursuing this path Mao acted on his faith, unsupported by evidence, that tapping the spontaneous energy and supposed socialist instincts of the peasantry would unleash new productive forces in the countryside. His skeptical colleagues objected to Mao's insistence on haste and on a single policy applied to China's diverse agricultural conditions. This "adventurism," they warned, had China racing toward socialism faster than the country's still short economic legs could carry it. Mao dismissed these objections for their excessive caution: "Some of our comrades are tottering along like a woman with bound feet, always complaining that others are going too fast."[1]

By the late 1950s Mao's discontents had reached a boiling point. He blamed an ossifying and privileged party and state bureaucracy for favoring urban intellectuals and the experts, while the rural poor lagged ever farther behind. The 1956 upheavals in Poland and Hungary strengthened his fear that Communist parties could lose touch with the people. Mao was also turning against the Soviet model of economic development, formally copied in 1953 with the PRC's first five-year plan and backed with Soviet aid and advisers. Instead of slavishly copying the Soviets by nationalizing private enterprise, building up state-controlled heavy industry, and promoting technical expertise, Mao wanted a distinctly Chinese model of development.

Once aroused, Mao took the offensive. In 1957 he invited intellectuals to criticize CCP errors in what he described as letting "a hundred schools of thought contend, a hundred flowers bloom." But rather than simply questioning CCP methods, some among the educated began to question the party's very legitimacy. Their response convinced Mao that his revolution was in even greater danger than he had thought. He attacked intellectuals suspected of holding "rightist" views in what became a long, dark period for many educated Chinese.

In 1958 Mao took an even bolder step by launching the Great Leap Forward, a visionary economic plan for accelerating China's industrial production. He ordered a still higher, communal form of organization in the countryside with newly formed "people's communes" containing on the average 4,000 households. Peasants now shifted to shared living, eating, and child-care arrangements as well as production responsibilities and resources. They were to start up small-scale steel-making as a demonstration of an alternative to the Soviet model of centralized, large-scale industrial production. With the Great Leap Forward, Mao sought to launch the peasantry into a world of previously unimagined abundance. He argued that rapid socialist development could occur only if "the boundless creative powers" of the masses and their "inexhaustible enthusiasm for socialism" were brought into play.[2] Properly led and inspired, the "poor and blank" could become the main builders of his new society. Within 15 years a mobilized people could catch up with the West, while the communes with their rigorously egalitarian rules would create a classless society and thus take China to communism even before the Soviet Union.

At first hailed inside China as a magnificent success, Mao's experiment ended disastrously. The Great Leap had disrupted planting and harvesting. Flood and drought compounded the crisis. Worst of all was distorted information reaching leaders at the top. Lower-level officials under heavy pressure to meet targets perpetrated various frauds on their superiors to convince them misguided policies were actually working. They passed off specially prepared model plots as typical, and they reported soaring production at a time when it in fact was in free fall. Belatedly Beijing realized that it faced a calamitous situation. Between 1959 and 1961 by conservative estimates some 20 million died as a result of starvation or hunger-related disease. It was perhaps the greatest human disaster in Chinese history or in the annals of a century no stranger to disaster. When faced in 1959 with criticism of his costly economic experiment, Mao confessed, "I am a complete outsider when it comes to economic construction, and I understand nothing about industrial planning."[3] A chastened Mao retreated into a less active policy role between 1960 and 1962, leaving his chief lieutenants—Liu Shaoqi, Deng Xiaoping, and Zhou Enlai—to implement more flexible policies to restore production while preserving collectivization itself.

Mao was by this point deeply worried about the Soviet Union, and his doubts were to destroy the unity of the socialist bloc. He saw the Soviets undergoing a kind of corruption at home as their Communist Party became a new privileged class. This corruption set in doubt Soviet credentials as leader of the bloc and Soviet reliability as an ally to China. Mao had been unhappy with Khrushchev's unilateral denunciation of Stalin, a figure as important to the international communist movement as to the Soviet Union. Mao had resented the Soviet characterization of his Great Leap plans as harebrained and Moscow's reneging on an earlier pledge to supply nuclear technology. He had profoundly disagreed with Khrushchev's call for peaceful coexistence with the United States and chided the Soviets for not keeping up with China's support for national liberation movements in Asia, Africa, and Latin America. In Mao's view, while the masses around the world were putting imperialism on the defensive, the leaders of the Soviet party were cuddling up to the Americans. Mounting Sino-Soviet tensions resulted in a sudden cutoff of Soviet aid in 1960 and by 1963 in a permanent split between the two heavyweights of the socialist bloc. China's test of its first atomic bomb in 1964 added to Beijing's confidence and Moscow's fears.

The Great Proletarian Cultural Revolution, initiated in 1965, marked Mao's second major attempt to promote a distinct, Chinese revolutionary way. Mao still clung to his egalitarian vision—of reducing the differences between manual and mental labor, between peasants and workers, between agriculture and industry. His party colleagues had for the most part stayed on the wrong side of these issues. The exceptions were Lin Biao (the minister of defense) and Jiang Qing, a former actress who had become Mao's wife in 1938. With them behind him, he began making a familiar set of charges. A bureaucratic, bourgeois, "revisionist" spirit had infected his party just as it had the Soviet's. CCP officials were cut off from the people and afraid of criticism. As he graphically put it in 1962, the party harbored "degenerate elements who sit on the heads of people and piss and shit on them, behaving in a vicious and unrestrained way." At the same time he worried that young people were not carrying forward China's revolutionary tradition. He complained in 1963 that they "don't understand the bitterness, the hardships of the Revolution, and what sacrifices it took to get where we are today."[4]

To help cleanse the party and revitalize youthful idealism, the army distributed millions of copies of the "Little Red Book" containing the quotations of Chairman Mao. The pocket-sized guide to correct revolutionary thought and conduct acquired almost holy status and helped to mobilize youth known as Red Guards against party members whose lack of ideological fervor revealed their preference for "following the capitalist road." Mao claimed that these supposed capitalist-roaders were led by none other than his designated successor, Liu Shaoqi. The task of the Red Guards was, in the language of the times, to erase revisionist influences "in politics, in thought, and in theory." The first Red Guard campaign erupted at Beijing University in 1966 and soon spread throughout the country, setting off ever more severe attacks on party leaders, educators, factory managers, newspaper editors—indeed against almost every kind of authority. Mao believed that a little dose of anarchy was just the tonic that China's backsliding revolution needed.

But as authority declined, Mao got more anarchy than perhaps even he wanted. Local conflicts and resentments led to public beatings, torture, executions, damage to cultural treasures, and general insecurity. Many of Mao's old comrades perished in this grim period of persecution. Mao himself did nothing to save Liu Shaoqi or any other party leaders from abuse and death. Finally, in 1968 he ordered Lin Biao's army to restore order, but this proved easier said than done. The Cultural Revolution had degenerated into virtual civil war, with loss of life estimated conservatively in the hundreds of thousands and with millions subjected to persecution. By 1969 the Cultural Revolution as an official mass movement had come to an end, and one by one those who had supported it lost power. Lin Biao was the first to go in 1971 under mysterious circumstances. (Supposedly after a bungled coup

The Red Guards Who Waged Mao's Cultural Revolution
This assemblage of Red Guards reads from the talisman of the Cultural Revolution, the Little Red Book containing the political aphorisms of Chairman Mao. The young revolutionaries were not only armed with the writings of Mao Zedong; presiding over this gathering is the larger-than-life man himself, wearing an armband bearing the characters "Red Guard," leaving little doubt about his support. (Photograph by Camera Press London)

against Mao, Lin fled for the Soviet Union, only to have his plane crash en route.) Lin's demise led to the gradual restoration of the functions of the state and party. In 1972 the Red Guards that Mao had called to life were formally disbanded and sent into the countryside to be "re-educated through labor" alongside the peasants.

Mao's last years were a time of political disappointment and even bitterness. Mao had given his life to building the party and the nation, and he had seen those around him—both family and political associates—suffer for the cause. Yet his dreams of making China into a revolutionary utopia seemed no closer as his life drew to an end. Indeed, those dreams had twice—during the Great Leap and again during the Cultural Revolution—turned into nightmares. The Cultural Revolution had in addition ravaged the party that Mao had created and slain men with whom he had closely collaborated since the 1920s and 1930s. As the author of these disasters, Mao had become his own worst enemy.

Mao was by the early 1970s ill and isolated. He suffered most seriously from a disease that caused progressive degeneration of the nervous system. Lin Biao's betrayal had been a heavy psychological blow. Estranged from Jiang Qing, he found comfort in the young women put at his disposal. He kept at a distance his associates, now behaving like jealous courtiers, each seeking the chairman's favor and each eager to secure power after his death. In July 1976 a massive earthquake shook northern China, killing a quarter of a million people and reviving an old popular conviction that disorder in the natural world mirrored disorder in human affairs. Two months later Mao was dead.

Mao's passing from the scene in September 1976 set the stage for an early, major assessment of his reputation as party leader and founding father of the PRC. Many had reason for a revising of accounts. Each turn of the political wheel by the elderly autocrat had ruined careers and destroyed lives, but many Chinese also credited Mao with great achievements. He had led the CCP to power and laid the enduring foundation for the PRC. He had regained much of the territory once controlled by imperial China. He had forced the major powers to deal with China as an equal and pushed his way into the prestigious club of nuclear-armed powers.

Mao also deserved credit for having overseen a period of generally successful economic development. Despite all his talk of helping the countryside, industry dominated the economy, rising from 30 percent of total output in 1949 to 72 percent by the time of Mao's death in 1976. By that time China had become one of the world's top six industrial powers. Reflecting general economic progress, per capita income quadrupled between 1949 and 1978. Improvements in health care and nutrition raised life expectancy from 35 years before 1949 to 65 years in the mid-1970s.[5] Chinese enjoyed expanded educational opportunities, higher levels of literacy, and in general greater social mobility. The CCP managed to avoid a bloated urban population characteristic of much of the Third World. A strictly enforced pass system kept peasants working on the land rather than becoming marginalized city dwellers living in poverty or straining the welfare system. These achievements provided a basis for the stunning material gains that China would score in the 1980s and 1990s.

For the majority of Chinese—those living in the countryside—the Mao years overall delivered real and wide-ranging benefits. Peasants appreciated the party's success at bringing order and greater security against calamity. The new regime shored up dikes, sprayed against locusts, and provided food and tax relief in lean years. Gradually, the CCP state brought the hallmarks of modernity to the countryside. It promoted better production by introducing chemical fertilizers and new seed strains and by providing technical advice and education. It brought public health campaigns and clinics to villages and extended electricity to power engines, radios, and eventually televisions. It built and upgraded roads, canals, and communications lines that further opened villages to the outside world. Thanks to CCP initiatives, peasants lived healthier, longer, and in general better lives than they had before 1949. Little wonder that many who had suffered during the old order and had benefited from CCP programs grieved over Mao's death in 1976. A longtime village leader gratefully recalling "Chairman Mao's" legacy—"land, an end to banditry, a happy life"—was perhaps not simply parroting the party line.[6]

The rural gains were most marked between 1949 and 1958. Peasants had generally welcomed the early phase of land reform, which had redistributed land on a vast scale, including to land-poor and previously landless rural folk. Many had benefited at the expense of absentee landlords or abusive local bullies. The shift to cooperative arrangements appealed to the poorer peasant families, the overwhelming majority in most villages, who had the most to gain. Full collectivization in the mid-1950s proved a harder sell because it asked peasants to give up the one thing they prized above all else—ownership and control over their land. But peasants were forced to accommodate and hope that the party would once more deliver improvements.

During the Great Leap Forward, Mao rewarded peasants' trust with a famine. Survivors vividly recalled "the torment of hunger" and "the chronic pain in the stomach, the dizziness and emptiness in the head, and the constant craving to chew on something that is solid and edible."[7] Although the famine passed, peasants still had good grounds for complaint well into the 1970s. They were demoralized by central planning that constrained their initiative and judgment and by endless rounds of tiresome and unproductive political meetings. They did lackluster work on the collectives because individual effort bore no relationship to reward; an increase in total output would simply boost government claims on that output. Perhaps most serious of all, neglect of population control during the Mao years left villages with more mouths to feed from only minimally higher levels of agricultural output. As a result, peasants were no better off at the end of the 1970s than they had been two decades earlier on the eve of the Great Leap.

In weighing the achievements of the Mao years, peasant women deserve attention as special beneficiaries. Mao described women as "holding up half the sky," and the CCP had a history of promoting equal rights for women. Once in power, the party abolished a wide range of oppressive practices, including forced marriage, concubinage, infanticide, and foot binding. It legalized divorce and abortion. It made education open to all children. The shift to collective agriculture brought other benefits. Because women were able to earn work points, they helped raise overall household income. Their economic contribution, once taken for granted, received

THE MAOIST PROJECT IN CHINA	
1949	People's Republic of China created, proclaiming a moderate domestic program and pursuing an assertive foreign policy
1955	Mao implements collectivized agriculture
1957	Mao turns on intellectuals for "rightist" tendencies in the "Hundred Flowers" campaign
1958	"Great Leap Forward" inaugurated, resulting in famine and death of an estimated 20 million and Mao's temporary retreat from leadership
1959–60	Open split begins with the Soviet Union
1966	Mao launches the Cultural Revolution, resulting in persecution and violence by Red Guards
1969–71	Mao winds down the Cultural Revolution
1976	Mao's death

official recognition, and women's status in the family and in the community rose accordingly. But revolution hardly ended male dominance. Men still directed production units, and on the whole their work received greater rewards. Men were still the heads of families and village organizations. Sons remained important to continuing the family line, and so giving birth to a son remained a major family preoccupation. Daughters, who traditionally joined their husband's families, were regarded as drains on family resources, and this gender bias would continue well into the twenty-first century.

Vietnam's Fight for the South

While China's revolution could proceed apace after the victory of CCP forces in 1949, Vietnam's Communists had far to go. The triumph over the French in mid-1954 was a major step forward. The agreement reached at the Geneva conference in July of that year ended the colonial era. But the goal of independence for all of Vietnam was still unfulfilled. The great powers had imposed a line of temporary political division at the 17th Parallel (at the country's narrow waist). U.S. leaders wanted to make that division permanent and set aside the Geneva provisions for national elections by 1956 to unite the southern part of the country with the Communist-controlled Democratic Republic of Vietnam (DRV). It would take two decades of struggle and sacrifice to achieve Vietnam's unification.

Initially, between 1954 and 1959, Ho Chi Minh and his colleagues in the Communist capital, Hanoi, decided to delay the unification drive and thus avoid provocations that might draw the United States deeper into the contested South. They concentrated instead on their five-year plan to build socialism in the North, helped by about $1 billion in foreign aid from the Soviet Union and China. Predictably. that meant industrialization and nationalization of commerce and industry. In the countryside, the party pushed land reform to destroy the landlord class, although it also led to summary executions and injustices that embarrassed the party and drove some peasants into open revolt. After recovering from this setback, the party returned to the task of collectivization, which was essentially completed by the early 1960s.

In 1959 Hanoi shifted its attention back to the South, setting the stage for re- newed conflict. The catalyst for this shift was Ngo Dinh Diem, who had become head of the U.S.-backed regime in the main southern city of Saigon in 1954. As we saw in Chapter 4, the Eisenhower administration supported Diem's government with assistance that by 1961 totaled $7 billion. For a time Diem appeared to be a successful nation builder. Relying heavily on members of his immediate family, he crushed his opposition, consolidated his political position, and with U.S. backing ignored the countrywide elections agreed upon at Geneva.

Diem's very success put Ho in a difficult position. The cancellation of the elec- tions seemed to rule out peaceful unification, while Saigon's ruthless campaign of repression threatened the survival of the former Viet Minh who had organized the anti-French resistance and had stayed behind after the 1954 partition. Isolated and vulnerable, they warned that Hanoi's lack of support would cost them their lives. It would also cost Hanoi organizational structure and experienced personnel that would in time be essential to winning the South.

The leaders of the DRV finally responded by embarking on an active southern strategy, first authorizing in early 1959 military force by southern cadres to pro- tect themselves and their organization. Hanoi took another step on the road to full-scale civil war the next year when it created the National Liberation Front (NLF). The NLF would serve until 1968 as the main instrument of Hanoi's drive to win the South. Modeled on the Viet Minh, the NLF was a united-front organiza- tion meant to appeal broadly to South Vietnamese, including peasants, students, religious and labor leaders, and prominent nationalist politicians. By playing up the Ngo family's political oppression, dependence on the Americans, and regres- sive land policy, the NLF won broad southern support. Also like the Viet Minh, it operated under veiled Communist control. To sustain the southern resistance, Hanoi built up the Ho Chi Minh Trail running through the eastern part of Laos and Cambodia, and it used Cambodian territory along the South Vietnamese border as a sanctuary where NLF and later northern forces could rest and resupply (see Map 4.1 on p. 171).

The NLF fought during this period on three fronts as it attacked a politically vulnerable Diem and later an unstable Saigon military government. One front was in the cities, where the NLF underground promoted anti-government protest, won influential recruits, and infiltrated the Saigon bureaucracy and military command. The second front was on the battlefield, where the NLF had to learn to neutralize the new military technology such as helicopters and armored troop transports that the Kennedy administration provided to the South Vietnamese army. Villages scattered across the southern countryside constituted the NLF's third and most important front. The NLF built on the earlier successes of the Viet Minh at land reform, appealing to peasants with the promise of land for the landless, an end to exploitation, and opportunities for social mobility.

Diem had made mistakes that raised the NLF's popular appeal. He allowed landlords to return to the countryside to reclaim fields previously distributed by the Viet Minh. Once the NLF-supported insurgency began, the Diem government resorted to police raids and military sweeps that further antagonized a rural population already inclined to favor the NLF. This support was pivotal to the ability of Ho's southern forces to grow stronger and ultimately triumph. Saigon finally attempted land reform as a positive response to NLF inroads, but it came too late and was in any case half-hearted, in deference to the landlord element that supported Diem. The battle in key southern provinces for the control of "hearts and minds" (a phrase much invoked by Americans preoccupied with winning Vietnamese support) was settled by the early 1960s. Although many villagers were intimidated by the government's power, they generally did not see Saigon as a legitimate regime, while American involvement seemed simply a continuation of the repugnant French colonial presence.

During the early 1960s, even while supporting the NLF, Ho remained hopeful that he could sidestep a costly collision with U.S. forces. He trusted, he remarked in fall 1963, in the good sense of an American ruling class that was "more practical and clear-sighted than other capitalist nations." Surely, he argued, "they will not pour their resources into Vietnam endlessly. One day they will take pencil in hand and begin figuring. Once they really begin to analyze our ideas seriously, they will come to the conclusion that it is possible and even worthwhile to live in peace with us."[8] Ho's strong Marxist assumptions led him to these views about the rational bottom-line outlook of U.S. leaders and also to the conviction that the American "masses" would no more support a hard, distant war than the French had.

Between 1964 and 1968 Communist leaders in Hanoi stepped up their efforts in the South. Diem's overthrow, with American connivance, in late 1963 and the unstable military governments that followed suggested that the South was vulnerable. Hanoi decided to gamble on a quick victory before U.S. military intervention could save the collapsing Saigon regime. The first North Vietnamese combat units reached the South in December 1964 following the Tonkin Gulf clash in August (see Chapter 4). The inauguration of the U.S. strategic bombing campaign against the North and the appearance of American forces in the South raised the stakes through the first half of 1965. Hanoi moved quickly to match the Americans on the ground, intensifying the conflict while denying U.S. forces a quick victory. The Soviet Union and China both supported the DRV with substantial military aid. By mid-1965 the first of a quarter-million Chinese support troops began arriving in the DRV, and additional forces stood ready just across the border.

NLF Fighters Pose for the Camera
Members of a unit that had received special recognition project an air of professional nonchalance and combat readiness in this posed scene. The inclusion of the woman offers a reminder that women made up a substantial part of the NLF. Despite the lack of information about the identity of this group, their location, or the date, this photo gives a face to the NLF light infantry that U.S. forces found elusive. (Photograph by Van Phuong, in Tim Page, *Another Vietnam*, 2002)

In July, at the very time that LBJ and his advisers were debating massive intervention, Le Duan (the general secretary of the Communist Party and by now its effective leader) explained why Vietnamese could expect victory, even if outnumbered. "The U.S. rear area is very far away, and American soldiers are 'soldiers in chains', who cannot fight like the French, cannot stand the weather conditions, and don't know the battlefield . . . To fight for a prolonged period is a weakness of U.S. imperialism." The United States might even attack the DRV, Duan predicted, but that course would trigger direct Chinese or even Soviet involvement.[9]

Between 1965 and 1968 this escalating conflict visited death and destruction throughout Vietnam. The North absorbed a pounding from the air, while sending young men south to fight until victory. ("Born in the North to die in the South" was these recruits' favorite, sardonic slogan.) The South suffered extensively from bombing and defoliation, free-fire zones, and search-and-destroy missions. The violence disrupted all aspects of society, imposed widespread economic hardship, and sent floods of refugees into the cities.

The decisive encounter of the Vietnam War came in 1968 with the Tet Offensive (so named for the new year holiday in Vietnam's lunar calendar). Le Duan had decided despite Ho's doubts to employ virtually all the NLF forces in a general offensive intended to shake the Saigon government's hold on its urban strong points. The party appealed for a maximum effort by its rank-and-file in order "to avenge evil done to our families, to pay our debt to the Fatherland, to display our loyalty to the country, affection for the people and love for our families."[10] In early 1968 the NLF launched its surprise attack, seizing cities all over the South, including parts of Saigon. NLF forces were eventually beaten back with heavy losses, forcing northern troops to bear the brunt of the fighting through the balance of the war. But, as we have seen (Chapter 4), Tet deeply shocked and unsettled both U.S. policymakers and the public and finally cracked Johnson's resolve.

Still, the war raged on for another seven years, with the fighting in the South reaching its most destructive phase after Tet. Peace talks, begun in late 1968, deadlocked. Implacable as ever, Hanoi sustained its forces in the field despite high casualties and weathered Nixon's bombing campaigns and expansion of the ground war against its sanctuaries and supply lines in Cambodia and Laos. Finally, in January 1973 the two sides reached a compromise. Washington had as early as May 1971 dropped its insistence on North Vietnamese troop withdrawal from the South, and Hanoi finally gave up its demand for the end of the South Vietnamese military government. Nixon had to force Saigon to submit to this compromise.

With the American troops out, the war ended sooner than anyone expected. The strategy of "Vietnamization" of the war, begun by Johnson after Tet and continued by Nixon, had sought to strengthen the South Vietnamese army and air force so that they could cope on their own. But the Saigon government's forces remained hobbled by corruption and inept leadership. The North Vietnamese spring offensive in 1975 revealed how fragile that force was—and how empty were Nixon's assurances of continuing support. His successor, Gerald Ford, was like most Americans ready to write off Vietnam as a bad investment. South Vietnamese defenses collapsed rapidly, and Saigon fell in April. Hanoi had emerged victorious after a long and costly struggle.

Vietnamese patriots celebrated the realization of a dream of independence and unity that was a century old. The combination of strengths turned effectively against the French had also proven effective against the even more powerful Americans. Just as the French public had wearied, so too had the Americans. Just as the French had found themselves isolated, so too had Americans watched international sympathy evaporate.

NORTH VIETNAM TAKES ON THE UNITED STATES

1954	Geneva Conference agreement leaves Ho in control north of the 17th Parallel; U.S.-backed Diem takes charge to the south
1959	Diem's repressive policy prompts Hanoi to endorse military as well as political struggle in the South
1960	National Liberation Front for South Vietnam created
1963	Diem's overthrow and assassination; South Vietnamese army takes charge in Saigon
1964	Hanoi introduces combat units into South Vietnam and begins to line up Soviet and Chinese support
1968	Tet Offensive washes over cities all over the South, including Saigon; peace negotiations with United States begin; American policy of "Vietnamization" begins to turn the main war effort over to the South Vietnamese government
1973	Paris agreement on withdrawal of U.S. forces concluded
1975	South Vietnam falls to North Vietnamese forces

Ho Chi Minh did not live to see that victory, but his contributions, above all as a national symbol and party builder, helped make that triumph possible. His public image as a warm, conciliatory figure and his adherence to collegial decision making helped win broad popular support and keep the party leadership together through a series of lopsided struggles and difficult choices. Ho thus left as his legacy a leadership style that differed considerably from that of his Chinese contemporary Mao Zedong, whose later years were marked by erratic policies, growing estrangement from most of his colleagues, and the demise of collegial governance.

Shortly before his death in September 1969, Ho had appealed to compatriots in an almost lyrical celebration of the country that he had devoted virtually the whole of his life to liberating: "The American invaders defeated, we will rebuild our land ten times more beautiful."[11] But Ho had only to look around to see some of the costs, and others would become evident only at the end of the war. An estimated 1.7 million Vietnamese died during the last decade of the long Vietnamese struggle (1965–1975). The environment suffered lasting damage from bombing that was triple the total for World War II and from the extensive use of herbicides that destroyed not only plants holding down fragile tropical soil but also human genes, resulting in widespread birth defects to Vietnamese as well as Americans who had been exposed. Over 10 million South Vietnamese became refugees between 1965 and 1973, and by the war's end Vietnam had some 1.4 million disabled and half a million orphans to care for. Substantial parts of the southern countryside were depopulated, while urban industry and commercial activity had ground to a virtual halt. However sweet the victory, prolonged conflict had imposed a heavy price on Vietnam.

THE CARIBBEAN BASIN: BETWEEN REACTION AND REVOLUTION

In the Caribbean and Central America as in East Asia, the postwar period opened with a rising challenge to the old order. Reformist regimes and populist movements sprouted everywhere, drawing sustenance from Allied propaganda that victory over fascism was but the prelude to building more prosperous and open societies. Standing in the way were regimes traditionally dominated by strongmen backed by the military. These regimes had protected the interests of the small number of families who controlled the economy and had close ties to a staunchly conservative Catholic Church. This coalition of wealthy families, strongmen, the military, and the church had crushed groups attempting to break its grip on national life. Challengers to the establishment were committed to broader political participation, expansion of the right to vote beyond the ranks of propertied males, and the legalization of labor unions. They also concerned themselves with pressing questions of social justice and redistribution of wealth in societies marked by glaring inequalities. The urban middle class and the working class as well as students and intellectuals were the chief advocates of these changes. As dictators fell and repression lifted, parties on the Left, including Communist parties, began to play a prominent political role, and unions became more assertive and saw their membership increase. By the 1960s elements within the Catholic Church joined the call for reform. Radical priests articulating a doctrine of "liberation theology" viewed poverty not as the natural order but as a condition to be eliminated by education, community building, and state-sponsored social programs.

Sharpening the demands for change was pervasive nationalist resentment against U.S. hegemony. Already by the early twentieth century the United States had established itself as the dominant regional presence that left states, most independent since the 1820s, only nominally free to chart their own course. At times, especially between 1898 and 1933, U.S. control took the form of direct rule—over Cuba, the Dominican Republic, Haiti, and Nicaragua. But this sort of direct control, justified by the Monroe Doctrine with its longstanding claim to U.S. dominion over the Americas, was costly and an embarrassing contradiction to national principles of self-determination. So in the 1930s the Roosevelt administration promoted a "good-neighbor" policy rejecting colonialism and even direct military intervention. Nevertheless, Washington continued to protect its sphere of influence by working through friendly local elites, supplying military and economic aid, and applying diplomatic pressure. The memory of past U.S. interference and the continuing reality of pervasive U.S. constraints created fertile ground for radical politics in postwar Central America and the Caribbean (Map 6.1).

Nowhere in the broad Caribbean basin region did the radical impulse grow stronger than in Guatemala and Cuba in the course of the 1950s. In both cases demands for change sharpened longstanding internal divisions. Those demands also stimulated powerful U.S. fears of communist advances in the U.S. backyard.

MAP 6.1
Latin America and the Caribbean

Washington's forceful opposition would doom fundamental social and economic change in Guatemala, while Cuba's revolution would survive, but at a heavy cost.

Guatemala's "Ten Years of Spring"

Radicalism in Guatemala arose within a society that was, like others in the region, deeply divided. The Spanish conquest in the sixteenth century and the subsequent period of colonial rule had created the divide, and it had persisted beyond independence in 1821. On one side was a large underclass composed primarily of descendants of the Mayans, a people living in Mexico and Honduras as well as Guatemala. They had numbered as many as 14 million in the eighth century. The Mayan civilization, composed of strong city-states surrounded by farming communities, had reached the peak of its power in the tenth century before being overwhelmed by invasion, civil war, and natural disasters. Spanish conquest, followed by three centuries of Spanish rule, completed the abasement of this once-powerful people, while diseases introduced by the Spanish sharply reduced their numbers.

Some of the survivors were enslaved, while the rest took refuge in remote regions practicing subsistence agriculture. But even remote settlements were increasingly threatened in the late nineteenth and twentieth century as export-oriented agriculture expanded. An 1871 law expropriated Indian as well as Catholic Church land in order to make it available for well-to-do families building up the country's coffee plantations. Indians stripped of their land were forced to accept work tending and harvesting export crops. The steady encroachment of plantation agriculture at the end of the century further disrupted Indian communities and left rural laborers ever more poorly paid. To protect themselves culturally and economically, some Indian communities sought to isolate themselves in remote highlands, especially in the western part of the country. Still slightly over half of Guatemala's population of three million in 1950, the Maya suffered from poverty, malnutrition, poor health, short life expectancy, and an illiteracy rate of over 70 percent. Although living in scattered groups, each with its own language, they maintained a keen sense of their Mayan heritage and of their oppression as a conquered people and culture.

Ladinos occupied the other side of the Guatemalan social divide. Broadly understood, *Ladino* refers to anyone (including even descendants of Indians) who adopted the social standards and language of those of European descent. A Ladino minority—a small collection of powerful families—ran the country. Their ancestors had taken a leading role in the sixteenth-century Spanish conquest and in colonial governance, and they remained prominent after independence from Spain. Their ranks had been steadily reinforced by the arrival of Europeans and Spanish-descended peoples from other parts of Latin America.

This Ladino elite controlled an economy dominated by plantation agriculture. Two percent of landholders from that class owned roughly three quarters of agricultural land. They used their wealth derived from export agriculture to import finished products from industrial countries, to expand their holdings, or to make secure investments abroad. Their minority status and their dependence on Mayan labor gave rise to charged racial attitudes. Many Ladinos felt contempt for the Indians, who seemed to them more animal than human. They also feared Indian uprisings that could disrupt production and endanger the agricultural system. When these uprisings occurred, the army brutally repressed them. In the twentieth century this elite expressed its fear of popular unrest by labeling as communist any challenge to its control, even moderate calls for social reform and labor unions. This privileged class with much to lose gravitated to repressive, authoritarian rule as the best guarantee of order and stability. The vote was limited in the interwar period to literate males, and urban opposition parties then taking shape were crushed and their leaders exiled or killed.

This yawning gulf between the privileged and the poor—one of European descent and the other largely indigenous—created a society marked by gross inequalities and ethnic domination. Those conditions in turn bred resentment and fear and political tension that often spilled over into armed conflict, creating a climate inhospitable to long-term economic development. Because Guatemala and other countries in the region were overwhelmingly agricultural, control of land usually figured as the most sensitive political issue. Land represented patrimony and privilege for the upper class, while for peasants it was the stuff of survival and dreams for a better life.

In 1944 Guatemala entered what some have looked back nostalgically on as the "ten years of spring in the land of eternal tyranny." That decade witnessed the unfolding of a far-reaching reform program intended to promote national unity and popular welfare. This era of promise began with the overthrow in 1944 of Jorge Ubico Castañeda, a military dictator who had been in power since 1931. A revolt led by students, urban professionals (teachers, doctors, lawyers, and civil servants), and military officers drove him into exile and opened the way for two elected reformers—first Juan José Arévalo Bermejo and then Jacobo Arbenz Guzmán.

A prominent and eloquent intellectual untainted by the old regime, Arévalo proved an attractive leader for the new era. He won the presidency in December 1944 with 85 percent of the vote, and then legitimized political parties, opened up public debate, broadened the right to vote, and made it possible for workers to organize. Arévalo's successor as president, Jacobo Arbenz, broadened the reform agenda from 1951 to 1954, giving it a distinctly radical tinge. His father was a Swiss German who had settled in Guatemala in 1901. Arbenz was born in 1913. The bankruptcy of his father's pharmacy closed his avenue to university, so he turned to the military academy. He proved an excellent cadet and officer. In 1939 he married an upper-class Salvadoran, María Vilanova. She had a gregarious personality (in contrast to her somewhat introverted husband), was educated in the United States, and was interested in a broad range of social and cultural issues. In 1944 Arbenz had joined other young officers pressing for Ubico's removal. Thereafter he served as minister of defense, keeping the army loyal to Arévalo and actively encouraging the reform program. In 1950 Arbenz won the presidency with 64 percent of the vote.

Both Arbenz and his wife had by then developed a sensitivity to social injustice that pulled them to the political left. Exploring the sources of Guatemala's underdevelopment and extreme poverty, they determined that deep social and ethnic divisions were to blame. They were also perturbed by their country's economic dependence on the United States. The Boston-based United Fruit Company was Guatemala's largest private landowner and biggest employer. It occupied a privileged position that made it a state within a state. Backed by Washington, it defied postwar legislation that gave labor the right to organize and collect a minimum wage. Arbenz was not alone in resenting U.S. arrogance and in attributing Guatemala's economic backwardness, at least in part, to the dominant influence of American capitalists and their alliance with the landed elite.

In their quest to understand Guatemala's plight, the Arbenz couple turned to Marxist writings. Marxism offered hope that history was on the side of change—that in the end neither Guatemala's own reactionary classes nor the American imperialists could block progress. The record of the Soviet Union and other socialist states convinced them that it was possible to build a new Guatemala. But if Arbenz was becoming a Marxist, he was a cautious one, for he wanted to avoid provoking Washington, and he knew that he would get no significant Soviet support. Stalin's successors, like Stalin himself, approached the Third World cautiously, and realized the explosive implications of a direct challenge to the Monroe Doctrine.

Domestically Arbenz realized that socialism was a distant dream. Guatemala had first to develop capitalism and end the feudal conditions that defined the lives of so many of his compatriots. He thus wanted to promote education and private enterprise, improve working conditions, and bring the peasantry into touch with the broader world. He also sought to promote a shared national identity, and that meant drawing what he and other Ladinos saw as a superstitious and backward Mayan population out of its brutish isolation. He genuinely believed that helping Indians shed their indigenous values in favor of "modern" ones would improve their lives while promoting economic development and justice.

Arbenz's deepening convictions on domestic and foreign policy made the still-outlawed Guatemalan Communist Party his natural partner. While other political parties suffered from internal quarrels and corruption, the Communists commanded the only disciplined, honest political organization in the country. After they helped Arbenz in his 1950 election campaign, he legalized the party and made its leadership trusted presidential advisers.

Agrarian reform would prove the major tool by which Arbenz would try to push his country forward. His reform law passed Congress in June 1952. Its sponsors argued that peasants given their own land would work harder, boost agricultural production, lead better lives, and develop a more sophisticated, market-oriented mentality. The reform, which called for the expropriation and redistribution of land to peasants, largely exempted small and medium-sized holdings (estates of less than 224 acres). Large holdings with substantial idle land were subject to expropriation. Those losing land included Arbenz himself and some of his close advisers. Owners were to be compensated in bonds amounting to the declared tax value of the land taken. This provision penalized those, including the United Fruit Company, who had always grossly understated their land value in order to avoid taxes.

By June 1954 the Arbenz program had transferred one quarter of the arable land to the benefit of as many as half a million Guatemalan poor. Reformers went beyond handing out land to politicizing peasants—involving them in the redistribution process in order to overcome their political passivity and fear. To make sure that peasants prospered, the government provided credit, technical assistance, education to raise literacy, and roads to get crops to market. At the same time it encouraged rural wage laborers to unionize in order to raise their pay and to support the new order in the countryside.

This rural reform program exacerbated longstanding tensions, especially between Mayans and Ladinos. Land had become ever scarcer because of two long-term trends—population growth and concentration of holdings in the hands of the wealthy. The scarcity had ignited feuds within and between villages that could last for decades and create bitter divisions. Postwar democratization provided a political arena for the expression of this struggle for land, usually pitting Mayans (often landless laborers) against Ladinos (often the major local landowners). The injection of the land-reform process in 1952 added oil to a long-smoldering fire. Officials arriving in a town to redistribute land had to sort out an complex tangle of local alliances and decades-old rivalries. The more affluent Ladinos increasingly feared that popular unrest would, with the backing of the Arbenz government in Guatemala City, undermine their social control. In their view, the reform was a disguise for an emerging revolutionary threat.

By 1953 the Arbenz government was facing growing opposition. At home landowners and the Catholic Church were intensely hostile to reform. Already under Arévalo landowners had begun plotting coups, and the Arbenz land reforms made them even more determined to find a military dictator to beat back the supposed communist threat. The leading members carried their vivid fears to a receptive U.S. Embassy. Through the press and the radio stations it owned, this upper class gradually convinced the middle class of the danger of economic and social upheaval. This consolidation of opinion among the affluent urban classes left Arbenz heavily dependent on the support of peasant and labor organizations. The Catholic Church too feared a rising tide of Marxism that threatened Christian values as well as the Church's privileged status. Guatemala's strongly authoritarian archbishop warned, "Sad experience shows that liberty left to the caprice of each individual only disorganizes [our people] into opposing bands, weakens them, and begins to destroy them."[12] These views of the staunchly conservative native-born clergy were notably at odds with the position of foreign priests espousing liberation theology and working with the Guatemalan poor out of a commitment to social justice.

U.S. interests lined up behind the old order. The United Fruit Company had already under Arévalo been shocked to find a cool reception at the presidential palace, and worse still, they faced government attempts to renegotiate contract terms and enforce newly passed labor measures. The agrarian reform was the crowning blow, depriving United Fruit of three fourths of its holdings of about 600,000 acres. Washington soon joined the ranks of the opposition. As we saw in Chapter 5, U.S. leaders approached the region convinced that private capital was the key to creating prosperity. To attract investment from abroad and hold accumulated wealth at home, countries such as Guatemala had to maintain stability against leftist or populist agitation, limit state intervention in the economy, and in general respect the rights of private property. Already during Arévalo's tenure,

United Fruit was warning the Truman administration of trouble in Guatemala. By the time Arbenz became president, Washington's fears were fueled primarily by U.S. diplomats. The U.S. ambassador applied what he called his "duck test" for determining whether a country was undergoing a quiet communist takeover. Watch for the signs, he suggested: If the bird walks, swims, and quacks like a duck, then it's a duck "whether he's wearing a label or not."[13] His conclusion was that the Arbenz government met the test.

At first the Truman administration sought to push Arbenz from the clutches of the communists by applying diplomatic pressure and denying his government economic aid and weapons sales. Truman's successor, Dwight Eisenhower, embraced more aggressive measures late in the summer of 1953, authorizing the CIA to engineer a coup. On June 17, 1954, a rebel force of only several hundred men, trained in Nicaragua and led by Carlos Castillo Armas, crossed into Guatemala. The CIA planners wanted to shake the loyalty of the army and secondarily to demoralize the civilian population, so they backed up the invaders with clandestine radio broadcasts, a few aircraft that dropped leaflets and intermittently bombed and strafed the capital, and a U.S. Navy blockade.

In Guatemalan politics the army cast the swing vote on the fate of the reform project. Arbenz had respected the army's autonomy, pampered its officers, and received its loyalty in return. What finally strained the relationship was the prospect of a collision with the United States that would bring certain defeat and possibly the loss of the army's privileged position. The alternative to this potentially ruinous scenario was for officers to get rid of Arbenz. Faced with the defection of his own military, an exhausted president resigned on June 27. He explained in a public statement that "the sacrifice that I have asked for does not include the blood of Guatemalans." In private, American leaders exulted over the effectiveness of this low-cost covert operation, but publicly they were more circumspect. President Eisenhower proclaimed to the press, "The people of Guatemala in a magnificent effort have liberated themselves from the shackles of international communist direction and reclaimed their right of self-determination."[14] In Arbenz's place, Washington installed in power the reliably anticommunist Castillo Armas. His government severed diplomatic ties with the Soviet bloc, banned the Communist Party, and persecuted its members. Rural activists either fled or faced violent repression. Little of the domestic reform program survived. Eventually, 1.03 million of the 1.30 million acres expropriated under the 1952 law would be restored to their owners.

This return to pre-1944 conditions had different meanings to the winners and the losers. The well-to-do wanted a guarantee against anything like the Arbenz land reform, described by a leading newspaper as "the most monstrous act of robbery ever perpetrated by any ruler in our history."[15] This class looked to the military and police to check any challenge—democratic or otherwise—to the system and in effect to perpetuate the country's deep ethnic and class divisions. Washington was equally resolved after the Guatemala scare to keep tighter control. To forestall

GUATEMALA STILL DIVIDED

1821	Guatemala gains independence from Spain
1871	The government gives legal sanction to land consolidation to promote export agriculture
1944	Dictator Ubico overthrown; Arévalo elected as president and presses for democratization
1950	Arbenz elected president with help of the Guatemalan Communist Party
1952	Arbenz launches a broad-based program of land redistribution
1954	CIA-sponsored exile force invades Guatemala; armed forces topple Arbenz government; new U.S.-backed military government restores land to elites

leftist inroads in Central America and the Caribbean that might benefit Moscow, U.S. policymakers increased their support for right-wing regimes, and where the communists did threaten, Washington was prepared to intervene, confident of success after the easy victory against Arbenz. For his part Arbenz watched the collapse of his dream of a new Guatemala from exile. Haunted by his failure, he could at last join the Guatemalan Communist Party. On the Latin American Left the Arbenz reform effort became the stuff of mythology. The Chilean Communist poet Pablo Neruda wrote "In Guatemala," an elegy for the dashed hopes:

I saw the rose bloom in Guatemala.
I saw the poor man's land defended,
and justice arrive to every mouth.

. . .

The North American arsonists
dropped dollars and bombs:
death built its finery,
the United Fruit uncoiled its rope.
And thus Guatemala was assassinated
in full flight, like a dove.[16]

Others on the Left, most consequentially Cuban revolutionaries, studied Arbenz's failure for political lessons. They realized the importance of arming loyalists, the better to protect any reform program from its powerful enemies.

Cuba and the Revolution That Survived

Events in the island nation of Cuba took a dramatically different course from those in Guatemala in part because of differences between Arbenz and Fidel Alejandro Castro Ruz, the author of the Cuban revolution and its presiding presence through the last four decades of the twentieth century and beyond. He guaranteed at least a footnote for himself in Cuban history on July 26, 1953, when he staged an attack on a military barracks in Santiago de Cuba on the eastern end of the island. He hoped the attack would spark a nationwide revolt against the government of dictator Fulgencio Batista. The 26-year-old had no more than 150 young factory and farm workers behind him, and after more than an hour of fighting, the outmanned rebel leader fled to the mountains with a band of 60, only to fall into government hands within a week. This young upstart's political career seemed doomed—but it had only just begun. He would get the best of his foes and leave an enduring stamp on Cuban national life.

The other major difference can be found in the make up of these two societies. While Cuba suffered, like Guatemala, from deep inequalities that divided the countryside from the city and that favored those of Spanish descent, Cuba more resembled the rest of the Caribbean in the identity of its underclass, primarily descendants of the four million slaves brought from Africa to supply labor, usually on the sugar plantations that became the mainstay of the colonial economy. Slavery had persisted until 1886 in Cuba, one of the last places to embrace emancipation. Also unlike Guatemala, Cuba's bankers, business leaders, and prominent landowners did not constitute a cohesive, independent upper class resolute in defense of the status quo. Nor was there an isolated peasantry on the fringes of national politics. Large-scale cane sugar operations, which dominated the economy, had integrated peasants either as renters of company land, as landowners selling their limited production to the company, or as wage laborers (often seasonal).

Castro's revolution would develop under the shadow of its giant North American neighbor. U.S. expansionists had fantasized throughout the nineteenth century about making Cuba, then a colony within the decrepit Spanish empire, into a state of the union. The Spanish–American War in 1898, which made the United States the colonial master of the Philippines, also paved the way for lasting, although informal, control over Cuba. Before 1898, the island had been in a state of simmering revolt against Spanish rule from the 1860s on, but it had taken U.S. intervention in 1898 to finally break Spain's grip. U.S. troops occupied the island until 1902, when Cuba gained independence.

But that independence was highly qualified. Cuba had to accept the U.S. right to intervene militarily to maintain order and to hand over Guantanamo as a permanent military base, and the U.S. Embassy became the kingmaker in Cuban politics. In addition, Cuba's sugar economy had become tightly tied to the U.S. market and dominated by American investors. Already by the 1920s, two thirds of all arable land belonged to U.S. companies, and U.S. firms controlled Cuba's mineral wealth as well as its public utilities and transport. Trade reinforced this subordination. Cuba's sugar industry came to depend on privileged access to the U.S. market at prices above the world-market level, and (in a pattern that aroused advocates of import substitution) U.S. producers supplied Cuba with manufactured imports while a high U.S. tariff discouraged Cuban manufacturing.

A U.S.-backed strongman was essential to maintaining the status quo. From the 1930s until the late 1950s Batista filled that role. Reassuringly anticommunist, he used his control of government revenue to dispense patronage to political supporters and keep the army happy with generous funding. The middle class prospered, the North Americans were satisfied, and Batista successfully intimidated most of his critics—but not Castro. Like other Cuban nationalists, Castro charged the Batista regime with making Cuba a "neocolonial" dependency of the United States. He realized that so tight was the U.S. grip that he could not challenge Batista and seek internal reform without also ending that dependence. Complicating Castro's thinking was his intimate relationship to the United States. He was, for example, a baseball player of considerable skill and a long-time devotee of the Yanqui sport much beloved on the island, and he had chosen New York City for his honeymoon. He later visited Cuban communities in New York and Florida to raise funds during his periods of exile. So large did the United States loom in the imagination of Cubans that they tended to compare themselves not to other Latin American countries but to their rich northern neighbor. This complex entanglement with the United States had helped to shape Cuban nationalism and to give a special edge of resentment against U.S. condescension and intervention that Castro fully shared and politically mobilized.

In September 1953 Castro went on trial along with others implicated in his failed uprising and received a 13-year prison sentence. Before the court he delivered an impassioned address, "History Will Absolve Me," that attacked corrupt politicians and laid out a reform program to serve the interests of ordinary Cubans. He draped his appeal in the folds of Cuban patriotic mythology while omitting all reference to communism or socialism, making no attack on the United States, and raising no call for revolution. Secretly reprinted and widely circulated, this call for political democracy and social justice enhanced Castro's reputation as a moderate eager to create a broad-based opposition. In 1955 Batista issued a general amnesty that freed Fidel and his men, and Castro went into exile in Mexico. There he concentrated on building his political organization, named the 26th of July Movement (after the date of his 1953 revolt). There he also met an Argentine doctor, Ernesto "Che" Guevara, who become his chief adviser along with his younger brother Raúl.

In December 1956 Castro and 82 associates slipped back into Cuba on a small, overcrowded boat. The landing miscarried, but Castro, in one of his repeated strokes of good fortune, made it to the Sierra Maestra mountains (in eastern Cuba) with 18 of his men. He learned the terrain and enlisted the backing of local bandits. He also induced *New York Times* journalist Herbert Matthews to report that the rebels were a major force, thus scoring a propaganda coup in both Cuba and the United States. In fact, a wide range of Cubans was beginning to embrace the anti-Batista cause, and dozens of other opposition groups were springing up. By early 1958 the opposition movement numbered about 20,000 active supporters and 2,000 guerrillas in scattered bands. It was a force in cities, and in the countryside it had taken the military initiative against Batista's demoralized army.

On January 1, 1959, the dispirited dictator fled the country. The next day opposition forces entered Havana. Castro began a long triumphant pilgrimage across the island of seven million to the capital. He reveled in the popular adulation.

What had brought Castro so rapidly—within six years of his daring uprising—to this surprising victory? His origins give some clues. He was born in August 1927 on a farm in eastern Cuba. His father, Spanish by birth, was deeply religious, rough-hewn, and illiterate. He made his way, acquired his own farm, and eventually accumulated a net worth of half a million dollars. Young Fidel was energetic, athletic, and independent, with an outgoing personality. Attendance at a prominent Jesuit school in Havana for children of the upper crust inculcated Catholic teachings on social justice. In 1945 Castro entered the University of Havana to study law. He developed a passion for rough-and-tumble campus politics, demonstrated a talent for public speaking, and increasingly turned to national political issues. He charged corrupt politicians with failing to address popular welfare, especially the gap between privileged city dwellers and impoverished rural folk. He made his first run for elected office in 1952, only to have Batista seize power and close down the political process. The dictator came to represent in the eyes of this ambitious and impatient young man the two problems plaguing Cuba—its social ills and U.S. domination.

By the time of Batista's fall in 1959, Castro's political daring, charisma, and effectiveness as a guerrilla leader had established him as the dominant figure within a loose alliance of liberal-left opposition groups that included the Communist Party as well as the 26th of July Movement. Castro's striking capacity to tap popular sentiment made him the voice of the revolution and increasingly put his views beyond challenge. Castro himself appears to have had no revolutionary blueprint. Until 1961 he had avoided any clear statement of long-term policy that might alienate his broad coalition of supporters, which was as important to his anti-Batista struggle as it was to the Vietnamese in their anticolonial cause.

Castro made his first important decision in May 1959 when, in response to popular demands for vengeance, he approved the dramatic public trial and execution of Batista loyalists charged with the deaths of some 20,000 opposition figures. At the same time Castro failed to calm U.S. fears of communism gaining a foothold in the hemisphere. Worried that Washington would turn against any government that embraced meaningful social change, he plunged ahead anyway by nationalizing U.S.-owned oil refineries. When Eisenhower retaliated with an economic embargo, Castro responded by nationalizing additional U.S. property. In January 1961 the two sides broke diplomatic relations. As we saw in Chapter 4, John Kennedy endorsed CIA plans formulated under Eisenhower for an invasion by Cuban exiles modeled on the Guatemala operation. Che Guevara, who had personally witnessed Arbenz's overthrow, drew the appropriate lesson. He warned Castro that he must anticipate American intervention and prepare militarily against American intervention. Castro took the warning seriously, and when the U.S.-backed invasion force came ashore at the Bay of Pigs in April 1961, Castro's forces easily prevailed.

The Kennedy administration was shocked. Castro remained a problem not just for Kennedy but for all his successors in the White House.

American hostility gave Castro reason to further tighten his control. In the course of 1959 he banned liberal parties as enemies of the revolution, and liberals followed the old regime into prison or exile, mainly in Miami, Florida. Free elections were never held and free speech was severely curtailed. With the political situation polarizing, exile-sponsored raids only added to the crisis. Castro saw that he needed a reliable political instrument to carry out his policies. The Cuban Communist Party would be that instrument, even if Castro disliked its ideological rigidity and its subservience to Moscow. It had a well-organized mass base, and it shared his opposition to American imperialism and his vision of social justice. In December 1961 Castro publicly embraced socialism as the best way to promote the popular welfare. But there is some doubt about when his conversion actually took place, indeed even how thorough a conversion it was. Castro himself remarked in a 1964 interview, "It was a gradual process, a dynamic process, in which the pressure of events [after the revolution] forced me to accept Marxism as the answer I was seeking."[17]

In practice, Castro was like other Third World radicals including Arbenz and Ho. He acted on values that were as much populist and nationalist as Marxist. His domestic program aimed to eliminate abject poverty, promote literacy, make medical care widely available, and reduce the birthrate and infant mortality. He expropriated the land of wealthy property owners (both foreign and Cuban) and moved toward collective agriculture. As in China, the new regime limited migration from the countryside into the capital, Havana, to head off out-of-control urban growth that would become common in the Third World. And it expanded rights for women. The positive effects of Castro's policies quickly became evident. Economic redistribution raised ordinary Cubans' purchasing power and closed glaring gaps in welfare. But badly formulated economic policy and the flight of foreign capital plagued the revolution from the outset.

Expensive domestic policies and U.S. hostility turned Castro toward the Soviet Union. He would become increasingly reliant on that country as a market, a source of oil, and a military as well as economic patron. Relations with the Soviet bloc first developed from February 1960 on the basis of trade and aid agreements. The threat of a second invasion attempt, underlined by the Kennedy administration's militant rhetoric and U.S. naval maneuvers, prompted Castro to appeal to Khrushchev for military support. Soviet nuclear missiles were just the thing to deter an invasion. During the ensuing crisis of October 1962 (treated in Chapter 4), Castro seemed eager to see a Soviet–American clash of arms. When Khrushchev went behind his back to strike a deal with Kennedy, the Cuban leader was outraged. But even if Castro had had no say in the decision to remove the Soviet missiles, he could take comfort in the American pledge not to sponsor another invasion, although U.S. hostility (and covert operations) continued. A visit to the Soviet Union in May 1963 healed the breach with Khrushchev and signaled Cuba's full-fledged membership in the socialist bloc. In 1972 Cuba joined the bloc's Council for Mutual Economic

Fidel Castro Working the Crowd, 1965
This photo of an impromptu public conversation captures the populist charm that made Castro beloved to many Cubans. An 87-year-old man asks for a pension so he'll have the money to start a small business growing cocoa trees. Castro at first expresses surprise that the old man has no pension and promises to check into the matter but jocularly dismisses the idea of going into business so late in life: "What sheer madness!" When the old man persists, Castro finally surrenders, amidst much laughter from onlookers. "Help! No more, no more! You will have your pension, *viejo* [old man]. Ay, these *campesinos* [country folk], going into business when they are nearly ninety. They are never going to understand what socialism is all about, that's for sure!"[18] (Lee Lockwood/The LIFE Images Collection/Getty Images)

Assistance (COMECON) and became integrated into its system of economic planning.

During his first two decades in power, Castro thought of his revolution as the spearhead for Third World liberation. His victory at the Bay of Pigs had made him the hero of the Latin American Left. Castro enthusiastically embraced this new role, giving rebel groups from neighboring countries a secure base of operations on the island and supporting insurgencies in the Dominican Republic, Guatemala, Argentina, Bolivia, and Venezuela. None was successful, and Che Guevara, a close lieutenant who served as his overseas agent, was caught and killed in the jungles of Bolivia in 1967. Chastened for a time, Castro's hopes for revolution in the hemisphere revived in the late 1970s with the dictator Anastasio Somoza's overthrow in Nicaragua and the appearance of left-leaning governments in Grenada and Jamaica.

Castro's interest in exporting revolution extended well beyond the Western Hemisphere. He had given assistance to Algeria's independence struggle against France in 1960 and backed Kwame Nkrumah's call for black liberation by setting up guerrilla training camps in northern Ghana in 1961. In 1965 Guevara led the first small Cuban contingent to fight in the Congo, and soon Castro extended his

CUBA'S REVOLUTION

1898	The United States goes to war to end Spanish control of Cuba
1902	Cuba gains independence as a U.S. protectorate
1953	July 26 attack on a military barracks propels Castro to prominence as an opponent of Batista
1956–59	Castro builds an opposition movement that topples Batista
1960	Castro cements close ties to the Soviet bloc
1961	U.S.-sponsored invasion force defeated at the Bay of Pigs; Castro declares himself a socialist
1962	Castro accepts Soviet missiles, setting off a superpower nuclear confrontation
1991	Soviet collapse deprives Castro of his chief source of international political and economic support

support to other African liberation movements. These commitments became a source of friction with Moscow following Khrushchev's overthrow. In 1966 Castro accused the new Soviet leadership of turning its back on Third World struggles, thus positioning himself as their foremost advocate. In 1975 Castro would renew his engagement in Africa—in Angola and Ethiopia—and, as a result, end any chance for normalization of relations with the new U.S. administration under Jimmy Carter.

Why did Castro survive the American onslaught while Arbenz suffered defeat and exile? One part of the answer can be found in the lessons that the Cubans drew from the Guatemalan failure. Another part of the explanation is Soviet support proffered to Castro but not Arbenz. But perhaps above all we need to consider the role of Castro's personality. He combined self-confidence with a fatalistic sense of destiny in a way that gave him that intangible quality called charisma—the power to elicit hope and sacrifice from his followers. Those who came within his ambit found him irresistible. Someone who had known Castro during his Mexican exile recalled, "When he puts his hand on your shoulder . . . ten minutes later you are saying yes to everything."[19]

Castro's revolution offers the sobering reminder that even successful programs for radical change cannot easily solve the political and economic problems that provoked the effort in the first place. The Cuban revolution struggled to create a prosperous, just, and truly independent Cuba. On the plus side it made gains in social welfare, matched by no other country in the region, dramatically improving life expectancy and literacy rates and significantly lowering infant mortality (Table 6.1). But these achievements, however impressive, have to be seen in light of the relatively high standard of living and high literacy rates that Cuba already

TABLE 6.1 Castro's Revolution in 1990: A Comparative Balance Sheet[20]			
	Cuba	Latin America and Caribbean	Industrialized countries
Life expectancy (average years)	75	67	75
Infant mortality rate (deaths to age 5 per 1,000 live births)	14	70	18
Literacy (percent of population)	94	84	near universal
Military spending (percent of GNP)	11	2	5

enjoyed before the revolution. Moreover, Castro's revolution carried a cost. The continuing confrontation with the United States and the hostility of the large Cuban exile community forced him to spend heavily on military security and to deny a political opening that his enemies would exploit. This one-party state had little tolerance for public expressions of political dissent. Activists demanding political rights were jailed or otherwise restricted.

Finally, economic development in an embattled Cuba did not live up to its promise. Cuba remained tied to a single export crop—with the only difference that sugar no longer went to the U.S. market but to the Soviet bloc. Relentless U.S. sanctions and Castro's shifting policies pushed the economy into cycles of crisis and recovery from the early 1960s on. In the late 1960s Castro experimented (much as Mao Zedong had done in China's Great Leap Forward) with a shift in emphasis from industry to agriculture and reliance on mass mobilization to dramatically increase production. This strategy failed. Verging on economic collapse, Cuba became more dependent than ever on Soviet support. Castro retreated to a more moderate, market-oriented policy to revive the economy, but by 1985 shifted again out of fear of emerging "capitalist" tendencies.

The collapse of the Soviet Union in 1991 plunged the Castro regime into a crisis of unparalleled severity. Now without a powerful patron, Castro had to face alone the continuing U.S. policy of economic blockade and diplomatic isolation. Some North Americans and many in the exile community still hoped to bring down Castro, while the Cuban leader sought new trading partners and sources of investment. The attraction of a better life in the United States, made evident daily in television beamed from Miami, challenged the regime's legitimacy. Castro worried about how he would keep the spirit of revolution alive for a younger generation impatient for a higher standard of living.

DECOLONIZATION IN SUB-SAHARAN AFRICA

Africa south of the Saharan Desert—the bulk of the continent, excluding Morocco, Algeria, Tunisia, Libya, and Egypt—is a place of enormous diversity. Roughly

5,000 miles from north to south and 4,600 miles from east to west, it accounts for a fifth of the Earth's surface. Its size—three times that of the United States—is matched by the variety of its landscape, the range of its climates, and the richness of its natural resources. Yet the region fits in its own distinct way into the broad patterns previously attributed to the Third World. Like much of the rest of the Third World, the sub-Saharan region experienced foreign conquest and exploitation. In the late nineteenth century the European powers completed Africa's subjugation, carving it up into colonies (formalized at the conference of Berlin in 1884–1885). The only exceptions were Liberia (colonized by African Americans and independent since 1847) and the kingdom of Ethiopia. This subjugated region was the home of vital societies, sprawling empires, long-distance trade, warfare, and cultural interchange among a wide array of peoples. Europeans added new features. They diverted inland trade into imperial, maritime patterns; they shaped local economies to suit their short-term strategies of exploiting resource-rich land and cheap labor, especially in extractive industries and plantation agriculture; and they kept their costs low by minimizing investment in local economies and relying on locals for administration and police.

Also like other Third World peoples, Africans began in the wake of World War II a sustained drive against European colonial control. By the late 1950s and early 1960s they had made enormous strides toward throwing off that control (Map 6.2). In most cases colonial powers had worked out collaborative arrangements with indigenous elites. This was the favored British path. As we have seen in the case of India, London had consistently preferred a low-cost, light-rein approach to colonial administration that left substantial authority in the hands of local leaders, and even anticipated conceding greater autonomy to the "natives." When the cry for independence went up after World War II, London usually accommodated rather than engage in a costly defense of colonial authority that would radicalize postcolonial leaders. Former British colonies such as Ghana, Nigeria, and Kenya began their national life with parliamentary governments and a place in the association of former colonies known as the British Commonwealth. The French had, by contrast, pursed policies of assimilation intended to create a close, permanent bond with their colonies. But France had to retreat in the face of indigenous pressures and after 1958 offered its remaining sub-Saharan colonies a choice between full independence or an association with France that would preserve some mutually beneficial ties. A third pattern involving prolonged conflict over independence and majority rule prevailed in Zimbabwe, South Africa, and the Portuguese colonies of Mozambique and Angola. In these cases substantial numbers of European settlers supported the colonial status quo. Their tenacity set the stage for long, bitter struggles with African liberation movements. (Chapter 9 treats South Africa as the most extreme example of the persistence of European settler control.)

The ghost of Marx hovered over Africa during the early phase of decolonization. Many independence leaders were to tilt left for familiar reasons. Capitalism was a system that had brought them few benefits in the colonial era. Socialism, by contrast,

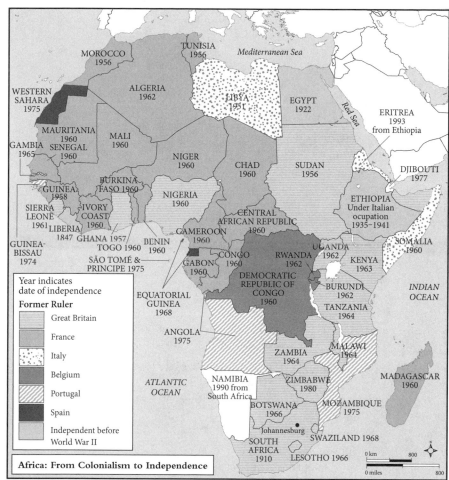

MAP 6.2
Africa: From Colonialism to Independence

seemed most relevant to their aspirations for rapid economic and social development. The Soviet Union proved more supportive of true independence and autonomous development than the West, and Mao's peasant revolution offered a model suited to Third World social conditions. Leaders in diverse settings—from Patrice Lumumba in the Belgian Congo to Nelson Mandela in South Africa—drew ideological inspiration and political support from the Left. The most influential figure in the heyday of African decolonization was Kwame Nkrumah, Ghana's founding father.

Ghana and Nkrumah's African Socialism

The land to which Nkrumah returned in late 1947 after his long sojourn abroad (see pp. 145–147) had come under British control. The process had begun in the late fifteenth century, when independent kingdoms had started trading with the Europeans, mainly in slaves and gold. Between 1874 and 1901 the British, with the help of local allies, took over Ghana's territory (then known as the Gold Coast). Just as the political consolidation was coming to a close, cocoa production for export took off. By 1910 Ghana controlled almost half the global market.

On arrival home, Nkrumah found the road to full independence blocked by a cozy alliance between the British and local elites consisting of tribal chiefs, merchants, crop brokers, and urban professionals. This minority of political notables—roughly a thousand in total—had worked closely with the British, traded with the British, and had received education under British rule. They strongly favored a gradual transition to independence that would allow them to take control without inviting dangerous social upheaval. As the first formal step in that direction, this elite organized the United Gold Coast Convention (UGCC) in 1947. By embracing this "responsible" established class of influentials, London hoped to guide the Gold Coast toward independence in a way that would maintain Britain's political and economic influence. Already in 1946 Britain's Labour government had given the colony a constitution as a first step toward what was supposed to be a long, peaceful evolution toward independence.

Nkrumah disrupted this comfortable arrangement. Working within the "establishment" UGCC, he set up a newspaper, schools, and a youth organization to create a base of popular support. Nkrumah's energy and success unnerved the UGCC leaders and the colonial administration. Sensing in increasing popular agitation a "communist" plot, worried colonial authorities had Nkrumah among others arrested in 1948. Soon released from jail, UGCC leaders attacked him as a "rabble-rouser." Now resolved to chart his own path, Nkrumah created his own Convention People's Party (CPP) to advocate immediate independence and a popular role in national politics. Although Nkrumah and others at the CPP forefront lacked wealth and close working ties with the British, they still had important assets—a familiarity with the West, political experience, and popular support.

Nkrumah pressed ahead with a nonviolent program to force concessions from the British, much as Gandhi had in India earlier. The response was at first repression, including his second arrest early in 1950. Now more popular than ever, Nkrumah ran for the legislature from prison and won a resounding victory in 1951, along with others of his party. London realized that, like it or not, it had to deal with Nkrumah and accelerate decolonization if it wanted to prevent a blowup. This decision was made easier by the absence of a substantial European community tenaciously clinging to the colonial order. The British government released Nkrumah, asked him to form a government, and promised to move the colony rapidly to self-rule. In 1957 the colony, with its almost seven million people, became a fully independent state within the British Commonwealth. It took the name of Ghana after an interior West African trading empire that had flourished a thousand years earlier.

As Ghana's first president, Nkrumah proved an articulate, internationally recognized figure bent on exploring an African road to socialism. This impatient modernizer envisioned a country quickly and drastically made over. He wanted for his people universal, free education and health care, safe water and good sanitation, affordable housing, and wide access to electricity. But he could not advance popular welfare without addressing the injurious economic impact of the colonial era and the continuing subordination in trade and finance to their former colonial masters. As Nkrumah saw it, Ghana was poor because of foreign exploitation. The British had profited from his country's wealth, while Ghanaians gained little as their natural resources and the fruit of their labor flowed abroad.

Like other leaders of the independence era, Nkrumah made "neocolonialism" a major issue. This system of influence by former colonial powers over formally independent, new countries was reinforced by the Cold War superpower, the United States, which for the first time took an interest in Africa as a region of instability that the Soviet Union might exploit. Washington pressed Ghana and other newly independent states to align with the West politically as well as economically and to eschew socialist policies. Nkrumah argued that these neocolonial pressures created a formidable obstacle to charting a path that would best serve his people.

Nkrumah devised a two-pronged prescription for achieving genuine independence and meaningful economic development. He first of all opted for a domestic policy intended to alter the pattern of foreign trade. As long as the country exported cheap raw materials and imported expensive finished goods, it would remain underdeveloped and exploited. To break this pattern Nkrumah implemented import substitution, promoting rapid industrialization so that Ghanaians could produce their own finished goods in place of imports, while also raising production of raw materials for processing within Ghana, thus increasing their export value. (See Chapter 5 on the emergence of this strategy of import substitution.) Impatient with private enterprise, Nkrumah created state-owned corporations to take over gold mines, plantations, processing industries, transport, and marketing. The government improved the road and rail network, built port facilities, established a national airline and shipping line, and constructed a major hydroelectric project. Ghana went deeply into debt, but the long-term benefits were expected to be large. In March 1964 Nkrumah inaugurated an ambitious seven-year development plan that would gradually restrict private enterprise in favor of a state-controlled economy. He had concluded that this was the surest way to create a prosperous Ghana free of foreign economic control.

The other part of Nkrumah's prescription was Pan-Africanism, with its dream of uniting black Africa politically, economically, and militarily. As Africans emerged from colonial rule, he hoped that they would recognize their common bonds, work closely together, and thus undo the divisions among them created by arbitrary European lines of partition. A great African union would transcend boundary issues and submerge ethnic differences that weakened individual African states. It would permit the creation of a unified armed force to fend off U.S. or European interference and to force decolonization on the European powers still struggling to hold on to their African possessions. It would help create an African market with the capital to finance its own development and the buying power to absorb its own production. This Pan-African idea may have been the sturdiest of Nkrumah's dreams, going back to the early 1940s and attracting to his country like-minded intellectual exiles from the United States and the Caribbean such as W. E. B. Du Bois and George Padmore. In a speech to a meeting of African leaders in Addis Ababa, Ethiopia, in May 1963 Nkrumah urged them to "unite in order to achieve the full liberation of our continent."[21] This speech heralded the creation of the Organization of African Unity (OAU). Nkrumah made good on his verbal commitment, serving personally as patron of independence movements and making training bases available for their use.

But by 1966 Nkrumah was in deep trouble. His Pan-African dreams were not shared by other heads of state, who shied away from integration. They wanted the OAU only as a consultative body. At the same time socialism was not bringing prosperity to Ghana. Population growth was outpacing food output, forcing Ghana to import food for the first time. At the same time, the price of the prime export, cocoa, fell on the world market, and Ghana experienced a foreign-currency shortage. Consumer products disappeared from shop shelves, and inflation soared. With an empty treasury, a heavy national debt, and a struggling economy, Nkrumah's promise of a better life and his calls for patience and sacrifice rang hollow.

Finally, the CPP was failing Nkrumah as a political tool in part because of Ghana's overlapping regional and ethnic divisions. The broad Northern Territories kept a distance from the CPP, while the central sections dominated by the Ashanti nobility, with its own proud tradition of kingship and system of chiefs, fought for autonomy against the CPP's centralizing tendencies. Cocoa producers in the Ashanti region, the source of nearly half of Ghana's output, added to the clamor against the CPP for its policy of purchasing the crop at prices well below the international market. In the southeastern region, the Ewe turned their back on the CPP, eager to unite instead with kinfolk in neighboring Togo. (See Map 6.3.)

Adding to these ethnic difficulties, the CPP had become faction-ridden and self-serving, with its members happily enriching themselves as party and government bureaucrats. A disillusioned Ghanaian novelist wrote of the corruption associated with CPP rule: "Men who know nothing about politics have grown hot with ideology, thinking of the money that will come. The civil servant who hates socialism is there, singing hosanna. The poet is there, serving power and waiting to fill his coming paunch with crumbs."[22] When Nkrumah's attempt to crack down on official corruption, nepotism, ethnic rivalry, and bureaucratic inertia failed, he began silencing his critics and moving in 1964 to a one-party state. By then Nkrumah had become a "big man" who dominated the political system with a style that became increasingly autocratic. A personality cult promoted by sycophants insulated him from criticism.

With internal tension building, powerful outsiders looked to hasten Nkrumah's exit. France was troubled by Nkrumah's help to its former colony, Guinea, then struggling to survive independence, while his support for liberation struggles in

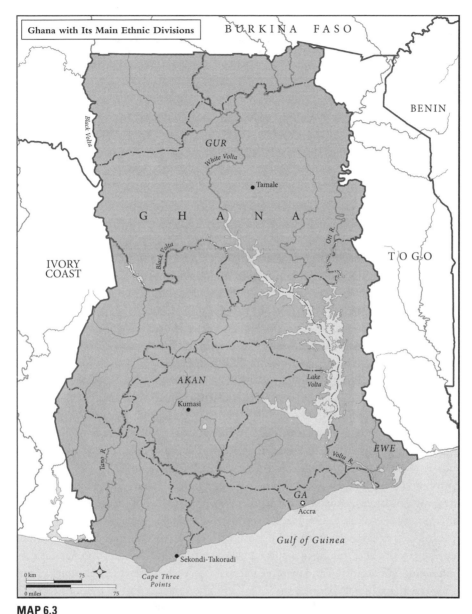

MAP 6.3
Ghana with Its Main Ethnic Divisions
Akans, located in the southern half of the country west of the Volta River, made up roughly half the population. They were not one group but a variety of groups, including Ashanti and Fante, with a common language and cultural patterns (including a generally matrilineal system). The Gur-speaking peoples of northern Ghana constituted about a third. Isolated from the rest of the country, they felt some resentment toward coastal peoples who benefited from British rule. The Ewe group accounted for 13 percent. They had become part of Ghana as the result of the post–World War I transfer of Togoland from Germany to Britain. The Ewe of Ghana lived in the resource-poor area east of the Volta River, with the majority of Ewe just across the border in what became the independent state of Togo. The fourth broad group, those speaking Ga, made up 9 percent. They lived along the coast around the capital, Accra.

GHANA'S NKRUMAH

1909	Nkrumah born on the coast of Britain's Gold Coast colony
1935–47	Nkrumah's political education in the United States and Britain
1948	Nkrumah plunges into the independence movement, splits with United Gold Coast Convention, and forms his own Convention People's Party
1957–60	Ghana moves to full independence, signaling the rapid end to colonial order in sub-Saharan Africa
1964	Nkrumah launches his seven-year economic plan and imposes one-party rule
1966	Nkrumah ousted (dies in exile in 1972)

Portuguese colonies, in Rhodesia, and in South Africa caused more general irritation in the West. He struck bilateral economic deals with eastern European regimes, the Soviet Union, and China, and he publicly attacked exploitation of the Third World by multinational corporations.

The ranks of Nkrumah's enemies were reaching formidable proportions by the mid-1960s. He had survived three attempts on his life. Finally in February 1966 he fell victim to a coup carried out by disaffected police and senior army officers (largely of Ewe origin) while he was visiting Vietnam. From exile in Guinea, he watched excitedly the growing militancy of blacks in the United States and imagined a global alliance of peoples of African descent advancing alongside other liberation movements toward the overthrow of capitalism, imperialism, and neocolonialism. While his old pan-African dream flowered for the last time, his plots to regain power in Ghana failed, and he died of cancer in 1972.

Whatever his failures, Nkrumah pursued a remarkable course. He ventured abroad and into another culture from one that was politically subjugated and branded inferior by the West. He explored a world of new ideas, seeking the ones suitable for his country. He maneuvered Britain into giving up colonial control without serious bloodshed, and his quest for a brighter future for Ghana and Africa commanded world attention and inspired enthusiasm in the region. His economic plans failed, perhaps largely because the CPP did not become the sort of tight, disciplined Leninist party-state critical to imposing change in the Soviet Union, China, Vietnam, and Castro's Cuba. Although his Pan-Africanism never took hold, the OAU still exists as the African Union, and his idea of a continent with a common interest in cooperation also survives.

Colonial Legacies in Ghana and Beyond

Nkrumah and other independence leaders faced serious limits on their freedom of action. Perhaps the most important of those limits were the legacies of the colonial past. The practices and decisions imposed by Europeans had consequences that carried over powerfully into the post-1945 period and help explain the difficulties that new states encountered in the postcolonial period. To be sure, Africa south of the Sahara is marked by a diversity that rules out simple, rigid generalizations. Ghana, featured above, is only one country of the 51 in the region, and more than most its early post-independence experience reflected radical currents flowing through the Third World generally. Even so, Ghana can tell us a good deal about the way the past weighed heavily on African countries whatever their political orientation.

One of the prime colonial legacies was a transformed rural economy. Commercializing agriculture altered the lives of rural people (the majority of the population) and created a gap between the city and the countryside. To understand this transformation we need to look back at least a century. Throughout much of Africa before the first Europeans reached the coast, peasants engaged either in subsistence agriculture or in trade along interior lines. The arrival of the Europeans, beginning with the Portuguese and the Spanish in the sixteenth century, marked a gradual reorientation of commerce toward the coast. Agricultural products, timber, minerals, and slaves were gathered in the interior and then shipped to the coast for export to Europe or the Americas. The slave trade alone had a deeply disruptive effect over a long period extending from the fifteenth to the nineteenth century. During that time not only were 15 million Africans forced into slavery but also two to five times that number may have died in the fighting that attended slaving.

By the time of the colonial carving up in the late nineteenth century, a clear economic pattern had emerged that would shape contemporary Africa. Powerful chiefs and merchants formed strong and profitable commercial networks with European business firms. These arrangements saw African peasants more and more involved in producing for the global market. Goods passed through growing port cities that connected internal commercial networks with the international trading system. Those same cities were also becoming the center of colonial administration and the home of a small but influential African elite that had accommodated to European dominance.

Ghana was a microcosm of this process of economic transformation. For example, the shift to cocoa production in the early twentieth century had enormous social effects. As it became central to the economy, cocoa production displaced the once-dominant crops of palm oil and rubber. The new crop drew migrants from far in the interior into the central region, where growing conditions were good. The newcomers either cleared their own land to farm or worked for others. This rush of activity gave rise to a more complex and fluid society. At the top were the larger farmers with command of capital, the brokers who purchased cocoa for sale to exporters (usually European) in the major ports, and the colonial bureaucrats who regulated and taxed the cocoa trade. Below them were smaller independent farmers. Still lower were sharecroppers and contract and wage laborers.

Within villages in Ghana, but also elsewhere in Africa and other parts of the Third World, the rise of export crops grown for cash initiated a profound shift in values. The new commercial ethos associated with this export crop encouraged more individualistic behavior and eroded the sense of moral community. As the sense of reciprocal responsibility declined under the pressures of the new trade, the tight village system with its strong welfare elements gave way to families and individuals pursuing their own interests and to the wealthy turning their backs on their poorer neighbors. Family and village lands once held in common passed into private control. The loss of communal land and the tendency toward concentration of land in the hands of those with the resources to grow and market the export crop in turn increased the number of landless who once could have made a claim on a portion of the communal holdings. As public land disappeared and the revenue from that land dried up, village chiefs lost control of resources that could be used for the common good. Thus their power declined relative to the new class of large entrepreneurs.

The loss of communal land and the fraying of social bonds proved especially detrimental to women. Before Western economic networks began penetrating into the rural interior, women had had an important voice in village affairs, while also bearing a special responsibility for family well-being and community harmony. Commercialization undermined the power and status of women at the same time that it expanded opportunities for men. Encroaching cash crops ate up land once dedicated to communal subsistence and deprived women of their say in the disposal of the crop, even as they continued with their old chores of planting, weeding, and harvesting. As village society fragmented, separation and divorce became more common. Abandoned women could no longer depend to the extent they once had on communal resources for help in caring for children.

Colonial administrators who promoted the growth and sale of export crops, as well as missionaries who spread new values, accentuated the crisis for women. In Ghana as elsewhere in the region, they applied European gender codes that gave formal authority to men. Convinced that women had no place in politics or the mainstream economy, British governors reserved for men alone the opportunity for education, professional advancement, employment in the modern sector of mining and industry, participation in long-distance trade, and decisions about lucrative cash crops. Colonial policies ignored flourishing women's associations and discouraged women from continuing to play their long-established role in marketing food and fabrics.

The elaboration of trade and the growth of port cities combined with the strains felt by villages to set in motion a major rural exodus typical of most of the Third World. Migrants (primarily men) set off to carve out a better life in the privileged urban sector. The human exodus depopulated villages and left behind disproportionately women, the very young, and the very old. Village women who carried a mounting burden of responsibilities depended on funds sent home by migrants. Some also found serving as a bridge between city and countryside a rewarding niche that built on their traditional role in petty trading. Market women in Ghana, for example, developed distribution networks and general trading savvy. Operating in associations defined by type of goods, they served as commercial intermediaries.

They purchased local produce, often perishable, in the countryside at prices that were sure to find buyers at the markets they ran in nearby cities. Thanks to this independent source of income, these women were able to support themselves and their children when husbands proved unreliable.

The second colonial legacy, closely related to the first, was a generally parasitic relationship of the city to the countryside. Functioning within an urban environment, colonial governments from Mali to Mozambique made scant economic contribution to the life of rural people. Indeed, they drained resources from the countryside in order to pay for administration and whatever projects were essential to external trade, such as roads, rail lines, and port facilities. Colonial administrators wanted otherwise to avoid the bother and expense of direct rule and thus left rural people to fend for themselves after paying taxes and providing labor.

In Ghana the chief instrument for the exploitation of the countryside was the cocoa marketing board, established by the British during World War II. The board assured producers a minimum price and pocketed the difference when world prices were higher, thus accumulating substantial reserves. Resentment against this blatant form of economic exploitation had helped to feed independence fever. Although the board and its reserves fell into Nkrumah's hands on independence, he did not abolish this unfair fiscal system, nor did he use the savings to help the rural producers who had been its source. Instead, like other African leaders, he pursued large-scale development projects such as dams and heavy industry designed to showcase the country's claim to being modern. While the reserves went into those projects, he at the same time intensified the effort to squeeze money from the countryside. As in China, agriculture represented an outmoded way of life yet also a national prime resource to exploit to the full in the interest of building a modern society. Since Nkrumah's projects did more to help the city than the countryside, cocoa farmers understandably felt exploited.

Behind this pervasive pattern of favoring the city over the countryside was the condescension toward the rural population felt by the Western-trained, urbanized elites who led the national independence movements. Like the Ladino elites in Guatemala and the Congress Party leaders in India, many were educated abroad, thus strengthening their attachment to Western ways. Exposure to the comforts of modern urban life and the power of the modern Western state during sojourns overseas engendered a stinging sensitivity to the backwardness of their own societies and a deep-seated impatience with the adherence of peasants to old ways of doing things. Overwhelmingly, the rank and file that joined in the independence drive were also city dwellers, while rural Africa remained politically peripheral.

Nkrumah strikingly illustrates these post-independence, pro-urban biases. Growing up on the coast among a commercial rather than an agricultural people, then studying with missionaries, and finally experiencing life in the United States and Britain had shaped his view of what Ghana should become. He wanted to transform the countryside, replacing small-scale, "backward" peasant production with "modern," mechanized, state-controlled agriculture. He repeatedly expressed his faith in science and technology wielded by rational people operating in a framework of socialist principles to create a new Ghana. It was the grand march of progress, not the daily struggles of rural folk, that excited him.

In according cities a privileged status, these indigenous leaders were following, perhaps unconsciously, the colonial lead. Cities throughout the colonial world had arisen as the site of European residence, political administration, and sometimes trade. The very independence leaders who denounced economic control by outsiders proceeded to practice a kind of internal cultural colonialism by favoring the city over the countryside. New African leaders focused their concerns on the modern urban sector where their political supporters and political institutions, along with industry and other major projects, were located. They invested in urban infrastructure and education and lavished food subsidies as well as housing and health care on the urban population. This favoritism placated urban elites and forestalled political discontent. The neglect of the countryside, combined with an improving urban living standard, not surprisingly acted as a powerful magnet for peasants. Rather than working productively in the countryside, they piled up in enormous shantytowns and added little to economic output.

This imbalanced development created long-term economic problems. To be sure, immediately after independence economic prospects seemed generally favorable. Although initial per capita income in most countries of sub-Saharan Africa was less than $100 per year, school enrollments climbed, life expectancy rose from 39 years to 49 years, and major construction projects moved ahead. But the first flush of optimism quickly passed. Per capita income growth was slow and, as we have seen, the large, urban-based state sector got the lion's share of resources while burdening agriculture.

The final major colonial legacy can be found in the ethnic patchworks that came to characterize sub-Saharan states. Although Africans account for only about a tenth of the world's population (three quarters of a billion in 1998), they were fragmented into at least a thousand ethnic and linguistic groups. When European colonizers arrived, they paid no attention to ethnic homogeneity and in some cases preferred a diverse population within one colony so administrators could exercise divide-and-rule tactics. Colonial officials created their own ethnic map, deepening old social divisions or fostering new ones. As a result of arbitrary decisions by nineteenth-century Europeans, newly independent states were not homogeneous nations. Each held a considerable variety of groups within its borders, with some of those groups spilling over into adjacent states. This ethnic pluralism made post-independence governance difficult.

Ghana's divisions were minor compared to some other African countries. For example, Zambia contained within its borders 73 ethno-linguistic groups, while Kenya had about 40. Nigeria, the most populous of the sub-Saharan states, was divided into 250 ethnic groups overlaid by major religious differences (with roughly half of the population Muslim and a third Christian).

States riven ethnically had to find ways to contain rivalry, although this effort often failed and led to violence. Nigeria provided early and bloody testimony to the dangers of these divisions. Growing ethnic and religious tension evident immediately after independence in 1963 erupted in open conflict three years later. Not until 1970 was a secessionist movement in the eastern, Ibo portion of the country finally crushed with the loss of more than a million lives. More recently, Rwanda has revealed the terrible potential for internal conflict created by colonial division of the continent without regard for ethnic homogeneity of individual states. In the colonial period, Belgian authorities not only combined diverse people but also accentuated differences by promoting the Tutsi (people with favored physical features) over the Hutu. Independence in 1964 found the majority Hutu in control, which in turn generated armed Tutsi resistance and finally in 1994 a genocidal campaign by militant Hutus opposed to any compromise power-sharing deal. At least 800,000, perhaps a million, mostly Tutsi, died in the course of several months of organized slaughter at the hands of their compatriots. Ghana has been spared ethnic warfare, but it has nonetheless faced interregional tensions. The Ewe, split by the border with Togo, have entertained secession. The political assertiveness of the Ashanti has worried other groups, while the Ashanti felt discriminated against when Nkrumah made them bear the burden of his development policy. His characterization of their mentality as "primitive" in some youthful writing suggests the deep-seated ethnic stereotypes that made political cohabitation difficult.

We should not think of sub-Saharan Africa as somehow peculiar in having to cope with internal divisions of this sort. Europe 500 years ago (not to mention modern-day Yugoslavia and Indonesia) offers parallels. State boundaries, drawn then at the pleasure of monarchs, contained multiple and overlapping language groups. The resulting disputes helped plunge European states into nationalist wars that tore apart empires and created new, more homogeneous political units. While African leaders professed support for the legitimacy of the inherited colonial administrative boundaries, already within the first decades after independence states were falling victim to centrifugal and secessionist forces that left some governments powerless and that opened predatory opportunities for local warlords and neighbors. Sierra Leone, Liberia, Chad, the Democratic Republic of the Congo, Angola, Togo, Sudan, Rwanda, and Somalia are all cases of the frightening potential of political and social disintegration to undermine states and invite outside intervention.

The impulse to hold divided states together and thereby stave off disaster helped give rise to an autocratic (often despotic) and parasitic political system—what some observers have called the "big-man" syndrome. Typically, a leader once in power would proceed to enrich himself, his family, and the ethnic group that was his base of political support. But, if he were to survive, he also had to use his access to the country's wealth to appease other ethnic groups. By widely distributing state largesse, the "big man" assured even those on the fringe of political power a share in the system and a stake in his continued rule. In that sense the state functioned as a prized resource for the father-leader to use to smooth over ethnic tensions among his children-subjects—in contrast to Central America, where it served to bolster the position of a few wealthy families, or in East Asia, where it functioned as the agent of either economic or revolutionary mobilization.

Nkrumah had big-man counterparts in most of the post-independence African states—figures who dominated the political landscape for years. Kenneth Kaunda controlled Zambia for its first quarter-century, relinquishing power only in 1991. Jomo Kenyatta not only led Kenya to independence in 1963 but also dominated until his death in 1978 and handpicked a successor, Daniel arap Moi (in power until 2003). Félix Houphouët-Boigny ruled Ivory Coast for 34 years until he died in 1993. The infamously corrupt and brutal Mobutu Sese Seko took power in the Belgian Congo (later renamed Zaire) in 1965, became president in 1970, and exploited his poor, mineral-rich country until driven into exile in 1997. In Nigeria, a string of military leaders occupied that big-man role through the bulk of the period following independence in 1960. Julius Nyerere, who led Tanzania to independence from Britain in 1961, ruled for 27 years.

Of all these legacies, the European creation of multiethnic states seems to have created the most fundamental constraints to political and economic development in sub-Saharan Africa. Divergent loyalties and competing values not only made a common national vision impossible but also proved a constant source of political tension and frequently armed conflict within newly independent countries. The persistence of ethnic division and jealousy in turn made the "big man" an attractive solution to the problems of integration, while the improvisation and shifts in policy to accommodate ethnic pressures and interethnic alliances virtually ruled out a coherent policy toward agriculture, migration, or development more generally. The alternative—breaking Africa into thousands of microstates along linguistic and ethnic lines—had scant appeal. Nkrumah grasped from the outset of his career the promise of African integration as a solution to the challenges deeply divided countries would face. His own attempt to act on a transnational vision and move Africa as a whole toward liberation and greater cooperation only partially succeeded. But among his last words was a familiar message: "When Africa is a united, strong power, everyone will respect Africans, and Africans will respect themselves."[23] The insight seems perhaps even more profound today than in Nkrumah's time.

REMAKING THE MIDDLE EAST AND NORTH AFRICA

The countries stretching from North Africa to the edge of the Indian subcontinent were in the 1950s and 1960s in as much upheaval as other parts of the Third World. The sources were the same: The experience of foreign domination gave rise to demands for full independence and a determination to explore new paths to prosperity and unity. However, bold dreams for recasting individual societies and even the entire region fell short of realization. For the most part, popular welfare improved only marginally. At the same time, Europeans fought a rear-guard defense of their interests, while the superpower rivals intruded on the scene, making North Africa and the Middle East one more part of the global Cold War battleground.

The European powers had begun incursions into the region in the fifteenth century, and continued with even deeper inroads during the nineteenth century. The climax came in a burst of colonization early in the twentieth century. The Ottoman Empire lost one territory after another. As it staggered toward collapse, Algeria became a French colony in 1848 and Tunisia a French protectorate in 1881. By the turn of the century, Iran as well as Afghanistan had fallen under the joint sway of Britain and Russia. Egypt came under British influence during the 1880s and became a formal protectorate in 1914. Italy colonized Libya in 1911, and the next year France and Spain divided Morocco. After World War I the victors took from a now defunct Ottoman Empire additional lands as mandates, nominally under the supervision of the League of Nations. As in Africa, Britain and France imposed borders for the new states of Syria, Lebanon, Iraq, Transjordan (later Jordan), and the mandate of Palestine without regard to ethnic and religious makeup (Map 6.4). Handpicked rulers served imperial interests, and when they did not, Paris and London were ready to intervene, militarily if necessary, to set matters right.

As elsewhere in the Third World, this imposition of foreign control gave rise to nationalist demands for independence and reform. The modern states that would define the region in the postwar years began emerging in the interwar period. Britain ended its Iraqi mandate in 1932 and gave Egypt limited independence in 1922 (although keeping military bases in both countries). In Iran a feeble dynasty collapsed under international pressures and domestic demands for reform. World War II intensified the colonial crisis in the Middle East. Weakened by conflict, the Europeans were less able to maintain their position in the region. At the same time, the Allied commitment to self-determination inspired nationalists with hopes for a new postwar order. A defeated Italy surrendered Libya, which became independent in 1951. France granted Syria its independence in 1944, and the next year Lebanon won its freedom. Morocco finally gained full independence in 1956. In Tunisia, France resisted independence demands in the late 1940s but then gave way in 1956 to prevent radical elements from taking power. Algeria, which witnessed the last stand of the old European order, finally forced France out in 1962.

These developments unleashed a complex set of political and ideological currents. While monarchies survived—some longer than others—in Morocco, Libya, Egypt, Jordan, Saudi Arabia, Iraq, and Iran, military regimes were on the rise as officers began to step forward as authoritarian national leaders, especially after the defeat of Arab armies by Israel in 1948. Communist parties and socialist critiques of the domestic and international order commanded an unprecedented appeal among politically active urbanites. Secular nationalism was ascendant, but conservative notions of a restored Muslim polity also won followers, especially among those alienated by the effects of long-term Westernization. Talk of pan-Arab

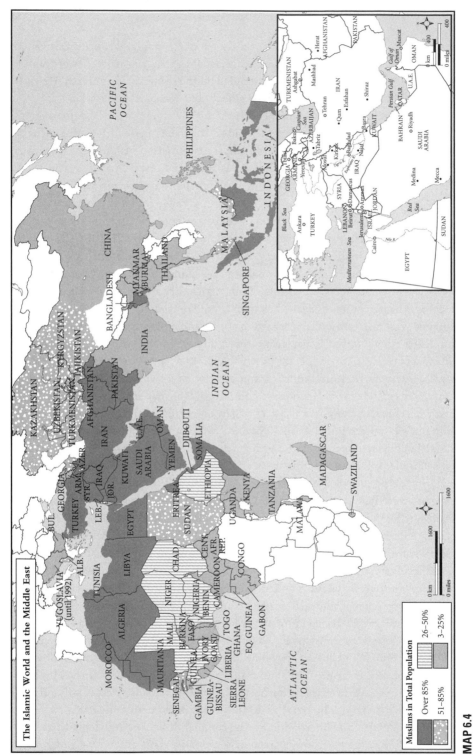

The Islamic World and the Middle East

Muslims in Total Population

- Over 85%
- 51–85%
- 26–50%
- 3–25%

MAP 6.4
The Islamic World and the Middle East

solidarity was widespread, spurred by European imperialism and the creation of the state of Israel in 1948 at the expense of the Palestinians living in the area.

Politically explosive questions of national or regional identity had to be answered in the context of intense Cold War pressures. The United States wanted to promote containment and to protect oil resources critical to the economies of its allies. The Soviet Union feared American influence on its southern border. Both powers thus recruited regional clients. The most important for the Americans were Israel and Iran; for the Soviets it was Syria and Iraq. Egypt shifted sides in an attempt to play the Cold War rivals against each other.

Economic Nationalism in Iran

Iran, one of the two most populous states in the Middle East, nicely illustrates the interplay between domestic differences over development and superpower pressures. Known until 1935 as Persia, Iran was a vast country that was largely arid and mountainous, with the exception of a lush and fertile strip along the Caspian Sea in the north. During the nineteenth century, this non-Arab people had increasingly fallen under European domination. Its agricultural system shifted to cash crops—chiefly cotton, silk, and wheat—for sale on international markets. Landlords consolidated their holdings to exploit this opportunity, rendering many peasants landless. A parallel political process of subordination had been completed by the turn of the century as Britain and Russia each asserted their sphere of influence. Britain enjoyed a privileged position in the south with its chief prize an oil concession held by the Anglo-Iranian Oil Company (AIOC; later British Petroleum). Russia was predominant in the north. A weak and unpopular native dynasty, the Qajars, ruled from the capital in Tehran. Its critics demanded modernizing reforms, above all the creation of a constitutional monarchy.

In 1921 Reza Khan, a tough officer who had risen through the ranks, marched his forces into Tehran. The old dynasty was failing, and the country had descended into social disorder, which the British exploited to extend their influence. Reza Khan began by restoring calm in the countryside and building up his military force. Then in 1926 he replaced the Qajars with his own Pahlavi dynasty. This autocrat, now known as Reza Shah (or king), strengthened the state bureaucracy, replaced Islamic courts with those following European legal principles, promoted industry and communications, and encouraged a strong sense of national identity. At the same time he ruthlessly repressed dissent and aggressively lined his own pocket. Only the British resisted his reach; their southern stronghold functioned as a virtual independent state within Iran, with the oil operation, the country's largest employer, remaining firmly in AIOC hands. The rule of this strong but unpopular autocrat came to a sudden end in 1941. Early that year Britain and the Soviet Union had sent troops into Iran to safeguard a supply route into the Soviet Union that was critical to the war effort. They agreed that Reza Khan was too pro-German and forced him to abdicate.

Reza Shah's successor was his son, Mohammad Reza, the man who came to be known at least in the West simply as "the shah." Mohammad Reza Shah ascended the throne in his early twenties just as World War II began to reshuffle the pattern of foreign influence over his country. U.S. troops joined in the Anglo-Soviet occupation and the United States established itself as the dominant power, pushing out the Soviets and marginalizing the war-weakened British. In 1946 the Truman administration confronted the Soviets over their troops still in Iran and over their support for a secessionist movement in the northwest corner of the country. Stalin withdrew his forces, the Iranian army crushed the secessionists, and Washington began to integrate Iran into the containment line stretching around the Soviet Union. A growing contingent of U.S. advisers arrived to get the Iranian army into proper shape.

Seriously complicating the plans of the cold warriors was a surge of postwar nationalist unrest. A wide range of political groups—from communists to middle-class professionals to religious conservatives—now demanded change. The common denominator among them was a desire to end British dominance. Nationalists resented pervasive interference in the country's political life, but they resented even more control of Iran's oil. While the AIOC output was the highest in the Middle East, the returns to Iran were measly. Like other Mideast oil companies at the time, the AIOC decided on the rate of extraction of oil, set oil prices, and thus controlled the level of revenues from royalties that Iran would receive. To add insult to injury, the AIOC management, whose views were distinctly colonial and racist, carefully limited the Iranian role in management and maintained poor pay and conditions that inflamed workers. A strike in 1946 led by Iran's Communist Party (known as the Tudeh or "Masses" Party) linked labor discontent with nationalization and highlighted the serious challenge Britain posed. A woman appealed at a party rally, "Oh brothers, the production of oil in our land is like jewels. We must try to get these jewels back. If we don't we are worthless."[24]

The widely respected Mohammad Mossaddeq emerged as the most prominent champion of a nationalist program. He was born in 1882 into a patrician family with close ties to the country's elite. He had gone to universities in France and Switzerland, earned a doctorate in law, and brought home Western notions of state building and economic development. Consistent with those views, this aristocrat argued during his long political career for shifting power from the royal court to the national legislature and for asserting greater control over the British-controlled oil industry. These positions had led him to lock horns with the shah's father and suffer imprisonment and internal exile between 1928 and 1941. His views put him on a collision course with the young shah as well. In 1951 this reform-minded nationalist with a reputation for honesty and public service rode to power on a wave of opposition to a new, one-sided contract with the AIOC. Amidst another major strike in the oil fields, the legislature defiantly passed a bill nationalizing AIOC holdings and made Mossaddeq the prime minister. His supporters were organized into a loose coalition known as the National Front; his chief aides were men of standing, many French-educated. The well-organized Communist Party, after a period of opposition to Mosaddeq, reversed itself and lent support, although it was not part of the National Front. The new prime minister at once put oil nationalization into effect. In June Iran regained full control of its prime resource. Mosaddeq then began to chip away at the shah's powers. He wanted to move the country toward a genuine constitutional monarchy in which the shah would reign but not rule. He also pushed for measures to improve popular welfare.

These initiatives ignited a crisis that would grip Iran for two full years. The consequences would reverberate for decades. The decision to nationalize the oil industry outraged the British government, which had a 50 percent stake in the AIOC. London did not want to lose this major fiscal resource and feared other countries might seize on the Iranian precedent to nationalize their own foreign-controlled industries in what might amount to falling imperial dominoes. Reflecting a pervasive and self-interested tendency to denigrate the Iranians, Anthony Eden, then the British foreign secretary, characterized Mosaddeq as a "fractious child" and a "megalomaniac."[25] London retaliated at once. It organized an international boycott of Iranian oil that damaged the economy, and it enlisted the support of a network of long-time Iranian political allies (notably the old landed elite, tribal leaders, courtiers, officers close to the shah, and businessmen) in an effort to turn back the clock on oil policy.

In the standoff over Iran's oil, the U.S. government's position was pivotal. The Truman administration joined the economic boycott but restrained London from taking military action in hopes of securing a diplomatic solution that stopped short of real nationalization. By the time Eisenhower came to office in 1953, London and Washington were well advanced in plotting a coup. The American president endorsed his covert operation nominally out of fear that Iran's Communists might exploit this crisis to take power, but he was no more prepared than the British to see a critical oil resource pass fully into Iranian hands. Launched in August 1953, the Anglo-American plot at first stumbled, but then officers loyal to the shah took control of the streets. Mosaddeq, fearing bloody clashes that might degenerate into civil war, refused to mobilize his popular support. Placed under arrest, he defiantly defended himself during his trial: "My only crime . . . is that I nationalized the Iranian oil industry, and removed the network of colonialism, and the political and economic influence of the greatest empire on earth from this land."[26] He endured several years of imprisonment followed by confinement to his home. Mosaddeq died in 1967, then in his mid-eighties and still defiant. His nationalism if not his secular outlook was an inspiration to a later generation.

The shah, who had fled abroad during the coup attempt, was its major beneficiary. With Mosaddeq gone, he proceeded to consolidate his family's hold on Iran with the long-range goal of restoring his country's imperial greatness. To buttress his own political authority, he purged dissidents from the army, built up the police force, including the feared secret police, and brought the legislature under tight control. At the same time, the shah cultivated close relationships with the U.S.

Demonstration in Support of Mohammad Mosaddeq, 1953
The large picture carried by the crowd is that of the premier. (New York World-Telegram and the Sun Newspaper Photograph Collection [Library of Congress])

government and oil companies, breaking AIOC monopoly of Iran's oil but leaving control in the hands of a foreign consortium with the British majority stakeholders. (Genuine nationalization would have to wait for the shah's overthrow.) A large influx of American economic and military aid helped secure the shah domestically and laid the foundation for one of the best military forces in the region. The long-term costs of the shah's victory were, however, considerable (as we'll see in Chapter 9). His rule witnessed the elimination of the secular political opposition. His accommodation to foreign powers, especially on the oil issue, served to delegitimize the monarchy itself. And the coup that had saved the throne deepened paranoia about hidden foreign hands shaping the destiny of Iran.

Confident that the shah was a reliable client and Iran a solid base for defending the Middle East, U.S. policymakers in the late 1950s and early 1960s turned toward a policy of modernization in Iran. The State Department and the CIA, the shah's warmest supporters in the American government, were convinced that the long-term prospects for internal stability depended on Tehran undertaking a program of social and economic reform. Bowing to U.S. pressure, the shah embarked on what became known as the White Revolution (so named to distinguish it from violent "red" revolutions). Formally launched in 1963, it was a top-down effort to transform Iran into a modern, secular country. Its major goals were to build up industry, liberate women, promote advanced education as well as basic literacy, carry out land reform, and establish civil law in place of Islamic law. These changes pointed to a transformation in Iran every bit as radical as the program Mosaddeq had championed, and in time would generate a backlash as potent as the one that had toppled Mosaddeq. The funding for this multifaceted program came from oil.

IRAN AND THE POLITICS OF OIL

1926	Reza Khan establishes the Pahlavi dynasty in place of the Qajars
1941	Mohammad Reza Pahlavi becomes shah after the ouster of his father by British and Soviets
1951	Mosaddeq champions a nationalized Anglo-Iranian Oil Company and a limited monarchy
1953	Coup orchestrated by London and Washington overthrows Mosaddeq; the shah regains control with U.S. support
1963	Shah launches "White Revolution" reforms
1970s	Soaring oil prices allow the shah to spend lavishly on industry, the military, and public works

As international oil prices rose in the 1970s, so too did government revenue. This oil money paid for urban and industrial development, military power, and courtly pomp. It also raised per capita gross domestic product (GDP) almost threefold between 1963 and 1977.

The 1970s seemed to prove the Tehran–Washington collaboration a great success. Iran's growing wealth encouraged the shah to dream of exercising more than regional power. He told a confidant in 1974, "To be first in the Middle East is not enough. We must raise ourselves to the level of a great world power." But rapid and unbalanced economic development together with autocratic rule was breeding increasingly serious internal discontents. The shah denounced critics as wild radicals and pawns of the superpowers plotting to block Iran's rise to power. Although he sensed that something was amiss in his relationship to his people, he could not conceive of a revolutionary outbreak. "Our farmers and workers are far too happy," he asserted in private in 1973.[27] Washington welcomed this ever-stronger Iran as a bulwark of stability in the oil-rich Persian Gulf, and beginning with Nixon gave the shah *carte blanche* to buy whatever arms he wanted. The shah spent lavishly to the benefit of the American arms industry and the U.S. balance of trade. Little did either the shah or Washington realize that they had planted the seeds for an Islamic revolution (treated in Chapter 9) that would shake the country and the region.

A New Order for Egypt and the Region

The radical impulse animating the Mosaddeq program in Iran also took hold in Egypt, and the stakes were equally high. Like Iran, Egypt was one of the most populous and influential countries in the region, and Gamal Abdel Nasser was one of its most influential figures during the 1950s and 1960s. He gave voice within his own country to strong nationalist and reform ambitions with a pronounced secular and socialist dimension while also championing regional unity, struggle against Israel, and nonalignment in the Cold War.

Egypt reached its radical moment by a familiar route. Like others in the region, it had been pulled tightly into the European orbit in the course of the nineteenth century. Commercial agriculture, above all cotton, reshaped life in the countryside by consolidating land holdings. More and more of the population were left with little or no land. At the same time, Britain was establishing its position as the dominant power in Egypt. The British textile industry came to rely on Egyptian cotton, while the Suez Canal, completed in 1869, provided an indispensable link to India, the jewel in the British imperial crown (see Map 6.4). Guided by economic and strategic interests, London in 1882 asserted informal control over Egypt, then an autonomous province of the Ottoman Empire. After the Ottomans aligned with Germany following the outbreak of World War I, London made Egypt a formal protectorate.

Simmering Egyptian discontent with these arrangements burst into the open in the interwar years. London responded to cries of "Egypt for the Egyptians" by granting limited independence in 1922, but continuing restrictions on Egypt's foreign relations and a major British military presence angered nationalists. As in other parts of the colonial world, World War II inspired Egyptian hopes for finally securing full independence.

The decade between 1942 and 1952 set the stage for the fall of the old regime and the rise of the new one. In February 1942 Britain imposed its choice for prime minister on the reigning monarch, Farouk. Thus discredited in the eyes of nationalists, the king made a bad situation worse after the war by cavorting on the French Riviera while corruption flourished at court and the country stagnated politically and economically. Groups across a wide political spectrum—from educated, liberal middle-class elements, to conservative Muslims, to a small number of Marxist intellectuals—protested their country's impotence and humiliation. Not only did the British continue to wield substantial influence but also Egyptian and other Arab armies failed dismally in a war to prevent the establishment of a Jewish state in Palestine, viewed as a fresh European intrusion into the Arab world. The culmination of these provocations came in January 1952 when British forces, now skirmishing frequently with nationalist guerrillas linked to the Egyptian military, attacked a police station and left over 50 dead. Cairo exploded in anti-British violence. The January riots set the stage for the emergence of the Free Officer movement. Consisting of about a thousand middle-level officers from modest backgrounds, this secret organization used the January riots as justification for overthrowing Farouk and the next year declaring Egypt a republic.

One of those officers, Colonel Gamal Abdel Nasser, emerged as the leading figure. He was born in 1918. His father moved from the countryside to the city of Alexandria to work as a postal clerk. As a high school student, Nasser participated in the interwar anti-British demonstrations. In 1936 he enrolled in the military academy. A career in the army offered an avenue to social mobility otherwise closed to someone of his limited means. He served in the war to prevent the creation of the Jewish state of Israel in 1948, and in the wake of that defeat had helped organize the Free Officer movement. After the king's overthrow, Nasser quickly established his preeminence. He restrained other nationalist groups, repressed those who challenged him, and gave charge of the state apparatus to his close military associates. Nasser, with his charismatic personality, came to embody nationalist hopes. Following an assassination attempt in October 1954, he proclaimed to a crowd on the spot his readiness for patriotic martyrdom: "My life is yours, my blood a sacrifice to Egypt. . . . I have lived for you, and will do so until I die, striving for your sake."[28]

Nasser blamed the attempt on the Muslim Brotherhood, creating a fateful split in Egyptian politics. Founded in 1928, the Brothers had from the start espoused a nationalism that held Islam critical to Egypt's future but also to the future of the region. Their populist call for land redistribution, workers' rights, broad access to education and medical care, and provision of emergency food aid created a basis for collaboration with the military in launching the revolution. But in the wake of the attempt on his life, Nasser repressed the Brothers and then in 1966 hanged its leading thinker, Sayyid Qutb. The result was a lasting rift between a secular military jealous of its power and a formidable Islamist group. Not only were the Brothers a well-organized and popular presence in Egypt, but the organization in general and Qutb's writings in particular also exercised a strong influence throughout the region. Offshoots of the organization operated in Tunisia, Algeria, Syria, Jordan, Palestine, and Sudan.

At the start of his rule, Nasser recognized how widespread was the "dream of a strong liberated Egypt." But making that dream reality was, he conceded, "the most complicated of our problems." From the start Nasser took an assertive, independent international position. He provided support for anti-French independence movements in North Africa and leadership in the Arab campaign to crush Israel. He resisted pressure to take sides in the Cold War, sought economic assistance from both superpowers, and joined India and Yugoslavia in championing nonalignment. At home his main concern was to relieve suffering in the countryside. About 5 percent of landowners held 65 percent of cultivated land, while the remaining 95 percent of the population had 35 percent (usually minuscule plots). By 1952 more than half of all rural families were landless. Shortly after seizing power, the Free Officers took a dramatic step toward addressing these inequities by redistributing the royal estates as well as large land holdings controlled by mainly absentee owners.[29]

Of all his policies, nonalignment would embroil Nasser in the most trouble, setting off a major international crisis in 1956 and pushing him sharply to the left. He tried to dissuade fellow Arab rulers from signing up as Cold War allies of the United States. In 1955 he worked out an arms deal with the Soviet bloc to bring the Egyptian army up to the level of Israel's, while securing a World Bank loan of at least $1 billion for his showcase domestic project, the Aswan High Dam. Nasser envisioned building a major project that would harness the Nile, control floods, expand arable land, provide electricity, and thus dramatically lift Egypt into the modern age. He boasted, "In antiquity we built pyramids for the dead. Now we build pyramids for the living."[30] The dam would also raise Nasser's prestige and Egypt's influence in the Arab world. The Eisenhower administration, provoked by Nasser's "neutralism," suddenly withdrew its support, thus killing the World Bank loan for his grand project.

The Egyptian leader struck back, nationalizing the Suez Canal Company owned by British and French interests and thus precipitating an international crisis. The British, French, and Israeli governments secretly plotted to cut Nasser down to size. In late October 1956 Israeli forces struck the first blow, followed by their European allies, on the excuse of "restoring order." Surprised and outraged by this aggression, Eisenhower demanded that the invaders pull back. He did not want to feed the fires of anticolonialism in the Middle East nor to create an opening for Soviet meddling. Nasser's prestige in the region soared. Where Mosaddeq had failed, Nasser had succeeded. But in the process he had become heavily reliant on Khrushchev's Soviet Union for economic and military aid. Khrushchev helped the first Soviet client in the Middle East complete the Aswan project, built up Egypt's army and air force, and provided access to technical training. Nasser justified his pro-Soviet tilt on the grounds that Moscow did not insist on drawing Egypt into the Cold War and did not support Israel.

In the wake of the Suez crisis, Nasser became a vocal exponent of Arab unity. He embraced the general view that Egyptians were bound to other Arabs by a shared religion and language, the experience of Western domination, similar domestic problems, and a common opposition to Zionism. This pan-Arab sentiment had especially strong appeal in Syria and Iraq as well as Egypt in the 1950s and 1960s. But Nasser's nationalist commitment to Egypt came first and led him toward a utilitarian conception of regional unity. Solidarity among Arab peoples would help in eliminating the last vestiges of colonial influence, blocking unwanted intrusions of the superpowers in the region, and ousting the Israeli presence. Progress on all these fronts would in turn make Egypt more secure and more independent. He remarked in December 1956, "Egypt must not live isolated from the rest of the Arabs, because once we are isolated, we shall be defeated separately."[31] His views carried far and convincingly because he had stood up to the West at Suez. In 1958 Nasser turned vague talk of unity into a dramatic political experiment linking Egypt to Syria to form the United Arab Republic. Nasser served as the union's president, and Egypt occupied the dominant position within the union.

Nasser's post-1956 domestic policies combined nationalism and social justice in what became known as "Arab socialism." Like Nkrumah and other Third World radicals, Nasser was drawn to socialism as a scientific, efficient way to provide a better life for his people, not as a doctrine of class conflict. The Suez crisis gave him an excuse to nationalize foreign businesses with French and British connections. In 1960 he shifted to a planned economy, launching his first five-year plan with a heavy stress on industrialization. During the 1960s, he further expanded state economic control to include all major industry and commerce, even foreign trade. Only small-scale trading and agricultural operations remained in private hands.

Mindful of rural poverty, he implemented further rounds of land redistribution in 1961 and 1969.

Nasser could boast major achievements. His government ran the Suez Canal efficiently, turning it into an important source of national income. The economy grew during his tenure, in clear contrast to the stagnation marking the first half of the twentieth century. Per capita income doubled by 1973. Improvements in living standards would have been greater had it not been for a large population increase.[32] Unrelenting tension with Israel also held the economy back by diverting scarce resources from the civilian sector to the military, while the state-run part of the economy spawned a large, inefficient bureaucracy. Women gained expanded work and educational opportunities, but restrictive family law remained unchanged because Nasser did not want to challenge the Islamic values underlying that law. And while women and men both made headway in gaining literacy, the gap between the two remained substantial during the Nasser years. The much-touted Aswan High Dam proved disappointing. It began silting up, while at the same time producing a variety of adverse environmental effects, including loss of fertile lands along the Mediterranean and poisoning of once-productive fields. The limits of Nasser's socialism were most evident in the countryside. Land reform had created greater equality and especially benefited a small group of middle peasants rather than the large numbers of rural poor still without land. A high birthrate further contributed to poverty and landlessness. As the agricultural system failed to support the rural population, migration to the cities and abroad accelerated.

Nasser's attempts to promote unity within the region and destroy Israel were the least successful parts of his program. He intervened fruitlessly on behalf of allies in Jordan, Yemen, and Iraq, and in the process wasted Egypt's resources and made enemies within the Arab world. The experiment in building a United Arab Republic collapsed in 1961, and the idea of Arab nationalism was further discredited in 1967 when Egypt, along with Syria and Jordan, went to war against Israel and suffered defeat. Preoccupied with protecting his prestige at home and in the region, Nasser had blundered into this Six-Day War and lost the Sinai Peninsula and the Gaza Strip (see Map 6.4). With Egypt and Israel still locked in a sullen confrontation punctuated by frequent armed exchanges, Umm Kulthum, a singer of enormous popularity in Egypt and elsewhere in the Arab world, gave concerts to raise funds and rally support. Her song, "The Ruins," expressed a widely felt sadness and grim determination in the face of victorious Zionism with its links to that old enemy, imperialism: "Give me my freedom. / Untie my hands. / I gave, I held back nothing. / Ah, your bonds have made my wrists bleed."[33]

Despite the shocking setback of 1967, Nasser retained his extraordinary popular appeal at home. His offer to resign evoked a groundswell of public support. His death from a heart attack three years later brought a million mourners onto the streets of Cairo in an emotional outpouring. Nasser's passing marked the end of an era of radicalism for Egypt in both domestic and foreign policy. The high hopes for Egypt and the region that had flowered in the postwar years began to dim. What

THE NASSER ERA IN EGYPT	
1882	Britain asserts control over Egypt
1922	Britain concedes limited independence
1952	Free Officers movement overthrows Egyptian monarch
1956	Crisis over the Suez Canal radicalizes Nasser
1958	Egypt and Syria join in a short-lived United Arab Republic
1960	Nasser embraces a socialist economic program
1967	Egypt suffers stunning territorial losses to Israel in the Six-Day War
1970	Aswan High Dam completed; Nasser's death

was said by a colleague of Nasser during his 18 years in power applied equally to Egypt during that time: "He was a strong starter, but a lousy finisher."[34]

Colonial Crisis in Algeria

In striking contrast to the case of Egypt, where the colonial power steadily if reluctantly retreated in the face of nationalist pressure, Algeria had the misfortune of becoming a battleground in the most violent process of decolonization that the North Africa–Middle East region would witness. An Algerian nationalist movement had taken shape between World War I and World War II in ways familiar from other Third World countries. Growing numbers of the poor and landless moved to the cities, where exposure to colonial practices and proximity to the settler community sharpened anti-French sentiments. At the same time, French education made the Algerian elite sensitive to the gap between Europe's professed liberal and nationalist ideas and the colonial reality. World War II added impetus to burgeoning independence sentiment, encouraged by the Atlantic Charter's commitment to self-determination. Wartime economic deprivation and clashes with police heightened the sense of grievance.

Demands for independence ran up against a wall of French resistance. By 1945 Algeria was home to one million French settlers resolute in their opposition to any concessions that might threaten their political dominance and economic privilege. The more vociferous the calls for independence, the more stubborn settlers became in defense of the status quo and the more repressive the French military. In putting down one round of demonstrations at the end of the war, colonial authorities killed some 20,000 to 40,000 Algerians.

Tensions building for several decades came to a boiling point in mid-1954 with the formation of the National Liberation Front (Front de Libération National or FLN). The Vietnamese victory at Dien Bien Phu that year demonstrated that armed resistance to French forces was a viable liberation strategy. The highly diverse

Front leadership included military men operating inside the country and those forming FLN armies in neighboring Tunisia and Morocco after those two countries gained independence from France in 1956. It also included leaders such as Ahmed Ben Bella, who spent most of the struggle in French prisons, and others who guided the FLN from a sanctuary in Cairo provided by the Nasser government. Some among the leadership wanted nothing less than unconditional independence, while others were ready to settle for a compromise. Some viewed the world through the prism of European left and liberal ideas; others championed indigenous Arab and Islamic values. Popular support came from an equally diverse range of groups—from migrant workers in France and French intellectuals to Algerian peasants, some newly arrived in the city. Women participated no less than men. The strategies of resistance were no less diverse. An underground organization challenged French administration. Guerrilla operations and cross-border raids by FLN forces threatened French control in the countryside. Urban terrorists struck at the settler population, against Algerians collaborating with the French, and within France itself. Street demonstrations and general strikes underlined the breadth of revolutionary support.

Paris responded to this bold defiance by deploying ultimately 400,000 troops. Increasingly frustrated and demoralized senior French military officers conducted the war with grim determination. They had surrendered to the Germans during World War II and more recently to the Vietnamese, had abandoned control of Morocco and Tunisia without a fight, and suffered humiliation in the Suez crisis. They were now eager to prove their mettle, vowing that they would not be deprived of this one victory. The army's strategy of mass arrests, sweeps in the countryside, resettlement and destruction of villages, sealing off the border, and meeting FLN terror with counter-terror and torture successfully contained the FLN threat. These actions would in the end result in deaths on the Algerian side estimated as high as 300,000 out of a population of about eight million. Some 10,000 of the French forces would die. The dehumanizing brutality of this struggle was captured in Frantz Fanon's liberationist masterpiece, *The Wretched of the Earth*, published in 1961: "Colonialism is not a thinking machine, nor a body endowed with reasoning faculties. It is violence in its natural state, and it will only yield when confronted with greater violence."[35]

The French could not turn this ugly stalemate into victory. Repression deepened Algerian alienation from French rule, brought new recruits to the FLN, and provoked international condemnation of French policy. Within France itself, the brutality of the highly publicized urban struggle and the costs of the war in life and property had by the late 1950s polarized the public and paralyzed the political system. Some regarded Algeria as a lost cause, while others felt an obligation to defend the imperiled settlers and the last shreds of imperial glory.

Resolving this domestic political crisis in France ultimately proved critical to resolving the war in Algeria. Charles de Gaulle returned to power in 1958 along with a constitutional makeover to strengthen the presidency. With his base at home assured by 1961, de Gaulle moved to negotiate an end to the war over the violent objections of rebellious officers serving in Algeria and their allies within the settler community. Their acts of terrorism and threats of a military takeover in Paris gave special urgency and peril to de Gaulle's peacemaking. Finally in March 1962 de Gaulle and the FLN reached an agreement to bring this long, bloody war to an end. France yielded on independence but got in return continued access to military bases and preservation of economic ties. The agreement included safeguards for European settlers, but by the end of the year virtually all but the poor and aged had fled.

Independence found the new Algerian government facing high public expectations but daunting circumstances. The educational system was rudimentary and the illiteracy rate high. Colonial policy had created an imbalanced economy. Agriculture, which provided employment for the majority of the population, had stagnated for half a century, while gas and oil production had developed rapidly beginning in the 1950s. Some three million rural people displaced by the war needed attention. The loss of capital and technical skills, resulting from the flight of the settlers, plunged the economy into crisis.

During the first years following independence, the FLN-controlled government followed an authoritarian and secular path under the leadership of Ben Bella and then Colonel Houari Boumediene, who took power in a 1965 coup. By 1967 Boumediene's position was secure enough for him to launch a state-directed economic development program. Determined to end economic subordination to France and other major powers, the Boumediene government nationalized foreign-controlled sectors of the economy such as gas, oil, and banking. It directed government investments into petroleum and heavy industry, leaving almost nothing for the consumer and agricultural sectors. Even with fresh land-reform measures, agriculture continued to stagnate. But GDP during the Boumediene years (1965–1978) doubled, providing some insulation against the regime's critics.

The similarities of Boumediene to Nasser, apparent in intensifying domestic reform, extended to international affairs. Like Nasser, the Algerian government insisted on a position of nonalignment in the Cold War and joined India, Egypt, and Yugoslavia in championing that position in the UN and at international conferences. It also expressed its commitment to Third World causes by strongly opposing imperialism in the Middle East and throughout Africa. It sharply criticized Israel and supported the claims of displaced Palestinians. And it was an outspoken foe of white-minority rule in South Africa and of surviving colonial regimes elsewhere in sub-Saharan Africa.

CONCLUSION

What is striking looking back on the Third World in the middle years of the Cold War is the strong appeal of Marxism to many of its leaders. To understand that appeal we need to put ourselves in their place. Marxism helped them explain, as no other ideology could, how a few foreigners had come to subjugate their peoples and demean their old and proud cultures. "Imperialism" had driven economically advanced countries to dominate and exploit just as "feudal" conditions had rendered the Third World weak, divided, and thus easy prey. As Third World leaders began to think about the practical problems of ousting entrenched foreign influences and neutralizing native collaborators, they came to prize the single-party model often patterned on the tight Leninist party organization. It would allow them, as no open political system or democratic process could, to mobilize popular support and direct it through the often long, arduous liberation struggle. To be sure, the prominence of peasants in the Third World ill accorded with the preoccupations of Western Marxism, and the impatience of leaders to effect change collided with the ponderous planning ethos associated with Soviet-style development. But Marxism and Soviet leaders eager for influence were to prove flexible enough to accommodate diverse societies and ambitious timetables.

The Soviet Union and then by the 1950s China as well reinforced this radical trend. Even if Stalin had been cautious in offering help to anticolonial struggles, at least the Soviet Union in his time had been bold in denouncing Western domination. Under Khrushchev, the Third World found Moscow more inclined to back its rhetoric with offers of aid and protection. Mao's China also stepped forward with support, even if on a more limited scale than the Soviets. In addition, both socialist powers followed a course of dramatic domestic development that inspired confidence in the capacity of a strong state to transform a backward economy into a modern one.

The disappointing American record further accentuated the marked leftward drift in the Third World toward socialist principles, state-directed economic development, and one-party politics. For a time elites had taken seriously public American professions of support for national self-determination. Woodrow Wilson had loudly proclaimed the principle during World War I. The Atlantic Charter in August 1941 had at Roosevelt's insistence included a sweeping commitment to "respect the right of all peoples to choose the form of government under which they will live."[36] But by mid-1945 British and U.S. leaders were expressing reservations about colonial peoples rushing toward freedom without a suitable period of European tutelage. Perhaps worst of all, as the independence fever spread throughout the Third World, American officials expressed a barely concealed sense of superiority. And their actions during the Cold War were consistent with their paternalistic and racist attitudes, sharpening the view within the Third World that the United States had betrayed its much-touted commitment to freedom. The United States either aligned with Britain and France on colonial issues or asserted its own restraining influence out of fear of instability and communist encroachment. Washington increasingly backed military dictatorships, launched covert operations against nonaligned or left-leaning governments (as in Iran, Guatemala, and Cuba), and occasionally dispatched U.S. forces (as in Lebanon, the Dominican Republic, and Vietnam). Repeated U.S. interventions to preserve the status quo created widespread disappointment and anger that further enhanced the appeal of radicalism so alarming to American leaders.

The ambitions associated with the radicalism of the 1950s and 1960s were proving difficult to realize. They encountered domestic obstacles, while U.S. hostility imposed costs that new and relatively poor countries could ill afford. East Asian success at integrating into the international market economy suggested an attractive alternative to development through import substitution and state planning. This combination of domestically inspired second thoughts, potent international pressures, and a booming international economy would break the spell of radicalism and push Third World countries in so many different directions that it would become increasingly difficult to find anything in common among them (see Chapter 9).

Part Three

FROM COLD WAR TO
GLOBALIZATION, 1968–1991

THE FABLED MOMENT in the history of the McDonald's Corporation came in 1954 when an innovative idea met its messiah. Ray Kroc, a 52-year-old salesman, walked into a Los Angeles-area restaurant run by the McDonald brothers, Richard and Maurice. What Kroc saw that so impressed him was the "McDonald's Speedee Service System." A carefully coordinated kitchen team quickly produced good 15-cent hamburgers and quality fries for drive-up customers in a clean, friendly environment. In Kroc's version of this tale, he at once envisioned restaurants serving up cheap, fast food just like this one "dotting crossroads all over the country."[1] He quickly secured from the brothers the rights to franchise the concept, and in 1961 borrowed $2.7 million to buy them out. The gamble paid off handsomely: By the time of his death in 1984 Kroc was a millionaire many times over.

Kroc had the pluck and energy associated with the American myth that everyone had a shot at riches. Born in 1902 just outside Chicago, he had dropped out of high school to work as a traveling salesman for everything from Florida real estate and paper cups to milkshake mixers and folding furniture. Following his 1954 encounter with the McDonald's operation, Kroc became a fervent advocate of the fast-food concept, championing it with dogged optimism, energy, and ingenuity. After pouring the rest of his career into the effort, this ambitious perfectionist would look back and observe, "Work is the meat in the hamburger of life."[2]

But Kroc also owed his success to the special postwar ethos that first took shape in southern California. Wartime defense plants had brought jobs and rising incomes to the area. The Cold War kept defense industries humming and the local economy booming in the 1950s. At the same time, with the initiation in 1956 of a network of interstate highways, federal dollars were helping to create a thriving car culture. Southern Californians exploited the mobility made possible by car ownership, moving to the suburbs and shopping at stores relocated from downtowns to outlying malls with ample parking and easy road access. Customers were ready for restaurants that were easily reached by car and that offered inexpensive, tasty, and dependable food produced using the very industrial, production-line techniques familiar from defense plants. Kroc banked on this wave of social change to realize his vision of a McDonald's at thousands of major intersections.

But would this system of food production and consumption, so peculiarly American, ever catch on overseas? When in 1968 Fred Turner, a Kroc protégé, took over the company, he turned his attention abroad. Efforts to set up in Canada, the Caribbean, and the Netherlands misfired. Turner made adjustments by sticking closely overseas to the approach that had succeeded in the U.S. market: Select managers willing to embrace the company's philosophy and direction; insist on adherence to the McDonald's formula for food preparation and service; and maintain strict oversight of each franchise. The first breakthrough came in 1971 when Japanese businessmen proved enthusiastic converts to the fast-food formula. McDonald's scored similar successes in Germany and Australia. By the late 1970s the Chicago-based corporation had established a solid beachhead outside the United States—almost 400 outlets operating in 20 countries (66 in Tokyo alone)— and had begun negotiating access to eastern-bloc countries. The outlets that soon opened across eastern Europe represented early breaches in the Cold War lines. In 1990, in a telling sign of the times, McDonald's planted itself in downtown Moscow, where the "Beeg Mek" attracted crowds larger than at the Kremlin or Lenin's tomb—15 million customers during the first year.[3] The opening in Beijing two years later broke the company record for the most transactions in one day.

McDonald's had become an economic powerhouse and a global icon. By the start of the twenty-first century it had over 30,000 stores worldwide, with half in North America, a fifth in Europe, and an eighth in Japan.[4] It held the largest collection of real estate in the world. And by spending more money on advertising and marketing internationally than any other brand, it had displaced Coca-Cola as the best-known commercial product. The corporate mascot, the clown Ronald McDonald, had eclipsed Mickey Mouse in fame.

McDonald's was also emerging as a lightning rod for debate over the complex and contentious issues raised by globalization. Its critics saw numerous sins. Industrially produced food inflicted cruelty on animals while imposing restrictions on farmers and ranchers that robbed them of their independence. An insatiable demand for disposable paper products and large-scale, intensive assembly-line agriculture damaged the environment. McDonald's imperiled local culinary traditions by substituting synthetic materials and flavors for natural ones. It endangered good health. High in calories and saturated fat, the McDonald's staple of burgers, fries, and shakes promoted obesity. Problems of weight and health, first evident in the United States, were soon showing up abroad, even in developing countries such as China, as fast food became a part of a younger generation's daily diet. Finally, McDonald's exploited its largely inexperienced, unskilled, part-time workforce, paying low wages and offering no benefits. When union organizers appeared, McDonald's headquarters joined with its restaurant managers in stubbornly fighting back. On occasion McDonald's subjected its critics to long, costly libel suits and even monitored and disrupted their activities. French cultural nationalists denounced this foreign interloper. Siding with the critics, French President Jacques Chirac declared, "I detest McDonald's." Israel's president, Ezer Weizman, wrote of the need to be "wary" of this threat to the country's culture and religion.[5]

McDonald's success overseas was due in part to the changing preferences of overseas consumers. They were in important ways becoming like their U.S. counterparts: Rising incomes made possible spending on non-essentials; working parents had limited time for food shopping and preparation; and children on their own after school had allowances to spend on diversions. In this sense, McDonald's was not an intruder forcing its tastes on customers but a pioneer, meeting a demand for fast, friendly service and cheap, dependable food in a sanitary setting. Having blazed the way, McDonald's time and again found itself facing serious competition from locals who had borrowed one or more elements of the McDonald's model. Imitation was an admission that the foreign interloper had correctly read changing social conditions and customer tastes.

McDonald's had the good sense to realize that not all overseas markets were the same and thus to make adjustments that varied from country to country. The most obvious was some tinkering with the standard McDonald's menu. When Hindus balked at eating meat from cows, McDonald's in India substituted lamb patties. If Germans wanted beer, then McDonald's went along. If Norwegians hankered for fish, then they got a salmon burger. No less important was the latitude owner-operators overseas had to select store sites, to work out arrangements with local suppliers, and to select locally appealing advertising themes. Subtler but no less significant, McDonald's sometimes had to compromise the fast-food model, which expected customers to eat quickly and go. For example, in East Asia, young people used McDonald's as a safe, comfortable setting in which to study or socialize. The elderly and women used McDonald's as a meeting place. Families came to celebrate birthdays and other family occasions. The curious from the countryside dropped in to check out this symbol of a modern lifestyle and even to pretend for a moment that they were urbane. These various kinds of accommodations made McDonald's seem less like an American firm and more like an indigenous one. Little wonder that young people overseas growing up with McDonald's reportedly exclaimed with surprise and delight when they visited the United States, "Look, Americans have McDonald's too!"

For good or ill, McDonald's expansion overseas was part of a relentlessly rising tide of global economic activity from the 1970s onward. International trade accelerated as tariffs worldwide came down, and capital began to move more freely as states rolled back restrictions. Increasingly integrated and powerful, the world economy exerted its influence over the domestic affairs of countries—whether developed or developing, whether free market or socialist—and shaped both public agendas and private taste. It hastened the rise of the consumer ethic that was so

McDonald's on Paris's Champs-Élysées
No gaudy drive-in, this restaurant was discrete and pedestrian-friendly. By looking like a café from the outside and obscuring the 400 seats within, McDonald's remade itself to fit in. Parisian customers came to refer affectionately to the restaurant with the golden arches that appeared in neighborhoods around the city as "McDo." (AP Photo/Remy de la Mauviniere, file)

beneficial to McDonald's. Consumers enthusiastically embraced a wide range of mass-market products. Many were American in origin, ranging from casual clothes and fast food to TV programming and popular music. But Bombay movies producers and Qatar television news programming demonstrated that others could also exploit the possibilities of broader cultural markets. At the same time intensified competition placed pressures on producers in all countries to become more efficient, pressures that in turn were socially disruptive as industrial jobs migrated to low-wage areas, employment in the service sector (including fast food) expanded dramatically, and the earnings of the poor lagged behind. Government spending fell under assault as the source of deficits that would scare away international investors and as an affront to the free-market principles that were becoming orthodoxy. These developments created their own backlash, leading to charges that uncontrolled economic growth harmed the environment, smothered local cultures, and accentuated inequalities. The resulting controversies over the impact of globalization would not only envelop McDonald's but also outlast the Cold War.

These developments playing out worldwide did not (as McDonald's had discovered) erase diversity within the main parts of the market-oriented international economy. Indeed, intensifying economic integration had as its counterpoint intensifying economic differentiation. The leading economies of Europe, East Asia, and North America continued the postwar trend toward consolidating into major blocs, each with its own understanding of how the market ought to operate. Global governance would increasingly if informally pass into the hands of the major economies of these three blocs. No longer able alone to orchestrate the flow of global goods and investments, Washington came to accept its relative decline and with it the need for collaboration with other bloc leaders.

Seen in broad terms, McDonald's success paralleled the last act of the Cold War and foreshadowed its conclusion: a resounding victory for consumer culture. The spread of franchises overseas developed apace with interest in calming super-power tensions. The negotiations for McDonald's franchises in eastern Europe and the Soviet Union were as much the herald of the Cold War's end as arms con-trol agreements. McDonald's would survive; the Soviet empire would not. On both sides of an increasingly porous Iron Curtain, popular preoccupations with the good life constrained superpower policy as much as it enriched McDonald's. In the United States, western Europe, and Japan affluence from the 1960s was taken as a fact of life—a right to be protected and enjoyed, especially by a new generation habituated to relative affluence, wearing blue jeans, drinking Coke, and listen-ing to rock. In the Soviet bloc, where state-run ("command") economies were falling palpably behind popular expectations, the good life was only partially realized, stirring not only dreams of better housing, more appliances, and a car but also alienation from a socialist system that had failed to deliver the goods as promised.

Soviet and American leaders during the final two decades of the Cold War took careful note of this popular aversion to sacrifice or talk of nuclear war. Acting on these concerns, President Richard Nixon initiated the era of détente, which then faltered and seemingly collapsed under presidents Jimmy Carter and Ronald Reagan only to suddenly revive in the late 1980s under Mikhail Gorbachev. Seeking to resolve the tension between guns and butter already evident in the Khrushchev years, Gorbachev launched a daring experiment meant to invigorate the economy and thus catch up with the abundance and technological innovation of a capitalist West. Ending the costly Cold War was an essential part of Gorbachev's plan. That policy part succeeded just as the overall economic plan failed, with unpleasant consequences for the Soviet political system and Russian society.

Finally, McDonald's was an indicator of strong economic currents fundamentally transforming the Third World. The revolutionary phase there had peaked in the 1960s, and increasingly thereafter the demonstrable success of countries integrated into the international economy began to make the socialist model look passé. Only a few, such as Cuba and North Korea, stoutly hewed to that model. And Marxist-inspired revolutions went out of fashion, with the notable exception of Cambodia. Indeed, the most significant revolutionary upheaval of the late twentieth century—that in Iran—looked to Mohammad, not Marx. To most in the developing world, the global economy held out the greatest promise—access to capital and technology and the chance for low-wage countries to shift to export-oriented manufacture. The countries of maritime East Asia such as South Korea and Taiwan and even China demonstrated that international economic integration was more than a promise; it was an effective development strategy.

The cumulative result of these changes was to undermine not only the appeal of radical programs in the Third World but also the very idea of a Third World as a coherent concept. Countries that had followed a similar trajectory from colonial control to anticolonial resistance to independence with its promise of rapid, socialist-inspired transformation now began moving in strikingly different directions with strikingly different results. Some, especially in East and Southeast Asia, successfully came to terms with the global economy. Others in sub-Saharan Africa and Latin America were less successful. Population growth and neglect of women as a critical resource hindered progress, but more burdensome still were the longstanding internal conflicts that consumed such places as South Africa and Guatemala. Those whose economy floundered found themselves having to turn for relief to international bankers every bit as ideological as the old socialist planners. The bankers' prescription was giving more scope to the market and less to state welfare, which spelled for the short term at least more social pain and political tension for states already in trouble. A rough gauge of the winners and the losers in an increasingly diverse postcolonial world was which had a McDonald's and which still lacked the purchasing power, good economic prospects, and political stability to make a franchise a safe bet.

7

THE COLD WAR COMES TO A CLOSE

ONCE BEGUN, the Cold War was not easily ended. After warily circling each other for a decade, Moscow and Washington had taken the first tentative steps toward putting their dispute on the negotiating table in the mid-1950s. Bolder action was needed if they were to break out of Cold War suspicions. The Cuban Missile Crisis and the deepening U.S. role in Vietnam had testified to the continuing power of those suspicions into the 1960s, and they persisted not only over Soviet-backed Cuba and North Vietnam but also over the Soviet invasion of Afghanistan in 1979 as well as insurgencies at multiple points in Central America and Africa. Nevertheless, a string of initiatives took shape beginning in 1969 that finally in the late 1980s brought the rivalry to an end. The forward motion was, however, slow and uneven, obstructed on both sides by deep doubts and strong institutionalized interests in preserving the Cold War status quo. And the two leaders who did the most to push the process forward, Richard Nixon and Mikhail Gorbachev, would be thoroughly discredited at home. But their efforts would be rewarded with success—a surprisingly sudden superpower peace in 1989.

The Cold War world then quickly turned upside down. Beyond the wildest imaginings of Western specialists and even of socialist-bloc leaders themselves, Moscow surrendered its grip on its client regimes in eastern Europe, and one after another they toppled in the face of domestic protest. At the same time a reform program introduced within the Soviet Union itself veered out of control. The empire created by the czars and restored by Stalin fragmented in 1991, and the Soviet Communist Party was discredited. These events not only transformed the scene in the old Soviet bloc but also dramatically recast the international landscape.

THE RISE AND FALL OF DÉTENTE

The 1970s witnessed a distinct lessening of Cold War tensions known as détente. It built on earlier efforts to avoid a superpower collision with its accompanying nuclear risks. To diminish tensions policymakers sought to promote greater dialogue, hold regular summit meetings, and negotiate arms control and other bilateral agreements. By the late 1970s, however, détente was under assault within the United States even as it retained support among American allies and even within the Kremlin. The Cold War seemed to have acquired a life of its own, and most observers assumed that the Soviet–American rivalry had become a permanent feature of the postwar world.

The Nixon Turnaround

President Richard Nixon was the unlikely author of détente. Anticommunism had carried him to political prominence. Elected to the House of Representatives in 1946, he made his name pursuing a former State Department official, Alger Hiss, suspected of espionage. In 1950 he won a seat in the Senate after charging that his liberal opponent, Helen G. Douglas, was "pink right down to her underwear."[1] He accused the Truman administration of appeasement in China and in Korea, and urged strong U.S. backing for the French during their last stand in Vietnam in 1954. By then he was embarked on a long course of serious schooling in the ways of the world. His education began as Eisenhower's vice president between 1953 and 1960. His "kitchen debate" with Khrushchev showed that already by 1959 he was thinking of the Cold War in fresh terms (see Chapter 5). His studies continued for an additional decade in two runs for the presidency and wide foreign travel. Along the way he became convinced of the truth of a syllogism that Franklin Roosevelt would have accepted: Great powers had legitimate interests; the Soviet Union and China as well as the United States were great powers; thus the task of diplomacy was to locate the areas of essential national interest (where mutual tolerance should prevail) and to concentrate negotiations on the areas of mutual interest (where compromise was possible).

Nixon took possession of the presidency in 1969 with a much-modified view of the Cold War. It was not to be conducted as a moral crusade to annihilate evil; it was to make room for dialogue with the Soviet Union and China as a matter of necessity. As he told his staff in 1971, "the world will not be worth living in if we can't get the great potential explosive forces under control." In any case, he pointed out, the relative decline of U.S. economic power meant that a world dominated by "just two superpowers" had given way to one under the sway of "five great power centers"—the Soviet Union, China, western Europe, and Japan as well as the United States—engaged economically in both cooperation and competition. In keeping with this shift away from Cold War thinking, Nixon limited the growth of U.S. nuclear weapons and made deep cuts in the military budget.[2]

Nixon's personality made him an unlikely policy innovator. He was closed off emotionally; his words were often rehearsed; and his smile was forced. He was prey to inner conflicts that occasionally burst through to the surface, often as part of the mood swings to which he was prone. He would then lash out at liberals, Jews, African Americans, the media, the Northeast establishment—any group that had offended him over the course of his political career. In one of his vengeful fits he told his staff how to handle critics: "Get them on the floor and step on them, crush them, show no mercy."[3] He worked hard and contrasted his own personal struggle with the privileges that came by birth to others such as John Kennedy. He could not enroll at Harvard for want of funds, and instead attended Whittier College close to home. Despite a Duke law degree, he did not get an offer from the Wall Street firms that he hankered to work for, and had to settle for a position with a hometown law firm. After service in the Pacific during World War II, he embarked on the political career that would bring him recognition and satisfaction. Nixon took pride in his capacity as a man of humble origins to make his way to public eminence.

When he became president in 1969, conditions in the United States posed challenges to the old policies and gave an advantage to a discerning political leader willing to adjust. The controversy over the deepening conflict in Vietnam had seriously eroded the Cold War consensus, the bedrock for the policies pursued by Nixon's predecessors. The shift in attitudes became evident in a Congress less and less inclined to defer to presidential leadership (see Chapter 4). No less serious, the country suffered from deep divisions. Even as he campaigned for the presidency in 1968, Americans seemed about to descend into civil war over Vietnam, race relations, and other issues accumulating over a decade. To round off the challenge, Nixon faced from the start of his presidency economic difficulties. The dollar was under attack internationally, and at home the economy was entering a period of stagnation and inflation ("stagflation"). The time was ripe to trim American ambitions.

Nixon entered the White House with three basic foreign policy goals that he pursued with the assistance of his chief foreign policy adviser, Henry Kissinger. The first was to end the unpopular Vietnam War as quickly as was consistent with American honor. Nixon publicly suggested that he had a secret plan to bring "a peace with honor," an objective that he grimly held to. As we saw in Chapter 4, Nixon calculated that a new campaign of bombing and an expansion of the ground war into North Vietnamese sanctuaries in Cambodia and Laos would give the U.S.-supported government in the South a reasonable chance of survival. And he continued the peace talks in Paris begun by President Johnson in 1968. Those talks would ultimately yield a compromise agreement in January 1973, in which Washington dropped its insistence on North Vietnamese troop withdrawal from the South and Hanoi gave up its demand for the end of the Saigon government. By spring 1975, when the North Vietnamese launched their final offensive, scandal had already forced Nixon from office, and neither his successor, Gerald Ford, nor the American public nor Congress showed any taste for investing more money or troops to block Hanoi's impending victory.

Nixon's second goal was to open up relations with China. Proponents of diplomatic recognition for the People's Republic of China had become more vocal during the 1960s, and Nixon himself had gingerly endorsed that position in public in

1967. After his 1968 election, Nixon secretly pushed ahead with diplomatic contacts. His China initiative arose from long-term considerations. Nixon had concluded that the United States would have to learn to live with rather than convert or destroy Communist China. He explained to an aide, "In 25 years you can't have a quarter of the people of the world isolated and have any chance of peace."[4] The president also hoped that his closer ties to Beijing would worry Moscow and Hanoi and nudge them toward concessions on arms control and in the Paris peace talks on Vietnam.

In early 1972 Nixon made a triumphal visit to Beijing to meet with Mao Zedong and lay the foundation for a new relationship. A joint statement issued at the end of the visit confirmed the new commitment to normalized Sino-American relations and set Taiwan aside as an unresolved bone of contention—as a part of China (as Beijing claimed) but not to be regained by force (as Washington insisted). This agreement provided the basis for the new relationship between the two Pacific giants. Nixon premised his approach on avoiding a repeat of the wars in Korea and Vietnam. In 1969 he had announced that Asian rather than American boys would henceforth have to bear the primary burden of defending noncommunist regimes, backed by preexisting U.S. defense arrangements, notably for South Korea, Taiwan, and Japan. These decisions to step away from but not completely dismantle the containment line in East Asia established by Truman was consistent with the experience of a president who twice in his political career had seen the electorate recoil at Americans fighting and dying on the Asian mainland.

For his part, Mao at 78 (more than 20 years Nixon's senior) was a disappointed and increasingly frail revolutionary, anxious to protect his political achievements at home. Whom was he to trust with his legacy? He was also increasingly concerned with China's enemies. His confrontational policy had antagonized both superpowers so that their forces now lodged right up against China's southern, eastern, and northern frontiers. Sino-Soviet tensions had been deepening through the 1960s, climaxing in armed clashes in 1969 along the inner Asian border. Particularly troubling to Mao was the threat posed by over one million Soviet troops and nuclear weapons deployed against China. At the same time he had provoked Washington by endorsing revolution in Asia and resuming aid to Vietnam in 1964. Korea was still divided and tense, with the South serving as a base for U.S. forces, and Taiwan was no closer to liberation thanks to an American blanket of protection. The Chinese leader decided to preempt a dangerous strategic encirclement by his two formidable enemies by improving relations with one. Nixon would become his partner in thawing Sino-American relations.

Nixon's third and most important foreign policy goal was to reduce tension in U.S.–Soviet relations and minimize the dangers of nuclear war. To achieve this, he worked with Soviet leader Leonid Brezhnev. They built on the two earlier steps toward bringing the strategic nuclear arms race under control: a 1963 ban on tests in the atmosphere and a 1968 agreement against proliferation of nuclear weapons. Their major achievement was the Strategic Arms Limitations Treaty (SALT I) concluded in 1972. It aimed for the first time at creating stability and capping the competition. It froze the number of launchers each side could have at 2,568 for the Soviet Union and 1,764 for the United States and limited each side to two anti-missile defense systems. It did not, however, limit the number of warheads on each launcher, thus opening the arms race on a new front. Nixon and Brezhnev also developed economic and cultural exchanges to promote understanding. While making the Cold War less dangerous, these initiatives did not in Nixon's view preclude forceful action where necessary. He thus felt free, for example, to heavily bomb the Soviets' Vietnamese allies, undermine the Soviet position in the Middle East, and topple the socialist regime of Salvador Allende in Chile.

Brezhnev Conservatism

Nixon's Soviet partner in détente, Leonid Brezhnev, embodied conservative impulses within the Soviet Communist Party. Like Khrushchev, he was a product of the Soviet system. He was one of many of working-class background who had advanced rapidly under Stalin. But much more than Khrushchev, Brezhnev was wedded to the status quo. He thought Khrushchev's reformist, anti-Stalinist tendencies misguided if not dangerous. This conservatism would define an era, from Brezhnev's accession to power in 1964 until his death in 1982. Brezhnev dropped the attacks on Stalin, pulled back on reform in key areas, and protected the position of party cadres.

Perhaps the most striking expression of this domestic conservatism was Brezhnev's intolerance for critical voices, many left over from the Khrushchev cultural thaw. Outspoken and sometimes harsh, these voices reveal how much intellectuals had recovered their position of moral authority and confidence after Stalin's attempt to crush them. A look at two of the most prominent provides a sense of the political hopes and moral passions that sought to break through the crust of official conservatism.

The novelist Aleksandr Solzhenitsyn was deeply antagonistic to the Soviet regime. Profoundly attached to pre-revolutionary Russian society and values, he provocatively called for the party to admit that it had taken the country down a blind alley lured by false Western notions of constant material progress and faith in technology and reason. In the process the party had cut Russia off from its cultural and moral roots, despoiled the land, and created a brutal urban society. Marxism seemed to him nothing more than "this grim jest of the twentieth century." Solzhenitsyn favored the restoration of Christianity as "the only living spiritual force capable of undertaking the spiritual healing of Russia." He also favored an enlightened authoritarian political system until the people were ready to govern themselves. At the very least he wanted the party to open the system to free expression. In 1973 he admonished the leaders in the Kremlin, "Let the people breathe, let them think and develop."[5]

The physicist Andrei Sakharov, the father of the Soviet hydrogen bomb, followed a much more cosmopolitan agenda. This star in the Soviet scientific establishment was driven to dissent initially by alarm over the dangers posed by the hydrogen bomb that he had helped develop. In 1968 he called for applying scientific norms of open discussion broadly to public life. He said what many in the scientific community had long thought—that science was a model of rationality and democracy that should shape the Soviet system. The publication of his views abroad led to the loss of his security clearance. His human rights campaign in the 1970s got him into still deeper trouble. By then he had concluded that a closed, authoritarian Soviet system could not address the nuclear danger and more broadly the problem of international insecurity. He began demanding greater intellectual freedom, thus striking directly at the party's control over political and cultural life: "As long as a country has no civil liberty, no freedom of information, and no independent press, then there exists no effective body of public opinion to control the conduct of the government and its functionaries."[6]

By the end of the 1970s the Brezhnev leadership had managed largely to silence these and other troublesome dissident intellectuals. Solzhenitsyn was deported in 1974 after circulating copies of his classic account of the Stalinist prison system, *The Gulag Archipelago*. (He settled in rural Vermont.) The leadership decided to get rid of Sakharov after he openly criticized Soviet military intervention in Afghanistan (treated later in this chapter). To isolate him from the international press, the Kremlin exiled Sakharov to the city of Gorky in 1980. Others promoting human rights, such as the Russian section of Amnesty International, were charged with "antisocial" and "anti-Soviet" activities and accused of being in league with the American enemy.

Despite the Soviet Union's problems, Brezhnev favored letting the system plod ahead. He sidestepped the main challenge that Khrushchev had wrestled with—the inability of an inefficient state-controlled, command economy to meet rising consumer expectations while also supporting a military with superpower aspirations. Far from catching up with and then surpassing capitalism, the socialist system was lagging, especially in science and technology. Industry as well as agricultural and service sectors suffered from low productivity.

There was a long list of reasons—all too familiar to Soviet leaders—for the poor state of the economy. The intrusive, all-inclusive system of planning inculcated passivity. Malingering on the job was commonplace. Management and workers alike became implicated in corruption and graft. The gap between the countryside and the city in terms of living standards and educational opportunities remained substantial and encouraged those who could to flee rural hardship for a richer life in the city. The resulting failure of the "official" economy to provide consumers with adequate goods and services gave rise to activity outside the control of the state planners—a "second economy" that was part "gray" (officially tolerated if not condoned) and part "black" (illegal).

Alcoholism seemed to officialdom a worrisome concomitant of these economic troubles. Between 1955 and 1979, per capita consumption of both legal and home-brewed alcohol, mainly vodka, rose steadily and dramatically—more than doubling

The Anti-Alcohol Campaign, 1985
This cartoon, which appeared in the popular Soviet humor magazine *Krokodil* has Eve asking, "Would you rather [have] an apple, Adam?" When Gorbachev shortly after taking charge in 1985 launched a far-reaching anti-alcohol campaign, production and consumption simply went underground, and the state lost significant revenue. After several years the campaign collapsed and alcoholism persisted as a serious problem into the post-Soviet period. (*Krokodil*, no. 27, 1985)

by conservative estimates. With working adults in cities drinking as much as a bottle a day of heavily alcoholic drinks, an unusually large share of family budgets went to alcohol, by one estimate 15 to 20 percent of disposable income. A growing proportion of young people and women began to drink regularly and heavily. University students were, according to a secret police report, drinking "every day . . . before lectures, after lectures, and now in the breaks as well." Excessive drinking was blamed on a variety of social stresses such as a shortage of consumer goods, rural poverty, and hectic urban life. Whatever the reason, the consequences were an appalling range of social problems, including illness, premature births and birth defects, divorce, domestic violence, accidents on the road and at work, and crime. Rampant alcoholism took a heavy economic toll in the form of absenteeism, theft, and shoddy work. "If vodka interferes with your work, quit working," counseled a cavalier piece of folk wisdom. Drunkenness may have cut overall productivity by 10 to 20 percent. All these manifestations of alcoholism threw into embarrassing doubt Soviet claims for progress toward "developed socialism." Critics called the Brezhnev years the time of "developed alcoholism." It and other social maladies that persisted were interpreted as signs of a moral crisis.[7]

Brezhnev's conservatism and his declining health from 1975 onward hindered his capacity to deal with this tangle of social and economic problems that demoralized Soviet citizens and constrained the Soviet Union in its competition with the United States. He would not repeat what he regarded as Khrushchev's "harebrained" attempts at economic reforms, and he insisted on honoring the claims of the military and the military-related heavy industry. But consumers would not let him off the hook. Workers engaged in sporadic protests over shortages and pay, while the secret police reported widespread popular discontent over the leadership's long-deferred promises for a better life. Images of Western lifestyles carried by media and observed by travelers underlined Soviet backwardness and whetted the taste for consumer goods. In a bow to public demands, Brezhnev presented a program to the party congress in 1971 for raising living standards.

That program helped carry the Soviet population further along the road toward a consumer culture that was already well rooted in the United States, western Europe, and Japan. The most pressing need was housing, since 40 percent of the urban population still lived in communal units by the late 1960s. Brezhnev devoted resources to increase substantially the number of single-family apartments. Citizens were quick to fill those private apartments with consumer goods such as refrigerators, telephones, radios, and televisions. TVs, for example, had been available to only 5 percent of the population in 1960. By the late 1970s TVs could be found in almost every home. Leisure time increased. Despite the lure of television, a public that was universally literate still loved to read, especially nostalgic writings about a rural way of life that was disappearing, historical novels set in imperial times, and detective fiction. Movie-going remained popular, and Western musical genres found their way into the country with official approval (except for rock and roll). Jazz, folk, and disco mixed with indigenous musical forms to create a hybrid popular music heard on radio, television, and recordings as well as in restaurants and clubs. Sports and drinking were other major leisure-time activities, particularly for males.

Despite these advances, the public wanted more goods and less party authoritarianism and inefficiency. Cynicism flourished in a political system in which officials no longer commanded respect. Jokes abounded about the slow, dogma-bound Brezhnev. One of those jokes began with the announcement that the Soviet Union was going to top the American achievement of getting a man on the moon by sending a space team to the sun. When a Soviet cosmonaut protested that the team would be "burned alive," Brezhnev was quick to reassure him, "Don't worry. We have planned every detail. We have arranged for you to land at night."[8] The political estrangement of youth was especially worrisome to party leaders. The Soviet Union had developed its own youth culture in stages roughly paralleling that in the West. As we have seen in Chapter 4, it had begun to take hold in the 1950s and 1960s with the relaxation of international tensions, and flourished in the 1970s and early 1980s. Its hallmark was a fascination with Western musical styles and, from the late 1960s onward, especially rock and roll. The first homegrown rock group, the Slavs, had appeared in imitation of the Beatles. By late in the 1960s there were 263 informal bands in Moscow bearing such unsocialist names as Soft Suede Corners, Young Comanches, and Little Red Imps. The best-known Soviet rock group, Time Machine, headed by Andrei Makarevitch, attacked social conformism, political hypocrisy, and the endless government appeals for popular sacrifice. Despite official disapproval and even police harassment, hippie culture—jeans, bell-bottoms, peace signs, miniskirts, and bare feet—spread through an underground of communes, hangouts, and clubs.

Brezhnev's foreign policy was as conservative as his domestic course. Within the eastern bloc, he crushed the 1968 Czech reform movement (described in

Chapter 4), sending a clear signal that Moscow would defend the status quo there. The Czech attempt to forge an independent path threatened not only bloc unity but also the Soviet Union itself. It inspired separatists in western Ukraine as well as Moldavia, Georgia, and the Baltic region. Dissidents within the Soviet Union expressed sympathy with the Czech experiment and began to circulate translations of key Czech documents. The outspoken Sakharov hailed the Prague Spring, and many Soviet college students also expressed sympathy for what the Czechs were attempting. Brezhnev's fears for the survival of the Czech Communist Party, reinforced by those expressed by hardline party leaders in Poland, East Germany, and Bulgaria, finally resulted in a Soviet-led Warsaw Pact intervention in August 1968. Brezhnev took the occasion to formally articulate the doctrine that the Kremlin had in fact been acting on since 1945: "when internal and external forces hostile to socialism are threatening to turn a socialist country back to capitalism, this becomes a common problem and a concern of all socialist countries."[9] This public declaration of the Soviet right to intervene to preserve the political character of nearby states would become known as the Brezhnev Doctrine.

The international costs of Soviet intervention proved high. It completed China's alienation, while Albania, already pursuing an independent course, responded by severing all ties with the Warsaw Pact and making China its chief patron. The intervention provoked vehement opposition from the Communist parties of Spain and Italy, where sympathy for the Prague Spring was especially strong, and in general gave a fresh boost to Eurocommunism. The crushing of the Czech reform movement also revealed serious morale problems among the Soviet-led Warsaw Pact forces, including Polish, Hungarian, and East German units. By then Romania was already disengaging from the alliance and by 1969 it had ceased active participation. Moscow's show of force may have cowed some Eastern Europeans, but anti-Soviet feelings were stronger than ever. Among Moscow's friends and clients in the Third World, the Czech intervention dealt a damaging blow to Soviet prestige.

Brezhnev's partnership with Nixon fit within his generally cautious, conservative approach. The Soviet leader wanted in broadest terms to establish his country as an equal to the United States. To that end, he wanted Washington to accept as legitimate the Cold War lines separating the superpower spheres in Europe and to cooperate in limiting the dangers and costs of the nuclear arms race. He remarked in a May 1972 party meeting that even though the United States remained the "main force of imperialism," the danger of nuclear war made good relations critical. Thus he, like Khrushchev, sought a relationship of "peaceful coexistence." Brezhnev could embark on this policy because he felt more secure against U.S. nuclear blackmail thanks to the post-Cuban Missile Crisis buildup of Soviet strategic forces. In this new situation of rough nuclear parity, both sides had to recognize, Brezhnev publicly observed in 1975, "the senselessness and extreme danger of further increasing tension." He underlined the impact that Soviet parity had had on the thinking of its adversaries: "Now the leaders of the bourgeois world can no longer seriously count on resolving the historic conflict between capitalism and socialism by force of arms."[10]

Western European Pressure

Western European leaders joined Mao and Brezhnev in the overseas contingent of détentists. Washington's NATO partners were tiring of Cold War tensions; influential segments of their publics demanded East–West measures to promote peaceful relations. Driving this demand was the knowledge that a superpower misstep could set in motion the troops of the two powerful alliances facing each other across the German border. War might come without even a word from Europeans whose lands would serve as the battlegrounds, perhaps even be reduced to nuclear cinders.

The first pointed official European critiques of the Cold War confrontation came from the formidable Charles de Gaulle, the dominant figure on the French political scene from his election as president in 1958 until his retirement in 1969. His foreign policy was driven by an abiding concern with establishing French leadership in a western Europe that could act as an independent force in world affairs. This goal entailed a rejection of any bipolar notion of how the postwar world should operate; it particularly meant resisting American attempts to work with Britain to determine the fate of Europe; and it led him to a close working relationship with West Germany's Konrad Adenauer.

De Gaulle thus became for a decade the bane of U.S. policymakers, ready to frustrate them at every turn. In 1959 he began distancing France from NATO while developing an independent nuclear force to set his country on a symbolic par with the superpowers and Britain, the only other states with nuclear weapons at that time. In 1963 he blocked Britain's admission to the European Community in part because London would be a rival for European leadership but also because he believed that Britain would represent U.S. views in European councils. He rebuffed U.S. free traders intent on opening the European market to American farm products. He criticized U.S. intervention in Vietnam. And he accelerated the descent of the dollar into crisis by demanding gold in exchange for the large dollar reserves that a prosperous France had been piling up (see Chapter 5).

The stirrings within the NATO alliance took fresh form just as de Gaulle retired from the political scene in 1969. The West German elections of that year ended two decades of control by Adenauer's Christian Democratic party. That party had given priority to integration of West Germany into NATO to achieve security from attack and to gain international acceptance from neighbors still mindful of past German aggression. In keeping with early Cold War rigidities, Adenauer and his associates had refused to formally accept Germany's division or for that matter the broader pattern of Soviet domination in eastern Europe. The 1969 election produced a center-left coalition led by Willy Brandt—and with it a major shift in West German Cold War policy.

In what became known as *Ostpolitik* (literally, a policy oriented toward the east), Brandt sought to reduce tensions by accepting the division of Germany and the dominant Soviet role on its side of the European Cold War line. But his goal was not to freeze the status quo. To the contrary, he argued that the prospects for internal economic and social changes in socialist societies were dim as long as fear and repression prevailed. He sought to promote conditions that would lower political and military tensions and thus set in motion significant changes in the eastern bloc. The measures that Brandt promoted in pursuit of this goal included high-level exchanges with Soviet leaders, a lowering of military tensions between the armed forces facing off across the Iron Curtain, and the promotion of cultural, economic, and technological exchanges. Brandt calculated that as contacts multiplied and tensions diminished, the prospects would increase for a loosened Soviet grip on its European allies and for closer links between the two Germanys.

Brandt's fresh approach bore fruit. He signed formal agreements with East Germany, Poland, and the Soviet Union accepting postwar boundaries as legitimate, and gained an agreement for the free movement of peoples between the two German states. Thanks to this warming trend, West Germany became the Soviets' largest trading partner in the West. Brandt's agenda got a major boost from the Helsinki accords signed by the superpowers and the Europeans in 1975. The accords legalized the European borders that prevailed at the end of World War II, encouraged trade between the two sides of the Iron Curtain, and promoted the free movement of peoples and ideas. Perhaps most important of all, they stipulated respect for the full range of human rights. Brezhnev and leaders in the Soviet bloc accepted the agreement as a harmless piece of paper, but they soon had reason to regret making this international commitment. Just as Brandt anticipated, Helsinki gave legitimacy to the activities of human rights groups within eastern Europe and the Soviet Union and inspired external pressure and monitoring that Communist regimes resented and resisted but could not simply crush without paying a public relations price.

The Brandt policy initiatives reflected changes going on within Germany itself and Europe more broadly. The physical division of Berlin, created by the construction of the Wall in 1961 while Brandt himself had been mayor of West Berlin, had become a symbol of the human costs of the Cold War, cutting off contact between German families on the two sides. At the same time the West German state was riding high. It had won the gratitude of its citizens and impressed foreign observers by engineering an economic miracle in a land devastated at war's end. It had also neutralized much of the international hostility left over from the war, and gained acceptance as a full-fledged alliance partner in NATO. Other European governments favored the Brandt policy as a welcome step toward relaxing Cold War tensions and reducing the chance of war. Polls revealed deep public anxieties about the arms race. For example, a survey done in early 1963 in the aftermath of the Cuban Missile Crisis already then registered lopsided support in Italy, France, West Germany, and Britain for completely eliminating nuclear weapons.

The détente-minded Nixon administration found *Ostpolitik* troubling despite Brandt's insistence that he would maintain close ties to NATO and consult regularly with the Americans. While publicly supportive, Nixon and Kissinger worried in private that the Brandt government in Bonn might be exploring an independent and more nationalistic course or even that West German–Soviet contacts might upstage Washington's talks with Moscow. In mid-1970 an irritated Kissinger dressed down a West German emissary, "Let me tell you something! If anyone is going to pursue détente with the Soviet Union, it will be us."[11] This growing European independence would continue to trouble Washington, especially after U.S. leaders shifted back to a more militant Cold War stance during the late 1970s and early 1980s.

The U.S. Retreat

A policy shift as fundamental as Nixon's was bound to come under fire within a U.S. political culture still deeply anticommunist and viscerally afraid of seeming weak in the eyes of the world. Thus even before Nixon's resignation in 1974, détente had come under assault, and the domestic opposition would continue to grow during the presidencies of Gerald Ford (1974–1977) and Jimmy Carter (1977–1981).

Of all Nixon's domestic enemies, he was himself perhaps the worst. He made his policy vulnerable in part because he failed to build a public consensus or create support within the foreign policy bureaucracy. Secretive and impatient, Nixon preferred to keep policy out of sight of what he saw as an ignorant public, a jealous bureaucracy, an opportunistic Congress, and irritating special interests. He extended his telling comment on the public—"You don't take the people where they want to go, you take the people where they ought to go"[12]—to include the other potential participants in the policy process. Nixon was also limited by an inability to break completely with Cold War thinking. He remained obsessed with the maintenance of American prestige and worried that his country might seem "a pitiful, helpless giant." His stunted ethical sense proved most directly his undoing during the Watergate affair. By authorizing "dirty tricks" against his political enemies, including the attempted burglary of the Democratic National headquarters, he committed crimes that led to a cover-up and drew relentless congressional scrutiny. Threatened with removal through impeachment, the embattled Nixon resigned in August 1974. Henry Kissinger, now serving as secretary of state, sought under Ford to preserve the gains of détente, but by then even that term had fallen into disrepute.

Nixon's policy initiative finally lost all momentum during the presidency of Jimmy Carter. That genial Southern Baptist, U.S. Navy nuclear engineer, and Georgia governor had no foreign policy experience. He was, moreover, gripped by conflicting impulses on broad foreign policy goals. He shared Nixon's dissatisfaction with the earlier, overly militarized containment policy. He pursued a new round of arms negotiations, capped in 1979 by an agreement (SALT II) with

Brezhnev to limit each side to 2,400 launchers and reduce each side to one defensive antiballistic missile system. (There were still no limits on the number of warheads that a single missile might carry.) But Carter also sought to make the United States the guardian of human rights everywhere, even in the Soviet Union. He eyed Soviet involvement in the Third World with concern. Brezhnev supported Cuba, drew close to North Vietnam from 1965 onward, cultivated Mozambique, Angola, and Ethiopia as footholds in Africa, and drew neighboring Afghanistan into a dependent relationship. These decisions, following along the same activist track pursued by Khrushchev, disturbed the American president. To make matters worse, Carter's chief advisers, Secretary of State Cyrus Vance and White House adviser Zbigniew Brzezinski, were themselves at odds on how to deal with the Soviet Union. The result was what the Soviet ambassador in Washington perceptively described in a report for his bosses in mid-1978 as "a selective, half-hearted conception of détente."[13]

Increasingly the anti-Soviet Brzezinski prevailed in White House councils. He pushed normalization of diplomatic relations with China as a way to put the Kremlin on the defensive, and gave higher priority to standing up to the Soviets than reaching agreements with them. His ascendancy was complete by 1979 as a new Cold War chill set in. The Soviet invasion of Afghanistan did the most to make the temperature plunge. The actions of two Soviet allies—the Vietnamese invasion of Cambodia and the dispatch of Cuban troops to Africa—combined with the Iran hostage crisis (see Chapter 9) and the Afghanistan invasion to leave the Carter administration shaken. Both Brzezinski and a new, more militant Carter saw a dangerous "arc of crisis" running from Afghanistan, through the Middle East, and into the heart of sub-Saharan Africa. They were alarmed by pro-Soviet regimes and insurgent groups making headway in all these areas as well as in Central America, particularly Nicaragua and El Salvador.

The president toughened his tone, began a dramatic increase in defense spending, and shelved the SALT II agreement awaiting ratification in the Senate. In August 1980 the administration announced a major shift in nuclear war strategy—making the enemy's nuclear weapons and communications systems rather than cities and industries the main target. The threat of massive loss of life and economic disruption under the old policy was supposed to deter an attack on the United States. Since the number of urban and industrial targets was fairly stable, the number of warheads did not need to grow beyond a certain point. The new policy, by contrast, was less stable and more costly. It required a constantly increasing number of nuclear weapons first to match the many warheads on the other side and then to keep up as the Soviets increased their arsenal to avoid getting wiped out by an American first strike and losing their retaliatory capability. Advocates of the new policy seemed to regard nuclear war as a game, which a skillful player might win by outpacing any rival in the production of nuclear weapons.

What Carter and Brzezinski could not grasp were the problems besetting the Soviet Union. China's transformation from ally to enemy had been a terrible blow to Soviet security, forcing the military to stand watch on two widely separated fronts. Romania and Poland were drifting from Soviet control in defiance of the Brezhnev Doctrine, and the rest of eastern Europe was also in ferment. The Communist parties of western Europe were publicly challenging Moscow's claim to lead the international socialist movement. And as we have seen, disaffection was no less a problem within the Soviet Union among intellectuals, youth, and national minorities. Economic difficulties were deepening. On top of all this the Kremlin launched an ill-fated campaign of pacification in Afghanistan that U.S. cold warriors interpreted as a serious Soviet challenge (see Chapter 9 for additional detail).

Carter's shift toward a hardline stance seemed to vindicate longstanding criticisms of détente as politically naïve and morally misguided. The Committee on the Present Danger was at the forefront of that criticism. It had been organized in 1975 in reaction against Nixon's "sellout" to the Soviet Union and China, and it kept up the fire on what it saw as Carter's fuzzy-minded, ineffectual policy. Its prominent members included Paul Nitze (drafter of NSC-68, the alarmist 1950 articulation of the containment policy), Norman Podhoretz (editor of the organization's mouthpiece, *Commentary*), and Jeane Kirkpatrick (Georgetown political scientist). They believed in a strong military establishment, a boldly interventionist foreign policy, and presidential leadership unimpeded by congressional restrictions or public hesitations. They suspected that the Democrats had lost their nerve, and so turned to the Republican Party to close the strategic "window of vulnerability" and defeat Moscow's strategy of expansion.

Ronald Reagan embraced the Committee's arguments and made them central to his 1980 presidential campaign. This actor and Hollywood labor leader turned two-term California governor promised that he would stand up to the communists and make the tide of history flow again in favor of freedom. This promise of restored national pride and power, along with a commitment to smaller government, helped Reagan defeat Carter in 1980. Once in the White House, the new president launched initiatives that smashed Nixon's plans for détente, and his landslide reelection victory in 1984 in a campaign that proclaimed "Morning Again in America" left scant hope for reassembling the pieces anytime in the foreseeable future. Reagan was not strong on policy details. (He long believed that missiles once fired could be recalled.) He did not make good use of his staff. (The intense battles at the highest levels to influence Reagan's thinking damaged his presidency.) And he husbanded his energy. (Reagan liked to joke that hard work never killed anyone, but then why take a risk.) But despite all these deficiencies, the president had a strong and simple vision of America's place in the world, and he could articulate it with charm and conviction that played on nationalist themes popular with the public. America was, in a phrase he frequently invoked, "the last best hope of man on earth."[14]

The new president sustained Carter's military buildup. His public pronouncements suggested a depth of enmity toward what the president called "the evil empire" not seen since the darkest days of the Cold War in the late 1940s and early 1950s. He gave members of the Committee on the Present Danger prominent places in his administration. He continued Carter's counter-targeting strategy, expanded the nuclear weapons arsenal, talked about a "winnable" nuclear war, and in 1983 committed the country to forging a high-tech shield against missile attack (the Strategic Defense Initiative, popularly known as Star Wars). He denied critics' claims that missile defense would prove unworkable and costly, would provoke Soviet countermeasures, and (most serious of all) would create a dangerously unstable relationship between Soviet and American nuclear forces. Only on China did Reagan retreat: After promising confrontation, he instead kept the lines to Beijing open.

Reagan's Third World policy was as hardline as his approach to the Soviet Union. His administration funded "freedom fighters" in Central America, Afghanistan, sub-Saharan Africa, and Cambodia. Especially alarming for the Reagan administration was the communist onslaught in the Americas. In Nicaragua the Sandinista revolutionary movement (named for Augusto Sandino, who had opposed U.S. occupation between 1912 and 1933) had taken power in 1979 after overthrowing the long-time U.S.-backed dictator. Reagan authorized a CIA campaign of pressure, armed anticommunist exiles known as the "Contras," and imposed a trade embargo. These measures, controversial at home and internationally, slowly ground down Nicaragua's government as well as its economy, and in elections in 1990 U.S.-backed candidates would oust the Sandinistas. In El Salvador, where an insurgency was gathering strength when he entered the White House, Reagan supplied money, weapons, and advisers. With the assistance of death squads and U.S. aid, the conservative government was able to stalemate the opposition in a bitter, brutal civil war costing the lives of 75,000. In 1983 U.S. forces invaded the island nation of Grenada, making quick work of its Marxist regime aligned with Cuba.

In these and other Third World cases, the Reagan team made no pretense of supporting economic development or nation building. Kirkpatrick, now Reagan's representative at the UN, had explained why stopping radical revolutions was so important even if it meant backing dictators on the Right. In a swipe at Carter's failure to protect long-time U.S. allies in Nicaragua and Iran, Kirkpatrick observed in late 1979 "that traditional authoritarian governments are less repressive than revolutionary autocracies, that they are more susceptible of liberalization, and that they are more compatible with U.S. interests."[15] Supporting strongmen could help advance the free-world cause.

True to its conservative instincts, the Brezhnev leadership clung to its earlier preference for détente. Brezhnev himself was by the late 1970s showing signs of failing health, and senility would become increasingly evident. But whether speaking his own words or those of his colleagues, Brezhnev reiterated his earlier argument about the dangers of nuclear war. In 1981, with Reagan on the ideological offensive, Brezhnev bluntly told a party congress, "To count on victory in a nuclear war is dangerous madness." The next year, he pledged that the Soviet Union would

THE SHORT CAREER OF DÉTENTE

1968	Soviet-led forces intervene in Czechoslovakia (justified by the Brezhnev Doctrine)
1969	Sino-Soviet border clashes break out; Nixon initiates "détente" with the Soviet Union, opening to China, and "peace with honor" in Vietnam; Brandt presses *Ostpolitik*
1972	Nixon and Brezhnev sign SALT I; Nixon makes groundbreaking visit to China
1973	Paris peace accords end U.S. combat role in Vietnam
1975	Helsinki accords are concluded; Committee on the Present Danger is organized
1979	Carter and Brezhnev conclude new strategic weapons treaty (SALT II); Soviet forces invade Afghanistan, resulting in Carter boosting U.S. military budget and shelving SALT II treaty
1980	Reagan elected president as foe of communism and big government
1983	Reagan announces plans to build a shield against missile attack

not be the first to use nuclear weapons and thus risk destroying "world civilization" and even "life itself on earth." His successors would stick with what had now become virtually an article of faith in Soviet policy.[16]

THE GORBACHEV INITIATIVES

The 1980s witnessed a revival of the reform spirit in the Kremlin—and soon a campaign to breathe life into détente. Brezhnev's death in 1982 brought a pair of transitional figures to power—first Yuri Andropov for two years and then Konstantin Chernenko for barely more than a year. They wanted to invigorate an economy suffering from a slowing growth rate and to address social problems such as workplace indiscipline and alcoholism. But both men were cautious reformers. Their successor, Mikhail Gorbachev, began with a similarly cautious approach, but then gradually developed a more intense and wide-ranging program for change, one that would lead not only to the end of the Cold War but also to the collapse of the Soviet bloc and then the Soviet state itself.

Glasnost, Perestroika, and a New Foreign Policy

The last Soviet leader was born in 1931 into a peasant family in southern Russia. The family had carried black political marks as "enemies of the people": One grandfather was sent into exile in 1933 and another suffered arrest, imprisonment, and torture in 1937. Gorbachev's father, on the other hand, had won honor during World War II at the front, where he was twice wounded. In the immediate postwar years young Mikhail compiled an outstanding record as a student and worker in collective agriculture. He went on to study law at Moscow University between

1950 and 1955, a time of transition from the lean, repressive Stalinist era. He later recalled how much he had then preferred Tarzan movies over dreary documentaries idealizing Soviet life. In 1952 he joined the Soviet Communist Party. In 1953 he married Raisa Titorenko, a gifted classmate. From 1955 to 1978 Gorbachev rose through the party ranks. His first official posts were in his home region, but his appointment in 1978 as Central Committee secretary with responsibility for overseeing agriculture brought him full time to Moscow. By then Gorbachev had prudently veiled views on the need for reform going back at least to the Twentieth Party Congress in 1956. Khrushchev's speech on Stalin had made a strong impression on him, as it did on others of his age: "I was shocked, bewildered and lost. It wasn't an analysis, just facts, deadly facts."[17]

Between 1980 and 1985 Gorbachev operated within the upper reaches of the party, gaining support and experience as a full Politburo member. Andropov's succession to party leadership in 1982 worked to Gorbachev's advantage. Worried by lagging technological standards and slowing economic growth, Andropov enlisted Gorbachev's help in shaking up the system and extended his authority from agriculture to the entire economy. Gorbachev pushed for decentralization, with greater autonomy to be given to lower-level managers. After Andropov's death, Gorbachev served as the frail Chernenko's vigorous second-in-command and made an impressive international debut, traveling to Canada, Italy, and Britain. At the same time he positioned himself as an advocate of reform in carefully worded public statements. He offered a franker assessment to his wife: "We cannot go on living like this, we must change."[18] Upon Chernenko's death in March 1985, the Politburo voted Gorbachev the party's new General Secretary.

As party head, Gorbachev set in motion a major generational shift in the Soviet leadership, what his biographer has described as a "revolution from within."[19] He began slowly, but soon enough was calling for a major transformation of the party-state. Within six years he had converted virtually without violence a communist dictatorship into a system that mixed authoritarian and democratic elements. The turning point came in January 1987 at a meeting of the entire Central Committee. Putting aside narrow economic goals, Gorbachev made the case for an ambitious makeover of the system as the only way to stimulate technological innovation, improve consistently poor agricultural performance, and end official corruption. He got Politburo backing for these and other reform goals by bringing in like-minded leaders and removing doubters. By summer 1988 Gorbachev had completed his shift away from piecemeal reform to sweeping domestic change. By then he had espoused democratic socialism closely akin to a western European model of political pluralism and mixed economy.

One part of his emerging program was *glasnost* (openness), reflecting a commitment to getting Soviet citizens to discuss publicly the problems of their system and seek solutions. Gorbachev wanted to promote a freer flow of information with the outside world in science, technology, and culture. It was important to make leaders accountable, and so he encouraged popular scrutiny and criticism, even the airing in the mass media of social, economic, and environmental problems that those responsible might otherwise seek to sweep under the rug. As the champion of *glasnost*, Gorbachev ended the persecution of dissidents, even lent them his backing. He paved the way for publication of Solzhenitsyn's works for the first time in the Soviet Union, and he arranged Sakharov's return to Moscow.

The other part of Gorbachev's domestic program was *perestroika*, the restructuring of the economy and the closely linked state bureaucracy that planned and controlled production. The fundamental problem, as the new Soviet leader saw it, was a failure to keep up with the West. "We are encircled not by invincible armies but by superior economies," he declared at a party meeting in May 1986.[20] *Perestroika* had as its general goal invigorating the system of production through a gradual reduction in the size of the state-administered (or command) economy and the creation of more scope for market forces. Industry would become more accountable and self-supporting. In agriculture, Gorbachev wanted to give more responsibility to farmers but stopped short of privatizing the land. He proposed the removal of subsidies for food, housing, farm machinery, and other goods that ate up nearly a fifth of the state budget. *Perestroika* would make prices reflect the real cost of production, thus bringing more efficiency to the economy. It anticipated cutting the central planning bureaucracy in half. And it sought to give wide scope for private property and privately owned enterprise, especially for the supply of consumer goods and services.

Determined to make his foreign policy serve his domestic program, Gorbachev launched the crowning initiative to end the Cold War. To some extent he acted on the old logic of Khrushchev and Brezhnev—that the rough nuclear balance with the United States and the unthinkable destructiveness of nuclear war made arms control negotiations imperative. Easing the way forward, Sakharov had convinced Gorbachev that the U.S. Star Wars program was vulnerable to cheap countermeasures and thus no reason to hold up arms control agreements. The new Soviet leader also acted on the premise that domestic reform required a more relaxed international environment as well as reform in eastern Europe to make regimes there more popular and less dependent on Soviet aid for survival. He regarded greater foreign trade and investment, technology transfers, and reduction of the military budget all as important to advancing his domestic agenda. Finally, Gorbachev had to shed some of the massive costs of maintaining the Soviet international position. The military budget, the subsidies to client states, the war in Afghanistan, and the like were consuming 25 to 30 percent of GNP.[21]

In short order, Gorbachev moved to create the international conditions conducive to reform. One key step was to liquidate the costly and unpopular conflict in Afghanistan. Soviet forces would complete their evacuation in 1989. On the European front, Gorbachev launched a dual effort. He cultivated western Europeans and especially West Germans, entrancing them with his urbane style and vision of Russia as part of the European family. At the same time he prodded eastern European clients toward liberalization. He warned that if they did not begin their own programs of *glasnost* and *perestroika* the Soviet Union would not block the rise of popular leaders who would. He thus in effect repealed the Brezhnev Doctrine's threat of military intervention to preserve the status quo. Enthusiastic receptions during his tours of eastern Europe suggested that the peoples there shared his commitment to a revitalized socialism.

Perhaps the most important part of Gorbachev's international initiative was winning Reagan to arms control. In meetings beginning in 1985 Gorbachev quickly convinced the American president to renew the policy of détente. Faced with this new kind of Soviet leader, Reagan found irresistible the chance to make his own mark in history. His impulse was reinforced by an American public whose nuclear anxiety had been revived by talk in Washington about strategies for fighting and winning nuclear war. Reagan was himself increasingly alarmed by the potential for nuclear war and increasingly aware of its disastrous consequences.

Reagan and Gorbachev at a Summit in Reykjavik, Iceland, November 10, 1986
This first meeting between the two superpower leaders began cordially but turned sour after Reagan agreed in private to accept steep reductions in nuclear weapons, only to reverse himself under pressure from incredulous advisers. Subsequent meetings in which Reagan was more carefully scripted moved toward more modest cuts, subsequently embodied in formal agreements. (Courtesy Ronald Reagan Library)

He stopped referring to "the evil empire," and got down to work with Gorbachev in four summit meetings between 1985 and 1988. In 1987 the two leaders completed an agreement to eliminate 1,836 intermediate-range Soviet and 867 U.S. missiles in Europe. They pushed ahead on Strategic Arms Reduction Talks (START) that would sharply cut back strategic nuclear weapons.

As Reagan's successor, George H. W. Bush continued to work with the Soviet leader to relax tensions, although he remained suspicious of Moscow's intentions, and the phrase "the Cold War is over" seemed to stick in his throat. That momentous point finally came at the first summit meeting between Gorbachev and Bush, held in December 1989 on a Soviet cruise liner docked in Malta harbor and buffeted by gale-force winds and high seas. Gorbachev had no difficulty saying simply to the U.S. delegation, "We don't consider you an enemy any more." He was equally definitive in the closing press conference: "The world leaves one epoch of Cold War and enters another epoch." Bush, still cautious, pronounced the two powers at "the threshold of a brand new era."[22] Deeds counted more than words. Two years later they signed the START agreement. That July 1991 accord committed Washington and Moscow to significant reductions in warheads on long-range missiles. Both sides were soon talking about substantial additional cuts.

The Demise of the Soviet System

By 1989, with foreign policy successes piling up, Gorbachev was beginning to discover how destructive were the forces that his program of liberalization had unleashed. They destroyed not just the Warsaw Pact but also the Soviet grip over its neighbors to the west. Winds of change that he had encouraged began blowing down rickety socialist regimes. His calls for reform had shaken the confidence of ruling old-line Communists. Their critics, often tapping a deep anti-Russian and antisocialist sentiment, realized that Moscow would no longer intervene. When those critics took power and began to move out of the Soviet camp, Gorbachev could only watch. More consequentially, liberalization set in motion forces that would tear the Soviet Union apart. The world that Gorbachev sought to remake had a place neither for him nor for the communist system he had sought to save.

The Kremlin's hold on its European clients had been slipping for at least two decades, largely as a result of economic problems. After strong growth in the 1950s, eastern Europe encountered in the 1960s the first hints of trouble ahead. The labor supply ran short and productivity failed to increase. At the same time the Soviet economy, to which the region was tied by COMECON, started to slow, and Soviet subsidies fell. Eastern European economists began to question the rigid, ponderous Soviet model. They urged instead seeking efficiencies through the market mechanism, new technologies, and trade with the capitalist economies. Some governments followed this advice and concluded loans to create an export industry. This strategy backfired. After piling up international debt, their foreign trade did not grow because their products were of poor quality, and in any case the economies in the West suffered a temporary slowdown and thus were importing less. From the mid-1970s growth rates in Soviet satellite states slumped, and in some years Poland, Hungary, and Czechoslovakia suffered an absolute decline in national output.

Eastern Europeans could see that their standard of living was stagnating. To make matters worse, visits abroad and exposure to foreign media made it clear that those standards compared poorly with levels in the West. As vaunted "social rights" seemed increasingly hollow, popular resentment was directed against the *nomenklatura*, party officials who enjoyed special access to goods and services while talking of shared sacrifice and worker sovereignty. The governments in the region kept calling for popular patience and sacrifice as officials sought to get their economies moving. By the 1980s they had little to show for their efforts, while critics began to focus on workplace safety, outdated technology, shoddy products, and accumulating environmental damage. Pollution from outdated heavy industry created acid rain that killed forests, contaminated waterways, fouled urban air, and gave rise to an epidemic of cancer and respiratory diseases. The catastrophic failure of a nuclear power plant at Chernobyl in neighboring Soviet Ukraine in 1986 dramatized the mounting region-wide environmental danger. A cloud of radiation from the melting reactor spread across eastern Europe and then the EU, poisoning soil, air, and water as it went.

At this moment of vulnerability for European socialist governments, Gorbachev's intervention opened the floodgates of change. (See Map 7.1.) Poland and Hungary were the first to feel the effects. A labor organization (Solidarity) had taken form in Poland in 1980, propelled by worker discontent. Muttered one striking worker in 1988, "Forty years of socialism and there's still no toilet paper!"[23] Gorbachev's thaw created favorable conditions for Solidarity under the leadership of an electrician in Gdansk's Lenin Shipyard, Lech Walesa, to press for fundamental economic and political reform. The beleaguered Communist Party headed by Wojciech Jaruzelski finally agreed to hold parliamentary elections in June 1989. Solidarity won handily, signaling the beginning of the end for Communist control in Poland. In Hungary memorial demonstrations for Imre Nagy, executed by the Soviets after the 1956 revolt (see Chapter 4), shook the government. By October 1989 Hungary had a new constitution, and elections in March–April 1990 brought non-Communists to power.

In East Germany, tremors in the neighborhood together with strong signals from Gorbachev set off a wave of demonstrations that shattered the nerves of already demoralized Communist leaders. The police violence failed to stop peaceful protestors from growing rapidly—from hundreds in the epicenter of open discontent in Leipzig in September to half a million marching in East Berlin on November 4. The crowds sang the U.S. civil rights favorite, "We shall overcome," as well as the "*Internationale*," the old anthem of the political Left. They chanted "Gorbi, Gorbi," "We are the people," and "We are one people," while carrying signs that ranged from "Stop privilege" to "I want to visit my girlfriend in Holland."[24] The climax came on

The Wall Comes Tumbling Down, 1989
This photo, taken on November 7, captures the early assault on the hated Berlin Wall. Men hammer away on the western side even as East German border guards fire water cannons through the cracks in the vain hope that a little cold water would stop the assault and preserve the status quo. (© Alexandra AVAKIAN/Contact Press Images)

November 9 when, amidst official confusion, East Germans broke through a border checkpoint to West Germany, went on a shopping spree, and returned home with bags filled with consumer goods.

The death throes of the East German party-state intensified popular pressure in Czechoslovakia. The catalyst was the arrest of dissidents, including playwright Václav Havel, the leader of an organization of independent intellectuals known as Civic Forum. In late October 1989 student protestors publicly challenged the old regime. The government responded with police repression but then in November conceded the need for reform. This retreat turned almost at once into a rout. At the end of November a rehabilitated Alexander Dubček, the hero of the Prague Spring (see Chapter 4), appeared alongside Havel before an exultant crowd of hundreds of thousands chanting his name, a sure sign that with the Soviet brakes off the political wheel was finally turning. In December Havel was elected president, and six months later candidates from the Civic Forum and its Slovak counterpart organization won the first free elections and with it control of the government. Ousting the Communists had been so smooth and fast that it was called the "velvet revolution."

In Romania and Bulgaria the events of 1989 did not mark so dramatic a break with the past. In both countries officials prominent in the old socialist regime clung to power under the banner of reform Marxism. Romania witnessed what was the most violent repression. Challenged by demonstrations against Nicolae Ceauşescu, the despot in power since the mid-1960s, the military fired into crowds in two cities, setting off protests elsewhere. The crisis abated when a palace coup ousted Ceauşescu and his powerful wife, Elena. They were executed on Christmas Day. The new government was led by high-ranking officials from the old one, and although it faced continued protests well into 1990, this old guard preserved its power. Communists in Bulgaria made a smoother transition to the new order, perhaps in part because they had not been compromised by the popular anti-Soviet feeling so prominent elsewhere in the eastern bloc. By late 1989, the government had lost control to demonstrators and opted for talks with the opposition. In January 1990, the Communist Party agreed to surrender its monopoly of political power. Elections in mid-1990 brought strong support for reform Marxists leading a now renamed Communist Party.

The destabilizing effects of liberalization were by 1989 also becoming apparent in the Soviet Union itself. By that spring so much had changed that the main structural and ideological features defining a Communist country had vanished. The leading role of the party was gone. So too was democratic centralism, the ultimate goal or legitimizing myth of building a communist society, and a sense of membership in (if not leadership over) an international socialist community. State ownership of the economy was still largely intact, but Gorbachev had begun the process of creating a mixed economy, thus stimulating fresh popular economic demands.

The parliamentary elections in March 1989 began the unraveling of the Soviet Union. Those elections unleashed centrifugal forces, especially ethnocultural sentiments, that firm (even brutal) central control had for decades held in check. The Soviet Union contained 22 different ethnic or national groups with two million or more members. When each gained a voice, political disintegration and economic confusion not surprisingly soon followed. Already Armenia-Azerbaijan and the Baltic region had begun to slip beyond Moscow's control. Cities, republics, and regions used the March elections to assert their interests and in some cases even claim autonomy or independence. Following Boris Yeltsin's election as president of the Russian Republic in June 1991, Russia declared itself independent. Gorbachev had fought to preserve the union but now faced a resounding defeat as others of the 15 Soviet republics also opted out. Critics thought the failed reformer looked like "someone who has missed his train and is scurrying around the empty platform."[25]

Paralleling this political disintegration went a failure on Gorbachev's part to push hard on the economic restructuring envisioned by *perestroika*. As the old centralized system of state planning fell apart, Gorbachev was not able to put a new system in its place that could even equal old production levels. Soviet GNP began a steep decline in 1990 and 1991. Despite the incentives of the market, production in agriculture, industry, and energy all fell, and inflation soared. With supplies disrupted, hoarding of goods became commonplace, and cities and regions had to implement rationing. Workers became militant in their demands for higher wages and resorted to crippling strikes. For example, during the summer of 1989

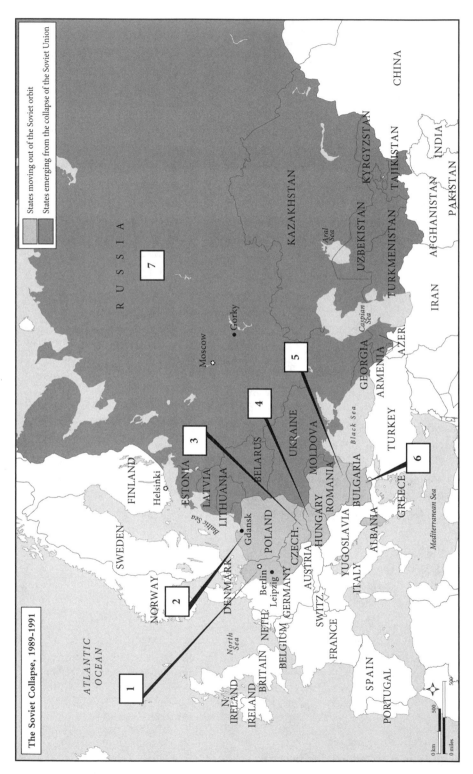

The Soviet Collapse, 1989–1991

States moving out of the Soviet orbit

States emerging from the collapse of the Soviet Union

ATLANTIC OCEAN

North Sea

NORWAY

SWEDEN

FINLAND

Helsinki

Baltic Sea

ESTONIA

LATVIA

LITHUANIA

N. IRELAND

IRELAND

BRITAIN

NETH.

BELGIUM

DENMARK

Gdansk

POLAND

Berlin

Leipzig

GERMANY

CZECH.

AUSTRIA

SWITZ.

FRANCE

SPAIN

PORTUGAL

HUNGARY

YUGOSLAVIA

ITALY

ALBANIA

GREECE

ROMANIA

MOLDOVA

BULGARIA

BELARUS

UKRAINE

Mediterranean Sea

Black Sea

TURKEY

GEORGIA

ARMENIA

AZER.

Caspian Sea

Aral Sea

IRAN

AFGHANISTAN

PAKISTAN

INDIA

CHINA

KAZAKHSTAN

UZBEKISTAN

TURKMENISTAN

TAJIKISTAN

KYRGYZSTAN

R U S S I A

Moscow

Gorky

1

2

3

4

5

6

7

0 km   500

0 miles   500

322

coalminers walked out in what was the first major public protest since 1962. Gorbachev bowed to their demands, an unprecedented retreat by the Soviet state in the face of working-class protest. The economic slide resulting from bungled economic reform would prove prolonged and deeply painful to many through the 1990s. The hard times were reflected in a sardonic tale that went the rounds in Moscow about a Russian boy. Asked by his mother what he wanted to be when he grew up, he replied: "I want to be a foreigner."

Growing political upheaval and economic deprivation now propelled Gorbachev toward the end of his career and the Soviet Union to collapse. Consumers standing in long lines looking at empty shelves were unhappy. So too were party leaders who stood to lose their power and privileges, bureaucrats doomed to unemployment, and the military facing deep cuts. A desperate Gorbachev tried to salvage a deteriorating situation in 1990 by bringing hardliners into his inner circle, scaling back economic reform, and acquiescing in a military crackdown in the Baltics. He thus stumbled into still greater danger. In August 1991 elements of the Soviet Communist Party, including some of his own associates, staged a coup with hopes of strengthening the center and preserving the union. Gorbachev, confined to his vacation house, furiously denounced them as "adventurers and criminals." In downtown Moscow Yeltsin rallied popular opposition to the coup. In the face of resistance at home and criticism abroad, the coup collapsed, and several of its leaders committed suicide. The chief of staff of the Soviet armed forces, a 50-year veteran who had collaborated closely with Gorbachev in arms control negotiations with the United States, left a note: "I cannot live when my motherland is dying and everything that I ever believed in is being destroyed."[26]

This bungled effort to turn back the clock destroyed Gorbachev's fading authority, administered a serious blow to the legitimacy of the Communist Party itself, and gave full vent to autonomist and independence movements already tearing the Soviet Union apart. On December 25, Gorbachev resigned. In his parting words, he defended his record on domestic reform and détente but conceded, "The old system

◄ **MAP 7.1**
The Soviet Collapse, 1989–1991
The unraveling of the Soviet empire began in eastern Europe in 1989 and had by 1991 worked its way home.
1) Nov. 1989: Berlin Wall falls—Oct. 1990: East and West Germany reunified
2) June 1989: Solidarity wins elections
3) Oct.–Nov. 1989: Protests overwhelm Communists—Dec. 1989: Vaclav Havel elected president
4) June 1989: Reform Communists come to power and open talks with opposition—March–April 1990: Free elections sweep Communists from power
5) Dec. 1989: Nicolae Ceauşescu overthrown and executed
6) Nov. 1989: Reform Communists take power and open talks with opposition—June 1990: Communists win in free elections
7) March 1989: Parliamentary elections spur autonomy and independence demands—Dec. 1991: Soviet Union dissolves

THE GORBACHEV EXPERIMENT

1982	Brezhnev's death brings briefly to power Andropov and then Chernenko
1985	Gorbachev emerges as reform-minded Soviet leader, championing *glasnost* and *perestroika*
1986	Reagan and Gorbachev revive arms control talks
1987	Gorbachev and Reagan agree on reducing nuclear forces in Europe
1989	Soviet elections release regional and nationalist impulses, fragmenting the Soviet Union; socialist regimes collapse in Europe
1990	Germany is reunited
1991	Bush and Gorbachev sign the START agreement on reducing warheads on long-range missiles; coup against Gorbachev fails, discrediting Communist Party; Yeltsin emerges as the leader of Russia as the Soviet Union collapses

collapsed before a new one had time to start working."[27] This impersonal verdict clouded Gorbachev's own responsibility for the failure of reform and even more importantly for the destruction of the state and party that might have survived sometime longer without his ministrations. An experiment intended to make the Soviet Union stronger instead extinguished it. Of all the stunning events of 1989–1991, none was more incredible than the sight of Mikhail Gorbachev leading the Soviet Communist Party into the dustbin of history (where the capitalists were supposed to end up) and pushing the state created by his hero Lenin into extinction less than 75 years after its creation. There was a real irony in Gorbachev's role. He failed disastrously as a reformer at home but was lionized abroad for his success as an international peacemaker. Indeed, the collapse of the Soviet Union, the result of his failed reforms, was the definitive signal that the Cold War was over.

EXPLAINING THE COLD WAR OUTCOME

The sudden end to the long, costly, and dangerous U.S.–Soviet contest, soon followed by the demise of the Soviet Union, is so bizarre that its begs for an explanation. In tackling this task we need to keep in mind that we are still quite close to this complex set of events and so should proceed tentatively. One key point deserves emphasis. Gorbachev has been identified in jest as a tool of the CIA used to undermine the Soviet system and more seriously as a closet capitalist-democrat in no way averse to Soviet collapse. He was not a clone of Reagan or Thatcher or even of Brandt, and there is no evidence that he envisioned or desired the crisis that gripped his country between 1989 and 1991. He was rather a product of the reform impulses active in the Soviet system since Khrushchev's time. He believed that it contained good elements worth preserving as well as defects that required reform.

The outcome of those reforms is a reminder that leaders, however powerful, cannot control what happens when they translate their dreams into action. Gorbachev's experience may well suggest that the bolder the dreams, the more unpredictable the results.

The Role of Leaders

Gorbachev's role in the events of 1989–1991 was of central importance. He represented a generational shift among the ranks of the Soviet leadership. The Khrushchev and Brezhnev generation preceding him had grown up amidst the traumatic social upheaval of 1905–1921 and embraced the Bolshevik cause around the time of the revolution of 1917 and the civil war that followed. They came from peasant, working-class, or lower middle-class backgrounds. And they had little formal schooling, usually limited to some technical education. While party members were by the early 1980s distinctly better educated than most Soviet citizens, at the time of Brezhnev's death none of the Politburo members (aside from the relatively youthful Gorbachev) had a full college-level education. This aging leadership was exhausted intellectually as well as physically.

Those of the Gorbachev generation had grown up entirely within the Stalinist system. It had structured their lives and given them education and privilege. The seminal political event for them was Khrushchev's secret 1956 speech. It encouraged them to believe in the possibility of a more humane, open socialism. For that reason this generation of political activists and intellectuals was known as the "Children of the Twentieth Congress." Some of them operated within the system; others, such as Solzhenitsyn and Sakharov, operated outside it. Even during the dark Brezhnev years, foreign travel and foreign contacts fed the reformist impulse among the young influentials in the state and party bureaucracy. They could see the discrepancy between Soviet propaganda and the capitalist reality, and they watched with interest the experiments in reform socialism in eastern Europe.

In a generation predisposed to embrace change, Gorbachev himself stands out for his boldness. On the international front, he decided simply to reject the old rules of the game and call the Cold War over. He was determined to concentrate on domestic renewal, so he simply walked away from the rivalry with Washington. Reagan seized the chance to shift from confrontation to cooperation. The Soviet leader's charm as well as his concessions made it difficult to say no, while Reagan's own easy optimism and unimpeachable anticommunist credentials facilitated the switch even while his more ideologically rigid associates fumed. Even so, Reagan as well as Bush responded to the new Soviet policy with considerable hesitation. One student of Soviet reform has wryly noted that "Gorbachev served up the severed head of his superpower on a silver platter and still had to employ all his artifice to cajole two U.S. administrations to the banquet."[28]

The Soviet leader was no less bold domestically, although with quite different consequences. His domestic reforms proved fatal to the Soviet economy and ultimately to the Soviet Union itself. Arguably reform went haywire because Gorbachev tried too much, too fast, with vague slogans but no coherent plan. His speeches consisted of mushy generalizations, and his policy relied on improvisation. There is much merit in the notion that Gorbachev was not driven by some popular groundswell and that Soviet collapse was accidental, not inevitable. Gorbachev may thus represent, as one of his aides put it in retrospect, "a genetic error of the system."[29] Could a more skilled reformer have saved the system? The case of China (treated in Chapter 8) suggests yes. There cautious Communist leaders focused on moving from a command to a market economy, put political liberalization on hold, and successfully managed sweeping reform. Or was there such resistance to change within the Soviet system that any reform effort had no chance? Perhaps Gorbachev had only two choices as a reformer: to admit defeat or to press forward on a front so broad that it was bound—whether he liked it or not—to put the entire Soviet system in peril.

Impersonal Forces

However important leadership may have been, Gorbachev as well as Reagan acted within a web of constraints and pressures that also deserve examination if we are to understand the end of the Cold War and Soviet collapse. Perhaps the most important was broad popular disaffection with the costs and risks of the Cold War. Nuclear anxieties and the longing for a better life ate away at Cold War orthodoxies in both camps, but nowhere more consequentially than in the thinking of the U.S. electorate. Western European and Japanese opinion had only a marginal effect on American leaders; Gorbachev was well ahead of his own still ill-articulated public opinion; but Reagan had to heed popular preferences if he and his party wanted to retain power.

Throughout the Cold War, even in times of détente, the destructive nuclear arsenals of the superpowers continued to grow. (See Fig. 7.1.) The nuclear buildup fed suspicions on both sides, drained away national resources, and inflicted widespread, lasting environmental damage. By the end of the Cold War the rivals had together over 50,000 warheads of all types in their arsenals when 500 were enough for either to destroy the other. Soviet and American leaders accompanied by black boxes that could instantly initiate nuclear war were worried and sought a way to limit if not eliminate the danger. We now know that their fears were well grounded. Nuclear planners on each side were plagued by misperceptions of the other that stoked anxieties about a first strike and raised the chances of a deadly miscalculation.

Even as the multiplication of destructive power drove leaders to arms control, crafting meaningful and lasting agreement was fraught with difficulties. The habits of worst-case thinking and the relentless development of new technologies of destruction continually hindered cooperation. With national survival at stake, policymakers were wary of taking risks on questionable arms control deals. Moreover, they and their technical experts had to cope with ever more complex strategic systems on both sides that made it difficult to strike a balance and to deal with

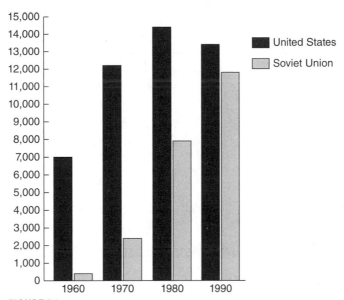

FIGURE 7.1
Superpower Nuclear Arsenals, 1960–1990
The bars on this graph measure only the number of warheads on longer-range "strategic" weapons. Adding smaller, "tactical" warheads would raise the count substantially. For example, in 1990 the United States had 7,800 tactical warheads and the Soviet Union 21,600.[30]

problems of verification. Even the most carefully worked out agreement was soon undercut by new technologies.

Whatever the difficulties, arms control efforts continued because of popular pressure. Two bouts of nuclear fear had built to politically significant levels and given impetus to negotiations. The first, evident in the United States and western Europe by the late 1950s (Chapter 4), had been quieted by cooperative measures taken by Soviet and American leaders in the wake of the Cuban Missile Crisis. The second bout came in the early 1980s. Loose talk in the Reagan administration about fighting a nuclear war, accompanied by the deployment of American missiles to Europe, sparked an intense reaction overseas. Europeans on both sides of the Iron Curtain knew full well that in even the most limited war the ever more numerous nuclear-armed missiles in the region would devastate them. By late spring 1981 northern Europe was the scene of large demonstrations and intense political polemics. The Japanese were even more solidly in the antinuclear camp. A national consensus had existed since the mid-1950s, sustained by memories of Hiroshima and Nagasaki. Even in the Soviet Union dissidents such as Sakharov openly voiced concern.

In the United States antinuclear sentiment grew distinctly sharper. Scientists were outspoken in expressing their fears, none more so than Carl Sagan, a Cornell astrophysicist. He popularized the concept of a deadly "nuclear winter" resulting from a nuclear war shrouding the earth in debris and cutting off sunlight essential to human life. George Kennan, an influential voice in policy circles, joined the chorus of alarm: "We have gone on piling weapon upon weapon, missile upon missile, new levels of destructiveness upon old ones. We have done this helplessly, almost involuntarily: like the victims of some sort of hypnosis, like men in a dream, like lemmings headed for the sea."[31] Nuclear war was soon at the forefront of public discussion, and nuclear fear began to influence popular culture. Jonathan Schell's *Fate of the Earth*, a bestseller in 1982, drove home to millions of readers the horrible effects of even limited nuclear war in powerful, personal terms:

> *Now we are sitting at the breakfast table drinking our coffee and reading the newspaper, but in a moment we may be inside a fireball whose temperature is tens of thousands of degrees. Now we are on our way to work, walking through the city streets, but in a moment we may be standing on an empty plain under a darkened sky looking for the charred remnants of our children. Now we are alive, but in a moment we may be dead. Now there is human life on earth, but in a moment it may be gone.*[32]

In 1984 Dr. Seuss, the author of popular children's books, published the *Butter Battle Book* about an escalating arms race between the Yooks and the Zooks, who deployed ever more impressive weapons such as the Triple Sling Jigger and the Bitsy Big Boy Boomeroo. The work with perhaps the widest impact was a 1983 made-for-television docudrama, *The Day After*. It gave a hundred million viewers a taste of the death and suffering that a nuclear attack would inflict and compelled Reagan's secretary of state, George Shultz, to appear on television to calm the public.

The hopeful twin to this corrosive nuclear fear was the dream of the good life. A preoccupation with consumer goods increasingly gripped the public in both the East and the West and inspired an aversion to ideological crusades and nuclear adventurism. Everywhere leaders could hear popular demands that they address problems of livelihood. Workers in the East no less than electorates in the West wanted vacations, health care, and better pay, not international tensions and possibly war.

The constraints were especially marked in the United States after the Vietnam War. The call for "no more Vietnams" reflected the public's preference for giving priority to problems at home. Military and congressional leaders shared this aversion to military adventures that might go wrong. The result was that even the most militantly anticommunist of the late Cold War presidents felt constrained. When Ronald Reagan discovered that American forces in Beirut were vulnerable to attack, he quickly pulled them out. In Central America he had to fight communists by proxy (the right-wing Contras) or through the CIA because the public and Congress would not support direct U.S. military intervention. So strong was public skepticism that the Reagan administration had to fund that battle by secretly selling weapons to Iran, resulting in the Iran–Contra scandal that shook Reagan's presidency.

Soviet leaders also faced consumer expectations and at the same time tried to wage a Cold War—all while drawing on an economy that was smaller and far less efficient than that of the United States, produced goods of lower quality, and was slow to innovate, especially in the critical area of technology. These disparities left the Kremlin at a constant disadvantage and straining to catch up. Current data indicate that the Soviet economy grew at a low but fairly steady rate in the Brezhnev and Gorbachev years (in the 2 to 3 percent range). But that rate was trending downward, and between 1979 and 1981 the economy probably shrank before resuming its expansion until 1989, when it was overwhelmed by the disruptions brought on by the Gorbachev reforms.[33] The sardonic jibe often attributed to Soviet workers—"We pretend to work and you pretend to pay us"—captured the fundamental alienation and inefficiency that plagued the system and that was especially worrisome to urban professionals.

It is tempting in this connection to consider the argument that the accelerating U.S. arms expenditures in the 1980s won the Cold War. Some have contended that Carter and Reagan had shrewdly pushed the Soviets into spending themselves into the ground. However, this appealingly simple cause-and-effect explanation has yet to be documented. Indeed, current evidence indicates that Moscow did not respond to the U.S. buildup in kind but rather held military spending fairly steady (measured as a proportion of GNP). But on the other hand, it is true that Moscow had long strained to make the smaller, less dynamic Soviet economy carry the weight of global aspirations, while Washington had the luxury of being able to draw on a larger, more dynamic economy. Even after the Carter–Reagan buildup, military outlays accounted for at most a modest 6.5 percent of U.S. GNP. In the end it was the very reforms intended to make the Soviet economy more productive that proved its undoing and helped push the Soviet Union over the edge into oblivion.

Finally, we need to consider the argument that the Soviet Union was so flawed in principle that it was bound to fail both in its competition with the United States and as a working political and economic model. Of the several forms this argument takes, the most common and obviously ideological is that Gorbachev collided with the irresistible tide of freedom. It could be argued that, like his Bolshevik predecessors, he was tied to a morally bankrupt and thus doomed system. But this interpretation seems more a leap of metaphysical faith than a historically grounded explanation. The case is certainly easier to make after the Soviet collapse; beforehand virtually no Western observers saw the Soviet Union as tottering, and to most it looked impressively sturdy. In any case, no groundswell of popular pressure drove Gorbachev to take his democratizing initiatives, and it is not yet clear even today how democracy will fare in Russia. Large parts of the former Soviet Union remain distinctly authoritarian in their politics.

This argument about the deficiencies of the Soviet system takes a second form: Gorbachev was overwhelmed by the global capitalist economy. He needed access to new technologies and the international market, but to get that access he had to open the country and ultimately to transform the economy and with it the entire system. Although the Soviet Union made only limited headway during the Gorbachev years in building links to the outside world, the domestic opening weakened the hold of the central government, threw out of kilter an already faltering, inefficient planned economy, and gave a boost to the internal forces that tore the Soviet state apart. There was no halfway position, so this argument goes, between involvement in the international economy and staying out. While there may be some truth in this point of view, it is important to recall once more the case of China. During the 1980s and 1990s, it demonstrated that deepening international economic involvement need not lead to domestic political instability. The Chinese leaders preserved party power and domestic stability while integrating China with global markets.

The most sophisticated of the arguments about the flaws in the Soviet system contends that Gorbachev was doomed to fail because he was shackled to a monolithic and rigid party. The Communist Party had served as an effective instrument for Lenin's revolution and Stalin's economic development drive. But, as Khrushchev first discovered and then Gorbachev after him, it was a poor instrument of reform because its leading members, the *nomenklatura*, had become a self-interested, privileged class.

This line of analysis is compelling. One of the most discerning of communists, the Yugoslav Milovan Djilas, had already in the mid-1950s identified the rise of this powerful new class. He had noticed that wherever Communist parties had come to power—whether in the Soviet Union or eastern Europe—members came to command all the resources even while claiming to promote equality and an end to class distinctions. He had predicted that they, like capitalists, would tenaciously defend their privileges. By one rough estimate *nomenklatura* in the mid-1980s enjoyed a standard of living nearly four times as high as the Soviet average (with their low salaries offset by a rich array of benefits). The gap between the top 1.5 percent of the population who were *nomenklatura* and the Soviet average was probably about the same as between the top 1.6 percent of the wealthiest in the United States and the average American.[34] Caught between popular criticism and resentment on the one side and fear of losing its privileged control over the economy on the other, the party elite became paralyzed. It could neither accommodate change nor effectively defy the reform-minded leader of what was still in the mid-1980s a centralized, authoritarian party.

CONCLUSION

The Cold War's final phase provides no finer illustration of history's unpredictability. Anyone who might in early 1969 have imagined locking Nixon, Mao, and Brezhnev in the same room would have justifiably predicted general mayhem, not some kind of rough accord, among these three toughened cold warriors. The threesome was divided not just by political beliefs but also by personal background and age. But, as it turned out, the American, Soviet, and Chinese leaders shared a recognition that the time was ripe for fundamental changes in the Cold War. They proceeded to do the completely unexpected, diminishing confrontation and promoting détente. Similarly, observers in 1985 did not imagine that Gorbachev and Reagan might form a partnership that would end the Cold War just before the Soviet Union itself disappeared. These major surprises serve as a salutary reminder of how history seldom sticks for long to the same course and how difficult predicting the future can be.

The vision of leaders, especially Nixon and Gorbachev, played a large role in shaping this outcome. So too did pressures within the societies of the superpowers and within their alliance systems. But to the list of reasons for the end of the Cold War should be added the international economy, which began in the 1970s and 1980s to show signs of greater international integration and at the same time increasing consolidation of the major developed economic regions. In contrast to the bipolar Cold War, the international market economy was becoming, as Nixon recognized, multipolar and less subject to U.S. control. It was also becoming, as Gorbachev came to see, a striking contrast in its productivity to the old Stalinist command economy. Important in its own right, the international economy that had once been subject to Cold War pressures was making itself felt as a force pushing the United States and the Soviet Union away from the Cold War.

8
GLOBAL MARKETS: ONE SYSTEM, THREE CENTERS

THE MARKET-DRIVEN international economy tightened its grip on the globe in the 1970s and 1980s, penetrating into almost every place on the planet. In the process it blurred state boundaries, overwhelmed the competing socialist model, and imposed on national economies a sometimes painful discipline enforced by bankers and other masters of international finance. Leaders in the Third World and even in the socialist states had to recognize the market's capacity for wealth creation: $4.5 trillion added to the world's economy in the 1980s alone.

At the same time that the world economy was moving toward greater integration, the differences among its foremost centers of production and investment stood out in increasingly sharp relief. The international economy could be three as well as one. A U.S. economy buffeted by domestic and international pressures was a diminished yet still key part of this growing regional differentiation. Further altering the landscape was the ascent of the Japanese and the Europeans to something like equal status thanks to a long stretch of growth within the Anglo-American-designed international economic framework. These three defined a new configuration of power. The United States occupied a preponderant place in North America. Close trade and investment ties and a shared approach to economic policy created a loose community of interests between Japan and its partners in maritime East and Southeast Asia. Europe was launched on a far-reaching integration. While the trade among these three blocs flourished, trade within each of them rose even more rapidly, suggesting that the trend toward inward integration was at least as strong as outward global integration. Globalization at least in this case was having the paradoxical effect of creating more distinct regional economic groupings.

Each of the three blocs had its own distinct, closely linked economic and cultural style. What people within each region considered appropriate economic behavior had a lot to do with prevailing social values: a faith on the part of

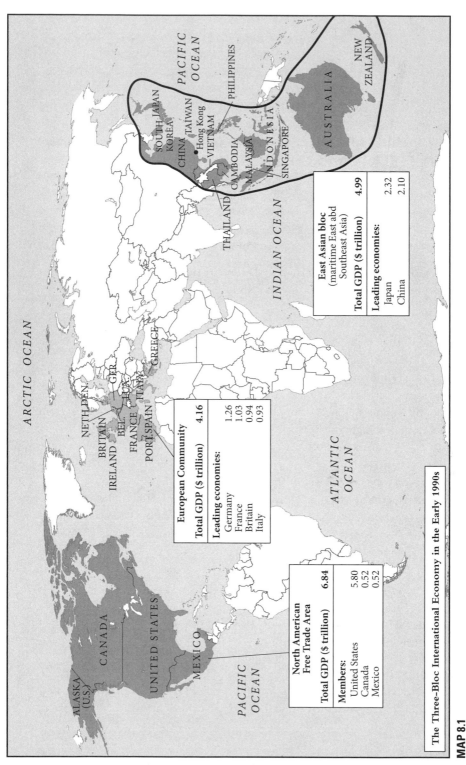

North American Free Trade Area	
Total GDP ($ trillion)	**6.84**
Members:	
United States	5.80
Canada	0.52
Mexico	0.52

European Community	
Total GDP ($ trillion)	**4.16**
Leading economies:	
Germany	1.26
France	1.03
Britain	0.94
Italy	0.93

East Asian bloc (maritime East abd Southeast Asia)	
Total GDP ($ trillion)	**4.99**
Leading economies:	
Japan	2.32
China	2.10

The Three–Bloc International Economy in the Early 1990s

MAP 8.1

The Three-Bloc International Economy in the Early 1990s

The gross domestic product (GDP) data show that the blocs were of roughly equal size in 1990 and that the United States was far and away the largest single national economy.[1]

individualistic Americans in the free market, a constellation of Confucian values prevailing in eastern Asia, and a European belief in tempering the free market with strong welfare programs. These attitudes reflected sturdy, persistent preferences about which was better: production or consumption, individualism or community, equality or hierarchy, small government or big, efficiency or justice.

THE UNITED STATES IN TRANSITION

For roughly a quarter-century—from the late 1960s to the early 1990s—Americans traveled a bumpy economic road. Inflation, slow growth, loss of international competitiveness in a range of key industries, and mounting trade and government deficits suggested deep-seated problems and put in question long-term U.S. economic dominance. Some observers saw a relative decline that was inevitable as other powers grew economically stronger; others saw disaster ahead. Others had a more alarmist view of an economy in needless crisis because of flawed Keynesian policies. Their solution was greater reliance on the market mechanism and less on state intervention.

By the early 1990s these advocates of a neoliberal course were riding high. They had created a political consensus behind their views. They could also point to signs of returning domestic prosperity. Moreover, U.S. regional dominance was confirmed with creation of a North American trading bloc that integrated the United States with Canada and Mexico. Internationally the dollar remained the prime reserve currency and Washington the indispensable first responder to any of the increasingly frequent financial crises abroad. The U.S. economy seemed assured of its place as first among equals in the three-bloc world.

The Stagflation Crisis

The gathering problems in the U.S. economy, already evident in the late 1960s, set the country up for a fall. Trade and federal government deficits, low savings, pressure on the dollar, and the onset of inflation had created economic vulnerability to any severe pressure from outside (see Chapter 5). That pressure came in the form of a pair of sharp oil shocks in the course of the 1970s that left Americans mired in a prolonged period of stagflation marked by stagnant growth and inflation. Usually one precluded the other, with low growth containing costs and high growth fueling it. It was perplexing that, in this case, the two economic ills came together in a single package.

The sharp blow to the U.S. economy came from the Organization of Petroleum Exporting Countries (OPEC). Middle Eastern leaders had organized this oil cartel to diminish the control that the major multinational corporations, such as Standard Oil of New Jersey, Royal Dutch-Shell, and British Petroleum, had exercised in the Persian Gulf oil fields through the 1950s. These producers held the whip hand thanks to strong backing by U.S. and western Europe governments determined to guard access to this critical economic and strategic commodity. A unilateral decision in 1959 by these producers to cut prices angered the shah of Iran (see Chapter 6 for the CIA-backed coup that restored him to power) and the king of Saudi Arabia whose country held at least one quarter of the world's oil reserves), and in 1960 they sponsored a meeting to organize oil-rich countries. Kuwait, Iraq, and Venezuela joined them at once, soon followed by eight other producing countries. The goal of OPEC, which by 1971–1972 controlled two thirds of all crude oil exports, was to coordinate policies with the long-term goal of fixing production and price levels and thus increase the rewards to countries in possession of this valuable resource. The steady climb in the demand for oil in the industrial countries through the 1960s strengthened OPEC's position. Prices began slowly to rise.

The United States and the rest of an energy-hungry world, already under price pressure, were soon in full crisis. They absorbed the first oil shock in 1973 when Arab producers shut off exports to the United States, Israel's major backer, in response to the outbreak of fighting between Arab states and Israel. Simultaneously, they dropped oil production, sending prices soaring to four times the prewar level and precipitating a recession in the industrial economies. Although the boycott ended in 1974, rising demand and strict production limits held prices up. Revolutionary turmoil in Iran in 1979 (see Chapter 9) gave another major boost to oil prices by disrupting supply. The price spikes of 1973 and 1979 combined to send prices to a level painful for developed countries and devastating for developing countries. By late fall 1980 oil was selling at $32 a barrel, compared to below $2 at the highest point in the late 1960s.

As higher basic energy costs passed through the U.S. economy, they created a multiplicity of problems. The immediate consequence was to fuel smoldering inflationary fires. Once ignited, inflation kept burning as shaken producers and consumers got used to rising prices and so rushed into purchases, thus accelerating the very trend they feared. Between 1968 and 1975 the price of consumer goods rose 62 percent. This higher consumer prices accentuated a decline in savings, already at a rate below that of other major economies. This low savings rate in turn had damaging effects on overall economic performance. It drove up the cost of borrowing capital and in turn discouraged investment in the areas that could make the economy more productive—in infrastructure, research and development, plants, and machinery. Weak productivity gains, inflation, and low savings combined to slow the rate of economic growth, giving rise to popular discontent expressed at the ballot box against elected leaders expected to do better. (See Fig. 8.1.)

A sluggish U.S. economy created trouble on another front: It intensified fiscal troubles by constricting government revenues. Federal budget deficits in the 1970s and 1980s became a persistent, worrisome feature of the economic scene. Americans were faced with a choice of either raising taxes or paring back government spending, but the electorate and its representatives in Washington refused to do either. Indeed, the deficit soared during the Reagan-era experiment with supply-side economic theory (what the elder George Bush called "voodoo" economics

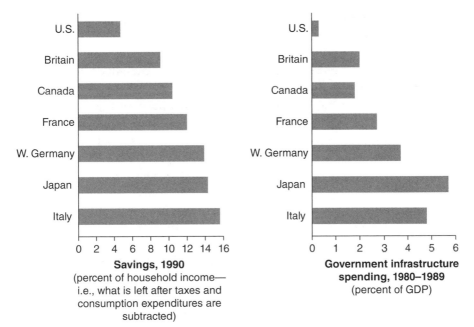

FIGURE 8.1
The U.S. Economy Falls Behind, 1980–1990
These two graphs measure U.S. performance against its competitors in two key measures commonly used by economists.[2]

before he became Reagan's vice president). Reagan cut taxes, certain that the additional money in the hands of Americans would boost investment and stimulate the economy. However, the lower tax rates did not result in the higher government revenue that supply-siders had predicted. Reagan compounded the fiscal woes by doubling military spending between 1981 and 1986, even as the members of Congress refused to make offsetting cuts in domestic programs valued by their constituents. Combined, these budget decisions opened a yawning gap between the federal government's income and expenditures. A young supply-sider charged with implementing Reagan's economic revolution emerged from the experience convinced that it had been "radical, imprudent, and arrogant."[3]

Each year's deficit added to the federal debt with cumulative effects that were dramatic. When Reagan became president in 1981, the total was $1 trillion. By 1986 it had risen to $2 trillion, then in 1989 when Bush senior entered the White House to almost $3 trillion, and finally by the time he handed the presidency over to Clinton in 1993 to $4 trillion (with interest payments on the deficit now claiming about 15 percent of the federal budget). Alarmists liked to point out that the accumulated debt apportioned on a per person basis amounted to about $16,000, and combined with corporate and consumer debt added up to something in the range of $10 trillion—or twice the nation's GNP. Third-party candidate Ross Perot complained during his 1992 presidential campaign that the persistent debt problem was "like a crazy aunt we keep down in the basement. All the neighbors know she's there, but nobody wants to talk about her."[4]

Popular expectations about consumption made these interlocking problems difficult to resolve. Americans already burdened with personal debt and hard pressed to maintain their lifestyle in the face of stagnating personal income resisted higher taxes to pay for the government programs that they continued to demand. While the average worker failed to gain significant ground during the 1970s and 1980s, blue-collar workers actually experienced a fall in real wages. These trends stood in sharp contrast to the first 25 years of the postwar period, when real wages for the average worker had more than doubled. The economy was failing to deliver on the promise of abundance that postwar Americans had come to take for granted, and many felt cheated. Disillusionment was particularly strong among young adults denied the opportunities available to their parents. Bruce Springsteen, a rock star with a pronounced populist streak, expressed the pessimism in "Born in the U.S.A.," his popular anthem from 1984: "Down in the shadows of the penitentiary/Out by the gas fires of the refinery/I'm ten years burning down the road/Nowhere to run ain't got nowhere to go."[5]

The accumulation of intractable internal problems in turn left domestic producers more exposed to rising competitive pressures from western Europe and Japan. Industry suffered a marked decline. For example, American steel, which had accounted for 39 percent of the world's production in 1955, had fallen to 15 percent by 1981, while automobile production had plummeted over that same period from 68 percent to 21 percent of world output. By 1980 Japan was not only outstripping the United States in the quantity but also the quality and fuel efficiency of its Toyotas and Hondas, and one major American manufacturer, Chrysler, was teetering on the edge of bankruptcy. The U.S. television industry, a giant with 90 manufacturers making seven million sets in 1951, had totally disappeared by 1995 with the sale of the last company (Zenith) to a South Korean firm. Older, heavily labor-intensive industries such as textiles moved production abroad to stay competitive. As international competition ate away at U.S. manufacturing, well-paid workers lost their jobs by the thousands, and the entire northern tier of industrial states turned into a "rustbelt" of closed factories, declining neighborhoods, and high unemployment. Chicago steelworkers, like blue-collar workers all around the country, saw opportunities closing for them that had been open to their parent's generation. "I'm workin' harder, makin' less money, got less of a future," lamented one. Another confessed, "It's the fear about maybe takin' a step down in society. Everyone's got that fear."[6]

The growing American taste for foreign goods and the difficulty American products were having winning foreign customers led to mounting trade deficits, which tripled between the late 1970s and the late 1980s ($153 billion by 1987). Those recurring annual deficits put ever more American debt in foreign hands, with the result that the country suffered a dramatic shift from creditor to debtor standing. By 1982 the United States had lost its surplus as foreign investments in the

United States came to exceed U.S. investments abroad. By 1987, in a stunning reversal, the United States had earned the dubious distinction of becoming the world's leading debtor nation.

This national fall from economic grace put strains on the consensus that had developed around free trade since the 1950s. Influential supporters, including journalists, economists, exporters, policymakers, and some labor leaders, could point to the fact that the General Agreement on Tariffs and Trade (see Chapter 2 on GATT) had made possible new jobs and a wider range of consumer goods at lower prices. But by the 1980s, with the country entering its second decade of economic difficulties, more Americans were questioning whether global trade was indeed good for the country.

Japan became the lightning rod for chagrin and anger over this rapid national decline. At the height of the Cold War, Americans had welcomed Japan's recovery. It seemed to affirm the U.S. model of economic development, vindicate U.S. international leadership, and strengthen the free world in its struggle against communism. However, American attitudes shifted dramatically in the 1980s as Japan laid claim to the status of "number one" in the economic sphere, where Americans had long prided themselves on primacy. At the same time that Japanese automobiles and electronics were flooding the U.S. market, American industry was having difficulty penetrating the Japanese market. The cumulative effect of a persistent trade imbalance was to put more and more American IOUs in the hands of Japanese business and banks. They in turn poured money into the American stock market and real estate, including such national icons as New York City's Rockefeller Center. Pointing to Sony's purchase of CBS Records in 1988 and Columbia Pictures the next year, a *Newsweek* magazine cover announced: "Japan Invades Hollywood."

By the early 1990s the tensions in U.S.–Japan relations had reached a postwar peak, and some alarmists claimed to see in Japan a successor to the now-defunct communist menace. Business and labor led the call for protectionist measures, and some disgruntled Americans charged that the Japanese had become an economic juggernaut because they did not play fair. They imposed informal obstacles to foreign goods and services or unnaturally suppressed consumer demand. Some even traced Japanese economic success back to a sinister conspiracy or a deformed society's resistance to the "natural" desire for individualism and consumer debt. Japan-bashing became politically popular. A 1992 poll revealed that 40 percent regarded Japan as an unfair competitor, and 55 percent suspected that Japanese secretly looked down on Americans.[7]

Nevertheless, mutual self-interest limited the gathering tensions. For the United States, trade across the Pacific had by 1984 surpassed trade across the Atlantic, making Asia the largest U.S. foreign market. Japanese investors buoyed Wall Street and property values. And when Washington asked Tokyo to remove barriers to trade, including tariffs and other obstacles to foreign business, and to offer inducements for higher spending on U.S.-made imports, Tokyo gave enough ground to calm U.S. ire, although not to eliminate the trade gap.

The battering of the 1970s and 1980s had seriously eroded U.S. economic dominance and weakened the dollar's pivotal role in international finance assigned it at
Bretton Woods. Poor economic performance had gradually undercut the value of
the dollar, which was accumulating in foreign hands, and caused a flight into other
currencies, chiefly the German mark and the Japanese yen. Unable to sustain the
fixed dollar–gold price ratio at $35 per ounce, Nixon took the dramatic step in
1971 of breaking the dollar's fixed link to gold that had made the U.S. currency the
single point of reference for international trade and investment since the end of
World War II. The "greenback" now "floated" ingloriously, subject like any currency
to the tides of the market.

U.S. policymakers were confronted with new limits. They now had to engage in
greater coordination with the other economic powerhouses. They began meeting
ad hoc as the Group of Six in 1975. Finance ministers, central bankers, and sometimes heads of state of Japan, the United States, Britain, France, West Germany,
and Italy, representing the leading economies in the North Atlantic region along
with Japan, began to meet on a regular basis to coordinate industrial, trade, and
financial policies, to give direction to the original Bretton Woods institutions,
and to promote free trade and currency stability. This body of influentials was
expanded to include Canada; the G-6 thus became the G-7. U.S. policymakers also
now found they no longer had the deep economic pockets to which they had
become accustomed. It was as a result harder for Washington to throw money at
global problems. For example, there were no generous grants of the sort given
western Europe after World War II for post-socialist eastern Europe and Russia
struggling through the transition to democracy and free markets. Similarly, to
counter Iraq's invasion of Kuwait in 1990 (see Chapter 11), a fiscally pinched but
muscle-bound U.S. government had to ask its affluent partners—the Japanese,
Kuwaitis, and Saudis—to subsidize the American military effort.

The Free-Market Solution

Two decades of economic stress helped bring about an important shift in fundamental economic philosophy in the United States. A strong free-market faith came
into vogue, confirming the truth of Keynes' famous observation about the subtle
influence "some defunct economist" can have in the world of practical affairs.
The gurus of the new faith were the Austrian economist Friedrich Hayek and the
American Milton Friedman. They might be best described as neoliberal because
they wanted to revive what they regarded as the true liberalism of the nineteenth
century, with its robust faith in free markets. They argued that the free market
was not only the most efficient way of arranging economic activity but also an
essential feature of a democratic society.

These neoliberals saw themselves in sharp opposition to the "false" liberalism
that John Maynard Keynes had promoted (see Chapter 2). They concluded that
much of the economic malaise of the time was due to excessive government intervention in the international no less than the domestic economy. Hayek had formed

his ideas in reaction against the pre-1945 German and Italian fascist experiments as well as the Soviet model. He and like-minded economists had hoped that a war fought for freedom was a prelude to a postwar drive to turn back the inroads of the statist model. To them it was abundantly clear that governmental control over the economy, however laudable its objectives, was neither politically wise nor economically effective. They watched with dismay as Soviet-backed regimes imposed state planning in eastern Europe, radical Third World regimes pursued state-sponsored industrialization, and Keynesian ideas prevailed in the West. Even the United States in the 1960s seemed to be going down a dangerous collectivist road as welfare spending dramatically increased. In calling for shifting power from the state back to the market, the neoliberals laid the intellectual groundwork for a conservative political resurgence in the United States as well as Britain.

The most influential neoliberal was Milton Friedman. Born in 1912 in Brooklyn, New York, he taught economics at the University of Chicago from 1946 to 1977. Through much of his early career, Friedman criticized Keynes and advocated the virtues of the free market. However, as long as the economy was doing fine, the Keynesians could take credit and keep the upper hand in policy circles. But by 1978, when Friedman received the Nobel Prize in economics, the Keynesians were on the defensive, and he had gained a wide hearing among economists and politicians looking for fresh solutions to U.S. economic malaise. His own students spread the gospel, and some became influential in policy circles in the United States and abroad. (For example, Chile's post-Allende military government was heavily staffed with his disciples.) Conservative politicians increasingly drew on Friedman's ideas in their drive to dismantle the welfare state and political obstructions to free enterprise.

Friedman's *Capitalism and Freedom*, written in close collaboration with his economist wife, Rose D. Friedman, was the best known of his works. Published in 1962, it made a special point of rescuing the term "liberal" from the corruption that Friedman believed it had undergone in the twentieth century. That the Roosevelt administration and its Democratic successors down to Lyndon Johnson had used state intervention to promote welfare and equality made them (as Friedman phrased it) "men of good intentions and good will" yet still dangerous. In his estimate, they had surrendered freedom as the ultimate good and developed a faith in the state to achieve social change that aligned them with the coercive tendencies of totalitarian systems. This recast liberalism was thus a corruption, even a betrayal, of an older classical liberalism that had recognized "freedom as the ultimate goal and the individual as the ultimate entity in the society." Starting from that premise, they had "supported laissez faire at home as a means of reducing the role of the state in economic affairs and thereby enlarging the role of the individual." They had seen "free trade abroad as a means of linking the nations of the world together peacefully and democratically." Friedman called for a return to this older tradition that recognized the close relationship between economic and political freedom. A free economy "gives people what they want instead of what a particular group thinks they ought to want." It thus encouraged social and political diversity. It reduced "greatly the range of issues that must be decided through political means," thus minimizing the range of government intervention. And finally, "if economic power is kept in separate hands from political power, it can serve as a check and a counter to political power."[8]

Mounting difficulties in the U.S. economy through the 1960s brought these neoliberal ideas into political fashion. Keynesian fiscal policy had failed to end stagflation. Proponents of neoliberal programs pressed the case for taking the problem out of the hands of the president and Congress, where political concerns prevailed, and handing it over to the Federal Reserve Board, which served as the U.S. central bank. There economists could make decisions about the size of the money supply on technical grounds and thus provide a more stable, less politically influenced context for the functioning of the economy. With the bias toward inflation removed, markets would work better to achieve real growth. Neoliberals looked beyond monetary policy to a broader restructuring of the American economy. They believed that the state imposed a heavy burden on businesses by taxing too much to fund wasteful programs like welfare and siphoning off capital otherwise available for productive investment. Bureaucratic red tape got in the way of market transactions, raising costs often with no appreciable gain. Downsizing the government was the neoliberal mantra—and it became the mantra of every president after Richard Nixon, Democratic as well as Republican. It is tempting to see the calls for cuts as a kind of magical incantation; in fact, the federal budget continued to climb (to a fifth of GDP by 2000).

Looking abroad, these neoliberal economists also advocated greater reliance on markets to keep the international economy healthy and growing. The most general change that they championed was the liberation of international currency and capital movements. This represented a major departure from the attitudes promoted by the Bretton Woods architects, who had regarded currency speculation as dangerously disruptive and linked the sustained downturn of the 1930s to its destabilizing effects. By putting the dollar in a pivotal role and by allowing states to keep currency controls, they raised a significant barrier to speculation and instability. Nixon's decision to unhitch the dollar from gold meant that the U.S. currency would now float in value relative to other currencies. Neoliberals pressed for taking the next step—removing state restrictions hindering the freedom of the currency market and capital movement.

Nixon's decision on convertibility of the dollar and cuts in government spending carried him only partway toward the neoliberal position. As part of his attack on the country's economic woes, he imposed a 15 percent import surcharge as well as wage and price controls. These measures did not produce a turnaround, as the neoliberals were quick to point out, so Nixon soon removed them. Inflation surged, consumer spending fell, and the Federal Reserve raised interest rates in a failed attempt to control inflation. In 1974 real GNP declined 2 percent, and unemployment reached 7.2 percent. The country was in the grip of the most severe economic downturn since 1945.

The failure of Nixon's heavy-handed intervention emboldened neoliberals. Now was the time to try a new regimen on the sick economy: Get the government out of the economy except for controlling the money supply, and let the markets find a cure for the national economic ills. Major banks hoping for greater freedom from government regulations supported these views, and U.S. industry shifted in this direction as its growing multinational operations aligned its interests closer to those of banks. Only labor expressed sustained, serious opposition.

Winning popular support for the neoliberal position involved above all else a cultural campaign couched in terms of freedom applying as much to firms, no matter how large, as to individuals. Spearheading the campaign were conservative think tanks, corporate-owned media, favored academic economists, and public intellectuals. By the 1980s, with Ronald Reagan leading the Republicans to victory in the United States and with the Conservative Party under Margaret Thatcher in power in Britain, proponents of neoliberalism occupied the Anglo-American high ground and continued to press their claim that the dynamism of the market would restore prosperity and safeguard freedom internationally no less than at home.

They set to work overturning the grand postwar bargain that gave the state and labor a place alongside capital in determining the direction of national economies and that imposed restrictions on both the activities of corporations and the movement of capital in the name of stability and public welfare. As neoliberals took the offensive, they sought to weaken labor unions, shrink government, and reduce state-sponsored social security programs. With the popular tide shifting, opposition parties—the Democrats in the United States as well as Labour in Britain—made their peace with the new neoliberal consensus. The market was the solution, while governments just got in the way. They expected the Federal Reserve to tighten control of credit in order to check inflation. This bitter medicine produced a deep recession in 1981–1982 and another brief bout of recession in the early 1990s. At the same time these Republican administrations, true to supply-side principles, lowered taxes, expecting Americans to spend and invest more and thus to stimulate the economy and ultimately raise revenue sufficient to offset the cuts. Those cuts did strongly stimulate the economy, but the federal deficit continued to balloon. During this same period American corporations made themselves more competitive internationally, going on a frenzy of consolidation, holding down wages, and investing significantly to upgrade plants and equipment and thereby raise productivity.

By the early 1990s Americans were headed into a decade of prosperity thanks to a convergence of developments. Alan Greenspan, appointed to head the Federal Reserve in 1987, succeeded in beating down inflation. As a result, Greenspan, who was a musician before turning to economics, became an oracle. His speeches, supposedly composed in his bathtub, were carefully studied for insight on the new neoliberal policy dispensation with its emphasis on fiscal discipline and market freedom. Greenspan got a considerable assist from moderating oil prices. Energy conservation measures and greater efficiency had gradually lowered oil demand at the same time that the opening of new oil fields increased supply. Even the OPEC cartel had helped douse inflationary fires. Kuwait and Saudi Arabia, which had accumulated an enormous pool of capital, had billions invested in the real estate and stock markets of the advanced economies. The OPEC moguls now set oil prices with care so as not to hurt the very economies in which they had so substantial a stake. Under these auspicious circumstances, a formerly ailing American giant turned into the most robust of the world economies. Growth held steady, and inflation and unemployment dipped to levels previously thought unsustainable for a prolonged period. Wages for most Americans began to grow once more, and the stock market boomed. American goods were more competitive internationally. While U.S. firms no longer dominated such industries as automobiles and consumer electronics, they were strong in such high-tech fields as aircraft, entertainment, biotechnology, computers, and telecommunications. Even the venerable steel industry, victimized by competition, slimmed down, upgraded, and staged a comeback. More competitive goods helped to narrow but not close the trade gap and to dampen frictions with trading partners.

Technological innovation played a critical role in the U.S. comeback. The star of the new class of technology was the computer, which could handle massive amounts of data, facilitate communications (including the Internet), and bring more automation to the production line. The computer and other innovations were the product of a postwar system of collaboration among government agencies, university research teams, and corporations. In the Cold War era Washington wanted to keep on the cutting edge of science and technology for reasons of national prestige as well as advantage against the Soviet foe. But rather than impose a centrally run program, Cold War leaders opted for a diverse and decentralized approach better suited to American values. Out of this security-driven collaboration emerged breakthroughs in such areas as nuclear weapons, jet aircraft, and antibiotics. The government also created agencies such as the National Science Foundation to channel funding into pure research and the National Aeronautics and Space Administration (NASA) to keep the United States ahead in the space race. As the available R&D funding expanded, so too did the ambition of university scientists. They competed for big grants and carried out large-scale research as a team effort. Corporations watched closely for promising discoveries to come out of this government–university collaboration while at the same time underwriting their own research. The infusion of new technology, greatly facilitated by government money and initiative, had an important economic payoff: It made old industries more productive and thus more competitive, and it gave a strong impetus to cutting-edge firms in the electronics, telecommunications, aeronautics, and biopharmaceuticals sectors.

The U.S. economic revival helped shore up the country's position as the premier player on the global stage. GDP doubled between 1970 and 1993. The U.S. economy still accounted for a quarter of world output and almost a fifth of world trade. The dollar retained its worldwide appeal as the currency of choice. In the mid-1990s

nearly 60 percent of the foreign exchange holdings of central banks and governments was in dollars, while over 80 percent of foreign-exchange transactions involved the purchase or sale of dollars.[9]

The worldwide appeal of a popular culture generated by American corporations
further bolstered the U.S. position. Hollywood continued its drive toward domination of foreign markets. Its feature films in 1971–1972 accounted for roughly a
third of the market in West Germany, Spain, and Hong Kong, around a half in
Italy, the UK, Japan, Mexico, and Egypt, and a little over two thirds in India. The
share in the especially lucrative European market continued to grow, reaching
70 percent in 1996. As TVs became onmipresent in homes throughout the developed
world, programming for the new medium proved equally successful. The advance
of the music industry added yet another layer to U.S. culture influence abroad. Tin
Pan Alley led the way during the 1950s popularizing big-band croners such as
Frank Sinatra, Tony Bennett, and Rosemary Clooncy. They were in turn overtaken
by the Rockers led by Bill Haley and Elvis Presley. Music no less than films and
TV bore the hallmarks of consumer culture: corporate dominance and careful
attention to marketing and to new technologies (for example, enhanced amplifi-
cation and sound manipulation). This rising tide of U.S. entertainment was not
only profitable; it also consolidated the primacy of English as the global language.
Japanese spoke of *biiru* (beer) and *terebi* (television)—to cite the top two English
loan words—just as the French referred to *le weekend*.[10]

Popular American products such as blue jeans and T-shirts became omnipresent.
A thirsty Che Guevara was caught on film in 1961 with a bottle of Coke in hand.
Despite fears that the drink was "capitalism concentrated in a bottle," Chinese Communist leaders opened the doors in the 1980s ostensibly to keep the tourists happy.
In an evermore prosperous Europe, Disney opened a theme park outside of Paris in
1992. Pummeled by the cultural mandarins and plagued at first by poor attendance,
the park eventually gained popular acceptance. Japanese who grew up in the 1950s
and 1960s raptly watched the Mickey Mouse Club and found in Disney films simple,
vivid stories of virtue vindicated. Their children were in turn treated to Bambi wall
clocks, Sleeping Beauty wristwatches, Donald Duck and Minnie Mouse mugs, and
visits to the stunningly successful Disney theme park, which opened in Tokyo in
1984. The millions who visited it annually encountered a purportedly American
world whose very exoticism served to highlight their own unique national character
and history. As China opened in the 1980s, it too embraced Disney film and paraphernalia. During the spring 1989 protests Chinese coeds could be seen sporting
outfits that mixed nicely tailored skirts and jackets with Mickey Mouse T-shirts.
Children at Beijing birthday parties squealed in delight at adults wearing elaborate
mouse costumes. The opening of a Disney theme park in Hong Kong in 2005, with a
second soon to open in Shanghai, marked an important new step in the peculiarly
American pop-culture conquest of the China market.[11]

This combination of economic power and cultural reach a exercised a strong
gravitational pull over Canada and Mexico and drew them into the emergent North

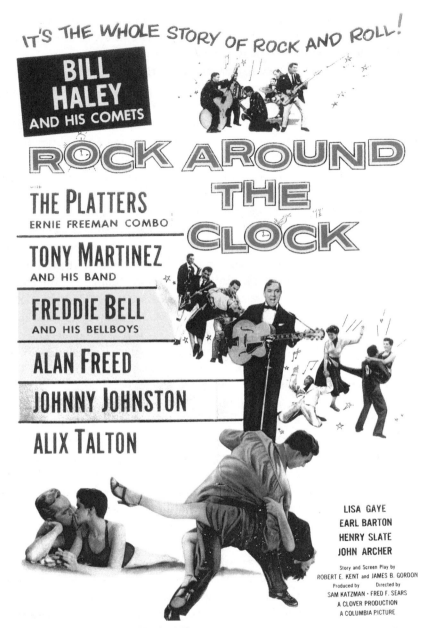

Poster for *Rock Around the Clock*, 1956
Rock around the Clock, a film featuring Bill Haley and directed by Fred F. Sears, helped inaugurate what became the first genuinely global music culture. Rock with its roots in the African-American community acquired an aura of rebellion that would win it a fervent following among young people around the world, even on the other side of the Iron Curtain. The performers who followed Haley and Presley in the late 1950s and 1960s created a diverse Anglo-American rock scene with enduring influence. Some of the leading lights were (in chronological order) Ike and Tina Turner (U.S.), the Beatles (UK), Rolling Stones (UK), Jimi Hendrix (U.S.), the Who (UK), Jefferson Airplane (U.S.), the Doors (U.S.), Grateful Dead (U.S.), and Led Zeppelin (UK). (© Pictorial Press Ltd / Alamy)

American bloc. In 1989 Canada had consolidated its ties to the American economy by signing a free trade agreement. A similar agreement, negotiated by the first President Bush, extended the arrangements to Mexico in 1994 under what was now formally known as the North American Free Trade Agreement (NAFTA). This North American free trade bloc was the largest in the world ($6.84 trillion in GDP in 1990). Reflecting the values of its dominant economy, the NAFTA bloc shared neither the social policies that were integral to the development of the European community nor the mechanisms of state guidance commonplace in East Asia.

For Mexico more than Canada, a formal link to the American economic giant involved profound changes. Canada, already heavily export-oriented, embraced NAFTA as a guarantee of access to the large, rich, U.S. market. As a developing country, Mexico entered the pact with its authoritarian political system intact, with wide disparities of income and considerable poverty, and with a legacy of state intervention dating back to the days of import-substitution policies. In 1994, even as Mexico embraced NAFTA, reminders of its underdeveloped status came in the form of a peasant, predominantly poor Indian rebellion in the southern state of Chiapas and a severe financial crisis that required a $20 billion U.S. bailout. NAFTA accelerated the trend toward neoliberal economic policies set in motion by a major debt crisis in 1982 and promoted by a string of U.S.-trained Mexican government officials. NAFTA also ignited a Mexican export boom, while workers hungry for jobs crossed an increasingly porous U.S.–Mexican border. With free trade, heavy U.S. investment, and sizable migration went a marked shift toward democratization. Just as the period of import substitution and single-party rule had transformed Mexico, so too now was neoliberalism reshaping the country.

Neoliberals had good reason to feel vindicated. Reagan's turn to market-friendly policies, which Clinton continued, seemed to have restored U.S. economic vitality and global preeminence, and it had pulled neighbors more tightly into the U.S. orbit. By the start of the 1990s policymakers and pundits alike looked to the future with confidence. Not only had they prevailed over the communist threat but they regarded the new free-market orthodoxy as a demonstrable success that offered a guide to the future at home and abroad. In domestic policy, the free-market gospel assigned a privileged place to corporations on the assumption that a business model would resolve thorny problems in American life, from education to social welfare to military logistics to health care. In global terms, they were confident the United States represented a globally tested and applicable model of modernity. It had prevailed over one set of European ideological rivals—Nazism and fascism— and then overwhelmed the socialist variant on modernity. From this position of hegemony, the United States could press for an international regime congruent with its values. The U.S. economy, better than any other, exemplified the neoliberal faith in market mechanisms, strong individual property rights, low taxes, and limited state interference. Determined to lay down the terms for how the world should work, a country in thrall to neoliberalism was ready to stand against authoritarian regimes and inefficient statist economies. Americans in the years ahead would

TURBULENCE AND TRANSITION FOR THE U.S. ECONOMY

1959	Iran's shah and the Saudis take the lead in creation of OPEC
1962	Friedman publishes *Capitalism and Freedom*
1971	Nixon ends the fixed gold–dollar exchange rate, allowing the dollar to float
1973	Boycott by Arab members of OPEC deals oil shock to U.S. and other industrial economies
1979	Iran's revolution disrupts oil supplies and creates second oil shock
1981	Reagan administration promotes neoliberal economic policy
1987	U.S. overseas debt becomes highest in the world; Reagan appoints Greenspan to head the Federal Reserve
1989	U.S. and Canada sign free-trade agreement
1990	U.S. federal debt hits $3 trillion
1993	Clinton enters White House and presides over a decade of prosperity
1994	NAFTA integrates Mexico into the regional bloc

double down in their faith in the free market that gave the North American bloc its distinguishing character.

THE RISE OF AN EAST ASIAN BLOC

While Americans struggled to find their way during the 1970s and 1980s, the Japanese sailed ahead, carried along by their continuing economic miracle. Nearly four decades of high growth rates had made Japan one of the top three world economies and its people among the most prosperous. Japan's neighbors closely watched this unfolding success story. Taiwan, Singapore, and South Korea were the first to adopt important aspects of the state-led economic growth strategy to their own situations. As smaller craft traveling toward prosperity in the 1970s and 1980s in the wake of the great Japanese vessel, they too would experience high growth rates. China, Vietnam, and the rest of Southeast Asia would be close behind. With Japan as the model, the region would come to constitute a loose regional bloc united less by formal institutional arrangements than economic interdependence resulting from high levels of intraregional trade and investment and a common economic outlook.

Taken together, the economies of the entire region running from the Korean peninsula to Indonesia and Thailand put on a display of productivity, technical innovation, and enterprise that rivaled that of the United States and Europe. The four leading economies alone had a total GDP in 1990 of $5 trillion. At the same time the region was becoming a pivotal part of world trade. By the early 1990s both the United States and the EC were beginning to do more business with East and Southeast Asia than either did across the Atlantic, long the major avenue for international trade and investment. And in this trade the surplus ran substantially in favor of Asia. These vibrant Asian economies made dramatic improvements in the lives of their peoples. Between the mid-1970s and the mid-1990s, households suffering from the severe deprivation associated with absolute poverty had fallen dramatically.[12]

Japan Stays on Course

Despite heavy dependence on imported energy supplies, the Japanese economy showed considerable resilience in weathering the OPEC oil shocks of the 1970s. While the jump in prices early in the decade ignited inflation and squeezed profit margins, it also encouraged investment in energy efficiency that stimulated the economy and made Japanese products more cost-competitive. By the late 1970s the Japanese were embarked on a prolonged period of stable growth, Japanese goods were as competitive as ever, and the home market was as difficult for foreigners to penetrate. The trade surplus and investment holdings abroad would soar. Between 1955 and 1985 Japan's share of world exports had quadrupled (to 10.1 percent). Its GNP had grown over the quarter-century ending in 1984 at 3.5 times the U.S. rate. By the late 1980s per capita income had climbed to U.S. and West German levels and far outstripped the British. This gathering economic momentum eventually fed a speculative fever. Land prices boomed along with the Tokyo stock market. (See Fig. 8.2.)

The Japanese were proud of their success in reaching the position of the leading economic performer, and they bristled over American attacks in the 1980s and early 1990s on such flaws in the Japanese model as "oversaving," informal protectionism, and export subsidies. The strongest reaction came from the economy's "iron triangle" of powerful government bureaucrats, Liberal Democratic Party politicians, and leaders of *keiretsu* (the enterprise groups that united large corporations). They cautioned against reforms that would not only hurt economically but also undermine Japan's social cohesion and throw into chaos a stable, ethically attuned society rooted in a thousand years of tradition. They worried particularly that an American-style open economy would lead to crime and social breakdown. A prominent Finance Ministry official warned against unleashing "naked market forces." "It would be the end of Japanese-style capitalism if we pushed this kind of change too far. Japan would be split, as America is split."[13]

A widely read response to American criticisms appeared in the 1989 book *The Japan That Can Say No*, co-authored by Sony's Morita Akio and Ishihara Shintaro, a popular and outspoken politician. They conceded that "whites, including Americans, have built the modern era." But the authors insisted that the "pride [of whites]

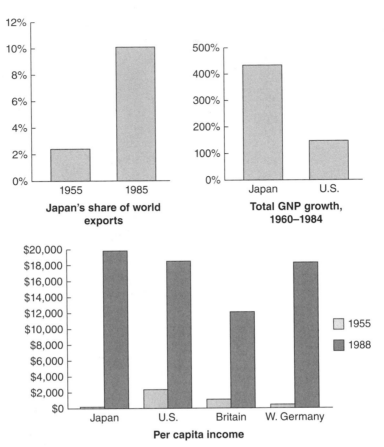

FIGURE 8.2
Japan Catches Up, 1955–1988[14]

is too strong" and their ignorance of the cultural achievement of Japanese and other Asians over the last five centuries was appalling. The authors wondered "if the historical pride has gone to the length of inerasable arrogance. Right now, the modern civilization built by whites is coming close to a period of practical end."[15] Behind this confident and defiant Japanese reaction was a widely shared feeling of vulnerability. As they saw it, their small, resource-poor island nation had struggled since the late nineteenth century to catch up with the West and win international respect as an equal. Despite stunning economic success, other countries and above all the United States continued to treat Japan as a second-rate power.

Japanese commentators, businesspeople, and government officials countered American demands on Japan with an agenda of changes for the United States to implement. They wanted an end to U.S. free-trade hypocrisy; it was time to give Japanese steel and autos full access to the U.S. market. They suggested that Washington address its own economic problems, especially endemic debt, rather than telling the Japanese what to do. Americans might learn from the Japanese such

Japanese Nurse a Sense of Grievance, 1990
This cartoon, which appeared in a leading Japanese newspaper in March 1990, shows a small, vulnerable Mount Fuji (symbol of Japan and its purity) facing an overbearing, militaristic United States demanding reform. Mount Fuji is labeled "The Japan that cannot say no," playing off the popular critique of Japanese subservience to the United States titled "The Japan that Can Say No." The caption reads: "Isn't 'postwar' over?" suggesting that it was time to end the dependent relationship established during the U.S. occupation after World War II. (Yokoyama Taizo, *Asahi Shimbum*)

fundamental economic virtues as personal sacrifice and social cooperation. The Japanese public, proud of their country's success, agreed, and many resented the U.S. making Japan a scapegoat for its own economic problems.

The "Little Dragons"

By the 1990s a distinct economic bloc was taking shape in East Asia. Japan's success had been followed first by the "little dragons" (South Korea, Taiwan, and Singapore) in the 1960s and 1970s. (Hong Kong is often included among the little dragons, but its unusual niche role as a free-trade center handling goods moving between China and the outside world distinguished it from the others.) That they could develop vibrant economies with vital export industries was due to more than imitating Japan's guided capitalism. Taiwan and South Korea both built on infrastructure and an educational foundation laid by Japanese colonial administrations. Both along with Singapore had, moreover, benefited significantly from Japanese investments drawn by low labor costs and the prospect of getting around host country and U.S. import restrictions. Finally, they had benefited from U.S.

Cold War policies favorable to foreign trade, U.S. cold warriors' preference for strong leaders who could maintain political stability, and the economic stimulation from U.S. military spending (the equivalent to the role the Marshall Plan had played in Europe). Thanks to this set of favorable conditions, the little dragons had moved successfully into household electronics such as radios and televisions and then on to semiconductors. The addition of the big dragon (China) in the course of the 1980s followed by Vietnam broadened the zone of Asian prosperity while diluting Japanese influence.

Of the early adopters of the Japanese model, South Korea was far and away the most significant with the largest economy and population. Disturbed by halting political and economic recovery after the Korean War, the military seized power in Seoul in 1961. The dominant figure, Park Chung-hee moved aggressively in the mid-1960s to promote export-oriented industrialization. Guided by technocrats, Park's single-minded, heavy-handed pursuit of growth turned a poor, agricultural economy into a rising economic powerhouse by the time of his assassination in 1979. By that date GDP was more than four times higher than it had been in 1965. His military successors and then elected civilian governments built on this foundation in what proved a continuing success story, with the broad population increasingly sharing in the benefits. The major instruments as well as chief beneficiary of this sustained drive were the *chaebols*, family-controlled industrial conglomerates resembling the Japanese *zaibatsu*. Park had given strong government support to them as the prime engine of industrial, export-oriented development. The top ten accounted for nearly a quarter of South Korea's total output by 1978 and three quarters by the early 1990s. The Asian financial crisis winnowed the *chaebol* ranks, but the survivors led by Samsung and Hyundai went on from strength to strength. Samsung's sales in 2012 alone accounted for a quarter of the country's output.[16]

South Korea embodied the regional pattern of resorting to strong state direction. The advocates of this approach started from the premise that the international free-trade regime offered significant opportunities for growth but that success required more than outdated technology and low wages. The state had to provide promising industries with incentives in the form of subsidies and capital available on easy terms. The state also had to buffer these industries against outside competition by raising tariffs and other barriers to imports. At the very time that neoliberals in the West were mounting their attack against state intervention, these economies were demonstrating that state capitalism did work.

The cultural-economic characteristics of this East Asian bloc might best be summed up by the term "Confucian capitalism." The values underlying bloc success arose from long-dominant social and political patterns often described as Confucian. Political legitimacy rested not on abstract laws or constitutional arrangements but rather on the virtue evident in the ruler's character. A well-ruled state was marked not by ideological diversity and debate but rather by broad acceptance of a state-sponsored sociopolitical orthodoxy. Finally, society was in Confucian terms not a collection of competing, self-interested individuals. Members of society were rather mutually dependent, with common goals that transcended individual interests and that required a modicum of group cooperation and sacrifice. This strong and widely shared set of values helped sustain the very conditions that made East Asian economies work so well, including notably authoritarian politics, a stress on public order, loyalty to family and organization, an ethic of hard work, and a faith in the importance of education. The Japanese and their neighbors operated on the principle that a market mechanism driven primarily by self-interest would not create a decent, moral society and might not even make for an efficient economy. Individualism with its rejection of group obligations seemed from this Asian vantage point a dysfunctional trait to be frowned upon.

Some outside observers saw in Japan at the head of this Asian bloc a new imperial presence in the world about to subordinate the once-dominant West. What such fears overlooked were old regional animosities that drained any political will for the tight economic integration of the sort that Europe had embraced. Some in the region, such as the Chinese and Koreans, vividly recalled Japan's wartime brutality and its attempt in the late 1930s to impose its economic as well as political control (see the Introduction), and others feared China's growing power.

Capitalism with Chinese Characteristics

Of all the additions to the East Asian bloc, China was the most important. Beijing's turn to capitalism and the international market dramatically expanded the geographical scope of the bloc and created a dominant regional presence. Gradually, beginning in the late 1970s, China abandoned central planning in favor of state-guided growth while preserving the dominant role of the CCP. The result might be described as capitalism with Chinese characteristics, although the Chinese themselves called it socialism with Chinese characteristics. The resulting economic transformation of China, the world's most populous country and once the region's most prominent revolutionary standard-bearer, stands in importance on a par with Japan's "miracle" of the 1950s and 1960s.

Deng Xiaoping was the party leader who sharply reoriented the direction of China's development path. Deng was born in 1904 in the interior province of Sichuan, the son of a landlord. In 1920, after schooling in Confucian classics as well as Western studies, the 16-year-old set off for France to participate in a work-study program then popular among young Chinese. Like other future leaders, such as Ho Chi Minh and Kwame Nkrumah, the sojourn would prove critical to his cultural as well as his political outlook. In France Deng made a commitment to the CCP that would endure a lifetime, and his labors at publishing party material earned him the nickname "Doctor of Duplication." (Those years also created an abiding passion for soccer, coffee, and croissants.) In 1927, after training in Moscow, he arrived back in China.

Over the following decades, as the CCP fought its way to power (see Chapter 3), Deng played an increasingly prominent role. He participated in the fabled Long March that carried Mao to leadership, built one of the CCP's armed base areas, won critical battlefield victories during the civil war, and administered China's south-west after the CCP came to power in 1949. In 1956, now one of Mao's chief lieuten-ants, Deng assumed the prominent position of general secretary of the CCP. He brought to the post experience in political and military affairs. His grasp of eco-nomic issues was tenuous, so he would later have to rely on advisers in shaping his reform program. By the early 1960s, with Mao less active following the Great Leap Forward disaster, Deng shared leadership with Liu Shaoqi and Zhou Enlai.

Years of loyal service no more saved Deng from attack during the Cultural Revo-lution than it did others close to Mao. But unlike many at the top accused of "taking the capitalist road," Deng survived denunciation and imprisonment and won reha-bilitation in 1973. Purged again in 1976, Deng this time sought the protection of military leaders in the south. Mao's death in September 1976 marked the end of an era. A month later the "gang of four," the radical Maoist group led by Mao's wife, Jiang Qing, were arrested and later sentenced to long prison terms. Deng's stand-ing as a senior party leader and his extensive political and military relationships built up over half a century of party service now paid off. Colleagues rallied to Deng's support, and he quickly established himself as China's new leader, elbowing aside Mao's own choice as successor, Hua Guofeng. Even as his health failed, Deng would remain China's "paramount leader" down to his death in 1997.

The man holding the destiny of China in his hands had abilities long recognized within the CCP. Mao is supposed to have pointed Deng out to Khrushchev during a 1957 meeting in Moscow: "See that little man there? He's highly intelligent and has a great future ahead of him." Round-faced and standing barely five feet tall, Deng was neither a deep thinker nor a charismatic public figure. He was rather a skilled, no-nonsense administrator, a pragmatic problem-solver, a fierce party loy-alist, and a thorough patriot committed to making China strong and its people prosperous. He was a man of few and simple words. (Asked by his daughter to de-scribe his experience during the epic Long March, Deng responded laconically that he "went along.") He was, finally, a devoted family man. Deng's 1939 marriage—his third—created a tight-knit family that provided a sanctuary during a bruising up-and-down political career.[17]

Deng decided that he could not lead the party forward without first confronting its past. He and his colleagues needed above all else to examine Mao's record for the lessons it might yield, for the mistakes to be avoided or corrected, and for the legitimacy Mao's genuine achievements might confer. In June 1981 party leaders offered a public reassessment that praised Mao's early leadership but condemned his later errors, notably the Great Leap Forward and the Cultural Revolution, and his imperial style of governance with its frequent and ill-considered policy shifts. The CCP's efforts at coming to terms with its past invites comparison with Khrushchev's own attempt earlier to deal with the legacy of Stalin.

Deng's highest priority was reinvigorating the CCP, above all restoring the early commitment to give-and-take at the top of the party pyramid and firm but moder-ate party discipline that Mao had undermined beginning in the 1950s as he started turning viciously on his comrades. Deng wanted a return to open, frank discussions among the leadership. Out of negotiations and compromise among the top leaders would emerge consensus decisions. Deng expected loyal party members to abide by those decisions and maintain party discipline (just as Deng himself had stoically done throughout his career). For party members who strayed, Deng preferred to apply education and rehabilitation. The chief task of a restored party was in Deng's estimate to implement a practical, careful program of economic development.

Although lacking a grand strategy, Deng gradually committed the CCP to a rapid, market-driven economic strategy linked to greater openness to the outside world. He described his approach as "building socialism with Chinese characteristics," but "four modernizations" is the term that finally stuck. To develop, so the proponents of this course argued, China had to advance on four major fronts—by promoting advanced technology and science, a modernized military, competitive industry, and productive agriculture.

In the greatest surprise of all, the new policy lent support to the emergence of a market economy. Dissolving communes and returning individual plots to peasants was the first striking step, taken in 1978. This initiative came not from Beijing, but from below—from peasants in Anhui province—and was only cautiously and reluctantly approved by Deng thereafter. Although peasants did not own their land under the new policy, they exercised formal control as long as they sold a contracted portion of their crops to the government. The rest was for them to sell on their own account at market prices. Responding to the new incentives, peasants raised production by 25 percent between 1975 and 1985, and China exported grain for the first time in recent memory. The liberation of rural entrepreneurs set a precedent for privatizing other parts of the economy. At the same time businesses still part of the government-controlled public sector gained greater autonomy in decision-making. The result of these changes was a mixed economy in which market forces played a generally broader role and in which the state-controlled sector accounted for an ever-smaller portion of national economic activity. To ensure that unchecked population growth did not erode material gains, Deng gave birth control high priority. He instituted a one-child policy that offered incentives such as health and educational benefits for those who complied and criticism, fines, harassment, and coercion for those who did not.

These reforms were accompanied by a deepening involvement in the international economy. Foreign investors first began testing the water and then plunging in with greater enthusiasm as the 1980s wore on. The effects of this new global orientation could be seen in the vogue of copying foreign management techniques and in Chinese exports carving out a place in foreign markets. Intellectuals, above all those in technology and the sciences, won expanded opportunities to speak out and to travel abroad. Under the new dispensation CCP leaders held that cultivating China's best minds and giving them some latitude was more likely to hasten economic development than persecuting them as in the past.

Although Deng was able step by step to gain acceptance of his economic policy within the CCP's Politburo, his initiatives did encounter resistance from some of his closest and oldest associates. During the 1980s and early 1990s they expressed fears that he was going too far too fast. They worried that privatization would create social inequalities, weaken the party's control, and negate the achievements of the revolution. Critics also worried that the erosion of the state sector and loss of subsidies would rob workers of their job security and leave them prey to impersonal market forces. Finally, critics feared that the promotion of foreign trade and investment and access to foreign education would give rise to "spiritual pollution," a term that referred to the spread of Western bourgeois values and practices such as individualism, conspicuous consumption, and immoral behavior such as prostitution and drug addiction. In articulating these fears, Chinese were echoing concerns felt earlier by Japanese and other East Asians reluctant to sacrifice core social principles in the name of the unrestrained free market.

Deng and his allies in the leadership responded that the new economic initiatives represented the creative application of Marxism, not its abandonment. The reforms were in one view the necessary updating of the insights of Karl Marx to a world much changed since his death over a hundred years earlier. Deng's approach, his supporters explained, represented a blending of Marxism with elements from capitalism, especially the market principle, to make Chinese-style socialism work better. Reformers argued that building socialism required a developed modern economy and that the long-term hope for socialism was thus best advanced by tapping whatever techniques worked to create that economy. Deng himself seemed to take this tack when he had observed that whether the cat is black or white is not important as long it catches mice. So too with the economy: Whatever produced growth was good.

Whatever the justification, the reform program was on the whole a success, in marked contrast to the other major socialist reform program initiated by Gorbachev, which was already foundering by the late 1980s (see Chapter 7). China's economy began to boom in the early 1980s, although it had a tendency to overheat, forcing the government to implement a slowdown, quickly followed by recovery, a new round of inflation, and imposition again of government restraints in what became a familiar cycle. China's overall growth rates—the fastest in the world—averaged over 9 percent from the initiation of the Deng reforms down to 1993. This impressive performance pushed GDP (adjusted for inflation) from $1 trillion in 1979 (the year after Deng launched his reforms), to $2 trillion in 1988, then to $3 trillion in 1994, and finally to over $4 trillion in 1999.[18]

Chinese leaders took special pride in their achievements. They liked to stress how their focused, incremental, party-directed economic reforms had succeeded unlike Gorbachev's broad assault on both the Soviet political and economic system, which had failed. They had proven that a CCP-led China could do well in an increasingly competitive, technologically driven international economy. They could look ahead to having, after another two decades of comparable growth, an economy larger

than that of the United States. They could even boast that infant mortality and literacy data already looked better for children born in Shanghai than for those in New
York City.

In Deng's China there was room for only four modernizations, not a fifth—
democratization. Political dissidents and some urban intellectuals argued that
democracy was essential to China's development. China could not modernize economically and socially if it did not modernize politically or at least take a step
toward political liberalization by loosening party control. They pointed out that
centralized power, especially when exercised by one leader, had repeatedly led the
CCP to arbitrary and costly decisions. They called for more government autonomy
from the CCP in the implementation if not the formulation of overall policy. They
also asked how relevant party ideology was to a rapidly changing Chinese society.

Deng responded to these critics by linking his program of economic modernization to a stand-pat political program. He insisted that the CCP retain its monopoly
of political and military power and that the CCP's interpretation of socialism
remain the country's official orthodoxy. Deng's adamantly authoritarian stance
reflected worry that chaos might erupt if political restrictions were removed. It
may also have reflected the fear that a more open system would stimulate independence movements in the inner-Asian border territories occupied by majorities of
people who were not of the dominant ethnic Chinese group, especially in Xinjiang
and Tibet.

While Deng's tolerance for dissent was greater than Mao's, any direct attack on
the commanding position of the CCP was sure to rouse him. In 1979 he closed
down Beijing's Democracy Wall where dissidents were posting their criticisms of
the CCP and their calls for political pluralism. The most outspoken were subject
to harassment, arrest, and imprisonment. Wei Jingsheng, a former Red Guard
working at the Beijing zoo, was imprisoned for 15 years when he called for a fifth
modernization, namely democracy. Clashes with students and intellectuals testing the limits of the new system carried over into the 1980s as Deng launched
campaigns against dissent in the name of checking "spiritual pollution" and "bourgeois liberalization."

The spring 1989 "democracy" demonstrations brought to a climax tensions
building over a decade both between the party and its critics and within the party
leadership itself. The demonstrations began in mid-April following the death of
the former CCP general secretary and reformer Hu Yaobang. Under the guise of
mourning, students voiced their dissatisfaction with party corruption and with
the effects of inflation on students and others trying to live on fixed incomes.
Demonstrations on campuses quickly snowballed into major marches to the city
center demanding greater party accountability to the public. By early May the government and the students were locked in a standoff. Emboldened by a stream of
replacements arriving from schools in other cities, by rising worker activism, and
by the vocal support of ordinary Beijing residents, the student leadership took a
distinctly more confrontational approach toward government officials. When the

A Nameless Young Chinese Halting a Tank Column, Beijing, June 5, 1989
This iconic photo, taken immediately following the brutal crackdown on protests in central Beijing, carried two warring messages. American critics of the CCP saw a courageous individual standing up to the brute power of a repressive state. Chinese TV provided the government perspective: "Anyone with common sense can see that if our tanks were determined to move on, this lone scoundrel could never have stopped them. This scene . . . flies in the face of Western propaganda. It proves that our soldiers exercised the highest degree of restraint."[19] (AP Photo/Jeff Widener)

official response to student demands proved insufficient, the students made the fateful decision to occupy Tiananmen Square in a direct challenge to a party headed (as one of their declarations phrased it) by "an emperor without a crown, an aged, fatuous dictator."[20] Alarmed by this "chaos" in central Beijing and by the demonstrations breaking out in many cities across the country, party elders resolved in late May to crack down. Troops struck on the night of June 3–4, killing at least several hundred protesters, appalling party reformers, and outraging foreigner observers. Although seen at the time as an Asian analogue to the popular revolt against socialist regimes then gaining headway in eastern Europe (see Chapter 7), this upheaval played out differently. China's government enjoyed considerably more legitimacy and proved considerably more effective in holding its ground against protest.

The controversial 1989 crackdown (still officially a taboo topic in China) should not obscure the achievements of the Deng era. Whether viewed as nation builders or the architects of a development strategy, CCP leaders could claim remarkable success. They had managed to move dramatically closer to realizing the dream of making China "prosperous and powerful," in effect lifting it to a position of parity with the modern West and Japan fervently embraced by Mao's generation and a generation of leaders before that. Viewed in comparative global terms, the CCP's eclectic approach to economic development had produced results with few if any equals in the Third World. It is hard to imagine another Third World case where national weakness was so dramatically turned around, and certainly the scale of the enterprise—whether measured in territory or population—puts China's experiment in development in a class by itself.

But the success of the Deng "revolution" came at a price of which the repression of 1989 was only a small part. Popular resentments over the brutal repression in 1989 and over party members trading on their insider connections continued to fester, keeping alive the question of the fifth modernization. Rapid development created marked regional inequalities and tensions. While China's coastal areas were beginning to behave like and integrate with its prosperous neighbors such as Hong Kong, Taiwan, South Korea, and Japan, peasants in interior regions deprived of the opportunities to ride the recent wave of economic growth seethed under agricultural stagnation and exploitation by local party bosses. Many set out to look for employment in the cities, swelling a great floating workforce mounting into the tens of millions. Employees in the struggling, debt-ridden state sector of the economy faced an uncertain future as the social compact that once gave them security unraveled. Dissidents kept their heads down and continued to organize, sustained by a burgeoning free-enterprise system and by hopes that the next political spasm would find the Communists more vulnerable. China's "growth-at-any-cost" philosophy was, moreover, incurring a hidden but steep and pervasive cost in environmental degradation. The manifestations, to be found virtually everywhere, included severe water pollution, water shortages in the north, and pollution from heavy use of high-sulfur coal for energy production. China's cities were wrapped in smog, and China's contribution to global atmospheric pollution was growing ever larger.

On the Southern Periphery

The burgeoning economic activity spreading from Japan across East Asia had ripple effects felt with special force in much of Southeast Asia. By degrees governments there absorbed the lessons of state-directed development and confirmed in the development of their policies the efficacy of that approach. Though not predominantly Confucian in their social values, the states in the region had available proxy Confucians in the form of a small but wealthy and highly entrepreneurial Chinese community operating within strong international networks of trade and investment. The most dramatic economic gains occurred in Vietnam, Thailand, Indonesia, and Malaysia where an influx of foreign investment (mainly from Japan, South Korea, and Taiwan) stimulated export-led growth. Their success not only added to the reach, heft, and vitality of the Asian bloc; it also stimulated a sense of regional solidarity. Thailand, Indonesia, and Malaysia together with Singapore and the Philippines had formed the Association of Southeast Asian Nations (ASEAN), in 1967. Despite its loose consultative framework, ASEAN became an increasingly important forum for promoting economic development as well as resolving political issues. The addition of Brunei, Vietnam, Laos, Myanmar (Burma), and Cambodia had by 1999 raised ASEAN's population to 500 million, its combined GDP to $737 billion, and its total trade to $720 billion.

Vietnam—Communist, Confucian, and no stranger to emulating the larger, culturally related land to the north—stands out as an example of the move toward a more market and export-driven economy. Hanoi's decision to shift in a dramatically new direction in the late 1980s was made under intense internal pressure. Already battered by intense warfare since 1965, a newly united Vietnam had to make the transition to peacetime production. Demobilized soldiers flooded labor markets. At the same time, China cut off aid, the Soviet Union reduced its support, and the southern economy suffered from the total loss of once-generous U.S. assistance.

A Vietnamese Communist Party good at organizing a popular revolution and waging war against strong powers had compounded these problems by mishandling the integration of the heavily French- and American-influenced South. Early in 1978 the government in Hanoi headed by Le Duan ordered the South to fit the northern economic mold. Agriculture was collectivized, industry was nationalized, and central planning put in place. The reaction was intense. Southerners, remembering the NLF's promise of gradual integration, felt betrayed. Peasants who had supported the NLF to win, not surrender land, balked at the new policies. Some resorted to sabotage to express their opposition, and newly formed agricultural collectives collapsed. By 1979 the economy was in a tailspin. Mismanagement by the planners as well as the lack of incentives and a fair market price for produce led to a fall in rice production. Shortages of food and other products necessitated rationing and the import of foodstuffs. Per capita income declined. Unemployment and inflation were both high. The flight of merchants and entrepreneurs of Chinese descent—some 700,000 between 1978 and 1982—further disrupted the economy while swelling the ranks of the "boat people" (those fleeing the country in small and often unseaworthy crafts). A social malaise took hold as the old wartime solidarity began to dissolve into a scramble for advantage, with party cadre now grabbing at the spoils of victory. Vietnam was experiencing a familiar phenomenon. Much like the Soviet *nomenklatura*, a party elite benefited from its privileged access to scarce consumer products, quality medical care, personal transportation, and subsidized materials that could be sold on the black market at a handsome markup.

Driven by crisis, the Vietnamese Communist Party installed a reformer, Nguyen Van Linh, as party leader in December 1986 following Le Duan's death. Linh incrementally instituted a far-reaching policy of "renovation" (*doi moi*) that closely resembled the program already under way in China. Linh's long service in the South during the war had taught him the importance of tapping its considerable economic potential, both its entrepreneurial spirit and its rich natural resources. He looked to private enterprise to spur agricultural output, increase the production of consumer goods, and help Vietnam move as a competitive player into international markets. Linh's reforms encouraged foreign investment to overcome Vietnam's lack of capital and poor infrastructure. Linh also cut back support for state enterprises, abandoned central administrative direction in favor of indirect control exercised through tax and fiscal measures, let the currency trade at international market values, and gave peasants virtual ownership of the land that they worked. He moderated policies toward ethnic Chinese in hopes that they would resume their important middleman role in the economy.

The reforms began to brighten the prospects for Vietnam's 71 million people. Stores began to fill with consumer goods. By 1990 light industry and agriculture were growing at a good pace, and Vietnam reemerged as a significant rice exporter for the first time in decades. New oil production covered the country's energy needs. Tourism began to develop as an industry. Foreign trade expanded, with Japan the major trading partner, and more foreign investors (with Taiwan and Hong Kong capital in the lead) were finding their way to Vietnam. Inflation was brought under control and living standards were on the rise. Although still one of the poorest countries in the world measured by annual per capita income (about $200), Vietnam was on track to taking a place in the vibrant East Asian economic zone. While party leaders continued to insist that their ultimate goal was socialism, they did not pretend that they would get there anytime soon.

Like Deng's reform program, Linh's was largely economic and only marginally political. Although the national assembly gained more power to shape policy and journalists and intellectuals had more scope to expose political corruption and abuse of power, few critics dared openly advocate the overthrow of the ruling party or the creation of a multiparty system. Even the most enthusiastic proponents of markets among the leadership worried that too much economic freedom might compromise political stability and national security. Linh himself even while still in power was increasingly explicit in his attacks on sweeping political liberalization. Western-style democracy would lead to chaos, he argued. Unrest in 1989 in eastern Europe, the Soviet Union, and China reinforced these fears about the destabilizing effects of an open political system.

In Nguyen Van Linh's Vietnam as in Deng Xiaoping's China, Communist leaders had effected a dramatic shift. They had long taken as an article of faith the decline and inevitable collapse of capitalism, and they had behind them a lifetime of practical schooling in the hostility of capitalist powers to their national independence and socialist development. Despite all this, they had come to embrace the rules of an international system defined by a seemingly still vital capitalism. Economic growth came at a price. They had to accept some considerable loss of control of the economy and an openness to the outside world that threatened to change, perhaps fundamentally, the political and cultural environment at home. "Spiritual pollution" from abroad would prove a formidable and on going challenge to party orthodoxy and socialist values.

EAST ASIA AS ZONE OF ECONOMIC VITALITY	
1967	ASEAN formed
1970s	Japanese economy rebounds from OPEC oil shock; South Korea, Taiwan, and Singapore enter second decade of rapid growth
1976	Vietnam unified politically
1978	Hanoi imposes a socialist economy (including collectivized agriculture) on the South; flight of the "boat people" begins. Deng secures primacy in CCP, offers a mixed verdict on Mao's legacy, and launches the policy of "four modernizations."
1986	Linh adopts a market-oriented economic strategy
1988	Japanese per capita income overtakes that of the United States and West Germany
1989	Deng crushes protests but holds to course of economic reform
1990	Reforms in Vietnam begin to spur strong, steady economic growth
1997	Deng dies, but his economic and political policies survive

REVIVED BLOC BUILDING IN EUROPE

Like Americans, the Europeans in the 1970s and 1980s suffered an economic slow-down. Inflation had taken hold in the late 1960s, and the subsequent escalation of oil prices compounded the problem. Thus, for example, between 1968 and 1975 the cost of consumer goods in France and Italy climbed about 90 percent. These rising costs in the major western European economies between 1973 and 1989 contributed to lower per capita growth—roughly half of what the region had experienced between 1950 and 1973.[21]

Where Europeans could count unmatched progress was in pushing forward with regional economic integration. They had given renewed attention during the 1980s to deepening internal ties, but they were also quick to exploit the socialist collapse of 1989 to extend the sway of the distinctive European way. By the 1990s they had gone considerably farther than either the North Americans or the East Asians. Geographically coherent but without a single dominant power, this emergent community was one of rough equals with a shared interest in finding a common response to internal problems and sometimes antagonistic global currents.

Renewed Integration and the EU

The road toward integration and growth on which the western Europeans had set with the Treaty of Rome in 1957 turned for a time distinctly bumpy. As we saw in Chapter 7, through much of the 1960s French leader Charles de Gaulle had obstructed British membership in the European Community (EC) and stymied attempts to breathe some independent life into its institutions. He could not bear the thought of a proud France ruled "by some sort of technocratic body of elders, stateless and irresponsible."[22] The first of the oil shocks in 1973 posed a new kind of challenge to the Community. The rapid price increases hurt a region heavily dependent on oil imports. Quickening competition from high-tech, low-cost competitors, especially in East Asia, compounded the problem of weakening international demand for important European exports such as automobiles and steel. These economic blows were exacerbated by political inertia. Rather than retrench, most European governments sought to maintain their full array of social programs. The result was ballooning budget deficits as revenues from slowing economies faltered at the very time that the economic downturn created a demand for more, not less, government welfare. Like their American counterparts, European politicians had no taste for imposing fundamental reforms needed to restore international competitiveness. Economic investment declined dramatically, leaving European firms even worse off.

By the late 1970s and early 1980s, with voters registering their discontent, political leaders began to put forward austerity programs. These included notably higher taxes and curbs on government spending in order to close the budget deficit and bring down inflation. Even left-leaning governments had to tighten their belts, and more conservative governments launched campaigns to privatize inefficient state-owned companies.

Nowhere was the shift in political tone as well as policy more dramatic than in Britain during Margaret Thatcher's years as conservative prime minister (1979–1990). "There is no such thing as society, only individual men and women and their families," observed the "iron lady" in an assertion of her strong neoliberal philosophy.[23] Consistent with that view, she tamed the unions, cut welfare programs, and denounced dependency on the "nanny state." The political and social warfare was bitter, but Thatcher won. Along the way she demonstrated that the British still had a spark of martial ardor by defeating the Argentines in a war for control of the Falkland Islands (a remnant of empire in the South Atlantic near the southern tip of Argentina).

West Germany typified the continent's continued preference for an activist state to manage the economy. To soften the oil shocks, the government in Bonn promoted energy efficiency. Oil consumption quickly fell by 20 percent. At the same time Bonn encouraged an export drive that especially targeted the now cash-rich OPEC countries. This combination of initiatives soon turned a trade deficit into a surplus. At the same time the West German central bank took vigorous steps to contain inflation, with the result that West Germany's inflation rate between 1968 and 1975 was the lowest of Europe's major economies. But keeping inflation in check meant slower growth and rising unemployment.

Concerned over the persistent sluggishness of western Europe's economy, EC members embarked on a series of discussions out of which emerged a consensus in favor of intensifying regional integration. The new course rested in part on hopes of stimulating economic expansion, just as the creation of the Coal and Steel Community and the EC itself had in the 1950s. European leaders were also aware of their region's slipping competitiveness in areas such as computers and military technologies. Concerted research programs and shared production might improve Europe's international position in the increasingly important high-tech sector. In 1986 EC members resolved to take steps to create a single market by the end of 1992. German unification in 1990 accelerated the timetable by convincing nervous neighbors that further integration would offset the greater influence wielded by a larger Germany. These trends culminated in a decision in December 1991, quickly formalized by a treaty signed in Maastricht in the Netherlands, to create from the EC a new, tighter European Union (EU). Its principal sponsors were France's François Mitterand and the leader of the new Germany, Helmut Kohl. The Maastricht Treaty called for the creation of a common currency and a European central bank. It also looked ahead to political union that would build on EC institutions and expand their responsibilities. Finally, the treaty, which went into effect in 1993, provided for a common citizenship for all members of EU countries, free movement within the EU, and the creation of a common currency. The implementation of these provisions was major leap forward. In 1993 the EC became the EU. The formal introduction of the single currency (the "euro") followed in 1999, a widely celebrated landmark event. By early 2002 the euro was in full circulation.

While intensifying integration among its core economies, the European bloc was also steadily expanding in scope, adding layers like an onion. In 1973 Britain, Ireland, and Denmark joined. Subsequently, the EC brought in Greece (1981) and Spain and Portugal (1986) after those three embarked on a course of democratization following the fall of right-wing dictatorships in the 1970s. In 1995 Austria, Sweden, and Finland joined the EU, bringing the total membership to 15 (with 13 applicants eager to join and further extend the EU's scope). (See Map 8.2, p. 370.)

Within the EU, no single national economy occupied a role comparable to either Japan or the United States in terms of size of output or magnitude of influence. Although West Germany was often regarded as dominant, in fact three of its neighbors—Italy, France, and Britain—were quite close in output even after East and West Germany merged. The four contributed almost equally to a combined output of $4.16 trillion in 1990. And while German conservative fiscal policy and the attractions of the mark gave Germany prominence and power, the shadows of the Nazi past inhibited the vigorous exercise of that influence. British hands were also tied by a reluctance, shared by British leaders as well as the public, to fully embrace a continental destiny. When Britain finally did join the EC in 1973, it was a move prompted largely by economic problems, including the highest rate of inflation of any of the major European economies and lagging growth. EC membership did not prove a panacea. Britain's per capita growth over the ensuing sixteen years (1973–1989) fell at the low end for the major European economies while doing marginally better than the United States (Fig. 8.3 on p. 367). Hesitation about a closer relationship to the continent again came to the fore during the talks leading to the Maastricht Treaty. British leaders repeatedly voiced objections and finally opted out of the plans to create a single currency. The British pound was a reminder of past glories and a symbol of a distinct national identity that was not to be lost in the EU mixer.

Social and Cultural Developments

This emergent European community experienced significant social and cultural changes that left it quite different in the 1990s from what it had been at the beginning of the postwar boom, when integration had begun to gain headway. In general the trends were strikingly similar in the core economies across the region.

The most obvious and perhaps important of these was the deepening grip of consumer culture. Rising income levels caught up with the United States, permitting families more and more discretionary spending. Perhaps even more than Americans, Europeans prized the leisure that affluence made possible. They enjoyed shorter workweeks and took longer vacations (roughly a month for most industrial workers compared to 11–12 days for their American and Japanese counterparts). In a 1994 poll, workers ranked family, leisure time, and friends ahead of their jobs. Consumerism advanced in tandem with a pronounced turning away from formal religion. In Italy, for example, the once-powerful Catholic Church suffered repeated defeats—the legalization of divorce in 1972 and abortion in 1980 and the end of Catholicism as the state religion in 1985.

Consumerism also promoted homogenization, eroded class distinctions once evident in speech and dress, and dampened class conflict. Children of industrial workers moved into white-collar service jobs. A youth culture promoted tastes in entertainment, language, and dress that cut across class lines. Unions in France, Italy, and Britain, once militant and powerful, shifted from demands for sweeping political and economic change to a stress on bread-and-butter issues. German unions took the lead in making the case for moderation. They avoided inflammatory rhetoric, worked with management to make their industries competitive instead of going on strike, gained a voice on actual production procedures, and provided retraining for workers in declining industries. Thanks to this strategy, German workers led the continent in wages.

This consumer society witnessed basic shifts in the workforce. Agriculture and industry declined in overall importance, while white-collar employment in the service sector moved the western Europeans toward what has been tagged a postindustrial economy. Agriculture suffered the steepest drop, as labor left the countryside for the city. For example, in Italy the portion of the workforce in agriculture fell from 40 percent in 1954 to 8 percent in 1992. With these changes went a dwindling of small-town life and a once-influential class of small shopkeepers.

Despite these tendencies toward cultural homogenization, working-class moderation, and changes in areas of employment, class differences did not disappear. Even though education became increasingly the ticket to employment and advancement in an ever more technology-based economy, family prominence and wealth were the best predictors of who would get the best schooling and hence the most important jobs. In Britain those who attended prestigious and expensive private schools and then went on to university at Oxford or Cambridge tended overwhelmingly to come from privileged backgrounds. This educational track created influential networks of classmates and smoothed their way to the top in government and business. Similarly, in France exclusive *lycée* schooling (comparable to the British private schools) and then highly selective professional schools (known as *les grandes écoles*) produced high-level government and business leaders. In the somewhat less confined Italian and German systems, law degrees tended to be the ticket to high status and high pay. In general the top rungs of government and corporations were at the end of the century as much dominated by elites as they had been early in the postwar period. The major exception was Scandinavia and above all Sweden, where democratization of schooling led to major strides toward democratization of the elites.

Societies marked by a high degree of ethnic homogeneity at the outset of the postwar period had become strikingly more diverse by century's end. Immigrants, largely unskilled labor from Turkey as well as North Africa and other areas earlier colonized by Europe, flocked to Britain and the continent to fill the many open service and industrial positions created by the early postwar boom. Friction between foreigners and long-time natives remained low-key until the economic downturn of the 1970s. As unemployment soared, so too did resentment over the burden associated with this foreign workforce. German and French nationalist politicians responded with calls for immigration controls. For example, in Germany a strong backlash developed against "guest laborers" (*gastarbeiter*), especially Turks, who had flocked to the country during more prosperous times. Some demanded the departure of these longtime foreign residents, and a fringe element occasionally turned to violence. But a return to prosperity in the 1980s and 1990s blunted nativist sentiment. So too did falling birthrates among the native-born and workers shifting to the white-collar service sector, which combined to leave less attractive jobs unfilled. Workers from outside the EC continued to arrive, increasingly from an economically troubled eastern Europe. By 1986 foreigners had come to account for 7 percent of the German and French populations and 15 percent of the Swiss.

Despite economic austerity and rapid social change, the western European bloc retained a distinct economic culture biased in favor of a mixed economy with a strong state role and a strong commitment to social welfare. While governments began to retreat from state control in banking, communications, and transport as well as some industries, they continued to provide citizens with social welfare benefits that remained far ahead of those in the United States and Japan. As a result, taxes remained relatively high. For example, in 1990 tax receipts as a percentage of GDP in Germany, France, and Italy hovered around the 40 percent mark compared to about 30 percent for the United States and Japan. Britain was in the middle—above the figure for the United States and at the low end for this sample of EU countries.[24]

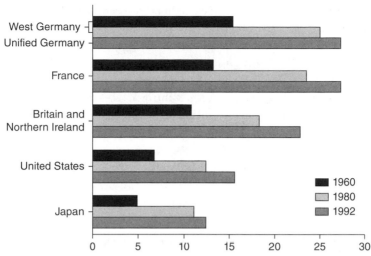

FIGURE 8.3
Social Security Spending in the Three Blocs, 1960–1992 (as a percentage of GDP)
In the three major European countries, social security expenditures have steadily grown over the last half-century and outpaced the United States and Japan, usually by a factor of two. Here, as in other matters of political economy, Britain was in between: below the continental states but ahead of the United States and Japan.[25]

"Welfare capitalism" is the term that best captures the regional expectation—within the EU as well as along its periphery—that the state was supposed to soften the hard edge of capitalist competition and defend vulnerable groups in the name of social justice. Traditional *laissez-faire* parties that had resisted welfare capitalism had virtually disappeared, and conservative parties either converted (as in Britain) or had actually themselves taken the lead in developing a rich array of social programs (as in the case of the Christian Democrats in Germany and Italy). A 1990 poll revealed continuing, widespread European support for the state playing an important, multifaceted economic role. In West Germany, Italy, France, Spain, and Hungary as well as the former Soviet Union, the system that won the highest support was "democratic socialism" or "social democracy." Predictably, those same polls registered reservations about unbridled "capitalism" (or an unconstrained free market). Only in Poland and Britain were reactions to "capitalism" more positive than negative.[26] This persistent regional concern with the commonweal was reflected in steadily rising levels of welfare spending among major western European countries since 1945. The upward trend persisted even into the 1990s, when the strong winds of global competition were supposedly sweeping away all before them.

Post-'89 and the Opening to the East

Already the most integrated of the blocs, western Europe found itself facing fresh opportunities for expansion and consolidation with the sudden collapse in 1989 of socialist states previously propped up by the Soviet Union. Although usually regarded as the last act in the Cold War drama, the political upheavals in the old Soviet-controlled bloc paved the way for significantly expanded EU influence, a healing of the political divisions imposed by the superpowers after World War II, and perhaps even the rise of a greater Europe. Americans may have won the Cold War, but the western Europeans were the major beneficiaries. The one significant exception to this trend came from a surprising quarter—not one of the collapsing Soviet clients, but an independent socialist Yugoslavia, which dissolved in open ethnic conflict just as its neighbors were following a peaceful path toward collaboration with the EU (see Chapter 11).

The post-Communist states of eastern Europe looked to their neighbors to the west for a variety of reasons. The most economically advanced, including Poland, Hungary, and the Czech Republic (a product of the peaceful 1992 breakup of Czechoslovakia), had developed under the cultural and economic shadow of the German and Austrian empires and France. Further inclining the new states westward were shared political aspirations. The dissidents who toppled socialist regimes had demanded free elections, genuine parliamentary government, and civic pluralism in place of Soviet-style political repression and economic constraints.

Among ordinary citizens, freedom implied something no less important—the promise of shopping in well-stocked stores with full pockets, owning a home, buying a car, and traveling abroad on vacation. This freedom to consume was one of the most attractive features of Western societies that eastern-bloc citizens had gotten to know through travel, trade, television, and pop music long before 1989. In East Germany the lure of a better standard of living—closer to that of their German cousins on the other side of the Berlin Wall—may have been the single most important factor motivating the protests of 1989. For example, the banana—so commonplace in the grocery stores of the free-market western part of the country but scarce and costly in the eastern section—became a symbol used by protesters of the socialist failure to deliver what its leaders had promised and what western Europeans took for granted.

Finally, the two halves of Europe discovered a common commitment to welfare capitalism. The cries for freedom during 1989 did not signal the victory of neoliberal values. Nor did the end of socialism bring a smooth economic transition and the rapid realization of a Western standard of living. It instead brought eastern Europeans face to face with something new—the rigors of the free market and the wrenching adjustments of economic reorientation. The removal of price controls set off inflation, which in turn necessitated government austerity measures to bring the inflation under control. Despite rising prices, wages did not increase, while food and other subsidies on which many depended disappeared. At the same time, unemployment rose as a result of closing down the almost invariably inefficient, debt-ridden state-run industry. The economy contracted for the first several post-socialist years. Businesses had to refashion themselves in order to win western European markets, including attracting investment capital, integrating new technology, and instituting new management techniques. The rapid erosion of the old socialist welfare system and the strong International Monetary Fund (IMF)-administered free-market medicine together prompted a new appreciation for the role of the state and a consensus in favor of something like western Europe's welfare capitalism.

The most important development during this time of transition was the rapid reunification of East and West Germany. Once demonstrators had shaken the resolve of East German Communist leaders, no broad-based, well-organized opposition was ready to fill the political vacuum. With elections looming in March 1990, West Germany's Christian Democrats touted rapid unification as the key to prosperity. This appeal brought them victory and allowed Bonn to control events. The 16 million East Germans became citizens of the West German state; overnight East Germany ceased to exist. With unification went a costly process, paid for by West Germans, of rehabilitating the East's infrastructure and production facilities. With more than 36 percent of the workforce in the endangered public sector, unemployment soared in the East. By mid-1991 industrial production there had fallen by 70 percent, and 3.5 million workers out of a total workforce of 8.5 million were unemployed. Although the move toward unity imposed a heavy social and economic burden in the short run, it promised to establish Germany as first among equals within the EU and as an influential intermediary between the EU and formerly socialist eastern bloc.

Of those countries, Poland, the Czech Republic, and Hungary made the most rapid turn westward, although the transition carried a price: widening income inequalities and painful social dislocation for those who were ill suited to the new market-oriented economy. All three countries were soon on track to joining the EU. Part of the reason for this northern tier's quick adjustment was its easy access to the EU market and its ability to attract substantial foreign investment. Poland led the way, achieving an economic recovery in 1992. By then roughly three quarters of Poland's trade was tied to western Europe. These countries were also helped by a smooth transition to post-socialist politics, in which former Communists played a major role. Nothing was more surprising than the durability of seemingly discredited politicians. Their parties had been at first in disarray after 1989, stunned by public repudiation expressed through the ballot box in Poland and Hungary and through massive demonstrations in Czechoslovakia. But in both Poland and Hungary Communists could take credit for having contributed even before 1989 to the gradual rise of multiparty democratic politics. In those two countries as well as the Czech Republic, they had by the 1994 round of elections made a striking comeback, presenting themselves as social democrats and promising a mix of market reform and social welfare. They had managed to retain a base of support that other parties, led by dissident-era intellectuals, lacked. There was no little irony in old-line Communists having failed at creating "socialism with a human face" now helping to build a kinder, gentler capitalism.

Romania and Bulgaria followed a different pattern, moving so haltingly into the post-socialist era that their relationship to the EU was not resolved until 2007. In Romania holdovers from the old Ceaușescu regime cobbled together a cautiously

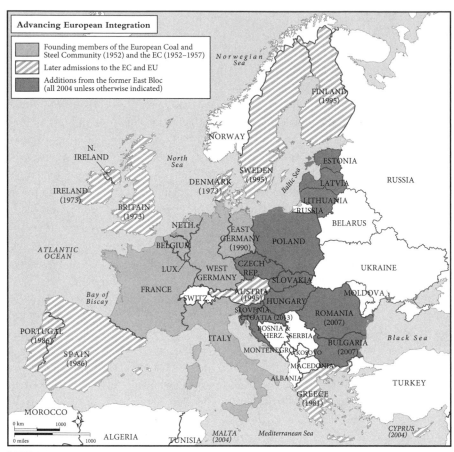

MAP 8.2
Advancing European Integration

reform-oriented National Salvation Front. In Bulgaria Communist leadership was only briefly interrupted; party leaders made a quick comeback in 1990 elections. Despite taking the "shock" therapy prescribed by the IMF, the economies of both struggled. Bulgaria was the last of those in the region attempting economic reform and showed no signs of economic recovery until 1995. Romania's transition to a market economy, launched in 1990, attracted little of the foreign assistance that reformers had hoped for, and as a result already difficult economic conditions did not improve significantly.

CONCLUSION

By the late twentieth century the three centers of the global economy were locked in a relationship marked by both cooperation and conflict. They shared a stake in a smoothly functioning system that could generate an increasing output of goods and services. They thus had good reason to work together in formulating a widely accepted set of economic rules, overseeing their implementation, and resolving problems and containing disputes. But the North American, East Asian, and EU economies differed significantly over how the one-world market should operate. They had differing views over such issues as the proper role of the government in economic policy and regulation, the degree and kind of protection against outside competition, and the appropriate level of welfare provisions for citizens. When one party tried to universalize rules at odds with another's fundamental assumptions about the nature of the good life and social justice, the resulting tensions could slow or threaten the trend toward global integration.

These three major economic blocs provide a reminder that the international system remained pluralistic. The U.S. economic model has not generally prevailed, nor was it likely to in less-developed economies still searching for an appropriate path. European and East Asian practices are just as likely to appeal as American ones. Asian growth rates make a powerful argument for giving the state ample power to promote and sustain economic competitiveness. At the same time, the European example argues for the virtues of state-promoted economic inclusion of all citizens and generous welfare provisions.

The American, European, and East Asian models do not constitute fixed, stark alternatives. Rather, they offer a range of choices that can be combined in almost endless ways. Each has evolved over time and contains significant internal tensions. For example, the United States may be the paragon of the free market, but the portion of GDP claimed by the government has been steadily growing, and government regulation, unemployment insurance, monetary and tax incentives, and bailouts of troubled corporations have played an important role in policing, directing, and at times even suspending the operation of the market. The advanced economies taken collectively offer a great buffet of goals and strategies among which peoples around the world are likely to choose according to their traditions and values.

9
DIVERGENT PATHS
IN THE THIRD WORLD

THE THIRD WORLD was never a monolith. The colonial impact, the course of the liberation struggle, and the choice of development models began to distinguish one place from another quite early in the postwar era. The distinctions among former colonial regions and even within regions were to grow steadily greater. By the 1970s and 1980s, those distinctions—whether measured by per capita income, life expectancy, infant mortality, or levels of literacy—had grown so large that they strained beyond credibility the idea of a coherent Third World.

One major source of this growing diversity was the decline of a radical vision. The hope for national liberation and for a more equitable international system that had served to bring much of the Third World together in the 1960s faded in the following decades. The Stalinist and Maoist development model lost favor. The leading disciples of Marx and Lenin in Asia, the Communist parties of China and Vietnam, moved to embrace the capitalist free market (see Chapter 8). The collapse of the eastern European socialist regimes amidst economic stagnation (treated in Chapter 7) confirmed for Third World observers that command economies and five-year plans were not a promising development model. Finally, the Cold War record demonstrated to Third World leaders that any leftist upstarts were likely to encounter strong, even potentially deadly American opposition. In East Asia alone, conflict in which the superpowers were implicated in the 30 years following the end of World War II had already cost the lives of 10.4 million people.

In the developing world from the 1970s onward, authoritarian regimes committed to stability and order were far more common and long-lived than those devoted to fundamental social change. The revolutionary outbreaks that did appear at century's end took forms that would have surprised Marx and Lenin. They arose in reaction against regimes of ethnic or religious oppression (for example, in Guatemala, South Africa, and Palestine) or gave expression to long-smoldering ethnic or religious impulses toward social purification (as in Cambodia and Iran). The most common trend was a turn from inward-looking models of state-dominated economic development to approaches allowing greater room for market forces. This experiment worked for some, especially in East Asia, but for most the outcome was problematic. Markets often promised more than they could deliver. Population growth nullified much of whatever gains the shift to markets yielded. And women in countries making the transition to the market frequently found their status and welfare diminished, thus shackling half of the workforce and undermining long-term economic prospects.

THE CHANGING FACE OF REVOLUTION

Left-leaning revolutionary regimes continued to appear toward century's end in places as diverse as Ethiopia, Grenada, Cambodia, and Nicaragua. Few had any staying power, and most amply confirmed the hardnosed observations of the Italian political philosopher, Niccolò Machiavelli, over four centuries earlier: "There is nothing more difficult to carry out, nor more doubtful of success, nor more dangerous to handle, than to initiate a new order of things."[1] Cambodia serves as an example of the rocky terrain that late-arriving revolutionaries had to cross. The racial hatreds that informed that revolution provoked Vietnamese countermeasures that proved fatal to its survival. Astonishingly, the most revolutionary regimes of the era would emerge not from a Marxist tradition but from a potent strain of Islamic political thinking. In Iran a clergy committed to a faith much older than Marxism led a revolution that secured its firm grip on power. Iran's revolution would transform that country, send powerful reverberations through the Islamic world stretching from North Africa to Southeast Asia, and stun the superpowers.

Cambodia's Genocidal Revolution

A seemingly quiet political backwater, Cambodia became the improbable scene for the most radical and destructive revolution of the late twentieth century. Prince Norodom Sihanouk's long rule created the illusion of calm and set the stage for the upheaval that would engulf him and his people. Sihanouk led his country to independence from France in 1953, riding on the coattails of the Vietnamese struggle. Until the mid-1960s he held power virtually unchallenged, thanks in large measure to the popular deference to the monarchy that was especially strong among the peasantry, some four fifths of the population.

Sihanouk pursued a nonaligned course in the Cold War in hopes of securing development assistance but also of insulating a weak country with a proud past from outside pressures. Cambodia had once been a power in the region—a great Buddhist kingdom that flourished between the tenth and fourteenth centuries and that is best known for the architectural marvels of Angkor. But it declined rapidly. Early in the nineteenth century, Thailand and Vietnam had squeezed Cambodia territorially from either side. Then the French arrived and in 1863 imposed a protectorate, making Cambodia a part of their Indochina holdings.

Escalating conflict in neighboring Vietnam placed Sihanouk's policy of neutrality in peril. Cambodia had become a critical part of Hanoi's war strategy as both supply route and troop sanctuary (see Map 4.1 on p. 171). Washington responded by trying as early as 1963 to get Sihanouk to live up to his claims to nonalignment or to replace him with a leader more responsive to U.S. direction. In March 1969 a frustrated President Richard Nixon launched a secret campaign of B-52 carpet-bombing in Cambodia, at first along the border and then deeper into the interior. Over half a million tons of bombs would fall over the following four years, tearing apart the lives of Cambodians below.

As Sihanouk's rule began to unravel during the late 1960s, Pol Pot seized the opportunity as head of the Cambodian Communist Party (generally referred to as the Khmer Rouge—literally red Khmers or Cambodians). He was born in 1928, the offspring of a middling peasant family in a town north of the country's capital, Phnom Penh. Drawing on family connections with the royal palace, he won a scholarship to study in France, where he arrived in 1949. Those who knew Pol Pot then remembered him as charming and self-effacing. "He would not have killed a chicken," noted a fellow Cambodian.[2] Like other prominent Third World figures such as Nkrumah, Ho, and Deng, and like other youths later influential in Cambodian revolutionary politics, he was radicalized by communist and anticolonial ideas.

Pol Pot's revolutionary career began in 1953 when he returned home to join the Khmer Rouge. When Sihanouk's secret service drove senior party leaders to take refuge in North Vietnam, their younger comrades, including Pol Pot, were left in Phnom Penh to run a struggling Khmer Rouge. By the early 1960s he had advanced to the top of this internal wing of the party. He shifted operations from the capital to the safety of rural base areas in eastern Cambodia under the protection of Hanoi. In January 1968 Pol Pot called for armed struggle against Sihanouk, setting off an intricate and deadly political dance between the two men. Representing an old elite tradition and a populist and egalitarian approach, the rivals would alternately fight and ally over the next 30 years. In starting this first civil war, Pol Pot defied Hanoi's pressure on the Khmer Rouge to do nothing to undermine Sihanouk, who was acquiescent to the North Vietnamese presence in his country. In any case, Pol Pot's prospects seemed poor. He had behind him only some 5,000 ill-equipped and poorly led guerrillas whose appeal to peasants was limited.

The local repercussions of the Vietnam War created the opening for the Khmer Rouge. In March 1970 a pro-U.S. military junta led by Sihanouk's defense minister, Lon Nol, seized power in Phnom Penh. The Nixon administration at once threw substantial military backing to the new, anticommunist regime and authorized a military "incursion" into Cambodia by 80,000 U.S. and South Vietnamese troops. The operation was meant to destroy the North Vietnamese command center, but it mainly served to push North Vietnamese forces deeper into Cambodia and into a one-sided collision with Lon Nol's poorly trained army. Sihanouk himself, now in exile in Beijing, threw his support to the Khmer Rouge against Lon Nol and the Americans. So too did China and North Vietnam. The Khmer Rouge got an additional boost from the effects of the U.S. carpet-bombing and the intensifying conflict on the ground. Together they disrupted rural life, reduced agricultural production, and flooded the cities with refugees. Khmer Rouge propaganda blamed the Lon Nol government for Cambodia's misery, while young, poor peasants blazing with anger flocked to its guerrilla forces.

Attacking from its rural bases, the Khmer Rouge defeated Lon Nol and took Phnom Penh in April 1975, just as the war in Vietnam came to a close. Now in power, Pol Pot launched Cambodia (renamed Democratic Kampuchea) on a draconian and destructive revolutionary course. Its strong utopian and violent qualities made it quite different from the revolutionary path followed by the neighboring Vietnamese. The new regime summarily emptied the cities. Pol Pot's aim was to crush not just the wealthy and influential tied to the old regime but the entire bourgeois class by destroying their urban strongholds. He also initiated a ruthless

Victims of Cambodia's Descent into a Frenzy of Revolutionary Repression
The notorious Tuol Sleng prison in Phnom Penh functioned as a grim death factory, taking in suspect elements within the population, meticulously photographing them, torturing them, and finally killing them. Most if not all of the individuals looking out at us from this assemblage of prison photos were doomed. (Photo: Ben Kiernan, July 1980)

persecution of ethnic minorities (including Vietnamese), some 20 percent of Cambodia's population. Any signs of resistance doomed to death entire families and communities. Finally, Pol Pot initiated a hunt for suspect elements within the Khmer Rouge itself. The prison in Phnom Penh took in thousands of these "tainted" party members; virtually none survived.

Most extraordinary of all, Pol Pot set in motion an experiment in social mobilization unmatched in twentieth-century revolutions. The Khmer Rouge pressed the entire Cambodian population into mobile work teams laboring under party direction. The brutal labor regime, the exercise of terror to secure compliance, starvation diets, forced resettlement, and the collectivization of land and living arrangements alienated even the most supportive of peasants. The party that many had embraced took from them what they most prized—land, family, and religion. One mocked the new government's promises of a better life to be achieved through heavy labor on water control projects: "Before, we cultivated the fields with the heavens and the stars, and ate rice. / Now, we cultivate the fields with dams and canals, and eat gruel." Cambodian society had become what survivors of the revolution would describe as "the prison without walls."[3]

Finally, Pol Pot pushed his revolution in an anti-Vietnamese direction that would prove its undoing. Long resentful of Vietnamese paternalism toward the Khmer Rouge, he now became suspicious that moderates within his own party were traitors working for Vietnam. Trained and aided by Hanoi, they were, he feared, acting as agents of Vietnamese ambitions. As early as 1971 Pol Pot had struck at the Vietnamese patron by conducting the first of a string of party purges and by soliciting China to serve as the Khmer Rouge's new patron. Once in power, he injected into revolutionary policy his bitterness toward Vietnam, which he described as "a black dragon" spitting poison at Cambodia.[4] With China already by 1976 committed as his protector and major source of aid, he turned on his old enemy with fury, demanding the immediate withdrawal of all Vietnamese troops from Cambodia. He drove over 150,000 ethnic Vietnamese living in Cambodia across the border, and he sent troops to reclaim from Vietnam disputed borderlands and islands in the Gulf of Thailand. By June 1978 his cross-border attacks had forced three quarters of a million on the Vietnamese side to flee their homes.

By 1978, with tensions high, Vietnam's leaders moved toward a decision to overthrow Pol Pot. That prospect in turn forced the major powers interested in the region to take sides. Beijing issued stern warnings to Hanoi, and Washington aligned with China against Vietnam. These developments in turn deepened Vietnam's dependence on the Soviet Union as a counterweight to a hostile China and as a source of aid as Hanoi rebuilt its army and organized Cambodian units made up of the survivors of Pol Pot's successive purges.

In December some 150,000 Vietnamese and 15,000 Cambodian troops crossed the border. In short order, they installed a new government in Phnom Penh, headed by Heng Samrin, a former Khmer Rouge military commander. Pol Pot retreated to the countryside, where he resumed the kind of guerrilla warfare that had won him power in the first place. He won support from Thailand, and China continued to back him because it did not want Vietnam to dominate Cambodia and to ally with the Soviet Union. Deng Xiaoping launched an invasion into northern Vietnam to underline his unhappiness. The Carter administration also retaliated by withholding diplomatic recognition, embargoing trade and investment, and vetoing assistance by the World Bank and the International Monetary Fund. Despite revelations of the horrors of Pol Pot's rule, the Khmer Rouge enjoyed backing by Prince Sihanouk and the Association of Southeast Asian Nations (ASEAN) as well as China and the United States. The Vietnamese and their Cambodian allies retained the upper hand militarily, but Hanoi found Cambodia a quagmire requiring a costly 10-year occupation (1979–1989) that in turn perpetuated tensions with Beijing and Washington.

Talks on ending the fighting began in late 1987 among the exhausted contenders for power, and in September 1989 the Vietnamese withdrew their troops, leaving behind the government of Hun Sen (another of the former Khmer Rouge who had returned with the Vietnamese in 1979). In 1991 the rival groups finally arranged a ceasefire. To help secure the peace, the UN dispatched a multinational force of over 20,000 to disarm the warring factions and arranged for refugee resettlement. An election held under UN auspices in 1993 resulted in a coalition government dominated by Hun Sen's party of ex-communists and the royalist party run by Sihanouk's son. Sihanouk remained on the political scene, a symbol of national reconciliation. The peace process left the Khmer Rouge politically isolated and crippled by splits among its leadership. Before the last bit of Khmer Rouge strength dwindled away, Pol Pot died in 1998, supposedly peacefully in his sleep and never to be held to account for his crimes.

The Cambodia that emerged from this era of revolution, foreign occupation, and three civil wars was devastated. During the bombing and fighting between 1970 and 1975, up to half a million died and some two million became refugees. Once set in motion, Cambodia's revolution turned genocidal with an unprecedented speed and impact as the new regime turned on Vietnamese and other minorities, descended into deadly political infighting, and (most significant of all) embarked on a ruthless social mobilization with no care for human consequences. The spasm of violence and inhumanity between 1975 and 1979 resulted in about 1.7 million deaths. In other words, about a fifth of the population perished from overwork, starvation, or execution. The survivors faced grim economic conditions, demolished educational and health care systems (only 300 doctors for the entire country), and a reduced life expectancy of 48 years (one of the lowest in the world). It is easy to look back and feel sympathy for Sihanouk's failed attempt to prevent regional and superpower conflicts from engulfing his country with destructive consequences even he could not have imagined.

For Vietnam, the end of its Cambodian intervention gave a welcome boost to hopes for prosperity and regional peace. In 1990 Beijing and Hanoi began to shift from confrontation to cooperation. To improve relations with the United States,

CAMBODIA CONVULSED

1951	Cambodian Communist Party (Khmer Rouge) organized
1953	Cambodia gains independence from France under Sihanouk
1964–65	Escalation of war in Vietnam raises importance of Cambodia as a supply route and troop sanctuary
1969	Nixon launches massive bombing campaign in Cambodia
1970	Lon Nol overthrows Sihanouk
1975	Khmer Rouge, led by Pol Pot, takes power
1979	Vietnamese forces oust Pol Pot regime and put in power former Khmer Rouge aligned with Hanoi
1989	Vietnamese forces withdraw, leaving Hun Sen in control

key to gaining access to advanced technology and loans for infrastructure development, Hanoi began in 1985 to help in search for the several thousand Americans missing in action from the Vietnam War. This cooperation, together with the end of the Cambodian occupation and the shift toward a free-market strategy, led President Bill Clinton to normalize trade relations in 1994, and the next year he restored full diplomatic relations. To round out the new regional diplomacy of peace, Vietnam began improving ties with Thailand and Indonesia and moving toward membership in ASEAN.

Religious Challenge in Iran

In contrast to the relatively short-lived Cambodian revolution, the Iranian revolution of 1978–1979 had considerable staying power. It swept the old contenders for political power from the board, beginning with the U.S.-backed regime of Mohammed Reza Shah Pahlavi, in control since 1953 (see Chapter 6). It then eliminated secular allies in the anti-shah revolution. Once in full control, the mullahs in Tehran pressed their vision of a society aligned with Islamic values while at the same time fending off U.S. pressure and fighting Saddam Hussein's Iraq to a draw.

The Shi'i clergy ('ulama) were by default the most promising of revolutionaries in Iran. The consolidation of the shah's power had left other groups coopted, marginal, or in exile, while Islam remained the most popular alternative to the secular course pursued by the shah. The clergy built on a tradition going back to the seventh century, when Arab conquerors had introduced the Shi'i branch of Islam to the country. Shi'a meant literally "faction," referring to those devoted to Ali, the prophet Mohammed's son-in-law and successor. From the Shi'i perspective, Ali's murder broke the legitimate line of descent within Islam. The opposing Sunni branch won a position of dominance in the Muslim world that it retains today.

(Nine out of ten of the world's 1.2 billion Muslims are Sunni.) The Shi'a became an embattled minority in the Middle East outside Iran, Iraq, Yemen, and Bahrain. While the shah and Washington sought to break the grip of feudal, traditional ideas and institutions, Iran's Shi'a clergy clung to a faith that represented to many stability in a time of rapid social change and continuity in the face of challenges to indigenous cultural values from Western ideologies, mainly capitalism but also Marxism. The clergy's popular appeal arose from a long tradition of wielding moral and political authority at the local level. They had, for example, collected and spent taxes, maintained large landholdings, dispensed justice, managed basic education, and attended to social welfare.

Some disaffected clergy became increasingly activist in response to the tide of Western influence and the shah's anticlerical policies. This politicized clergy began to argue that the only legitimate state was one that strictly followed Shi'i religious ideals as interpreted by religious authorities (the ayatollahs). In their determined stance and leadership hierarchy, they came to constitute something like a revolutionary party. Their long-established theological schools developed and popularized their doctrine of resistance to unjust civil authority, in effect creating a revolutionary ideology—populist and xenophobic. In those schools were some three to four thousand students who could serve as organizers. The activist clergy and their students would prove a potent political combination.

Alone, the clergy would have been a troublesome but not formidable opposition. However, the clergy won many followers as a result of the political alienation produced by the far-reaching impact of the shah's modernization program. Land reform, begun in 1962, initially improved the lot of some peasants, but increasingly it served to consolidate land into large mechanized farms at peasant expense. Many projects associated with the shah's modernization program were dramatic and visible—large dams, airports, grand avenues, modern military equipment, and new government buildings—but did little for economic development or popular welfare. At the same time, corruption and patronage were widespread throughout the government. Unsettling Western influences, promoted by the shah's program and symbolized by some 50,000 American residents by 1978, provoked a backlash. For many outside the charmed circle of the royal court and the expanding middle class, modernization seemed to bring hardship, waste, and moral decline.

While Iran as a nation became wealthy on oil, the actual distribution of that wealth was marked by extremely wide disparities. These disparities were especially glaring in the capital, Tehran, and other large cities where by 1979 half of the population resided, including an alienated and unemployed underclass driven from their rural homes by the consolidation of land holdings. Peasant loss of land had begun in the nineteenth century when landlords had assembled large estates in order to grow cotton and opium for the international market. By the mid-1930s land consolidation had by one estimate left 96 percent of the rural population landless. In the wake of the White Revolution's failure to help the landless, desperate peasants streamed into the cities seeking a new life. But the newcomers suffered from inflation, poor housing, government neglect, and the cultural shock of urban ways at odds with values carried from the countryside.

Growing resentment among Iranians over cultural defilement and economic exploitation was reinforced by memories of the 1953 coup (widely attributed to the Americans), and contributed to the view that the shah was the political tool of American and Israeli interests. While the shah did not try to hide his U.S. ties, he preferred to conceal his trade, military, and intelligence links to Israel, not wanting openly to defy the Arab policy of no contact. But his critics were not fooled. By the 1970s political discontent had spread to a wide range of social groups. They included uprooted peasants, students and educated professionals committed to greater democracy and more balanced economic development, and an influential merchant class (the *bazaari*).

Ruhollah Musavi Khomeini was the inspirational figure who would combine these varied discontents into a successful revolutionary movement. He would articulate the Islamic values of the clergy and echo the reformist and nationalist complaints of the other alienated groups. One of his admirers described that charismatic cleric as a person of "spirituality and erudition, asceticism and self-discipline, sobriety and determination, political genius and leadership, compassion for the poor and deprived, and relentless hatred of oppression and imperialism."[5] Whatever its truth, that assessment came to be widely accepted in Iran.

Khomeini was born in 1902 into a well-to-do, respected family in a town about 200 miles southwest of Tehran. Both his father and grandfather had been religious scholars. At 17 he left home to study religion. Later in Qum, the center for Islamic studies, he gained distinction as a teacher of ethics and philosophy. In 1943 he authored a tract that openly criticized Reza Shah, "that illiterate soldier," and those who backed his secularizing policies, but otherwise remained silent on politics, playing no role in the Mosaddeq crisis of the early 1950s. In the early 1960s he recovered his political voice. With backing from a nationwide network of clerics and influential bazaar merchants, he led the opposition to Reza Shah's son as he pressed new measures of secularization. In 1963, amid antigovernment protests, he delivered a sermon denouncing the White Revolution that reflected the shah's commitment to Westernizing Iran. He charged the shah with tolerating corruption, immorality, and materialism and undermining the religious values at the heart of Iranian life. He also censured the shah for his humiliating ties to the United States and Israel: "The government has sold our independence, reduced us to the level of a colony, and made the Muslim nation of Iran appear more backward than savages in the eyes of the world!" To this point he demanded reform, not the regime's overthrow.[6]

This attack had a nationwide impact and marked the beginning of a prolonged and bitter struggle. The shah immediately countered, raiding religious centers and imprisoning Khomeini. After vociferous, often bloody protests, the Shah released Khomeini, but the cleric continued to speak out on political issues. When in 1964 he attacked the regime's subservience to the United States, the shah exiled him.

For the next 14 years, Khomeini lived abroad but maintained contact with the domestic opposition, offering encouragement and guidance in a cause he came to define as the overthrow of "the tyrannical regime imperialism has imposed on us" and its replacement by "an Islamic government."[7] His clear, direct pronouncements circulated widely in Iran and established him as the leading critic of the shah. As earlier, the shah responded with police repression and the exile of opponents. But now spreading disaffection left him with a shrinking base of political support, even within the urban middle class and within the royal court and its clients, the primary beneficiaries of Iran's new wealth.

In January 1978 Iran entered a period of sustained, open conflict, culminating late in the year with nationwide protest led by militant youths serving as anti-shah shock troops. Bloody government repression fed the outrage and led to more massive protests until the police and army were powerless to defend the regime. From Paris Khomeini declared the anti-shah resistance a holy cause and those killed martyrs. In January 1979 the shah fled, and on February 1 Khomeini, the central figure in the loose coalition of opposition groups, returned to Tehran in triumph. The Pahlavi dynasty was at an end, as was the U.S. strategy of using the shah as a regional surrogate. An American position built up over a quarter-century had swiftly collapsed.

Once back in Iran, Khomeini held adamantly to his vision of an Islamic Iran and soon began to translate that vision into an Islamic republic. Initially he depended on moderates within the anti-shah coalition to lead the government, but increasingly clerics took charge. In effect, autocratic rule by the clergy would replace the shah's autocracy. Under clerical rule Iran experienced a real social and political revolution. Revolutionary courts, a revolutionary council, and revolutionary guards exercised power and enforced the will of the clergy. Parliament was restricted in its membership, and its laws were subject to review by a veto-wielding Council of Guardians, consisting of six clerics and six laypersons. The government set out to make public behavior conform to religious ideals. Alcohol and coeducational classes were banned, and the media was purged of offensive Western cultural influences spread by imported movies, music, and literature. Women were enjoined to return to the veil in public and to abandon business and public affairs. The new government provided social services to the urban poor, carried out some land reform, nationalized major financial and industrial enterprises, and extended clerical control down to the village level.

These changes were effected in the face of considerable domestic turmoil. Members of the old regime as well as left-wing Islamic militants earlier allied with Khomeini fought the drift toward clerical rule. They assassinated leading clerics and bombed the headquarters of the Islamic Republican Party. The clerics struck back and began to purge moderate allies. Some were exiled; others were executed. Between 1979 and 1981 thousands died amidst the violence and half a million (mostly middle-class professionals) fled abroad. At the same time Iran became locked in a real war with Iraq and a propaganda war with the United States (treated below). Both were debilitating but neither shook the commanding position of the leaders of the Islamic Republic.

Revolutionary Aftershocks in the Middle East

The revolution that convulsed Iran also created international shockwaves. The United States and the Soviet Union were both alarmed by the specter of "Islamic fundamentalism," and both were as a result drawn into regional conflicts. Superpower intervention would prove costly for all concerned.

The administration of President Jimmy Carter was the first to feel the impact. Initially in 1978–1979, the president and his top aides tried to find a middle way between what they saw as strident and hostile "religious fanaticism" and the collapsing regime of an old ally, the shah. When the shah fled the country in early 1979, Carter faced a Khomeini-dominated government demanding that the shah be brought to justice and that the United States end its interference in Iranian politics. In October the Carter administration, acting on the pleas of American supporters of the deposed ruler, admitted him to the United States for cancer treatment. Early the next month Revolutionary Guards retaliated by taking 60 U.S. diplomats in the Tehran Embassy hostage. The condition for their release was the return of the shah for trial along with the riches he had accumulated. The American media fixated on the hostages, as did Carter himself. A desperate president launched a secret rescue mission in April 1980, but the attempt failed, and a frustrated electorate helped doom Carter's bid for a second term. In a final twist of the knife, Iran ended the hostage ordeal in January 1981, just hours after Carter had vacated the White House for Ronald Reagan.

Moscow too felt the effects of Iran's revolution. In December 1979 a Soviet leadership headed by the ailing Brezhnev sent Soviet combat forces into Afghanistan. This decision was prompted not by expansionist ambitions but rather fear of Islamic sentiments spreading into the southern and heavily Muslim Soviet republics. Moscow in fact shared Washington's alarm over the sudden surge in Islamist sentiments. The leaders in the Kremlin saw a friendly Afghan government as a firewall against the spread of a disruptive "fundamentalism" from Iran into the Muslim populations of Soviet Central Asia. That government also provided a strategic buffer along a vulnerable Cold War frontier. Moscow knew the costs of decisive intervention to prop up a failing and ineffective pro-Soviet regime in Kabul would be high. As Foreign Minister Andrei Gromyko summed it up at a meeting early in 1979, "The army there is unreliable. Thus our army, when it arrives in Afghanistan, will be the aggressor. . . . Afghanistan is not ripe for a revolution. And all that we have done in recent years with such effort in terms of detente, arms reduction, and much more— all that would be thrown back. China, of course, would be given a nice present. All the nonaligned countries will be against us."[8] Even so, with the situation deteriorating, Moscow finally resolved late in the year to send in Soviet troops.

The Soviet effort to prop up its Afghan allies strikingly parallels the American effort in Vietnam in the 1960s. Moscow inherited a situation of political upheaval following the murder in April 1978 of long-time strongman Mohammad Daud, who had charted a nonaligned course while accepting Soviet aid. In a story familiar to U.S. officials in Saigon, Moscow then looked to the local Communist Party to take charge. But despite Soviet aid and advice, the Afghan Communist Party launched a far-reaching reform program at odds with Islam and the prerogatives of village and tribal elders. Uprisings cost the government control of the countryside, and party leaders soon fell to battling among themselves. Facing a stark choice of military intervention or the loss of a client regime, Moscow marched its forces into Afghanistan. The Soviet intervention galvanized a broad-based Afghan resistance whose center of gravity was Islamic and whose support was international, including strong backing from Pakistan and Iran as well as Saudi Arabia, China, and the United States. The Carter administration provided almost $2 billion in covert support while also imposing economic sanctions on the Soviets and boycotting the 1980 summer Olympics in Moscow.

Over 100,000 Soviet forces and a third that many Afghan government troops failed to defeat the resistance. Again parallels to Vietnam are striking. Soviet forces occupied the cities, which were assumed to be strategically decisive. But when Soviet units sallied forth to search for the enemy in the countryside, the guerrillas simply dispersed into the mountains, attacked the Soviet flanks and communications lines, and then returned to their base areas after the Soviet sweeps. Simultaneously, Soviet advisers sought without success to "build a nation" united and stable. By 1987 the Soviets had assumed a passive posture in a war that was unpopular at home and demoralizing to the troops in the field. In 1988 Gorbachev finally resolved to get out and in 1989 completed troop withdrawals. As Soviet troops disengaged, the conflict became once again an internal struggle. By then over a million Afghanis and 50,000 Soviets had fallen.

Iran's revolution also helped spawn war with Iraq (1980–1988). Saddam Hussein struck in September 1980 when Iran was still distracted by revolutionary conflict, seizing disputed oil-producing territory near the Iran–Iraq border. Zealous Iranian forces rallied, thus setting the stage for a prolonged bloodletting. Adding to the horrors was the Iraqi use of poison gas for the first time on a wide scale since World War I. This stark violation of longstanding international law evoked no outcry from the world community. Indeed, Iran was all but isolated internationally, with support coming only from Syria, while Iraq received arms, intelligence, and economic aid from the United States, the Soviet Union, and France as well as neighboring Kuwait, Saudi Arabia, and the United Arab Emirates. A mix of nationalism and faith in Islam sustained popular support in Iran through this long, costly struggle. A father whose sons had died fighting Iraq revealed that faith when he observed, "In the markets of martyrdom they sell their souls very cheaply."[9]

Finally in 1988 Iran agreed to peace, driven by economic exhaustion and heavy losses that had climbed as high as 300,000. Even so, the clerics retained firm

THE IRANIAN REVOLUTION	
1963	Shah jails Khomeini for public opposition and then exiles him in 1964
1978	Khomeini backs mounting anti-shah protests
1979	Shah flees abroad; Khomeini returns and consolidates power of the Islamic Republic; shah admitted to United States for medical treatment; U.S. diplomats taken hostage (held until January 1981); Soviet forces intervene in Afghanistan
1980	Iran–Iraq war begins (ends in 1988)
1989	Khomeini dies; revolution enters a more moderate phase; Soviet forces retreat from Afghanistan

control. Iraq had also paid dearly: Some 300,000 troops had died, and the country's debt had soared to $100 billion. Saddam Hussein had a strong army and an empty treasury. This second war in the wake of the Iranian revolution left Tehran still regionally embattled and Baghdad moving toward its own collision with Washington (see Chapter 11).

OPPOSITION TO SETTLER COLONIALISM

By century's end a phenomenon known as "settler colonialism" had tied some complicated knots in parts of the Third World and had given rise to struggles of a sort that marked a further diversification of conditions in postcolonial states. (See the Introduction for a discussion of this among other types of colonies.) These new battlegrounds looked different from communist-inspired revolutions in Cambodia or China, from the culturally defensive impulses that animated the Iranian revolution, and from the liberation movements that broke the fragile colonial grip in India and Ghana. A high living standard, social status, and a powerful sense of identity gave settlers good reason to fight to preserve the status quo and to keep subject peoples down, in particular by denying them advanced education, administrative office, and access to land. The ever-present threat from the majority indigenous people tended to stimulate among the European minorities a bunker mentality, strong racial or religious justifications for inequality, and a heavy reliance on armed force to sustain their position. The results were societies marked by deep social divisions that made political compromise and social cooperation difficult.

The settler problem had been at the heart of some of the most tangled cases of decolonization early in the postwar period. French settlers in Vietnam were a potent voice for maintaining colonial control just after World War II, while French residents in Algeria provided influential support for a bitter war in the late 1950s and early 1960s to preserve their way of life (see Chapter 6). In parts of sub-Saharan Africa where the settler presence was strong, the decolonization battle continued into the 1970s and 1980s. Mozambique and Angola, each home to about a quarter-million Portuguese residents, witnessed prolonged conflicts. In Rhodesia (now Zimbabwe), English settlers declared independence in 1965 and held out against majority rule until 1980.

No less difficult were the three cases that moved to prominence in the last decades of the century—that of the Dutch settlers in South Africa, Zionist state builders in Palestine, and the elites of Spanish descent in Central America. Each fought tenaciously against indigenous opposition forces, resulting in conflicts that were cruel, exhausting, and intractable.

South African Apartheid under Siege

South Africa stands as perhaps the starkest example of settler colonialism. In what became a carefully regulated racial hierarchy, a minority of whites (16 percent of South Africa's 29 million people in 1980) stood on top. A majority of blacks (72 percent) were on the bottom. "Coloureds" (people of mixed race) and "Asians" (primarily Indians), totaling together about 12 percent, fell in between.[10] The mythology of white supremacy masked the diversity of the population. Whites were not monolithic but broke into Anglos and Afrikaners, with the latter accounting for more than half of all whites. Blacks were also diverse, with most belonging to one of five groups. The Zulu was the largest, followed by the Xhosa.

European settlers, primarily Dutch but also French Protestants and Germans, came to southern Africa's Cape of Good Hope beginning in the mid-seventeenth century under the auspices of the Dutch East India Company, which sought a way-station to its colonies in South and Southeast Asia. In the course of the eighteenth century, these settlers developed a distinct national identity and their own Afrikaans language. As these settlers moved into the countryside to produce goods for local consumption, they set off a brutal frontier struggle with indigenous peoples, whom they drove from their land and coerced into farm labor on terms quite close to slavery. And just as in the European colonization of the Americas, diseases introduced by the foreigners ravaged the local populations. During the nineteenth century the British, drawn by diamond and gold deposits, constituted a new and aggressive presence, crushing resistance from the Zulu kingdom along the east coast and then engaging the Afrikaners in an armed conflict known as the Boer War (1899–1902). This struggle ended with the British prevailing militarily but resolved to move toward a political accommodation. The Union of South Africa, set up in 1910, was the first step toward the creation of an Afrikaner-controlled state in which British residents would run mining and industry and enjoy the privileges Afrikaners demanded for all whites.

Afrikaners resisted the post-World War II trend toward decolonization. They had made South Africa their home and so had everything to lose by conceding majority rule. The 1948 election victory of the Afrikaners' National Party established *apartheid* (literally "apartness") as the guiding principle in South Africa's domestic affairs, rationalizing and regulating a regime of white supremacy. The party promoted the view, sanctioned by the Dutch Reformed Church, that Afrikaners were a chosen people working out their destiny in a God-given land. The pious early settlers had justly swept away a scattering of "heathen natives," preserved their way of life, and made the land blossom into the most economically developed country in Africa.

Apartheid was a rigid and intricate system whose chief goal was to isolate whites from nonwhites insofar as modern industrial life and white comfort made it possible. Blacks were to live in government-designated tribal homelands (*bantustans*) scattered across South Africa. This scheme assigned blacks (nearly three quarters of the population) their own states occupying a bit more than a tenth of South Africa's land, most of it poor. Although in fact only half of all South African blacks ever lived in their assigned homeland, they nonetheless legally ceased to be citizens of South Africa. Afrikaners could now claim that there was no black majority, only collections of black "tribes," each of which had its own land. These pseudo-states operated under the close supervision of the South African government in Pretoria, and none was recognized internationally. A developed, industrial economy depended on black labor, so apartheid had to tolerate black settlements near all the major cities. But the system compensated by imposing an intricate system of pass laws that strictly controlled blacks' movement and kept them from settling too close to whites. The pass laws required that blacks carry written permission to travel from homelands, to live in makeshift townships, and to travel from those townships to work. Apartheid also made interracial contact—whether public or private—illegal. On the job blacks were restricted to menial work. They had limited opportunity to advance to more skilled positions or to acquire education. Pay was dramatically lower for blacks than for whites doing the same work. Blacks could not participate in national political institutions. State repression and censorship protected the system from critics, and a vigilant, ruthless security force silenced dissidents and responded violently to demonstrations.

As a system of control, apartheid rested ultimately on violence. Black children quickly learned this basic fact. One later recalled an early morning raid in 1966 when a pair of black policemen enforcing the pass law had burst into his family's shack in a black township just outside Johannesburg.

> *Before I knew what was happening one of them had kicked me savagely on the side, sending me crashing into a crate in the far corner. . . . [M]y knees had turned to Jell-O, my eyes were cloudy and my head pounded as if it were being split with an axe. As I tried to gather my senses, another kick sent me back to the floor, flat on my face. . . . My head burned with pain. Blood began oozing from my nostrils and lips. Several of my teeth were loose. I started screaming, . . . begging for forgiveness from my assailant for whatever wrong I had done. My bloodied hands reached out and clung to his legs, but he shoved me away. I again lost control of my bladder. My muscles tightened and beads of sweat with blood covered my body.*[11]

A six-year-old had learned a hard lesson about the power of apartheid to effect social control through terror.

South Africa also depended heavily on violence to control its neighbors. The government in Pretoria was first roused to action by the rise of independent, black-ruled states sharply critical of apartheid. Growing international criticism further increased Pretoria's sense of isolation and its grim determination to protect its way of life. To ensure that it could defend itself in the face of an international arms embargo, South Africa developed its own arms industry and an advanced nuclear weapons program, both in cooperation with Israel. To maintain a security buffer, South Africa sought to intimidate its neighbors. It retained control of Namibia (a German colony before World War I), defying UN calls for independence and fighting a Namibian resistance movement (SWAPO) operating out of Angola. Elsewhere it intervened to overthrow or destabilize governments that provided refuge for anti-apartheid activists, including recently independent Angola, Mozambique, and Zimbabwe.

The African National Congress (ANC) would emerge as the chief foe of apartheid. Established in 1912, it sought democratic freedoms and an end to segregation in all forms. It was guided at first by middle-class blacks committed to nonviolent struggle. In their approach they had been influenced by the direct example of Mohandas K. Gandhi, who had during his time in South Africa fought for civil rights in this way, just as he would later employ nonviolent tactics in the movement for India's independence (see Chapter 3). Following the victory of the National Party in 1948, the ANC became ever more militant. The Sharpeville massacre in March 1960 marked a turning point. The killing of 67 unarmed blacks protesting the pass laws made clear that the white-controlled state would not bow to peaceful demands for change. Moreover, the incident was followed by the banning of the ANC and the arrest of 18,000 people. The ANC, now operating underground and in exile, shifted to a strategy of armed struggle. An ANC flyer explained, "The choice is not ours; it has been made by the National government which has rejected every peaceable demand by the people for rights and freedom and answered every such demand with force and yet more force!"[12] ANC leaders conducted the struggle in a way that would limit loss of life. They discarded deadly terror tactics as too likely to produce bitterness that would make it difficult for whites and nonwhites to live together in a post-apartheid society. The ANC also rejected open rebellion as too costly in terms of black lives.

The ANC program contained three main elements. It looked to a united South Africa in which the artificial homelands would be eliminated. It sought black representation in the national parliament on a one-person, one-vote basis. And it anticipated a continued white presence in a society accepting of all races. What was not clear was how far the ANC would go in redistributing wealth and how far in general it might want to take control of the economy. The leadership did not agree on these delicate issues, and in any case did not want to take a stand on a matter of no urgency and risk alienating white allies and overseas supporters and investors.

Nelson Mandela emerged as the leader of the ANC. Born in 1918, he was the son of a minor chief. After attending a mission school, he enrolled in 1938 in a black university but in 1940 was expelled after heading a protest with another future ANC leader, Oliver Tambo. In 1942 Mandela got his law degree, and in 1952 he and Tambo formed the first black law partnership in Johannesburg. In 1957 his first marriage ended in divorce; his second wife was Nomzamo Madikizela (better known as "Winnie"), who would in time play her own independent role in ANC politics.

Over a 20-year period Mandela rose to political prominence. In 1944 he had joined with Tambo and others to organize the ANC's Youth League, and in 1949 this new generation of leaders took over the whole organization. They insisted on the vision of a multiracial South Africa. (Blacks opposed to this multiracial vision left the ANC in 1959 to create the Pan-Africanist Congress.) The new leadership also insisted on moving beyond talk and petitioning to public protest and civil disobedience. After the Sharpeville massacre, Mandela joined in the decision to abandon nonviolence and was arrested in 1962. He used his trial as a platform for ANC goals, telling the court, "I have cherished the ideal of a democratic and free society in which all persons live together in harmony and with equal opportunities. It is an ideal which I hope to live for and to achieve. But if needs be, it is an ideal for which I am prepared to die."[13]

Convicted and given a life sentence, Mandela spent the first 18 years in a harsh maximum-security prison, and then from 1981 enjoyed more comfortable confinement with increasingly free access to visitors and information. During his long imprisonment Mandela served as the symbol of the ANC's steadfast resistance, while Tambo headed the organization in exile. A defiant Mandela turned down offers by the government to release him if he promised to abstain from politics. He warned that demands for an end to apartheid and power sharing would eventually prevail—if possible through negotiations but if necessary through violence. Looking to a post-apartheid future, he sought to reassure whites: "Unlike white people anywhere else in Africa, whites in South Africa belong here—this is their home." On this point he was emphatic: "We want them to live here with us and to share power with us."[14]

Vigorous government efforts to crush the anti-apartheid movement failed. The ANC enjoyed strong support from a younger generation, apparent in the 1976 Soweto riots in which 575 were killed and again in the riots through the summer of 1985, in which unrest reached for the first time from black townships into white residential areas. Other groups joined the ANC in pressing the anti-apartheid cause. The Black Consciousness Movement, devoted to the idea of separate black development, flourished in the late 1960s, part of a broader trend in the African diaspora. At first the National Party approved, but in the early 1970s Pretoria repressed the movement, and its leader Steve Biko was murdered in police detention in 1977. Peaceful opposition to apartheid now fell to the United Democratic Front (a moderate, multiracial organization), churches, and religious leaders such as Anglican bishop Desmond Tutu. But they too ran afoul of government restrictions and were banned from political activities. Finally, labor organizations became more influential as they incorporated an increasingly politically aware black industrial working class. Black unions, legalized in 1979, had leverage because white owners recognized their vulnerability to disruptive protests and strikes.

This mounting domestic pressure on the white government was reinforced by outside pressure. Neighboring territories were moving during the 1970s toward independence and open support of the anti-apartheid movement. Portugal was ready after 1974 to give up control of Mozambique and Angola, while the white settler government in Rhodesia failed in 1979. Criticism from the United States and other Western countries culminated in the 1980s in an international sanctions and divestment movement to isolate the apartheid regime and get corporations to sell off ("divest") their holdings in South Africa. As international pressure mounted, the Reagan administration responded half-heartedly with a "constructive engagement" policy aimed at modification but not overthrow of apartheid. U.S. officials most feared instability that communists might exploit, they worried about loss of access to strategic minerals, and they wanted to protect the significant U.S. investments in South Africa. The Nationalist government was a long-time Cold War friend while those who supported the ANC included such U.S. foes as Cuba and Iran. Black liberation could wait.

The combination of internal protest, international pressure, hostile neighbors, and capital flight created intense pressure on the South African government and sent the economy into an alarming decline during the 1980s. P. W. Botha, the leader of the National Party and prime minister between 1978 and 1984, responded by offering the first limited concessions—what he called the "modernization" of apartheid. He was prepared to allow limited power sharing with some nonwhites but not blacks. He wanted to revise the rules on segregation in order to accommodate the need for a black workforce near the site of industry, and he was ready to cut back on "petty apartheid" dividing the races at movie houses, beaches, and other public gathering places. Botha warned his white countrymen that South Africa had to "adapt or die."

These reforms spelled the beginning of the end of apartheid. They created divisions among Afrikaners and opportunities for greater organized resistance under the umbrella of the United Democratic Front. In 1985, in the face of rising protest, Botha (now president of the republic) began to crack down. While still promising reforms, he unleashed his security forces, which carried out mass arrests, engaged in torture, and conducted assassinations. In 1986 Pretoria declared martial law, and an uneasy truce descended on the country. But the ANC remained popular; it became increasingly well organized and retained a headquarters in nearby Zambia. Influential whites more and more recognized that repression had failed and that the government would have to talk with the ANC if the transition to a new order was to be achieved without destroying the economy and their privileged lifestyle with it.

Botha's successor, F. W. de Klerk, accepted this line of thinking and moved boldly to work out an accommodation. In 1989, de Klerk began dismantling major elements in the apartheid system, disengaging from costly interventions in neighboring states, and accepting independence for Namibia. He was even prepared to legalize the ANC and begin negotiations with it. But at least initially he was not willing to give blacks the vote. In 1990 de Klerk took the dramatic step of releasing Mandela from prison and discussing terms for a transition to full democracy. Under a one-person, one-vote system, blacks would be the overwhelming majority, so the minority whites sought safeguards. In February 1993 the ANC reached an agreement with de Klerk on a five-year transitional period of power sharing. During that time minority parties would have a guaranteed voice in the government. White monopoly of political power was to end with elections in April 1994 for a 400-seat assembly that would in turn elect the president. The gradual approach was justified within the ANC as essential to avoiding a backlash among whites, who still controlled the state bureaucracy, the security forces, and the economy.

The April 1994 national elections successfully inaugurated the new democratic system while yielding, as expected, a victory for the ANC and the election of Mandela as president. But a South Africa in which blacks had finally won freedom

Nelson Mandela on His Release from Prison in 1990
He appears here with his wife, Winnie Mandela. They had married in 1958 just as the ANC was entering the prolonged period of fierce struggle against the apartheid regime. Winnie valiantly supported Mandela and the ANC cause during his 28 years of imprisonment and developed her own political following. Her more militant views, controversy over violence by her loyalists, and a personal gulf created by the long separation would finally destroy the marriage. (Allan Tannenbaum/The LIFE Images Collection/Getty Images)

had to grapple with the social and economic legacies of *apartheid*. Mandela and his ANC successors, first Thabo Mbeki and then Jacob Zuma, can point to significant improvements for blacks in income, educational opportunity, quality of housing, and provision of public services such as electricity and water. But social and racial segregation persists to a high degree, and income inequality is stark and growing. In broad terms South Africa faces issues familiar to sub-Saharan states that had gained their independence some three decades earlier: how to reconcile imposed Western economic and cultural forms with the values and institutions of the majority population.

But South Africa's long experience with apartheid was cumulatively transformative in a way that sets this case apart from others on the continent. A developed and diverse economy was one distinguishing feature. The movement of blacks into mining and industry had eroded local loyalties, so influential in other sub-Saharan states. As migrants left homelands for jobs in the modern sector, black urban residents increased from 4.9 million in 1960 to 9.2 million in 1980. Black labor had grown over those years from 0.5 million to 1.1 million, or three quarters of the workforce. Prolonged political struggle also contributed to a distinctly South African outcome. It had helped to blur ethnic lines. ANC membership from the start had

SOUTH AFRICA EMBATTLED

1652	First European settlers arrive
1898–1902	Boer War pits British against Afrikaners
1912	ANC created
1948	Nationalist Party representing Afrikaners begins constructing a formal apartheid system
1960	Sharpeville massacre followed by the banning of the ANC and the arrest or exile of its leaders; ANC abandons nonviolence
1962	Mandela sentenced to life imprisonment
1976	Soweto riots set off broad protest in South Africa
1978	Botha begins limited reform of apartheid
1984	Protest becomes endemic in black townships, forcing Botha to declare state of emergency (1986)
1989	De Klerk begins dialogue with ANC; South Africa withdraws forces from Namibia
1990	Mandela's release from prison speeds move to power sharing
1994	First post-apartheid elections put the ANC in power and Mandela in the presidency

transcended "tribal" identity, and the long exile and imprisonment of ANC leaders intensified their tendency to see the future in nonsectarian terms. Finally, the anti-apartheid cause triumphed in a world in which free-market forces rather than Third World radicalism were riding high. The ANC leadership once in power rejected a socialist quick fix in response to the profound frustration of blacks over their living standards. Mbeki and Zuma agreed with Mandela that a significant redistribution of wealth would alienate skilled whites, scare off foreign investment, and thus undermine the advanced sectors of the economy. South Africa would have to live with the divisive and potentially dangerous legacy of segregation and inequality bequeathed by apartheid if it hoped to prosper economically and function politically.

Conflict over Palestine

Palestine, a land hugging the eastern coast of the Mediterranean, has multiple claims to historical fame. Three of the world's major religions—Judaism, Christianity, and Islam—have venerated its chief city, Jerusalem, as a holy place. Palestine has also been the crossroads of empires for several thousand years—from the ancient Jewish kingdom 3,000 years ago, to Roman overlordship dating back 2,000 years, to Islamic conquest during the seventh century, and finally to European dominance in the nineteenth and early twentieth centuries. The last half-century has brought another chapter in Palestine's history with striking similarities to the case of South Africa. Here too settler colonialism took shape, championed by Europeans and justified by nationalism bearing strong religious overtones. In Palestine as in South Africa, European success came at the expense of indigenous people, and it would give rise to fierce and determined opposition. In this case the creation and expansion of the Jewish-dominated state of Israel, itself an expression of nationalism, would provoke Arabs, for the most part Muslim and long settled in the region, and sharpen their own distinct Palestinian nationalism.

The contest for the land occupied by the state of Israel began well before its creation in 1948. On the Jewish side, a Zionist faith sprang up in the late nineteenth century that inspired dreams of winning a homeland. Jews scattered throughout the Mediterranean world and across Europe had lived as second-class citizens, often discriminated against and sometimes brutally persecuted. Theodore Herzl and other leaders of the early Zionist movement argued that only when Jews had their own state would they be free from discrimination and violence. The nationalist movements taking shape in nineteenth-century Europe provided an even more important spur; Jews had either to embrace the identities decreed by these movements or to construct their own distinct national identity. The appeal of Zionism was strongest among Jews in western Russia and Poland, where both anti-Semitic violence and combat among nationalist groups were most intense. The first Zionist congress, held in 1897, sought a safe place outside Europe to settle. It focused on Palestine (the site of the kingdom of David centuries earlier and of the twice-destroyed Temple of Jerusalem) and persuaded the Ottoman

Empire to allow Jewish immigrants into this part of its domain. One early settlement proponent, a Russian Jew who reached Palestine in 1882, made clear Jews' determination to become "masters of their ancient homeland." The task, he explained, was clear: "We must establish agricultural settlements, factories and industry. We must develop industry and put it in Jewish hands. And above all, we must give young people military training and provide them with weapons."[15]

During World War I, Britain took Palestine from the Ottomans. This apparent imperial asset quickly turned into a liability as British authorities became caught between two conflicting populations. On the one side were some 80,000 Jewish settlers by 1914 representing Zionist aspirations. On the other side was an Arab majority, in excess of half a million, resentful of the foreigners pressing in on them. In 1917 the wartime government in London put itself squarely in the middle of this emerging ethnic conflict by issuing what was known as the Balfour Declaration. That document raised Zionist hopes by endorsing the idea of "a national home for the Jewish people" in Palestine, but at the same time promised not to "prejudice the civil and religious rights of existing non-Jewish communities" there. Indeed, British officials indicated in the course of the war that it favored the creation of an Arab state.[16]

After World War I, tensions in Palestine grew as Zionist organizations in Europe continued to finance a growing Jewish presence. Persecution of Jews in Germany and elsewhere in Europe in the late 1930s gave a special urgency to immigration. By 1939–1940 some 467,000 Jews were in Palestine, representing 30 percent of the population. The newcomers steadily encroached on Arab land and threatened majority rights. Zionist leaders expected Arab resistance and saw no choice but to overcome it. As one put it candidly, "I don't know of a single example in history where a country was colonised with the courteous consent of the population."[17] By the mid-1930s Palestine was the scene of growing social unrest. The climax came with an uprising between 1936 and 1939 in opposition to the settlement project. It cost the lives of 3,000 Arabs, 2,000 Jews, and 600 British and made Zionism an explosive issue in the Arab world. Britain tried to calm by limiting Jewish immigration and instituting strict control of land sales to Jews. London also announced plans to end its control within a decade, adding that it did not support the creation of a Jewish state.

Arab–Jewish relations in Palestine, already under severe strain, collapsed after World War II. The accumulated costs of war undercut Britain's capacity to control the situation. At the same time the Zionist drive intensified as a result of the Holocaust. The death of six million European Jews gave fresh international moral force to long-standing Zionist aspirations. Sympathy in the United States was particularly strong, and American Jews became vocal and generous supporters of the homeland drive. At the same time many Holocaust survivors were struggling amidst the chaos of the early postwar to reach Palestine. Anticipating British retreat and eager to receive these desperate refugees, armed Zionist groups began in 1944 to assert territorial claims. Jewish political leaders such as David Ben-Gurion, the leading figure in the independence struggle, were determined to make Palestinian Arabs accept Zionist predominance. If they refused, then the Jews had to persuade them by force. The logic of military force was central in Zionist homeland strategy.

With tensions mounting and the British on their way out, the newly established United Nations tried in 1947 to devise a compromise solution. The proposal was to split Palestine into an Arab and a Jewish state, with Jerusalem designated an international city. The United States and the Soviet Union both supported this proposed partition, as did the Jews of Palestine. But Arabs facing loss of their land adamantly refused to accept any Zionist political entity, and their irregular forces began attacking Jewish settlements. When in May 1948 Jewish leaders formally proclaimed the founding of the state of Israel, a league of Arab states (Egypt, Syria, Transjordan, Lebanon, and Iraq) attacked. Although outnumbered, Israeli forces were well armed and well led, and managed to defeat the Arab coalition. The fighting finally ended in 1949 under UN auspices with Israel gaining more territory than originally envisioned in the partition plan (including half of Jerusalem). The conflict had driven 700,000 Palestinians to take refuge in neighboring countries. Many were driven from their homes by Israeli forces; some fled in fear. About 150,000 were still left in Israel, but they were now a minority in a state dominated by a Jewish majority of nearly 700,000. The settlement process had created facts on the ground: a state with Jews firmly in political control. The first phase of this settler project was over.

A determined Zionist vision and the generosity of the Jewish community abroad, key ingredients to the birth of the new state, were also key to the state's survival and expansion amidst hostile neighbors. Born in war, Israel faced almost constant border conflicts with its neighbors and repeated wars. In 1956 Ben-Gurion's government plotted with Britain and France to attack Gamal Abdel Nasser's Egypt. In June 1967 Israel passed through its next major test of arms, known as the Six-Day War. With tensions building on both the Egyptian and Syrian frontiers, the Israeli military launched a surprise attack, confident of its superiority. In six days of fighting, it scored a stunning victory, taking the Sinai and the Gaza Strip from Egypt, the West Bank (including East Jerusalem) from Jordan, and the Golan Heights from Syria.

The 1967 conquests not only deepened Arab hostility throughout the Middle East but also cast Israel into the difficult role of an occupying power exercising control over a substantial and resentful Palestinian population in the West Bank and Gaza. On the West Bank, Israel would make strenuous efforts to encourage Jewish settlements, seize Palestinian lands, and destroy Palestinian homes. But despite new settlements and military and bureaucratic repression, Israelis could not keep up with natural Palestinian population increase. While Jews accounted for 75 percent of the population of Israel by 2011, they were less than half of the total population under Israeli control, and projections had their portion falling steadily further. Israel's leaders faced difficult choices: whether to embark on a new phase of settlement in which annexations would make Jews a minority in

MAP 9.1
Israeli Territorial Expansion

Israeli-controlled land or whether to abandon conquered land and thereby pre-serve a Jewish majority in the core territory.

The future of these occupied lands became the single most divisive issue in Israel's fractious democracy. The Labor Party, which had dominated during Israel's early years, advocated trading occupied land as part of a peace deal while also

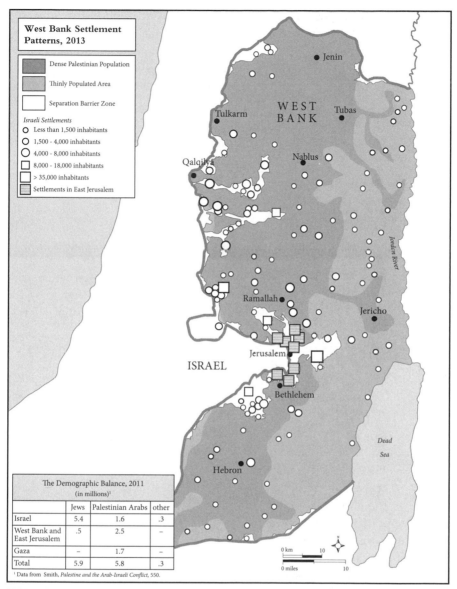

MAP 9.2
West Bank Settlement Patterns, 2013
(Based on a map by Jan de Jong appearing on the Foundation for Middle East Peace website [www.fmep.org])

promoting West Bank settlements. Without resolving the Palestinian problem, so Labor leaders argued, Israel would remain a garrison state that could not focus its resources on domestic development, cultivate cooperative relationships with neighbors, and end the cycle of violent protest and brutal repression. In the 1970s an alternative, more religious and expansionist position articulated by the Likud

Party gained popular support, and Likud has remained the single most influential party. Likud governments, dreaming of a "Greater Israel," pushed Jewish settlements on the West Bank (calling them by the Biblical names of Judea and Samaria) and resisted concessions that might compromise control of the occupied lands. Expansionists denigrated the locals as backward and terrorists, and denied their claims to a distinct political identity and state. As Israel's prime minister, Golda Meir, famously observed in 1969, "It was not as though there was a Palestinian people . . . and we came and threw them out and took their country away from them. They did not exist."[18]

The success of Jewish settlement, state building, and military conquest helped push Palestinians to consolidate their own sense of identity and find ways to give that identity political and cultural expression. The chief vehicle for this gathering nationalist movement was the Palestine Liberation Organization (PLO), created in 1964 by Palestinians living in exile. The PLO charter, issued in the aftermath of the Six-Day War, called for armed struggle by the "Arab nation" to liberate all of Palestine from a "racist and fanatic" Zionist presence backed by "international imperialism."[19] In 1969 Yasir Arafat, head of the PLO's Al Fatah faction, took the helm of this coalition of guerrilla organizations and launched a campaign of terror within Israel and attacks along its border.

But Arafat's PLO encountered setback after setback. It was first forced out of Jordan as a result of political crisis there in 1970. Lebanon became its new base. Israel responded by launching an invasion in 1982 aimed at eliminating the PLO and creating a security zone in the southernmost part of that country bordering Israel. (The intervention intensified a civil conflict that had since 1975 divided Lebanese along religious and political lines and would claim the lives of 144,000 until finally, in 1990, Syrian forces imposed peace.) Under Syrian pressure in 1983, Arafat and his PLO associates abandoned Lebanon for Tunisia. At the same time, Egypt and other Arab states were deserting the Palestinian cause. Egypt's defection from the anti-Israel united front was an especially serious blow. Egypt's leader, Anwar Sadat, had confronted Israel militarily in October 1973 with the hopes of drawing the United States, Israel's main source of international support, into a more balanced, mediating role in regional disputes. In the talks that followed the war, Sadat conceded the right of Israel to exist, and in return Israel agreed to return the Sinai but retain the other fruits of the 1967 war. Sadat's dramatic visit to Israel in 1977 marked his country's formal abandonment of the anti-Israel united front. Four years later Muslim militants retaliated by gunning Sadat down.

These blows to the externally based PLO during the 1970s and 1980s undermined its authority and at the same time created an opening for a campaign of resistance by Palestinians in the West Bank and Gaza. Their uprising (or *intifada*, literally "shaking off") began in the Gaza Strip in December 1987 after an Israeli truck hit and killed a group of Palestinians, and quickly spread to the West Bank. It was inspired by a desperate realization that neither the Arab states nor the PLO had made any headway against an oppressive Israeli occupation. Those who daily bore the indignities and losses at the hands of that occupation resolved to act. Rock-throwing and other public acts of violence against Israeli forces as well as campaigns of civil disobedience such as withholding of taxes and general strikes became the main expression of this new strategy of resistance.

The *intifada* brought to the fore a fresh set of Palestinian activists. They included on-the-ground figures aligned with the PLO. Prominent among them was a new generation of Palestinian nationalists with advanced education (sometime in foreign universities). They promoted a nationalist faith among a population with rising literacy levels thanks in part to educational opportunities in refugee camps. This Palestinian nationalism--promoted in art, literature, and education as well as politics—built on longstanding attachment to land, raised Zionism to the level of an existential threat, and depicted a collective past of heroic struggle against overwhelming odds. The repeated social upheavals and military defeats from the late 1930s right down to the late 1960s had paved the way for a common national vision by diminishing old, debilitating lines of social division, by helping new leaders of poor and middle-class background to push discredited old elites aside, and by imposing a common and unifying experience of oppression and loss. The traumatic defeat in the Six-Day War made Palestinians more aware than ever of themselves as a separate people with their own roots in the land. A poem by Hanan Ashrawi, a PLO spokesperson and educator, articulated the importance of places— of fields that had belonged to her family and streams, rocks, and paths that she had known as a child—now subject to Israeli expropriation and to bulldozers that demolished home after home:

> *Have you seen a stone house die?*
> *It sighs, then wraps itself*
> *Around its gutted heart and lays*
> *Itself to rest to become*
> *One with the earth who's in*
> *The process of giving birth to*
> *Yet more stones.*[20]

Impatience with the PLO and the relentless restrictions and humiliations of the Israeli occupation gave rise to Hamas (short for the Islamic Resistance Movement). A branch of the Egyptian Brotherhood, it came to prominence during the 1987 *intifada*. It called for open, even violent resistance as the only language the Israelis would understand. Its appeal a month into the *intifada* breathed defiance: "We will burn the ground under the feet of the occupiers. Let the whole world know that the eruption . . . by the Palestinian people will not be extinguished until the achievement of independence in a Palestinian state with Jerusalem as its capital."[21]

The *intifada* seemed to set the stage for some kind of negotiated settlement. In 1988 Arafat extended an olive branch by recognizing Israel's right to exist. He now became a more eligible negotiating partner. In 1993 representatives from the PLO and Israel's Labor government headed by Yitzhak Rabin (the commander of Israeli forces during the Six-Day War) finally met in secret. In what became known as the Oslo accords, they agreed to formally recognize the existence of the other and attempt to reach a mutually acceptable resolution of the status of the West Bank, Gaza, and occupied East Jerusalem. Thanks to these contacts, Arafat was able to return home in July 1994 and organize a de facto government known as the Palestinian Authority. His initial area of control was limited to Gaza and the city of Jericho on the West Bank. He did not get Jewish settlements stopped, nor did he secure any clear timetable for the creation of a Palestinian state. The administrative and military initiative was still in the hands of the Israelis.

By the end of the 1990s, with negotiations going nowhere, the conflict resumed, but now with the lines on both sides redrawn. Palestinians split politically and geographically. To some the price Arafat had paid for his return seemed nothing less than a sellout. Once ensconced in the West Bank, he and his successor, Mahmoud Abbas, offered only weak protests to continued occupation and expansion of Israeli settlements, roads, and closed security zones. The corruption and factionalism of the PLO further discredited it as a resistance movement. Hamas emerged as an alternative with a strong appeal to Palestinians deeply frustrated by the status quo. Ready to confront Israel, Hamas took the lead in the second *intifada* inaugurated in September 2000. Following Israel's military withdrawal from Gaza in 2005, Hamas consolidated its control there, winning an election in 2006, ousting the remnant presence of a decrepit Palestinian Authority, and repeatedly challenging Israel with armed resistance and with rockets fired into Israel proper. Continuing tension erupted in 2014 with Israel launching retaliatory attacks against Gaza. Several thousand Palestinians died, and half a million residents were displaced. At the end Hamas was still firmly in control of the territory's 1.8 million people—and still defiant toward Israel.

On the Israeli side, meaningful support for a negotiated two-state solution evaporated while a dominant Likud Party pursued its settlement policy, sometimes on the sly, sometimes openly. Many Israelis now saw Palestinians as terrorists, Hamas as even worse, and a *modus vivendi* hard to imagine. Jewish settlers were more vociferous than ever in branding any move to surrender their West Bank land as a historic betrayal, and regarded even Jews as illustrious as Rabin who were ready to trade land for peace as traitors deserving of death. (A Jewish extremist did in fact assassinate Rabin in 1995 for precisely this reason.) The Likud and its hardline religious allies resolved to meet resistance with military retaliation in Gaza and harsher administration of the occupation in the West Bank. Isolated within the region and in international fora and facing campaigns for applying sanctions and charges of violating international law, Israel depended heavily on U.S. support. An Israeli lobby kept leaders in Washington in line so that generous aid kept flowing (about $3 billion a year), and the U.S. veto kept sheltering Israel from any concerted challenge in the UN Security Council.

Israeli Army Operating in the West Bank, April 8, 2002
This image from Nablus during the second *intifada* highlights the degree that armed force continues to govern the relations between Palestinians and Israelis. (Israel Defense Forces)

With all parties dug in, the future seemed to promise the kind of prolonged bloodletting all too familiar from other cases of settler colonialism. Palestinians seemed to pay the price of continued resistance in death and privation. In a lopsided military conflict, Israel had the advantage, but each round of conflict made the country more of an international pariah, disrupted daily life, and depressed the economy. Increasingly the most likely outcome seemed a one-state solution in which a Palestinian majority would come under the de facto political control of a militant Jewish minority. It is hard to imagine how either Israeli security or commitment to democracy—both now already compromised—could survive.

Repression and Resistance in Guatemala

Stubborn systems of internal oppression drawn along racial lines in South Africa and along national lines in Palestine assumed yet a third form in Guatemala. In this third case of settler colonialism, the European conquest came in the form of the Spanish conquest of the Mayan people, thus deeply dividing the country into two groups (Ladino and Maya) astoundingly unequal in power and wealth and creating an enduring fault line. The Maya had intermittently resisted, but not effectively until the latter third of the twentieth century, when they gained Ladino allies driven by a sense of class injustice and determined to work with the Maya to change the system. This transethnic coalition challenged Ladino elites accustomed

THE STRUGGLE FOR PALESTINE

1897	First Zionist congress calls for a Jewish homeland in Palestine
1917	British forces take Palestine after promising support to Arabs and Jews
1948–49	Britain abandons Palestine; Israel declares independence, turns back attack by Arab neighbors, and expels Palestinians
1956	Israel joins Britain and France in an abortive attack on Egypt
1964	PLO formed
1967	Six-Day War ends with Israel's defeat of Egypt, Jordan, and Syria; Israel gains the Sinai Peninsula, the West Bank, the Gaza Strip, and the Golan Heights
1969	Arafat assumes leadership of the PLO
1970	PLO ousted from Jordan
1973	Israel defeats Egypt in the October War
1978	Egypt's Sadat defects from the Arab united front, makes peace with Israel, and gains return of the Sinai Peninsula
1982	Israeli forces invade Lebanon, create security zone in the south, and put the PLO on the defensive
1983	PLO forced by Syria to abandon Lebanon, relocates in Tunisia
1987	*Intifada* begins in Gaza and the West Bank
1993	Israel and the PLO initiate direct contacts, paving the way for the creation of a Palestinian Authority for the West Bank and Gaza
2000	*Intifada* resumes
2005	Israeli forces unilaterally withdraw from Gaza
2006	Hamas wins election in Gaza
2014	Israel attacks Hamas in Gaza

to privilege and deference. They proved as determined and brutal in defense of their position as Afrikaners and Zionists.

During Guatemala's era of reform and even after the 1954 coup against Arbenz (see Chapter 6), the majority Mayan population had sat on the sidelines of national politics. But beginning in the 1970s, they began to enlist in a smoldering rural insurgency launched by dissident Ladinos. During what proved to be one of the longest of Central America's civil wars—lasting into the early 1990s—the insurgents with their base of Indian support never came close to toppling the government, but sabotage and armed clashes left Guatemala disrupted and tense.

The first signs of open internal conflict appeared in 1962. Junior military officers, angry over the government's rollback of the Arbenz reforms and inspired by the Cuban example, launched an insurgency. They failed to build a base of popular support, so when the army finally in 1966–1967 moved decisively against them, the insurrection collapsed and the leaders fled to Mexico to regroup. After a brief period of calm, the insurrection resumed on a broader, more popular base. In 1972 the Guerrilla Army of the Poor inaugurated operations just across from the Mexican border under the leadership of Ricardo Ramírez. The son of an army officer, he had as a teenager supported the Arbenz reforms. The 1954 coup and the ensuing repression drove him to join the insurgency in the early 1960s. The failure of that effort convinced him that the ethnic struggle of the Indians was as important as class struggle. Thus concerns about working and living conditions for peasants and workers going back to the reform period joined with issues of cultural autonomy and respect that appealed to Mayan communities. The Guerrilla Army's focus on cultural as well as economic issues would draw the Indian population into the insurgency for the first time and ensure it a broad base.

The Guerrilla Army was joined in 1982 by other, smaller resistance groups under the umbrella organization the Guatemalan National Revolutionary Unity, headquartered in Mexico, with Ramírez the leading figure. Also participating were newly militant labor unions and dissident Catholic priests and nuns espousing a "liberation theology" of helping the poor through social action. It was not enough to save souls, they insisted; the church should attack the sources of oppression and poverty. Long-festering social discontent sharpened by an economic crisis that began in 1973 and by the destruction wrought by a massive earthquake in 1976 created a sympathetic audience for groups calling for a new order in Guatemala.

This time Indians were ready to embrace the opposition. Indian political activism arose initially within peasant associations organized by the Committee of Peasant Unity, known by its Spanish acronym CUC. It had emerged in 1978 to stem the steady loss of Mayan land holdings. For the first time Indians made contact with each other across language divides, began to engage in sustained political organizing and education, and even developed ties with poor Ladinos. Government repression finally pushed newly politicized Indians into the arms of the guerrillas.

Faced with growing rural as well as urban unrest, the regular army emerged as the guarantor of the status quo and eventually became the dominant institution exercising control over the country. The army was assisted by civil defense patrols and vigilante groups and by the Johnson and Nixon administrations, which supplied military aid and advisers. Officers were becoming privileged, isolated from society, and above the law. When U.S. officials counseled restraint, army leaders responded defiantly: "If we want to kill each other off its our business. The United States has no right to interfere."[22]

The army-controlled government conducted a campaign of violence against both guerrillas and labor activists that became most ferocious under General

Romeo Lucas García, president between 1978 and 1982. He was alarmed by the leftist surge in neighboring countries that threatened to leave Guatemala more exposed to subversion. Sandinistas were about to overthrow the Nicaraguan dictator Somoza, while in El Salvador insurrection battered the government. The first rural repression occurred in the village of Panzós, where in May 1978 the army used indiscriminate killing of civilians as a counterinsurgent tool.

The high point of the repression came in 1981–1983. The army launched an intense campaign to eliminate any basis for insurgency among Mayan communities, especially in the western highlands, and to integrate pacified communities into the nation on the army's terms. The army would in practice do its nation building through violence, including systematic rape and wholesale massacres. Thus isolated, the rural resistance would surely collapse. Two years later the security forces began systematically "disappearing" labor leaders. Seized on the street or at home, they were usually tortured and executed, their bodies left on remote roadsides as a warning to others. If treated with sufficient brutality, the army leaders argued, peasants would turn their backs on the rebels and anyone with subversive ideas would think twice.

By the early 1980s the army had blunted this second round of insurgency, but at the price of alarming international investors and stirring up widespread international condemnation. In 1977 President Carter had cut off aid because of human rights abuses. In 1982 a military coup replaced Lucas García with General Efraín Ríos Montt, who tried to soften the counterinsurgency policy with the slogan "beans and bullets" and professed concern with popular needs. But the military remained deeply suspicious of popular organizations such as the CUC. Army units continued to attack entire villages suspected of sympathizing with the guerrillas, while the security forces and civil defense patrols abducted, tortured, and murdered suspected opponents. Ríos Montt noted candidly, "We have no scorched-earth policy. We have a policy of scorched Communists."[23]

In the face of this repression, many fled deep into the mountains or to Mexico. But the insurgents were able to maintain a force of several thousand in the field, while women's organizations sprang up (first GAM—Grupo de Apoyo Mutuo or Mutual Support Group—in 1984 and then Conavigua in 1988) and sponsored demonstrations that boldly challenged the government. They demanded an accounting for "disappeared" husbands, sons, and other male relatives. They also pursued a program familiar to social feminists (see Chapter 5) of demanding help in their daily effort to make a living and raise their children. They wanted food, medical care, housing, and clothing; government assistance in meeting education costs; and legislation to protect the interests of widows and poor women. In a society deeply divided along ethnic lines, widows and other women came together on the basis of common experiences of gender oppression and common grievances against the government. As one activist observed, "Our suffering has helped us to understand our social situation and it encourages us to be more active in changing it. We know that if women don't do something, this killing is never going to end."[24]

Woman in Mayan Garb Protesting "Disappearances"
The sign says, "Enough trampling on the dignity of our brothers! Immediate release of students detained yesterday!" The woman belongs to GAM, one of two major activist groups organized by women. (Jenny Matthews)

Guatemala's crisis of violence began to ease during the late 1980s. Changes in the upper-class composition and outlook contributed. An elite that at midcentury had consisted of some 200 families had over the decades expanded its ranks while also extending its holdings from land into banking, industry, and commerce. It still had good reason to fear that concessions to the poor—higher wages, improved sanitary conditions, better education, and help for agricultural cooperatives—would only intensify popular demands. But to reject change was to lock Guatemala in underdevelopment and leave the upper class to face a resentful and militant underclass on the one side and an out-of-control army on the other. An exhausted resistance coalition was also ready to rethink its course. Peace negotiations might be the only way out of the destructive deadlock that had intensified suffering. Two thirds of the population by 1986 were in poverty and illiterate, and at least half were unemployed or underemployed. Finally, the receding radical tide in neighboring states left elites feeling less exposed and the resistance more isolated. In 1990 the Sandinistas were voted out of power in Nicaragua, and two years later peace talks in El Salvador brought an end to the civil conflict there.

The army took the first step toward breaking Guatemala's costly deadlock. In 1986 it made way for the first elected civilian government in 20 years. The new president had promised social reform but had backed off in deference to a military that still regarded itself as the ultimate arbiter of the nation's destiny. The election

THE PRESSURE BUILDS IN GUATEMALA

1962	Junior officers launch an insurrection
1972	Guerrilla Army of the Poor restarts resistance with appeal to Indian population
1978	CUC emerges; government of Romeo Lucas García intensifies repression against guerrillas and labor unions
1982	Guatemalan National Revolutionary Unity (GNRU) formed to coordinate resistance groups
1984	First of women's organizations (GAM) takes to the streets
1986	Army leaders step aside in favor of an elected civilian president
1991	Government opens talks with GNRU
1996	Peace accords concluded

in 1991 put Jorge Serrano Elías, an evangelical Protestant, in power. Serrano believed that economic development depended on peace, which in turn meant negotiating a ceasefire and drawing guerrillas into the electoral process. Talks between the government and the resistance began that year and finally produced an accord in 1996 that promised social reforms, free elections, and respect for Mayan languages and traditions. The return of Arbenz's remains for burial with honors in 1995 and the creation of a truth commission to bring to light past abuses were significant if symbolic steps toward reconciliation.

Guatemala had gained relief from the violence that had caused the death or disappearance of 200,000, attributable almost entirely to government forces. But the country still faced the formidable challenge of creating a shared sense of nationhood and a working consensus on economic development. As in Palestine, so too in Guatemala, settler colonialism had generated a conflict by entangling two very different peoples yet leaving little grounds for compromise. Guatemala remained a deeply divided society.

DREAMS OF DEVELOPMENT IN DISARRAY

While revolution of one sort or another continued to convulse some parts of the developing world and bitter internal conflict engulfed others, the siren call of integration into the international economy gripped a third substantial segment. A wide sweep of the Third World had in the early postwar period embraced extensive state control and rapid industrialization and then found that it yielded disappointing economic growth rates. But transition to the market also proved in most cases disappointing due to weak world demand for commodities or protectionism practiced by developed countries on behalf of their own agricultural sector. But

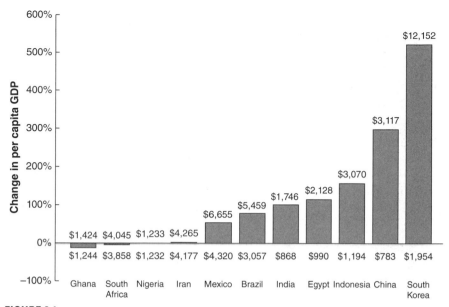

FIGURE 9.1
A Scorecard on Economic Performance in the Developing World, 1970–1998
This graph shows the strikingly different rates of growth of selected developing countries over a quarter-century measured in per capita GDP (in constant 1990 dollars), with 1970 figures along the baseline and 1998 figures at the end of the bar. Those countries at the far left failed to make headway in increasing the size of their economies enough to improve the lives of their rising populations. The performance of individual countries listed here mirrors the overall performance within the main regions of the developing world. East Asia and parts of Southeast Asia did far and away the best. South Asia and Latin America followed with moderately strong growth. The economies of the Middle East and Africa were flat, showing either negligible increases or small declines. Some relatively well-to-do developing countries such as South Africa stagnated, while others, such as China, began this period poor and made dramatic headway.[25]

internal problems—notably the adverse effects of rapid population growth, the neglect of women as an important human resource, and deepening environmental degradation—also put a drag on economic growth. This plunge into the market left many developing countries adrift with growth frustratingly low, even negative in some cases, and without a galvanizing vision to replace the once-appealing socialist and revolutionary models. (See Fig. 9.1.)

Stalemated Economies

The widespread shift during the last decades of the century from inward-looking, usually socialist policies to outward-oriented market principles had several sources. The Soviet economic model was losing its appeal, and then Soviet assistance declined and finally disappeared along with the Soviet Union itself. The palpable success of the "little dragons," those capitalist outposts on Asia's maritime periphery, strengthened the case for the free market. China underwent a gradual economic transformation that left it socialist in name but increasingly market-driven in fact, and Vietnam was close behind (see Chapter 8). Chile's economy thrived after the military seized power and technocrats backed by bayonets imposed market reforms. These profitable adaptations undermined the notion that capitalism was an inherently exploitative dead end for the Third World.

But it soon became apparent that the turn to international markets worked only for some. Countries heavily dependent on one or two crops or minerals for export (such as Kenya with its coffee and tea, Nigeria with its oil, and Honduras with its coffee and bananas) remained especially vulnerable to swings in international markets. A sudden drop in prices on international markets could quickly turn prosperity into hard times for producers of raw materials. Moreover, developed countries continued to protect their own farmers from exports produced in developing world. International investors added another dimension of risk: They could decide overnight to pull out, paralyzing production and undoing years of progress. Finally, the transition to the market required domestic sacrifices that fell heavily on the poor, generated pressure on elected leaders to pull back from painful market reforms, and imperiled the investment in infrastructure on which long-term competitiveness depended.

The case of Ghana illustrates the ways hopes for salvation through the global market gave way to sober reflection. A country could do all the right things and still measure progress in painfully small increments.

A leader in the era of independence for sub-Saharan Africa, Ghana suffered through two decades of troubled economic policy. The difficulties had begun with Nkrumah's socialist project, which had fed ethnic suspicions and exhausted the country's financial reserves without generating sustainable growth (see Chapter 6). However, Nkrumah's successors between 1966 and 1981, through eight changes of government and five military coups, followed an erratic and ineffective course that was even more harmful to the economy. Average annual GDP growth dropped from 2.8 percent in the 1960s to a negative 5.2 percent in the early 1980s. With the economy falling and the population rising from 6.2 million in 1957 to 12.2 million in 1984, Ghanaians watched their standard of living decline by about a third. High infant mortality and low life expectancy indicated that development no less than democracy was in crisis.[26]

Finally, a junior air force officer, Jerry Rawlings, ended the political merry-go-round in 1981 and dramatically shifted the country to free-market principles championed by the World Bank, the IMF, and other international lenders. The man who would dominate Ghanaian politics over the next two decades had himself espoused Nkrumah's socialist vision. Ghana's accumulating problems after Nkrumah's fall increasingly worried him. Those problems were in his view rooted not in economic exploitation by the West but rather in the misbehavior of Ghana's own elites—infighting among political parties, corruption among top military leaders, and mismanagement of the economy. He felt the need for a government that would focus on improving material welfare and increasing mass political participation (including a greater role for women).

The first step taken by the Rawlings-led military government was to impose an austerity budget favored by Western financial advisers, slashing subsidies and producing hardship in both the city and countryside. In 1985 Rawlings pushed his policy forward yet another step by privatizing parts of the state-controlled economy, relaxing government regulations standing in the way of production, and cutting government budgets and bureaucracies. He tempered these measures by promoting rural development and reforming education to focus on building skills. His reward was better economic performance. Agricultural production rose and food imports fell. Duly impressed, international investors made new loans available, and Ghana was able to import goods to develop industry and infrastructure. Economic growth turned strong, averaging 5 percent annually for six years running. To effect his economic reforms Rawlings resorted to the devices of the strongman. In 1982 he banned all political parties and used detention to silence his critics. Finally in the early 1990s, with the reforms securely in place, he called for a transition to democracy. In 1992 Rawlings won the presidency in a five-way race. Charges of fraud blemished that election but not the one in 1996, when he was reelected in a strong multiparty campaign overseen by a vigilant press.

However, prosperity still eluded Ghana. Production continued to lose its race with population increase. Even with the improved economic performance, by 1992 per capita income was still slightly lower than it had been some 40 years earlier.[27] The steady drop in cocoa prices on the world market compounded Ghana's economic problems: By 1989 the commodity sold for only a fifth of its 1977 value. At the same time the price of imported goods was rising, and Ghana was still burdened by heavy external debt. Clearly, embracing the international economy was not a cure-all.

What little Ghana had achieved with good luck and strong leadership was far from the grasp of much of the rest of the continent. Indeed, nowhere in the developing world was the transition to the market less fruitful than in sub-Saharan Africa. Grinding poverty was more than ever a problem. With its population of 559 million in 1987, Africa had a total GDP about the size of Belgium's (a country of 10 million people). By the 1980s, 29 of the world's 34 poorest countries were in Africa. One quarter of its population (over 100 million people) faced chronic hunger. Prolonged civil war or several years of drought could leave many starving. The highest population growth rate in the world guaranteed that the situation would get worse and inspired troubling forecasts of a doubling of the continent's population to about 1 billion by 2010. Compounding the poverty were endemic health problems. Malaria and dysentery were common. Two thirds of Africa's population lacked safe drinking water. An HIV/AIDS epidemic had killed 14 million people by 2000 and accounted for over 29 million cases by 2002, 70 percent of the world's total. With almost a third of the adult population testing positive in some countries, the epidemic was putting severe strains on families, economic productivity, and health systems. Africa's fragile ecology was under stress, thus threatening food production. For example, the need for firewood caused the loss of millions of acres of forest each year. Much of the continent's dry lands and rangelands were gradually becoming more desert-like.

This grim state of affairs was if anything intensified by integration into the international economic system in the course of the 1980s. Long-term neglect of the countryside was compounded by a downward slide in the international market price for raw materials. This spelled serious trouble for already stagnant sub-Saharan economies, hurt rural producers, and meant that countries with already high levels of international debt would either face defaulting on those debts or have to limit domestic programs, creating in turn public protests and military mutinies. As a result of this combination of adverse developments, living standards across sub-Saharan Africa fell by 15 percent between 1979 and 1985. This decline was serious for countries already close to the margin, and in places it wiped out the middle class.

The World Bank and major creditors began intervening in the course of the 1980s, setting limits on loans and demanding austerity. Debtors had to accept an export-driven development strategy. The elements in the new program included notably implementing price incentives to promote agricultural production, improving distribution systems, making investments in the rural sector, privatizing the economy, and cutting subsidies to public enterprises. In return for these reforms African countries received funds to help them through this crisis. International loans were supplemented by foreign assistance amounting to $13 billion a year between 1980 and 1987.

Economies remained in trouble even after acting on World Bank advice. The prescribed cutbacks in government spending hurt health and education. Austerity also increased unemployment, sharpened inequalities, and created popular unrest among the privileged city residents (particularly over rising food prices). And the pain did not bring economic gain. Between 1980 and 1987 per capita income fell by 10 percent, thus deepening poverty. Foreign investors did not come in as anticipated. International commodity prices remained low. And Africa's share of the world market declined to 1.5 percent. Africa became the most heavily indebted region of the world, with external obligations equal to total GNP and with payments on the debt eating up half of export earnings. With the end of the Cold War and of the superpower competition for clients, aid programs declined sharply.

Prospects for democratization on the African subcontinent were equally poor. While Rawlings was promoting democracy in Ghana, much of the region remained in the grip of strongmen and the military. Moreover, political sentiment was not foursquare behind Western-style democracy. To be sure, some argued that free elections would bring stability, more accountable government, and less corruption. Authoritarian politics and military-dominated governments were, according to these pro-democracy advocates, at the root of Africa's economic woes. But some skeptics wondered whether democracy might stir up ethnic or religious rivalries better contained under a strongman, and they noted a regional preference for "traditional" forms of decision making by elders though consensus building and an antipathy to dissent and permanent opposition parties. Finally, doubters argued that democracy was a product of economic development, not its source. From this point of view, African states were better off following the example of Japan, Taiwan, China, and South Korea, where authoritarian politics and state-guided economies geared to international trade had put economic growth first and let democracy follow behind.

The Population Explosion

The problem of rapid population growth plagued not just sub-Saharan Africa but also Latin America and South Asia. Viewed globally, three quarters of the additional population at the end of the twentieth century belonged to the developing world, especially in those three regions, where it seriously burdened attempts to create a better life by substantially offsetting or even canceling out economic growth. Overpopulation also added to the pressure on limited land in densely settled rural areas, degrading the environment and feeding civil unrest, itself harmful to production and investment and the provision of government services such as health care and education. The African state of Rwanda offers perhaps the most chilling example of the potential consequences. Growing population pressure had over three decades reduced farm size by a third—from 5 acres for the average family to 1.8 acres. The struggle for land contributed to interethnic tensions, climaxing in the slaughter of as many as a million Tutsi and their supporters by their Hutu neighbors. But even as population growth surged in much of the developing world, some areas were showing the first signs of a slowing in the birthrate. This trend promises to make economic development easier because there will be fewer mouths to feed and fewer demands on natural resources.

The population boom of recent decades is part of a long-term trend curving ever more dramatically upward. By about 1804 world population had reached 1 billion. By 1927 (123 years later) it had doubled. Then in rapid succession it jumped to 3 billion (1960), 4 billion (1974), 5 billion (1987), and 6 billion (1999).

Why did population, particularly in the Third World, increase with such speed? Part of the answer is that Western medicine had a major impact over the long term. During the late nineteenth and early twentieth centuries colonial administrators promoted public health projects to safeguard foreign residents, with benefits that ultimately trickled down to local populations. They put in proper sewage disposal that helped check cholera outbreaks. They attacked insects that carried malaria and typhus. They built hospitals in major administrative centers, while working with missionary groups to introduce modern medicine to remote, rural areas. Colonial schools and Western universities diffused medical techniques among the indigenous population. Progress continued into the post-1945 period. New UN agencies were especially helpful in maintaining the momentum in public health improvements. Major achievements in this postwar period included the virtual eradication of polio and smallpox and the control of malaria. As a result of these favorable developments, infant mortality declined dramatically. In India, for example, infant deaths per 1,000 live births fell from 237 in 1900 to 65 in 2000. At the same time, life expectancy in developing countries such as Mexico and India was rising dramatically—and catching up with the developed world (Fig. 9.2). Even though much of the developed world also experienced significant increases (usually somewhat short of doubling across the twentieth century), the developing world scored the most spectacular gains.[28]

The other part of the explanation for a soaring population was to be found in birthrates, which remained high throughout the developing world well into the postwar period. Even as the conquest of such longtime killers as malaria saved infant lives and extended life expectancy, peasants and poor city dwellers continued to have babies at the old high rate as though mortality levels had not changed. High infant mortality meant a large number of births were needed to ensure survivors. Moreover, large families had traditionally been an asset rather than a liability in the countryside. Children were valued as laborers in the field, as caretakers of younger siblings and aging parents, and as a new link in the chain of family and village life. The prevailing wisdom was thus that the more births, and hence the more survivors, the better off the family and the community would be. The value placed on producing at least one male heir gave an additional impetus to childbearing. Catholic and Islamic values reinforced a bias toward large families. In Latin America, South Asia, the Middle East, and northern Africa, religious leaders warned that birth control would encourage promiscuous sexuality. Political

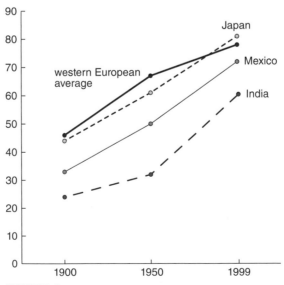

FIGURE 9.2
Lives Grow Longer, 1900–1999
Years of life expectancy at birth, averaging both sexes.[29]

fears in the developing world further strengthened doubts about birth control: The Mexican government in the 1950s, China under Mao, and the heads of some sub-Saharan Africa states denounced family planning as a Western plot to weaken their countries.

During the 1960s and 1970s the population tide began to turn as the idea of restricting family size gradually took hold. Worldwide fertility fell from five children per woman in 1960–1965 to three in 1990–1995. Reproduction rates started to drop in the developed world in the 1960s. At about the same time the runaway population growth in Asia and Latin America began a steady, long-term decline. The demographic turnaround was slowest in Africa, but even there in the 1980s and 1990s a drop became evident for the first time.

Driving this demographic transition everywhere were both new medical technologies and changes in attitudes. A widening choice of safe, effective, easy-to-use contraception, including rubber condoms, diaphragms, intrauterine devices, hormonal contraceptives, and surgical sterilization, gave couples more power to limit family size and to space children. Peasants were beginning to learn, especially as they moved to the city, that education was the key to opportunity. Now that each child required more of an investment from scarce family resources, poor people saw an incentive to have fewer children. The declining demand for agricultural labor and the unmistakable evidence that more children were surviving reinforced this trend toward smaller families. Spacing pregnancies also improved the health of the mother.

Political leaders once doubtful about birth control began to appreciate the burden that a growing population put on the economy and the environment. The new common wisdom held that economic progress in the developing world depended on reducing the birthrate, opening government-sponsored family planning clinics, and organizing educational campaigns about contraception. Not surprisingly, socialist states had the tools to impose the most far-reaching and effective population controls. For example, in China by 1987 three quarters of all couples used some form of contraception; stiff penalties were imposed on those exceeding the one-child limit. Nonsocialist states were slower to embrace birth control measures and more tentative in their implementation. In Catholic Mexico, for example, the government had dragged its heels even though the economy could not grow fast enough to ensure employment for all those seeking work and even though women were increasingly interested in obtaining contraceptives openly rather than on the black market. Finally in the mid-1970s the government launched a vigorous population control effort, including a media campaign and a network of family planning clinics. The use of contraceptives rose dramatically and birthrates fell from 7 children per woman in 1965 to 2.5 in 1999. Where states put neither education nor financial resources behind birth control, the use of family planning was low and the progress on curbing growth slow. Guatemala, with a 23 percent contraception rate in 1987, was one of these laggards, and some parts of Africa registered below 15 percent.[30]

The new consensus on controlling population growth inspired international initiatives. Beginning in 1975, the United Nations sponsored conferences and funded programs that highlighted the important link between population control and provision of education and autonomy for women so that they could play a more active role in reproductive decisions. To that end, the UN as well as nongovernmental organizations set up health clinics and schools and arranged small business loans for women breaking into the market.

Women and Development

If sputtering economies and growing populations were the most obvious problems hobbling developing countries, glaringly inequitable gender relations hurt in ways less frequently noticed. Those celebrating the market have tended to see it as a liberating force creating opportunities for human development at the same time that it stimulated material abundance. But in fact its contributions to the welfare of women in the developing world were distinctly limited and in some cases actually regressive. Despite encroaching global trade and finance, male social and economic domination persisted, above all in South Asia, West Asia, and Africa. Even where female literacy and life expectancy rates rose, they were still generally lower than those for men. Half the population was limited, often severely, in the contributions it could make to social well-being or for that matter to economic production in a world economy that rewarded education and a capacity to innovate.

The reasons that the broad pattern of "life chances" had long been stacked against women are multiple and daunting. Most Third World cultures valued male over female offspring. Males usually carried the family line forward, whereas women married out of the family and thus did not count as long-term family assets. A son would remain at home to work in the fields and care for elderly parents, while a daughter in most cases became part of her husband's family. Immediately after birth, female infanticide was practiced in some rural areas such as in India and China. Once modern medical tests became available that could reveal the sex of the fetus, gender-based abortion took the place of infanticide. The discrimination against women persisted into childhood. Under conditions of scarcity, poor parents had to decide how to allocate limited resources, and almost invariably they gave their sons better health care and more food. These various forms of discrimination translated into a cumulative loss of female life reflected in skewed gender ratios within the general population. For example, in India in 1995 there were 927 women for every 1,000 men—a 7 percent gap.

As girls matured, their families further disadvantaged them by cutting them off from public activities on the grounds of protecting their daughters' virtue as well as the family's reputation and resources. Daughters as a result received less education than sons and thus suffered from low literacy rates. In most of sub-Saharan Africa, for example, those rates were 20 percent below those for men, even though more education would have made women more productive in the agricultural sector in which they predominated.

Restrictions carried over into marriage, where control of the woman and whatever property she brought with her passed from her father to her husband or her husband's family (often a mother-in-law exercised direct daily supervision within the enclosed family domain). The wife had no independent standing; her status derived from her husband and his family. The husband made the decisions that defined her life. A poor peasant woman from northern India described her sense of this sorry state of affairs. "We women stay at home and do back-breaking work even if we are feeling ill or if we are pregnant. There is no sick leave for us. But we do not have any money of our own and when the men come home we have to cast our eyes down and bow our heads [submissively] before them."[31] The husband's control extended to how many children to have and whether birth control was appropriate. A woman's failure to have at least one child (ideally a son) could reduce her to a pitiable failure in the eyes of the entire community. Barrenness could serve as legitimate grounds for abandonment or divorce. A pronounced double standard applied to relationships outside marriage. The woman was bound by strict standards of fidelity, and any breach was severely punished. Husbands by contrast enjoyed more latitude for liaisons outside the home and greater impunity if found out. Given the considerable power that husbands possessed, they often exercised it violently against women as well as children.

Women who sought to break out of this iron cage of social restrictions found their way blocked by rank upon rank of males—within the family, the village, the courts, and the political system. Most men were tied by custom or self-interest to the status quo. Women attempting to become economically self-supporting were told to attend to household tasks. Those working outside the home did so on the condition that they were to supplement the husband's earnings, not supplant them or establish personal independence from him. Moreover, women's work was in the main limited to peripheral economic activities such as small-scale agriculture or petty trades in the informal sector of the economy. (We have seen the example of Ghana's market women in Chapter 6.) Access to the capital and credit needed to run a business was limited if not entirely closed off. Formal restrictions often reinforced informal ones. For example, the law often constrained women wanting to enter into contracts, a major commercial hindrance.

What explains this pervasive pattern of male dominance in predominantly rural societies in the face of considerable social and economic flux over the last half-century or more? Whatever the upheavals, males have managed to preserve their dominant position within the family, the political system, and the economy, and in some cases they have strengthened their dominance. Their success can be explained by the imposing package of assets that men brought to changing conditions. These included greater literacy, a near-monopoly on decision-making power, far superior political connections, and economic experience. In many cases men's traditional position of dominance had been enhanced by Western influence. Colonial administrators and missionaries introduced Victorian notions of domesticity that restricted women's access to the public sphere. Combined, these substantial advantages put men in a better position to make the most of periods of change, while women who took on new economic responsibilities assumed them on top of their traditional domestic duties of birth and child care. The resulting double burden accentuated already substantial gender disadvantages.

Commercialized agriculture, the leading catalyst for rural change, offers a prime illustration of how men could seize the opportunity for profit—and in the process significantly widen the gender gap. Men would make the decisions on how family resources, including the labor of women, would be used and what crops would be grown. The pattern was surprisingly similar around the globe. For example, we saw in Chapter 6 the impact that the arrival of cocoa as a commercial crop in Ghana had on women's lives. While this cash crop opened doors for men, it diminished the socially sanctioned rights of women and left them scrambling for sources of income to care for their families, whether in petty trades or small-scale cocoa growing using their own and their children's labor. In rural Iran, women found that after husbands were forced to find jobs in the city, they carried a staggering burden of domestic work while still cut off from the public sphere of activity. One woman in a village in central Iran lamented, "Only a dead woman is a free woman."[32]

Where men gambled on cash crops and won, they controlled the additional resources. If the gamble failed, women were left to cope with the consequences. A Kenyan village that converted from corn to sugar cane offers an example of how commercialization could hurt women. Under the contract concluded by the men, women were to tend the cane, outside crews with mechanical harvesters were to take it for processing, and the men were to collect a cash payment. After one growing cycle, the women protested that they still worked in the field but now without ultimate control of the crop, and that cane had squeezed out corn so that there was no available food once the men had spent the cash. In a public meeting the village chief acceded to the women's call to hold back some land for corn and to give them some say in the disposal of the cash. The sugar contract, it soon turned out, prevented this reallocation of land use, and men, disgruntled by this challenge to their authority, were unwilling to make any substantive concessions. The women had lost out.[33]

Women suffered disproportionately when free-market economies went into crisis. Debt-ridden countries such as Guatemala and Nicaragua in the 1980s and 1990s received financial relief from the international banking community at the price of programs of fiscal austerity that added significantly to burdens already carried by women and their families. Food and education subsidies disappeared. Health care and child care became more expensive. Living costs rose while income stagnated or fell.

Paradoxically, it was precisely under the discredited socialist regimes that women had made the most progress. Socialist revolutions took equality as a fundamental goal and promised to end gender no less than class oppression, both evils attributed to the old feudal and capitalist orders. Those revolutionary parties on the Left that won power did address women's welfare. The results were evident, for example, in Cuba, where women enjoyed a literacy rate of 95 percent by the 1990s (46 points ahead of women in Guatemala). Chinese women, to take another revolutionary case, were significantly ahead of Indian women on literacy (by 35 percentage points). The Sandinista revolution in Nicaragua in the 1980s pushed women to the fore with lasting consequences, evident in high levels of political and economic participation and prominence in government ministries, parliament, and the non-profit sector. Even quite localized struggle over community welfare such as access to land could transform the position of women through their engagement in village mobilization and public protest. A Bangladeshi woman after just such a local drive by the rural poor noted the gender consequences with pride.

> Before the village elders and union-council members abused and threatened us for joining the group, now they are silent. . . . Before we did not understand our wages, now we understand profit and loss. . . . Before we did not know our rights to rations or medical services, now we are conscious and exert pressure to receive our due. . . . Before we did not go outside our homes, but now we work in the fields and go to the town. . . . Before our minds were rusty, now they shine.[34]

But even under socialism men dominated. During the period of revolutionary struggle, the Chinese and Vietnamese Communists were reluctant to press issues of gender equality too hard for fear of alienating males who did most of the grass-roots fighting and organizing. In the post-liberation period the political system remained male-dominated, and rural males were still better off. If any group of women fared especially well in the aftermath of revolution, it was urban women. This was true in China and Vietnam but also in Iran, where revolutionary leaders were not comparably friendly to the cause of equality. In all these cases better-educated urban women had valuable skills to apply to the post-liberation process of economic development and state building and thus had a better chance of overcoming at least some of the well-rooted prejudices standing in their way.

This tendency for patriarchy to powerfully perpetuate itself became the subject of international debate in the 1980s and 1990s. While feminists agreed that removing the extensive disabilities placed on Third World women was important to human welfare and economic development, they disagreed on the best solution. Some, especially in the developed world, argued for an agenda of equal rights informed by a faith in unfettered personal opportunity. This individualistic feminism, particularly influential in the United States and Britain, had little appeal for many Third World feminists, however. Their preferences were closer to the social feminism popular on the European continent (see Chapter 5) that honored women's unique role in procreating and nurturing children. Thus, securing individual rights and opportunity was less important than promoting the interests of the family and the ability of women to contribute to societal well-being. Social feminists in the developing world, like those similarly minded women in Europe, gave high priority to government programs critical to women's lives such as family planning, health care, education, and social security.

Social feminists in the developing world often got caught in a crossfire between men in their own societies and equal-rights feminists in the developed world. Their countrymen, defensive and often angry, told them to steer clear of public affairs, ignore meddling foreign reformers, and attend instead to their "natural" domestic realm of family, reproduction, household management, and marriage arrangements. At the same time those Western feminists who were convinced that gender was constructed and not fixed urged their sisters in the developing world to shape a fresh identity guided by ideas of individual autonomy and rights. Developing world women thus found the counsel of their men at odds with their own pressing bread-and-butter family preoccupations, while the foreign advice collided with their collectivist concerns. This debate raised a question of the first importance for all countries embracing the market-based international economy: How important were matters of family livelihood and social welfare to successful and sustainable development?

CONCLUSION

By the 1990s the pressures of a vibrant but unforgiving international economy were dissolving the commonalities of outlook and interests that had given the Third World its unity and meaning. Revolutionary impulses, once anticolonial and Marxist in origin, were now more likely to take shape as a reaction against the cultural baggage that came with integration into the global economy. The most important of the late-twentieth-century revolutions fits this pattern. Iran's Islamic clerics successfully followed a course consciously at odds Western materialism and secularism. Regimes built on the foundation of settler colonialism—as in South Africa, Israel, and Guatemala—found themselves in the grip of internal crises that were likely to scare away investors, provoke boycotts in important markets, and in the end diminish the prospects for development. Elites with cultural roots in Europe clung with determination to their positions of power and privilege, but their response to the challenge of politically disenfranchised and economically marginalized indigenous peoples was constrained by the pressures of the international economy and by suasion exercised by the leaders of that economy. Finally, as the Third World increasingly tried to make foreign trade and investment into an engine of significant, sustained growth, the results registered winners and losers. Autocratic Communist parties like China's were as likely to succeed as right-wing military regimes like Chile's. The deeper the countries of the old Third World got into the postcolonial era, the more varied the problems they faced and the directions they took.

Part Four

INTEGRATION AND FRAGMENTATION, THE 1990s AND BEYOND

THE DESTRUCTION VISITED on New York's World Trade Center on September 11, 2001, was a particularly American trauma but with global resonance. Between 8:46 a.m. and 10:28 a.m. two airplanes struck the Twin Towers and ignited an inferno that reduced both to giant piles of smoldering rubble. Well over 2,700 people died that morning in southern Manhattan, including those going about their morning routine, those in two hijacked jetliners, and those who rushed to the rescue, while more than 200 lives were lost when another plane, also under the control of a suicide team, crashed into the Pentagon and a fourth was brought down by passengers before reaching its target.[1] The disaster shook Americans as no event had since the attack on Pearl Harbor some six decades earlier. But the grim scene unfolding in lower Manhattan contains a larger tale that brings into sharp relief the contradictions at the heart of a new phase in the history of the post-1945 world.

From one perspective the World Trade Center—its rise, its fall, and its rise again—was linked intimately to the workings of globalization in an eminently global city. The Center had been conceived as a way of rejuvenating a part of lower Manhattan by making it a locus of activity for firms dealing in the flow of goods, services, and capital in an integrated world market. The name given the proposed site—the World Trade Center—was no accident, nor was the name of the restaurant eventually placed at the top of one of the two towers. "Windows on the World" self-consciously played on the sense of a city with a global vantage point. Reflecting the project's modern, cosmopolitan spirit, a Japanese-American, Minoru Yamasaki, was the lead architect, and his plans took advantage of new lightweight materials that allowed for building higher and more cheaply by dispensing with old-style heavy masonry. The two tallest buildings in the world that would define the Center and make it visible for miles had no match in any metropolis around the world.

Globalization helped make the Center a success. After completion in 1970–1971, it filled slowly with tenants until the late 1970s, when it began to attract firms specializing in international trade, investment, currency trading, mergers, shipping, litigation, and insurance. The estimated 17,000 people in the towers at the time of the attack were as global as the business they conducted. They were themselves part of the worldwide movement of population set in motion by the rising global age. Some were mobile cosmopolitans prized for their skills in management, finance, communications, and technical analysis; others were immigrants who did the manual labor that kept the building running. Roughly one in ten who died in New York on 9-11 were foreign-born. Even many of their several thousand dedicated rescuers on 9-11 had their own ties to globalization—as offspring of immigrants to the United States during a phase of globalization more than a century earlier.

In a variety of ways the attack itself took advantage of the opportunities a more integrated world afforded. Osama bin Laden, a Yemen-born Saudi businessman with a family fortune, had built a transnational organization—al-Qaeda (literally "The Base")—extending across the Middle East and into South Asia in the course of mobilizing Arab opposition to the Soviet occupation of Afghanistan during the 1980s. Following the Soviet defeat, the United States became the new target. He learned to exploit to the hilt the ease of communications and transport afforded by the new age to move volunteers, direct their training and deployment, and keep himself safe. As his cause gathered momentum and cells around the region multiplied, he became a hunted man, on the move from country to country for his own safety. No matter, as one perceptive student of political Islam has noted; he could depend on "Internet websites, satellite television links, clandestine financial transfers, international air travel, and a proliferation of activists ranging from the suburbs of Jersey City to the rice paddies of Indonesia." Even his television performances with their "soap opera costumes" tailored to their Arab audiences "owed a debt to the electronic revolution and American-style globalization."[2]

Not satisfied with attacks against American diplomatic and military targets in the region, bin Laden devised a plan to take the conflict to the enemy. Where better to strike than the vulnerable symbol of global finance? The World Trade Center had already survived the detonation of a massive bomb at the base of one of the towers in 1993. The next attempt would involve an attack from the air and would also target the government in Washington. This dual blow would terrorize the enemy, lift the pride of Muslims, and win fresh recruits to the struggle.

To carry out his plot, bin Laden selected well-educated and determined agents who could exploit the links holding together a globalized world. One profile of al-Qaeda recruits, prepared in 2004, found them strikingly privileged and cosmopolitan. Well educated, including time spent studying abroad, they had become upwardly mobile professionals, often in the fields of science and technology with a command of multiple languages. In other words, they were some of their societies' "best and brightest," with the intelligence and skills to wage a transnational struggle with considerable effectiveness.[3] Once the members of bin Laden's 9-11 team had ensconced themselves in the United States, they set to work on the details of a plot masterminded from Germany and coordinated in meetings in Spain. They got the necessary aviation training, said their prayers, and turned the most sophisticated of transport systems to their own destructive ends—with stunning results.

The response to the attack also speaks to the globalized nature of the age. The incredible news traveled widely and almost instantly on the morning of September 11. Radio reports of an airplane hitting the first tower were on the air minutes after the event. A networked world was soon flooded with photos and videos of the towers in flames, accompanied by interviews with those on the scene, even as the disaster unfolded. With smoke still rising from the ruins of the two massive structures, expressions of sympathy and goodwill were arriving from people in many lands who associated New York with vitality, modernity, and wealth. Crowds in major cities around the world gathered in impromptu demonstrations of solidarity; governments sent messages of condolence and support. *Le Monde*, a leading French newspaper not known for its enthusiastic embrace of the United States, captured the general sense of sympathy with an editorial headline that famously declared, "We are all Americans now!" Mainstream Muslim religious leaders joined in condemning this suicide attack. As the details of the plot became clear, bin Laden became infamous, and his al-Qaeda jumped to the top of the "worry list" of nervous state security services.

As the dust settled, reception around the world turned distinctly ambivalent. In surveys conducted late in 2001, opinion leaders in media, politics, business, and culture in a wide range of countries expressed resentment against past U.S. policy transgressions and blamed the United States for contributing to the global gap between the rich and the poor. They generally saw the United States as a self-interested power acting on its own without accomplishing a lot of good in the world. While this set of influential and well-informed respondents might feel sympathy for American victims, they also welcomed the fact that Americans had been made to feel vulnerability of the sort that peoples in other lands had experienced. Over two thirds of the elite respondents thought people in their country were glad to see the 9-11 attack knock Americans, with their pretensions as a special people, down to the level of the rest of humanity. A bit more than half cited American actions in the Middle East as the reasons for the attack. In the Middle East the response was higher—four out of five. No surprise, many politically engaged young Muslims regarded bin Laden as a charismatic crusader. An Egyptian graduate student in his mid-twenties attending the American University in Cairo expressed a widespread sentiment: "I like America so much. I like the American people. I want to go to America to study computer science, but I hate American policy in the Middle East and against Afghanistan. I hate it so much."[4]

The Statue of Liberty against the Backdrop of a Lower Manhattan under a Shroud of Smoke, September 11, 2001

This image creates a striking juxtaposition. The new global age made it possible for terrorists half a world away to inflict a terrible blow, but the statue, created as a tribute to a world open to immigration during the late nineteenth and early twentieth centuries, speaks to a more benign facet of globalization. It serves as a constant reminder of the historical U.S. openness to free labor and of the racial and ethnic diversity that has come to define Americans' special sense of themselves in the world. (AP Photo/Daniel Hulshizer, File)

The attack in 2001 had destroyed a symbol of globalization but not the process itself. International markets quickly regained their balance, and just as quickly New York reclaimed its accustomed place as the center of global financial activities. Plans to rebuild the World Trade Center were under way just two months after the attack. The world was still firmly lodged in a new age of globalization. The 1970s and 1980s had marked the time of transition. The Cold War contest, perhaps the most enduring feature of the postwar world, had sputtered to a close, first in the early 1970s in East and Southeast Asia and then abruptly between 1989 and 1991 with the collapse of the Soviet Union and its eastern Europe clients (see Chapter 7) No less important, the separate national economies that had emerged from World War II had begun a slow but steady march toward regional integration, with Western Europe in the lead (see Chapter 8). Finally, the conception of a Third World that emerged in the early postwar era in the imagination of many had by the 1970s and 1980s begun to dissolve as the countries supposedly part of that entity moved along strikingly diverse paths (see Chapter 9). Some developing countries were benefiting from international markets; others that had tried were not faring well. Some had succeeded at controlling population growth; others had neglected it and were paying the price. Some had a strong, centrally administered state, whereas others were divided and fell prey to civil war and foreign intervention. Democracy had taken root in some places, but many remained autocratic.

That the world of the 2000s looked so different from previous decades had much to do with the ascendant force of globalization. As it gathered force and sweep from the 1970s, global economic integration drew national economies more tightly together with astonishing consequences. It widened gaps in wealth and welfare among the world's peoples, raised to prominence a neoliberal economic and political ideology, pushed the environmental crisis to an alarming new level, and stimulated efforts to create new rules and institutions to bring order to proliferating international contacts. While Karl Marx and Friedrich Engels had proven prophetic about the effects of globe-girdling trade and investments, they had erred along with contemporary pundits in failing to see that globalization was not an irresistible force driving all before it or an inevitable outcome following some predetermined trajectory. Their misreading of the future is particularly evident in their prediction that "national one-sidedness and narrow-mindedness become more and more impossible." Their anticipation of a world drawn together not only economically but also culturally has been given the lie by durable local and regional differences that fragment the one world of globalization.

This last point should not be overlooked. The desperation, determination, and organization it took to bring the towers down is a reminder of how a stubborn diversity among the world's major regions could generate tension, suspicion, and even hostility. One world of trade and finance did not create one world of vision and values. Different creeds, different family and gender roles, different political outlooks, different ideological attachments, and different expectations about the future gave each major region of the world its own profile. These differences did not amount to a simple "West vs. Rest" division of the globe but rather played out in diverse ways, with the precise dynamics varying from region to region. While globalization unleashed powerful pressures on states to conform to a new set of rules and promoted ideas and practices across national lines, it also opened up avenues for individual expression, communication, and action not previously available. An intricately wired system in which people, goods, and capital moved fast and freely within a circuit of major cities also provided means for mobilization, organization, protest, and resistance against that system, sometimes violently.

Surprisingly, some of these counter-trends were most dramatically at work in the New World. The United States, the hemisphere's preeminent power and leading champion of globalization, appeared at its zenith, confident after its Cold War victory and certain of the advance of democracy and free markets. Yet this international supremacy was eroded by debilitating trends at home and challenged by potent resistance abroad. That resistance found expression right in its backyard. The century-old U.S. grip on lands to its south and especially the Cold War pattern of militarization and dictatorship came into question. Brazil took the lead in replacing the military with elected governments, giving popular welfare priority, and exploring a domestic alternative to rigid neoliberalism while also championing a conception of regional and international governance that defied U.S. dominance.

The Middle East stands out as the most restive region in the new era. Nowhere was the relationship with globalization and the attendant U.S. dominance more awkward. There resistance took on its most overt, calculated, sustained, and violent form. Bin Laden was not alone in feeling humiliation and anger in the face of the imposition of Western political ideologies, repeated rounds of foreign intervention in regional affairs, and the spread of Western materialism and lax moral standards. However, deep divisions developed across the region over an effective response. Those divisions followed cross-cutting lines of religion, ethnicity, class, and nationality. Foreign penetration and internal division were turning the Middle East into a pressure cooker.

Asia stands out as the great success story of the new global age. Continuing its steady resurgence, the region had by the start of the new century gone a long way toward restoring the economic prominence and cultural prestige it had lost two centuries earlier. Asia boasted the most dynamic economies of any around the world, with total output rising at a stunning rate. At the center of this regional dynamism was China, but its rapid growth and ambitions spawned regional rivalries with worrisome potential. China cast a shadow over the two Koreas, alarmed Japan, made the countries of Southeast Asia uneasy, and troubled India. Old resentments and new rivalries jostled with fresh opportunities to promote regional trade, investment, and cooperation on issues such as the environment and education and clouded the future of a promising region.

Taken together, the Europeans and Russians found themselves entangled in a set of historical afflictions seemingly resolved over the course of the Cold War. After World War II the Old World on both sides of the Iron Curtain had sought to maximize wealth and welfare and minimize the prospects of regional conflict. Western Europe governments had almost at once after the war made a strong commitment to popular needs that had been so badly neglected during the previous half-century, and Soviet leaders had taken that path from the 1950s onward. For a half-century levels of livelihood rose improssively and interstate conflict was avoided. But by the 1990s that commitment was in trouble across Eurasia. The European Union was under stress, and the Soviet collapse precipitated a crisis as much social as political. Adding to the stress were globalization's challenge to the EU's social and political compact and a resurgent Russia's geopolitical claims.

These themes—of a world in the grip of global forces and yet still divided by fundamental values as well as vastly different levels of wealth and welfare—define the last stage in this narrative of the post-1945 world. Transnational forces, visions, problems, and organizations were stronger than they had ever been, yet at the same time the dominant regions of the world pursued their own set of aspirations and wrestled with their own set of challenges that together pointed them in directions different one from the other. These differences generated conflict in some cases and at times threatened to destabilize the great power system and send an already dynamic international economy out of control. Chapters 10 and 11 offer windows on a world integrated yet also divided by a complicated geography of power and identity. Together these two tendencies provide the key to understanding the major issues that are likely to confront humanity over the coming decades.

10

THE POWER AND PERILS OF GLOBALIZATION

MANY RECENT OBSERVERS of world affairs have embraced the view that globalizing trends, unprecedented in scope and depth, are erasing national borders, eroding the authority of states, and creating a radically new order. This view took hold during the 1990s, nowhere more enthusiastically than in the United States, with the help of popular commentators, the daily news, and advertisements. Those trumpeting the arrival of globalization did differ in their appraisals of it, however. In 1995 Benjamin Barber's *Jihad vs. McWorld* warned that globalization was spiritually hollow, conflict prone, and undemocratic. *New York Times* columnist Thomas Friedman countered four years later with a snappy, enthusiastic endorsement in *The Lexus and the Olive Tree*. Others painted a dark picture of a world fragmenting under mounting social, demographic, and environmental pressures or saw in a dynamic international economy contradictions that could bring it down.[1]

This diversity was strikingly evident in the reaction to the iconic image of globalization. In 1972 U.S. astronauts took a photo of the Earth that would become ubiquitous. The "blue marble" appeared on T-shirts, commercial products, book covers, and bumper stickers. For some it evoked wonderment at the beauty of a lonely planet floating in a great void. Alienation was the response for those who could now imagine the home planet as an extraterrestrial might see it or as a place bereft of any obvious human presence. The environmentalist reaction was to see confirmation of the apparent fragility of Earth as a super-organism. This sense of an ecosystem tightly but tenuously tied together suggested the bumper sticker proclaiming "Good planets are hard to find." Finally, it was possible to see in a globe without evident national, ethnic, or other differences affirmation of a single human community. Here for enthusiasts of globalization was an encapsulation of their dream of peoples of the world coming together, their lives and outlooks more and more running along similar lines.[2]

The Earth Taken by the Crew of Apollo 17, December 7, 1972
The Mediterranean Sea, the Arabian Peninsula, and the Red Sea appear at the top, Madagascar and Africa (with the southern part cloud-covered) are in the middle, and Antarctica is at the bottom. In a photo that came to symbolize the new era of global consciousness, these geographical details got lost amidst the preoccupation with assigning grand significance to the "blue marble." (NASA - AS17-148-22727)

Most of these responses to globalization—whether popular or punditry—were simply impressions, and many of the claims were vaguely formulated, promiscuously invoked, and (most worrisome of all) historically anemic or distorted. Skeptics even dismissed the underlying preoccupation as "globaloney." To help us get a better grip on what's been happening down on the surface of this singular planet, we might think of globalization systematically—as a constellation of features. It has a history. What began to preoccupy the public in the 1990s was only the most recent act in a long-running drama that began in the nineteenth century, paused in the era of war and depression between 1914 and 1945, and then resumed in the post-World War II years. (The preliminary stages in the rise of a globalized world are covered in the Introduction and Chapters 2, 5, and 8.) Globalization in its most recent phase also depends on particular technologies, ideologies, and institutions. Operating together, they have made possible intricate networks of trade, finance, and labor migration. Those networks have raised overall levels of wealth, consumption, and geographical mobility and in turn generated far-reaching cultural and social effects, including the emergence of a global consciousness (as one historian puts it) "as a matter of practice, not just wishful thinking or ideal aspiration."[3] Finally, we need to keep in mind that globalization has imposed costs that have come to preoccupy a wide variety of groups determined to tame its excesses while preserving its benefits. Foreign trade, foreign labor, and foreign investment have increasingly figured in debates within countries over social welfare and national identity. In sum, for good or ill, this highly dynamic, worldwide system has had broad and powerful ramifications.

THE DIMENSIONS OF A NEW GLOBAL ORDER

Globalization was not inevitable, and it was certainly not technologically determined. To be sure, new means of communications made Earth-spanning integration possible. But who would use these innovation and for what ends depended on the distribution of economic power and on the power of ideas about political economy (the interrelationship between economic activities and the broad contours of politics and society). Leaders in the government and the corporate world had an outsized say, and their preferences were embodied in national legislation and regulation as well as international agreements. These arrangements in turn rested on broad notions articulated by public intellectuals and given broad currency by the popular media. The animating idea behind these developments was neoliberalism. It held that a market-oriented society would facilitate production, maximize wealth, and sustain freedom. By extension, a market-oriented world would best serve all its peoples by bringing greater prosperity and peace among interdependent states.

The Pieces Fall into Place

As in the earlier era of globalization at the end of the nineteenth century, technological innovations were key to "shrinking the world" and spurring economic activity. In the post-World War II period technology had the same broad, stimulatory impact. From the late 1950s onward, propeller-driven commercial aircraft were overtaken by jets, which were several hundred miles per hour faster and carried ever-larger payloads of people and goods. Container ships, tankers, and bulk carriers ballooning in size began to feed supply chains stretching over vast distances. Telephone and radio—technologies that had established their broad utility in the interwar years—provided the communications foundation on which postwar globalization was to build.

From a technological point of view, what supercharged the process of global integration was the digital revolution, above all the development of the Internet and the innovations that attended its rise. The rudimentary idea of an Internet came in 1960 to Paul Baran, an engineer working in a think tank. The Internet was then to emerge in the United States thanks to a steady stream of U.S. Defense Department funding. The initial goal was to devise a robust communications system that could survive a nuclear war. The money went to a select group of computer science specialists, most notably at UCLA, Stanford, and MIT, who operated with considerable autonomy. Also drawn into the network of government-funded activity were private contractors. The British government attempted a similar public–private approach, but the initiative foundered as a result of limited funding and a preoccupation with short-term commercial payoff. The Americans would lead the way.

Gradually it became apparent that the Internet was not about national security or even the flow of data among university-based researchers working on military projects but rather regular, rapid communications open to a wide variety of uses and users. The arrival of mini-computers in 1975 had an immediate impact, providing more convenient access than afforded by the large computers that had previously dominated Internet design. The first computers had weighed tons, took up thousands of square feet of floor space, cost millions of dollars at today's prices, and offered a fraction of the calculating power of a current personal computer. The arrival of minicomputers opened the way for amateur enthusiasts and significantly broadened the community of users and innovators. Quick email communications was already proving more important to the Internet community than the connections among large computer-based research projects that the new digital system was supposed to facilitate.

During the 1980s the Internet began to grow up. Businesses began to explore commercial applications while at the same time computer specialists worked out ways to link the different kinds of computer networks emerging in the United States and western Europe. The community of computer users was growing rapidly. In 1985 only 2,000 had Internet access; four years later the number had risen to 159,000 as computers as well as local area networks attached to the Internet multiplied. Together these trends broke the Internet's ties to defense research (ended in 1990); spurred commercial activities, especially among software and hardware producers and telecommunications companies; and brought new players—national and international regulatory agencies—into the mix. The World Wide Web began to take shape with its familiar "http://," domain names (those ending in ".com," ".org," and so forth), ".html" for composition, and competing browsers and search engines—all soon to be followed by such banes of the digital age as malware, phishing, industrial espionage, and cyber-warfare, not to mention cellphone attention disorder and online addiction.

The Internet was on its way to going global as people around the world discovered this sensational "new" technology whose modular nature made it highly adaptable to different and rapidly expanding institutional, business, and personal interests. The number of users rose sharply as the cost fell and both states and corporations multiplied points of access through telephone lines, fiber-optic cable, cell towers, and satellites. Some 16 *million* users in 1995 had by early 2014 increased to approximately 2.9 *billion*. Increasingly, Internet use expanded beyond the wealthy, developed countries. In 1995 only 0.04 percent of the world's population had access, with well over half of those living in the United States. By 2014 41 percent of the world's people had Internet access, with usage in the developing world much expanded compared to two decades earlier.[4] In response, new products flooded the world of digital communications. Personal computers, tablets, and smartphones became commonplace appliances, and "going online" became a daily activity for many. The digital revolution reached into every facet of contemporary life: music, movies, television, manufacturing, finance, politics, warfare, medicine, science, education, journalism, and everyday social activities.

Translating the enormous potential inherent in new technology into real-world applications was a task ultimately taken in hand by neoliberals. They would above all others shape the world that innovation made possible. Their views not only provided the ideological foundation for the new order but also set the parameters in which new technology would develop and function and the priorities that would govern it. This marketplace philosophy took hold in the 1970s and 1980s in the two countries—the United States and Britain—steeped in the exercise of global hegemony and possessed of leading centers of international finance (see Chapter 8). What began there as a domestic political project gained a pronounced global dimension. Overseas no less than at home neoliberals campaigned to free banks, investment houses, and corporations from old restraints. They demanded that the international economy and the international agencies that oversaw it adopt these principles.

Building on the success of the General Agreement on Tariffs and Trade (GATT) in reducing obstacles to trade, neoliberals called for freeing capital. They convinced the U.S. government to press for a general opening in the international financial markets. Already in the early 1970s Washington was putting pressure on western Europe and Japan while also lifting the last U.S. capital restrictions. Britain soon got into step, eliminating in 1979 its 40-year-old regulations on capital movement. Australia and New Zealand soon followed. Both western Europe and Japan were now under pressure to embrace the new orthodoxy. Resistance seemed unwise. The creation of national financial markets to handle large, unregulated capital flows could be profitable, as the American and British bankers had already shown. Moreover, states that did not embrace the principle of free capital movement would not be able to compete effectively for international investments. As a result, both western Europe and Japan initiated financial liberalization measures beginning in the 1980s.

By the 1990s neoliberalism was in the saddle. The advanced sector of the global economy was marked by a degree of freedom not known since the 1920s, and the free-market position was beginning to have an impact on policy in a wide range of countries. On the European continent, neoliberals began to challenge the social welfare state created by Christian Democratic parties working with Socialists and Communists. They also went to work in the developing world—in places such as Mexico, Chile, Argentina, and Egypt—and following the socialist collapse between 1989 and 1991 reached into eastern Europe, Russia, and the other Soviet successor states. This advancing program of the market fundamentalists had a name that reflected the site of its strongest support: "the Washington consensus."

It reduced the key neoliberal points to a formula for successful economic develop-ment and global growth. It started with the fundamental notion that markets were the most efficient mechanism to allocate resources and thus deserved consid-erable freedom of action. In this formulation, unions were a troublesome obstacle to market efficiency while states were too often a disruptive presence. The job of political leaders was simple: Keep budgets balanced, sell off nationalized firms, end popular subsidies and transfers, trim back economic regulations, and other-wise stay out of the way. Countries whether developed or developing that had dab-bled in socialist experiments in the postwar decades were told to accommodate to the new neoliberal formula. With the market thus cleared of obstructions, multi-national corporations and banks could go to work as the engines of prosperity and as the creators and suppliers of consumer dreams.

The remaining piece of the neoliberal order was institutional. The Bretton Woods trio of the World Bank, the International Monetary Fund (IMF), and GATT supplied the foundation on which the neoliberals could build (see Chapter 2). The World Bank and the IMF fully embraced the new orthodoxy under pressure from the United States and its ideological allies. In 1995 GATT was given a makeover so that it better served the neoliberal agenda. It ceased its strikingly successful career as an ad hoc sponsor of repeated rounds of multilateral trade talks that had re-duced world tariffs to an average of 5 percent, an eighth of what they had been right after World War II. It became instead a bureaucracy known as the World Trade Organization (WTO) whose task was to adjudicate disputes and press for an end to obstructionist measures whether prompted by local producers, environmentalists, or labor unions.

Operating behind these bulwarks of the neoliberal order were the leaders of the established economies. Their ad hoc meetings in the mid-1970s became regular affairs, and in the spirit of collaboration they welcomed to the table the rising eco-nomic powers, particularly Russia, China, India, and Brazil, into what became in 2008 the G-20. But the wealthy economies continued to dominate decisions on matters critical to the international economy whether in the World Bank, the IMF, or the WTO or in regular leadership meetings. In the globalized order as before, the developed world set the rules and interpreted them so that multinational cor-porations and international finance might roam freely while fixing states and democratic movements in an iron cage of neoliberal rules.

President Bill Clinton in the United States and Prime Minister Tony Blair in the UK, both leaders of nominally left-leaning parties, reflected the emergence of a pro-market consensus that was at heart Anglo-American. In their policies and pro-nouncements they proved worthy successors of Ronald Reagan and Margaret Thatcher. Labor unions were impediments to economic efficiency. Government should be slimmed down by turning functions over to the private sector. Keynes-ian ideas about government intervention in the economy were outmoded. Financial markets would operate better if freed from the burden of regulation. Dismantling welfare programs would spur the indigent to greater individual effort. Any problem of inequality could be left to the market to work out. Leaders in Washington and London were insistent that these neoliberal "best practices" had application to the wider world no less than at home.

This globalized economy that neoliberals helped shape had a distinct geography defined by urban centers tightly tied to the international circuit of trade and finance. Usually listed in the first tier were New York, Chicago, and Los Angeles in North America; London and Paris within the European Union (EU); and Tokyo, Hong Kong, and Singapore in Asia. These critical nodes of intense economic activity with their rich capital and intellectual resources were linked to each other and to lower-tier urban nodes by a dense network of cheap transport and rapid electronic communications over which moved the products of leading multinational corporations. Such products were less and less manufactured goods for mass consumption and more and more innovative financial services such as accounting, advertising, legal support, telecommunications, insurance, and securities. These cities hosted corporate headquarters and boasted a highly specialized, skilled, mobile, and well-paid workforce with the transcultural skills critical to navigating the rapid and diverse interurban flow. These skills included a command of English, critical in finance as well as science and technology, plus one or more other languages. From these sites, the goods, services, and values of the neoliberal order spread from Europe and North America into the maritime periphery of the developing world.

The life of a T-shirt provides a window on an intricate system of global production that even in the case of a humble, low-tech product knit together far-flung people and places. Imagine it originating in the cotton fields of a highly mechanized west Texas farm that could produce half a million pounds of cotton a year, enough for about 1.3 million T-shirts. The Texas cotton might then take a long trip to Shanghai in a country that by 1993 had become the largest apparel-exporting country and that by 2007 accounted for nearly a third of the world's total. There an actual T-shirt appeared after a labor-intensive process of spinning the Texas cotton into yarn, knitting the yarn into cloth, cutting the cloth into pieces, and sewing the pieces together. Once complete with a screen-printed image, it might end up as one of the items sold to a U.S. distributor for a couple of dollars. Even after it was sold, used, and finally discarded, our T-shirt might well have an afterlife as part of a stream of clothing and worn textile products going into a fluid, fast-moving global market. American consumers who discarded clothing on a profligate scale were the main source for the small operators who collected, sorted, and sold it. The United States was the leading world exporter, with sub-Saharan African markets the main destination.[5]

The trade in used T-shirts, like other aspects of globalization, had distinct winners. Geofrey Milonge was one of them. He had left his village to seek his fortune in Dar es Salaam, the capital of Tanzania. He started small as a *mitumba* trader, buying on credit small bundles of T-shirts, which he peddled on the sidewalk. He learned the tricks of the trade—how to sort through a *mitumba* (Swahili for the bundles of plastic-wrapped clothes) and spot profitable items. He knew that male customers liked the names of sports teams or brand names like Nike or Reebok, and they had to pay more because foreign men, who bought fewer clothes than foreign women, discarded fewer items and fewer still free of the signs of long and hard wear. Milonge's women customers were interested in items that they recognized as stylish from the media. Large sizes poorly suited to African frames were worth less. Milonge would wash, iron, and neatly lay out the promising items in his stall, one of hundreds in the main market. Although his profit on items that sold for a couple of dollars was small, by 2008 Milonge had managed to acquire seven shops and had branched into importing and real estate. His business now took him abroad and required that he master English.

To focus only on commerce and capital is to miss the broad impact of globalization. It has also served as a conduit for culture and knowledge and thus shaped consciousness. Globalization has thus been a good deal more than about promoting brands and encouraging borrowing and spending. Consider the rise of soccer as a sport with genuinely worldwide appeal. The 2010 World Cup final had almost a billion people watching their TV sets, while three times that number tuned in at some point to the games played in the host country, South Africa. (The preliminary audience count for the 2014 World Cup in Brazil was even higher.) Think about the thriving international cinema, which offers a space for the imagination that transcends nationality in its conception and consumption. An inspired Iranian director such as Abbas Kiarostami is hardly unusual. He established his international reputation on the basis of work done in his home country and then moved abroad to make movies in Italy and then Japan to be seen around the world. Popular music was no less global. Hip-hop, with its African and Jamaican roots, traveled far from its home in urban America and became a vehicle for expressing all sorts of cultural and political concerns in places as diverse as Tel Aviv and Tokyo. Higher education also bears the distinct mark of globalization with its MOOCs (massive open online courses), its booming study-abroad programs, and its proliferating branch campuses overseas. Even the worrisome realm of weapons of mass destruction has felt the effects. The neoliberal world with its porous borders has made it easier than ever for clandestine operatives and skilled technicians to carry sensitive information, technology, and materials and thus to dramatically expand the number of states with the capability to build and deliver an atomic bomb or a chemical or biological agent.

The Magic of the Market

New technologies applied within a world-spanning neoliberal economic and political order yielded impressive economic gains—just as neoliberals had promised (Table 10.1). Total gross domestic product (GDP) at the beginning of the new century (2003) was 2.5 times greater than in 1973, 8 times greater than at the start of the postwar period (1950), and 41 times larger than 1870 at the outset of the first era of globalization. World per capita income had dramatically increased despite the fact that there were many more people on the Earth. By 2010 it was almost double the figure in 1973 and nearly four times the immediate post–World War II

TABLE 10.1 More Wealth for More People, 1870–2010			
	World GDP (trillions of 1990 dollars)	World Population (billions)	World Per Capita GDP (1990 dollars rounded to nearest 100)
1870	1.1	1.3	900
1913	2.7	1.8	1,500
1950	5.3	2.5	2,100
1973	16.0	3.9	4,100
2003	40.9	6.3	6,500
2010	53.2	6.9	7,800

The increase in worldwide economic output since the late nineteenth century is striking, but so too has been population growth. Although the rate of population increase is slowing, it still has a momentum of its own that is likely to push the total number of humans on the planet to about nine billion by 2050. This would represent just short of a fourfold increase in less than a century. Whether the economy can keep up with the material needs of that larger population is a major question. On the answer hangs the prospects for social welfare and political stability, especially in the developing world, where the fertility rate is projected to be the highest.[6]

level. This performance in wealth creation was roughly on a par with the first era of globalization, which managed to almost double per capita GDP during the 43 years between 1870 and 1913. Behind all these dry data were lives that were longer, tables that were fuller, and work that was more rewarding. The cumulative effects of globalization over a century and a half, and especially over the past 40 years, were to raise living standards to levels unprecedented in human history and at a pace that was also unprecedented. Wealth opened amazing possibilities for people to work, travel, and have leisure, without the choking material limits long considered the natural fate for most inhabitants of the planet.

Underpinning postwar economic gains were steadily rising levels of trade and an accelerating pace of capital movement (Figs. 10.1 and 10.2). Global trade in 2013 ($4.7 trillion) was 10 times higher than it had been in 1980. Money was also on the move. Between 1970 and 2012, foreign direct investments in productive assets overseas increased 100 times (to $1.4 trillion). Sustaining this intense level of international economic activity, the daily (not annual) turnover in the markets for foreign exchange catapulted from about $15 billion in the 1970s to $5.3 trillion in 2013. The 1970s had marked the beginning of good times for international finance. High oil prices had resulted in large accumulations of petrodollars to invest. Banks and other financial entities in the United States and Europe offered good returns and in turn sought places to invest these funds. Some ended up in the developing world, while another part moved speculatively around the world.[7]

However eye-popping these trade and finance figures, they need to be seen in relation to the levels of a century ago so that we don't exaggerate the degree of global economic integration. One astute review concludes overall, "By most measures,

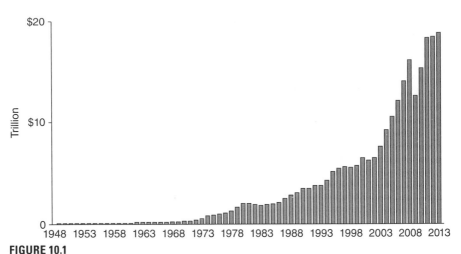

FIGURE 10.1
Global Trade, 1948–2013
Total exports (in US dollars at current prices and current exchange rate).[8]

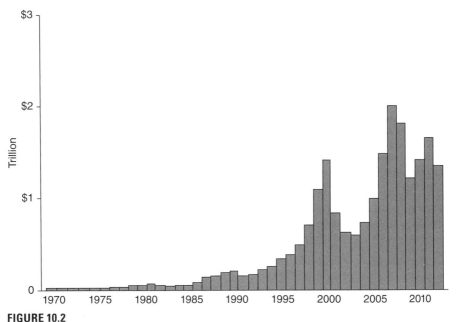

FIGURE 10.2
Global Foreign Investment, 1970–2012
Direct inward flows (in US dollars at current prices and current market exchange rates).[9]

today's world economy still does not match the integration of a century ago."[10] Trade despite its dramatic rise is still comparable to levels reached during the first era of globalization. The volume of trade is held down by the pick-and-choose nature of recent globalization compared to the first phase. Agricultural goods had in the earlier period moved freely. Not so in the postwar era: The very countries that have championed the principle of free trade have also insisted on protecting their farmers. The United States and the EU have both been especially resolute in shielding their agricultural sector. This one-sided approach has hit rural producers in developing economies particularly hard and finally paralyzed the most recent round of GATT negotiations on tariff reductions that began in 2001 (the so-called Doha Round). The poorer countries refused to make more concessions until their agricultural products could move freely into the markets of the rich countries.

Tanzania, where Milonge sold his secondhand T-shirts, illustrates the disadvantageous position into which the trade regime put developing countries. Cotton growers there could not compete with the Texas farmer who produced the cotton for our T-shirt. American cotton producers not only received generous federal and state support and university-based agricultural research; they were also shielded from direct foreign competition by federal regulations. Tons of cheap secondhand imported clothing arriving duty-free, whatever the gain to consumers, hurt economic development. IMF rescue packages—"structural adjustment programs"—had ended protections for established textile factories and thus eliminated one of the tried-and-true starting points for countries wanting to climb the industrial ladder to more capital-intensive, profitable production. Like a great river, the imports swept away the local textile producers. With the loss of each factory went thousands of job. "We've made the mistake of confusing the free market with development," observed a newspaper editor in neighboring Zambia. In the case of Milonge's Tanzania, which had swallowed the bitter pill of neoliberal reform in the 1990s, per capita GDP by 2013 was at the same level it had been three decades earlier.[11]

Further deflating the relative significance of latter-day global trade is the fact that only a small proportion of the output of today's most export-oriented economies actually goes abroad, and none of those economies sends goods abroad to the same degree as did the export leaders of the late nineteenth and early twentieth centuries. In addition, exports have tended in recent decades to travel from one developed country to another or within one region, such as the EU or East and Southeast Asia. In other words, trade is more intraregional than global and does not dominate national economies. In fact, only 20 percent of total global output of $36 trillion in 2003 was linked to exports.

Similarly, the impressive international financial figures should be taken with a grain of salt. Finance in the nineteenth and early twentieth centuries tightly linked British banks with a half-dozen financial centers on the European continent and with New York. The result was highly mobile capital that was more closely integrated than today. Moreover, investments today, like trade, tend to move in regional rather than global circuits, and for most countries the current levels of overseas investments do not exceed the high point during the first globalization era. In addition, much of the trillions of dollars on the move daily involves purely speculative plays on changing currency values and is in any case concentrated in its movement among the upper-income countries.

The overall achievements of the neoliberal era have to be weighed against the decelerating pace of international economic growth over the last half-century.

During the 1990s and into the new century, global growth has been a relatively low 1.0 percent annually overall, with a substantial number of countries suffering a decline in real income. This growth rate represents a steady drop from the recent past: 3.5 percent during the 1960s, 2.0 percent during the 1970s, and 1.2 percent during the 1980s. Whatever the reason, this decline puts in question the mantra that freer markets will deliver better growth. If rising world population is brought into the picture, the neoliberal promise becomes even more doubtful.

An even more fundamental problem in assessing the neoliberal performance is the narrow nature of GDP as a gauge of progress. GDP tells us about the output of goods and services but not about national welfare, social justice, human happiness, or hidden environmental costs. A variety of alternatives have been devised to broaden the conception of growth so that a distinction is made between how the economy is doing and how the people in it are doing. One of these is the social GDP, which includes on the plus side unpaid work in the home or by volunteers and deducts for loss of natural resources, ecological costs not built into conventional pricing, and damage to groups and communities inflicted by impersonal economic forces. A rough social GDP estimate makes economic growth look less impressive. For example, U.S. GDP per capita calculated along these broader lines was essentially flat from the late 1970s to 2004.[12] Another crude measure of progress that attempts to go beyond simple GDP calculations is the Human Development Index. Championed by the UN, it takes account of such indicators of social progress as education, health care, sanitation, nutrition, and environment to produce world rankings. A variety of subjective global "happiness indices" take another tack: They use surveys of popular attitudes to arrive at a more fine-grained sense of what money can't buy. These quality-of-life measures indicate that countries at the same GDP level can experience very different levels of overall welfare and that more GDP does not after a certain point translate into higher popular satisfaction. More things may not mean more happiness.

Finally, the neoliberal order has been strikingly one-sided in a way seldom mentioned. A world generally open to goods and services has been severely limited for workers. The recent immigration regime is decidedly restrictive in contrast to the relatively open, unhindered regime around the end of the nineteenth century. Since World War II nation states attractive to immigrants have closely policed their borders, accommodating only a limited number of newcomers, primarily those with needed skills or with family connections. For most poor people looking for opportunity to move to the developed world, the global economy is not so much open and integrated as sticky and obstructive.

While other parts of the global economy are recorded precisely to the dollar, migration numbers are exceedingly imprecise. Not every government has kept careful immigration records, and the statistics that are kept can vary in quality and kind from one to the next. A recent conservative estimate shows immigration slowly increasing after World War II, trending sharply upward from the late 1970s, and peaking in the mid-1990s even as trade and financial activity continued to rise. A 2009 estimate put those leaving the developing world for somewhere in the developed world at about five million immigrants a year out of a total of about six to seven million people on the move.[13]

What does seem certain is that postwar immigration pales by comparison with the first era of globalization at the end of the nineteenth century and the beginning of the twentieth. Figure 10.3 makes clear the difference in raw numbers, but those numbers need qualifying. Since the data provided here are based on passage across national boundaries, the increase in the number of states, from 54 in 1850 to 202 in 2008, has a decided inflationary effect on the count for the last half-century. The fact that there are more nations—for example, those that emerged from rapid decolonization during the 1960s and 1970s and from the collapse of the Soviet Union and Yugoslavia in the early 1990s—has meant more borders, which in turn results in counting more people who might earlier have simply been internal transplants. The relative importance of postwar migration diminishes further when measured as a percentage of a growing world population. The emigrant stream was smaller relative to total population in recent decades than a century ago. During the peak immigration year of 1913, the approximately 5.4 million people who moved across borders represented 3 percent of the world's population, while the recent peak figure of almost 8.8 million in 1994 was slightly less than 1 percent.

Formal immigration figures tell only part of the story of populations set in motion by recent globalization. An accurate count would include illegal immigration, although how many sneak across borders or overstay their visas is impossible to know. To round out our picture, we would need also to include peoples uprooted by humanitarian crisis who end up in a foreign country and, like conventional

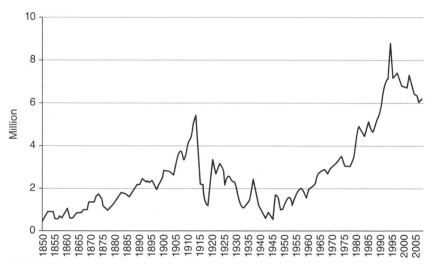

FIGURE 10.3
A Tale of Two Eras of Globalization: Migration across National Borders, 1850–2008
Based on statistics gathered by states on departures to another country[14]

immigrants, seek to make a life there or resettle somewhere else. At the end of 2013 those in flight from dire conditions at home—above all the crossfire of conflict, food insecurity, and infrastructure collapse—totaled nearly 17 million.[15]

No matter how dire their situation or how high the gamble, migrants knew that reaching one of the metropolises prospering under the influence of globalization would likely pay off. There they would have better access to gainful employment, education for their children, family medical care, and personal autonomy. Even if the work was menial—taking care of domestic chores, cleaning streets, serving food, selling trinkets, or doing casual construction work—migrants stood to raise almost at once their income level to a point many times higher than before. The flow of remittances, most often sent to family members in distant homelands, reveals the potential rewards of migration (Map 10.1). In 1980 the world total was $41.7 billion; by 2012 remittances had risen to $527.7 billion (with over two thirds going to developing economies).[16]

But moving carried a risk: An aborted passage or a period of detention could deplete limited resources and leave family members back home in the lurch. Were the transplanting process to go awry, it could extract a high material and emotional toll on both the migrant and the dependents at home. To diminish their risks, immigrants tended to travel in particular circuits between poor and rich countries that relatives or acquaintances were familiar with. For example, the poor beat a well-worn path connecting the Philippines to the oil-rich states of the Persian Gulf and to prosperous Hong Kong and Taiwan. They trekked from North Africa and Turkey to the more affluent economies of southern Europe and Germany. They moved from Mexico and Central America back and forth across the U.S. border.

The case of "Vicky Reyes," a Filipina domestic in Rome, illustrates how migration worked under relatively benign circumstances. While many Filipinos went abroad to support the family, Vicky was from the group that sought to escape personal problems (in her case a bad marriage). The price was to leave four children behind in the care of various relatives and give up a job as a registered nurse. She picked Italy, not her first choice, because she had two sisters settled there since the 1980s. They were part of a rapidly growing and well-networked Filipino community drawn by Italy's Catholic culture and worker safeguards. Without papers to get into the country legally, Vicky Reyes had to pay a "fixer" $6,400, which came from her savings and a loan from a sister. Smuggled through former Yugoslavia, she arrived in 1991 and thus became part of a massive Filipino diaspora. By then more

MAP 10.1 ➤

Remittances and the Developing World, 2014

Remittances have come to figure as an important source of national income in the economies of the developing world. For 2014 the worldwide total is estimated at $435 billion, more than three times official development assistance. This total has to be taken as a minimum since it reflects only officially recorded movement of funds. The map indicates the absolute value of remittances (expressed in billions of dollars) for the major regions and the relative share of GDP those remittances supply for the eight countries that most benefit within those regions.[17]

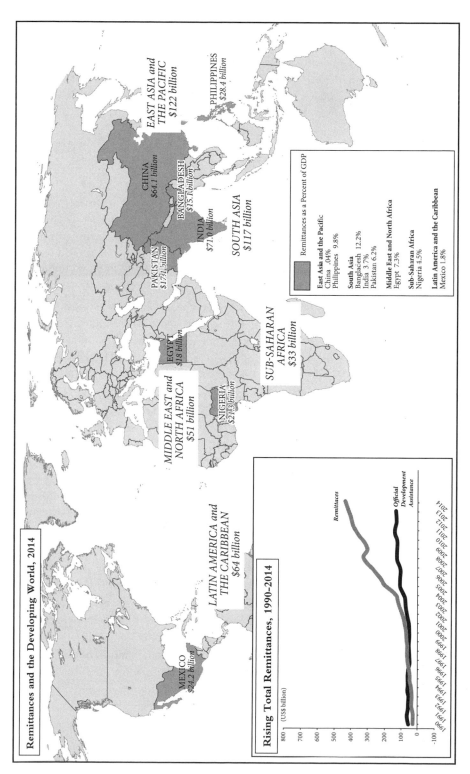

Remittances and the Developing World, 2014

EAST ASIA *and*
THE PACIFIC
$122 billion

PHILIPPINES
$28.4 billion

CHINA
$64.1 billion

BANGLADESH
$15.1 billion

INDIA
$71.0 billion

SOUTH ASIA
$117 billion

PAKISTAN
$17.1 billion

EGYPT
$18 billion

SUB-SAHARAN
AFRICA
$33 billion

NIGERIA
$21.3 billion

MIDDLE EAST *and*
NORTH AFRICA
$51 billion

LATIN AMERICA *and*
THE CARIBBEAN
$64 billion

MEXICO
$24.2 billion

Remittances as a Percent of GDP

East Asia and the Pacific
China .04%
Philippines 9.8%

South Asia
Bangladesh 12.2%
India 3.7%
Pakistan 6.2%

Middle East and North Africa
Egypt 7.3%

Sub-Saharan Africa
Nigeria 4.5%

Latin America and the Caribbean
Mexico 1.8%

Rising Total Remittances, 1990-2014

(US$ billion)

800
700
600
500
400
300
200
100
0
-100

Remittances

Official
Development
Assistance

1990 1991 1992 1993 1994 1995 1996 1997 1998 1999 2000 2001 2002 2003 2004 2005 2006 2007 2008 2009 2010 2011 2012 2013 2014

441

than half a million were leaving the Philippines annually (more than half women, and most of them like Vicky Reyes in domestic service). The pain of separation from her children—the youngest was two months old at the time of her departure—made the adjustment to new surroundings hard: "The first two years I felt like I was going crazy. . . . Every moment, every second of the day, I felt like I was thinking about my baby." Once established, she began sending back for her children's support $300 to $500 a month (about half of her income that fed into a stream of remittances by Filipinos amounting to roughly 10 percent of their country's GDP in the mid-1990s). She stayed in contact by regular phone calls home while dreaming of eventually reuniting with her children and moving to the United States or Canada, where she thought the economic opportunities for them were greatest. For her at least, the door of opportunity was closing. While the Philippines lost skilled workers like Vicky Reyes (most with a least some college-level education), the migrants settled for unskilled work abroad that earned them five or six times what most women made back home but that left them "stupid" (as another Filipina in Rome put it), with no new skills that could be applied once back in the Philippines.[18]

Even the poor who did not or could not join the international stream of labor gravitated toward prosperous cities integrated into global trade and finance. They moved from the countryside in numbers that not only made the flow of international migrants look puny but that also fundamentally altered the urban–rural balance in most developing countries. In 1975, 62 percent of the world's population lived in the countryside; by 2013 the number had fallen to 47 percent (although in absolute numbers the rural population had in the interim risen by nearly a billion as a result of overall population growth).[19] Tales of urban affluence conveyed by television, cellphones, and returning migrants helped to set hard-pressed peasants into motion. As villages emptied, the population of cities swelled. For example, Mexico City—to take one of the most dramatic examples of urban explosion—grew from a third of a million in 1900 to 21 million in 2013. Iranian villagers, like their Mexican counterparts, turned their back on limited opportunities in the countryside. They began swelling the shantytowns of major cities during the oil boom of the 1970s and by 2006 had pushed the population of Tehran to 8 million. China's poor rural interior supplied a migratory army of urban workers numbering in the tens of millions by the 1990s. Freed from Mao-era restrictions, they formed an army of second-class citizens moving among prosperous coastal cities thriving on export production, including the Shanghai factories that processed American cotton into T-shirts. They accepted the drudgery and regimentation of factory life in order to escape rural conditions that were still harder and for women more constricted.

This rural exodus—whether moving internationally or within national boundaries—resulted in an explosive growth of cities that was a prime feature of the new global era. In 1900 only 2 cities could claim at least 5 million inhabitants, but by 2000, 71 cities on the planet were at the 5 million mark or higher (with 5 of those reaching at least 20 million).[20] Southeast Asia offers a good illustration of the magnitude of this change wrought by this flight from the countryside. In 1910 the region had no cities with over half a million people, and by 1930 there was only one. By 1960 the number had grown to 8 and then by 1980 to 20, of which 12 had a population of over a million. The two largest of the region's booming cities, Bangkok in Thailand and Jakarta in Indonesia, had a population of a bit over half a million in 1945; 50 years later they were both in the range of 10 to 11 million. Today their populations are 14 million and 28 million respectively.

CREATION'S DESTRUCTIVE SIDE

The very process that spurred economic growth also had adverse effects. Globalization disrupted societies, set off recurrent financial crises, widened inequalities, undercut democracy, and poisoned the planet. This paradox was captured by the phrase "creative destruction" coined by the Austrian economist Joseph Schumpeter. Marketplace-induced innovation by definition imposed widespread disruption. Jobs changed, skills shifted, production moved, and investors sought better returns—all with a potent impact on social stability, individual welfare, and the political process. No less problematic, globalization in its neoliberal guise perpetuated disparities in wealth between the developing and the developed worlds. Those in the developed world benefited disproportionately from the system as consumers, producers, and investors. Finally, ever-higher levels of economic activity and living standards created deepening environmental dangers. Good evidence suggests that "creative destruction" was putting the planet in peril.

Disrupted Lives, Torn Societies, Hollow Politics

Globalization unleashed strong economic forces that carried human and social costs. These are most palpable in the experience of people on the move and above all in the millions caught up in the rural–urban transfer. Whether the move was within a country or from a developing to a developed country, the effects were disruptive. These shifts in population—almost invariably to cities—stripped villages of healthy young men and young, unmarried women. Their departure tore the social fabric of villages, leaving wives, young children, and the elderly behind to struggle to preserve the tattered threads of economic and social life amidst a diminished circle of kin and compatriots. Hardship was also the fate of rural folk arriving in cities already swollen with the rural poor seeking economic opportunities. In general, peasants in the city had no capital and only rudimentary skills to draw on. Unemployment rates could be high. Many jobs were low-paying. Basic services (running water, sewage, waste disposal, electricity, education, and public health) were lacking. Housing on the neglected margins of city life was rudimentary and sometimes perilous. Rio de Janeiro serves as a current example: About a fifth of its population of six million live in several hundred settlements (*favelas*) situated on steep, neglected land largely beyond the control and services of city authorities.

The lucky migrant would find a job on production lines in the export sector. Work in the global factory system meant distinctly better income, but the gains came at a cost. Factory owners, themselves under intense price pressures as sub-contractors to global firms searching for the best deal, worked their employees hard and cut corners on health and safety. Local government regulations were weak, and officials often sided with management. As a result, conditions in assembly plants or in textile mills were often poor, hours were long, and the risks of injury were high. The worst consequences are evident in a string of disasters that struck Bangladesh garment factories. In April 2005, one collapsed, killing 75 workers. In February 2006, another collapsed, killing 18. In June 2010, a third collapsed, killing 25. In November 2012, a factory fire killed at least 112 workers. The worst event came in April 2013, when 1,100 workers died and approximately 2,500 were injured in the collapse of a garment factory that produced for internationally famous name brands. The same story of death and injury has been repeated since the 1990s in factories that have sprung up as part of the global supply chain along the U.S.–Mexico border, in Haiti, in Sri Lanka, and in other places where rural workers agreed to produce cheap products under deplorable conditions while multinational firms and their affluent customers turned a blind eye.

Migrants who had to cross international borders faced the greatest difficulties. The illegals put their savings and very lives at risk in dangerous journeys in overcrowded boats or across treacherous terrain. Those who were successful in that perilous passage faced discrimination that made their prospects even more precarious. The illegals had to live in the shadows, with no recourse against swindlers, thieves, or unethical employers. Whether illegal or not, newcomers ran the constant risk that local sentiment would turn against them. The charges lodged against them were well worn: They depressed wages; they burdened social welfare services; they spread crime and disease. Perhaps the most volatile of all the charges was that they carried values threatening to the host country's identity and social cohesion. France offers a good example of this backlash. Openings in low-skilled, low-paying jobs had drawn millions of North Africans to France during the 1950s and 1960s. These newcomers began to change the ethnic composition of some cities such as Marseilles, and their high birthrate meant they would be a growing presence well into the future. The number of practicing Muslims began to catch up with those who were practicing Catholics, and controversy arose over cultural practices such as schoolgirls' headscarves and female circumcision. Right-wing nationalists such as the French politician Jean-Marie Le Pen and later his daughter Marine Le Pen charged that these outsiders threatened France's national identity. The antipathy to migrants became a *leitmotif* of European politics, especially as fear of radical Islam intensified early in the new century and as national economies experienced downturns after 2008.

If immigrants were like a glacier that reshaped the landscape as it crept along, global finance could behave more like a tsunami. Capital movements were often connected not to the production of real goods and services but to currency or securities speculation The masters of finance prowled the globe seeking quick returns. Investors might flock to a country with attractive yields and then flee as the speculative bubble started to pop or suddenly redirect their interest to some other more attractive investment target. A preoccupation with short-term yields made the financial sector a fickle and for some dangerous source of capital. Once doubtful about the prospects for a particular currency, stock market, or country, investors could retreat with blinding speed and set financial and stock markets crashing. The resulting retreat of capital could capsize small economies and threaten large ones.

Instability had been part of globalization from its modern inception, but in its latest phase financial crises became more commonplace. Mexico, burdened by bad debts and attacked by speculators, set off an international debt crisis in 1982. The global stock market crash of October 1987 created far-reaching alarm. Mexico succumbed again in 1994. A full-blown crisis hit Asia in 1997. A panicked retreat by investors from Thailand spread within the region, with South Korea, Thailand, and Indonesia falling especially hard. Indonesia rapidly lost over half of its GDP. As foreigners sold off their stakes, regional stock markets and currencies lost 30 to 70 percent of their value within a year, and unemployment doubled or tripled in Indonesia, Thailand, South Korea, Malaysia, Hong Kong, and Singapore. South Korea's GDP fell by a third.[21] From Asia financial troubles spread to Russia, Brazil, Argentina, and Turkey. More recently, Greece was the first in a string of countries in southern Europe that toppled like dominoes after financial pressures escalated. They submitted to a prolonged bout of austerity rather than affront the financial market.

The capacity of states to resist the financial herd was limited. Developing countries were more vulnerable to the rapid and unhindered transfer of funds than their more affluent cousins, cushioned by their larger economies and by the resources at the disposal of their central banks to respond to sharp swings in financial markets. But financial speculation gone wrong could bring even the rich down. The 2008 global financial crisis began in U.S. investment houses ostensibly constrained by market forces and calculations of self-interest. They nonetheless embraced lucrative but complex mortgage-based investments that their leaders barely understood. Few saw that they had built a house of cards, and fewer still realized how deeply damaging the collapse would prove. Alan Greenspan, the former head of the U.S. Federal Reserve revered by neoliberals for his free-market views, confessed in October 2008, in the face of financial collapse, "Those of us who have looked to self-interest of leading institutions to protect shareholders' equity, myself included, are in a state of shocked disbelief."[22] Governments that sought to curb or defy foreign investors found themselves facing a "capital strike." Investors quickly wound up their accounts one place and moved their money elsewhere. Politicians with a financial gun to their heads then faced a hard choice: Accede to the investment community's demands or risk plunging their economies into crisis. The smaller the economy, the greater the vulnerability and the deeper the potential damage.

Once political leaders acceded, as they almost invariably did, their countries faced a cure that was as bad as the disease. The IMF and other international agencies, backed by private international bankers and the political leaders in the G-7, arrived in the troubled country as the healers. Their prescription was thoroughly neoliberal: cuts in government economic regulation and spending on social programs, privatization of state-owned industry, and greater openness to foreign trade and investment. These so-called structural adjustment programs reduced sovereignty to a shadow and imposed the greatest pain on women and poor families, who lost education, health care, food, and housing. Countries subject to these cures often failed to see the promised economic recovery and in any case resented the heavy-handed outsiders. While South Korea quickly regained its footing, South Koreans still groused that the price of their $60 billion rescue package concluded in December 1997 was a humiliating IMF makeover of their economy. After the IMF bailout of Thailand, one newspaper there grumbled that the terms were "a subtle triumph of U.S. financial imperialism," while another warned against "economic colonialism" developing as a result of this outside intervention.[23]

The propensity of the financial world to take risks has only increased in recent years within the major centers of finance thanks to the demonstrated willingness of governments to rescue them from investments gone seriously bad. The solvency of major banks became linked in the thinking of policymakers with the welfare of the broader economy. A relatively limited number of financial institutions had, in other words, secured such a commanding strategic position that they could pursue profitable deals, however risky, confident that states would bail them out rather than chance an economic meltdown. They had become (in the phrase popularized in 2008) "too big to fail." Profit was private; risk was social.

Less dramatic but no less damaging than social displacement and financial upheaval has been the growing power of corporate and financial entities to narrow democratic choice, to undercut local autonomy, and to capture or escape state oversight. Corporations that were multinational—in other words, had production and distribution scattered across many countries in a complex network—were formidable mobile giants. The pioneering nineteenth-century multinationals were in

A CRISIS-PRONE INTERNATIONAL ECONOMY

1980s	Debt crisis in Latin America (Argentina, Bolivia, Brazil, Chile, Colombia, Ecuador, Mexico, Paraguay, Peru, and Venezuela) spreads to Africa (Ivory Coast, Nigeria, and Morocco)
1994–95	Mexico plunges into crisis, U.S.-led rescue operation.
1997–98	Crisis in Thailand spreads to Indonesia, Malaysia, Philippines, and eventually South Korea and Russia. IMF steps in with bailouts.
2001–02	Argentina in crisis again along with Russia. IMF demands provoke popular resistance and political deadlock.
2008–12	Panic on Wall Street plunges U.S. economy into worst recession in the postwar period that spreads to the EU; Greece, Spain, Portugal, and Italy are hit hard. IMF demands austerity.

trade and resource extraction. They then branched out into manufacturing and more recently financial and other services. The recent growth of multinationals has been explosive—from 7,300 in 1969 to 63,000 in 2000.[24] So too their economic heft. The top 50 exceeded most nations in output; Exxon Mobil and Walmart each generated more income than Austria. But unlike any nation, the multinationals had the option of picking up and moving depending on labor costs, resource availability, tax laws, and changing consumer demands.

In this world of predatory finance and mobile multinationals, national electorates have lost substantial control over the direction of their economies. In the prevailing neoliberal order, a hyperactive state and "do-good" politicians are seen as the enemy, while popular choice on matters of consumption (of course guided by advertising) is regarded as an unalloyed good and a fundamental right. That choice does not extend to policies that might violate the neoliberal rules of the game or restrict the freedom of its major economic players. As a result, electorates may vote for whomever they please, but their hands are tied on the big issues of industrial policy, protection of unions, capital control, environmental safeguards, and job protection. Democracy remains formally intact but in many respects becomes a hollow shell. Shareholder fixation with returns trumps public goods. Thus, for example, corporate leaders can offload the environmental costs of their operations and let someone else address the damage. Similarly, CEOs can move production overseas without having to worry about political backlash or the hemorrhaging of jobs that can over time destroy families and neighborhoods, diminish social mobility, and slow overall domestic economic growth.

Corporate capacity to run roughshod over local objections expressed itself in a variety of ways all over the world. The eruption of opposition to McDonald's (discussed in the Introduction to Part Three) was a preview of controversy that corporations both created and quelled. As in the case of the Golden Arches, popular criticism caused the economic giants to pause before continuing their advance. In the EU a campaign against genetically modified food led by French farmer-activist José Bové collided with the WTO. The French government fell into line, having little choice but to enforce free trade agreements whatever the cost. Nigeria offers an even more blatant example of corporations running roughshod. A half-century of Shell operations in the Niger Delta, including oil spills, gas flaring, and dumping of waste, had despoiled the landscape while also draining the region's wealth without local benefit. Leaders of the Ogoni people, a million or so longtime residents of the area, organized protests in the early 1990s. A corrupt military government heavily dependent on oil revenues from this prime area of production responded with displays of armed force, arrests, show trials, and executions, including the hanging in 1995 of one of the protest leaders, playwright Ken Saro-Wiwa. Shell profited handsomely; not so the Ogoni, despite international condemnation directed at both the government and the oil company.

The critics of a world cut to corporate dimensions have sounded a common set of themes. They opposed a world emptied of spiritual and collective meaning in which market forces and market metaphors shaped society and individual consciousness. They insisted that the environment had significance far greater than the bottom line. They refused to see people's lives as merely a set of monetary transactions attended by reveries of an endless stream of shiny products and "indispensable" services. They attacked the tendency to deny labor intrinsic social value. They decried as spiritual deserts societies that conceived themselves as little more than the sum of their production and consumption. These views raised fundamental questions about the nature of a good society and the value of a corporate- and market-defined life.

The Specter of Inequality

The gap between rich and poor has emerged as a second kind of problem generated by the international economy. It was already a simmering issue in the early postwar decades (see Chapter 5), but inequality has risen in prominence as globalization has gathered force, animating critics and setting off controversy. Out of the reams of data and the multiplicity of approaches to analyzing them emerge some patterns that might be best treated as a map of privilege and poverty.[25] The broadest view is that of the global population as a whole, with the best recent generalizations based on household surveys conducted from the 1980s onward. They reveal high levels of inequality, with the richest 10 percent claiming over half of the global income (51.5 percent in 1988 and 55.5 percent in 2005) and the remaining 90 percent taking the rest.

Within this broad generalization lurk some important variations. Inequality viewed globally was not a simple matter of those at the top extending their advantage over those at the bottom. Three groups were the main winners over the two decades between 1988 and 2008. One was the top 1 percent (about 60 million people, mostly in Western Europe, North America, and Japan) and to a lesser degree the top 5 percent. That top 5 percent enjoyed an income gain of more than 60 percent over two decades. Also winners was an emerging global middle class (notably 200 million Chinese, 90 million Indians, and 30 million each from Indonesia, Brazil, and Egypt). The third group to benefit was the bottom third of the global income distribution, who experienced a jump in real income ranging from over 40 percent up to nearly 70 percent. This gain reduced the percentage of absolute poor (those living on a dollar a day by the World Bank definition) from 44 to 23 percent. The major losers were the poorest 5 percent, whose income was unchanged, and also perhaps surprisingly the global upper-middle class (those between the 75th and 90th percentile, i.e., the affluent near but not at the top), whose income stagnated. This last group was located above all in rich countries, in Latin America, and in former Communist countries going through the throes of economic transition.

Another way to trace the contour lines of inequality is to compare the distance between the low-income and high-income regions in recent decades (Fig. 10.4). Between 1980 and 2010 that gap remained roughly the same. This leveling off may

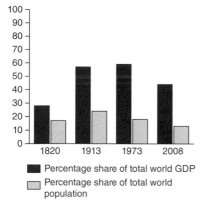

FIGURE 10.4

Concentration of Wealth in the Developed World, 1820–2008

■ Percentage share of total world GDP
▢ Percentage share of total world population

The developed world is defined here as western Europe, the western European offshoots (the United States, Canada, Australia, and New Zealand), and Japan.[26]

mark the end of a long-term trend of the developed world gaining and maintaining a long lead over the developing world. The Euro-American economies centered on the North Atlantic, together with Japan, came to constitute a privileged club thanks to high growth rates during the nineteenth and early twentieth century that doubled the share of the world's wealth under their control. They preserved their advantage into the twenty-first century, even as their relative share of the world's population shrank. Rapid growth in China and to a lesser degree in India is the main reason for the leveling off of inequality in recent decades and may fore-shadow a return to a regional distribution closer to what prevailed before the first era of globalization.

But for the moment at least the inequalities among regions remain large. While in absolute terms latecomers to economic development generally managed to im-prove their conditions during the most recent, post-World War II phase of global-ization so that each generation lived better than the previous one, in relative terms low or uneven economic growth left much of the developing world ever farther behind. Parts of Latin America lost ground during the financial crises of the 1980s (the "lost decade"). So too did countries in Eastern Europe and the former Soviet Union during the 1990s as they suffered a rocky transition to a more market-oriented economy.

Sub-Saharan Africa was the most troubled of all the regions. Over three decades (from 1980 to 2010) GDP per capita increased a paltry $59 from $594 to $653. Average per capita GDP in 2010 was one fourteenth of that in the EU and a twenti-eth of that in the United States. Even as the economy stagnated, population was rising the fastest of any region in the world. Sub-Saharan Africa's population of 0.9 billion in 2014 was projected to increase to 2.3 billion by 2050. All the recent measures of well-being testified to the consequences of pervasive, stubborn pov-erty. Life expectancy at birth was stunningly low (54 years in 2010), with only small gains over the previous 30 years (the lowest in the developing world). Child mortality in sub-Saharan Africa accounted for more than two thirds of all child deaths worldwide. Malnutrition was more acute than in any region except South

Asia. It was the home of half of the 57 million children worldwide not enrolled in school in 2011. Conditions in cities, where slum dwellers constituted 62 percent of the population, were singularly unfavorable, and adult mortality actually rose from the 1990s to late 2000s. Behind these doleful numbers on material deprivation and disease was a failure of states to supply even basic services such as clean water, electricity, transportation, public health systems, and public security all essential to human welfare.[27]

The global economic gap translated into glaring contrasts—pervasive suffering in places and general comfort in others. On the one side millions were chronically hungry. Malnourishment was the fate of more than 800 million people according to the most recent (2014) UN count.[28] Children suffered an especially high death toll, especially those without safe drinking water, adequate sanitation, and crucial vaccinations that left them vulnerable to diseases. Countries and regions on the short end of the development stick had no meaningful role in global governance, were captive to a sometimes disastrously fickle international economic system run by outsiders, and despaired of realizing the dreams associated with the early postwar years of decolonization. This last spiritual loss is as serious as the material setbacks. Genuine independence and prosperity, a domestic regime of social justice, and an end to foreign dominance had once seemed achievable. But by the end of the twentieth century these goals were beyond the reach of much of the world's population.

On the other side, the developed world retained its considerable privilege, with its wealthiest members controlling astounding assets. A handful of the super-rich individuals could claim income equal to the combined annual income of several billion of the world's poorest. Even the poorest in the developed world lived far better than most in the developing world. Countries within the circle of privilege had a commanding voice in international governance, maintained substantial control over their own internal affairs, and had some hope of realizing cherished goals particular to their societies.

Yet a third perspective on inequality comes from looking within countries. The divide between rich and poor so evident globally and regionally is apparent here too, although once more with notable variations. Developed countries with few exceptions watched internal divisions widen significantly between 1990 and 2012. So too did some of the large developing countries, accounting for two thirds of the world population. This rising inequality was in both cases substantially due to those at the top capturing more income. For example, in the United States, the top 22 percent gained control of half, leaving the other half to the remaining 78 percent of the population. Joining the United States on the list of the countries with the highest levels of inequality were Argentina, South Africa (higher since the end of apartheid), and the United Kingdom. Even more traditionally egalitarian countries such as Germany, Denmark, and Sweden have seen inequality grow. Asian countries, which began the recent phase of globalization with relatively low income inequality, have also seen the gaps among their people widen. China stands out for the way the economy and inequality have grown together. On the other hand, 14 of 20 Latin American countries narrowed their income gaps, including Brazil, which has long had one of the world's widest gaps. Those that have had success in closing inequalities have followed a fairly clear formula that is anathema to neoliberal purists. The key has been making the state the engine for welfare as well as development. Rather than giving the market free rein, the activist state has not only set industrial policy but also made provision for public goods, including expanded educational access, infrastructure investments, social insurance against economic instability inherent in a mobile, integrated world, minimum wage requirements to protect the poor, and protection for labor organizations.

Yet a fourth way of seeing the inequality problem is to map it from a rural–urban perspective. A group of major cities stretching around the world formed the backbone of global privilege. The privileged were to be found within urban outposts of the modern global economy. As they assumed the lifestyle of their overseas counterparts, they became increasingly divorced from the sentiments of their less privileged countrymen. Rural residents, by contrast, had less access to education, health care, and basic services such as safe drinking water, adequate sanitation, transportation, and communications. Given the importance of education to narrowing inequality, it is significant that rural children were nearly twice as likely to be out of school as urban children. These differences show up in gross terms: People living in the countryside around the world in 2002 accounted for 75 percent of those in extreme poverty, even though they constituted only 52 percent of the world population.

The sources of this growing income and wealth gap were much the same both within countries and among them. In general, the higher the educational level, the more disproportionate the rewards. The less skilled did not have a place in the most productive and high-paying sectors of the national and global economy. For countries at the top or on their way up, technology played an increasingly important part in raising productivity and maintaining international competitiveness. Scientific research was a critical part of the process, and general basic education was essential for a productive workforce. To sustain technical progress, the high achievers constantly built up their physical capital, including plants, schools, and communications systems, and workers regularly upgraded their skills. When the elements critical to success came together in a stable, sustained way, they set in motion a reinforcing cycle of productivity and plenty.

Developing countries too often found themselves trapped in a vicious cycle that doomed any drive to catch up with the developed world. Illiteracy was commonplace, thus rendering the workforce better suited to the export of raw materials or agricultural products than to technologically driven production. As we saw in Chapter 9, women were often not able to fulfill their economic potential, and swelling population put pressure on existing resources. Ethnic or class divisions like those in Guatemala, Nigeria, and India fed a sense of economic and social injustice and prevented the emergence of any kind of national consensus on promoting economic competitiveness and hence national welfare. Often these divided countries suffered from weak governments that failed to create critical economic infrastructure and from corruption, political instability, social violence, insecure property rights, and ineffectual commercial codes. In these cases, those with the greatest needs had the fewest resources to work with and thus the dimmest prospects for building a better life.

An Environment under Stress

The most dangerous consequences stemming from globalization have been mounting environmental dangers and the prospect of catastrophe. Those dangers have increased in direct relation to expanding population, rising standards of living worldwide, and the almost universal appeal of a consumer lifestyle. In 1990 industrial output was 40 times higher than a century earlier; energy use had increased by a factor of 16, carbon dioxide emissions by a factor of 17. Overall water use was nine times greater, driven in part by a quadrupling of irrigated area. Thirty-five times more fish were being caught at the same time that bird and mammal species and forest area decreased. These trends persisted into the new century and in most cases accelerated. Those in the developing world tasting for the first time real prosperity combined with the already affluent in the developed world to push the Earth's resources to the limits. Producers treated the environment as a dump, while consumers addicted to a way of life abetted this tendency by demanding more and more goods at the lowest possible price heedless of the hidden costs. Under this arrangement, waste byproducts have accumulated in the commons—in the rivers, lakes, seas, atmosphere, and landfills. As one environmental historian has put it, "Humankind has begun to play dice with the planet without knowing all the rules of the game."[29]

Some of the end-of-century environmental problems were essentially regional in nature. In the more developed and the high-growth developing economies, one of the most serious was the accumulation of toxic contaminants. They fouled ground, air, and water. In the developing world, land-hungry peasants, ranchers, loggers, and plantation owners cleared mountainsides and rainforests. Since the 1970s some 40 percent of rainforests have been lost, thus damaging soil, reducing species diversity, imperiling indigenous cultures, and feeding CO_2 into the atmosphere. Only three great blocks of forests and woodlands remain—in northern North America, in northern Europe and Siberia, and in the Orinoco and Amazon basins in South America—and the last of these is under steady human assault.[30]

Environmental stress was also beginning to manifest itself in global terms. One was declining biodiversity, as species disappeared at a rate far higher than at any time in the recent past. Farming and logging were destroying rich forest habitats, and unregulated harvesting drove economically valuable wild plants and animals to the brink of extinction. The factory-like production of genetically altered crops added to the threat to ecological diversity and raised the specter of catastrophic food shortages if one dominant strain were to fail. Climate change was also a danger, putting in peril areas of habitat on which particular species depended. Scientists warned that the extinction of a wide range of plants and animals would

Amazon Rainforest Burning, 1983
The human figure in the foreground gives a sense of the scale of destruction inflicted by human encroachment on an invaluable natural resource. This photo captures a commonplace scene: the burning to clear land for cattle pasture. Within a few years tropical rains will erode the ground and leach the nutrients, leaving the environment depleted, the pasture valueless, and ranchers looking for new habitat to clear. (© R. Bierregaard, 1983)

create imbalances in nature with consequences that were hard to predict for the web of life of which humans are a part. They also warned against the loss of species whose value to humans could not be foreseen; for example, a yet-undiscovered wild plant might have life-saving pharmacological properties. Finally and more broadly, proponents of diversity pointed to species loss as evidence of an arrogant human assertion of dominance over the natural world. They suggested that all species have a right to survival and that humans had an obligation to leave the Earth no poorer for their descendants.

Ozone depletion commanded wide attention as well. Chlorofluorocarbons (CFCs), used in refrigerators, air conditioning, aerosol sprays, and industrial cleaning agents, rose into the upper atmosphere, where they broke down ozone molecules and allowed ultraviolet radiation, harmful to plants as well as animals, to more easily penetrate to the surface of the Earth. Developed in the 1930s by General Motors and Du Pont, these ozone-destroying compounds had been heralded as some of the most useful ever invented. But scientists now proclaimed them a deadly threat to life on the planet's surface. An international protocol signed in 1987 began to limit the production of destructive compounds and gave impetus to the development of alternatives. While ozone levels have on the whole stabilized and may in decades recover, radiation levels remain dangerously high in places.

Finally, and most serious of all, the Earth was suffering from global warming (also known as the greenhouse effect) caused by burning coal, oil, and natural gas to meet rising energy demands. These fossil fuels yielded carbon dioxide (CO_2) and sulfur along with various metals, which accumulated in the air and trapped heat created by the play of infrared radiation from the sun on the Earth's surface. Methane (produced in significant quantities by domestic livestock and rice paddies) and CFCs were additional sources of greenhouse gas. Computer models of global warming trends yielded a nightmare scenario. As the average temperature inched toward the highest point in 10,000 years, glaciers would melt, raising the sea level, inundating coastal areas inhabited by an estimated one billion people, and altering ocean currents. Rising temperatures would also introduce greater variations in climate patterns and increase rainfall. The risk was thus high for serious disruption of agricultural production, with horrendous results for global food supply. The long-term stakes were incredibly high. An environmental scientist with an eye for the big picture has put it this way: "Global warming could be one of humankind's longest-lasting legacies."[31]

Increasingly dire and confident predictions came from the Intergovernmental Panel on Climate Change, an authoritative international body of several thousand leading scientists in multiple disciplines operating under the auspices of the United Nations. Its assessments were inherently conservative because of the consensus-based process of reaching conclusions, and its reports necessarily lagged several years behind the latest peer-reviewed research findings. Even so, skeptics questioned the scientific evidence and its interpretation. Was global warming the result of human activity or fluctuations within a normal temperature range? How was it possible to predict with any accuracy the impact of rising temperatures on a climate system as complex as the Earth's? These doubts, reinforced most potently in the United States, Russia, and China by popular attitudes, collided with the increasing confidence of the scientific community in their alarmist findings.[32]

To mounting environmental threats in the new era of rapid globalization, a neoliberal approach can offer only partial solutions. The demand-driven increase in prices for some goods has prompted conservation as well as the search for new supplies and alternatives. Thus, feared scarcities of fossil fuels, minerals, timber, and food have not materialized. But can environmental protection meet the magnitude of the challenge unless governments impose constraints on the market, for example by insisting that producers or consumers cover the true cost of exploiting the environment? The ultimate barrier to effective action may be less neoliberal assumptions than the headlong consumer drive. The very fact that so many people are now on the growth escalator, wanting ever more goods, raises profound questions not just about how to protect the environment but how to organize societies now in the grip of powerful material aspirations. The consumer society as a culture, an ideology, and an economic system may well be unsustainable in the long run, and its foundational notion that income will rise constantly across a lifetime and from generation to generation is probably outmoded. As noted earlier, GDP may no longer be a good gauge of progress. Not only may attachment to GDP growth be self-destructive in the impossible demands it makes on the Earth's resources and in the peril it places on the planet, but it may also not serve consumers themselves well. As recent studies suggest, after a certain point, higher levels of income do not yield higher levels of individual happiness.

SAVING PEOPLE AND THE PLANET

Globalization, at least in its neoliberal version, promised a steadily improving international order, but its claims were challenged from two directions. On the one side were sins of commission. As critics were pointing out with increasing frequency and intensity by the late 1990s, unchecked globalization did serious damage that had to be addressed. The growing activism called to mind the "double movement" that Karl Polanyi described for the late nineteenth century as the damaging effects of globalization provoked a popular backlash. On the other side were sins of omission—long-term problems such as intrastate and interstate violence that the neoliberal faith in practice paid little attention.

Those bent on creating a global order that was more humane and sustainable were not easily pigeon-holed politically. When the French conservative Charles Pasqua denounced globalization in 1999 as a nice-sounding term that was in fact "this new totalitarianism of our time," it was hard to tell which end of the political spectrum he came from.[33] Moreover, the advocates for the global community could claim a long pedigree. The effort to write rules of conduct and to address problems outside the scope of any one country or even region can be traced back to the first phase of globalization in the late nineteenth and early twentieth centuries when conferences and treaties addressed such concerns as the law of the sea, terms for the conduct of civilized warfare, and the protection of minorities. The process gained increased attention and legitimacy after World War II. In the last several decades this effort to ameliorate international life gathered significant force and breadth, spurred by an ever-more-tightly integrated world. The very integration that globalization created has facilitated a sustained and complex international conversation in which no issue has loomed larger than human rights and the environment.

Agents of Reform

A diverse set of players took up the cause of a more secure, equitable, and humane international order. Of these, national governments were the oldest and best established. They had played a central role in channeling globalization, and they could also limit its damage, although how much they were prepared to do varied considerably from case to case. The divergence among countries—from those in favor of full-throttle neoliberalism to those profoundly doubtful—meant that truly international reform would move ahead slowly and selectively, always the subject of difficult negotiations. International organizations, especially those attached to the

UN, had a shorter pedigree, a narrower mandate, and a thinner power base, but they could point to a record of considerable success of reform. Finally, the newcomers to the task of protecting people and the planet were a motley crew of surprisingly effective nongovernmental organizations (NGOs) often acting in concert with social movements. From this striking variety of directions came a broad range of initiatives to curb the process of globalization unfolding under the neoliberal aegis.

Governments were as much as ever the first line of defense against the damage globalization could do. All the talk of once-sovereign states rendered impotent in the new age does not stand up to scrutiny. They retained the power to mitigate, resist, and redirect globalization, thanks in no small measure to the considerable growth in state capacity since the end of the nineteenth century. Reflecting the continued belief in sovereignty as the foundation of international relations, the UN Charter stipulated up front that the organization had no authority "to intervene in matters which are essentially within the domestic jurisdiction of any state or shall require the Members to submit such matters to settlement."[34] As the post-1945 regime-building efforts proceeded, advocates for state sovereignty insisted on limits to outside interference and a respect for domestic standards. They saw dangers to giving outsiders, even benignly intentioned ones, control over national destiny. This stance obviously created a major obstacle to reform, whether in economics, the environment, or human rights. While individual governments would remain the primary defender of their citizens' welfare, the actions they have taken and the effectiveness of those actions have varied considerably.

Nowhere has state resistance to globalization been more potent than in the developing world. There the neoliberal project looked like something constructed by and for the leading economies, with developing countries expected to accommodate to the neoliberal straitjacket. Neoliberalism seemed to perpetuate the old Cold War pattern of great-power domination in a new guise. No surprise, the strongest doubts about the neoliberal model came from developing countries associated with the Group of 77 created in 1964 (see Chapter 5). The G-77 summit in Cuba in April 2000, which brought together leaders representing 133 countries and some 80 percent of the world's population, provides a good example of the intensity of the feeling. The host, Fidel Castro, compared the effects of neoliberal's global dominance to the Nazi Holocaust. Malaysia's equally outspoken Prime Minister, Mahathir Mohamad, attacked a global system that had allowed "rogue currency traders" to bring disorder to East Asian economies and had exploited the ensuing crisis to effect a neoliberal takeover. Nigeria's leader, Olusegun Obasanjo, warned that the great and widening wealth gap between the rich and the poor posed "a major threat to international peace and security."[35] Regional groupings such as the Arab League, the African Union, the Association of Southeast Asian Nations, and the Union of South American Nations have provided other fora for states in opposition to the one-size-fits-all approach championed by the neoliberal globalizers.

Poorer countries have long held that a strong, activist government was essential to serving the interests of their people, and this task could not be left to foreign interests. Critical programs included effecting land redistribution and developing better credit and extension services for small-scale enterprises run by the urban and rural poor neglected by commercial banks. The governments needed in addition to build infrastructure, promote education, and address soil erosion, water pollution, malnourishment, and inadequate shelter. Steps such as these were likely to reduce economic inequalities and social tensions while also improving economic prospects. Rich countries were expected to do their part by debt reduction that would get the poorest states out from under almost impossible payment conditions and enable them to concentrate on serving urgent human needs. One-sided trade deals and reliance on fickle finance were not a panacea and were even fundamentally at odds with the dreams spawned during the era of decolonization of an end to outside control and exploitation.

Developing countries have, not surprisingly, been suspicious of the neoliberal crusade and its insistence that all people—rich as well as poor—benefit from getting the market incentives right and keeping state intervention minimal. Even so, those needing emergency IMF loans have had to accept strict austerity measures and fully embrace the free market. Poor countries struggling under heavy debt have become familiar with the neoliberal opposition to "handouts" and "short-cuts." They have won only minimal relief, and even then it has usually been conditioned on cuts in state health, education, and infrastructure spending. At the same time, official development assistance from rich countries has actually fallen relative to the income at their disposal. In 1960 the leading donor countries contributed 0.51 percent of GDP. In recent decades it has fallen to the range of 0.21 to 0.35 percent, even as inequalities grew. The figure for 2013 was 0.31 percent with only five countries hitting the target of 0.7 percent (Denmark, Luxembourg, Sweden, Norway, Denmark, and the UK).[36]

Compounding the alienation of developing states has been the economic hypocrisy of the rich. They violate their own neoliberal principles, by shutting out (as noted above) agricultural products and workers from the developing world. To make matters worse, the foremost neoliberal powers—above all the United States—have repeatedly wielded an economic stick against countries in the developing world guilty of serious geopolitical defiance. During the Cold War Vietnam, Algeria, Cuba, and Iran were prime targets; recently it has been the turn of Iraq, Iran, North Korea, Syria, and Cuba. This repeated resort to sanctions seems peculiarly at odds with the neoliberal American faith in the power of markets to promote cooperation and also heedless of the indiscriminate harm sanctions inflict on the general population of targeted states.

Historical precedent is on the side of the advocates of strong state action in the developing world. The strategy, adopted by emerging states in the nineteenth century and maintained well into the twentieth century, was unabashedly protectionist. The records of Germany, Sweden, France, Finland, Austria, Japan, Taiwan, and

South Korea, not to mention the United States, reveal a common pattern of long-term growth resulting from policies designed to direct the currents of globalization in a nationally beneficial direction. Protectionism and other measures to encourage strategic industries were only part of the answer; promoting technology and education, both critical to a skilled workforce, was even more important over the long haul. For those lagging economically, sidelining the state and handing over the national destiny to putatively benign foreign banks and corporations made sense neither in the abstract nor in the historical record. Only the rich who have already climbed the ladder of state-directed development think that kicking it away is a good idea.

Where states have proven ineffective or passive in responding to looming economic, environmental, and other global and regional problems, the United Nations has proven to be a remarkably active and effective venue for action. The Security Council has been at best of mixed value precisely because of the divergent perspectives and interests of the leading states. The major powers have dominated its proceedings and used their veto power to stymie action. The major exceptions here are the peacekeeping operations, which the Security Council has endorsed with increasing frequency over the past several decades (Table 10.2). These initiatives had a worldwide scope, including missions to separate belligerent forces or head off war in Kosovo, South Sudan, Somalia, Mozambique, Cambodia, East Timor, El Salvador, and Haiti.

Even more impressive have been the achievements of the UN's many functional agencies and committees. They have done the most to advance the goals of the UN Charter, which formally articulated the postwar hopes for building a better world. Operating across a remarkable range, they have significantly raised the level of global governance by promoting a just and equitable international society and by drawing attention to problems in a highly dynamic and highly unequal international economy.

Some of the functional agencies have a long pedigree. The International Labor Organization, the World Health Organization, and the UN Educational Scientific and Cultural Organization all got their start under the League of Nations. Others emerged in the immediate aftermath of World War II as part of an effort to rehabilitate war-torn regions, especially Europe. For example, the emergency refugee work done by the UN Relief and Rehabilitation Administration laid the basis for

TABLE 10.2 The Dramatic Expansion of UN Peacekeeping Operations, 1988–2014[37]		
	1988	2014
UN budget for peacekeeping (in billions)	$0.3	$7.1
UN peacekeeping forces	13,000	116,400
Number of ongoing missions	7	16

the UN High Commissioner for Refugees, and the UN International Children's Emergency Fund emerged as part of the effort to confront the suffering of a war-torn Europe.

From the 1960s, the UN mandate expanded significantly to include a striking range of fresh concerns. The General Assembly, pushed by new member states, began to articulate welfare concerns neglected by the Security Council while UN agencies took up the tasks that states would not or could not tackle. The UN Economic and Social Council, the UN Conference on Trade and Development, and the UN Development Program worked on a wide front, ranging from literacy programs to technology transfers, to farming assistance, to disease eradication. The preoccupation with development and inequality persisted beyond the Cold War era and has been most evident recently in the Millennium Development Goals, which include eradicating extreme poverty, cutting infant mortality by two thirds, halting the spread of HIV/AIDS and malaria, achieving universal primary education, and promoting gender equality. (These ambitious targets, laid down in 2000, were supposed to be realized by 2015, but in fact were likely to fall short.)

In another sign of the UN's responsiveness to the problems of the times, it turned its attention to environmental issues. The UN Environmental Program, established in 1972, has become increasingly active. It has sponsored major international meetings and scientific investigation, none more important or controversial than the work of the Intergovernmental Panel on Climate Change.

NGOs have emerged in recent decades as a third force for global activism. They specialized in pressing problems that states refused to address or the UN could not adequately deal with alone. These ranged from inequality and stalled development to human rights violations, to succor for refugees, to global warming. Thanks to the elaborate and rapid communications network available in a globalized world, they could draw attention to their causes, mobilize support, and coordinate action in a way impossible in an earlier time. The number of NGOs granted the right to participate in the UN Economic and Social Council suggests their rising importance. The number rose from 132 in 1969 (little changed from earlier) to 367 in 1989, and then to well over 1,000 by the end of the century. The total of all NGOs was far higher, reaching nearly 44,000 by 1999. These NGOs were incredibly diverse in their funding, membership, organization, and of course objectives. In general they have evolved with the times. For example, CARE (Cooperative for Assistance and Relief Everywhere) International and the British-based Oxfam were created to succor a Europe ravaged by war but then shifted focus to other regions and embraced a broader relief and development agenda, often acting in league with the EU or international institutions such as the World Bank.[38]

Amnesty International illustrates the capacity of NGOs to raise the visibility of neglected problems of human welfare and to press for solutions. Founded in 1961 by Peter Benenson, a London lawyer, Amnesty International challenged the prevailing international etiquette, which frowned on NGOs' making direct public accusations of human rights violations by states. Amnesty was not afraid to speak up. It sought to bring those violations to light in a nonpartisan, apolitical fashion, initially scrutinizing all countries, whatever their position in the Cold War or their level of economic development. As it gained credibility for its factual reports, added members (up to some 300,000 in the course of the 1970s), and extended its international network, the organization expanded its concerns to include protection against torture, disappearance, and extrajudicial execution. In each of these areas this particular NGO, like others, helped to create international consensus, which it pressed to have formalized in international agreements. Amnesty International demonstrated that states could not claim a monopoly over the international system and that citizen-activists employing techniques of publicity could command government attention and engage the UN and other international organizations. Reflecting the upsurge on interest in human rights, the Nobel Peace Prize went to this NGO in 1977.

The broadening activism of the UN's functional agencies and the multiplication of NGOs has created a kind of organizational synergy promoting worldwide action on major international problems. This development has left states in an ambivalent and sometimes awkward position. Programs congruent with their goals were fine, but in such basic matters of concern to the international community as the environment or human rights, states often found themselves resisting or providing only half-hearted cooperation.

This organizational synergy has been strikingly evident in relief for refugees. The growing incidence of low-level but socially disruptive conflict over the last half-century has led to a persistent refugee problem addressed by a range of international organizations. Of the UN agencies, the most important has been the UN High Commission for Refugees, which evolved from a temporary operation in 1951 to a permanent bureaucracy with a budget at almost $1 billion in 2001. Joining the relief effort were a wide variety of private, nonprofit organizations such as Doctors Without Borders (Médecins Sans Frontières), Oxfam, and CARE. With humanitarian needs great and resources limited, these organizations and their sponsors in the developed world have fought a constant battle to save lives in those parts of the developing world caught up in the worst nightmares of violence and privation.

The growing capacity of UN agencies and NGOs has been matched by the magnitude of the refugee problem. The numbers of people in flight climbed dramatically during the late twentieth century—from 1.7 million in 1960s to a peak of 17.4 million in 1992. Between 2002 and 2013 the numbers plateaued around 9-11 million. Hardest hit were the peoples of Afghanistan, Palestine, the Kurdish-inhabited region of the Middle East, the Horn of Africa, Angola, Mozambique, Liberia, Rwanda, Bosnia, Central America, and Indochina. Syria is the most recent refugee hot spot, sending by late 2014, 3.3 million of its people into exile as the country imploded. In this case as in others, the displaced became a burden on neighbors, often themselves with limited resources and under their own internal strains. By official count of those formally registered, over a million Syrians ended up in Lebanon and

Turkey, over a half million in Jordan, and almost a quarter of a million in Iraq. Add to these numbers those internally displaced within Syria, estimated at 6.5 million. Those coming to the rescue of refugees whatever the time or place have found themselves caring for a melancholic lot with a lasting sense of trauma. One who had fled the violence of Bosnia spoke for many when she lamented, "My soul is empty and cold. What is left is a 40-year-old woman in a 20-year-old body. I cannot even see the graves of my friends, the grave of my native village."[39]

Synergy has also been evident in efforts to combat disease, nowhere more strikingly than in the AIDS epidemic. Although it probably had its origins in the 1930s, HIV did not become widespread in parts of Africa until the late 1970s and early 1980s. Thanks to the technology that made airplane travel commonplace and tourism a mass phenomenon, the disease traveled far and fast. An estimated 36 million people have died of AIDS; the majority were in the epicenter of this catastrophe, sub-Saharan Africa. The growing scale of this disaster soon engaged researchers in a quest for a treatment. To ensure equitable medical care, UN Secretary General Kofi Annan called in 2001 for help for poor countries with weak governments and fragile societies. The World Health Organization and the UN Programme on HIV/AIDS (UNAIDS) gathered information on the state of the epidemic, pressed for effective countermeasures in the poor countries worst hit, and lobbied the affluent for funds to support their programs. By 2010 in sub-Saharan Africa, the infection rate among adults had been contained at just below 5 percent.[40]

The Ebola outbreak in 2014 has followed a similar script. Once more sub-Saharan Africa was the epicenter, with the west African states of Guinea, Liberia, and Sierra Leone—all already at the bottom of the Human Development Index and with extremely limited resources—hardest hit. The international community began to respond as reporting turned alarmist and as infected international travelers began to arrive in the developed world. NGOs such as Doctors Without Borders were early on the scene and quick to sound the alarm; the rich states and the WHO reacted more slowly. Scientists went into overdrive to devise an antidote for a disease far more infectious than AIDS. With deaths hitting 10,000 by early 2015, optimists talked of containing the epidemic in the course of the next year, but only after a dramatic increase in the number of those afflicted (worst case in excess of a million) and after serious economic damage had been done to already vulnerable economies.

A third example of synergy can be found in the international pushback against the excesses of globalization. In a networked world, critics have been able as never before to mobilize publics within countries and link like-minded people in transnational coalitions. Establishment voices began in the late 1990s to join NGOs in attacking the neoliberal turn. George Soros, who had himself made a killing through financial speculation, argued that societies had a legitimate need to protect themselves from markets, which in his view meant measures "to keep markets stable, to impose some degree of regulation and supervision, and to find a political extension to match the extension of the markets—some international political cooperation to match the globalization of markets." A World Bank insider, the

Ebola Treatment Center in Paynesville, Liberia
Here a staffer with Doctors Without Borders carries a child suspected of having contracted Ebola. The leaders of this medical NGO were quick to call for rapid international action against this deadly virus, prodding the World Health Organization and leading states to join in shoring up rudimentary health-care systems in West Africa. (Photo by John Moore/Getty Images)

economist Joseph E. Stiglitz, lashed out at the IMF for pursuing "a cookie-cutter approach" to economies in crisis and then stubbornly sticking to measures that patently did more harm than good. The secrecy surrounding IMF policy prompted Stiglitz to observe: "Smart people are more likely to do stupid things when they close themselves off to outside criticism and advice." Amartya Sen, another reform economist preoccupied with balanced development, cautioned that free markets had their limits: "Global capitalism is much more concerned with expanding the domain of market relations than with, say, establishing democracy, expanding elementary education, or enhancing the social opportunities of society's underdogs."[41]

The most broad-based and wide-ranging indictment appeared in 1998. The International Forum on Globalization, a broad coalition of advocates for the developing world as well as for the environment, human rights, and indigenous peoples, issued a sharply critical attack on the destructive system of globalized finance. They charged the IMF, the World Bank, the WTO, and other powerful but aloof international bureaucracies with operating on the basis of the fatally flawed assumption of "a never-ending expansion of markets, resources and consumers." The results were "massive economic breakdown in some nations, insecurity in all nations, unprecedented hardships for millions of people, growing unemployment and dislocation in all regions, direct assaults on environmental and labor conditions, loss of wilderness and biodiversity, massive population shifts, [and] increased ethnic and racial tensions." In general, the declaration argued, not only states but also communities needed to reclaim power accumulating in the hands of distant and unaccountable "corporate-led global trade bureaucracies."[42]

Perhaps appropriately, Seattle—then the home of Microsoft, Boeing, and Starbucks—found itself the scene of the first major antiglobal protest in the developed world in November 1999 during a meeting of the WTO. Angered by its position on environmental protection, industrial-scale agriculture, and labor standards, some 40,000 protesters flooded the street, catching the police off guard and paralyzing the WTO proceedings. The critics came from colleges, labor unions, religious organizations, and a variety of environmental and human rights NGOs. Their complaints were equally diverse—from the rich–poor divide to the fate of the planet. For example, Jennifer Krill, an environmentalist activist, charged that WTO policies promoted logging of environmentally important forests and thus were at odds with "long-term human sustainability on the planet. The WTO is only representing long-term corporate and economic interests."[43] The champions of full-throttle globalization continued to face a backlash, forcing them in subsequent meetings in Quebec, Genoa, and Cancun to retreat behind police phalanxes or to remote enclaves. Forced to hide well away from the public eye and the wrath of demonstrators, they effectively confirmed the critics' charge that globalization was at heart secretive and antidemocratic.

Even before Seattle, one of the most dramatic expressions of antiglobal sentiment took shape in Chiapas state in Mexico. The implementation of NAFTA posed a threat to Mayan communities in the far south of the country by allowing U.S. corn imports to compete with a staple crop that had an important symbolic as well as commercial place in Mayan life. NAFTA had also prompted the politically dominant People's Revolutionary Party, in power since early in the twentieth century, to make agricultural output more competitive by promoting land consolidation and setting aside constitutionally mandated land redistribution. Simmering discontent in Chiapas exploded on New Year's Day in 1994, the occasion of NAFTA coming into force. The Zapatistas, an armed force named after an early-twentieth-century revolutionary populist, seized ranches and took control of villages. The army counterattacked, inflicting heavy casualties. An uneasy peace followed. Having gotten the attention of Mexico City as well as the world, the Zapatistas shifted to a form of guerrilla theater in which local autonomy, indigenous rights, the wealth inequality gap within Mexico, and gender equality figured prominently. Subcommandante Marcos, a masked, pipe-smoking Latino, served from the start as the movement's voice. Zapatista demands for democracy and social justice were conveyed widely at home and abroad through a sophisticated media campaign and won tacit support from the local Catholic Church and the backing of prominent NGOs. An uneasy truce has prevailed for nearly two decades, longer than the Ogoni people in Nigeria were able to hold out, giving this remarkable social movement time to build a network of local governments and deepen its social base.

In the Name of Human Rights

The drive to define and apply global standards of human rights proved the most sustained and successful facet of the push for a more humane global order. The conception of rights had its origins in the seventeenth and eighteenth centuries when it took form in Britain, the United States, and France. By the end of World War II, the idea of human rights as understood today—applying to people of all stations everywhere—had developed clear if still circumscribed appeal. The UN took the lead in codifying the emergent human rights consensus. The ground-breaking document was the 1948 UN declaration, which enumerated a long list of human rights that deserved worldwide respect.

Like virtually all of the major postwar agreements contributing to the international regime, the 1948 declaration was the product of a sustained effort involving considerable negotiation and compromise. Eleanor Roosevelt, earlier an activist First Lady, played a critical role, chairing the commission that crafted the declaration and adroitly transcending the ethical, cultural, philosophical, and political differences to create a consensus. The declaration was prompted by revulsion against the recent "barbarous acts which have outraged the conscience of mankind" and a realization that "the world of man is at a critical stage in its political, social, and economic evolution. If it is to proceed further on the path towards unity, it must develop a common set of ideas and principles." In late December 1948 the UN General Assembly gave its approval by a lopsided margin (48 in favor, none opposing, and 8 abstentions coming from South Africa, Saudi Arabia, the Soviet Union, and its eastern European clients). That the declaration garnered such broad support was due in large measure to its lack of teeth.[44]

The final document took a stand on a striking range of issues. Political rights figured prominently: freedom of speech, conscience, thought, and assembly as well as the right to vote, to receive fair legal treatment, and to enjoy privacy. But the declaration also spoke to social and economic concerns such as the right to basic education, to work, to earn a living wage, and to have opportunities for rest and leisure. It looked ahead to gender rights by stipulating not only nondiscriminatory employment and universal suffrage and education but also marriage with consent and the right to initiate divorce. Finally, it cast protection over dissidents by asserting the right of those persecuted to seek asylum in other countries.

The declaration carved out a position that was potentially revolutionary in its long-term significance: In a world society in transition, states could no longer hide their misdeeds behind the shield of sovereignty. State leaders were responsible for criminal conduct. Even before the 1948 declaration the trials of German and Japanese leaders in Nuremberg and Tokyo had established the notion of war crimes and crimes against humanity (see Chapter 2). The sweeping claims made by the declaration became the basis for bringing over time the needs and interests of individuals, coherent groups such as ethnic and racial minorities, and even categories of people such as women, children, and migrants under the rights umbrella. Those protections were buttressed by major human rights treaties and agreements concluded in the following decades, dealing with such varied subjects as genocide, torture, racial discrimination, forced labor, migrant workers, stateless persons, the rights of children and women, and the right to economic development.

The 1970s proved a turning point in turning potential into reality. Human rights ceased to be a peripheral concern of states and of the UN. Disillusion with the Cold War struggle and the fading promise of socialism helped elevate human rights as an alternative vision with wide appeal and broad application. The result was remarkable progress in consolidating old claims and advancing new ones. Among the notable advances in broadening the application of rights were the cases made for covering sexual orientation, the developmentally disabled, those who had contracted HIV/AIDS, indigenous peoples, and victims of environmental degradation. Going even further, some stretched the idea of rights to justify international intervention in cases of humanitarian disaster (the so-called responsibility to protect) and to condemn government interference in the flow of digital information ("the right to connect").

Along with an expanding application of the human rights went fresh mechanisms for their enforcement. Revelations from the genocidal revolution in Cambodia (see Chapter 9), news coverage of brutal ethnic warfare waged by regimes in Rwanda and Yugoslavia (see Chapters 6 and 11), and investigations into state-sponsored terror elsewhere created pressure to bring to account those responsible. While the UN Security Council had proven ineffectual in stopping the killing in Rwanda and in the former Yugoslavia, it did after the fact affirm international standards by creating the International Criminal Tribunal for the Former Yugoslavia in 1993 and the International Criminal Tribunal for Rwanda in 1994. The arraignment of Slobodan Milošević, the leading figure behind Serbian atrocities during the 1990s, was a landmark event. (Five years into his trial he died in custody in 2006.) Other prominent figures responsible for the killings in former Yugoslavia as well as in Rwanda did not escape the judgment of the court. Elsewhere—in Guatemala, Chile, Argentina, and South Africa—truth commissions played an important role in vindicating internationally recognized standards of civilized conduct. They brought past wrongs to public light while also creating a new shared civic sense likely to forestall a recurrence of abuse. The capstone to these institutional innovations was the creation of an International Criminal Court to handle on a permanent basis charges of war crimes, crimes against humanity, and genocide. A coalition of NGOs had campaigned for such a court. A treaty based on a draft they produced at a conference in Rome in 1998 finally secured enough international backing in the face of U.S., Russian, and Chinese opposition to bring the court to life in 2002.

The states of western Europe, operating individually and in common, have emerged as the most insistent champions of a robust rights regime. Its leaders came into the postwar period with a visceral grasp of the evil that states left to their own devices might do, both to their own people and to others. The supranational path Europeans then traveled made them even more attuned to the notion of universal rights that existed beyond the ambit of state authority. They sought to steadily deepen their own rights provisions. European states began concluding their own set of conventions in 1950 in what would accumulate into a robust set of provisions. These included agreements in the 1980s directed against torture and the death penalty. In 1996 the EU created an impressively comprehensive and detailed convention on rights. (This European Social Charter was approved and went into force in 1999.) To ensure respect in member states, the EU created a dedicated human rights court in 1959.

Not coincidentally, the EU was at the forefront of efforts to promote rights internationally and to bring violators to justice. It was the home of Amnesty International, it served as the host for the International Tribunal for the Former Yugoslavia and the International Criminal Court, and it witnessed the arraignment of the former Chilean dictator, Augusto Pinochet, on charges of involvement in kidnapping, torture, and assassination. (The remarkable Pinochet affair was initiated by a Spanish judge and conducted before a British court but ended with the accused claiming failing health and being released to return home.) On top of all this, the EU was outspoken in pressing for total abolition of the death penalty around the world and in criticizing those such as the United States, China, Iran, and Saudi Arabia that still resorted to it.

Human rights was a double-edged sword that grew sharper as it gained acceptance and carved the rights field along several contentious lines. One was over how broadly human rights should be conceived and in particular over which articles of the UN declaration to privilege. The narrow conception, essentially Anglo-American, held that human rights were to be understood primarily if not exclusively in civil and political terms. According to this perspective, the major human rights concerns should be free speech, voting, and removal of such constraints on political activity and individual expression as arbitrary arrest and censorship. This insistence on respect for the autonomy of the individual and especially limits on state coercion seemed tailor-made for the advancing neoliberal order. Advocates of the alternative view wanted to make economic and social provisions equal to, if not more important than, the civil and political ones. The corollary to their view was that governments should have latitude to act in order to promote the security, livelihood, health care, gender equality, and education that all citizens deserved;

the right to vote every four years was meaningless without solid guarantees to food, shelter, and work.

A second major fault line has developed over whether human rights transcended the particularities of culture and politics. Skeptics on this point have asked whether the understanding of rights did not vary from region to region. Islam was the source of values and judicial procedures that were arguably as valid as a Western-based legal code. A tradition of political authoritarianism left some in East Asia at odds with sweeping claims of individual rights, especially at the expense of the state as the voice of the collective good. Still others have resisted the notion that individual rights should take precedence over such collective interests as the family, clan, or village. Social solidarities and socially defined roles (for example, the different position ascribed to women because of their unique role in physical and social reproduction) should in this view take precedence over individual preferences.

A third point of controversy has turned over whether human rights crusaders apply a double standard depending on the geopolitical context. During the latter stages of the Cold War, American and western European leaders pressed human rights principles into service to stimulate political change behind the Iron Curtain and embarrass the Kremlin. The Helsinki accords of 1975 (treated in Chapter 7) is the best example of this geopolitical opportunism. The call to respect rights was taken less seriously on the "free world" side. While Communist regimes might face censure and even economic restrictions, U.S. allies who blatantly violated international standards got a free pass. The same charges of applying a double standard have arisen in regard to the international courts, which do not in practice hold to account the most powerful states. These tribunals seemed benign as long as they confined themselves to "bad men from small countries." This complaint about using a double standard continues to apply with special force to the United States, which refused to join the International Criminal Court and threatened those who did, violated the UN prohibition against wars of aggression by invading Iraq in 2003, tortured suspected terrorists, and committed judicial killings.

In Defense of the Planet

Perhaps the most urgent of all the issues that the international community wrestled with was the crisis of the environment. No problem of the global age was more threatening to humanity and at the same time more intractable. Global solutions presupposed agreement among states at varying stages of development—and hence with very different notions of who should sacrifice. Any solution required in addition a fundamentally revised notion of growth and consumption; neither could be endless if the planet were to remain habitable. But if its capacity to absorb pollutants imposed limits to growth, how to make the transition to greater sustainability?

Between the 1962 appearance of Rachel Carson's *Silent Spring* (see Chapter 5) and the present, thinking about the environment has undergone a revolutionary transformation. Within a single generation, environmental values became an integral part of popular attitudes in the developed world. They gained such wide acceptance that they had come to constitute (in the words of the *New York Times* in 1990) "a modern secular religion."[45] As environmentalism gained ground, it became the subject of domestic politics and administrative regulations as well as frequent and often-contentious international negotiations.

Round after round of unsettling news kept alive the popular and political concerns expressed on the first Earth Day in April 1970. OPEC's 1973 embargo drove home to consumers the notion of finite resources. In 1974 newspapers began to report the danger posed by CFCs to the ozone layer. The meltdown of the U.S. nuclear plant at Three Mile Island in 1978 stirred alarm, as did repeated oil spills, the worst of which was the 70 million gallons that leaked from the *Amoco Cadiz* off the French coast in 1978. In 1979 the U.S. Environmental Protection Agency reported the existence of as many as 50,000 major hazardous-waste sites across the country. And throughout the 1980s and 1990s, environmental activists expressed a rising anxiety over rapidly rising population pressures in the developing world and high consumption levels in the developed world.

These accumulating environmental dangers not only pushed higher popular environmental consciousness but also spurred social and political activism. "Green" parties impatient for a bolder environmental agenda sprang up in western Europe and elsewhere in the developed world. While New Zealand's was the first, Germany's proved the most politically influential. Founded in 1980, the German Greens won a place in the national parliament and in the late 1990s in the ruling coalition. While in western Europe environmentalists fought to be heard alongside other major organized groups such as labor and business, in eastern Europe environmental concerns, sharpened by the Chernobyl meltdown and industrial pollution, were helping to undermine socialist governments (see Chapter 7). In the United States, the largest and most wasteful of the world's economies, environmental issues became a matter of growing public concern and political conflict during the 1970s. Congress passed major environmental bills, and the environmental movement became more deeply involved in the legislative and regulatory process. Support for new environmental groups such as Greenpeace and for the long-established ones such as the Sierra Club rose dramatically, and local activists made their presence felt. By 1990 three out of four Americans professed support for the highest possible environmental standards.

The issues that inspired all this consciousness and controversy commanded more and more attention around the world as it became clear that environmental problems showed no more respect for borders than economic transactions did. International treaties and conventions on the environment multiplied. In this age of growing environmental concern, the United Nations emerged as the leading sponsor of fresh initiatives. The first major UN-sponsored conference on the environment, held in Stockholm in 1972, created a forum in which an expanding network of NGOs could lobby for their favored causes.

By the time of the next major UN conference—the 1992 "Earth Summit" in Rio de Janeiro—not only had anxiety over environmental deterioration intensified but also the conviction had grown that the problem had passed well beyond the power of a single country to resolve. Norway's Prime Minister Gro Harlem Brundtland put the case for international cooperation succinctly: "Our Earth is one, our world is not."[46] It had also become clearer since Stockholm that the environmental agenda had to go well beyond attacking physical pollution and protecting a few highly visible species such as whales; now it seemed that the whole biosphere and entire ecosystems were in peril. Finally and perhaps most important, in the 20 years between Stockholm and Rio, a consensus took shape that environmental protection on a worldwide basis was closely tied to economic development in poorer countries. If developing countries went into crisis, the developed world would lose trade and feel the pressure of refugee populations. If the developing world destroyed its forests, then the effects would be felt globally in the contribution to the greenhouse effect. The new notion was "sustainable development," which emphasized striking a balance between the current material needs of all the world's people and the preservation of the vital resources on which future generations would depend.

The delegations from 178 countries as well as some 2,500 NGOs attending the Rio conference were ready to make formal agreements on protecting biodiversity, cutting back gases linked to global warming and loss of upper-atmosphere ozone, and regulating the exploitation of undersea resources. But the ensuing negotiations revealed serious obstacles to sweeping action or meaningful regulation that a maturing environmental movement now faced. The fundamental environmental quandary was trying to square the circle—reconciling unbridled consumer desires in both the developed and the developing worlds with the preservation of environmental values.

Sharp differences separated the rich and poor over how to deal with the environment. Those speaking for the developing countries had their eyes on national economic growth and regarded environmental restrictions as an obstacle to ending poverty. India's Prime Minister Indira Gandhi made the point provocatively at the 1972 Stockholm conference: "Are not poverty and need the greatest polluters?" Poorer countries thus resisted across-the-board cuts in pollution favored by the most developed. Governments in the developing world pointed out that the advanced economies got to where they were at a time when regulations were few or none, and they asked why those who came late to the industrialization process had to accept burdensome limits. Not only had the advanced countries brought the environment to a critical point, but in addition their current high levels of consumption contributed disproportionately to the crisis. For example, carbon emissions associated with the greenhouse effect came overwhelmingly from the developed world (more than four fifths of the output at the time of the Rio conference in 1992) despite the far larger population in the developing world (Map 10.2). Thus, poorer countries argued that the developed world had a responsibility to apply its ample financial and technological resources to the solution of a problem largely of its own making. A critical part of that solution was generous development aid. If the developed world did not help, desperate people all around

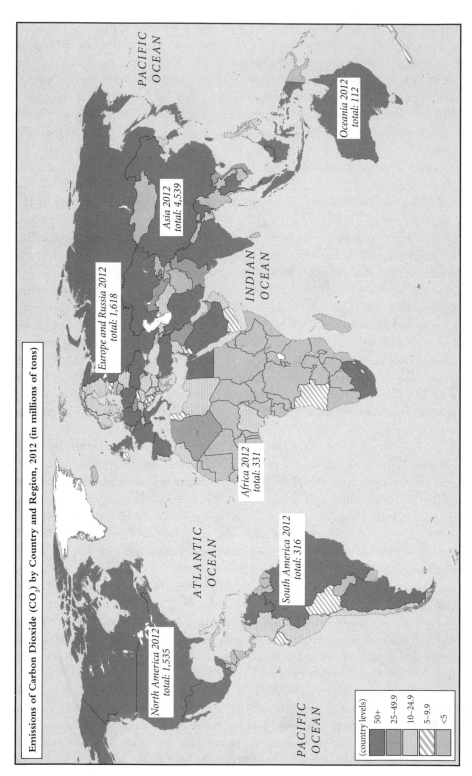

Emissions of Carbon Dioxide (CO$_2$) by Country and Region, 2012 (in millions of tons)

PACIFIC OCEAN

Asia 2012
total: 4,539

Oceania 2012
total: 112

Europe and Russia 2012
total: 1,618

INDIAN OCEAN

Africa 2012
total: 331

ATLANTIC OCEAN

North America 2012
total: 1,535

South America 2012
total: 316

PACIFIC OCEAN

(country levels)

50+
25–49.9
10–24.9
5–9.9
<5

the world would take from the Earth what they could heedlessly—to the detriment of all.[47]

The priority that poor countries gave to economic development found its match in a reluctance among the rich to make sacrifices, even though they used resources on a profligate scale and fouled the environment on an equally large scale. The United States, as the world's third most populous country, its largest economy, and the land with the most avid consumers, was arguably the most serious offender. U.S. policymakers were cool to environmental activism. Republican neoliberals in Congress, in tandem with the Reagan and first Bush administrations, led a counterattack in the 1980s. Reagan's secretary of the interior famously compared environmentalists to Nazis and Bolsheviks, and a high-level Bush appointee huffed, "Americans did not fight and win the wars of the twentieth century to make the world safe for green vegetables." Washington rejected the main Rio agreements regarding biodiversity, sea resources, and climate change that had been endorsed by virtually all other countries. Behind this U.S. stance was an unusually powerful and well-funded coalition with a material or ideological stake in unrestricted marketplace activity. Publicists and lobbyists for major industries, free-trade advocates, and conservative think tanks such as the Heritage Foundation mounted a well-funded assault on environmental "hysteria." The public was hardly enthusiastic about initiatives that might impinge on national and consumer sovereignty. "We see the train coming," President Clinton observed on the problems of the environment, "but most ordinary Americans in their day-to-day lives can't hear the whistle blowing." Small cars were fine as long as gas prices remained high. Homes got more energy-efficient even as "McMansions" multiplied. This American ambivalence persisted into the new century. The massive 2010 oil spill in the Gulf of Mexico, coastal communities endangered by rising sea levels, and shifting rainfall patterns posed fresh challenges yet failed to push the country toward a consensus on the environment.[48]

These divisions between the rich and poor and the reluctance of some of the rich to take significant action stymied action on climate change. Skeptics asked whether changes were part of a natural process, not the result of human activity. They wondered if a warmer climate might actually have benefits, such as larger

◄ **MAP 10.2**

Emissions of Carbon Dioxide (CO₂) by Country and Region, 2012

Carbon dioxide (CO_2) has been the major driver for both global warming and ocean acidification. It has entered the atmosphere in ever greater amounts primarily as result of human activity, either burning fossil fuels or destroying forests. Deciding which humans are most responsible for rising CO_2 levels depends on point of view. As the map makes clear, some countries have much higher total output than others. Viewed regionally, there are also marked differences. For example, by 2010 East Asia's total emissions of carbon dioxide amounted to twice that of North America and three times that of the European Union countries. Finally, calculating emissions on a per person basis tells yet another story. To take one telling comparison, North Americans in 2010 accounted for twice what Europeans produced and more than three what East Asians were responsible for.[49]

harvests or faster-growing forests. They wondered whether it made sense to spend heavily in order to head off some potential threat and speculated that technological innovation might save the day. Despite all the skepticism, a conference in Kyoto in 1997 did produce a fresh agreement, but the targets for CO_2 reduction were relatively low and the signatories slow to act. The United States for its part simply refused to sign on. Even on paper the Kyoto agreement seemed less and less adequate in the face of mounting evidence of the severity of global warming. A follow-up conference in Copenhagen in 2009 failed to heal the rifts dividing the wealthy from those intent on poverty reduction and left the major oil and gas exporters, such as Russia, Saudi Arabia, and Iran, feeling threatened. While the globe warmed and NGOs and the UN scolded ineffectually, states heavily dependent on a fossil fuel economy continued to dally. On this most pressing of threats to the planet, humanity seemed unable to organize to protect itself.

CONCLUSION

The inhabitants of the world today are better off in fundamental terms than they were in the middle of the twentieth century. The Cold War, with its regional conflicts and threat of nuclear annihilation, has ceased to spread fear and dissension. Subjugated peoples have thrown off rule by distant powers that viewed them solely as markets to be exploited, plastic societies to be remolded, and cannon fodder to be expended. The international economy has brought great material abundance to already privileged countries and opened up a markedly better future to some poorer countries. Even those in the most economically troubled states are living longer lives under improved conditions. In this much-transformed world, few people living today would want to trade places with the generation that came of age in 1945.

But these significant advances have come at a high, perhaps unavoidable price. Rising population levels have combined with rising levels of production to spawn new problems such as environmental degradation and to intensify old ones such as major gaps in wealth and welfare, especially along regional and gender lines. Instability remains a prime feature of the international economy. With the busts that seem inevitably to follow the booms come economic hardship, social stress, and sometimes political unrest. These problems have stirred up an increasingly serious backlash that itself has assumed global dimensions. Critics ask whether the benefits spawned by the system outweigh the costs and whether the corporate interests controlling the system and profiting from it have slipped beyond public control and accountability. It remains to be seen whether these negative features could singly or in some combination threaten globalization or whether they are merely incidental or temporary growing pains in what will be seen someday as an essentially benign process of worldwide growth and integration. It also remains to be seen whether the critics of globalization in its current incarnation, with its striking variety of profoundly serious problems, will form into an effective coalition. Their task is difficult: They have to carve out an ideological space in competition with potent nationalist attachments and popular consumerist commitments that together now dominate the cultural landscape. Those seeking a coherent, overarching alternative to the current system face a challenge of the first order.

Globalization has spawned along with these problems a dangerous illusion that cellphones, cable modems, and other appurtenances of the new age have created one world moving relentlessly toward a neoliberal future. In fact, globalization's impact and prospects vary enormously from country to country and from region to region. The next chapter tackles the ways the world remains stubbornly variegated and often sharply at odds with the integrating tendencies of globalization. People in different places continue to dream different dreams, national leaders still diverge over fundamentals, and the possibilities of daily life—the opportunities and constraints—vary enormously from country to country and region to region.

11
A REGIONALLY CONFIGURED WORLD

THE GLOBALIZED WORLD is neither flat nor uniform nor fixed. Regional distinctions remain strong—surprisingly so to those who have taken up the gospel of neoliberalism as an irresistible force. The differences have manifested themselves at multiple levels: the values intrinsic to societies, the distinct dynamics of particular regions, and the relentless reconfiguring among those regions. These trends, already apparent during the Cold War, have since become even more pronounced.

Perhaps the most notable trend has been the redistribution of power among states, creating as a result a more multipolar world. In long-term perspective this redistribution of power has diminished the influence of what might be called the Anglosphere—Britain, the United States, and the other countries of British settlement. They not only set globalization in motion in the nineteenth century but also revived it and gave it fresh impetus in the latter half of the twentieth. But by the start of the twenty-first century the leading Anglo power, the United States, showed signs of relative decline. Strains at home together with imprudent adventures abroad had compromised the U.S. position. Even in Latin America, a longtime sphere of influence, the U.S. grip weakened as Brazil took the lead in moving beyond an era of dictatorships and toward more populist, democratic politics. In the Middle East Islamists challenged the status quo built on the legacy of British colonialism and sustained by U.S. intervention. In the reshuffle of the regions, Asia posed the most direct challenge to the dominance of the North Atlantic powers, with China and India at the forefront. Finally, Europe was caught in the backwash of the past. Old problems of security and welfare seemingly settled in the latter half of the twentieth century resurfaced, while Russia's recovery from post-Soviet collapse raised big questions about Eurasia's future. (Sub-Saharan Africa with its problematic development record is treated in Chapters 9 and 10.)

THE NEW WORLD'S NEW ERA

A Western Hemisphere previously under U.S. dominance was in the midst of significant changes. On the one side, U.S. power appeared to be eroding as a result of adverse trends playing out on a remarkably broad front. The 2008 economic crisis inflicted broad damage, while pressing long-term domestic problems eluded solution. Foreign interventions, notably in Iraq and Afghanistan, went awry, while regional powers from Iran and Russia to China and North Korea proved frustratingly resistant to U.S. preferences. One historian, after a detailed survey of the state of the nation, saw a future in which "at a minimum, the United States will suffer decline in wealth, standard of living, and global influence."[1]

The neighbors to the South were not waiting to see how far that decline would go or how soon or with what consequences. The Monroe Doctrine, which had through much of the twentieth century embodied U.S. claims to act as overlord, lost its purchase. Latin Americans began to explore development paths defined neither by Washington nor by the Cold War pattern of dictatorship and repression.

Hegemonic Pretensions

The ancient Greeks had a name—*hegemon*—for a state that occupied a position of overwhelming dominance over all other states. This term comfortably fit the United States as the Cold War came to a close. Americans could claim political leadership on the world stage, an unmatched military prowess that underwrote their claim, and unequaled economic and cultural influence. The perpetuation of this hegemonic position depended above all on a robust domestic base that could sustain global prestige and power. Media mogul Henry Luce, in an influential essay titled "The American Century" published in early 1941, had identified the essential elements.[2]

In Luce's formulation, U.S. standing rested most obviously on its claim to represent a model democratic order. But in recent decades the model has been tarnished. Voter participation has fallen significantly since the 1960s and pales by comparison with turnout in other advanced democracies. Voter awareness of the issues is shockingly deficient. Underlying both low participation and awareness is a pervasive cynicism and alienation from the political process. "Don't vote—it only encourages them" expressed a widespread view about not only politicians but also the democratic process. Popular disapproval of Congress has recently risen to the 80 percent range from the 50 percent range that prevailed from 1975 to 2005. The deep doubts about the efficacy of the very state essential to addressing national problems are reflected in the popular if mistaken conviction that half of every dollar the federal government spends is wasted.[3]

This woeful state of affairs has been exacerbated by big-money elections and lobbying by powerful interest groups and corporations. Corporations have used their power and connections to sidestep or neutralize state oversight and to capture government officials and agencies. What better example than Washington's record of failed oversight of a banking community by regulators who had deep personal, professional, and political ties with it and who in 2008 rescued the bankers from their own folly? Corporations have managed to perpetuate their favorable situation with the aid of the Supreme Court's grant of political personhood with the right to spend freely to influence elections and legislators. The Court has further opened the door to big-money politics by rejecting campaign financing restrictions, thus allowing the wealthy to flood the airwaves and forcing officeholders desperate for funds into increasingly expensive reelection contests to appeal to anyone with deep pockets. Politics in neoliberal America has thus turned into the special preserve of the rich and powerful. Globalization has intensified the crisis of democratic control as technocrats have laid down sweeping rules that were not subject to review or recall by any electorate, even though those rules might have a greater impact than any piece of national legislation. As one critic put it, American democracy was yielding to "a supergovernment of unelected trade bureaucrats."[4]

The second pillar supporting Luce's conception of the American century was a large, vital, growing economy that distributed its benefits widely and that could support at the same time welfare at home and the exercise of power abroad. A demonstrably successful economic system also served as a model that others might emulate while also underwriting U.S. claims to virtual veto power within the major international economic institutions (discussed in Chapter 10). Money is the mother's milk of great powers; when the supply dries up, capacity and ambition alike wither. U.S. economic standing had already begun by the late 1960s and 1970s to suffer in relative terms as the Europeans and Japanese got back on their feet. Since then a set of middle powers known collectively as the BRICs—Brazil, Russia, India, and China—have further undercut the U.S. position. Hastening this long-term decline are structural problems within the U.S. economy that have left it sclerotic. Savings rates are low. Neglect of investment in schooling has translated into lagging skills important in global economic competitiveness. American students not only at the K–12 but also the better funded college level compare poorly to those in other developed countries. Infrastructure investment has dropped significantly as a percentage of gross domestic product (GDP). Bridges awere crumbling. Public transport was anemic. Air terminals looked dilapidated compared to the sparkling facilities built in other countries. Underinvestment in the public sector has meant slower growth, slower increase in median income, slower job creation, slower productivity gains, and slower rates of technological change. Perhaps above all, a manufacturing sector that made U.S. international dominance and a consumer society possible has collapsed, resulting in (according to one informed observer) "a debt-ridden, import-dependent state."[5]

These adverse trends have been exacerbated by rising levels of inequality, both wealth and income, relative to earlier periods in U.S. history and by the social and political tensions inequality has generated. The income gap is now as wide as at any time since 1917. Recent reports indicate that the top 20 percent of income earners claimed slightly more than half of all income generated in the United States, and the top 1 percent laid claim to nearly a fifth. The share of this top group has grown steadily since the 1980s, capturing much of the national income increase over that time.[6] As in other countries, this trend toward greater inequality was the product of neoliberal policies, which flattened the tax rate, denigrated government social policies, and favored corporations (especially in the financial sector). Globalization helped to deepen the divide by distributing rewards disproportionately to those with intellectual, social, and real capital. Those with education, broadly marketable skills, and geographical mobility won while those who came from low-income families and received only minimal education lost out. No national consensus has emerged on fighting social inequalities by adopting distributive and educational policies to limit the disproportionate rewards that otherwise have gone to the skilled and to high finance. The one organized attack on inequality, the Occupy Wall Street movement, failed to strike a national chord and disappeared without a political trace.

The third pillar as Luce conceived it was the internationally appealing consumer-oriented social model that had already made the United States "the intellectual, scientific, and artistic capital of the world." By the time Luce wrote this, this consumer society, marked by mass production and mass consumption and an assertive individualist creed, had made deep inroads into the middle class, and it would broaden and deepen its appeal in a postwar golden age of abundance for many Americans. But that promise of abundance and social mobility has dimmed. The net worth of the median family fell by a third between 2003 and 2013 (down to $56,000) even as the top 5 percent of families enjoyed a 14 percent increase. The captains of industry and finance who were supposed to deliver on the dream failed to even live up to their professed free-market principles. Corporate leaders beholden to shareholders and mesmerized by performance bonuses took excessive risks, hollowed out large segments of the national economy, suppressed information critical to transparent market operations, set off speculative crises, and created combinations and concentrations inimical to competition.[7]

This spectacle has undercut the international appeal of the American social model to a degree that would have shocked Luce. Observers noted that American society was marked by the widest economic disparities between the richest and the poorest parts of the population found anywhere in the developed world. Despite spending more than anyone else on health care (around 17 percent of GDP and nearly double the outlays by many other developed countries and three times that of some), U.S. health outcomes were relatively poor on such basic measures as life expectancy, infant mortality, maternal mortality, and poverty among children. Even some developing countries did better. U.S. expenditure on social services such as housing, job training, unemployment benefits, old-age assistance, and family support was about half the level of many developed countries. The United States could also claim the dubious distinction for its deaths from gunfire as well as overall murder rates and for the highest number and percentage of the population in prison. Far from standing out as a model to emulate, the United States better served foreign observers as a cautionary tale about the consequences of a highly individualistic, neoliberal ethos.[8]

Even as its domestic foundations have weakened, U.S. hegemonic pretensions have doggedly persisted. The collapse of the socialist states between 1989 and 1991 opened a debate about what form American dominance should take. One position cast the United States as the defender of Western civilization against an awakened Islam and an assertive Confucian Asia. A second imagined the country as the embodiment and presiding presence in a world moving relentlessly toward economic and cultural integration. Yet a third stance saw the U.S. triumph over communism as signaling the definitive victory of liberal values in the world and guaranteeing a smooth path ahead for U.S. dominance.[9]

The vision that actually prevailed was none of the above but a fourth that took the shape of a hard-edged commitment to holding down regional challengers and crushing any overt opposition to U.S. dominance. Dick Cheney, part of a generation schooled in Cold War precepts and devoted to unchallengeable U.S. military power, was the leading proponent of this approach. This consummate bureaucratic in-fighter and certified Washington insider got off to an unsteady start. He left Yale after two suspensions, took up and then abandoned a doctoral program, and declined military service in Vietnam on the vague grounds that he had "other priorities." Like Truman, he eventually found politics his true *métier*. After serving in the Nixon and Ford administrations and the House of Representatives, he landed the job of Secretary of Defense under the first president Bush. There he formulated a doctrine that explained why regional mastery was essential to U.S. security. The declassified version of the Cheney document, toned down to minimize controversy, called for using dominance to "secure and extend the remarkable democratic 'zone of peace' that we and our allies now enjoy."[10] Washington would take the world as its sphere of influence, and to police it would keep the military budget at Cold War levels and well in excess of what any single challenger or combination of challengers spent (Fig. 11.1). NATO and other allies as well as the United Nations were to follow the U.S. or get out of the way. The Cheney doctrine became Washington's governing strategic concept.

The U.S. response to Iraq's invasion of Kuwait in August 1990 revealed the primacy of that concept but also its limits. The devastating Iran–Iraq war of 1980–1988 had left Iraq's economy reeling, and Kuwait compounded the problem by pushing oil production up and thus oil prices down and resisting settlement of a dispute over an oil-rich border area. With desperately needed oil revenue at risk, Saddam Hussein seized Kuwait. The Bush administration, with Cheney running the Pentagon, quickly resolved to discipline this regional challenger, even though he had only recently received U.S. help in his war against Iran. Bush ordered 200,000 U.S. troops positioned in Saudi Arabia. When the Iraqi strongman refused to surrender his trophy, Bush decided in January 1991 to attack. Heavy bombing followed by a U.S.-led ground attack quickly secured Kuwait's liberation. In contrast to minimal deaths on the U.S. side, Iraqi losses ranged from 10,000 to 150,000.

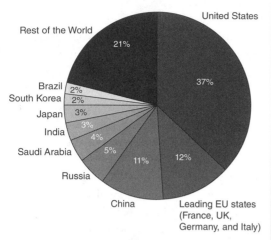

World-wide military expenditures, 2013

Inventory of nuclear warheads, 2013

	number of warheads	signed nuclear non-proliferation treaty
Russia	8,000	yes
U.S.	7,700	yes
France	300	yes
China	250	yes
UK	225	yes
Pakistan	100–120	no
India	90–110	no
Israel	80	no
North Korea	6–8	yes but withdrew 2003

FIGURE 11.1
Preserving U.S. Global Military Dominance

Commitment to military prowess can be measured in terms of annual spending by countries around the world. In 2013 that spending amounted to $1.75 trillion (a minimum since some countries do not supply information). The United States was the clear leader of the pack with outlays matching the combined total of the next nine. Relative to earlier years, the U.S. and European percentage had declined as a result of cuts imposed in the wake of the 2008 financial crisis, while Asian and Middle Eastern outlays were up. Another revealing way to measure military prowess is in terms of nuclear weapons. The United States and Russia had far and away the largest arsenals (a carry over from the Cold War). They together with a second tier of smaller nuclear powers (France, China, and the UK) had agreed to cooperate in restricting the spread of nuclear weapons. The third tier composed of relative newcomers—Pakistan, India, Israel, and North Korea—stood outside the non-proliferation regime.[11]

Bush exulted, "By God, we've kicked the Vietnam Syndrome once and for all."[12] But in fact the Iraq invasion highlighted the continuing national skittishness over military interventions and the limits of U.S. hegemony. To avoid the risks of going it alone, Bush had assembled a 30-nation coalition, including two Arab states, Syria, and Egypt. But the Middle East partners drew the line at American troops invading an Arab state, and the president did not want to incur the political risk of heavy U.S. casualties. Although he was defeated and his country was subjected to UN arms inspections and severe economic sanctions, Saddam Hussein remained in power, a thorn in the American side.

Bill Clinton pursued the policy of regional intervention, although with more caution. He pulled U.S. forces out of Somalia after they took casualties but sent them into Haiti and the former Yugoslavia. (Yugoslavia is discussed below in the context of the European Union.) Clinton's caution riled Cheney as well as other Cold War holdovers known as neoconservatives. They campaigned for a more forceful regional policy—what an influential 1996 essay called "benevolent global hegemony." In their view "military supremacy and moral confidence" provided the basis for dominance; preempting potential challengers would guarantee the United States its favored position over the long haul.[13]

These hawks got their way soon after George W. Bush restored the family claim to the White House in the 2000 election. The 9-11 attacks created an opening—an electorate that was angry, vengeful, and expecting tough action from the White House. In short order, Bush launched a fresh round of small wars in distant places. A clear doctrine and forceful advisers gave the president, a born-again Christian with a hankering for simple certitudes, just what he wanted. Cheney, selected for the vice presidency, would serve as the president's chief adviser, while neoconservatives made up a who's who in the administration's diplomatic and military establishment. Bush invoked the Cheney doctrine in a June 2002 address at West Point: "We must take the battle to the enemy, disrupt his plans, and confront the worst threats before they emerge. In the world we have entered, the only path to safety is the path of action."[14]

The president's first act was to dispatch an expeditionary force to Afghanistan while American agents fanned out seeking to excise the cancer of terrorism. The war in Afghanistan, after a quick success in overthrowing the Taliban, did not go well. Pacification failed for want of an effective central government. While the Taliban regrouped, U.S. NATO allies grew weary of even their token contribution to nation building. To make matters worse, Pakistan, described by one wag not as a country that had an army but as an army that had a country, complicated the U.S. mission. Nominally an ally, Pakistan backed elements of the insurgency opposing U.S. forces.

In March 2003 the younger Bush opened a second front, this time in Iraq, where the family had unfinished business. He proceeded despite grave public reservations, despite criticism from a wide range of U.S. pundits and former policymakers, despite overwhelming popular opposition around the world, and despite criticism from the governments of all the other major powers save Britain's. He was going to provide a clear answer to Cheney's characteristically blunt, impatient question: "Are you going to take care of this guy [Saddam Hussein] or not?"[15] But to what end was not clear: liberating Iraq and the entire region, putting in place a new doctrine of regime change, blocking the development of weapons of mass destruction, shutting down support for terrorism, securing cheap oil, or showing the United States would not suffer defiance.

Even as the fighting raged, the wisdom and consequences of the invasion remained the subject of heated debate. Developments on the ground badly betrayed confidence in the White House that "when we act, we create our own reality." Despite the investment of roughly a trillion dollars and the loss of 4,400 American lives, the Iraq project proved a disaster. It left Iraq's 25 million people badly divided and impoverished. Malnutrition—a good marker of social stress—affected a quarter of the population in 2014, substantially up from 8 percent in 1990–1992. The government in Baghdad, an American creation, was weak, closely tied to the

The Bush War Cabinet in a Videoconference on Iraq, June 2006
President George W. Bush is flanked by his key advisers, Dick Cheney to his right and Condoleezza Rice and Donald Rumsfeld to his left. The expressions on their faces make clear they now know full well that their project to remake Iraq and defeat what Bush called "Islamo-fascism" was going badly. (Brendan Smialowski for The New York Times)

U.S. arch-rival, Iran, and so sectarian in nature that it lacked genuine national authority. The U.S. public expressed mounting impatience with costly, open-ended campaigns in Iraq and Afghanistan. Four out of ten surveyed toward the end of the Bush presidency thought the United States "should mind its own business internationally and let other countries get along the best they can on their own."[16]

Any hegemony depends on legitimacy—the capacity to elicit international acceptance if not cooperation rather than provoking expensive, possibly debilitating resistance. By that standard America's standing as a global leader was in deep trouble by the end of the Bush presidency. The invasion of Iraq aroused international opposition, the mismanagement of the occupation inspired contempt, and the many violations of international norms—with aggression against a sovereign state, torture, handing prisoners over to states prone to torture ("rendition"), and judicial killings topping the list—created resentment and revulsion. The way that the United States conducted its war on terrorism seemed to many not only ham-handed but also counterproductive.

More broadly, U.S. leaders came under fire for their lopsided notion of leadership. They gave primacy to military force, dealt with others in a unilateral, my-way-or-the-highway fashion, and downplayed if not denigrated global governance exercised through the very international organizations, above all the UN, that an earlier generation of U.S. leaders helped create. Washington had rejected membership in the International Criminal Court and refused to join conventions against the use of antipersonnel mines, on the rights of children, and on exploitation of undersea resources. Washington resisted binding environmental regulations, with global warming getting the most hostile reception of all. In international fora U.S. policymakers were isolated in their support for Israel, acquiescing in its expansionist policies and paying only lip service to the rights of Palestinians. Adding to the reputational injury, an American-built house of cards collapsed on Wall Street in 2008, with damaging consequences around the world. The U.S.-championed neoliberal order seemed to many observers more of a problem than a solution.

Criticism worldwide was sweeping. By 2008 surveys in Britain, France, Germany, and Spain—all countries closely associated with the United States—found distrust of Bush registering at 81 to 88 percent. These results complemented earlier surveys that revealed a strong preference for seeing a power emerge that could offset U.S. military might. The U.S. economy, in its own deepening meltdown as the year unfolded, was thought to have a negative impact on other economies (the position of seven out of ten in Britain, Germany, Australia, France, and Turkey). While views of Americans as a people remained favorable, tellingly when asked about the country boasting the best lifestyle, the United States did not fare well. Canada and Australia dominated the list; only in India did the United States come out on top.[17]

Barack Obama, the "change candidate" for president, hewed to the policy of taming regional powers and troublemakers even though the approach looked less and less viable. He gave high priority to the containment or pacification of North Korea, China, Cuba, Venezuela, Iran, Syria, Iraq, Afghanistan, and Russia. The Middle East, the focal point of the open-ended "global war on terrorism," demanded his closest attention. Nowhere did he worry more about nuclear proliferation—and achieve less—than in his confrontation with Iran. His embrace of the one-sided U.S. policy toward the Palestine question made all his talk of brokering a deal empty. While pulling the last U.S. troops out of Iraq in 2011, he kept American Afghanistan policy on automatic pilot, sending more troops and more assistance to rescue a country that had become what he described as "the epicenter of violent extremism."[18] Building a nation around the Karzai government in Kabul was foundering, his ambassador warned, obstructed by the country's ethnic divisions, by an ineffective army, and by strong regional power holders.

Perhaps weary of slogging through the Middle East quagmire, Obama professed eagerness to "pivot" to an East Asia with its own set of problems that seemed to cry out for U.S. solutions. North Korea's nuclear program remained a source of great frustration. China was developing regional ambitions and a military to make them reality, while its leaders continued defiant in the face of criticism of their democracy and human rights record. The pivot proved problematic. Even as China grew more powerful and confident, U.S. leaders became more dependent on Beijing's cooperation on a host of issues—from nuclear North Korea and Iran, to trade, to the environment. Meanwhile the Middle East continued to generate crises that demanded attention: conflict in Gaza, coups in Egypt, civil war in Syria, and fragmentation of Iraq. The United States had become like the little boy rushing about

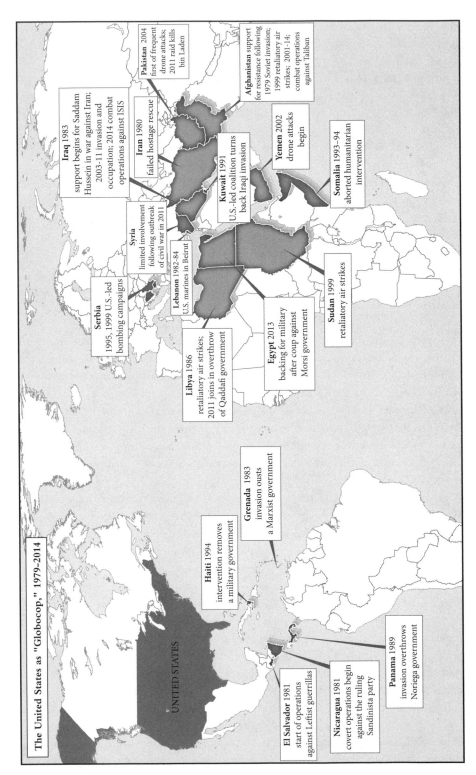

The United States as "Globocop," 1979–2014

Pakistan 2004 first of frequent drone attacks; 2011 raid kills bin Laden

Afghanistan support for resistance following 1979 Soviet invasion; 1999 retaliatory air strikes; 2001–14; combat operations against Taliban

Iraq 1983 support begins for Saddam Hussein in war against Iran; 2003–11 invasion and occupation; 2014 combat operations against ISIS

Iran 1980 failed hostage rescue

Yemen 2002 drone attacks begin

Somalia 1993–94 aborted humanitarian intervention

Kuwait 1991 U.S.–led coalition turns back Iraqi invasion

Syria limited involvement following outbreak of civil war in 2011

Lebanon 1982–84 U.S. marines in Beirut

Serbia 1995, 1999 U.S.-led bombing campaigns

Sudan 1999 retaliatory air strikes

Libya 1986 retaliatory air strikes; 2011 joins in overthrow of Qaddafi government

Egypt 2013 backing for military after coup against Morsi government

UNITED STATES

Grenada 1983 invasion ousts a Marxist government

Haiti 1994 intervention removes a military government

El Salvador 1981 start of operations against Leftist guerrillas

Nicaragua 1981 covert operations begin against the ruling Sandinista party

Panama 1989 invasion overthrows Noriega government

to plug holes in leaky dikes. So many were the dikes that he became not only over-extended and hyperactive but also easily distracted and often caught off guard.

Latin America beyond the Cold War

Nowhere was the unsettled U.S. relationship with other parts of the world more striking than in its very backyard. Latin America began to emerge in the 1990s from the long shadow of the Cold War and the even longer shadow of the Monroe Doctrine. Constant U.S. pressure and repeated rounds of direct intervention had left their mark. Economies were stumbling and societies had been torn by civil war and repression. The challenge in the new era was to find a path toward democracy, social reconciliation, and sustainable development. For those on the immediate U.S. doorstep there was still limited room for maneuver. To take the most blatant example, a still-defiant Cuban government remained locked in a seemingly end-less confrontation with Washington (see Chapter 6). Even the transfer of power from Fidel Castro to his brother Raúl in 2006 and modest internal liberalization did little to soften the impasse. But Latin American states at a greater remove had greater room for maneuver. Brazil, a hemispheric giant, was the most notable of these. A country with the seventh largest economy in the world and with a popula-tion estimated at 196 million in 2013 (a third of all of Latin America's) had ample latitude to decide its own future.

In charting its political course, Latin America had first of all to put behind it an era of dictatorship that had made the region into the graveyard of democracy in the post-World War II period. Even absent Cold War pressures, democratization was no easy task in fractured societies. The Spanish conquest of indigenous peoples had cre-ated one enduring fault line. Laborers imported to work on plantations created an-other. Strong class, ethnic, regional, and ideological differences generated sharp struggles over land and over control of the state. Wealthy families with European roots and conservative elements in the Catholic Church continued in the post-World War II period to lord it over their societies, supported by a military that claimed for itself a privileged place in national life. Torture, abduction, and mass murder became the answer to encroaching subversive ideologies and demands of the poor and indi-genous peoples. Washington endorsed this arrangement, cultivated the military, and intervened directly to protect the status quo—by persuasion and aid if possible, but by covert operations and military force if necessary. Repression did not end social conflicts but rather intensified them as those demanding more open and

◄ **MAP 11.1**
The United States as "Globocop," 1979–2014
The most notable feature of this map is the quickening tempo of U.S. engagement. Following the end of the Cold War, the sheriff was busier than ever, with attention shifting from Latin America miscreants to Middle East terrorists. Aside from the overt use of force identified here, the sheriff also kept order by training the personnel of U.S.-aligned governments and maintaining a robust military presence in the western Pacific.

equitable societies resorted to violence in the face of counter-violence. Guerrillas squared off against security forces, death squads, and right-wing paramilitary groups. Criminal gangs and drug lords joined the battle for social control and economic resources.

The Caribbean basin had the most troubled past to escape. Guatemala (treated in Chapter 9) is perhaps the most dramatic case of how thoroughly dictators and U.S. cold warriors had crushed democratic hopes. Washington's fixation with countries long in its sphere of influence did not abate even as the Cold War gave way to the new global era. Ronald Reagan, with his fear of communist inroads, had stoked the fires of conflict in El Salvador, Nicaragua, and Grenada (see Chapter 7). George H. W. Bush invaded Panama in 1989, toppling the government of General Manuel Antonio Noriega and carting him off to an American prison. Clinton dispatched U.S. forces to Haiti to remove a military government in the name of democracy. All three kept up the pressure on the Cuban government, even though its social achievements were considerable and its political transgressions paled by comparison with those of some U.S. clients. The gunboats were showing up less often and the dictators were leaving the scene, but the region remained socially conflicted, democratically unstable, and generally poorly governed.

South America, which had also felt the effects of U.S. pressure and internal divisions, proved more successful in bringing democracy back from the grave. In Chile, Argentina, and Brazil the generals had killed and buried democracy with the support of long-dominant elites, the Catholic hierarchy, and U.S. policymakers (see Chapter 5). Right-wing regimes there as well as in Bolivia and Uruguay collaborated with each other to eliminate any trace of left-wing opposition. But by the 1980s the transition from military rule was well under way. The generals in Argentina and Brazil had alienated even their well-to-do supporters and mismanaged their economies, while the political Left there as well as in Chile, Nicaragua, and Guatemala shifted to a nonviolent strategy of relying on human rights, the law, and coalition building. Elections began going off without a hitch, and in resuscitated democracies parties started passing power from one to the other as a matter of routine. As a sign of changing times, by 2010 Argentina, Brazil, and Chile had each elected women to the presidency, and two of the winners had the distinction of having suffered torture and imprisonment under the rule of the generals.

Truth and reconciliation commissions played a critical role as bridges between the eras of dictatorship and democracy. They examined the death of democracy the better to resurrect it. As elsewhere around the world, these Latin American truth commissions functioned in ways that reflected national conditions. In Argentina and Chile commissions delivered reports in 1984 and 1991 respectively that sought to spread the blame. They explained violations of human rights in terms of a social breakdown in which extremists on the Right and Left had provoked each other. A recognition of past excesses, the reports suggested, would lay the basis for reknitting society and for creating a new legal framework within which democratic politics could play out. These commissions left it to the courts to decide individual culpability through criminal proceedings involving only a few of the leading of-fenders among the military.

Guatemala's Truth Commission was more forthright and judgmental even though it operated under significant constraints. A still-powerful military limited the Commission to broad analysis (no naming of names) and ruled out any crim-inal proceedings. Administered by the UN, the Commission delivered a report in 1999 that was surprisingly blunt in identifying the social divisions that had plunged Guatemala into violence and in charging the military with genocide at the height of its campaign against the insurgency in 1981–1983. The report found that overall the military had committed some 626 massacres and 200,000 political murders. The Commission concluded that popular demands for change had been met with terror: "State violence has been fundamentally aimed against the ex-cluded, the poor, and the Maya."[19] Along with this verdict, which shocked the gov-ernment and the military, the report warned that there was still no social basis for a new, cohesive Guatemala. The old order that had given rise to conflict in the first place survived: a dominant landed class whose interests were defended by the mili-tary against any serious challenge.

The notable if uneven advance of Latin American democracy was matched by an uneven move toward more market-friendly economies. Mexico and Chile went far-thest in embracing neoliberal policies championed by United States and advanced by International Monetary Fund (IMF) bailouts, although with distinctly different social consequences. Mexico found integration with its neighbor to the north through the North American Free Trade Agreement (NAFTA) to be disruptive (see Chapter 8). The long dominant Institutional Revolutionary Party saw its position eroded during the 1990s and broken in the 2000 presidential election. Mexico had entered a period of multi-party competition. At the same time state institutions were atrophying and social order was breaking down. Criminal activity was soon on the rise, with gangs dealing in drugs bound for the U.S. market engaging in un-checked violence. With Mexico unable to offer gainful employment to its soaring population, some 12 million pushed northward from the late 1970s onward look-ing for work.[20] At the other extreme, Cuba and Venezuela clung to a state-directed economy that promoted welfare and equality if not growth at home.

Argentina's and Brazil's complex, ambivalent, and shifting relationship with neo-liberalism put them in a middle category. Despite a history of deep state interven-tion, elected governments following the return of the military to barracks had little choice but to move toward more market-friendly policies to achieve economic stabi-lization. In Argentina a new civilian government had to shoulder heavy debts in-curred by the military. To secure financial rescue from the international banking community, the government in the early 1990s embraced neoliberal policies, slash-ing tariffs, selling off state enterprises, opening the door wide to multinationals, and pegging the currency to the dollar. Despite these steps, Argentina found itself in a financial crisis in 2001 that turned into a severe, long-lasting, deeply deflationary, and politically explosive economic collapse. With the economy finally recovering by late in the decade, a government that traced its pedigree back to Juan Perón reversed the trend toward privatization. By 2014 the country was again in trouble with foreign investors and at risk of the second default in 14 years.

Brazil's embrace of neoliberalism began earlier, was more restrained, and proved less erratic. The return of an elected civilian government in 1985 after 20 years of military rule marked the beginning of a shift toward neoliberal economic policy. Brazil had by then accumulated the world's largest foreign debt. When interest rates rose and markets in the developed world for natural resources shrank, the civilian government faced a payment crisis that threatened to bankrupt the country. Like many African and Latin American countries such as Argentina and Mexico in debt difficulties at this time, Brazil had to turn to international banks and the IMF for help. The price was a move to the market. That meant limiting state intervention in the economy, lowering tariffs that protected domestic industry, privatizing state-owned companies, cutting welfare programs, and in general creating conditions favorable to foreign capital and corporations.

Between 1992 and 2010 this neoliberal turn moderated as Fernando Henrique Cardoso and then Luiz Inácio Lula da Silva moved policy distinctly to the Left. Their goal was to secure both prosperity and welfare within the confines of the global economy. Cardoso had established his reputation during the era of military dictatorship, doing distinguished academic work in exile on the policy of import substitution (discussed in Chapter 5). He turned policymaker in 1992, first as finance minister and then two years later as president. Surprisingly, he cut back on protectionist trade policies so that producers of raw materials, autos, and aircraft would have better access to export markets. He also bowed to neoliberal principles by following fiscal austerity to bring hyperinflation under control and to privatize inefficient state monopolies. Foreign investors began to funnel money into a more productive Brazil. But Cardoso still had a progressive side. He removed subsidies that went to the middle class and began experimenting with direct payments to help poor families. He initiated race-based affirmative action programs. And he put restrictions on the development of ecologically priceless Amazon rainforest.

This mix of market expansion with social spending, which resembled the course followed by western European economies, would continue under Lula da Silva. From an impoverished family, he had been a shoe-shine boy, then an entry-level metalworker, and by the 1970s a spokesman for the labor movement and a prominent figure in the Workers' Party. In 2002 this left-wing activist, popularly known simply as Lula, won the presidency. He built on Cardoso's achievements. Lula and his Workers' Party accepted some free-market policies and some privatization of state enterprises as necessary to stabilize and invigorate the economy, but they kept the major petroleum producer, Petrobras, under state control and continued the effort to check environmentally dangerous development of the Amazon basin. Even more important, Lula considerably extended his predecessor's social programs. Social welfare and minimum wage policies targeted deep and persistent wealth inequalities, and special funding promoted development in poorer regions. These measures including the world's largest conditional cash transfer program reduced the gap between the rich and poor that had topped the global charts. Government programs helped raise some 36 million people out of extreme poverty and broadened the middle class. Affirmative action plans and quotas targeted the widespread social and economic discrimination against people of color. Improved living standards and better opportunity among lower-income earners created a loyal following for Lula's Workers' Party. By the end of Lula's presidency, the Left had become the political mainstream, and Brazil had become more urban (over 80 percent), freer of old social hierarchies, more open politically to the poor and working class, and more plural in the range of interest groups jockeying for advantage. (For Brazil's overall development record compared to the other BRIC's, see Figure 11.3 on p. 528.)

Of all the countries of Latin America, a democratic Brazil with a bustling economy, enormous natural resources, and a large population has nursed the biggest regional and international ambitions. These ambitions, with roots going back to the early twentieth century, today seem closer than ever to realization. One arena for raising Brazil's profile has been regional. Brazil joined Argentina, Uruguay, and Paraguay in 1991 in creating a regional free trade zone known as MERCOSUR (Southern Cone Common Market). It took the lead in 2008 in creating UNASUR (Union of South American Nations), covering all the countries of South America and broadening the cooperative agenda to include infrastructure, energy, finance, and technical matters. These regional initiatives effectively conceded Mexico to the American sphere and avoided involvement in Central America and the Caribbean, where social and political stability was in question. But South America would operate outside U.S. control. Determined to contain and counterbalance U.S. influence, Brazil blocked an American-sponsored plan to extend NAFTA to the rest of the hemisphere and gave Washington heartburn by maintaining close ties to left-leaning parties in Cuba, Venezuela, Colombia, Bolivia, and Chile.

The other arena in which Brazil has asserted itself is international. Lula himself was an outspoken advocate for reform of international institutions to better address the needs of the Global South and for action to meet the deepening climate change crisis. All the while, he delighted in denouncing neoliberalism as "the absurd doctrine that markets could regulate themselves, with no need for so-called 'intrusive' state intervention." He pointedly rejected "the thesis of absolute freedom for financial capital, with no rules or transparency, beyond the control of peoples and institutions."[21]

Big problems still confront this giant of the Southern Hemisphere. They include urban violence that has pitted well-entrenched urban gangs against ill-disciplined police. Reining in environmental destruction in the Amazon basin remains a major challenge. Political corruption is deeply rooted in the bureaucracy and in the regional governments. The educational system, now universal in its coverage, is of low quality. Heavy dependence on commodity exports and foreign capital has left the country especially vulnerable to the vagaries of distant markets and investment houses. The end of the export boom in 2011 lowered growth rates to a mediocre 2 percent range and forced Lula's successor, Dilma Rousseff, to moderate social programs at home; delay improvements in health, education, and infrastructure; and cut back on Brazil's substantial support for regional integration projects. Protesting workers, students, and middle-class professionals have demanded improvements in public sector performance while at the same time demonstrating the democratic vitality of a country in which debate is vigorous, elections are closely

Street Artist Paulo Ito on the Cost to Brazil of Hosting the 2014 World Cup
This piece of public art captured the widespread resentment in Brazil over the costs incurred in preparing for the World Cup. In the run-up to the event, demonstrators took to the street to complain that health, education, and public transport needed attention, not special sports facilities built to the high specifications of the world soccer authority. In the end the investment in the World Cup failed to pay off in the way that mattered to most Brazilians; their team experienced an embarrassing meltdown. (Paulo Ito)

LATIN AMERICA IN TRANSITION

1983	Alfonsín elected Argentina's first civilian president in postmilitary era
1984	First of Latin American truth commission reports issued in Argentina
1985	Brazil elects first civilian president after two decades of military rule
1989	Chile elects first civilian president in post-Pinochet era
1991	Founding of MERCOSUR
1994	Mexico bound to U.S. economy by NAFTA; Cardoso elected president of Brazil and introduces economic reforms and limited welfare measures.
1995	Mexico's economic crisis requires U.S.-led bailout
2001	Argentina enters financial crisis
2002	Lula da Silva follows Cardoso as Brazilian president and accelerates welfare programs
2008	UNASUR formed

fought, and the electorate is engaged. How Brazil handles the demands of a public with rising expectations will do much to determine whether the country continues its rise as a regional and global player.

CROSSCURRENTS AND CONFLICT IN THE MIDDLE EAST

An entire region stretching from North and sub-Saharan Africa to Central Asia is in flux, buffeted by crosscurrents stronger and more confusing than at any time since 1945. The old order has become unglued and neoliberal solutions hold no promise of producing stability or addressing the issues that now agitate the region. Whether a little "creative destruction" might help is not at all clear. The states prominent in the early postwar period—modernizing secular elites and monarchies— have found themselves challenged frontally and forcefully over recent decades by the emergence of Islam as a political force. All politics has to have grounding somewhere, and so what form the Islamist variant takes and how it evolves depend heavily on place. Conditions vary considerably, ranging from western sub-Saharan Africa to South and Southeast Asia and into the immigrant communities of Europe and North America.

Overlaying this mounting confrontation has been rivalry among the regional powers—Turkey, Iran, and Saudi Arabia. Their competing agendas have generated additional tension and instability. They have unsettled Syria, Lebanon, and Iraq. They have marginalized Egypt, diminished and disoriented by its own internal divisions. They have sharpened the ethnic and religious identity of Sunni, Shi'a, Alawite, Christian, and Kurd and fueled civil conflict. And they have left Israel anxious about its own military and political future in a region evolving rapidly and beyond its control.

The Rise of Political Islam

The appeal of political Islam is in broadest terms best understood in the context of the Middle East's troubled relationship with globalization. In the most obvious, material terms the region has become a backwater of the global economy with profound effects on popular welfare. Per capita income in the region that once compared favorably with Asia's has fallen well behind. In Egypt in 1965 it was almost triple China's but now is less than half. Iran and South Korea were on a par in 1965, but now South Korea's per capita income is eight times higher. The region's economic ills are reflected dramatically in its small share of global merchandise trade. The Middle East (excluding North Africa and Turkey) accounts for just 4 percent, less than Germany alone. Whereas other regions have a vigorous internal trade (two thirds of all imports in the case of Europe), only 9 percent of Middle East trade stays within the region. This woeful record is in large measure the fault of government policies that constrain and distort enterprise. The public sector is a large burden (for example, in Egypt almost 30 percent of the workforce). Fuel subsidies, large government deficits and accumulated debt, corruption, and costly regulations are other drags on production. Women participate in the workforce at a rate lower than in any other major region. Education and programs to help the poor and raise overall levels of income and welfare have been underfunded.[22]

The economic failures of the postwar order and the social problems that have attended them were most glaring in the cases of the secular, westernizing governments. Usually guided by some mixture of socialism and nationalism, they promised a brighter future—but in fact they failed to deliver. At home they left the urban poor especially in distress. In their external relations these governments fell into dependence on outside support (chiefly from the United States and the Soviet Union). They were further discredited by their ineffectual if noisy opposition to Israel.

Egypt under Nasser's successors is a good case in point. Anwar Sadat, a long-time Nasser associate, launched one last military challenge against Israel with Soviet support in 1973. When initial success turned into a military stalemate, he shifted in a pro-U.S. direction. He pulled Egypt out of the anti-Israel coalition of Arab states and moved toward a peace agreement that restored the Sinai to Egyptian control. At home he privatized parts of the economy in a nod to pro-market pressures. When both the foreign and economic policy shifts proved unpopular, Sadat responded by adopting a more tolerant policy toward the Muslim Brotherhood. Sadat's successor, Hosni Mubarak, maintained non-confrontational relations with Israel while working to curb Islamic critics at home who objected, like many in the region, to a future conceived primarily in Western, secular terms.

The monarchies bordering the Persian Gulf, above all Saudi Arabia, have done better economically at least in general terms thanks to their oil resources. Predating the rise of the secular regimes, these oil states have profited richly from the international demand for oil, but they have largely played a *rentier* role in the global economy, investing accumulated petrodollars primarily in developed countries rather than at home or in the region. Their societies were hardly models of economic dynamism. For example, Saudi society has suffered from high levels of inequality, a high incidence of poverty, high real unemployment, and high functional illiteracy that is especially marked among women.

The problematic regional relationship with globalization is as much a matter of attitude as material welfare. At the heart of that attitude is a powerful historical mythology that holds up an age of regional grandeur as a contrast to the recent experience of domination by the West. For a thousand years—from the seventh to the seventeenth century—the Islamic world could boast of its learning and prosperity as well as power that extended deep into Spain and Central Europe. The rise of strong European and Russian states checked the advance of Islam. At the time of the partition of the Ottoman Empire in 1920, the Middle East was a weak and vulnerable backwater, the prey of European empire builders. The depth of this fall has bred deep and abiding resentment, while the failure to make progress from cultural and political subordination and humiliation to equality and pride has proven frustrating after a century of effort.

This long and unhappy history of Western encroachment is intimately associated with globalization in its most recent post-1945 phase. While the colonization projects of the Europeans collapsed in the face of independence movements, an increasingly assertive United States stepped in to assert a new kind of dominance. The U.S. advocacy of neoliberal values, its outspoken support for egalitarian gender relations, its close ties to the monarchies and the more accommodating secular regimes, its highly militarized solution to regional challenges, and its four-square support for the "Zionist entity" have all served as reminders that the age of subordination was not yet over.

From the regional perspective, this U.S. involvement looks a lot like an updated version of the old imperialism where European powers drew the maps, controlled the politics directly or through clients, infiltrated the culture, and facilitated a beachhead for Jewish settlements. The pattern of military intervention stands out in especially stark relief. Stunned by the Iranian revolution and then the Soviet invasion of Afghanistan, President Jimmy Carter began making military commitments to protect the oil-rich Persian Gulf. Washington has since then assembled a system of bases, training programs, and covert capabilities. Those accumulated assets have supported an accelerating pattern of intervention across the region, including frequent attacks from the air and the insertion of combat forces in Lebanon, Kuwait, Somalia, Iraq, and Afghanistan. Politically, U.S. policymakers have closely aligned with monarchies and strongmen, none more closely than Saudi Arabia, as a barrier to Islamist advances. Popular movements in Algeria, Lebanon, Gaza, Turkey, and most recently Egypt have at minimum made Washington as well as the monarchs nervous and in some cases prompted overt resistance. Given a choice between more moderate Islamists demanding majority rule and monarchs clinging to power, Washington has opted for the latter. For example, the Obama administration turned a blind eye when the ruler of Bahrain, backed by Saudi forces, suppressed a peaceful protest movement calling for rights for the Shiʻa majority. Washington had a naval base there as well as stability to protect; democracy mattered less.

Not surprisingly against this record, recent public opinion surveys record overwhelmingly negative views of the United States. In 2014, for example, 85 percent of Egyptians and 73 percent of Turks professed unfavorable views of the United States as a country. Attitudes toward U.S. policy were equally unfavorable. To a large extent these views rest on a widely perceived contradiction (as one scholar has put it) "between Western pronouncements on freedom, justice and democracy and the actions of Western states in the dealings with the Muslim world."[23]

Only in recent decades has the political path opened up for champions of Islam. Although participants in the campaigns for independence, they were in the post-independence order relegated to the sidelines. Secular states were interested in Islam primarily as a symbol to reinforce their legitimacy. But "old-fashioned" religious commitments were not to stand in the way of the advance of the "modern" values in political discourse, education, the courts, and social standards. The Cold War further accentuated the tilt toward secularism as states in the region aligned with the Soviet Union or the United States. The campaign to minimize Islam as a political force played out all across the Muslim world in the early postwar decades. Iran and Egypt (both treated in Chapter 6) are good cases in point, but the pattern of conflict also applied to Algeria, Tunisia, Turkey, Iraq, Afghanistan, and Indonesia.

A perceptible shift occurred in the 1970s. The failure of the secular states created an ideological and political vacuum, which political Islam has increasingly filled. At the same time, Saudi oil wealth generated by booming prices began to fund grassroots efforts to promote Islamic institutions and values. Together the effects of these developments were evident in the rise of a more militant politics bent on creating moral societies free of foreign political and cultural influences. In some places, such as Muhammad Zia-ul-Haq's Pakistan and Anwar Sadat's Egypt, state authorities managed to coopt the new religiosity temporarily at least. But in others, such as Iran, Afghanistan, and Lebanon, the emergence of Islamist parties led to conflict with state authorities. The Iranian revolution coming at the end of the decade dramatized the power of the Islamist surge even as it gave impetus to revival elsewhere (see Chapter 9).

It should be no surprise that a politically charged Islam would at the end of the twentieth century become a potent force for removing discredited elites and turning back outside interference. Religion has continued to play a central place in the daily life of ordinary people, rural and urban, and in the life of the community, from charitable organizations to schools to women's centers to publishing houses. A faith shared by all sorts of people in different countries across several continents provided the basis for the expansive notion of the *umma*, a transnational community of Muslims. However much they might differ in the practice of their faith, they tended to hold in common conservative social values, especially attitudes toward gender equality, abortion, divorce, and homosexuality. These attitudes translated into a conception of governance rooted in religious morality and expressed in some form of Sharia law. This legal system was administered by clerics trained in a venerable tradition of Islamic jurisprudence, which they applied to civil matters such as divorce, to criminal conduct such as theft and murder, and to grievous affronts to social standards such as adultery or impiety. Region-wide surveys underline the high regard many have for Islam as a political as well as spiritual force. In Egypt, for example, 85 percent of those polled in Spring 2010 (a time when Hosni Mubarak's government demonized the Muslim Brotherhood) had a positive view of Islam's role in politics in their country.[24]

The resort to political action to create a society more in line with Muslim values has in broad terms developed along three lines. The most familiar are the militant transnational networks best represented by al-Qaeda. It sprang to prominence as part of the anti-Soviet resistance in Afghanistan in the 1980s and rose to greater fame with the 9-11 attacks as well as the bombings in Madrid in 2004 and London in 2005. Its recruits often came from the ranks of *jihadis* repressed within their own societies, notably in Egypt, Algeria, Saudi Arabia, and Morocco. They enlisted in the Afghan conflict, gaining training that could be used back home. Later, as the points of conflict multiplied, they moved from one battlefront to another.

Osama bin Laden himself embodied a pronounced tendency to link domestic struggles with outside threats. In broadest terms the threat came from a fundamentally immoral Western civilization disfigured by drinking, gambling, usury, sexual license, homosexuality, and exploitation of women as commercial sex objects. But the threat that preoccupied him more was the actual intrusion of outside powers bent on domination of Muslim peoples. He justified his shift from the local to international in terms that made sense to other *jihadis* on the move. He saw two kinds of foes. The "near enemy" was the regional governments standing in the way of more godly societies, while the "far enemy" was the United States and the other great powers that were propping up those regimes. The latter, he realized, were more important. Force the foreigners out, and the old order in country after country would succumb.

Frustrated in his calls for reform of his own government in Saudi Arabia, he had turned his attention to the Soviets in Afghanistan and later to the Americans after their military forces moved into Saudi Arabia in 1990 as part of the response to Iraq's invasion of Kuwait. To prosecute his war against the United States he set up training camps in Afghanistan in 1996 under the protection of the Taliban government. Using the Internet and television, he joined other leading radical Islamists in proclaiming: "To kill the American and their allies—civilians and military—is an individual duty incumbent upon every Muslim in all countries." The indictment of a people who had facilitated the repression of the Palestinian people, sent troops into the holy lands of the Arabian peninsula, and devastated the lives of Iraqis with economic sanctions had strong resonance even among those averse to indiscriminate violence. He announced in the wake of the 9-11 attacks, "What the United States is tasting today is nothing compared to what we have tasted for decades. Our *umma* has known this humiliation and contempt for over eighty years. Its sons are killed, its blood is spilled, its holy sites are attacked, and it is not governed according to Allah's command. Despite this, no one cares." Bin Laden's assassination in his Pakistani hideout in 2011 at the hands of a U.S. team did nothing to dampen the appeal of his message. Bin Laden's successor, Ayman al-Zawahiri, an Egyptian physician and long-time al-Qaeda ideologue and mouthpiece, conveyed the same message.[25]

A second expression of political Islam has assumed the form of armed liberation movements. They operate within a distinct territorial framework that defines their goals and recruitment. Hamas (short for the Islamic Resistance Movement) in Gaza is a good example of this second tendency. It originated as a branch of Egypt's Muslim Brotherhood and got a boost in the 1980s from the Israelis, who wanted to create a challenger to the secular PLO. The first *intifada* (uprising) in 1987 marked the turning of Hamas toward armed resistance to Israeli occupation. Along with an armed wing, it deployed a network of charitable organizations and gained wide popular support. After playing an active role in the second *intifada* in

2001, it won power in Gaza through the ballot box in 2006. Since then Hamas has gone through repeated if inconclusive rounds of open conflict with Israel forces, most recently during the summer of 2014. Despite heavy losses, Hamas appears to maintain its broad base of support.

The list of the territorially bound Islamist movement is fairly long. Hezbollah (Party of God) developed a stronghold in southern Lebanon after the Israeli invasion of Lebanon in 1982. Its guerrilla resistance, conducted with Iranian and Syrian backing, forced the Israeli military to withdraw in 2000. By then Hezbollah had become a major player in Lebanon's intercommunal political system, giving voice to a previously marginalized Shi'a community. The Taliban, which has proven a resilient force in Afghanistan, is another case in point. This Pakistan-backed political and military organization fought its way to the top during the civil war that followed Soviet withdrawal in 1989. Once in power in the late 1990s, it imposed a semblance of order to a war-torn land and instituted a strict Islamic code. Although its primary concerns were with Afghanistan, its sympathies for the transnational ideology and struggle led to giving bin Laden refuge. The success of one of those missions—the 9-11 attacks—led to the Taliban's overthrow but not its destruction. It has retained its capacity to mobilize, especially among the Pashtun part of the Afghan population. Still other territorially focused Islamist movements include Pakistan's own Taliban, the Moro Liberation Front in the Philippines, which has battled to realize the dream of a homeland that goes back to the Spanish colonial era; Chechen fighters locked in battle with Russia forces; militant groups fighting to free Indian-controlled Kashmir; Boko Haram challenging government control in northern Nigeria; and Al Shabab struggling for power in Somalia against outside resistance, including Kenyan, Ethiopian, and African Union forces.

The first and second forms of political Islam overlap in several critical ways. To begin with, they often share a willingness to use force—whether conventional guerrilla operations, suicide bombings, or targeted assassinations. While some have developed loose ties with the core leadership of al-Qaeda and more recently with the Islamic State in Iraq and Syria (ISIS, also known as the Islamic State in the Levant or ISIL), the local organizations tend to pursue their own agendas. Coordination is at a minimum and tensions with al-Qaeda Central are commonplace. These two radical Islamist currents also share a far-reaching and urgent notion of social transformation. Influenced by the writings of Sayyid Qutb, they take *jihad* as an enduring obligation that rests on the individual and that has to take an offensive form against an impure society and ungodly rulers. This stands in distinction to the more orthodox position that *jihad* was a collective obligation, undertaken in defense and taken up only intermittently. This commitment to *jihad* was embedded within a socially conservative Wahhabist faith that prescribed the application of Sharia law, resistance to Western cultural inroads, and removal of infidels and apostates to the social margin or expelling them altogether.

The two versions of political Islam are also linked by their recruits, who often moved between the national and the transnational movements. Islamists defeated in their own country turned to transnational organizations as an alternative path of resistance. Such was the case with some members of Egypt's Muslim Brotherhood who grew so frustrated with government corruption, economic inequality, and lack of democracy that they launched a campaign of violence, including the assassination of President Anwar Sadat in 1981 and other government officials as well as attacks on tourists, Christians, and prominent secularists. Sadat's successor, Hosni Mubarak, countered with a successful campaign of state repression that drove militants abroad where they enlisted in foreign struggles. Veterans of those struggles have later returned home with redoubled commitment and new skills to turn against regimes that had previously frustrated them. Returnees from the war in Afghanistan had considerable impact on developments in Egypt, Algeria, and Tunisia.

Finally among our types of political Islam are the more moderate movements that have pursued state power within clearly demarcated territorial bounds and by nonviolent means. This third line of political Islam is related to the second by virtue of its distinct national set of concerns. Both might be properly labeled Islamo-nationalism since both aspire to exercise state power within currently demarcated boundaries. But those embodying this third tendency have pursued power through persuasion and the electoral process and given higher priority to

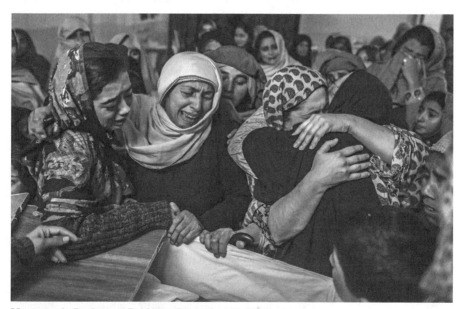

Mourners in Peshawar, Pakistan, December 16, 2014
These relatives of Mohammed Ali Khan, a fifteen-year-old student, grieve over his coffin. He died along with 133 others students and 10 staff in an army-run school in retaliation for military operations against Pakistan's Taliban. The attack was mounted by a Taliban team reportedly made up of non-Pakistanis, including two Afghans, a Chechen, an Egyptian, and a Moroccan. The targeting of children and the heavy loss of young lives provoked widespread public expressions of outrage and was condemned even by al-Qaeda. This photo is a reminder of the mounting costs of a multi-front and often indiscriminate war waged within the Muslim world. (REUTERS/Zohra Bensemra)

popular welfare and participation. The borders between the two kinds of Islamo-nationalists can shift. The Islamic Salvation Front in Algeria is a case in point. It rose to prominence in the early 1990s in the wake of student and worker protests against the secular post-independence military-run government. The Front's leader, Abbassi Madani, called for completing the Algerian revolution. The previous generation had in his view taken the first step of expelling France "*physically*"; now the time had come "to banish it *intellectually and ideologically*, to break with its supporters who have sucked its venomous milk."[26] The Front swept to victory in 1990 and 1991 in the country's first free elections since independence. Its demands for restricting the rights given women and more generally for instituting an Islamic state frightened the more secular and Europeanized part of the population and prompted the military to intervene. It nullified the results and rounded up Islamist leaders. The Front turned to guerrilla resistance in a bloody civil war that would consume most of the decade and ultimately exhaust the Islamists.

This third line of Islamist politics scored its earliest successes in Iran, well before the better-known examples of Turkey and the even more recent Arab Spring that erupted across North Africa. The Islamic Republic, founded in a violent struggle both before and immediately after the Shah's fall from power, evolved into a constrained democracy following Khomeini's death in 1989. The new supreme religious leader, Ali Khamenei, was a longtime associate and favorite of Khomeini. He faced a public that had revered his predecessor but was becoming impatient with clerical rule. Khamenei set to one side sharply anti-imperialist rhetoric and focused instead on recovery from the terribly destructive war with Iraq. The government promoted more market-oriented policies to improve the economy, called for respect for private property, and loosened cultural restrictions (for example, allowing more latitude in women's dress and a greater variety of music). The political system became increasingly a battleground over reform. Khamenei as the Supreme Leader and the Council of Guardians and the judiciary have combined to keep troublesome candidates off the ballot, overturn objectionable legislations, censor the press, restrict cultural activities, and intimidate reformers through selectively applied violence.

But popular pressure, expressed through elections for the president, the parliament, and local councils, has steadily favored reform. The parliament enjoyed special legitimacy thanks to a century-old commitment (at least in theory) to constitutional government. Mosaddeq had fought for it, the Shah had to pay it lip service, and Khomeini had adopted it to his own cause. Elections have become regular, competitive affairs that offered real choices to an engaged electorate (with 72 percent turning out in the 2013). Youth and the middle class were particularly restive. They wanted a more vigorous economy that would create jobs, and they wanted a more open social and cultural life. Prominent clerics themselves were divided over whether on the one hand a stand-pat approach would create so much popular alienation that it might threaten the entire experiment in Islamic government or whether on the other hand an increasingly pluralistic and democratic system would erode popular commitment to Islamic values.

The result has been a seesaw battle. The election in 1997 of Mohammad Khatami as president by an impressive 67 percent of the vote seemed to promise additional political liberalization amid an explosion of creativity in Iranian literature and film, the rise of a women's movement, and a popular resentment of the restrictions imposed by the clerics. Khatami the candidate had declared that "state authority cannot be attained through coercion and dictatorship. Rather it is to be realized through governing according to the law, respecting the rights and empowering people to participate and ensuring their involvement in decision-making."[27] Supreme Leader Khamenei, however, used his growing authority to check the reformers and to usher in a period of retrenchment under President Mahmoud Ahmadinejad (2005–2013). The election of Hassan Rouhani in 2013 was testimony to the persistence of the reform impulse and set the stage for another round in the contest over clerical control.

In Turkey a cautiously Islamist party has had signal success under Recep Tayyip Erdoğan. The Islamists, initially organized as the Turkish Virtue Party, began to make electoral inroads in the 1990s. After they were banned in 1999, a splinter group decided to circumvent a stoutly secular military that still regarded itself as the guardian of the country's founding principles. They organized the Justice and Development Party in 2001 and campaigned as "conservative democrats" who took Islamic values seriously but accepted a state grounded on secular principles. Party leaders liked to compare themselves to Christian Democrats in Europe who combined religious ethics with liberal democratic ideals. The party, under Erdoğan's leadership, quickly won the first of a string of electoral victories that gave it comfortable control in Ankara. Once in office, party leaders put into effect popular economic reforms while also leashing the military.

Most recently the Arab Spring promised to spread democratic change across the Middle East. A single incident set events in motion. A Tunisian fruit seller, Tarek (Mohamed) Bouazizi, had his cart and wares seized by officials, and he was harassed. Humiliated and deprived of a means to support his family, he protested by immolating himself. This dramatic event in December 2010 resonated among Tunisians fed up with official corruption and the long rule of strongman Zine El Abidine Ben Ali. Within a month street demonstrations had forced Ben Ali into exile, paving the way for elections that gave Islamists a leading role.

The shock waves created by this people's movement carried widely within the region, with consequences varying considerably from place to place. In Egypt demonstrations in 2011 toppled Mubarak from the presidency. In the elections that followed, the well-organized and popular Muslim Brotherhood scored major victories. The movement spread to Libya in an uprising that toppled the Gaddafi regime but left the country badly divided and headed toward civil war. In Morocco the monarch was quick to preempt reformists with a cautious opening of the political system. In Syria protests against the Assad regime led to a crackdown and the rise of armed resistance by the Sunni majority, with both transnational and nationally oriented groups playing a leading role. In Bahrain the monarchy faced a challenge from a restive but marginalized Shi'a majority (three quarters of the population). Repression by security services with the help of Saudi troops preserved a tense status quo.

Nothing better illustrates the perils of the democratic transition and the durability of the old order than the case of Egypt. Demonstrations in Tahrir Square in downtown Cairo against the regime of Mubarak started in late January 2011, quickly attracted massive crowds, spread throughout the country, and finally prompted the military to force Mubarak out after 30 years in power. In elections later in the year the Muslim Brotherhood gained control of the parliament in alliance with a more conservative Islamist party. It scored another victory in the June 2012 presidential election captured by its candidate, Mohamed Morsi. Extended controversies over the drafting of a new constitution, together with Morsi's exercise of presidential power, alienated groups committed to a secular order, set him against the conservative judiciary, drew criticism from international human rights groups, and ignited sustained street protests. Strikingly, Morsi had neither challenged Mubarak's neoliberal domestic policies, nor the peace agreement with Israel, nor the power of the old state bureaucracy. In mid-2013 the generals ended the crisis. They detained Morsi, appointed a compliant replacement, banned the Brotherhood, closed its media, put its leaders on trial, and clamped down on dissent of any kind. The head of the army, Abdel Fattah el-Sisi, staged an election in 2014 that put him in the presidency. What some have called "the deep state" had survived the popular Islamist challenge and regained its hold over the Egyptian political and economic order.

This signal failure of democracy in one of the preeminent Arab countries reverberated across the region. While Turkey's leaders, who had earlier voiced strong support for Morsi, forcefully condemned the military coup as well as the muted reaction of Western governments, Islamist radicals pointed to Morsi's fate as confirmation that their enemies—the old regimes and the great powers behind them—would not give up without a grim struggle.

Flash Points

Islamist currents have not only unsettled the old order but also aroused the major regional players while also implicating the great powers. Turkey has positioned itself as an advocate for regional reform and as an economic and political bridge to Europe. The ghost of Ottoman preeminence lives in a vision of restored Turkish prestige and influence. Iran has continued the pursuit of regional prominence initiated by the regime of the Shah, and in keeping with that goal has continued his drive to develop as a nuclear power. Tehran has regarded its nuclear program as a matter of national sovereignty, pride, and common sense in a neighborhood in which India, Pakistan, and Israel were already armed with nuclear weapons. The Islamic Republic has, however, added its own particular concerns: the defense of Shi'a interests in Lebanon, Iraq, Bahrain, and Saudi Arabia and the backing of non-Shi'a allies in Gaza and Syria. Finally, Saudi Arabia deserves a place on the list of regional influentials for the resources it has put into a conservative if ultimately contradictory agenda. On the one hand it has sought to promote political stability by protecting the other monarchies and containing Shi'a influence, whether coming from Iran's Islamic Republic, Shi'a-controlled Iraq, Bahrain's restive Shi'a majority, or a marginalized Shi'a minority in Lebanon and Saudi Arabia itself. On the other hand, the ruling family has funneled funds to groups and institutions aligned with its officially sanctioned form of Sunni Islam known as Wahhabism. Saudi funding has gone to religious schools and clerics all over the world as well as groups fighting nonbelievers from outside, notably in Afghanistan during the 1980s, and heretical offshoots of Islam, most recently in Syria. In this way Saudi Arabia has contributed to doctrinal and armed conflict and thus has fed instability. The actions of these three regional powers, together with the intrusion of outside powers, have created a crazy-quilt pattern of conflict that pits forces within and outside the region against each other in widely diverse ways depending on the particular flash point.

The oldest of those flash points centers on the Palestinian conflict with Israel bent on expansion into occupied territory (treated in Chapter 9). Increasingly a conflict with Palestinians spanning better than a half-century came to focus on Gaza, which suffered through repeated rounds of fighting between Hamas and the Israeli military. Three outside powers entered the fray. Washington, swayed by strong pro-Israeli domestic pressure, continued to provide robust support for Israel and wrote off Hamas as a terrorist organization. Iran has offered moral and material support to Hamas while also applying pressure on Israel through its Lebanese ally, Hezbollah. Egypt's role has been ambivalent. Sticking to the peace treaty that Sadat had concluded with Israel was the condition for continued U.S. military aid that was second in size only to what Israel received. On the other hand, the Palestinian cause was popular in Egypt, and depending on the vagaries of Egyptian politics, Cairo could open the border crossings critical to Gazans' livelihood and Hamas' supply of weapons.

Afghanistan took its place in the pattern of regional conflict with the Soviet invasion in 1979 (see Chapter 7). With the Soviets gone by 1989, the fighting became largely an internal matter. The victory of the Taliban, one of Pakistan's favorites, further calmed the conflict until 9-11 made the country again the focus of outside intervention. U.S. military operations, conducted in loose alliance with warlords, quickly overthrew the Taliban government. Hamid Karzai, backed by a U.S.-led NATO coalition, took charge, but his writ did not extend far beyond Kabul. Regional strongmen remained firmly ensconced, and the Taliban was still strong enough to mount a comeback campaign. Pakistan, guided by a long-term strategy of cultivating friendly elements among the warring parties, played a double game. It cooperated with the United States in controlling its own branch of the Taliban active in tribal areas along the Afghan border while the Pakistani security services continued to surreptitiously support the Afghan Taliban. To ensure Karzai's survival in this snake pit, U.S. forces took the lead in conducting counter-insurgency operations against Taliban resistance and funding long-term development projects. The Americans imagined that they could deliver "a government in a box" and that their military and economic initiatives would help Kabul win popular support, consolidate control, and stabilize the country.

Surveys in 2010 of nearly a thousand Afghan men scattered across the hotly contested southern provinces of Helmand and Kandahar indicate not only that the Karzai regime was an empty box but also that military operations had failed to win hearts and minds. Two thirds or more regarded NATO forces unsympathetically, judged NATO operations as harmful as well as ineffective, opposed a NATO presence either locally or nationally, and disliked countrymen who work with NATO forces. The respondents held the Taliban in considerably higher regard than the Kabul government security forces. Tellingly, 84 percent viewed the ongoing contest for hearts and minds in the context of their ultimate loyalty, which was to Islam (with attachment to the nation of Afghanistan a distant second). Even more tellingly, three out of four in this key region thought foreigners were disrespectful of local "religion and traditions."[28]

Washington's invasion of Iraq in 2003 added a fresh element to regional instability. After handily defeating Iraqi forces and overthrowing Saddam Hussein, the Americans went to work remaking the country as the first step toward reshaping the politics of the entire region. But nation building miscarried. What the occupation authorities lacked in experience and local knowledge they unfortunately more than made up for in ideological zeal. They purged elements of the old regime, disbanded its armed forces, alienated the Sunni by putting Shi'a in charge of the government even while fighting Shi'a militia, and tolerated the emergence of an autonomous Kurdish region. The U.S. occupation thus unleashed simmering but previously contained tensions, watched some five million flee abroad for safety, and created an opportunity for outside intervention. Iran and Saudi Arabia have lined up behind the Shi'a and Sunni respectively, while Turkey has kept a nervous eye on the nascent Kurdish state adjoining its own territory, heavily populated by restive Kurds. Transnational Islamists soon joined the fray. As U.S. forces prepared to leave in 2010, not only was the country in a state of chaos, but its people felt national humiliation and longed for a normal life but faced a grim future.

Syria was the next to get swept into the maelstrom of regional conflict. The country had been unsettled by protests inspired by the Arab Spring. Reformers

MAP 11.2 ➤

Lines of Conflict in the Muslim World

Two deeply contentious fault lines have emerged within predominantly Muslim areas. One is friction between Sunni and Shia populations. Shia majorities have run roughshod over other faiths in Iran and Iraq. In cases such as Bahrain, Saudi Arabia, and Pakistan the situation is reversed, with Shia minorities suffering discrimination and violence at the hands of Sunnis. Sunni insurgents have opened a second fault line with their challenge to the political status quo represented by monarchies as well as secular and military regimes. Al-Qaeda's transnational operations together with more territorially focused insurgents pose a threat to states from Nigeria, to Syria and Iraq, to the Philippines.

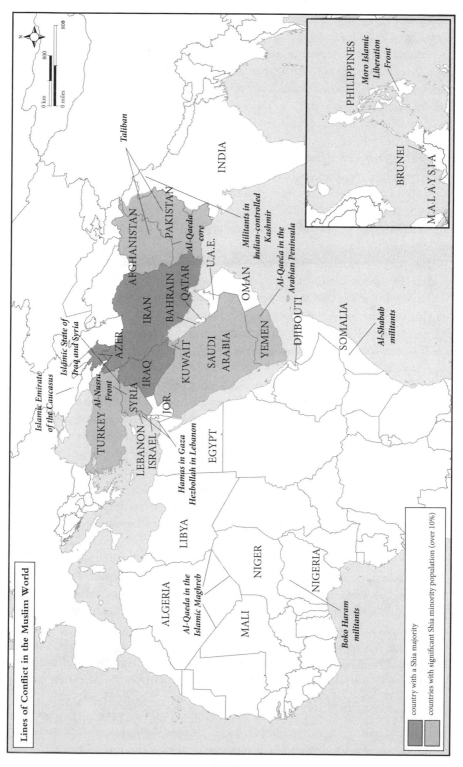

Lines of Conflict in the Muslim World

Islamic Emirate of the Caucasus

Taliban

Islamic State of Iraq and Syria

Al-Nusra Front

Al-Qaeda core

Militants in Indian-controlled Kashmir

Al-Qaeda in the Arabian Peninsula

Hamas in Gaza
Hezbollah in Lebanon

Al-Qaeda in the Islamic Maghreb

Boko Haram militants

Al-Shabab militants

Moro Islamic Liberation Front

TURKEY
AZER.
SYRIA
LEBANON
ISRAEL
JOR.
IRAQ
IRAN
AFGHANISTAN
PAKISTAN
INDIA
KUWAIT
BAHRAIN
QATAR
U.A.E.
SAUDI ARABIA
OMAN
YEMEN
DJIBOUTI
SOMALIA
EGYPT
LIBYA
ALGERIA
MALI
NIGER
NIGERIA

PHILIPPINES
BRUNEI
MALAYSIA

N

0 km   800
0 miles   800

- country with a Shia majority
- countries with significant Shia minority population (over 10%)

called for the regime in Damascus, based on the Ba'ath party and controlled by the Assad family, to democratize. Once more a regime that was determined to cling to power and the accumulated resentments of a repressed majority (in this case Sunni) led to civil war. A variety of resistance groups ranging from moderate Islamists to al-Qaeda affiliates and lesser-known groups of *jihadis* sprang into action, encouraged by Saudi funding. The Iranians working with Hezbollah rallied in support of the Assad regime. The Turks, the Russians, and the Americans were all concerned but largely stuck to the sidelines. The conflict was brutally conducted and socially devastating, with cities ravaged, several hundred thousand killed, and the largest refugee population in recent memory seeking safety.

As Syria descended into chaos, tension spread across the border. Hezbollah's, direct military intervention in support to the Assad regime together with the influx of refugees strained Lebanon's already fragile intercommunal accommodation. In Iraq ISIS launched a surprisingly successful offensive. ISIS had its origins in an Iraq-based organization headed by the Jordanian Abu Musab al-Zarqawi and nominally linked to al-Qaeda. Zarqawi, who was violently opposed to U.S. occupation forces and the Shi'a rulers in Baghdad, was able to mobilize a resistance that (as one gifted reporter on the scene described it) mixed "a visceral nationalism" with religious ideas: "Islam provides the vocabulary, the imagery and the faith in death itself as a cause."[29] After Zarqawi's death in 2006, the leadership passed to an Iraqi, Abu Bakr al-Baghdadi, who worked closely with officers from Saddam Hussein's army. The loss of support among tribal leaders in the western part of the country forced a shift of attention to Syria as it descended into civil conflict. Gains there provided a secure base of operations and the resources to return to Iraq in 2014 and overrun large areas inhabited by a Sunni minority still disaffected with the Shi'a-dominated government. The sudden ISIS advance—attended by a gory display of suicide bombings, mass executions, and public beheadings—seemed a step toward the realization of what had seemed an anachronistic dream: the creation of a Caliphate across portions of Syria and Iraq. The ISIS advance put in deeper question Iraq's survival as a state and created conditions favorable to an increasingly autonomous Kurdistan moving toward independence.

Today the relationship between the Middle East and a globalized world seems more problematic than ever. The Islamist sentiments now so much to the fore are challenged by neoliberal values with their strong secular and consumerist facets. Turkey's application for EU membership, facing opposition from the start and now practically abandoned, suggests a cultural divide not easily negotiated. So too does the unease felt in both the United States and Europe over the advance of even moderate Islamists and repeated rounds of intervention to "manage" developments in a region increasingly resentful of outside control. Globalization has created unprecedented possibilities for communications and travel that cut in several different ways. Those determined to strike against the West have taken advantage, but so too have Muslim migrants moving in unprecedented numbers into Europe and thus expanding the geographical scope of the community of faith to which activists can appeal, while also creating European unease over a potentially subversive presence immediately at hand. The encounters between globalization and regional struggles are nowhere more turbulent—and harder to predict—than in the case of the Middle East.

A REGION IN FERMENT

1979	Islamist-led revolution topples Shah in Iran
1985	Hezbollah organized in southern Lebanon
1987	First *intifada* against Israeli occupation
1988	Hamas founded in Gaza
1989	Iranian revolution moderates following end of war with Iraq and Khomeini's death; National Islamic Front seizes power in Sudan.
1990–91	Saddam Hussein invades Kuwait but is then pushed back by U.S.-led coalition; Islamist resistance drives Soviets from Afghanistan; electoral gains by Islamic Salvation Front in Algeria prompt a military crackdown.
1996	Taliban takes control in Kabul, Afghanistan; Israel–Hezbollah conflict begins.
1998	Osama bin Laden declares all Americans a target
2000	Bashar al-Assad takes control in Syria after death of father; second *intifada* against Israeli occupation.
2001	Al-Qaeda attack against U.S.; Taliban overthrown by Afghan warlords backed by U.S. forces; Karzai takes charge in Kabul.
2003	Saddam Hussein overthrown; U.S.-occupied Iraq begins to fracture.
2005	Israeli military withdraws from Gaza, taking settlers with them
2006	Hamas election victory in Gaza; Hezbollah forces Israeli withdrawal
2007	Hamas seizes full control in Gaza
2008–09	Israeli assault on Gaza
2011	Arab Spring breaks out in Tunisia; Egyptian protesters overthrow Mubarak; protests in Syria turn into armed resistance to Assad regime; protesters in Bahrain demand political opening; Gaddafi regime toppled in Libya; bin Laden killed by U.S. forces in Pakistan.
2012	Muslim Brotherhood candidate Morsi wins presidential election
2013	Army coup in Egypt
2014	ISIS launches offensive into Iraq from base in Syria; Israeli assault on Gaza.

THE RETURN OF ASIA

Asia, with China in the lead, is in the midst of reconfiguring the global economic landscape and in the process undermining a century and a half of global dominance by the North Atlantic economies. By the middle decades of the twentieth century the United States and western Europe had come to account for over half of global output. By the beginning of the twenty-first century China in particular had made a striking comeback. It could claim 12 percent of world output and together with the other two major Asian powers (Japan and India) accounted for a quarter of world output. From the start of the Deng Xiaoping era in 1978 to 2010, its per capita GDP had increased nearly eight-fold, and its annual growth rate was extraordinary—just shy of 10 percent.[30] At mid-century China is projected to displace the United States as the number-one economy, and India will become number three, pushing Germany down a notch. Together China and India are by then likely to account for half of global output (Fig. 11.2).

Asia's rise has so far done little to perturb the international system. Its leading economies have accommodated to the international institutions governing global trade and finance, and its delegates glide smoothly about the corridors of the United Nations. But the region was inexorably laying the material foundation from which to exercise considerable geopolitical clout. No longer could the North Atlantic community be confident in its capacity to lay down the terms on such key issues as free trade, human rights, environmental regulations, international peacekeeping, the status of women, nonproliferation of weapons of mass destruction, and economic

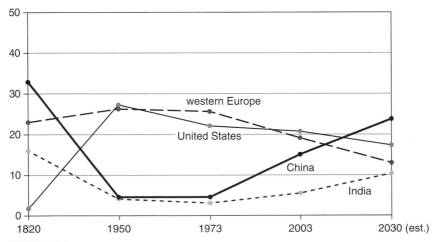

FIGURE 11.2
Changing Shares of Global Output, 1820–2030
China and India, which occupied a position of dominance early in the nineteenth century, had regained some lost ground by the end of the twentieth century, while the North Atlantic economies suffered a relative decline. These trends are likely to carry well into the twenty-first century.[31]

models for developing countries to follow. How Asia will figure globally will much depend on developments within the region. China's dramatic rise has given neighbors concern and notably put Japan on the defensive and India on edge.

Competing Development Models

China casts an especially long shadow as the most recent incarnation of the Asian model of state-guided capitalism. China's success has depended heavily on an active state. During the Mao years the party-state paved the way for prosperity by ending a century of economic stagnation and internal warfare and by firmly securing political and social control. Beijing promoted industrialization, invested in infrastructure, and set limits on urbanization. Income doubled between 1950 and 1973. To be sure, party control led to costly experiments and colossal errors. Even so, the booming output, changing skylines, and mushrooming consumerism from the late 1970s onward are hard to imagine without the state capacity and nationalist vision nurtured during the 1950s and 1960s (see Chapters 3 and 6).

The Chinese takeoff during the Deng Xiaoping years followed an already proven development approach. The economy operated as a variant on the state-guided capitalism practiced in Japan and adopted by South Korea and Taiwan. Like these forerunners, the Chinese state would take the lead in directing the economy. This involved a familiar set of measures: state protection of "infant" domestic industries, subsidies to encourage them, limits on foreign ownership, required technology transfer and local purchasing by foreign firms, control of foreign exchange markets, encouragement of the export sector, and heavy investment in research and development (see Chapter 8).

Deng's successors at the helm of the party-state have kept the economy on the previously marked-out track. But in background and style, they represented a distinct departure from the Mao/Deng revolutionary generations. The new crop of leaders have been gray, cautious figures, often from prominent Communist families, who have carefully picked their way up the hierarchy. They call to mind the privileged class of *nomenklatura* denounced by Milovan Djilas in the 1950s. Taking to heart the slogan from the Deng years "to get rich is glorious," they have traded on political influence to build up family wealth and opened the door to party membership to successful entrepreneurs who could in turn open economic doors to political benefactors. The current party head, Xi Jinping, exemplifies the new pattern. His father was a Mao associate, and the son was raised in the privileged confines of the party leadership compound in central Beijing. Although swept away in the Cultural Revolution, Xi quickly bounced back, becoming a party member in 1974 and by the late 1990s serving as a high-level official in the prosperous coastal area. By the time he was called to Beijing in 2007, Xi was being groomed for bigger things. Well schooled in the ways of party politics and convinced of the legitimacy of princeling rule, Xi has taken as his own the well-established and altogether conventional party objective of economic growth with political stability. On the side and out of sight, his relatives have become multimillionaires; in public Xi seeks to calm popular discontent with anticorruption campaigns and talk of closing the growing income gap within China. His views on foreign affairs have had a distinct nationalist flavor. For example, he asserted in mid-2014, "It is for the people of Asia to run the affairs of Asia," leaving unstated his expectation that China would be the presiding regional presence.[32]

The flaws of the current political system pale by comparison with its overall economic success. That success has established China as the poster child for a compelling development model distinctly at odds with neoliberal preferences. In much of the developing world states have been too weak or too much under the control of self-serving elites to impose the free-market orthodoxy—or for that matter to follow any coherent economic policy. The Philippines is a good case in point. A predatory elite has kept the state weak, resulting in relatively poor economic growth, endemic social discontent, and serious environmental degradation. The considerable material advantages of the Philippines relative to China at mid-twentieth century have vanished as the state apparatus in Manila has failed to promote education, develop physical infrastructure, or apply a long-term development strategy. Beijing has not been shy in drawing attention to its successful alternative to the neoliberal model and underlining its relevance by offering pragmatic, no-strings development assistance, especially in Latin America and Africa. Aid and investments of this sort further Beijing's hope of winning friends, markets, and raw materials.

To be sure, Deng Xiaoping's mixed economy, like Mao's command economy before it, had significant problems. Official misbehavior continued unchecked by courts, the media, or meaningful elections. Indeed, all the earlier forms of abuse have persisted down to the present—repression of dissent, official corruption, and pervasive cronyism—even if now in less horrific form. The Chinese state also faces new challenges brought on by its very economic gains. While the incidence of poverty has markedly declined over the past 30 years, inequality has in fact increased, above all between rural hinterlands and thriving coastal areas. China's pell-mell development has also ravaged the environment and left the country heavily dependent on fossil fuels, notably coal, that poison the air and warm the planet.

The overall success of the Chinese development model has produced an increasingly strong and self-confident country once denigrated as the "sick man of Asia." At century's end, nationalists could feel considerable pride over the successful drive toward "wealth and power" at home and prestige and influence internationally. Young urbanites have been especially prone to vociferous patriotic outbursts, celebrating their country's march toward international prominence and denouncing anyone standing in the way. A poem written by a student in 1999 amidst the furor over the U.S. bombing of the Chinese embassy in Belgrade captures the sense of outrage, solidarity, and destiny that this nationalism could inspire:

> *1.2 billion people shout together:*
> *The Chinese race will not be insulted!*

> *The giant dragon has woken to take off in the Orient,*
> *How can your kind of paper tiger resist?*[33]

The allusion to a "paper tiger," a dismissive term applied to the United States during the Mao era, suggests market inroads have done little to expunge old resentments.

China's success has sharpened a longstanding rivalry with India, that other Asian giant. Throughout the postwar era, China and India have represented divergent paths (see Chapter 3). Even as both in recent years have made a partial peace with the market and the global international economic order, the manner in which they have done so and the consequences that have followed provide a study in contrasts. (Figure 11.3 on p. 528 offers a side-by-side comparison of the development record of these two most populous of the BRIC's.)

India's move to the market has been both cautious and problematic. Change came slowly because the leaders of the long-dominant Indian National Congress were wedded to the notion of a mixed economy in which the government exercised a major, multifaceted role. This dominant view reflected the experience of Gandhi, Nehru, and the party's other early leaders, who associated capitalism and international trade with colonialism. The British socialist critique of capitalism to which they had been exposed during their schooldays reinforced this connection, while the perceived Soviet economic success confirmed the efficacy of state planning and regulation. In practice the Congress favored its industrialist supporters, and the state bureaucracy with its plethora of regulations became entrenched.

India's mixed economy had a distinctly mixed record. It could claim some notable gains in the first decades after independence. A series of five-year plans had boosted the country into the ranks of the top 10 industrial countries, and the large nationalized sector provided good jobs for 20 million people. But despite state intervention and a large influx of foreign aid, India's overall economic record down to the mid-1980s was unimpressive. For example, by 1985 about 55 percent of the population was still below the poverty line (most were extremely poor) compared to 20 percent for China. Jawaharlal Nehru as the first prime minister, followed by governments led by his daughter, Indira Gandhi, and then her son, Rajiv, failed to check increases in the population, which soared from 359 million in 1950 to an estimated 839 million by 1990 and which in turn depressed per capita income. While China by 1990 enjoyed a per capita income level four times that of 1950, India's had barely doubled. India's growth continued to lag so that by 2008 its per capita GDP was less than half of China's and roughly on a par with that of sub-Saharan Africa. In the face of more and more people to feed, India was saved from disaster by the "green revolution," the introduction of high-yield varieties of wheat and rice in the mid-1960s. By the 1970s India could feed itself, but the challenge was hardly over: Recent projections have the population increasing to 1.7 billion by 2050, double the 1990 level.[34]

India lagged in other areas as the result of a largely passive social policy. The government failed to manage the massive exodus of the landless from the poverty-plagued countryside. The result was an accumulation of great pools of unproductive urban poor in the slums of such major cities as Kolkata, Mumbai, and Delhi. Even more serious, the government failed to invest in public services, notably education. The infrastructure, from highways to public transportation to electricity grids, was weak. Improvements in social welfare, measured for example by life expectancy and literacy, lagged. While focusing on heavy industry and the cities, the government neglected rural development, even though roughly three quarters of the population still lived in the countryside, and malnutrition was rampant.

The first hints of a turn to a more market-friendly approach came from Indira Gandhi before her assassination in 1984. She and her son and successor, Rajiv Gandhi, gingerly explored deregulation. Growth rose to a respectable range of 3.5 to 5.0 percent, but it was attended by serious problems, including rising inflation and a large external debt. Despite criticism, the move toward the market accelerated following Rajiv's death in a bomb blast in 1991. The new prime minister, a lackluster Congress Party loyalist, P. V. Narasimha Rao, moved with surprising speed and determination. He trimmed the considerable influence wielded by state bureaucrats over the economy and forced formerly sheltered Indian producers to compete with foreign imports.

These measures invigorated the economy but had serious side effects of the sort associated with neoliberalism. The educated and affluent benefited, thus perpetuating a wide gap between the rich and poor. The economic bright spots—the booming information technology and pharmaceutical sectors—employed a minuscule portion of the workforce. In addition, deregulation brought greater pollution by sanctioning a rush to exploit resources and by limiting government oversight. Finally, the new economy intensified longstanding social, religious, and political divisions. Tensions between the Hindu majority (four fifths of the total population) and the large Muslim minority (only 12 percent but still some 110 million) exploded in periodic outbreaks of deadly communal violence. Cutting across the Hindu–Muslim divide were clashing class and regional identities. Privileged Hindu upper castes faced increasingly outspoken lower castes demanding a better life, stirring upper-caste resentment and setting off riots, while disputes over water and land were the source of endemic violence among the castes at the village level. Economic inequalities separated wealthy states such as Punjab from poor backwaters such as Bihar. More threatening were multiple demands for autonomy or independence coming most notably from Kashmir, Assam, and Punjab (see Map 3.3 on p. 130).

This broad-based ferment helped propel India's transition from dominance by a single party with a penchant for highly centralized government to a multiparty system in which regional governments figured prominently. This shift belatedly accommodated the country's diversity. The venerable but creaky and out-of-touch Congress definitively lost its four-decades-long lock on power. Its electoral base was badly eroded; the Nehru family control had become stultifying; and its centralizing, top-down approach to policy was at odds with regional or enthnolinguistic demands for a political voice. As parties with a multiplicity of views proliferated, coalition governments became the order of the day. At the national level, the Bharatiya Janata Party (BJP) became the Congress's main rival. The BJP originated as a champion for Hindu nationalism but has had to moderate its sectarian position in order to win broad electoral support and build governing coalitions, first in 1997 and again in 2014.

India faces major challenges. It will have to exploit its full potential not just for economic growth but for growth that is equitable if it is to feed, house, school, and provide health care for its booming population. Prosperity needs to reach beyond urban enclaves into the countryside. The strong class and caste distinctions sustaining wide inequalities need to be addressed. While the pronounced trend toward politics grounded in region and social identity reflects India's diversity, the centrifugal forces in play pose a danger if not counterbalanced by a shared sense of national belonging. Success in meeting this set of challenges could catapult India into the ranks of the leading states. Failure could leave the lives of a major fraction of humanity sharply diminished.

China's Long Regional Shadow

A China revived and robust casts another kind of shadow—one that reaches deep into Asia's core and out to its now-dynamic maritime zone. Most important in China's expansive geopolitical position has been preserving the world's last great continental empire despite minority discontent and international disapproval. Deng and his successors have jealously guarded the borderlands that Mao brought under Beijing's control (see Chapter 3). Inner Mongolia, Xinjiang, and Tibet were in the view of most Chinese important national patrimony. Those regions were also important for their natural resources and strategic position along the long and vulnerable inner-Asian frontier. Beijing has conceded little to minority peoples there, promoted Han Chinese settlement, and ruthlessly repressed separatist movements in the two most restive regions, Tibet and Xinjiang. China's leaders have been no less stubborn in insisting on sovereignty over Taiwan. Thanks to economic integration and military intimidation, they have virtually guaranteed that there will be no attempt to make the island independent. They have fully reclaimed Hong Kong from British control.

Northeast Asia comes a close second in importance in China's regional priorities. It is economically dynamic but also riven with tensions. Over several decades, China, Japan, and South Korea have developed a cooperative relationship built on substantial and intensifying intraregional trade and shared concerns with the environment and other transnational problems. But Korea is also dangerously divided between a prosperous South and a dysfunctional North, with conflict a constant prospect. Chinese leaders have responded by continuing a decades-old policy of supporting the introverted, fragile dynastic regime in Pyongyang, which passed in 2011 with the death of Kim Jong-il from the second generation to his son Kim Jong-un, representing the third. This support has been especially important over the past two decades as North Korea has suffered from severe economic decline and international isolation. At the same time, Beijing has cultivated the considerably more open and robust South Korea while also seeking to defuse tensions by serving as an intermediary in international fora devoted to the management of a bellicose, nuclear-armed regime in the North.

China's relationship with Japan, the most important one in the region, is more fraught than ever, with one country on the rise and the other declining. The economic wonder of Asia during the high-flying 1970s and 1980s, Japan thereafter lost its way. A massive credit binge pushed stock and real estate prices skyward, made Japanese free spenders, and astounded foreign observers. But the speculative bubble burst in the early 1990s, leaving the economy plagued by deflation and stagnant growth. The government and banks were heavily in debt. Large firms had to break their pledge of lifetime employment and fire workers, and unemployment rose to levels that were high by Japanese standards (although still low for western Europe and the United States). South Korean and Chinese industrial rivals began pushing once-dominant Japanese firms aside. The population was not only aging but also shrinking, so a smaller workforce had more retirees to support. The new generation faced a clouded future. Plagued by scandals and blamed for an ailing economy, the Liberal Democrats finally in 1993 lost their vise-like grip on the government after a nearly 40-year run. Economic troubles, together with a combined tsunami and nuclear crisis in 2011, undercut their rivals in power, and in 2014 the Liberal Democrats once again took the helm. Backed by a strong majority, the prime minister launched a Keynesian stimulus program. But even if it succeeds in shaking the economy back to life, Japan's relative standing in global output, already behind China's, is fated to continue to fall—back toward the 3.0 percent level it had occupied in 1820.

This shift of fortunes has made Japanese dispirited and neuralgic. China's growing national confidence and military might have made matters worse. Beijing's extensive maritime claims have become a flash point. Japanese leaders have bristled at Chinese attempts to control a motley assortment of islets as well as the sea lanes carrying China's exports and energy supplies. Despite the article in the U.S.-drafted constitution renouncing war, Tokyo has been spending more on its "self-defense forces," which has in turn fed anger among Chinese still harboring memories of the outrages Japan's military inflicted between 1937 and 1945 and fed fears that right-wing militarism was once more on the rise in Japan. In this awkward relationship, military anxieties and budding competition have raised the risks of serious military confrontation, but those risks are balanced by the continuing importance both sides attribute to intraregional trade and investment.

Southeast Asia has constituted for China a maritime as well as a land frontier that by comparison with Northeast Asia has been in recent decades relatively calm. Chinese goods and capital flow into the region, while overseas Chinese continue to play a major economic role there. The main irritant has been a complex of boundary and island disputes, some involving oil and natural gas deposits, that have pitted China against its neighbors, notably Vietnam, the Philippines, and Malaysia. China has sought to blunt criticism by playing up common economic interests and by joining in the deliberations of the leading regional organization, the Association of Southeast Asian Nations.

All along its maritime frontier China has had to face one overriding problem: the persistence of an American claim to a significant say in the future of Asia. The claim is supported by alliances with Japan, South Korea, and the Philippines and by a system of military bases, both dating back to the early Cold War. Even after the retreat from Vietnam in the early 1970s, U.S. troops continued to patrol Korea's 38th Parallel, a deterrent against any North Korean invasion, the U.S. Pacific fleet remained on call to protect Taiwan, and U.S. aircraft continued surveillance along China's coast. As earlier, the security alliance with Japan was the keystone for U.S. strategy in the western Pacific. It provided invaluable bases for American land, sea, and air forces while also ensuring the cooperation of a significant Japanese military establishment. Beijing's resentment of this intrusive American presence has generally been restrained, but patience on both sides will be tested as China's military grows stronger and more assertive, as the U.S. global position weakens, and as perennial irritants such as human rights and the future of Taiwan persist.

Here once more economic interdependence has helped to keep resentments in check. To be sure, disputes over intellectual copyright violations and denial of market access have become perennials. But on the other hand, fully one fifth of China's burgeoning exports by 2000 went to the United States. U.S. corporations profited from doing business in China and wanted to keep relations calm. And Chinese holdings of dollars—the largest of any country, at over $1 trillion—allowed Americans to run a heavy trade deficit and at the same time made Chinese dependent on the continuing strength of the U.S. economy and currency.

In this distinctly high-stakes relationship, some American opinion leaders express impatience with the China as a rising "totalitarian" power. The suppression of the 1989 demonstrations made clear that Communist leaders stood in the way of their country's "natural" democratic development. The critics recycled the well-worn view that a regime so morally wrong—"repressive and bloodstained," as the editors of the *Washington Post* put it—could not survive.[35] They imagined that an internal crisis or popular pressure was bound sooner or later to bring the Communist regime down or that economic liberalization would ultimately break the Communists' iron grip on political power. Vivid journalist accounts gave wide currency to the picture of a deeply flawed political system that was a standing affront to U.S. values and international leadership.

The relentless and widely retailed attacks have helped to create a fundamentally contradictory U.S. approach to China. Virtually all of Richard Nixon's successors in the White House have accepted the logic of his realpolitik course. They valued China as an ally against the Soviet Union late in the Cold War. They have wanted to protect the economic relationship. And they have more and more needed Beijing's cooperation on regional and even global issues of common interest. But so politically potent were the cries of the critics that presidential candidates have had to in-dulge in a bit of China-bashing, whether they believed what they said or not. And once in the White House they have engaged in a straddle. While following the es-sentials of the Nixon policy, they have also continued to supply substantial mili-tary aid to Taiwan, lent verbal support to the cause of Tibet, and publicly pressed Beijing to open up. Neoliberals were confident that in time the pressures of a high-tech global economy would break the grip of the Communist Party. "In the new century, liberty will spread by cell phone and cable modem," so Bill Clinton opti-mistically opined.[36]

These contradictions have left Chinese leaders perplexed. Deng Xiaoping and his successors have sought from the U.S. relationship trade, investment, techno-logical transfer, and scientific education. Deng calculated that the lure of the China market would overwhelm Washington's political scruples about dealing with com-munists and lay the basis for sound working relations: Didn't Washington always talk about how trade lubricated the wheels of peace? The U.S. response to Deng's brutal repression of the 1989 demonstrations—the sharpest and most enduring outrage expressed anywhere around the world—put that assumption in question. But then the first Bush administration in a line followed by subsequent adminis-trations affirmed China's international importance, the difficulty of imposing polit-ical change, the wisdom of supporting a development policy bringing prosperity and in time greater freedom to China, and the harm sanctions would inflict on American business and consumers. Communist rulers, who were proving frustratingly dur-able, were for their part finding American leaders frustratingly inscrutable—or at least inconsistent.

With India as with its western Pacific neighbors, Beijing has had an ambivalent relationship. A growing level of commerce as the two complementary economies prosper has helped to offset long-time tensions over disputed borders and over Chinese control of Tibet as well as China's support for Pakistan in a bitter quarrel with India that dated back to their division at the time of independence. The India–Pakistan rivalry, centered on Kashmir, has put China in a difficult position. The entrance into the "nuclear club" of India in 1974 and Pakistan in 1998 has made the rivalry considerably more dangerous. A showdown between the two in 2002 made the dangers all too clear.

Indian leaders, who harbor their own ambitions to cut a large figure on the regional and world stage, have watch anxiously as China's looms larger. Unlike India, China can now make a credible claim to have a major say in the way the U.S.-defined and -dominated regime of global economic and political governance evolves in the years ahead. Already China figures prominently as a trade and geopolitical partner for the EU, for Russia, and for the developing world. The return of China to a place of international power and pride is bound to have broad reverberations and give globalization in this century an increasingly Asian cast. The precise nature of that deeper Asian imprint may well depend on the kind of role that India manages to play alongside China.

CHINA AND INDIA IN A NEW ASIA

1965	India–Pakistan war over Kashmir
1966	Indira Gandhi's nearly two decades of political dominance begins
1971	India intervenes militarily to secure independence for Pakistan's West Bengal (Bangladesh)
1974	India's first nuclear test
1975–77	Indira Gandhi imposes state of emergency, suspending constitutional government, and is then ousted in 1977 election
1976	Mao's death opens the way for new policy line championed by Deng Xiaoping
1980	Election returns Indira Gandhi to power
1984	Indira Gandhi assassinated; succeeded by son, Rajiv Gandhi.
1989	Student-led popular protests in China violently repressed
1990	U.S.–Japan economic friction peaks and then Japanese stock and real estate markets collapse and economy sputters
1991	Rajiv Gandhi assassinated; leadership of Congress passes to wife, Sonia Gandhi.
1997	BJP breaks Congress's hold on power; Deng dies but his policy line is continued.
1998	Pakistan nuclear test
2001	China joins WTO
2002	India–Pakistan nuclear confrontation
2014	BJP returns to power

THE OLD WORLD'S OLD PROBLEMS

The end of the Cold War and the collapse of the Soviet Union seemed to mark an important step toward realizing what Mikhail Gorbachev had called "our common European home." When he first used that phrase in 1987, he had in view the reduction of military tensions in lands stretching across western Eurasia—from the Iberian peninsula and the British Isles to the Urals. But by 1990 he was thinking more broadly—about an economically interdependent Europe that was also tolerant of different paths of social and political development. The EU role was critical to any hopes for making a new Eurasia. While Russia stumbled economically and politically in the wake of Soviet collapse, the EU could point with pride to its creation of democratic societies dedicated to popular welfare and allergic to anything reminiscent of the old, pre-1945 pattern of great power rivalry and warfare.

Hopes for the creation of a "common European home," highest in the early 1990s, were soon considerably dimmed as old questions that the Europeans and their Russian neighbors had grappled with for virtually the entire century returned in new form. The EU encountered serious problems of governance. Member states clung to power, leaving the EU burdened with an awkward architecture that entailed a ponderous process of decision making. Those problems were accentuated by the pressures globalization applied from outside and exponents of neoliberal values championed from within. These trends eroded social solidarity and diminished welfare. At the same time nationalist rivalry and geopolitical tensions persisted in new form. The implosion of Yugoslavia revealed the continuing potency of nationalism while Russia, prostrate during the 1990s, became a more assertive and thus more difficult partner, especially in territory along its border, what Moscow called the "near abroad." The new century was raising problems of welfare and security thought banished to history but now at odds with the notion of a "common European home."

The EU Project in Trouble

Of all the world's major regions, Europe was the most deeply globalized and thus on its face at least in the best position to benefit as the process unfolded. European economies were heavily oriented toward production for export, and they boasted some of the world's leading financial markets. The EU was a magnet for immigrants both from adjoining regions and from distant former colonies, and those newcomers entered a culturally tolerant milieu. Europeans themselves were perhaps the most cosmopolitan people in the world, at home in multiple languages, addicted to travel, culturally curious, and quick to relocate. The EU states devoted a higher proportion of GDP to foreign aid than anyone else, and they took a leading role in promoting international norms and institutions. Human rights was a signature European cause. NGOs found a welcome home, ready volunteers, and generous support in Europe. It was the seat of the only institutionalized religion with a world-wide reach, the Catholic Church. This picture of a continent so deeply embedded in a globalized world contrasts sharply with insular Americans with their strong nationalist outlook, Asians only beginning to come into their own as global players, and a Middle Eastern population torn over how to respond to global trends.

But paradoxically, rather than prosper in a global environment for which it seemed perfectly suited, the EU was beset by problems. The steady advance of the European experiment—the introduction of a common currency and the admission of new members from the east—hid problems that only gradually became apparent. Even as the fresh initiatives were moving ahead during the 1990s, the collapse of Yugoslavia right on the EU doorstep and the costly integration of East Germany into the prosperous West Germany were signals that the transition of the former socialist states would not be smooth. More troubling, a close fiscal integration with the introduction of the euro was not matched by institutional oversight. Attempts to find solutions to these problem, and more generally to make the

EU itself a more efficient and coherent mechanism, had only limited success. As economies turned sluggish, once-welcome immigrant laborers became fiscal burdens and social lightning rods. Nativists focused on their Muslim populations (in total over 10 million in western Europe at the start of the new century) as a troubling cultural presence, vulnerable to the appeal of radical Islam. Europe thus confronted transnational and international challenges even as its experiment in multinational governance stumbled.

The 28 member states of the EU working through an assemblage of institutions with many moving parts were not in a good position to tackle the problems of the new era. "Far from building the United States of Europe," one historian has pungently noted, "the EU would be lucky to create the United Europe of States."[37] A parliament, based on popular elections held within member states every five years, was a weak bow to democracy, but it was a relatively toothless body. National governments were careful to keep preponderant control in their own hands, working through three different bodies with a mix of executive and legislative powers: the EU Council, the Council of Ministers, and the Commission that served as the executive for the parliament. The EU Council, which had the most clout, was composed of heads of government or state and chaired by one of its members on a six-month rotating basis. In addition, a strong court system, a court of auditors for the EU budget, and a central bank (considerably strengthened after the recent financial crisis) provided oversight. Finally, a bureaucracy in Brussels made the regulatory wheels go round. It acquired a reputation, perhaps exaggerated, for making exceedingly fine-grained decisions at a lumbering pace in splendid isolation from on-the-ground conditions. In a nutshell, the EU, despite having a single market, a single currency, and increasingly a single body of law, still left decisions on critical social and fiscal policies at the national level.

The expansion of the EU to include the formerly socialist states of eastern Europe introduced a fresh level of complexity and discord into EU governance. Poland, Hungary, the Czech Republic, Slovakia, the Baltic states (Lithuania, Latvia, and Estonia), and Slovenia were admitted in 2004. Romania and Bulgaria followed in 2007. Croatia entered in 2013 (see Map 8.2 on p. 370). As a result, not only have the governing EU bodies had to incorporate more states, but those states brought to EU discussions a fresh set of perspectives shaped by their unhappy experience with socialism and Soviet control, by lower levels of economic development, and by hardship inflicted by the "shock therapy" deemed the best medicine for economies diagnosed deficient in freely operating markets. Amidst painful social and economic adjustments, right-wing parties came back to life while reformed Communist parties fought for a place in the new eastern European order. Respect for human rights and the environment lagged behind the views in the longer-established member states. Countries rebuilding after a failed socialist experiment brought into the EU their own distinctive sense of what welfare entailed and how much it should cost, thus accentuating an already diverse approach that distinguished the Scandinavian countries from the big continental economies

(Germany, France, and Italy) from those admitted in the 1980s (Portugal, Spain, and Greece). The legacy of anti-Soviet feelings poisoned the new members' views of relations with Russia. From the perspective of the more affluent, established EU states, the expansion east was a gratifying but costly vindication of their experiment in integration. With an obligation to raise the standard of living in the former socialist states, the EU paid a price in subsidies and the opening of more prosperous areas to migrants from the east.

By the late 1990s disenchantment with EU governance was already marked. After nearly four decades the drive to integrate the region rested more heavily on elite than popular support. In a 1996 survey, civil servants, elected politicians, business and labor leaders, and academic, cultural, and religious figures gave EU membership high marks: Fully 92 percent regarded it favorably. By contrast, surveys conducted across the entire population in 1999 revealed that only half judged the EU a "good thing"; the rest responded it was a "bad thing" or had no opinion. A similar split appeared in response to the question of whether the EU had benefited the respondent's country. Of the elite group, 90 percent said "yes" and only 8 percent said "no." Among the general public, "yes" got 43 percent and the rest either said "no" or had no opinion.[38]

The strains within the EU were accentuated by its incorporation into the U.S.-championed neoliberal conception of the global economy. It left European economies vulnerable to the erratic swings of the financial markets and the whims of Wall Street banking houses. Moreover, the neoliberal economic model supported by the European industrialists and financiers was at odds with the EU's welfare model. Workplace protections ranging from minimum wage to collective bargaining came under pressure on the grounds that they were an obstacle to competitiveness. Subsidies distributed in the name of social welfare and the public good collided with demands for fiscal orthodoxy. Public industries and public services would, champions of the market claimed, be better run by the private sector.

European vulnerability came into sharp and punishing relief during the prolonged euro crisis beginning in 2010. The EU had put its fate in the hands of outside forces without creating effective national or regional mechanisms to counteract those forces or to compel member states to honor their formal obligations to keep budget deficits in check. Greece proved an egregious offender. It blatantly violated its deficits commitments, piling up large debts while covering up with deceptive accounting and outright misrepresentation. When financial markets got wise, the entire Mediterranean tier of the EU—Spain, Portugal, and Italy as well as Greece—along with Ireland fell under suspicion and then punishing pressure. Even the euro, which had appreciated beyond all expectation after its introduction, suddenly seemed in risk of collapse.

In meeting a crisis resulting from its own passivity, the EU proved predictably slow and unwieldy. Its leaders at first agonized over whether and how to rescue Greece. Who would guarantee the debt, how was Athens to get its fiscal house in order, and what institutional changes would keep the 18 Eurozone states in line and preclude another fiscal crisis? Germany's Angela Merkel finally took control. Her country, which had recovered from its own costly process of integrating East Germany, had the resources to move decisively. Backed by a strong economy, the Germans would set the terms for meeting the crisis in exchange for ensuring that the bailout effort had sufficient financial backing. Greece got a lifeline, a combination of temporary IMF and European bank support. The price was painful austerity, which Greece and all the other states under pressure had to accept. Devaluation of the local currency had once been an option for states in financial trouble, but after the introduction of the euro, their only option was belt tightening or leaving the common currency.

The crisis transformed the relationship among the EU member states. Berlin staked out its leadership, confidently in economic matters but more cautiously in matters of politics and foreign relations. France and Italy, the other leading continental powers, were too economically troubled to take a strong hand. Britain, habitually ambivalent about its relationship to the continent, became more Euro-skeptical than ever. Facing a fresh surge of anti-EU feeling that gripped his own Conservative Party and that buoyed the fringe United Kingdom Independence Party, Prime Minister David Cameron responded by scheduling a referendum on membership for 2017. The outcome could well result in Britain's abandoning or scaling back its EU ties, whatever the damage to British trade and Britain's claim to serve as a bridge between the United States and Europe.

The crisis also put downward pressure on the entire European economy with the kind of social stress last seen in the 1970s with its fiscal austerity and nativist agitation. Greece was the epicenter. Greece suffered from a prolonged and severe economic downturn, from political polarization, and from grievous social damage. Not only there but throughout the southern tier of the EU social welfare commitments that had been its pride and distinguishing feature were eroded. Temporary employment rose. Labor unions could no longer protect their members. Youth unemployment hit record highs. Street demonstrations against fiscal austerity became a regular occurrence, and governments struggled to stay in power in the face of popular anger. By 2014 most of the troubled economies were still struggling even after a long treatment of austerity, and public reservations about the EU project had become more pronounced. In surveys conducted in 2013, only 28 percent thought integration had strengthened the economy. Trust in the EU had fallen to 31 percent from a high of 57 percent in 2007. Those with a positive view of the EU had fallen from 52 percent in 2007 to 30 percent in 2013 (with 29 percent negative).[39]

Symptomatic of hard times, anti-immigrant sentiment flourished, colliding with longstanding multicultural trends within the EU. A rising tide of immigration both within and from outside the EU had created an unprecedentedly diverse European society. The tension that went with that diversity seemed manageable as European states worked (in the words of a specially commissioned French report) to balance "recognition of the right to an individual identity with the necessary effort to weave the individual convictions into the social fabric."[40] Hard times put

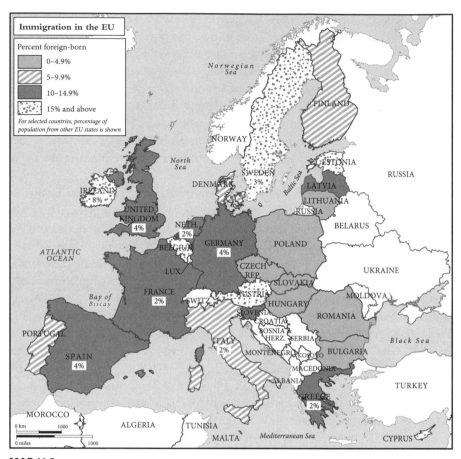

MAP 11.3
Immigration in the EU

The nativist picture of a continent overwhelmed by outsiders is too simple. First, by the conventional gauge used to measure immigration—the percentage of people who were foreign born—the EU stands at 7 percent in 2013. That figure falls well short of the level for countries traditionally open to immigration (13 percent for the United States, 21 percent for Canada, and 27 percent for Australia). Second, as the map makes clear, foreign-born people figure most prominently in the EU states whose advanced economies have attracted—and indeed depend on—fresh supplies of cheap labor. The main destinations for the 1.7 million arrivals in 2012 were thus Germany (accounting for a third), the UK, Italy, France, and Spain. These newcomers, divided almost equally between men and women, were overall considerably younger than the EU median of 42 years and thus injected some vigor into an aging population. Third, our calculations need to take into account those arriving in against those departing from the EU, which in 2012 was also 1.7 million. Finally, as the map indicates, immigration was not just a matter of people coming from outside the EU; it also included to a considerable degree those in the EU taking advantage of the principle of free movement to seek employment in another EU state. (Data from Eurostat and the Organisation for Economic Co-operation and Development)

pressure on this balancing act and gave rise to angry charges that foreigners were taking jobs that citizens needed. Nativists turned on refugees and migrants with special ferocity in the Mediterranean region. For example, Greece's Golden Dawn movement, an openly neo-Nazi party, targeted immigrants and to a lesser extent homosexuals, corrupt politicians, and bankers linked to austerity. Immigrants and anyone who looked non-Greek risked physical assault. Anti-immigrant parties put on a strong showing elsewhere in Europe, including Britain, France, Italy, Sweden, Norway, and the Netherlands.

Immigration was an indicator of how far Europeans had gone in enmeshing themselves in a neoliberal world. During the immediate postwar decades a battered Europe had served itself well by integrating into the U.S.-sponsored international economy. But the benefits diminished as the neoliberal values gained global ascendancy and posed an ongoing threat to financial instability and to the commitment to popular welfare on which the EU was built. To protect itself against a corporate-dominated order, the EU would have to embark on a risky renegotiation of the international economic order so that it operated in a way less at odds with European values. Alternatively, Europeans could turn their back on globalization American-style and instead pursue a regionalized trade and finance policy, perhaps in league with other economic groupings in Asia and South America that were also uneasy with neoliberal predominance. There would be economic risks and costs either way, but the Old World would stand a chance of gaining more control over its own destiny.

The Geopolitical Pygmy

The same awkward decision-making mechanisms and divided outlooks among the member states that afflicted internal policy also plagued the EU's external relations. Possessed of the world's largest economy, the EU seemed geopolitically more like a pygmy. Not only did its leading members continue to pursue their own foreign policy agenda, but they also guarded jealously their freedom of action. EU institutions claimed to speak for all but had limited success in arriving at, not to mention projecting, a common policy. Adding to the confusion was the influence exerted by U.S.-dominated NATO. European leaders were often unhappy with the style of U.S. leadership, but they were not prepared to abandon the alliance as long as they could not agree on something to replace it.

The collapse of Yugoslavia and the genocidal campaigns that followed revealed the EU's immobility even when the crisis was unfolding right on its doorstep. To be sure, dealing with the most virulent display of violence that Europe had seen since the end of World War II was no easy matter. Yugoslavia, with its unusual cultural diversity, was a tinderbox. Since the Roman Empire, conquerors had brought new faiths to the area, resulting in a jumble of religious and ethnic identities—Catholic Croats, Orthodox Serbs (subdivided into those living in Serbia, Montenegro, and Macedonia), and Muslims in Bosnia and Kosovo. Josip Tito had suppressed the resulting resentments and rivalries, but his death in 1980 gave ambitious nationalist leaders, foremost Slobodan Milošević as the champion of a Greater Serbia, the chance to apply a match to the tinder. Soon the federation—composed of the republics of Serbia, Montenegro, Croatia, Slovenia, Bosnia, and Macedonia as well as the autonomous republics of Kosovo and Vojvodina—was burning.

Europeans looked on in horror as Yugoslavia rapidly unraveled and descended into violence. In March 1989 Milošević, whose nationalism (one friend observed) was "like a heated stove,"[41] asserted full control over Kosovo, celebrated as the original Serb homeland but now with only a minority of Serbian residents. Croatia and Slovenia responded by declaring their independence in 1991, in turn setting off fighting between Serbian forces (both the national army and militias) and Croatians. This first round of "ethnic cleansing" led to a second in 1992 in the ethnically mixed Bosnian region among Muslims, Serbs, and Croats. In each case the process began with intimidation of the local population (for example, murder of its leaders and mass rape) followed by seizure of property, internment, the deportation of some, and the execution of others. All sides practiced ethnic cleansing but none on a wider scale or more viciously than the Serbs. By 1995 some 3.5 million people (at least 1 million of them Serbs) had fled their homes. The madness disrupted lives and destroyed dreams on a massive scale.

The crisis gave rise to profound fears within the EU. The continent could find itself awash in refugees fleeing the conflict zone. More worrisome still was the prospect of a general resurgence of ethnic enmities and an explosion of separatist and nationalist claims threatening the integrity of virtually all European states. This prospect was especially worrisome in eastern Europe, with its patchwork of discontented minorities no longer under the thumb of repressive socialist governments. The demise of a federated Czechoslovakia contributed to the alarmist view. There the post-socialist era had brought to the surface strains between the more economically developed Czech region, with about two thirds of the population, and the Slovak region. However, the two were able to reach an amicable decision in 1992 to divide the old state into two new ones, the Czech Republic and Slovakia.

Although western European leaders had claimed from the start that the Yugoslav conflict was a European problem, they could not formulate a coherent response. Germany took the most decisive action, getting an EU summit in December 1991 to accept independence for Slovenia and Croatia. Otherwise unable to agree on concerted action, the paralyzed European giant now resorted to its default position: It looked to the United States for a solution. After considerable indecision in Washington over whether to tackle what the administration liked to call a "problem from hell," Clinton bowed to mounting international outrage and pressure at home. Bombing by U.S. aircraft of Serb positions in 1995 paved the way for a peace agreement that preserved Bosnia as a state of three federated ethnic groups and provided for NATO troops to keep the peace. Four years later Clinton repeated the exercise after Serbian forces went on the rampage in Kosovo to crush demands there for independence. U.S.-led NATO forces went into combat. Bombing of Serbia finally forced Milošević, who had once more overplayed his hand, to capitulate. UN-authorized NATO peacekeeping forces occupied that strife-torn province and guaranteed the safe return of refugees.

By decade's end Milošević's campaign for a Greater Serbia would look like one of the most misguided expansionist drives in recent memory. At its peak in 1992 Serbia controlled one quarter of Croatia, two thirds of Bosnia, and all of Kosovo. But after nearly a decade of campaigning Milošević had lost most of this land, and

CHRONOLOGY: THE EU'S GROWING PAINS

1989	Eastern European socialist regimes collapse, their economies orient toward the European Community
1991	Collapse of Yugoslavia begins
1993	EU formally created with tight finance and currency ties
1995	Serbian offensive halted
1999	Euro instituted as a common currency but without British participation; NATO bombing of Serbia to protect Kosovo.
2000	Milošević falls from power in Serbia
2004	First wave of former socialist states admitted to EU
2009–10	Euro crisis engulfs Greece, Italy, Spain, Portugal, and Ireland

Serbia itself had suffered international economic sanctions and bombing. The economy was devastated, the country was isolated internationally, and its leaders were wanted for trial as war criminals. An opposition movement finally ousted Milošević in 2000 and turned him over for trial for his part in Serbian atrocities during his deadly decade in power. Serbia was then further diminished territorially when Montenegro went its own way in 2006 and Kosovo declared its independence in 2008. The postwar European order was, for the moment at least, safe, but the EU's weakness even in its own neighborhood was dramatically exposed.

Russia's collapse during the 1990s, and its subsequent revival, has presented the EU with an even more consequential challenge. Hopes for creating a common European home and even the expectation of a post-Cold War relaxation of tensions depended on the EU's reaching a *modus vivendi* with Russia. Instead EU leaders seemed to operate on the happy premise that Russia would remain debilitated forever or that a revived Russia would magically renounce its old ambitions and play the pygmy much as the EU did. As developments over the past decade have undercut both assumptions, the EU has fallen back on its familiar non-strategy of letting the United States handle the problem and has once again exposed Europe's incapacity to manage its own external relations.

Russia's fall was so deep and precipitous that it was easy to imagine the disarray lasting long into the future. The Soviet Union had offered security and a better life, at least into the 1970s, when economic growth slowed markedly and standards of living stagnated. Following the dissolution of the Soviet Union, the new Russian state led by Boris Yeltsin attempted a rapid transition to a market economy, abetted by loans and advice from the IMF. But the process turned into feast for the former Communist Party elite and their friends, who set about cannibalizing a stricken Soviet-era economy. After a deep and painful decline, a recovery began late in the decade only to absorb a heavy blow from the global financial crisis of 1998. Most Russians suffered as inflation ate away at purchasing power, state workers were either laid off or not paid, and pensions disappeared. Longevity plunged, infant mortality soared, and total population declined. By century's end 40 percent of the population fell below the poverty line. A formidable set of obstacles stood in the way of a return to the relative security and prosperity of Soviet times: corruption by insiders; an outdated industrial plant; an inefficient agricultural sector; flight of capital as well as talent abroad; and heavy dependence on the export of primary products such as oil, metals, and timber, whose international market prices were volatile. Russia was hardly alone in its ordeal; between 1990 and 2003 the 15 states formerly constituting the Soviet Union saw per capita GDP fall on average by a fifth.[42]

The loss of the international prestige and respect that the Soviet Union had once commanded was galling to Russians. No longer was their country a superpower, even though it was the largest of the Soviet successor states, with the bulk of the Soviet nuclear arsenal in its possession. Yeltsin had failed in the first years of his presidency to reassemble a shadow of the Soviet empire in the form of a Commonwealth of Independent States, while also facing ethnic unrest along the Russian border in such places as Tajikistan and the Caucasus region and even within Russia itself. A secessionist movement in the republic of Chechnya precipitated a prolonged and brutal conflict. Some 25 million Russians who had settled in non-Russian parts of the Soviet Union suddenly found themselves strangers with an uncertain future in one of the post-Soviet states. Adding to Moscow's woes, NATO advanced from the west while the Americans, in the name of their "war on terrorism," inserted their forces in the south in former Soviet Central Asia.

The EU's response to this moment of weakness was to fall in line with the United States and treat Russia as a country of marginal importance even in matters most relevant to its long-term security. When Russian leaders objected to the U.S. treatment of Serbia, the Europeans went along with the Americans in effectively ignoring them. Over strong Russian protests, NATO admitted Poland, the Czech Republic, and Hungary to full membership in 1997. Other former eastern-bloc states soon followed. Only when the Americans proposed admitting Ukraine and Georgia did Germany and France see danger and block the move.

Soon Russia under the aegis of Vladimir Putin was getting back on its feet. The new master of Moscow had his roots in Leningrad. There he grew up, went to university, and in 1990 began his rapid rise from university administrator and city government official to Yeltsin's designated successor as president in 1999. Putin's career was also rooted in the Soviet security agency, the KGB, for which he worked from 1975 to 1990 and which he headed briefly in 1998–1999.

Both as president and prime minister (a tenure that began in 1999 and will continue to 2018), Putin has followed a back-to-the-future policy that has had broad political appeal. It played effectively off popular anger over an economy and society in disarray, humiliation over the loss of international standing, and nostalgia

Vladimir Putin on Vacation in Southern Siberia, 2009
Putin spoke in his 2012 presidential election campaign in favor of "Russia muscling up." He seems to have taken this advice personally, to judge from photographs of him in a variety of manly poses. For a former KGB agent trained in discretion, he has proven surprisingly effective in projecting a macho media image. (Alexsey Druginyn/AFP/Getty Images)

for what seemed like a golden age under Stalin. Polls revealed a nostalgia for the Soviet era, remembered as a time of domestic stability, national unity, continental security, and international respect. Perhaps more important, Putin reflected an elite's nationalist longing to see Russia escape from its new "time of troubles" (a phrase with historical resonance). The remedy was to restore strong central, even autocratic control in the Kremlin. He observed in 1999, "For Russians, a strong state is not an anomaly to fight against. Quite the contrary, it is the source and guarantor of order, the initiator and the main driving force of any change."[43] Putin reduced democracy to a shell, silenced dissenters, promoted conservative values, brought to heel the economic oligarchs who had gained broad powers during the Yeltsin years, and crushed internal unrest, most notably in Chechnya. Thanks to lucrative oil and gas export markets, he was at the same time able to undo some of the economic and social damage inflicted by shock therapy and restore a sense of prosperity. (See Figure 11.3 on p. 528 for Russia's performance alongside that of the other BRIC's.)

Goaded by humiliating treatment by the West, Putin has pursued a strong foreign policy. He insisted that Russia be taken seriously as a great power whose views counted on issues such as nuclear proliferation and humanitarian intervention and whose interests extended to adjoining territory once part of the Soviet Union. Like Soviet leaders before him, Putin has given especially high priority to

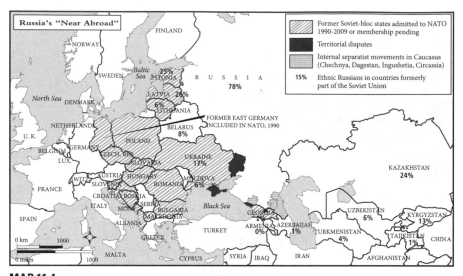

MAP 11.4
Russia's "Near Abroad"

Russian's "near abroad"—the lands once part of the Soviet Union or within the post-World War II Soviet sphere of influence—is a complicated place where the Soviet legacy weighs heavily. Demographically, that legacy is evident in the population of Russian ethnics, still substantial despite the departure of many since the Soviet collapse as a result of civil unrest, personal harassment, and legal discrimination. A rough total of those remaining ranges between 20 and 30 million, with the largest numbers in Ukraine, Kazakhstan, Uzbekistan, and Belarus. The Kremlin's involvement in neighboring states as well in Russian borderlands has generated a series of conflicts, most notably with Ukraine over Crimea and the eastern region, with Georgia over South Ossetia and Abkhazia, and with Moldova over Transnistria. NATO's advance right to the Russian border has accentuated Russian concerns. The Kremlin has taken a number of initiatives to reknit the old Soviet republics and thus bolster the Russian position. Of these initiatives, the most recent, most modest territorially, and the most viable is the Eurasian Economic Union, which consists of Russia along with Armenia, Belarus, and Kazakhstan, with membership pending for Tajikistan and Kyrgyzstan. (CIA's *The World Factbook* and BBC)

the "near abroad" (Map 11.4). He applied heavy pressure along Georgia's border. More recently he has maneuvered to keep Ukraine in the Russian sphere and outright annexed the Ukrainian territory of Crimea. Behind these moves was a determination to keep NATO at a distance and protect the millions of Russian nationals living in neighboring states. It made little difference that Washington fulminated over Russian meddling along its border and that, however reluctantly, the EU joined the chorus of criticism.

Deteriorating relations with Russia no less than the euro crisis pose an old question to the Old World: Where and what is Europe? This question hangs over the raft of security and welfare problems facing the EU acutely since the end of the Cold War. How to preserve the gains of a half-century of integration, to relate to a Russia no longer prostrate, and to fit into a globalizing world are big issues that remain unresolved and are not likely to fade away. How will a soft authoritarianism predominant in Russia and other parts of the former Soviet Union mesh with the values of a Europe aggressively dedicated to respect for democracy and human rights? Can the EU even hope to have a stable relationship with a Russia still constrained by the political and economic legacies of the Soviet era? How can Europe reconcile a frayed but still strong relationship with the United States with a Russia resistant to U.S. claims to moral leadership and police powers?

These questions highlight the problematic nature of close and longstanding ties between Europe and the United States. These ties persisted into the period after the Cold War even as the EU has made major advances in bloc building and even as the United States has turned into a declining if still exigent power. Letting the Americans take the lead in security affairs was, like the accommodation to their economic leadership, a postwar convenience that has turned into a habit. While subordination may no longer make sense, the EU clings to the logic of the Cold War era: It's better to keep military spending low, avoid entanglement in the militaristic passions so damaging during the first half of the twentieth century, and focus on welfare. But as a result, the EU has continued a satellite constrained by its orbit around the United States. While Washington has charged the Europeans with "free riding," they have responded that burden sharing was just another way to get them to pay for what Washington wanted—and much of what Washington wanted generated deep official, not to mention popular, opposition. The American invasion of Iraq created an uproar. The Afghan operation that Washington pulled NATO into had scant European support even though the NATO role was nominal. The permissive U.S. stance on Israeli expansion into the West Bank and oppression of Gaza has created widespread unease. The EU, which has professed the highest regard for human rights, international legal norms, and environmental protection, finds itself aligned with the United States, which is at best indifferent or selective in its response to these issues. By 2004 large majorities in France and Germany voiced support for setting the EU on a more independent course with as much power as the United States.[44]

To fundamentally reform a once-sensible but now-outmoded reliance on U.S. leadership in security matters would require further development of the EU itself. Europeans would in general have to accept a further degree of centralization at the expense of national autonomy. To make good on its potential as a great power, the EU would have to have the means to protect its economic as well as political influence in a string of volatile points along the southern and eastern Mediterranean; to work out an amicable, cooperative relationship with Russia; and to assert its voice in international fora. Rather than march to the U.S. drum, the EU would need to formulate a real foreign policy and replace NATO with a genuine, effective EU military. Both measures would require more centralization, a professional diplomatic service, an armed force strong enough to weigh in the great power balance, and a conventional command structure. Britain and France in particular would have to surrender the last tatters of their great power aspirations and their attachment to the glory of their colonial days. For them, there would be no more grand

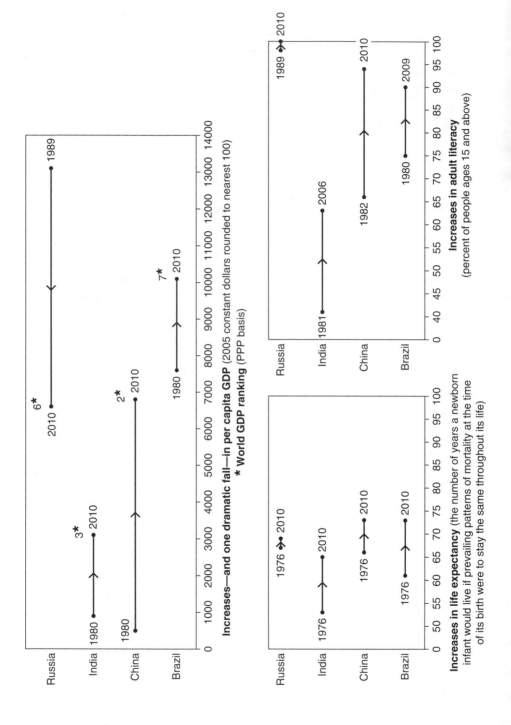

Increases—and one dramatic fall—in **per capita GDP** (2005 constant dollars rounded to nearest 100)
* World GDP ranking (PPP basis)

Increases in **life expectancy** (the number of years a newborn infant would live if prevailing patterns of mortality at the time of its birth were to stay the same throughout its life)

Increases in **adult literacy**
(percent of people ages 15 and above)

adventures as when they took the lead in bombing Libya in 2011 but then had to turn to the American when they ran out of munitions. All these measures would require higher levels of taxation and a popular acceptance of a new role for Europe in the world.

How the EU deals with its challenges—internal as well as external—turns heavily on how Europeans frame that challenge. Is the EU "an unfinished nation or an incomplete federal state," a pair of thoughtful observers have asked, or is it instead "a new type of cosmopolitan project"?[45] The choices Europeans make about their experiment in social welfare and social justice will determine what kind of life the common European home offers and how broadly it extends. The outcome will also help define the shape of the twenty-first-century world.

CONCLUSION

It may be tempting to think of global forces as eroding national and regional differences. Mammoth transnational corporations, along with powerful financial institutions, can overwhelm states and ride roughshod over local communities. Their goods and capital cross borders with ease and behind them come new knowledge, images, crime, pollution, drugs, fashion, and beliefs. Those who wish to resist run up against the rules formulated by transnational organizations such as the WTO and the IMF. This conception of a world moving inexorably toward a common destination inspires the neoliberal fantasy that economic interchange will bring together people of diverse cultural values and historical experiences and lay the foundations for the first integrated, truly global civilization.

This picture of globalization tearing down the old particularities of place is true—but only to a very limited degree. The effects of globalization are not so simple and uniform as its enthusiasts think. States continue to exercise considerable power, even if it is exercised in new ways. Evolution rather than decline of that power may be closer to the truth. Domestically, states may be reducing their direct involvement in the market. Selling off nationalized industries and reducing tariffs are the kinds of concessions made to neoliberal pressures. But at the same time the domestic role of the state has grown as governments seek to manage external economic pressures and rapidly changing economic conditions and to buffer citizens

◀ **FIGURE 11.3**
Changing BRIC Vital Statistics over Three Decades
These data highlight the enormous strides taken by China in both per capita income and social welfare. Brazil, which was in a strong position at the start of the new era of globalization, has not made comparable progress in literacy and life expectancy because of persistent inequality; it is now roughly on a par with the former laggard China. The striking drop in Russia's per capita income and its surprisingly low life expectancy reflect the dire conditions following the Soviet collapse, while its high literacy rate is a legacy of Soviet educational achievements. India remains at the bottom in terms of social conditions despite an impressive jump in per capita income. Its low level of literacy remains a serious impediment to economic growth. Data from World Bank, World Development Indicators.

against pressures of the market. At least in the more advanced economies, states have assumed regulatory, welfare, and infrastructural roles that require a substantial and generally rising level of spending. For example, central government spending on social programs increased between 1970 and 2011 in Japan from 5 to 23 percent of GDP, in the United States from 10 to 19 percent, and in the core EU countries from 13 to 25 percent.[46] (These figures would be higher if the budgets for regional and local government were included.)

The picture is further complicated by the persistence of cultural patterns. Societies on the receiving end of global forces have demonstrated resilience by variously resisting, blunting, or turning those forces to their own ends. Regional and national cultures have been altered but hardly erased by globalization. People in different parts of the world consume foreign goods each in their own way. Not only is this consumption highly selective, but it often results in the fundamental transformation in the way the product or practices are adopted. It may even set off a nationalist, religious, or ethnic reaction quite at odds with the assumption of rising uniformity. Just because the French adopted the term "le weekend" and ate at McDonald's did not mean that their outlooks had become American. Western Europeans and East Asians continued to live in distinct economic and political worlds. So too did Americans, even as they developed a taste for sushi, croissants and espresso, reggae and karaoke, Nintendo and Pokémon. In a globalized world there were still striking variations in what it means to be modern.

Edward Said, an American academic of Palestinian descent, made a good point when he warned against making "'civilizations' and 'identities' into what they are not: shut-down, sealed-off entities that have been purged of the myriad currents and countercurrents that animate human history, and that over centuries have made it possible for that history not only to contain wars of religion and imperial conquest but also to be one of exchange, cross-fertilization and sharing."[47] But cultures, wherever they may be on the globe, have demonstrated remarkable resilience and vitality and have inspired people to insist on some considerable say in their own fate. Even as the world becomes one to an unprecedented degree, it remains to a strikingly degree plural. Preserving integration while also respecting or at least accommodating difference will perhaps be the leading challenge of the decades ahead.

FINAL REFLECTIONS ON THE POST-1945 WORLD
The Limits and Uses of History

YOGI BERRA, THE LEGENDARY BASEBALL player and master of the fractured aphorism, reportedly declared, "It's tough to make predictions, especially about the future." Those inclined to worry can dwell on a long list of potential disasters. The international economy harbors a dazzling array of perils and problems that can erupt at any moment. Drug-resistant diseases may proliferate, transported by migration, trade, and tourists (some 700 million on the move annually in 2000), and set off epidemics that could cut wide swaths through the human population. Mutant genes made possible by modern scientific wizardry could create havoc in an almost infinite variety of ways. One of several thousand asteroids estimated to have a diameter of two thirds of a mile or greater could strike the Earth, sending enough debris skyward to block sunlight and lower the surface temperature, devastating agriculture and killing a billion or more people. Nuclear war—a more familiar human-made disaster—remains a specter, albeit less prominent than in earlier decades.

All these frightening possibilities could be part of our future, but precisely because so much hinges in these cases on chance, history cannot be of much help in predicting either the odds or the outcome. There are, however, important features of our world that are more amenable to historically grounded speculation about the decades ahead. Will the North Atlantic region, consisting of the United States and its European partners, still dominate culturally, militarily, and economically at the close of the twenty-first century? Will the transformations of this century prove as dramatic and far-reaching as those of the previous one? Will globalization continue its inroads on countries and cultures around the world and vindicate those convinced of its capacity to make the world not only better but also more uniform? Will inequalities between regions and within countries increase, setting off military conflict and social upheavals?

Anyone with a sense of history will realize the perils of prediction involved in answering even these more manageable questions and will recognize the capacity of events to evade expectation. The last seven decades provide some striking examples of surprises. The decolonization process came with a sweep and suddenness that often outpaced the anticipation of colonized and colonizer alike. Although the ghost of the Great Depression, with its falling prices and high unemployment, haunted people in the developed world at the end of World War II, their economies in fact experienced high and sustained levels of growth that greatly improved the lives of ordinary people. Into the 1980s Cold War commentators on both sides judged the Soviet bloc a sturdy structure—only to watch in amazement as it came rapidly tumbling down. Even the recent passage to the new millennium brought a reminder of how predictions can go awry. The portentous Y2K computer threat turned into an embarrassing fizzle for Americans and the British who had sunk substantial resources into heading it off while others had shrugged the threat off without serious consequences. Terrorism, a low-level preoccupation around the world before September 2001, suddenly jumped to the top of the lists of major menaces in what seemed to many a world turned upside down. Today's predictions stand a good chance of proving grossly ill founded and of being overtaken or overshadowed by developments entirely beyond current imagining.

Enveloped in uncertainty and disoriented by the daily rush of information, we have in history an indispensable tool. It can help us test the sweeping claims made by "authorities." It can tell cautionary tales about the limits of understanding and the dangers of jumping to bold or seemingly self-evident conclusions. Surface impressions, we learn, sometimes hide deeper meaning that we need to have the patience to look for. Wishful thinking can, if we are not on guard, lead us into false positions that subsequent events will expose. Historically grounded skepticism arms us against the overwhelming impact of apparently momentous events and against the absolute confidence of punditry. It reminds us to look for perspective and patterns in what otherwise may seem a blur of events. With history we cannot know the future. But without history we have no frame of reference for understanding the present, no basis for intelligent anticipation of what lies ahead, and no resource for coping with the surprises that we are bound to encounter along life's way.

Most important of all, history instructs us in the highly contingent nature of our world and the need to come to terms with the unavoidable fragility of life. The anxious prayer familiar to earlier generations remains pertinent: "From lightning and tempest, from plague, pestilence, and famine; from battle and murder, and from sudden death. *Good Lord, deliver us.*"[1] Our complex and dynamic world can indeed take unpleasantly surprising turns. We should not imagine for a moment that the current age is somehow immune from the patterns of the past or that passivity in the face of change is anything but a dangerous gamble with the stakes no less than a better, secure life on this planet.

RECOMMENDED RESOURCES

INTRODUCTION   THE 1945 WATERSHED
Doing Global History

For **general introductions**, see Peter N. Stearns, *Globalization in World History* (2010); Jürgen Osterhammel and Niels P. Petersson, *Globalization: A Short History*, trans. Dona Geyer (2005); Patrick Manning, *Navigating World History: Historians Create a Global Past* (2003); Bruce Mazlish, "Comparing Global History to World History," *Journal of Interdisciplinary History* 28 (Winter 1998): 385–395; A. G. Hopkins, ed., *Globalization in World History* (2002); and Jerry H. Bentley, ed., *The Oxford Handbook of World History* (2011). Robert B. Marks, *The Origins of the Modern World: A Global Ecological Narrative from Fifteenth to the Twenty-first Century*, 2nd ed. (2007), is a synthesis that builds on the influential "world systems" approach, treated in summary form in Immanuel Wallerstein, "The Rise and Future Demise of the World Capitalist System," in his *The Capitalist World-Economy* (1979), pp. 1–36. The contributions to "Essays on Global and Comparative History," sponsored by the American Historical Association and edited by Michael Adas, provide handy, authoritative introductions to major topics in a rapidly developing field. The advanced student will find Maxine Berg, ed., *Writing the History of the Global: Challenges for the 21st Century* (2013), instructive on approaches, issues, and methods.

Helpful for **news, commentary, and discussion related to global history**: the Toynbee Prize Foundation website (toynbeeprize.org/); the World History Association website (www.thewha.org/); the Big History Project website (www.bighistoryproject.com); and "World History Matters" maintained by the Roy Rosenzweig Center for History and New Media at George Mason University (chnm.gmu.edu/world-history-matters/).

On **global geography**, see Martin W. Lewis and Kären E. Wigen, *The Myth of Continents: A Critique of Metageography* (1997), and Edward W. Said, *Orientalism*, 2nd ed. (1994), on the ways each era has conceived the world to fit its own particular assumptions. The online map collection maintained by the Perry-Castañeda Library at the University of Texas at Austin (www.lib.utexas.edu/maps) is a rich resource for historical as well as current maps.

For **global economic data**, Angus Maddison left a wonderful legacy in *The World Economy: A Millennial Perspective* (2001) and in *Contours of the World Economy, 1–2030 AD: Essays in Micro-Economic History* (2007). His efforts to give historical dimension to economic data are being continued at the Maddison Project Database (www.ggdc.net/maddison/maddison-project/data.htm). Other rich and authoritative data collections include United Nations Development Programme, *Human Development Report*, issued annually, as well as the websites for the World Bank (data.worldbank.org/) and the United Nations Conference for Trade and Development (unctad.org/en/pages/Statistics.aspx).

Collections of primary materials pertinent to global history can be found at Peter Halsall's Internet History Sourcebooks Project at Fordham University (www.fordham.edu/halsall/), which includes links to other more specialized sites; the Marxists Internet Archive (www.marxists.org) for a range of left-wing leaders and intellectuals; the Avalon Project at the Yale Law School (avalon.law.yale.edu/), which favors formal, political documents; and the National Security Archive at George Washington University (www2.gwu.edu/~nsarchiv/), which features declassified documents on the U.S. role in the world.

Special studies on **key cultural and social topics** include Peter N. Stearns, *Consumerism in World History: The Global Transformation of Desire*, 2nd ed. (2006); Göran Therborn, *Between Sex and Power: Family in the World, 1900–2000* (2004); Leila J. Rupp, *Worlds of Women: The Making of an International Women's Movement* (1997); Ramachandra Guha, *Environmentalism: A Global History* (2000); and Allen Guttmann, *Games and Empires: Modern Sports and Cultural Imperialism* (1994).

Long-term perspectives on **migration** can be found in David Eltis, ed., *Coerced and Free Migration: Global Perspectives* (2002); Adam McKeown, "Global Migration, 1846–1940," *Journal of World History* 15 (June 2004): 155–189; and Patrick Manning, *Migration in World History*, 2nd ed. (2013).

The Rise of Trans-Atlantic Capitalism

Broad coverage of the first phase of globalization can be found in C. A. Bayly's masterpiece, *The Birth of the Modern World, 1780–1914: Global Connections and Comparisons* (2004); and in the lively and compelling four-volume history by E. J. Hobsbawm, especially *The Age of Empire, 1875–1914* (1987) and *Age of Extremes: The Short Twentieth Century, 1914–1991* (1994). See also Patrick K. O'Brien and Geoffrey Allen Pigman, "Free Trade, British Hegemony and the International Economic Order in the Nineteenth Century," *Review of International Studies* 18 (April 1992): 89–113; Patrick K. O'Brien, "International Trade and the Development of the Third World since the Industrial Revolution," *Journal of World History* 8 (Spring 1997): 75–133; Harold James, *The End of Globalization: Lessons from the Great Depression* (2001); Dwayne R. Winseck and Robert M. Pike, *Communication and Empire: Media, Markets, and Globalization, 1860–1930* (2007); and Steven Bryan, *The Gold Standard at the Turn of the Century: Rising Powers, Global Money, and the Age of Empire* (2010). Karl Polanyi's classic *The Great Transformation: The Political and Economic Origins of Our Times* (1944) remains important as a demystifying account of the rise of the market economy and the resistance it engendered. Vaclav Smil is a good guide to the technology that made the modern global economy possible. See for example his *Energy in World History* (1994) and *Two Prime Movers of Globalization: The History and Impact of Diesel Engines and Turbines* (2010).

Nationalism and the Modern State

Good places to begin are Lloyd S. Kramer's up-to-date introduction, *Nationalism in Europe and America: Politics, Cultures, and Identities since 1775* (2011); and Benedict Anderson's influential *Imagined Communities: Reflections on the Origin and Spread of Nationalism*, 2nd ed. (1991). Other notable treatments include Ernest Gellner, *Nations and Nationalism*, 2nd ed. (2008); Anthony D. Smith, *The Ethnic Origins of Nations* (1986); and E. J. Hobsbawm, *Nations and Nationalism since 1780: Programme, Myth, Reality*, 2nd ed. (1992).

For treatment of **the modern state** as a key element in the nationalist project, see Christopher Pierson's helpful primer, *The Modern State*, 3rd ed. (2011). For the capacity of states to inflict violence on an unprecedented scale, see James C. Scott, *Seeing like a State: How Certain Schemes to Improve the Human Condition Have Failed* (1998); Jonathan Glover, *Humanity: A Moral History of the Twentieth Century* (2000); Eric D. Weitz, *A Century of Genocide: Utopias of Race and Nation* (2003); and Yuki Tanaka and Marilyn B. Young, eds., *Bombing Civilians: A Twentieth-Century History* (2009).

Imperialism and Colonialism

Good places to begin: Heather Streets-Salter and Trevor Getz, *Empires and Colonies in the Modern World, 1500 to the Present* (2015), a clear-headed introduction to a slippery, controversial set of issues; Philip D. Curtin, *The World and the West: The European Challenge and the Overseas Response in the Age of Empire* (2000), which is especially helpful in identifying types of Western expansion and forms of counter-responses; Timothy Parsons, *The Rule of Empires: Those Who Built Them, Those Who Endured Them, and Why They Always Fall* (2010), a set of case studies that puts the spotlight on the problematic role of collaboration and nationalism in the making and breaking of empires; Herfried Münkler, *Empires: The Logic of World Domination from Ancient Rome to the United States* (2007), a wide-ranging, sophisticated, and stimulating theoretical treatment; Jane Burbank and Frederick Cooper, *Empires in World History: Power and the Politics of Difference* (2010), which takes as its concern large political units with an expansionist agenda and clear hierarchies among its peoples as distinct from nation-states; and John Darwin's *After Tamerlane: The Rise and Fall of Global Empires, 1400–2000* (2008), a fluent treatment of a succession of great powers, all designated "empire" because of their considerable span of control and significant impact on the making of the modern world. Frederick Cooper and Ann Laura Stoler, eds., *Tensions of Empire: Colonial Cultures in a Bourgeois World* (1997), is an influential exploration of new perspectives. See also Stephen Howe, *Empire: A Very Short Introduction* (2002); Jürgen Osterhammel, *Colonialism: A Theoretical Overview*, 2nd ed. (2005); Frederick Cooper, *Colonialism in Question: Theory, Knowledge, History* (2005); Alfred W. Crosby, *Ecological Imperialism: The Biological Expansion of Europe, 900–1900* (1986); and Michael Adas, *Machines as the Measure of Men: Science, Technology, and Ideologies of Western Dominance* (1989).

The comparative study of **the British and American empires** has emerged as an important subfield. Start with Julian Go's *Patterns of Empire: The British and American Empires, 1688 to the Present* (2011), an elaborate, systematic treatment that takes both theory and history seriously. Other helpful works include Bernard Porter, *Empire and Superempire: Britain, America and the World* (2006); Patrick Karl O'Brien, "The Pax Britannica and American Hegemony: Precedent, Antecedent or Just Another History?" and John M. Hobson, "Two Hegemonies or One? A Historical-Sociological Critique of Hegemonic Stability Theory," both in *Two Hegemonies: Britain 1846–1914 and the United States 1941–2001*, ed. Patrick Karl O'Brien and Armand Cleese (2002), 3–64 and 305–325; and Charles Maier, *Among Empires: American Ascendancy and Its Predecessors* (2006).

People on the Periphery

On the rising **challenge to Western domination**, see Michael Adas, "Contested Hegemony: The Great War and the Afro-Asian Assault on the Civilizing Mission Ideology," *Journal of World History* 15 (March 2004): 31–-63; Pankaj Mishra, *From the Ruins of Empire: The Revolt Against the West and the Remaking of Asia* (2012); and Rebecca E. Karl, *Staging the World: Chinese Nationalism at the Turn of the Twentieth Century* (2002). For an introduction to an influential interpretive approach, see Gyan Prakash, "Subaltern Studies as Postcolonial Criticism," *American Historical Review* 99 (December 1994): 1475–1490.

Excellent insights on **rural societies** emerge from James C. Scott, *Weapons of the Weak: Everyday Forms of Peasant Resistance* (1985); David Arnold, *Famine: Social Crisis and Historical Change* (1998); and Mike Davis, *Late Victorian Holocausts: El Nino Famines and the Making of the Third World* (2001). For a critical introduction to a debate over peasant outlook and motivation, see Jonathan Lieberson, *Peasant Values and Rural Development: An Unresolved Controversy* (1981). Eric R. Wolf's classic *Peasant Wars of the Twentieth Century* (1969) takes the side of that controversy stressing peasants' attachment to village solidarity.

CHAPTER 1 THE COLD WAR: TOWARD SOVIET-AMERICAN CONFRONTATION

General Works on Cold War Origins

On **the World War II backdrop**, see Gerhard L. Weinberg, *A World at Arms: A Global History of World War II*, 2nd ed. (2005); and Richard Overy, *Why the Allies Won* (1995). For **general guidance**, turn to Melvyn P. Leffler and Odd Arne Westad, eds., *The Cambridge History of the Cold War*, vol. 1: *Origins, 1945–1962* (2010); and Melvyn P. Leffler and David S. Painter, eds., *Origins of the Cold War: An International History*, 2nd ed. (2005). The Cold War International History Project (www.wilsoncenter.org/program/cold-war-international-history-project) is a leading source for newly released materials and current scholarly discussions from all sides of the global Cold War.

On **the dawn of the nuclear era**, see Campbell Craig and Sergey Radchenko, *The Atomic Bomb and the Origins of the Cold War* (2008), which is crisply written, international in scope, and helpful on scholarly controversies; and Gerard J. De Groot, *The Bomb: A Life* (2005), an engaging and wide-ranging synthesis focusing on 1940–1960. On the U.S. atomic bomb project, Richard Rhodes, *The Making of the Atomic Bomb* (1986); Martin Sherwin, *A World Destroyed: The Atomic Bomb and the Grand Alliance* (1975); and Samuel Walker, *Prompt and Utter Destruction: Truman and the Use of the Atomic Bombs against Japan* (1997), are standard accounts. The Atomic Bomb Museum (atomicbombmuseum .org/) and Nuclear Files (www.nuclearfiles.org) are well-curated sites that offer a wide range of materials on the bombings of Hiroshima and Nagasaki. The emergence of the Soviet nuclear program is treated in David Holloway, *Stalin and the Bomb: The Soviet Union and Atomic Energy, 1939–1956* (1994).

The U.S. Role

General surveys include William H. Chafe, *The Unfinished Journey: America Since World War II*, 7th ed. (2011); Norman L. Rosenberg and Emily S. Rosenberg, *In Our Times: America Since World War II*, 7th ed. (2002); and Michael S. Sherry, *In the Shadow of War: The United States Since the 1930s* (1995).

On **U.S. policy**, see Melvyn P. Leffler, *The Specter of Communism: The United States and the Origins of the Cold War, 1917–1953* (1994), a tighter and more interpretively explicit version of his *A Preponderance of Power: National Security, the Truman Administration, and the Cold War* (1992). Arnold A. Offner, *Another Such Victory: President Truman and the Cold War, 1945–1953* (2002), is a good interpretive counterpoint to Leffler. *Truman* (writ. and prod. David Grubin, 1997, 270 min.), a documentary prepared for the "American Experience" series on PBS, nicely evokes the challenges facing the first Cold War president. Campbell Craig and Fredrik Logevall, *America's Cold War: The Politics of Insecurity* (2010), is a handy policy survey that asks why the superpower rivalry did not start winding down in the 1950s. On the ideas that shaped U.S. Cold War thinking, see Michael H. Hunt, *Ideology and U.S. Foreign Policy*, 2nd ed. (2009); Abbott Gleason, *Totalitarianism: The Inner*

History of the Cold War (1995); and Michael Adas, *Dominance by Design: Technological Imperatives and America's Civilizing Mission* (2006).

On the **impact of the Cold War on American society and culture**, see Ellen Schrecker, *The Age of McCarthyism: A Brief History with Documents*, 2nd ed. (2002), a first-rate, fresh overview. See also her fuller account, *Many Are the Crimes: McCarthyism in America* (1998), as well as Richard M. Fried, *Nightmare in Red: The McCarthy Era in Perspective* (1990); and Penny M. Von Eschen, *Race Against Empire: Black Americans and Anticolonialism, 1937–1957* (1997). *Point of Order* (dir. Emile de Antonio, 1964, 107 min.) is a documentary that captures the drama of the McCarthy investigations. For the broader domestic impact of the Cold War, see Stephen J. Whitfield, *The Culture of the Cold War*, 2nd ed. (1996), an engaging treatment of the way anticommunism narrowed cultural as well as political expression; *Atomic Cafe* (dir. Jayne Loader, Kevin Rafferty, and Pierce Rafferty, 1982, 88 min.), which uses original footage to treat the origins of the nuclear age and the shadow it cast over American society; Elaine Tyler May, *Homeward Bound: American Families in the Cold War Era*, 2nd ed. (2008), exploring the impact on attitudes toward gender roles; and Michael J. Hogan, *A Cross of Iron: Harry S. Truman and the Origins of the National Security State, 1945–1954* (1998), highlighting the ramifications at home of the American state's anticommunist mobilization.

The Soviet Side

General treatments include Robert Service's balanced text, *A History of Modern Russia: From Tsarism to the Twenty-first Century*, 3rd ed. (2009); Raymond Pearson's treatment of the strategies accounting for *The Rise and Fall of the Soviet Empire*, 2nd ed. (2002); Vladislav M. Zubok's skilled synthesis, *A Failed Empire: The Soviet Union in the Cold War from Stalin to Gorbachev* (2007); and Richard Stites' brief but suggestive survey of *Russian Popular Culture: Entertainment and Society since 1900* (1992). *Seventeen Moments in Soviet History* is a rich online collection covering 1917–1991 assembled by James von Geldern and Lewis Siegelbaum and maintained at Macalester College (soviethistory.macalester.edu/).

For notable works on **Stalin and his foreign policy** that draw on new sources, see Robert Service, *Stalin: A Biography* (2005); Geoffrey Roberts, *Stalin's Wars: From World War to Cold War, 1939–1953* (2006), which gives pride of interpretive place to personality and worldview; and Anne Applebaum, *Iron Curtain: The Crushing of Eastern Europe, 1944–1956* (2012), which is sharply critical of the Soviet record. Vojtech Mastny, *The Cold War and Soviet Insecurity: The Stalin Years* (1996), is an older multiarchival study that depicts Stalin as both cautious and prone to miscalculation.

Domestic conditions in the Stalin era are treated broadly in John Channon, ed., *Politics, Society, and Stalinism in the USSR* (1998); and Elena Zubkova, *Russia after the War: Hopes, Illusions, and Disappointments, 1945–1957*, trans. and ed. Hugh Ragsdale (1998). Stephen Kotkin's social history case study, *Magnetic Mountain: Stalinism as a Civilization* (1995), gives a sense of what Stalinism meant on the ground. For the dark side of the Stalinist system, see Anne Applebaum, *Gulag: A History* (2003), and *Gulag: Many Days, Many Lives*, maintained by the Roy Rosenzweig Center for History and New Media at George Mason University (gulaghistory.org/).

The Cold War in the Third World

The impressively wide-ranging account by Odd Arne Westad, *The Global Cold War: Third World Interventions and the Making of Our Times* (2005), is **the place to begin**. For more on developments on the Korean peninsula, see Charles K. Armstrong, *The North Korean Revolution, 1945–1950* (2003); A. N. Lankov, *From Stalin to Kim Il Sung: The Formation of*

North Korea, 1945–1960 (2002); and Kim Dong-choon, *The Unending Korean War: A Social History* (2009). For **Korea** as the site of the first serious superpower collision in the Third World, see Sheila Miyoshi Jager's broadly cast, *Brothers at War: The Unending Conflict in Korea* (2013); and Steven Hugh Lee, *The Korean War* (2001), a tight international overview with documents. See also Burton I. Kaufman, *The Korean War: Challenges in Crisis, Credibility, and Command*, 2nd ed. (1997); and William Stueck, *Rethinking the Korean War: A New Diplomatic and Strategic History* (2002).

CHAPTER 2   THE INTERNATIONAL ECONOMY: OUT OF THE RUINS

Salvaging the International Economy

For **a general overview of the postwar economy**, turn to Daniel Yergin and Joseph Stanislaw, *The Commanding Heights: The Battle for the World Economy* 2nd ed. (2002), sprightly and impressionistic. **Bretton Woods** is set in the context of the U.S. approach to international reconstruction in Elizabeth Borgwardt, *A New Deal for the World: America's Vision for Human Rights* (2005), and is treated in detail in Benn Steil's accessible *The Battle of Bretton Woods: John Maynard Keynes, Harry Dexter White, and the Making of a New World Order* (2013). **John Maynard Keynes,** the most famous of the postwar reformers, is well served by D. E. Moggridge, *Keynes*, 3rd ed. (1993), and Robert J. A. Skidelsky, *Keynes* (1996)—both brief introductions. The contributors to Peter A. Hall, ed., *The Political Power of Economic Ideas: Keynesianism across Nations* (1989), do an excellent job of tracing Keynes' worldwide impact.

Postwar Recovery

Japan is given masterful coverage in John Dower, *Embracing Defeat: Japan in the Wake of World War II* (1999), the product of a lifetime of research. See also his *Empire and Aftermath: Yoshida Shigeru and the Japanese Experience, 1878–1954* (1979); Michael Schaller, *The American Occupation of Japan: The Origins of the Cold War in Asia* (1985); and Yukiko Koshiro, *Trans-Pacific Racisms and the U.S. Occupation of Japan* (1999). Andrew Gordon, ed., *Postwar Japan as History* (1993), contains a fine collection of essays, as does *The Cambridge History of Japan*, vol. 6: *The Twentieth Century*, ed. Peter Duus (1988). William M. Tsutsui, ed., *A Companion to Japanese History* (2007), Part 4 on the postwar period, contains good guides to debates and approaches in the literature.

For **broad treatments of postwar Europe**, see Tony Judt's widely acclaimed *Postwar: A History of Europe Since 1945* (2005); and Mark Mazower's much admired *Dark Continent: Europe's Twentieth Century* (1998); as well as Hartmut Kaelble, *A Social History of Europe, 1945–2000*, trans. Liesel Tarquini (2013); and Geir Lundestad, *The United States and Western Europe Since 1945: From "Empire" by Invitation to Transatlantic Drift* (2003).

On **European recovery**, begin with Alan S. Milward, *The European Rescue of the Nation-State*, 2nd ed. (2000). Other helpful works include Michael J. Hogan, *The Marshall Plan: America, Britain, and the Reconstruction of Western Europe, 1947–1952* (1987), which credits U.S, assistance with greater impact than Milward allows; Ian Baruma, *Year Zero: A History of 1945* (2013), an evocative treatment mainly concerned with Europe; and David W. Ellwood, *Rebuilding Europe: Western Europe, America, and Postwar Reconstruction* (1992), a synthesis that covers political and diplomatic developments into the early 1960s. Michaela Hönicke Moore, *Know Your Enemy: The American Debate on Nazism, 1933–1945* (2010), is essential on the postwar U.S, approach to the "German problem."

The Library of Congress online exhibit "For European Recovery: The Fiftieth Anniversary of the Marshall Plan" (www.loc.gov/exhibits/marshall/index.html) provides a mainly American perspective on a critical European development.

The U.S. Economic Model

For the rise of **a consumer-oriented U.S. mass market**, see Vaclav Smil, *Made in the USA: The Rise and Retreat of American Manufacturing* (2013), especially chaps. 1–3; Robert M. Collins, *More: The Politics of Economic Growth in Postwar America* (2000); Lizabeth Cohen, *A Consumers' Republic: The Politics of Mass Consumption in Postwar America* (2003); Susan Strasser, *Satisfaction Guaranteed: The Making of the American Mass Market* (1989); and Olivier Zunz, *Why the American Century?* (1998). On **Disney and Coke**, the most helpful works are Richard Schickel, *The Disney Version: The Life, Times, Art, and Commerce of Walt Disney*, 3rd ed. (1997); Steven Watts, *The Magic Kingdom: Walt Disney and the American Way of Life* (1997); and Mark Pendergrast, *For God, Country and Coca-Cola: The Definitive History of the Great American Soft Drink and the Company That Makes It*, 3rd ed. (2013).

The **American impact in Europe** is the subject of considerable excellent work. Jessica C. E. Gienow-Hecht, "Always Blame the Americans: Anti-Americanism in Europe in the Twentieth Century," *American Historical Review* 111 (October 2006): 1067–1091, and Rob Kroes, "American Empire and Cultural Imperialism: A View from the Receiving End," in *Rethinking American History in a Global Age*, ed. Thomas Bender (2002), pp. 295–313, are good points of entry. Important general treatments include Victoria de Grazia, *Irresistible Empire: America's Advance through Twentieth-Century Europe* (2005); Mary Nolan, *The Transatlantic Century: Europe and America, 1890–2010* (2012); David W. Ellwood, *The Shock of America: Europe and the Challenge of the Century* (2012); and Richard H. Pells, *Not Like Us: How Europeans Have Loved, Hated, and Transformed American Culture since World War II* (1997). Max Paul Friedman, *Rethinking Anti-Americanism: The History of an Exceptional Concept in American Foreign Relations* (2012), deals adroitly with the pronounced American allergy to foreign criticism.

For **the U.S. impact on particular countries**, see Richard F. Kuisel, *Seducing the French: The Dilemma of Americanization* (1993); Christopher Endy, *Cold War Holidays: American Tourism in France* (2004); Maria Höhn, *GIs and Fräuleins: The German-American Encounter in 1950s West Germany* (2002); Uta G. Poiger, *Jazz, Rock, and Rebels: Cold War Politics and American Culture in a Divided Germany* (2000); Jeff R. Schutts, "Born Again in the Gospel of Refreshment? Coca-Colonization and the Re-Making of Postwar German Identity," *Consuming Germany in the Cold War*, ed. David F. Crew (2003), 121–150; and Reinhold Wagnleitner, *Coca-colonization and the Cold War: The Cultural Mission of the United States in Austria after the Second World War*, trans. Diana M. Wolf (1994). A movie about Coke set in Berlin—*One, Two, Three* (dir. Billy Wilder, 1961, 108 min.)—captures amidst the gags some of the complexities of Americanization.

CHAPTER 3　THE THIRD WORLD: FIRST TREMORS IN ASIA

General Setting

Ronald H. Spector, *In the Ruins of Empire: The Japanese Surrender and the Battle for Postwar Asia* (2007), traces the regional ramifications of Japan's total collapse; while Michael H. Hunt and Steven I. Levine, *Arc of Empire: America's Wars in Asia from the Philippines to Vietnam* (2012), highlights both postwar ferment in the region and deepening U.S. involvement. For the growing impact of the Cold War in the Third World, see Westad, *The Global Cold War* (noted for Chapter 1).

China's Revolution

For a **general treatment**, see Odd Arne Westad, *Restless Empire: China and the World Since 1750* (2012); Maurice Meisner, *Mao's China and After: A History of The People's Republic*, 3rd ed. (1999); and Jeremy Brown and Paul Pickowicz, *Dilemmas of Victory: The Early Years of the People's Republic of China* (2007). On **Mao Zedong**, the recent and impressively researched treatment by Alexander Pantsov with Steven I. Levine, *Mao: The Real Story* (2012), captures the complexity of a protean figure. See also Odd Arne Westad, *Decisive Encounters: The Chinese Civil War, 1946–1950* (2003), an outstanding synthesis.

The **foreign relations of the Mao era** is treated in the excellent overview by Chen Jian, *Mao's China and the Cold War* (2001). See also Niu Jun, *From Yan'an to the World: The Origin and Development of Chinese Communist Foreign Policy*, ed. and trans. Steven I. Levine (2005); Michael H. Hunt, *The Genesis of Chinese Communist Foreign Policy* (1996); Dieter Heinzig, *The Soviet Union and Communist China, 1945–1950: The Arduous Road to the Alliance*, trans. David J. S. King (2004); and Odd Arne Westad, ed., *Brothers in Arms: The Rise and Fall of the Sino-Soviet Alliance, 1945–1963* (1998).

Writings on **the Chinese peasantry** in an age of revolution are rich. Peter Seybolt, *Throwing the Emperor from His Horse: Portrait of a Village Leader in China, 1923–1995* (1996); and Huang Shu-min, *The Spiral Road: Change in a Chinese Village through the Eyes of a Communist Party Leader*, 2nd ed. (1998), are two especially engaging accounts—one by a historian and the other by an anthropologist. *Yellow Earth* (dir. Chen Kaige, 1984, 89 min.) is a fascinating film by a leading director reflecting on village life in the area near Yanan in the late 1930s. Ralph A. Thaxton Jr., *Salt of the Earth: The Political Origins of Peasant Protest and Communist Revolution in China* (1997), offers in its conclusion some thought-provoking observations on village politics.

Modern Southeast Asia

Milton Osborne, *Southeast Asia: An Introductory History*, 10th ed. (2010), provides a good overview of a complex region. Clive J. Christie's, *Ideology and Revolution in Southeast Asia, 1900–1980: Political Ideas of the Anti-Colonial Era* (2001) and his *A Modern History of Southeast Asia: Decolonization, Nationalism, and Separatism* (1996) explore the antagonistic twin political impulses playing out in the region—the ideas animating state builders and the resistance issuing from a wide range of separatist movements. Richard Stubbs, *Hearts and Minds in Guerrilla Warfare: The Malayan Emergency, 1948–1960* (2004 [1889]), offers a careful treatment of a much-cited but generally misunderstood case.

Vietnam's Revolution

For **general perspectives**, begin with Mark Atwood Lawrence, *The Vietnam War: A Concise International History* (2008), notable for its lean and wide-ranging coverage; and Mark Bradley, *Vietnam at War* (2009), a fresh, crisp introduction to the Vietnamese perspective. For an outstanding visual overview offering a balanced treatment and excellent original footage, try *Vietnam: A Television History* (prod. WGBH, Boston; Central Independent Television, Great Britain; and Antenne-2, France; in association with LRE Productions; 1983, 13 episodes).

On **the origins of the Vietnamese revolution** see Huynh Kim Khanh, *Vietnamese Communism, 1925–1945* (1982); Hue-Tam Ho Tai, *Radicalism and the Origins of the Vietnamese Revolution* (1992); Christopher E. Goscha, *Vietnam or Indochina? Contesting Concepts of Space in Vietnamese Nationalism, 1887–1954* (1995); David G. Marr, *Vietnam 1945: The Quest for Power* (1995); Stein Tønnesson, *The Vietnamese Revolution of 1945: Roosevelt, Ho Chi Minh and de Gaulle in a World at War* (1991); and Tønnesson, *Vietnam*

1946: How the War Began (2010), are all helpful. The sweep of change in modern Vietnam is nicely captured in the family history by Duong Van Mai Elliott, *The Sacred Willow: Four Generations in the Life of a Vietnamese Family* (1999). The French film *Indochine* (dir. Régis Wargnier, 1992, 162 min.) evokes the social complexities of 1930s Vietnam. A good online resource is "The Indochina War, 1945–1956," maintained at the Université du Québec à Montréal (Indochine.uqam.ca/).

On **the revolution's leadership**, the obvious place to begin is with Ho Chi Minh: William J. Duiker, *Ho Chi Minh* (2000); Pierre Brocheux, *Ho Chi Minh: A Biography* (2007); and Sophie Quinn-Judge, *Ho Chi Minh: The Missing Years, 1919–1941* (2002). Another perspective on leadership can be found in Nguyen Thi Dinh, *No Other Road to Take: Memoir of Mrs. Nguyen Thi Dinh*, trans. Mai V. Elliott (1976), a peasant woman who rose to prominence within the southern resistance.

India's Independence

For general treatments, Stanley A. Wolpert, *A New History of India*, 8th ed. (2008), is an authoritative survey that gives substantial coverage to contemporary, mainly political developments. Judith M. Brown, *Modern India: The Origins of an Asian Democracy*, 2nd ed. (1994), is important for its attention to the continuities running from colonial to post-independence times. Ranajit Guha, *Dominance Without Hegemony: History and Power in Colonial India* (1997); and Partha Chatterjee, *The Nation and Its Fragments: Colonial and Postcolonial Histories* (1993), are leading examples of the influential subaltern studies approach.

On **Gandhi and Nehru**, Judith M. Brown has nearly cornered the market with a pair of skillful biographies: *Gandhi: Prisoner of Hope* (1989); and *Nehru: A Political Life* (2003). See in addition on Gandhi the movie version of the life, *Gandhi* (prod. and dir. Richard Attenborough, 1982, 188 min.), which wonderfully evokes the spirit and political acumen of the man; and the collection of Gandhi-related writings and audiovisual material at www.gandhimedia.org/, a website maintained by the GandhiServe Foundation. See also Nehru's own account of his life, *Toward Freedom: The Autobiography of Jawaharlal Nehru*, 2nd ed. (1941).

For **popular perspectives**, try the gripping fictional account, *Train to Pakistan*, by Kushwant Singh (1990 [1956]), which provides a sense of the hope and trauma that accompanied partition at the end of the colonial era. The novel *Nectar in a Sieve* (1954) by Kamala Markandaya and the contemporary classic film *Mother India* (dir. Mehboob Khan, 1957, 172 min.) bring the struggles of poor peasants vividly to life.

The Philippines

A **broad approach** is available in the distinctly comparative collection edited by Julian Go and Anne L. Foster, *The American Colonial State in the Philippines: Global Perspectives* (2003). More conventional overviews can be found in Stanley Karnow, *In Our Image: America's Empire in the Philippines* (1989); H. W. Brands, *Bound to Empire: The United States and the Philippines* (1992); and Stephen R. Shalom, *The United States and the Philippines: A Study in Neocolonialism* (1981).

Details on the critical **early postwar years** can be found in Nick Cullather, *Illusions of Influence: The Political Economy of the United States–Philippines Relations, 1942–1960* (1994), and in Luis Taruc, *He Who Rides the Tiger: The Story of an Asian Guerrilla Leader* (1967), an influential participant's perspective on the Huk appeal and ultimate collapse.

Good insights on **social divisions and conflict** emerge from Alfred W. McCoy, ed., *An Anarchy of Families: State and Family in the Philippines* (1993); Benedict J. Kerkvliet, *The Huk Rebellion: A Study of Peasant Revolt in the Philippines* (1977), a classic on the economic pressures pushing peasants into politics; and another classic, Benedict Anderson, "Cacique Democracy in the Philippines: Origins and Dreams," in *Discrepant Histories: Translocal Essays on Filipino Culture*, ed. Vicente L. Rafael (1995), 3–47.

CHAPTER 4   THE COLD WAR: A TENUOUS ACCOMMODATION

The Struggle to Stabilize the Cold War

For **general guidance**, see Melvyn P. Leffler, and Odd Arne Westad, eds., *The Cambridge History of the Cold War*, vol. 1: *Origins, 1945–1962* (2010) and vol. 2: *Crises and Détente* (2010).

On **the Soviet side**, begin with William J. Tompson, *Khrushchev: A Political Life* (1995), which offers a thoughtful scholarly appraisal of a pivotal figure; Aleksandr Fursenko and Timothy Naftali, *Khrushchev's Cold War: The Inside Story of an American Adversary* (2006), which exploits new documentation in great detail; and Robert Hornsby, *Protest, Reform and Repression in Khrushchev's Soviet Union* (2013), which offers good insights on state-society dynamics during the Khrushchev "thaw." *Khrushchev Remembers*, trans. and ed. Strobe Talbott and Jerrold L. Schecter with Vyacheslav B. Luchkov (3 vols.; 1970, 1974, 1990), lets the Soviet leader speak from his forced retirement. Lorenz M. Lüthi, *The Sino-Soviet Split: Cold War in the Communist World* (2008), and Austin Jersild, *The Sino-Soviet Alliance: An International History* (2014), taken together provide a rounded picture of the troubled relationship with China.

On **the American side**, see Robert R. Bowie and Richard H. Immerman, *Waging Peace: How Eisenhower Shaped an Enduring Cold War Strategy* (1998), a sympathetic treatment of perhaps the shrewdest Cold War president; Walter L. Hixson, *Parting the Curtain: Propaganda, Culture, and the Cold War, 1945–1961* (1997); Campbell Craig, *Destroying the Village: Eisenhower and Thermonuclear War* (1998); Lawrence Freedman, *Kennedy's Wars: Berlin, Cuba, Laos, and Vietnam* (2000); and Paul K. Conkin, *Big Daddy from the Pedernales: Lyndon Baines Johnson* (1986), which is a good place to begin on a larger-than-life leader.

On Key Points of Cold War Confrontation

The best single overview of **the Cuban Missile Crisis** can be found in Aleksandr Fursenko and Timothy Naftali, *"One Hell of a Gamble": Khrushchev, Castro, and Kennedy, 1958–1964* (1997). Michael R. Beschloss, *The Crisis Years: Kennedy and Khrushchev, 1960–1963* (1991), is good on context. In the light of recent scholarship, Robert Kennedy's popular and gripping insider account, *Thirteen Days* (1969), has (like many participant memoirs) to be taken with a large grain of salt.

For guides to an enormous and controversial literature on **the American commitment in Vietnam**, consult Gary R. Hess, *Vietnam: Explaining America's Lost War* (2009), as well as the website maintained by Edwin E. Moïse, "Vietnam War Bibliography" (www.clemson.edu/caah/history/facultypages/EdMoise/bibliography.html). Standard historical treatments are noted in Chapter 3, but see also on the U.S. role Robert J. McMahon, *The Limits of Empire: The United States and Southeast Asia since World War II* (1999); George C. Herring, *The Longest War: The United States and Vietnam, 1950–1975*, 4th ed. (2002), a longstanding favorite for its overview of U.S. policy; and Marilyn B. Young, *The Vietnam Wars, 1945–1990* (1991), which opens a broad window on the war. Fredrik Logevall has carefully chronicled the transition from the failed French struggle to mounting U.S. involvement in the late 1950s and early 1960s in *Embers of War: The Fall of an Empire and the Making of America's Vietnam* (2012) and *Choosing War: The Lost Chance for Peace and the Escalation of War in Vietnam* (1999). For an alternative appraisal, see Michael H. Hunt,

Lyndon Johnson's War: America's Cold War Crusade in Vietnam, 1945–1968 (1996). The documentary *The Fog of War: Eleven Lessons from the Life of Robert S. McNamara* (dir. Errol Morris, 2003, 107 min.) examines a key policymaker. The experience of Americans soldiers comes alive in Tim O'Brien's fictional *The Things They Carried* (1990) and in *The Anderson Platoon* (dir. Pierre Schoendorffer, 1966, 65 min.), which documents day-to-day combat operations.

The Social and Political Unrest of the Late 1960s

For a **broad perspective**, try Ronald Fraser et al., *1968: A Student Generation in Revolt* (1988), which uses oral history to explore the times as the participants saw it in western Europe as well as the United States; Jeremi Suri, *Power and Protest: Global Revolution and the Rise of Detente* (2003), an ambitious attempt at linking social ferment to Cold War developments; Gerd-Rainer Horn, *The Spirit of '68: Rebellion in Western Europe and North America, 1956–1976* (2007), excellent on context; and the forum on "The International 1968," *American Historical Review* 114 (February and April 2009): 42–135 and 329–404. Other overviews include Arthur Marwick, *The Sixties: Cultural Revolution in Britain, France, Italy, and the United States, c.1958–c.1974* (1998); and Robert V. Daniels, *Year of the Heroic Guerrilla: World Revolution and Counterrevolution in 1968* (1989). Lawrence S. Wittner's *Confronting the Bomb: A Short History of the World Nuclear Disarmament Movement* (2009) is an invaluable synthesis of a multi-volume project.

For **the United States**, David R. Farber, *The Age of Great Dreams: America in the 1960s* (1994), and Mark H. Lytle, *America's Uncivil Wars: The Sixties Era—From Elvis to the Fall of Richard Nixon* (2006), offer smart and accessible coverage of the civil rights movement and the erosion of Cold War social conformity. See also Terry H. Anderson, *The Sixties*, 3rd ed. (2007); Rhodri Jeffreys-Jones, *Peace Now! American Society and the Ending of the Vietnam War* (1999); and *Chicago 1968* (written and prod. Chana Gazit, 1995, 56 min.), which graphically conveys the anger and violence marking the antiwar demonstrations during the Democratic convention. The nuclear fears that both anticipated and fed the unrest of the 1960s serve as the subject of Allan M. Winkler's able synthesis, *Life Under a Cloud: American Anxiety About the Atom* (1993). *Dr. Strangelove, or: How I Learned to Stop Worrying and Love the Bomb* (dir. and prod. Stanley Kubrick, 1964, 93 min.), an irreverent film, marked a cultural watershed in attitudes toward nuclear war and more broadly the Cold War conflict. A good collection of materials on the Web can be found at the University of Virginia's "Sixties Project" (www2.iath.virginia.edu/sixties/HTML_docs/Sixties.html).

For a **more international view** of social unrest in the 1960s, see Thomas R. H. Havens, *Fire across the Sea: The Vietnam War and Japan, 1965–1975* (1987); Elena Poniatowska, *Massacre in Mexico*, trans. Helen R. Lane (1975); and Martin Klimke, *The Other Alliance: Student Protest in West Germany and the United States in the Global Sixties* (2010).

CHAPTER 5   ABUNDANCE AND DISCONTENT IN THE DEVELOPED WORLD

The U.S. Golden Age

For basic treatments encompassing the 1950s and 1960s, see the recommendations for Chapter 2.

A Revitalized Western Europe

General works to see aside from the items cited in Chapter 2 include Alan S. Milward with the assistance of George Brennan and Federico Romero, *The European Rescue of the Nation-State*, 2nd ed. (2000), and Philip H. Gordon and Sophie Meunier, *The French*

Challenge: Adapting to Globalization (2001), both of which make an important argument about postwar state survival and economic culture. On Fiat, see Alan Friedman, *Agnelli and the Network of Italian Power* (1988). For an empathetic look at how postwar prosperity changed the lives of a generation emerging from the shadows of depression and war, see Michael Apted's extraordinary long-term documentary series "Up" (8 episodes, 1964–2012 to date).

For the origins of **regional integration** and the resulting institutions and policies, see John McCormick, *Understanding the European Union: A Concise Introduction*, 6th ed. (2014). Wolfram Kaiser and Antonio Varsori, eds., *European Union History: Themes and Debates* (2010), offers a sophisticated introduction to the literature.

Japan's Leap into Prosperity

The classic general statement on **postwar political economy** is Chalmers Johnson, *MITI and the Japanese Miracle: The Growth of Industrial Policy, 1925–1975* (1982), but see also Shigeto Tsuru, *Japan's Capitalism: Creative Defeat and Beyond* (1993), which is especially good on the critical contributions of the Japanese government to economic growth; and the recent assessment by Frances McCall Rosenbluth and Michael F. Thies, *Japan Transformed: Political Change and Economic Restructuring* (2010). Laura K. Silverman, ed., *Bringing Home the Sushi: An Inside Look at Japanese Business through Japanese Comics* (1995), uses an extremely popular adult genre to convey a sense of the white-collar world of the "salary man."

The personalities and innovation that defined **Sony** come across in John Nathan, *Sony: The Private Life* (1999), and Akio Morita with Edwin M. Reingold with Mitsuko Shimamura, *Made in Japan: Akio Morita and Sony* (1986), while Simon Partner, *Assembled in Japan: Electrical Goods and the Making of the Japanese Consumer* (1999), provides valuable context.

Critics in an Era of Abundance

For overviews on the emergence of **environmentalism**, see J. R. McNeill, *Something New Under the Sun: An Environmental History of the Twentieth-Century World* (2000), especially strong in highlighting a period of unprecedented change, mostly for the worse; and John McCormick, *Reclaiming Paradise: The Global Environmental Movement* (1989). For developments in the United States, see Kirkpatrick Sale, *The Green Revolution: The American Environmental Movement, 1962–1992* (1993), an overview written from the perspective of an environmental activist; and Benjamin Kline, *First Along the River: A Brief History of the U.S. Environmental Movement*, 2nd ed. (2000), a compact and clear treatment of the last half-century of environmental concerns in the context of thinking about nature going back to the first settlements. Richard P. Tucker, *Insatiable Appetite: The United States and the Ecological Degradation of the Tropical World*, concise rev. ed. (2007), highlights the profound environmental impact of a leading consumer economy. On Rachel Carson, see Mary A. McCay, *Rachel Carson* (1993), and Linda Lear, *Rachel Carson: Witness for Nature* (1997). *Rachel Carson's Silent Spring* (written and prod. Neil Goodwin, 1993, 57 min.) brings to life an influential writer and her path-breaking book.

For **feminism in Europe and Japan**, see Claire Duchen, *Women's Rights and Women's Lives in France, 1944–1968* (1994), and her *Feminism in France: From May '68 to Mitterand* (1986). *Postwar Japan as History* (1993), edited by Andrew Gordon, contains excellent overviews by Kathleen S. Uno and by Sandra Buckley. Karen Offen, "Defining Feminism: A Comparative Historical Perspective," *Signs* 14 (Autumn 1988): 119–157, along with the responses in 15 (Autumn 1989): 195–209, makes the case for significant differences between the concerns of activist women in Europe and the United States. Developments in the **United States** emerge from Betty Friedan's colorful personal story, *Life So Far*

(2000). Joanne Meyerowitz, ed., *Not June Cleaver: Women and Gender in Postwar America, 1945–1960* (1994), and Amy Swerdlow, *Women Strike for Peace: Traditional Motherhood and Radical Politics in the 1960s* (1993), help set Friedan and her cause in context. Bonnie G. Smith, ed., *Global Feminisms Since 1945: A Survey of Issues and Controversies* (2000), examines through a social and political lens a good range of cases from the developed as well as the developing world.

Thoughtful introductions to critics of **global inequality** can be found in Cristóbal Kay, *Latin American Theories of Development and Underdevelopment* (1989), and Joseph L. Love, "Economic Ideas and Ideologies in Latin America since 1930," in *The Cambridge History of Latin America*, ed. Leslie Bethell, vol. 6, pt. 1 (1994), Chapter 7. The boldest and most accessible statement of the dependency position can be found in *Capitalism and Underdevelopment in Latin America* (1967) by the German-born and U.S.-educated André Gunder Frank. Ariel Dorfman and Armand Mattelert, *How to Read Donald Duck: Imperialist Ideology in the Disney Comic*, trans. David Kunzle (1975), first published in Chile in 1971, graphically develops the argument for seeing dependency in cultural as well as economic terms. Michael E. Latham, *Modernization as Ideology: American Social Science and "Nation Building" in the Kennedy Era* (2000), deals adroitly with the alternative U.S. approach.

For the **Latin American context** in which the dependency argument developed, see Greg Grandin, "Your Americanism and Mine: Americanism and Anti-Americanism in the Americas," *American Historical Review* 111 (October 2006); and Gilbert M. Joseph et al., eds., *Close Encounters of Empire: Writing the Cultural History of U.S.-Latin American Relations* (1998). The distinct authoritarian turn beginning in the 1960s is treated in Jerry Dávila, *Dictatorship in South America* (2013), and Tanya Harmer, *Allende's Chile and the Inter-American Cold War* (2011).

CHAPTER 6   THIRD WORLD HOPES AT HIGH TIDE

Third World Radicalism

On **the rise and fall of a transnational project**, see Vijay Prashad, *The Darker Nations: A People's History of the Third World* (2007), as well as Westad, *The Global Cold War* (cited for Chapter 1).

East Asia

For **general treatments**, see the items cited in Chapter 3.

On **the second phase of China's revolution**, see Jeremy Brown and Paul Pickowicz, *Dilemmas of Victory: The Early Years of the People's Republic of China* (2007); Roderick MacFarquhar and Michael Schoenhals, *Mao's Last Revolution* (2006), excellent on elite politics; and Joseph Esherick, Paul G. Pickowicz, and Andrew G. Walder, eds., *The Chinese Cultural Revolution as History* (2006), valuable for highlighting the diversity of social and regional perspectives. For engaging first-person accounts, see Jung Chang, *Wild Swans: Three Daughters of China* (1991), which details the life of a well-placed urban family during Mao's years in power; Li Zhisui, *The Private Life of Chairman Mao: The Memoirs of Mao's Personal Physician*, trans. Dai Hongzhao (1994), revealing on the daily life of the Communist emperor; and the sampling of perspectives in Feng Jicai, *Voices from the Whirlwind: An Oral History of the Chinese Cultural Revolution*, trans. Denny Chiu et al. (1991). For marvelous Cultural Revolution posters, most collected by Stefan R. Landsberger and housed at the International Institute of Social History in Amsterdam, go to chineseposters.net/.

On **the struggle for South Vietnam**, see Truong Nhu Tang with David Chanoff and Doan Van Toai, *A Viet Cong Memoir* (1985), which recounts the revolutionary awakening of a young, well-to-do southerner and his subsequent disillusionment. For local studies that are critical to understanding Vietnam's rural politics and rural conflict during the period of deepening American involvement, see Jeffrey Race, *War Comes to Long An: Revolutionary Conflict in a Vietnamese Province* (1972); David W. P. Elliott, *The Vietnamese War: Revolution and Social Change in the Mekong Delta, 1930–1975*, concise ed. (2007); and Pierre Brocheux, *The Mekong Delta: Ecology, Economy, and Revolution, 1860–1960* (1995). For perspective on the Saigon government, see Philip E. Catton, *Diem's Final Failure: Prelude to America's War in Vietnam* (2002).

The Caribbean Basin

For **general approaches** to a region in ferment, start with a pair of lively, balanced, up-to-date treatments: John C. Chasteen, *Born in Blood and Fire: A Concise History of Latin Latin America*, 3rd ed. (2011); and Franklin W. Knight, *The Caribbean, the Genesis of a Fragmented Nationalism*, 3rd ed. (2012). On **U.S. regional dominance**, see the fine survey by Lars Schoultz, *Beneath the United States: A History of U.S. Policy toward Latin America* (1998).

The best treatment of **Guatemala** is Piero Gleijeses, *Shattered Hope: The Guatemalan Revolution and the United States, 1944–1954* (1991), although it should be supplemented by Jim Handy, *Revolution in the Countryside: Rural Conflict and Agrarian Reform in Guatemala, 1944–1954* (1994); Greg Grandin, *The Blood of Guatemala: A History of Race and Nation* (2000); and Nick Cullather, *Secret History: The CIA's Classified Account of Its Operations in Guatemala, 1952–1954*, 2nd ed. (2006).

Insights on **Cuba's revolution** in long-term perspective emerge from Louis A. Pérez, Jr., *Cuba: Between Reform and Revolution*, 4th ed. (2011); Pérez, *Cuba and the United States: Ties of Singular Intimacy*, 3rd ed. (2003); and Pérez, *On Becoming Cuban: Identity, Nationality, and Culture*, 2nd ed. (2008). On Castro, turn to Tad Szulc, *Fidel: A Critical Portrait* (1987), and Peter G. Bourne, *Fidel: A Biography of Fidel Castro* (1986), both thoughtful treatments of a fascinating life. See also Piero Gleijeses, *Conflicting Missions: Havana, Washington, and Africa, 1959–1976* (2002), on Castro's sense of transnational revolutionary solidarity. *Memories of Underdevelopment* (dir. Tomas Gutierrez Alea, 1968, 97 min.), a classic of Cuba cinema, meditates on the aimless and melancholic life of a middle-class, middle-aged writer displaced by the revolution.

Sub-Saharan Africa

To set the subcontinent's **decolonization in broad context**, turn to Frederick Cooper, *Africa in the World: Capitalism, Empire, Nation-State* (2014), a taut, sophisticated, seasoned set of reflections; Donald R. Wright, *The World and a Very Small Place in Africa: A History of Globalization in Niumi, The Gambia*, 3rd ed. (2010) a deftly handled microhistory that nicely complements Cooper; Michael G. Schatzberg, *Political Legitimacy in Middle Africa: Father, Family, Food* (2001), delineating the political culture that made the "big man" possible and also constrained him; and Paul Nugent, *Africa Since Independence: A Comparative History*, 2nd ed. (2012), a detailed text treatment of political developments. A pair of websites are well worth a look: "African Online Digital Library" at Michigan State University (www.aodl.org/); and the BBC's "The Story of Africa," especially the section dealing with independence (www.bbc.co.uk/worldservice/africa/features/storyofafrica/14chapter3 .shtml).

On **Kwame Nkrumah and Ghana's early years**, see Basil Davidson, *Black Star: A View of the Life and Times of Kwame Nkrumah* (1974), a sympathetic account written from first-hand knowledge of the subject but in need of revision in light of the findings in Marika Sherwood, *Kwame Nkrumah: The Years Abroad, 1935–1947* (1996). Nkrumah speaks for himself in *The Autobiography of Kwame Nkrumah* (1957).

Fiction provides a window on **the hopes and frustrations of the post-independence period**. Ayi Kwei Armah, *The Beautyful Ones Are Not Yet Born* (1969), captures the corruption and general political demoralization afflicting Ghana by the time of Nkrumah's overthrow. Parallel developments in Nigeria emerge in two fine novels: Buchi Emecheta, *The Joys of Motherhood* (1979), which brings into focus the role of family and gender in a society in transformation at the close of the colonial era, and Chinua Achebe's *A Man of the People* (1966), which expresses deep political disillusionment over postcolonial developments.

The Middle East

Context on **the heyday of secular and radical nationalism** is available in William L. Cleveland and Martin Bunton, *A History of the Modern Middle East*, 5th ed. (2013), an accessible and sound textbook. Albert Hourani with Malise Ruthven, *A History of the Arab Peoples*, 2nd ed. (2002), traces the roots of modern developments going back to the seventh century while also providing a substantial section on the post-1939 era of the nation-state. Roger Owen, *State, Power and Politics in the Making of the Modern Middle East*, 3rd ed. (2004), and Adeed Dawisha, *Arab Nationalism in the Twentieth Century: From Triumph to Despair* (2003), develop the competing themes of state building and the appeal of a transnational ideology.

For a broad approach to the **nationalist impulse in Iran**, turn to Nikki R. Keddie with Yann Richard, *Modern Iran: Roots and Results of Revolution*, 2nd ed. (2006), an updated classic that provides topically and chronologically broad coverage; and Ervand Abrahamian, *Iran between Two Revolutions* (1982), which follows critical political and social developments from the late nineteenth century to the revolution of 1979. Abrahamian's *The Coup: 1953, the CIA, and the Roots of Modern U.S.-Iranian Relations* (2013), is a first-rate treatment—fresh and incisive—of a pivotal event. The rise and fall of a powerful and perplexing figure is the subject of a pair of recent and richly detailed biographies: Gholam R. Afkhami, *The Life and Times of the Shah* (2009); and Abbas Milani, *The Shah* (2011).

On **Egypt**, P. J. Vatikiotis, *Nasser and His Generation* (1978), does a splendid job of placing Nasser's life in the context of intense political and social change. Peter Woodward, *Nasser* (1992), offers a tight, fluent, measured assessment. "Umm Kulthum: A Voice Like Egypt" (dir. Michal Goldman, 1996, 67 min.), is an engaging film documentary of an immensely popular cultural figure whose career offers a window on the collective imagination of the Nasser era.

For **Algeria**, the place to start is John Ruedy, *Modern Algeria: The Origins and Development of a Nation*, 2nd ed. (2005), a careful, illuminating overview. Alistair Horne, *A Savage War of Peace: Algeria, 1954–1962*, 3rd ed. (2006), is the standard account of the prolonged and violent conflict leading to the end of French control. *The Battle of Algiers* (dir. Gillo Pontecorvo, 1966, 123 min.), provides a taut, nerve-wracking reenactment of the brutal struggle in 1956–1957 to control Algeria's main city.

CHAPTER 7 THE COLD WAR COMES TO A CLOSE

The Final Phase of the Cold War

For **overviews**, see Melvyn P. Leffler, and Odd Arne Westad, eds., *The Cambridge History of the Cold War*, vol. 2: *Crises and Détente* (2010), which includes coverage of the 1970s, and vol. 3: *Endings* (2010), treating developments from the late 1970s to Soviet collapse; Raymond L. Garthoff, *Détente and Confrontation: American-Soviet Relations from Nixon to Reagan*, 2nd ed. (1994), authoritative and suitably critical; and James Graham Wilson, *The Triumph of Improvisation: Gorbachev's Adaptability, Reagan's Engagement, and the End of the Cold War* (2014), which gives equal credit to Moscow and Washington. Wittner,

Confronting the Bomb (cited in chap. 4), and Matthew Evangelista, *Unarmed Forces: The Transnational Movement to End the Cold War* (1999), highlight the public pressures influencing policymakers.

On Shifting U.S. Policy

For the beginnings of **détente under Nixon**, see Stephen E. Ambrose's *Nixon*, vol. 2: *The Triumph of a Politician, 1962–1972* (1989), a fair assessment of a difficult subject. Irwin F. Gellman's multivolume biography (now well advanced) promises to considerably deepen our understanding of Nixon the statesman.

On the drift back to confrontation under **Carter and Reagan**, see John Ehrman, *The Rise of Neoconservatism: Intellectuals and Foreign Affairs, 1945–1994* (1995); Gaddis Smith, *Morality, Reason, and Power: American Diplomacy in the Carter Years* (1986), which builds on memoirs; Zbigniew Brzezinski, *Power and Principle: Memoirs of the National Security Adviser, 1977–1981* (1983), an engaging insider account; Frances FitzGerald's pungent *Way Out There in the Blue: Reagan, Star Wars and the End of the Cold War* (2000); and George P. Shultz, *Turmoil and Triumph: My Years as Secretary of State* (1993), which lays out the perspective of an influential moderate within the Reagan administration. William M. LeoGrande, *Our Own Backyard: The United States in Central America, 1977–1992* (1998) traces the deepening intervention under Carter, Reagan, and Bush.

The Gorbachev Era

On **Gorbachev and his reform project**, see Archie Brown's judicious assessment, *The Gorbachev Factor* (1996); Robert D. English, *Russia and the Idea of the West: Gorbachev, Intellectuals, and the End of the Cold War* (2000), tracing the rise of the "new thinking" that paved the way for reform; and Stephen Kotkin, *Armageddon Averted: The Soviet Collapse, 1970–2000*, 2nd ed. (2008), a postmortem done with flair and authority on a system destroyed by its own elite.

On the **ferment below the surface of Soviet bloc life** from the 1950s into the 1980s, see Donald J. Raleigh, *Soviet Baby Boomers: An Oral History of Russia's Cold War Generation* (2011); Timothy W. Ryback, *Rock Around the Bloc: A History of Rock Music in Eastern Europe and the Soviet Union* (1990), and Stites, *Russian Popular Culture* (cited in Chapter 1). Stephen White, *Russia Goes Dry: Alcohol, State, and Society* (1996), opens a fascinating window onto social strains and limits of official control. *Repentance* (dir. Tengiz Abuladze, 1986, 152 min.), an unsettling film fable about a Stalin-like dictator in a Georgian town, expresses late Soviet intellectuals' preoccupation with the Stalinist past, while *Little Vera* (dir. Vasili Pichul, 1988, 110 min.), with its focus on working-class life, was part of an outpouring of social commentary in the late Soviet period.

For a good sense of **the collapse of socialist regimes in eastern Europe**, see Stephen Kotkin with Jan T. Gross, *Uncivil Society: 1989 and the Implosion of the Communist Establishment* (2009), which examines the cases of East Germany, Poland, and Romania; Gale Stokes, *The Walls Came Tumbling Down: Collapse and Rebirth in Eastern Europe*, 2nd ed. (2012); and Timothy Garton Ash, *The Magic Lantern: The Revolution of '89 Witnessed in Warsaw, Budapest, Berlin and Prague*, 2nd ed. (1993), a vivid and historically sensitive piece of reporting. East Germany's collapse has evoked a run of thoughtful meditations on national identity and the old socialist regime: *Good Bye, Lenin!* (dir. Wolfgang Becker, 2003, 121 min.); *The Lives of Others* (dir. Florian Henckel von Donnersmarck, 2006, 137 min.); and *Barbara* (dir. Christian Petzold, 2012, 105 min.). "Making the History of 1989," available on the website for George Mason University's Center for History and New Media (chnm.gmu.edu/1989/), provides an array of helpful material.

CHAPTER 8   GLOBAL MARKETS: ONE SYSTEM, THREE CENTERS

The Evolving International Framework

For **overviews**, Eric Helleiner, *States and the Reemergence of Global Finance: From Bretton Woods to the 1990s* (1994), highlights how the freeing of international finance from the 1960s onward transformed the Bretton Woods system, while Jeffrey Hart, *Rival Capitalists: International Competitiveness in the United States, Japan and Western Europe* (1992), makes the case that states continue to play an important economic role in spite of the free-market tide. Sheldon Garon, *Beyond Our Means: Why America Spends While the World Saves* (2012), is excellent on divergent patterns of consumption and thrift from region to region. The PBS website "Commanding Heights: The Battle for the World Economy" (www.pbs.org/wgbh/commandingheights/) and the documentary of the same name (dir. William Cran and Greg Barker, 2003, 3 episodes of 115 min.) offer lively overviews.

The U.S.-Led Bloc

For **the ascendant neoliberal faith,** the place to start is Daniel Stedman Jones, *Masters of the Universe: Hayek, Friedman, and the Birth of Neoliberal Politics* (2012), with its focus on an Anglo-American ideological enterprise. See also the classics by Friedrich Hayek, *The Road to Serfdom* (1944), and by Milton Friedman with the assistance of Rose D. Friedman, *Capitalism and Freedom* (1962). Robert Solomon, *The Transformation of the World Economy*, 2nd ed. (1999), a compact insider account, follows the neoliberal policy trend around the world during the 1980s and 1990s, while Kevin Phillips, *Wealth and Democracy: A Political History of the American Rich* (2002), and Studs Terkel, *The Great Divide: Second Thoughts on the American Dream* (1988), contemplate the consequences of neoliberalism for U.S. society.

On **McDonald's** as a symbol of spreading U.S. economic and cultural influence, see John F. Love, *McDonald's: Behind the Arches*, 2nd ed. (1995), written with the company's cooperation; and James L. Watson, ed., *Golden Arches East: McDonald's in East Asia* (1997), which is suggestive on how an American export has accommodated to Asian consumer preferences and which is summarized in Watson, "China's Big Mac Attack," *Foreign Affairs* 79 (May-June 2000): 120–134.

The Asian Bloc

The recent rise of Asia is placed in historical perspective in Eric Jones et al., *Coming Full Circle: An Economic History of the Pacific Rim* (1993), and Andre Gunder Frank, *ReOrient: Global Economy in the Asian Age* (1998). Hilton L. Root, *Small Countries, Big Lessons: Governance and the Rise of East Asia* (1996), points to the importance of state intervention to make the market serve the goals of development, while Richard Stubbs, *Rethinking Asia's Economic Miracle: The Political Economy of War, Prosperity, and Crisis* (2005), relates Cold War rivalry to regional economic development.

On **Japan's consumer society**, Joseph J. Tobin, ed., *Re-Made in Japan: Everyday Life and Consumer Taste in a Changing Society* (1992), offers revealing examples of how foreign goods and practices became "domesticated." Mark Schilling, *The Encyclopedia of Japanese Pop Culture* (1997), drives home the point that such cultural products as movies, films, television programs, and toys need to be understood in terms of a complex interplay of international and domestic influences whose outcome is distinctly Japanese. Rosenbluth and Thies, *Transforming Japan* (cited in Chapter 5), provides essential background.

On tensions in **U.S.–Japanese relations**, see Michael Schaller, *Altered States: The United States and Japan since the Occupation* (1997), and John Dower, "Graphic Others/ Graphic Selves: Cartoons in War and Peace," in Dower, *Japan in War and Peace: Selected Essays* (1993), 287–300.

For **the Deng era in China**, begin with Alexander V. Pantsov with Steven I. Levine, *Deng Xiaoping: A Revolutionary Life* (forthcoming 2015), a broadly framed, richly researched biography that is the new standard. Geremie R. Barmé, *Shades of Mao: The Posthumous Cult of the Great Leader* (1996), graphically demonstrates Mao's continuing grip on the popular imagination even in the reform era. *The Gate of Heavenly Peace* (prod. and dir. Richard Gordon and Carman Hinton, 1995, 189 min.) is a penetrating, full-length documentary on the spring 1989 upheaval. The accompanying, high-quality website is at www.tsquare.tv/. For glimpses into daily life, see Zhang Xinxin and Sang Ye, *Chinese Lives: An Oral History of Contemporary China*, trans. and ed. W. J. F. Jenner and Delia Davin (1987), and B. Michael Frolic, *Mao's People: Sixteen Portraits of Life in Revolutionary China* (1980).

For **other Asian economies** on the move, see, Stephan Haggard, *Pathways from the Periphery: The Politics of Growth in the Newly Industrializing Countries* (1990); Gareth Porter, *Vietnam: The Politics of Bureaucratic Socialism* (1993); William J. Duiker, *Vietnam: Revolution in Transition*, 2nd ed. (1995); and Gregg Brazinsky, *Nation Building in South Korea: Koreans, Americans, and the Making of a Democracy* (2007).

European Integration

On the path followed by the Europeans, see the recommendations at the end of Chapter 5.

CHAPTER 9   DIVERGENT PATHS IN THE THIRD WORLD

Cambodia Convulsed

David P. Chandler, *The Tragedy of Cambodian History: Politics, War and Revolution since 1945* (1991), offers a helpful survey of events leading to Khmer Rouge revolution. Ben Kiernan, *The Pol Pot Regime: Race, Power, and Genocide in Cambodia under the Khmer Rouge, 1975–1979*, 3rd ed. (2008), brings a puzzling revolutionary movement into focus. The Cambodian Genocide Program at Yale, curated by Kiernan, offers a resource-rich website (www.yale.edu/cgp/). For the conflict surrounding the Cambodian revolution, see Odd Arne Westad and Sophie Quinn-Judge, eds., *The Third Indochina War: Conflict between China, Vietnam and Cambodia, 1972–79* (2006).

Revolutionary Iran

Baqer Moin, *Khomeini: Life of the Ayatollah* (1999), a splendid account, is revealing on **the revolution and the man who made it**. For a learned appraisal of Khomeini's powerful political ideas, see Ervand Abrahamian, *Khomeinism: Essays on the Islamic Republic* (1993). Roy P. Mottahedeh, *The Mantle of the Prophet: Religion and Politics in Iran* (1985), is an artful introduction to the world of the clerics. For an analytically acute treatment of their rise to power, see Charles Kurzman, *The Unthinkable Revolution in Iran* (2004). Abbas Milani, *Tales of Two Cities: A Persian Memoir* (1996), provides the perspective of a U.S.-trained intellectual who turned against the shah and ultimately the clerics. *Iran: Adrift in a Sea of Blood* (writ. and dir. Ron Hallis, 1986, 27 min.) provides a self-portrait of those supporting the Islamic Republic. On the revolution's regional consequences, see David W. Lesch, *1979: The Year That Shaped the Modern Middle East* (2001).

On **Iranian women**, see Erika Friedl, *Women of Deh Koh: Lives in an Iranian Village* (1991), an anthropologist's fascinating portrait of a community, and Haleh Esfandiari, *Reconstructed Lives: Women and the Iranian Revolution* (1997), featuring the accounts of well-to-do women in Tehran. *The Day I Became a Woman* (dir. Marzieh Meshkini, 2001, 78 min.), part of an outpouring of wonderful movies from Iran, is a poignant meditation on the straitened hopes and diminished lives of Iranian women in the wake of the revolution.

The Anti-apartheid Struggle in South Africa

Leonard Thompson, *A History of South Africa*, 4th ed. (2014), and William Beinhart, *Twentieth-Century South Africa*, 2nd ed. (2001), are balanced surveys. They should be supplemented by Patti Waldmeir, *Anatomy of a Miracle: The End of Apartheid and the Birth of the New South Africa* (1997), which captures the perspectives of the participants in the struggle. Nelson Mandela, *Long Walk to Freedom: The Autobiography of Nelson Mandela* (1994), allows the leader of the anti-apartheid struggle to tell his extraordinary story. *The Long Walk of Nelson Mandela* (dir. Clifford Bestall, 1999, 120 min.) follows the career of this extraordinary figure. On the main anti-apartheid organization, see Heidi Holland's accessible *100 Years of Struggle: Mandela's ANC* (2012) and the African National Congress website (www.anc.org.za/). For the impact of apartheid on everyday life for blacks, see Mark Mathabane's personal account, *Kaffir Boy* (1986).

The Struggle over Palestine

For **an overview** of a complex and controversial topic, start with Charles D. Smith's clear and balanced *Palestine and the Arab-Israeli Conflict: A History with Documents*, 8th ed. (2013).

On **Zionism** as an ideology and a political movement, see Shlomo Avineri, *The Making of Modern Zionism: The Intellectual Origins of the Jewish State* (1981), with its appealing and accessible biographical approach covering the rise to Jewish nationalism during the nineteenth and twentieth centuries; and Zeev Sternhell's analytic study, *The Founding Myths of Israel: Nationalism, Socialism, and the Making of the Jewish State*, trans. David Maisel (1998). For the recollections of a leader whose early years and rise to prominence offer a window on the Zionist movement, see Golda Meir, *My Life* (1975).

On **Palestinians and the PLO**, see Baruch Kimmerling and Joel S. Migdal, *Palestinians: The Making of a People* (1993), for its welcome attention to social as well as political developments; and Rashid Khalidi, *Palestinian Identity: The Construction of Modern National Consciousness* (1997), essential to understanding post-1967 developments. For the nuts and bolts of Israel's controversial regional policy, see Avi Shlaim, *The Iron Wall: Israel and the Arab World*, 2nd ed. (2014), which does an admirable job of sorting myth from history. *The Gatekeepers* (dir. Dror Moreh, 2012, 95 min.) catches on camera six heads of Israel's secret service between 1980 and 2011 reflecting candidly on the "management" of occupied Palestine. Hanan Ashrawi, *This Side of Peace: A Personal Account* (1995), provides insight into the first *intifada* from an academic who became its international voice. The Foundation for Middle East Peace (www.fmep.org/) and MidEast Web (www.mideastweb.org) offer resources for keeping track of settlement activity and the peace process.

The Guatemalan Civil War

For helpful general treatments, see the works cited in Chapter 6. Greg Grandin, *The Last Colonial Massacre: Latin America in the Cold War* (2004), uses a shocking instance of violence as a window on the process of revolution and counterrevolution in Guatemala. Margaret Hooks, *Guatemalan Women Speak*, 2nd ed. (1993), brings together a marvelous collection of oral histories highlighting gender perspectives as well as social divisions.

Guatemala: The Dream of Land (writ., prod., and dir. Lauren Drewery, David Hestad, and Randy Stringer, 1991, 28 min.) gives a sense of the importance of land as a source of livelihood and as a cultural symbol.

Development Patterns toward Century's End

For **broad treatments,** see Prashad, *The Darker Nations* (cited in Chapter 6); Vijay Prashad, *The Poorer Nations: A Possible History of the Global South* (2012), which follows the South's struggles into the new century; William Easterly, *The Elusive Quest for Growth: Economists' Adventures and Misadventures in the Tropics* (2001), tracing the fads and failures in the development field; and Gilbert Rist, *The History of Development: From Western Origins to Global Faith*, trans. Patrick Camiller (1997), a critique of a hegemonic idea.

On **the role of women,** Judith M. Bennett "Confronting Continuity," *Journal of Women's History* 9 (Autumn 1997): 73–94, followed by commentary (95–118), makes an argument about the persistence of patriarchy with broad implications. Therborn, *Between Sex and Power* (cited in the Introduction) argues for a general retreat of patriarchy but with enormous regional variations. Janet H. Momsen, *Women and Development in the Third World* (1991), surveys the major issues in brief compass, while Smith, *Global Feminisms Since 1945* (cited in Chapter 5), takes a case study approach. Sonia Kruks et al., eds., *Promissory Notes: Women in the Transition to Socialism* (1989), chides socialist regimes for their shortcomings while indicating areas of progress. Leila Ahmed, *Women and Gender in Islam: Historical Roots of a Modern Debate* (1992), traces changing gender discourses over millennia and finds no "true tradition" of subordinating women. See also Geraldine Brooks, *Nine Parts of Desire: The Hidden World of Islamic Women* (1994), whose engaging vignettes reveal the diversity of contemporary women's lives and the surprising turns negotiations over gender norms are taking. Bina Agarwal, *A Field of One's Own: Gender and Land Rights in South Asia* (1994), and *With These Hands: How Women Feed Africa* (prod. and dir. Chris Shepherd and Claude Sauvageot, 1987, 33 min.) both provide excellent insights on the interlocking themes of commercialization of agriculture and gender relations. The documentary *Asante Market Women* (dir. Claudia Milne, 1982, 52 min.) focuses on the Ghanaian women who link rural producers to urban markets.

On **Africa's post-independence crisis of development**, see the works cited for Chapter 6.

CHAPTER 10   THE POWER AND PERILS
OF GLOBALIZATION

Globalization in Recent Times

For **general treatments**, see Bruce Mazlish, *The New Global History* (2006), a crisp, vigorously developed introduction by a longtime student of the subject. For an excellent critical guide to the literature and the big issues, see Michael Lang, "Globalization and Its History," *Journal of Modern History* 78 (December 2006): 899–931. Lang's skepticism about some of the sweeping claims made about globalization is shared by Paul Q. Hirst and Grahame Thompson, *Globalization in Question: The International Economy and the Possibilities of Governance*, 2nd ed. (1999). David Held and Anthony McGrew, eds., *The Global Transformations Reader: An Introduction to the Globalization Debate*, 2nd ed. (2003), captures the extraordinary range of controversy in an exploding literature.

For good **sources of up-to-date information**, see Dan Smith, *The Penguin State of the World Atlas*, 9th ed. (2012), with its striking graphic format. Helpful periodicals include *Foreign Affairs*, the venerable quarterly put out by the Council on Foreign Relations;

Foreign Policy, a livelier bimonthly sponsored by the Carnegie Endowment for International Peace; *The Economist*, a British weekly that views the world through a free-market lens; *Far Eastern Economic Review*, a weekly out of Hong Kong that is indispensable to keeping up with a diverse and dynamic region; and *Current History*, a monthly (except during the summer) that puts present issues in the perspective of the past. Important perspectives on the current state of the peoples of the world are available on the websites of the Population Reference Bureau (www.prb.org/) and the UN Population Division (www.un.org/popin/data.html). The PRB's annual "World Population Data Sheet" (www .prb.org/Publications/Datasheets/2014/2014-world-population-data-sheet.aspx) is an especially handy reference.

The Dimensions of the Global Order

For a careful survey of **recent developments**, turn to Alfred E. Eckes, *The Contemporary Global Economy: A History Since 1980* (2011). Pietra Rivoli, *The Travels of a T-shirt in the Global Economy: An Economist Examines the Markets, Power, and Politics of World Trade*, 2nd ed. (2009), offers an accessible, pro-market case study highlighting the intricate patterns of production and trade. The technological and business basis for recent global integration and innovation gets its due in Janet Abbate, *Inventing the Internet* (1999); Alfred D. Chandler, with Takashi Hikino and Andrew von Nordenflycht, *Inventing the Electronic Century: The Epic Story of the Consumer Electronics and Computer Industries*, 2nd ed. (2005); and Louis Galambos and Eric John Abrahamson, *Anytime, Anywhere: Entrepreneurship and the Creation of a Wireless World* (2002). Robert Leeson, *Ideology and International Economy: The Decline and Fall of Bretton Woods* (2003), highlights the freeing of international finance from the 1960s onward. On the ideological dimensions, see David Harvey's deft treatment in *A Brief History of Neoliberalism* (2005), emphasizing the role of class, and Manfred B. Steger, *The Rise of the Global Imaginary: Political Ideologies from the French Revolution to the Global War on Terror* (2008), focusing on the threat new global visions pose to established nationalisms.

The Downsides of Globalization

The **costs and limits** are treated in Dani Rodrik's call for a retreat from "hyperglobalization" in *The Globalization Paradox: Democracy and the Future of the World Economy* (2011); Saskia Sassen's broad indictment, *Expulsions: Brutality and Complexity in the Global Economy* (2014); Joseph E. Stiglitz's critical insider critique, *Globalization and Its Discontents* (2002); and Ha-Joon Chang, *The Bad Samaritans: Rich Nations, Poor Policies and the Threat to the Developing World* (2007), an assault on orthodox neoliberalism as a guide to development.

Global inequalities are treated in a pair of accessible, up-to-date studies: Branko Milanovic, "Global Income Inequality in Numbers: in History and Now," *Global Policy* 4 (May 2013): 198–208; and UN Secretariat, Department of Economic and Social Affairs, *Inequality Matters: Report of the World Social Situation 2013* (2013), particularly Chapters 1 and 2. The research of Emmanuel Saez and Thomas Piketty has figured prominently, including most recently Piketty's data rich and analytically acute treatment of *Capital in the Twenty-First Century*, trans. Arthur Goldhammer (2014).

The **environmental crisis** is put in excellent historical perspective in J. R. McNeill, *Something New under the Sun: An Environmental History of the Twentieth-Century World* (2000). For recent developments see McNeill's update in "Earth, Wind, Water and Fire: Resource Exploitation in the Twentieth Century," *Global Dialogue* 4 (Winter 2002): 11–19; Lorraine Elliott, *The Global Politics of the Environment*, 2nd ed. (2004); and *State of the World*, an annual review by the Worldwatch Institute. David Archer, *The Long Thaw: How Humans*

Are Changing the Next 100,000 Years of Earth's Climate (2009), offers an accessible introduction to climate science. Osha Gray Davidson, *Fire in the Turtle House: The Green Sea
Turtle and the Fate of the Ocean* (2001), turns a case study into a broad and accessible
examination of ecological destruction and the effort to mitigate the effects.

Reforming the Global Order

General treatments of the leading issues and actors can be found in Mark Mazower,
Governing the World: The History of an Idea (2012), a fluent synthesis that emphasizes the
dominant role of the great powers; Paul Kennedy, *The Parliament of Man: The Past, Present,
and Future of the United Nations* (2006), which examines the institution's multiple moving
parts; David Clark MacKenzie, *A World Beyond Borders: An Introduction to the History of
International Organizations* (2010), a concise, clear guide to the evolution of a critical set
of institutions; and Akira Iriye, *Global Community: The Role of International Organizations
in the Making of the Contemporary World* (2002), notable as a pioneering work.

For insights on **key actors** in the struggle to curb and humanize globalization, see
Michael E. Mann, *The Hockey Stick and the Climate Wars: Dispatches from the Front Lines*
(2012), an engaging participant's account of the scientific community's battle with climate change skeptics; the Green Party website (www.greens.org/) for a window on a
global political movement; the revealing case study by Ann Marie Clark, *Diplomacy of
Conscience: Amnesty International and Changing Human Rights Norms* (2001); and the in-
formative website of this leading NGO (www.amnesty.org). *A Place Called Chiapas* (dir.
Nettie Wild, 1998, 89 min.) uses footage taken during 1996 and 1997 to provide a fascinating perspective on Mexico's Zapatista movement.

On **human rights**, good places to start are Paul Gordon Lauren, *The Evolution of International Human Rights: Visions Seen*, 3rd ed. (2011), which focuses on the UN Declaration
of Human Rights, including its origins and consequences; and Samuel Moyn, *The Last
Utopia: Human Rights in History* (2010), which treats the explosion of human rights activity in the 1970s. On the effort to hold state leaders accountable, see Michael R. Marrus,
ed., *The Nuremberg War Crimes Trial, 1945–1946: A Documentary History* (1997); Yuma
Totani, *The Tokyo War Crimes Trial: The Pursuit of Justice in the Wake of World War II* (2008);
and Kingsley Chiedu Moghalu, *Global Justice: The Politics of War Crimes Trials* (2006).

For the **politics of the environment**, see Joachim Radkau, *The Age of Ecology:
A Global History*, trans. Patrick Camiller (2014).

On better ways to **measure economic growth and social welfare**, see Tim Jackson,
Prosperity Without Growth: Economics for a Finite Planet (2009); and Diane Coyle, *GDP: A Brief
but Affectionate History* (2014). Leading welfare gauges include *World Happiness Report 2013*,
edited by well-regarded economists John F. Helliwell, Richard Layard, and Jeffrey D. Sachs
(available at unsdsn.org/wp-content/uploads/2014/02/WorldHappinessReport2013_online
.pdf); the UN Development Programme's Human Development Index (hdr.undp.org/en/
content/human-development-index-hdi); and the Organisation for Co-operation and
Development's Better Life Index (www.oecdbetterlifeindex.org/).

CHAPTER 11   A REGIONALLY CONFIGURED WORLD

For **up-to-date general information** on the current state of the states, see *The World
Factbook*, an excellent collection of profiles and maps compiled and regularly updated by
the CIA (www.cia.gov/library/publications/the-world-factbook/), and the BBC Country
Profiles (news.bbc.co.uk/2/hi/country_profiles/default.stm). The Pew Research Global
Attitudes Project (www.pewglobal.org/) and Gallup World (www.gallup.com/) are good
sources for public opinion around the world.

Transformation in the Americas

For **appraisals of U.S. hegemony** stressing decline, see David S. Mason's *The End of the American Century* (2009); Smil, *Made in the USA* (cited in Chapter 2), especially chaps. 4–6; and the essays in Andrew Bacevich, ed., *The Short American Century: A Postmortem* (2012). On the other side, Robert J. Lieber, *Power and Willpower in the American Future: Why the United States Is Not Destined to Decline* (2012); Zaki Laïdi, *Limited Achievements. Obama's Foreign Policy*, trans. Carolyn Avery (2012); Steven Weber and Bruce W. Jentleson, *The End of Arrogance: America in the Global Competition of Ideas* (2010); and G. John Ikenberry, *Liberal Leviathan: The Origins, Crisis, and Transformation of the American World Order* (2011), all profess optimism that the United States can retain its dominance. Vaclav Smil, *Why America Is Not a New Rome* (2010), makes a compelling case against those on both sides of the decline argument who invoke imperial comparisons.

For insights on the **post-9–11 plunge into the Middle East**, see Lloyd Gardner, *The Long Road to Baghdad: A History of U.S. Foreign Policy from the 1970s to the Present* (2008), which highlights the persistence of Cold War attitudes into the post-Cold War era; as well as Anatol Lieven, *America Right or Wrong: An Anatomy of American Nationalism*, 2nd ed. (2012); and James Mann, *Rise of the Vulcans: The History of Bush's War Cabinet* (2004). The consequences of Bush's wars are vividly on display in Rajiv Chandrasekaran, *Imperial Life in the Emerald City: Inside Iraq's Green Zone* (2006); Ahmed Rashid, *Descent into Chaos: The United States and the Failure of Nation Building in Pakistan, Afghanistan, and Central Asia* (2008); and the documentary *Restrepo* (dir. Tim Hetherington and Sebastian Junger, 2010, 93 min.), which captures the American war in Afghanistan through the eyes of the men who fought it.

On **Latin America**, see Brian McCann, *In the Throes of Democracy: Brazil Since 1989* (2008), an accessible and topically well-rounded treatment; the update in Matthew M. Taylor, "Brazil's Ebbing Tide," and Miriam Gomes Saraiva, "The Brazilian Soft Power Tradition," both in *Current History* 113 (February 2014): 57–67; Jerry Dávila, *Dictatorship in South America* (2013); and Greg Grandin and Gilbert M. Joseph, eds., *A Century of Revolution: Insurgent and Counterinsurgent Violence during Latin America's Long Cold War* (2010). *Cuba's Secret Side* (dir. Karin Muller, 2013, 57 min.) offers a charming and sympathetic glimpse of current everyday life.

The Middle East in Ferment

On **the U.S. role**, see Douglas Little, *American Orientalism: The United States and the Middle East since 1945* (2002); Rhashid Khalidi, *Resurrecting Empire: Western Footprints and America's Perilous Path in the Middle East* (2004); and Geoffrey Wawro, *Quicksand: America's Pursuit of Power in the Middle East* (2010). Anthony Shadid, *Night Draws Near: Iraq's People in the Shadow of America's War* (2005), is a classic of war reporting.

On **the Islamist challenge** to the regional status quo, see Beverley Milton-Edwards, *Islamic Fundamentalism Since 1945*, 2nd ed. (2014), an accessible overview of political Islam across the Muslim world with a stress on developments since the 1960s. See also the most recent of a string of authoritative works by Gilles Kepel, *The War for Muslim Minds: Islam and the West*, trans. Pacale Ghazaleh (2004), and *Beyond Terror and Martyrdom: The Future of the Middle East*, trans. Pacale Ghazaleh (2008). Jehane Noujaim has directed two gripping documentaries on recent developments: *Control Room* (2004, 84 min.) views the U.S. invasion of Iraq in 2003 from the perspective of the popular Al Jazeera news network, while *The Square* (2013, 108 min.) focuses on three protesters in Cairo whose struggle for fundamental change ended with the military back in control. For a broader context, see the excellent reportage by Juan Cole, *The New Arabs: How the Millennial Generation Is Changing the Middle East* (2014), which examines the cases of Egypt, Tunisia, and Libya.

Asia Rising

For **an overview**, see Melvin Gurtov, *Pacific Asia? Prospects for Security and Cooperation in East Asia* (2002), which considers the basis for regional integration.

On **China and Northeast Asia**, see Martin Jacques, *When China Rules the World: The Rise of the Middle Kingdom and the End of the Western World* (2009), which offers a more astute treatment than its breathless title suggests; Peter H. Gries, *China's New Nationalism: Pride, Politics, and Diplomacy* (2004), an examination of recent popular and official writings; Charles K. Armstrong, *The Koreas* (2007), a succinct, well-informed survey; and Steven Kent Vogel, *Japan Remodeled: How Government and Industry Are Reforming Japanese Capitalism* (2006), excellent on the persistence of old patterns that make Japan different.

On **India, see** Sumantra Bose, *Transforming India: Challenges to the World's Largest Democracy* (2013), especially Chapters 1 and 2, which provides a sure-footed survey of recent political history. For an accessible window on the single most pressing issue facing India today, try *Peepli [Live]* (dir. Anusha Rizvi, 2010, 104 min.), a film dramatization that evokes the desperation of the rural poor and satirizes the dysfunctional response of the political system and the media.

On the EU and Its Troubled Neighborhood

For **general coverage**, see McCormick, *Understanding the European Union* (cited in Chapter 5), and Luuk van Middelaar, *The Passage to Europe: How a Continent Became a Union*, trans. Liz Waters (2013). For a handy survey of the current state of the union, see John Pinder and Simon Usherwood, *The European Union: A Very Short Introduction*, 3rd ed. (2013). Richard F. Kuisel, *The French Way: How France Embraced and Rejected American Values and Power* (2012), treats one of the most nationalistically neuralgic of the EU countries.

On **the trauma in Yugoslavia**, Noel Malcolm, *Bosnia: A Short History*, 2nd ed. (1996), points to the key role of Serbian nationalist leaders in precipitating a prolonged and bloody crisis. Tim Judah, *The Serbs: History, Myth and the Destruction of Yugoslavia*, 3rd ed. (2009), tries to strike a balance between popular passions and elite decisions in explaining the rise of an aggressive nationalism.

On **Russia's transition** to a postcommunist era, see Kotkin, *Armageddon Averted* (cited for Chapter 7) as well as Rose Brady, *Kapitalizm: Russia's Struggle to Free Its Economy* (1999), strong on the wheeling and dealing involved with the shift to a market economy; and Fiona Hill and Clifford G. Gaddy, *Mr. Putin: Operative in the Kremlin* (2013), which makes good use of limited biographical material.

NOTES

The notes for this volume serve to identify sources for quotes appearing in the text and for data used in the graphs and tables.

PREFACE

[1] Quoted in *The New World History: A Teacher's Companion*, ed. Ross E. Dunn (Boston: Bedford/St. Martin's, 2000), 360.

[2] Vera Zamagni, *The Economic History of Italy, 1860–1990*, trans. Patrick Barr (New York: Oxford University Press, 1993), vi.

INTRODUCTION   THE 1945 WATERSHED

[1] John W. Dower, *Embracing Defeat: Japan in the Wake of World War II* (New York: Norton, 1999), 21.

[2] Michael H. Hunt, *Ideology and U.S. Foreign Policy*, 2nd ed. (New Haven, CT: Yale University Press, 2009), 134; Hunt, *Crises in U.S. Foreign Policy: An International History Reader* (New Haven, CT: Yale University Press, 1996), 47–48.

[3] Karl Marx and Friedrich Engels, *Basic Writings on Politics and Philosophy*, ed. Lewis S. Feuer (Garden City, NY: Doubleday, 1959), 43.

[4] Karl Marx and Friedrich Engels, *The Communist Manifesto*, ed. John E. Toews (Boston: Bedford Books, 1999), 164.

[5] Marx and Engels, *The Communist Manifesto*, 69.

[6] Observation by René Pleven, in charge of colonies in de Gaulle's Free French during World War II, quoted in Mark Mazower, *Governing the World: The History of an Idea* (New York: Penguin Press, 2012), 251.

[7] R. H. Tawney, *Land and Labour in China* (reprint of original 1932 ed.; Boston: Beacon Press, 1966), 77.

[8] James C. Scott, *Domination and the Arts of Resistance: Hidden Transcripts* (New Haven, CT: Yale University Press, 1990), v.

[9] Voltaire to M. Bertin de Rocheret, April 14, 1732, available at www.whitman.edu/VSA/letters/14.4.1732.html (accessed August 17, 2014).

PART ONE   HOPES AND FEARS CONTEND, 1945–1953

1 Michihiko Hachiya, *Hiroshima Diary: The Journal of a Japanese Physician, August 6–September 30, 1945*, trans. and ed. Warner Lee Wells (originally published 1955; reprint Chapel Hill: University of North Carolina Press, 1995), 16; Martin Harwit, *An Exhibit Denied: Lobbying the History of Enola Gay* (New York: Copernicus, 1996), 6 (quoting co-pilot).

2 Hachiya, *Hiroshima Diary*, 17; *Widows of Hiroshima: The Life Stories of Nineteen Peasant Wives*, ed. Mikio Kanda and trans. Taeko Midorikawa (New York: St. Martin's Press, 1989), 42, 45.

3 Quote from Haruko Taya Cook and Theodore Cook, *Japan at War: An Oral History* (New York: New Press, 1992), 403. Data on bomb victims from John W. Dower, *War without Mercy: Race and Power in the Pacific War* (New York: Pantheon Books, 1986), 325n21.

4 Quotes from Allan M. Winkler, *Life Under a Cloud: American Anxiety About the Atom* (New York: Oxford University Press, 1993), 36; and Michael B. Stoff et al., eds., *The Manhattan Project: A Documentary Introduction to the Atomic Age* (Philadelphia: Temple University Press, 1991), 5.

5 *Public Papers of the Presidents of the United States: Harry S. Truman, 1945* (Washington, DC: Government Printing Office, 1961), 199; Paul S. Boyer, *By the Bomb's Early Light: American Thought and Culture at the Dawn of the Atomic Age* (New York: Pantheon, 1985), 85 (public opinion).

6 Quotes from Michael H. Hunt, *The Genesis of Chinese Communist Foreign Policy* (New York: Columbia University Press, 1996), 150; and Paul Gordon Lauren, *The Evolution of International Human Rights: Visions Seen*, 3rd ed. (Philadelphia: University of Pennsylvania Press, 2011), 201.

7 David W. Ellwood, *Rebuilding Europe: Western Europe, America, and Postwar Reconstruction* (London: Longman, 1992), 4 (Carr); Elena Zubkova, *Russia after the War: Hopes, Illusions, and Disappointments, 1945–1957*, trans. and ed. Hugh Ragsdale (Armonk, NY: M. E. Sharpe, 1998), 34 (Soviet soldier); Alan Brinkley, "World War II and American Liberalism," in *The War in American Culture: Society and Consciousness During World War II*, ed. Lewis Erenberg and Susan E. Hirsch (Chicago: University of Chicago Press, 1996), 314 (MacLeish).

CHAPTER 1   THE COLD WAR: TOWARD
SOVIET–AMERICAN CONFRONTATION

1 Michael H. Hunt, *Crises in U.S. Foreign Policy: An International History Reader* (New Haven, CT: Yale University Press, 1996), 132.

2 Harry S. Truman, *Memoirs*, vol. 1 (Garden City, NJ: Doubleday, 1955), 5 (ER), 19 (HST).

3 Hunt, *Crises in U.S. Foreign Policy*, 136, 137.

4 Hunt, *Crises in U.S. Foreign Policy*, 136.

5 *Off the Record: The Private Papers of Harry S. Truman*, ed. Robert H. Ferrell (New York: Harper and Row, 1980), 80.

6 Hunt, *Crises in U.S. Foreign Policy*, 147.

7 Hunt, *Crises in U.S. Foreign Policy*, 148, 156.

8 David Holloway, *Stalin and the Bomb: The Soviet Union and Atomic Energy, 1939–1956* (New Haven, CT: Yale University Press, 1994), 292; *Khrushchev Remembers*, trans. and ed. Strobe Talbott (Boston: Little, Brown, 1970), 307.

9 *Khrushchev Remembers: Glasnost Tapes*, trans. and ed. and Jerrold L. Schecter with Vyacheslav B. Luchkov (Boston: Little, Brown, 1990), 101.

[10] Joseph Stalin, *The Great Patriotic War of the Soviet Union* (New York: International Publishers, 1945), 67.

[11] Milovan Djilas, *Wartime*, trans. Michael B. Petrovich (New York: Harcourt Brace Jovanovich, 1977), 437.

[12] Holloway, *Stalin and the Bomb*, 132.

[13] Hunt, *Crises in U.S. Foreign Policy*, 145–146.

[14] Hunt, *Crises in U.S. Foreign Policy*, 159.

[15] Estimates in Matthew A. Evangelista, "Stalin's Postwar Army Reappraised," *International Security* 7 (Winter 1982–1983): 110–138.

[16] Quoted in Ian Baruma, *Year Zero: A History of 1945* (New York: Penguin, 2013), 67.

[17] Russian Institute, Columbia University, ed., *The Anti-Stalin Campaign and International Communism: A Selection of Documents* (New York: Columbia University Press, 1956), 62.

[18] Elena Zubkova, *Russia after the War: Hopes, Illusions, and Disappointments, 1945–1957*, trans. and ed. Hugh Ragsdale (Armonk, NY: M. E. Sharpe, 1998), 86 (Soviet data); and Hunt, *Crises in U.S. Foreign Policy*, 166 (NSC-68).

[19] U.S. Department of Defense and Department of Energy, "Summary of Declassified Nuclear Stockpile Information" [June 27, 1994] available at www.osti.gov/opennet/forms.jsp?formurl=document/press/pc26tab1.html (accessed November 18, 2014).

[20] Holloway, *Stalin and the Bomb*, 204, 217.

[21] Michael H. Hunt, *Ideology and U.S. Foreign Policy* (New Haven, CT: Yale University Press, 1987), 163; Scott Lucas, "The Limits of Ideology: U.S. Foreign Policy and Arab Nationalism in the Early Cold War," in *The United States and Decolonization: Power and Freedom*, ed. David Ryan and Victor Pungong (Houndmills, Basingstoke, Hampshire, UK: Macmillan, 2000), 141.

[22] Steven Hugh Lee, *The Korean War* (Harlow, UK: Pearson Education, 2001), 34.

[23] Lee, *The Korean War*, 45, 131.

[24] R. W. Davis, "Economic Aspects of Stalinism," in *The Stalin Phenomenon*, ed. Alec Nove (New York: St. Martin's Press, 1993), 41.

[25] Data from Anne Applebaum, *Gulag: A History* (New York: Doubleday: 2003), 580, 581, 584.

[26] Zubkova, *Russia after the War*, 82.

[27] Zubkova, *Russia after the War*, 152.

[28] Zubkova, *Russia after the War*, 60.

[29] Zubkova, *Russia after the War*, 48.

[30] "Speaking Bolshevik" is a notion developed in Stephen Kotkin, *Magnetic Mountain: Stalinism as a Civilization* (Berkeley: University of California Press, 1995). Quote from Zubkova, *Russia after the War*, 142.

[31] Vasily Lebedev-Kumach, December 1937, quoted in Sarah Davies, "The Leader Cult: Propaganda and Its Reception in Stalin's Russia," in *Politics, Society, and Stalinism*, ed. John Channon (New York: St. Martin's, 1998), 121.

[32] Quote from Solomon Volkov, *Testimony: The Memoirs of Dmitri Shostakovich*, trans. Antonina W. Bouis (New York: Harper & Row, 1979), 156.

[33] Quoted in Ellen Schrecker, *The Age of McCarthyism: A Brief History with Documents* (Boston: Bedford Books, 1994), 211–212, 214.

[34] Quotes from Geoffrey S. Smith, "National Security and Personal Isolation: Sex, Gender, and Disease in the Cold-War United States," *International History Review* 14 (May 1992): 312 (attorney general); and Ellen Schrecker, *The Age of McCarthyism*, 119–120 (Hoover).

[35] Ellen Schrecker, *The Age of McCarthyism*, 144.

[36] Quotes from Smith, "National Security and Personal Isolation," 321 (tabloid); and Hunt, *Crises in U.S. Foreign Policy*, 159 (Kennan).

[37] This is Ellen Schrecker's summing up in *Many Are the Crimes: McCarthyism in America* (Boston: Little, Brown, 1998).

CHAPTER 2   THE INTERNATIONAL ECONOMY: OUT OF THE RUINS

[1] Quote from Richard N. Gardner, *Sterling-Dollar Diplomacy in Current Perspective: The Origins and Prospects of Our International Economic Order*, 2nd ed. (New York: Columbia University Press, 1980), xiii.

[2] John Maynard Keynes, *The Collected Writings of John Maynard Keynes*, vol. 7: *The General Theory of Employment, Interest and Money* (London: Macmillan, 1973), 383.

[3] Keynes, *The Collected Writings*, vol. 9: *Essays in Persuasion* (London: Macmillan, 1972), 311.

[4] Quote from David W. Ellwood, *Rebuilding Europe: Western Europe, America, and Postwar Reconstruction* (London: Longman, 1992), 21–22.

[5] Quote from John W. Dower, *Embracing Defeat: Japan in the Wake of World War II* (New York: Norton, 1999), 60.

[6] Quoted in Dower, *Embracing Defeat*, 550.

[7] Quote from Charles S. Maier, "The Politics of Productivity: The Foundations of American International Economic Activity after World War II," in *The Cold War in Europe: Era of a Divided Continent*, ed. Maier (New York: Markus Wiener, 1991), 180.

[8] Quoted in Eleanor M. Hadley, "The Diffusion of Keynesian Ideas in Japan," in *The Political Power of Economic Ideas*, ed. Peter A. Hall (Princeton, NJ: Princeton University Press, 1989), 298n.

[9] Ellwood, *Rebuilding Europe*, 31 (journalist); Victor Klemperer, *I Will Bear Witness: A Diary of the Nazi Years, 1942–1945*, trans. Martin Chalmers (New York: Random House, 1999), 434, 494.

[10] Claire Duchen, *Women's Rights and Women's Lives in France, 1944–1968* (London: Routledge, 1994), 9 ("sight of a uniform"); Ellwood, *Rebuilding Europe*, 34 (data on calories), 55–56 ("what hunger really meant").

[11] Elizabeth Heineman, "The Hour of the Woman: Memories of Germany's 'Crisis Years' and West German National Identity," *American Historical Review* 101 (April 1996): 374.

[12] Ellwood, *Rebuilding Europe*, 62.

[13] Ellwood, *Rebuilding Europe*, 167.

[14] Quote from Michaela Hönicke Moore, *Know Your Enemy: The American Debate on Nazism, 1933–1945* (New York: Cambridge University Press, 2010), 298.

[15] Ellwood, *Rebuilding Europe*, 118.

[16] Quote from Mark Mazower, *Governing the World: The History of an Idea* (New York: Penguin Press, 2012), 202.

[17] These advertisements, all from 1949, can be found at www.adflip.com.

[18] Quoted in Bob Thomas, *Walt Disney: An American Original* (New York: Simon and Schuster, 1976), 277.

[19] Quoted phrase from Richard Kuisel, *Seducing the French: The Dilemma of Americanization* (Berkeley: University of California Press, 1993), 52.

[20] Data from Victoria de Grazia, "Mass Culture and Sovereignty: The American Challenge to European Cinemas, 1920–1960," *Journal of Modern History* 61 (March 1989): 82.

[21] Quoted in Kuisel, *Seducing the French*, 65.

[22] Kuisel, *Seducing the French*, 55.

[23] Kuisel, *Seducing the French*, 63.

CHAPTER 3   THE THIRD WORLD:
FIRST TREMORS IN ASIA

[1] From Mao's autobiographical account in Edgar Snow, *Red Star Over China* (originally published 1938; New York: Grove Press, 1961), 131.

[2] Michael H. Hunt, *The Genesis of Chinese Communist Foreign Policy* (New York: Columbia University Press, 1996), 77.

[3] Quoted in Alexander Pantsov with Steven I. Levine, *Mao: The Real Story* (New York: Simon & Schuster, 2012), 172.

[4] Peter J. Seybolt, *Throwing the Emperor from His Horse: Portrait of a Village Leader in China, 1923–1995* (Boulder, CO: Westview, 1996), 7.

[5] Oral testimony in Seybolt, *Throwing the Emperor from His Horse*, 24.

[6] Stuart R. Schram, *The Political Thought of Mao Tse-tung*, 2nd ed. (New York: Praeger, 1969), 167, 350.

[7] Mao, "The Present Situation and Our Tasks," December 25, 1947, available at www .marxists.org/reference/archive/mao/selected-works/volume-4/mswv4_24.htm (accessed December 1, 2014).

[8] Quote from Chen Jian, *Mao's China and the Cold War* (Chapel Hill: University of North Carolina Press, 2001), 315n14.

[9] Mao, "On the People's Democratic Dictatorship," June 30, 1949, available at www.marxists .org/reference/archive/mao/selected-works/volume-4/mswv4_65.htm (accessed December 1, 2014).

[10] Ho Chi Minh, *Selected Writings (1920–1969)* (Hanoi: Foreign Languages Publishing House, 1973), 251.

[11] *Vietnam: A History in Documents*, ed. Gareth Porter (New York: New American Library, 1981), 29, 30.

[12] Truong Buu Lam, ed. and trans., *Patterns of Vietnamese Response to Foreign Intervention, 1858–1900* (New Haven, CT: Yale Southeast Asia Studies, 1967), 79 (poem); Huynh Kim Khanh, *Vietnamese Communism, 1925–1945* (Ithaca, NY: Cornell University Press, 1982), 29–30n (lullaby).

[13] Quote from Gérard Chaliand, *The Peasants of North Vietnam*, trans. Peter Wiles (Baltimore: Penguin, 1969), 143.

[14] Nguyen Thi Dinh, *No Other Road to Take: Memoir of Mrs. Nguyen Thi Dinh*, trans. Mai V. Elliott (Ithaca, NY: Cornell University Southeast Asia Program, Department of Asian Studies, 1976), 27.

[15] Figures on British presence around 1890 from Eric Hobsbawm, *The Age of Empire, 1875–1914* (New York: Pantheon Books, 1987), 81.

[16] Data from Mike Davis, *Late Victorian Holocausts: El Niño Famines and the Making of the Third World* (London: Verso, 2001), 311, 312.

[17] *The Indian Nationalist Movement, 1885–1947: Select Documents*, ed. B. N. Pandey (London: Macmillan, 1979), 142.

[18] Lionel Hastings Ismay, *Memoirs* (New York: Viking Press, 1960), 417.

[19] Mahatma Gandhi, *Hind Swaraj and Other Writings*, ed. Anthony J. Parel (Cambridge, UK: Cambridge University Press, 1997), 150–151.

[20] Judith M. Brown, *Modern India: The Origins of an Asian Democracy*, 2nd ed. (Oxford, UK: Oxford University Press, 1994), 350.

[21] Quoted in Brown, *Nehru* (London: Longman, 1999), 36.

[22] Data from Angus Maddison, *Historical Statistics of the World Economy: 1–2008 AD*, available at www.ggdc.net/maddison/Historical_Statistics/horizontal-file_02-2010 .xls (accessed October 9, 2014).

[23] Quoted in Benedict J. Kerkvliet, *The Huk Rebellion: A Study of Peasant Revolt in the Philippines* (Berkeley: University of California Press, 1977), 11.

[24] Kerkvliet, *The Huk Rebellion*, 51.

[25] Kerkvliet, *The Huk Rebellion*, 164, 269.

PART TWO   THE COLD WAR SYSTEM UNDER STRESS, 1953–1968

[1] Marika Sherwood, *Kwame Nkrumah: The Years Abroad, 1935–1947* (Legon, Accra, Ghana: Freedom Publications, 1996), 98, 141.

[2] Kwame Nkrumah, *Revolutionary Path* (New York: International Publishers, 1973), 426.

CHAPTER 4   THE COLD WAR: A TENUOUS ACCOMMODATION

[1] Amy W. Knight, *Beria: Stalin's First Lieutenant* (Princeton, NJ: Princeton University Press, 1993), 209.

[2] Nikita Khrushchev address reproduced in U.S. Senate, *Congressional Record*, 84th Cong., 2nd Sess. (Washington, DC: U. S. Government Printing Office, 1956), vol. 102, pt. 7, pp. 9391, 9395.

[3] Stephen F. Cohen and Katrina vanden Heuvel, *Voices of Glasnost: Interviews with Gorbachev's Reformers* (New York: Norton, 1989), 262.

[4] Elena Zubkova, *Russia after the War: Hopes, Illusions, and Disappointments, 1945–1957*, trans. and ed. Hugh Ragsdale (Armonk, NY: M. E. Sharpe, 1998), 185, 188.

[5] Richard Stites, *Russian Popular Culture: Entertainment and Society since 1900* (Cambridge, UK: Cambridge University Press, 1992), 133.

[6] William J. Tompson, *Khrushchev: A Political Life* (New York: St. Martin's, 1995), 246 (Yevtushenko poem), 257–258 (Khrushchev complaints).

[7] The notion of "bread-and-butter" socialism is central to Tompson's interpretation in *Khrushchev*.

[8] Zubkova, *Russia after the War*, 162.

[9] David Holloway, *Stalin and the Bomb: The Soviet Union and Atomic Energy, 1939–1956* (New Haven, CT: Yale University Press, 1994), 339 ("became convinced"), 343 ("feared us").

[10] Robert V. Daniels, ed., *A Documentary History of Communism and the World: From Revolution to Collapse*, 3rd ed. (Hanover, NH: University Press of New England, 1994), 124.

[11] Daniels, *A Documentary History of Communism and the World*, 170, 171; *New York Times*, November 5, 1956, p. 22 (newspaper message).

[12] Daniels, *A Documentary History of Communism and the World*, 166.

[13] Michael H. Hunt, *Crises in U.S. Foreign Policy: An International History Reader* (New Haven, CT: Yale University Press, 1996), 169.

[14] Hunt, *Crises in U.S. Foreign Policy*, 274.

[15] Hunt, *Crises in U.S. Foreign Policy*, 294.

[16] David Nordlander, "Khruschchev's Image," *Russian Review* 52 (April 1993): 262 (Khrushchev); Cohen and vanden Heuvel, *Voices of Glasnost*, 264 (Yevtushenko).

[17] Raymond L. Garthoff, *Reflections on the Cuban Missile Crisis*, 2nd ed. (Washington, DC: Brookings Institution, 1989), 133–134.

[18] Michael H. Hunt, *Lyndon Johnson's War: America's Cold War Crusade in Vietnam* (New York: Hill and Wang, 1996), viii (Greene), 60 (Kennedy).

[19] Michael H. Hunt, *A Vietnam War Reader: A Documentary History from American and Vietnamese Perspectives* (Chapel Hill: University of North Carolina Press, 2010), 84.

[20] Hunt, *A Vietnam War Reader*, 76 (Johnson), 79 and 83 (warnings of catastrophe).

[21] Data from UN Demographic Yearbook, U.S. Department of Commerce's Bureau of the Census, and National Center for Educational Statistics.

[22] William H. Chafe, *The Unfinished Journey: America Since World War II*, 3rd ed. (New York: Oxford University Press, 1995), 152.

[23] Chafe, *The Unfinished Journey*, 317 (Carmichael); Rhodri Jeffreys-Jones, *Peace Now! American Society and the Ending of the Vietnam War* (New Haven, CT: Yale University Press, 1999), 104 (Black Panther platform); Alexander Bloom and Wini Breines, eds., *"Takin' it to the streets": A Sixties Reader* (New York: Oxford University Press, 1995), 232 (King).

[24] Quoted in Terry H. Anderson, *The Movement and the Sixties: Protest in America from Greensboro to Wounded Knee* (New York: Oxford University Press, 1995), 138.

[25] Port Huron Statement" available on the University of Virginia's The Sixties Project website: www2.iath.virginia.edu/sixties/HTML_docs/Resources/Primary/Manifestos/SDS_Port_Huron.html (accessed February 18, 2015).

[26] Timothy Leary quoted in Todd Gitlin, *The Sixties: Years of Hope, Days of Rage*, 2nd ed. (New York: Bantam Books, 1993), 206.

[27] Data from Organisation for Economic Co-operation and Development.

[28] "On the Poverty of Student Life," first distributed in 1966 at the University of Strasbourg and available at library.nothingness.org/articles/SI/en/display/4 (accessed January 4, 2015).

[29] Cohn-Bendit quote from Ronald Fraser et al., *1968: A Student Generation in Revolt* (New York: Pantheon, 1988), 213.

[30] Quote from Thomas R. H. Havens, *Fire Across the Sea: The Vietnam War and Japan, 1965–1975* (Princeton, NJ: Princeton University Press, 1987), 205.

[31] Havens, *Fire Across the Sea*, 58.

[32] Havens, *Fire Across the Sea*, 186.

[33] Oral history in Elena Poniatowska, *Massacre in Mexico*, trans. Helen R. Lane (New York: Viking Press, 1975), 218.

[34] Gale Stokes, ed., *From Stalinism to Pluralism: A Documentary History of Eastern Europe Since 1945*, 2nd ed. (New York: Oxford University Press, 1996), 126.

[35] Quote from Jerzy Eisler, "March 1968 in Poland," in *1968: The World Transformed*, ed. Carole Fink et al. (Cambridge, UK: Cambridge University Press, 1998), 245.

[36] Quoted in Mark Kramer, "The Czechoslovak Crisis and the Brezhnev Doctrine," in *1968: The World Transformed*, 127.

[37] Quoted in Robert V. Daniels, *Year of the Heroic Guerrilla: World Revolution and Counterrevolution in 1968* (New York: Basic Books, 1989), 164.

CHAPTER 5   ABUNDANCE AND DISCONTENT IN THE DEVELOPED WORLD

[1] Data from Angus Maddison, *Monitoring the World Economy* (Paris: Development Centre of the Organisation for Economic Co-operation and Development, 1995), 73.

[2] Quotes from Richard M. Nixon, *Six Crises* (Garden City, NY: Doubleday, 1962), 253, 259–260; *Khrushchev Remembers: The Last Testament*, ed. and trans. Strobe Talbott (Boston: Little, Brown, 1974), 366.

[3] Robert M. Collins, "The Economic Crisis of 1968 and the Waning of the 'American Century'," *American Historical Review* 101 (April 1996): 416.

[4] Jacques Soustelle quoted in Richard F. Kuisel, *Seducing the French: the Dilemma of Americanization* (Berkeley: University of California Press, 1993), 24.

[5] Data from Maddison, *Monitoring the World Economy*, 83, and Vera Zamagni, *The Economic History of Italy, 1860–1990* (New York: Oxford University Press, 1993), 40.

[6] This notion is central to the interpretation in Alan S. Milward with the assistance of George Brennan and Federico Romero, *The European Rescue of the Nation-State*, 2nd ed. (London: Routledge, 2000).

[7] This encyclical, issued May 5, 1961, can be found on the Vatican website at www .vatican.va/holy_father/john_xxiii/encyclicals/documents/hf_j-xxiii_enc_15051961_ mater_en.html (accessed August 28, 2014).

[8] Data from Milward, *The European Rescue*, 33.

[9] Data from Angus Maddison, *The World Economy: A Millennial Perspective* (Paris: Development Centre of the Organisation for Economic Co-operation and Development, 2001), 135.

[10] Milward, *The European Rescue*, 208.

[11] Milward, *The European Rescue*, 390.

[12] Data from Alan Friedman, *Agnelli and the Network of Italian Power* (London: Harrap, 1988), 12–13, 85–86, 138.

[13] Data on German and Italian family business from Jeffrey R. Fear, "Constructing Big Business: The Cultural Concept of the Firm," in *Big Business and the Wealth of Nations*, ed. Alfred D. Chandler, Franco Amatori, and Takashi Hikino (New York: Cambridge University Press, 1997), 556.

[14] Data from Angus Maddison, *Contours of the World Economy, 1-2030 AD* (Oxford, UK: Oxford University Press, 2007), 380; Shigeto Tsuru, *Japan's Capitalism: Creative Defeat and Beyond* (Cambridge, UK: Cambridge University Press, 1993), 183; and Yutaka Kōsai, "The Postwar Japanese Economy, 1945–1973," in *The Cambridge History of Japan*, vol. 6: *The Twentieth Century*, ed. Peter Duus (Cambridge, UK: Cambridge University Press, 1988), 536.

[15] Akio Morita with Edwin M. Reingold and Mitsuko Shimomura, *Made in Japan: Akio Morita and Sony* (New York: E. P. Dutton, 1986), 79, 82.

[16] Sales and employee data courtesy of the Sony Corporation.

[17] Morita, *Made in Japan*, 189.

[18] Morita, *Made in Japan*, 180.

[19] *New York Times Magazine*, July 13, 1969, 10.

[20] Mary A. McCay, *Rachel Carson* (New York: Twayne, 1993), 23–24.

[21] McCay, *Rachel Carson*, 64.

[22] Rachel Carson, *Silent Spring* (Boston: Houghton Mifflin, 1962), 99, 297.

[23] Betty Friedan, *Life So Far* (New York: Simon & Schuster, 2000), 133.

[24] NOW "Statement of Purpose," adopted at the founding conference in Washington, DC, October 29, 1966, at now.org/about/history/statement-of-purpose/ (accessed August 28, 2014).

[25] Organisation for Economic Co-operation and Development data.

[26] Claire Duchen, *Women's Rights and Women's Lives in France, 1944–1968* (London: Routledge, 1994), 91.

[27] Duchen, *Women's Rights*, 185.

[28] Kathleen S. Uno, "The Death of 'Good Wife, Wise Mother'?" in *Postwar Japan as History*, ed. Andrew Gordon (Berkeley: University of California Press, 1993), 313.

[29] Gabriel Almond quoted in Tony Smith, "Requiem or New Agenda for Third World Studies?" *World Politics* 37 (July 1985): 537.

[30] Quote from one of the Argentine junta leaders, Admiral Emilio Massera, in Greg Grandin, "Living in Revolutionary Times: Coming to Terms with the Violence of Latin America's Long Cold War," in *A Century of Revolution: Insurgent and Counterinsurgent Violence during Latin America's Long Cold War*, ed. Grandin and Gilbert M. Joseph (Durham, NC: Duke University Press, 2010), 22.

[31] Estimated deaths from Jerry Dávila, *Dictatorship in South America* (Chichester, UK: Wiley-Blackwell, 2013), 3.

CHAPTER 6 THIRD WORLD HOPES AT HIGH TIDE

1 Stuart R. Schram, *The Political Thought of Mao Tse-tung* (New York: Praeger, 1963), 247.

2 Stuart R. Schram, ed., *Chairman Mao Talks to the People: Talks and Letters, 1956–1971*, trans. John Chinnery and Tieyun (New York: Pantheon Books, 1975), 92.

3 Schram, *Chairman Mao Talks to the People*, 142.

4 Schram, *Chairman Mao Talks to the People*, 104 (1962 comment), Sidney Rittenberg and Amanda Bennett, *The Man Who Stayed Behind* (New York: Simon and Schuster, 1993), 272 (1963 comment).

5 Data from Maurice Meisner, *Mao's China and After: A History of The People's Republic* (New York: Free Press, 1986), 436–440, 447n5.

6 Peter J. Seybolt, *Throwing the Emperor from His Horse: Portrait of a Village Leader in China, 1923–1995* (Boulder, CO: Westview, 1996), 75.

7 Huang Shu-min, *The Spiral Road: Change in a Chinese Village Through the Eyes of a Communist Party Leader,* 2nd ed. (Boulder, CO: Westview Press, 1998), 61–62.

8 Michael H. Hunt, *A Vietnam War Reader: A Documentary History from American and Vietnamese Perspectives* (Chapel Hill: University of North Carolina Press, 2010), 53.

9 Gareth Porter, ed., *Vietnam: The Definitive Documentation of Human Decisions* (2 vols.; Stanfordville, NY: Earl M. Coleman Enterprises, 1979), 2: 383–384.

10 Porter, *Vietnam: The Definitive Documentation*, 2: 477–478.

11 Ho Chi Minh, *Selected Writings (1920–1969)* (Hanoi: Foreign Languages Publishing House, 1973), 361.

12 Jim Handy, *Revolution in the Countryside: Rural Conflict and Agrarian Reform in Guatemala, 1944–1954* (Chapel Hill: University of North Carolina Press, 1994), 175.

13 Richard H. Immerman, *The CIA in Guatemala: The Foreign Policy of Intervention* (Austin: University of Texas Press, 1982), 102.

14 Handy, *Revolution in the Countryside*, 4; Piero Gleijeses, *Shattered Hope: The Guatemalan Revolution and the United States, 1944–1954* (Princeton, NJ: Princeton University Press, 1991), 369.

15 Piero Gleijeses, *Politics and Culture in Guatemala* (Ann Arbor: Center for Political Studies, Institute for Social Research, University of Michigan, 1988), 7.

16 Pablo Neruda, "In Guatemala," in *Song of Protest*, trans. Miguel Algarín (New York: William Morrow, 1976), 59.

17 Quoted in Peter G. Bourne, *Fidel: A Biography of Fidel Castro* (New York: Dodd, Mead and Company, 1986), 230.

18 Quote from Lee Lockwood, *Castro's Cuba, Cuba's Fidel* (New York: Macmillan Company, 1967), 42.

19 Bourne, *Fidel*, 119.

20 Data from Tim Golden, "Castro's People Try to Absorb 'Terrible Blows'," *New York Times*, January 11, 1993, A1, A6, supplemented by literacy figures from CIA's *World Factbook, 1991*.

21 Kwame Nkrumah, *Revolutionary Path* (New York: International Publishers, 1973), 240.

22 Ayi Kwei Armah, *The Beautyful Ones Are Not Yet Born* (New York: Collier Books, 1969), 104.

23 Quoted in Baffour Ankomah and Mike Afrani, "'If I Fall, Fall as a Man': Kwame Nkrumah 25 Years after his Death," *New African*, no. 351 (April 1997): 14.

24 Quoted in Ervand Abrahamian, *The Coup: 1953, the CIA, and the Roots of Modern U.S.–Iranian Relations* (New York: New Press, 2013), 19.

25 Quote from Tony Smith, *The Pattern of Imperialism: The United States, Great Britain, and the Late-Industrializing World since 1815* (Cambridge, UK: Cambridge University Press, 1981), 131.

[26] Mohammad Musaddiq, *Musaddiq's Memoir: The End of the British Empire in Iran*, ed. Homa Katouzian and trans. Katouzian and S. H. Amin (London: JEBHE, National Movement of Iran, 1988), 74.

[27] Asadollah Alam, *The Shah and I: The Confidential Diary of Iran's Royal Court, 1969–1977*, ed. Alinaghi Alikhani and trans. Alikhani and Nicholas Vincent (New York: St. Martin's Press, 1992), 360 ("world power"), 323 ("too happy").

[28] Quoted in P. J. Vatikiotis, *Nasser and His Generation* (London: Croom Helm, 1978), 145.

[29] Quote from Gamal Abdel Nasser, *Nasser Speaks: Basic Documents*, trans. E. S. Farag (London: Morssett Press, 1972), 29. Data from William L. Cleveland, *A History of the Modern Middle East* (Boulder, CO: Westview Press, 1994), 285.

[30] J. R. McNeill, *Something New under the Sun: An Environmental History of the Twentieth-Century World* (New York: Norton, 2000), 168–169.

[31] Vatikiotis, *Nasser and His Generation*, 228.

[32] Data from Angus Maddison, *Monitoring the World Economy*, 24, 63, 80, 103, 192.

[33] *Umm Kulthum: A Voice Like Egypt* (dir. Michal Goldman, 1996, 67 min.).

[34] Quote from Vatikiotis, *Nasser and His Generation*, 266.

[35] Frantz Fanon, *The Wretched of the Earth*, trans. Constance Farrington (New York: Grove Press, 1968), 61.

[36] The Atlantic Charter text is available at www.yale.edu/lawweb/avalon/wwii/atlantic/at10.htm#1 (accessed May 12, 2002).

PART THREE   FROM COLD WAR TO GLOBALIZATION, 1968–1991

[1] Ray Kroc with Robert Anderson, *Grinding It Out: The Making of McDonald's* (Chicago: Henry Regnery, 1977), 9.

[2] Kroc, *Grinding It Out*, 15.

[3] Data from John F. Love, *McDonald's: Behind the Arches*, 2nd ed. (New York: Bantam Books, 1995), 464.

[4] Data from "McDonald's Reports Global Results For 2002," released January 23, 2003, available at www.mcdonalds.com/corporate/press/financial/2003/01232003/index.html (accessed January 31, 2003).

[5] Quotes from "McAtlas Shrugged," *Foreign Policy*, no. 124 (May/June 2001), 26.

CHAPTER 7   THE COLD WAR COMES TO A CLOSE

[1] Quoted in Stephen J. Whitfield, *The Culture of the Cold War*, 2nd ed. (Baltimore: Johns Hopkins University Press, 1996), 19.

[2] Nixon remarks to White House staff, July 19, 1971, available at www.gwu.edu/~nsarchiv/NSAEBB/NSAEBB66/ch-41.pdf (accessed January 24, 2003); Nixon speech, July 6, 1971, *Public Papers of the Presidents of the United States: Richard Nixon, 1971* (Washington, DC: Government Printing Office, 1972), 804.

[3] Quote from Stephen E. Ambrose, *Nixon*, vol. 2: *The Triumph of a Politician, 1962–1972* (New York: Simon and Schuster, 1989), 660.

[4] Remarks recorded in H. R. Haldeman, *The Haldeman Diaries: Inside the Nixon White House* (New York: G. P. Putnam's Sons, 1994), 322.

[5] Solzhenitsyn quoted in *A Documentary History of Communism in Russia: From Lenin to Gorbachev*, ed. and trans. Robert V. Daniels, 3rd ed. (Hanover, NH: University Press of New England, 1993), 295, 297.

[6] Sakharov quote from Lawrence S. Wittner, "The Nuclear Threat Ignored," in *1968: The World Transformed*, ed. Carole Fink et al. (Cambridge, UK: Cambridge University Press, 1998), 455.

[7] Stephen White, *Russia Goes Dry: Alcohol, State, and Society* (Cambridge, UK: Cambridge University Press, 1996), 40 (police report), 172 (developed alcoholism); Isaac J. Tarasulo, ed., *Perils of Perestroika: Viewpoints of the Soviet Press, 1989–1991* (Wilmington, DE: Scholarly Resources, 1992), 182 (folk wisdom).

[8] Recounted in Hedrick Smith, *The New Russians* (New York: Random House, 1990), 25.

[9] Quote from Brezhnev doctrine in Mark Kramer, "The Czechoslovak Crisis and the Brezhnev Doctrine," in *1968: The World Transformed*, 168.

[10] Quotes from Raymond L. Garthoff, *Détente and Confrontation: American–Soviet Relations from Nixon to Reagan*, 2nd ed. (Washington: Brookings Institution, 1994), 40, 114–115.

[11] Quoted in Gottfried Niedhart, "Ostpolitik: The Role of the Federal Republic of Germany in the Process of Détente," in *1968: The World Transformed*, 181.

[12] Comment in interview with Serge Schmemann, "Moscow Journal: Who'll Speak Up for Russia Now? Nixon, No Less," *New York Times*, February 19, 1993, A4.

[13] The report quote appears in *Cold War International History Project Bulletin*, nos. 8–9 (Winter 1996/1997), p. 120.

[14] Quoted in Frances FitzGerald, *Way Out There in the Blue: Reagan, Star Wars and the End of the Cold War* (New York: Simon & Schuster, 2000), 31.

[15] Jeane Kirkpatrick, "Dictatorships and Double Standards," *Commentary* 68 (November 1979): 44.

[16] Quote from Garthoff, *Détente and Confrontation*, 70, 860.

[17] Quoted in Archie Brown, *The Gorbachev Factor* (New York: Oxford University Press, 1996), 39.

[18] Brown, *The Gorbachev Factor*, 336n152.

[19] Brown, *The Gorbachev Factor*, 94.

[20] Quoted in Geir Lundestad, "'Imperial Overstretch', Mikhail Gorbachev, and the End of the Cold War," *Cold War History* 1 (August 2000): 12.

[21] Data from Lundestad, "'Imperial Overstretch'," 3–5.

[22] Quotes from Don Oberdorfer, *From the Cold War to a New Era: The United States and the Soviet Union, 1983–1991*, 2nd ed. (Baltimore: Johns Hopkins University Press, 1998), 381 ("enemy"), 383 ("epoch" and "new era").

[23] Quote from Timothy Garton Ash, *The Magic Lantern: The Revolution of '89 Witnessed in Warsaw, Budapest, Berlin and Prague*, 3rd ed. (New York: Vintage, 1999), 16.

[24] Quotes from Gale Stokes, *The Walls Came Tumbling Down: The Collapse of Communism in Eastern Europe* (New York: Oxford University Press, 1993), 139, 140.

[25] Quote from Stephen Kotkin, *Armageddon Averted: The Soviet Collapse, 1970–2000*, 2nd ed. (New York: Oxford University Press, 2008), 92.

[26] Quote from Oberdorfer, *From the Cold War to a New Era*, 460 (Gorbachev), 465 (chief of staff).

[27] Quote from Daniels, *A Documentary History of Communism in Russia*, 392.

[28] Kotkin, *Armageddon Averted*, 170.

[29] Andrei Grachev quoted in Brown, *The Gorbachev Factor*, 88.

[30] Data from Natural Resources Defense Council Archive at www.nrdc.org/nuclear/nudb/datab9.asp and /datab10.asp (accessed January 25, 2003).

[31] Allan M. Winkler, *Life Under a Cloud: American Anxiety About the Atom* (New York: Oxford University Press, 1993), 212; George F. Kennan, *The Nuclear Delusion: Soviet–American Relations in the Atomic Age* (New York: Pantheon Books, 1983), 176.

[32] Jonathan Schell, *Fate of the Earth* (New York: Knopf, 1982), 182.

[33] Data from Angus Maddison, *Monitoring the World Economy, 1820–1992* (Paris: Development Centre of the Organisation for Economic Co-operation and Development, 1995), 186–187.

[34] Data from Stanley Lebergott, *Consumer Expenditures: New Measures and Old Motives* (Princeton, NJ: Princeton University Press, 1996), Chapter 5.

CHAPTER 8　GLOBAL MARKETS: ONE SYSTEM, THREE CENTERS

[1] Data from Angus Maddison, *The World Economy: A Millennial Perspective* (Paris: Development Centre of the Organisation for Economic Co-operation and Development, 2001), 272, 275, 284, 298.

[2] *New York Times*, January 27, 1992, C5, drawing on data from Organisation for Economic Co-operation and Development and from Bank for International Settlements.

[3] David A. Stockman, *The Triumph of Politics: How the Reagan Revolution Failed* (New York: Harper & Row, 1987), 429.

[4] Debt data from U.S. Bureau of the Census (www.census.gov/prod/2001pubs/statab/sec10.pdf); quote from Robert M. Collins, *More: The Politics of Economic Growth in Postwar America* (New York: Oxford University Press, 2000), 216.

[5] This Springsteen song is from his album *Born in the U.S.A.* (Sony; originally released 1984).

[6] Quotes from Studs Terkel, *The Great Divide: Second Thoughts on the American Dream* (New York: Pantheon Books, 1988), 175, 197.

[7] Poll results reported in *New York Times*, December 29, 1992, A6.

[8] Milton Friedman with the assistance of Rose D. Friedman, *Capitalism and Freedom* (Chicago: University of Chicago Press, 1962), 5, 15, 16.

[9] Data from Maddison, *The World Economy*, 275; and *New York Times*, April 28, 1998, C4.

[10] Jeremy Tunstall, *The Media Are American: Anglo-American Media in the World* (New York: Columbia University Press, 1977), 282, 299; "Culture Wars," *Economist* 348 (September 12, 1998): 97 (Hollywood market share in Europe for 1996); James Stanlaw, "'For Beautiful Human Life': The Use of English in Japan," in *Re-Made in Japan: Everyday Life and Consumer Taste in a Changing Society*, ed. Joseph J. Tobin (New Haven, CT: Yale University Press, 1992), 62.

[11] Randall E. Stross, *Bulls in the China Shop and Other Sino-American Business Encounters* (New York: Pantheon Books, 1990), 266 (*People's Daily* on Coke); Mary Yoko Brannen, "'Bwana Mickey': Constructing Cultural Consumption at Tokyo Disneyland," in *Re-Made in Japan*, 216; and Yukiko Koshiro, email to author, March 30, 1999.

[12] Data on total western Pacific rim exports from *New York Times*, November 24, 1993, A4.

[13] James Sterrngold, "In Japan, the Clamor for Change Runs Headlong Into Old Groove," *New York Times* (online ed.), January 3, 1995.

[14] Export and per capita data from Shigeto Tsuru, *Japan's Capitalism: Creative Defeat and Beyond* (Cambridge, UK: Cambridge University Press, 1993), 182–183.

[15] David Sanger, "Seeing a Dependent and Declining U.S., More Japanese Adopt a Nationalist Spirit," *New York Times*, August 4, 1989, A7.

[16] Data from Maddison, *The World Economy*, 298; Kwan S. Kim, "From Neo-Mercantilism to Globalism: The Changing Role of the State and South Korea's Economic Prowess," in *The Rise of East Asia: Critical Visions of the Pacific Century*, ed. Mark T. Berger and Douglas A. Borer (London: Routledge, 1997), 95; Donald Kirk, *Korean Dynasty:*

Hyundai and Chung Ju Yung (Armonk, NY: M.E. Sharpe, 1994), 11; and Eric Pfanner and Brian X. Chen, "Samsung: Uneasy in the Lead," *New York Times* (online ed.), December 14, 2013.

[17] *Khrushchev Remembers: The Last Testament*, ed. and trans. Strobe Talbott (Boston: Little, Brown, 1974), 253; David S. G. Goodman, *Deng Xiaoping and the Chinese Revolution: A Political Biography* (London: Routledge, 1994), 35.

[18] Data from Angus Maddison, "Historical Statistics of the World Economy: 1–2008 AD" available at www.ggdc.net/maddison/Historical_Statistics/horizontal-file_02-2010.xls (accessed December 4, 2014).

[19] Quote from *The Gate of Heavenly Peace* (prod. and dir. Richard Gordon and Carman Hinton, 1995, 189 min.).

[20] Han Minzhu, ed., *Cries for Democracy: Writings and Speeches from the 1989 Chinese Democracy Movement* (Princeton, NJ: Princeton University Press, 1990), 221.

[21] Per capita growth data from Vera Zamagni, *The Economic History of Italy, 1860–1990* (New York: Oxford University Press, 1993), 40.

[22] Derek W. Urwin, *The Community of Europe: A History of European Integration since 1945*, 2nd ed. (London: Longman, 1995), 111.

[23] Quoted in James H. Mittelman, *The Globalization Syndrome: Transformation and Resistance* (Princeton, NJ: Princeton University Press, 2000), 223.

[24] Data from Organisation for Economic Co-operation and Development reported in *New York Times*, December 22, 1992, C5.

[25] Data in Sheldon M. Garon, *Molding Japanese Minds: The State in Everyday Life* (Princeton, NJ: Princeton University Press, 1997), 216.

[26] *New York Times*, February 20, 1990, A6.

CHAPTER 9   DIVERGENT PATHS IN THE THIRD WORLD

[1] Niccolò Machiavelli, *The Prince*, trans. Luigi Ricci and E. R. P. Vincent (New York: Random House, 1950), 21.

[2] Quoted in Ben Kiernan, *The Pol Pot Regime: Race, Power, and Genocide in Cambodia under the Khmer Rouge, 1975–79* (New Haven, CT: Yale University Press, 1996), 11.

[3] Quotes from Kiernan, *The Pol Pot Regime*, 247 (gruel); Alexander L. Hinton, "Why Did You Kill?: The Cambodian Genocide and the Dark Side of Face and Honor," *Journal of Asian Studies* 57 (February 1998): 93 (prison).

[4] Quoted in Kiernan, *The Pol Pot Regime*, 111.

[5] Hamid Algar, ed. and trans., *Islam and Revolution: Writings and Declarations of Imam Khomeini* (Berkeley, CA: Mizan Press, 1981), 21.

[6] Baqer Moin, *Khomeini: Life of the Ayatollah* (New York: St. Martin's Press, 1999), 60 (on Reza Shah); Algar, *Islam and Revolution*, 182 (on Mohammad Reza Shah).

[7] Algar, *Islam and Revolution*, 132.

[8] Gromyko quoted in *The Fall of Détente: Soviet–American Relations during the Carter Years*, ed. Odd Arne Westad (Oslo: Scandinavian University Press, 1997), 301.

[9] Quote from the documentary, *Iran: Adrift in a Sea of Blood* (writ. and dir. Ron Hallis; 1986; 27 min.).

[10] Data from William Beinart, *Twentieth-Century South Africa*, 2nd ed. (New York: Oxford University Press), 353.

[11] Mark Mathabane, *Kaffir Boy* (New York: Macmillan, 1986), 33.

[12] Sheridan Johns and R. Hunt Davis, Jr., eds., *Mandela, Tambo, and the African National Congress: The Struggle Against Apartheid, 1948–1990, A Documentary Survey* (New York: Oxford University Press, 1991), 138.

[13] Johns and Davis, *Mandela, Tambo, and the African National Congress*, 133.

[14] Johns and Davis, *Mandela, Tambo, and the African National Congress*, 172.

[15] Quoted in Martin Gilbert, *Exile and Return: The Emergence of Jewish Statehood* (London: Weidenfield and Nicolson, 1978), 39.

[16] Charles D. Smith, *Palestine and the Arab-Israeli Conflict: A History with Documents*, 8th ed. (Boston: Bedford/St. Martin's, 2013), 25 (population data), 68 (quote).

[17] Smith, *Palestine and the Arab-Israeli Conflict*, 146 (population data), 116 (quote).

[18] Quoted in Helena Cobban, *The Palestine Liberation Organization: People, Power and Politics* (Cambridge, UK: Cambridge University Press, 1984), 246.

[19] The Charter is reproduced in Smith, *Palestine and the Arab-Israeli Conflict*, 340.

[20] Hanan Ashrawi, *This Side of Peace: A Personal Account* (New York: Simon and Schuster, 1995), 89.

[21] Shaul Mishal and Reuben Aharoni, eds., *Speaking Stones: Communiqués from the Intifada Underground* (Syracuse, NY: Syracuse University Press, 1994), 58.

[22] Quoted in Walter LaFeber, *Inevitable Revolutions: The United States in Central America*, 2nd ed. (New York: Norton, 1993), 256.

[23] Quoted in Piero Gleijeses, *Politics and Culture in Guatemala* (Ann Arbor: Center for Political Studies, Institute for Social Research, University of Michigan, 1988), 9.

[24] Margaret Hooks, *Guatemalan Women Speak* (London: Catholic Institute for International Relations, 1991), 125.

[25] Data from Angus Maddison, *The World Economy: A Millennial Perspective* (Paris: Development Centre of the Organisation for Economic Co-operation and Development, 2001), 288, 304, 307, 323, 325–326.

[26] Data from M. M. Huq, *The Economy of Ghana: The First 25 Years since Independence* (New York: St. Martin's Press, 1989), 46, 288.

[27] Data from Angus Maddison, *Monitoring the World Economy, 1820–1992* (Paris: Development Centre of the Organisation for Economic Co-operation and Development, 1995), 80, 103.

[28] Data from Tim Dyson, "Infant and Child Mortality in the Indian Subcontinent, 1881–1947," in *Infant and Child Mortality in the Past*, ed. Alain Bideau et al. (New York: Oxford University Press, 1997), 115; Maddison, *Monitoring*, 27; and CIA's *World Factbook 2000*.

[29] Data from Maddison, *The World Economy*, 30.

[30] Data from *New York Times*, June 8, 1999, A1 and A15 (Mexico), and *New York Times*, February 26, 1990, A11 (Guatemala).

[31] Quoted in Bina Agarwal, *A Field of One's Own: Gender and Land Rights in South Asia* (Cambridge, UK: Cambridge University Press, 1994), 431.

[32] Quote from Erika Friedl, *Women of Deh Koh: Lives in an Iranian Village* (New York: Penguin, 1991), 10.

[33] Depicted in the documentary *With These Hands: How Women Feed Africa* (dir. Chris Sheppard, 1987, 34 min).

[34] Data from the CIA's *World Factbook 1999*; and quote from Agarwal, *A Field of One's Own*, 463.

PART FOUR   INTEGRATION AND FRAGMENTATION, THE 1990s AND BEYOND

[1] Jim Dwyer and Kevin Flynn, *102 Minutes: The Untold Story of the Fight to Survive inside the Twin Towers* (New York: Henry Holt, 2005), offers a gripping reconstruction.

[2] Gilles Kepel, *The War for Muslim Minds: Islam and the West*, trans. Pacale Ghazaleh (Cambridge, MA: Harvard University Press, 2004), 112 (TV appearance), 120–121 (web of influence).

[3] Marc Sageman, "Understanding Terror Networks" from the website of the Foreign Policy Research Institute at www.fpri.org/enotes/20041101.middleeast.sageman .understandingterrornetworks.html (accessed September 11, 2005). Sageman, a forensic psychiatrist, was a CIA case officer in Afghanistan between 1987 and 1989.

[4] Pew Global Attitudes Project, report released December 19, 2001, and available at www.people-press.org/2001/12/19/america-admired-yet-its-new-vulnerability-seen-as-good-thing-say-opinion-leaders/ (accessed July 6, 2014), and a Cairo interview by Anthony Shadid, "In Arab world ally, anti-American feeling runs deep," *Washington Post National Weekly Edition*, October 14, 2001.

CHAPTER 10   THE POWER AND PERILS
OF GLOBALIZATION

[1] Benjamin R. Barber, *Jihad vs. McWorld* (New York: Times Books, 1995); Thomas L. Friedman, *The Lexus and the Olive Tree* (New York: Farrar, Straus, Giroux, 1999); Robert D. Kaplan, *The Ends of the Earth: A Journey at the Dawn of the 21st Century* (New York: Random House, 1996); and William Greider, *One World, Ready or Not: The Manic Logic of Global Capitalism* (New York: Simon & Schuster, 1997).

[2] Bumper sticker quote from Benjamin Lazier, "Earthrise; or, the Globalization of the World Picture," *American Historical Review* 116 (June 2011): 621.

[3] Bruce Mazlish, *The New Global History* (New York: Routledge, 2006), 4.

[4] Usage data from www.internetworldstats.com/emarketing.htm (accessed May 22, 2014).

[5] This account is based on Pietra Rivoli, *The Travels of a T-shirt in the Global Economy: An Economist Examines the Markets, Power, and Politics of World Trade*, 2nd ed. (Hoboken, NJ: John Wiley and Sons, 2009), especially 229–236 (the Milonge sketch that follows).

[6] Data from Angus Maddison, *The Contours of the World Economy, 1-2030 AD: Essays in Micro-Economic History* (New York: Oxford University Press, 2007), 376, 379, 382; and supplemented for 2010 from Jutta Bolt and Jan Luiten van Zanden, *The First Update of the Maddison Project: Re-Estimating Growth Before 1820* (Maddison Project Working Paper 4, 2013) available at www.ggdc.net/maddison/maddison-project/ abstract.htm?id=4 (accessed May 24, 2014); and from the Conference Board, Total Economic Data, 1950–2013, available at www.conference-board.org/retrievefile .cfm?filename=TEDI_Jan20141.xls&type=subsite (accessed July 26, 2014).

[7] Trade and investment data from UN Conference on Trade and Development: unctad-stat.unctad.org/ (accessed April 30, 2014). Data on daily turnover in foreign exchange from Bank for International Settlements.

[8] Data from UN Conference on Trade and Development website: "Values and shares of merchandise exports and imports, annual, 1948–2013" at unctadstat.unctad.org/ wds/TableViewer/tableView.aspx?ReportId=101 (accessed March 5, 2015).

[9] Data from UN Conference on Trade and Development website: "Inward and outward foreign direct investment flows, annual, 1970–2013" at unctadstat.unctad.org/wds/ TableViewer/tableView.aspx?ReportId=88 (accessed February 25, 2015).

[10] Quote from Michael Lang, "Globalization and Its History," *Journal of Modern History* 78 (December 2006): 909.

[11] Quote from Jon Jeter, "The Dumping Ground," *Washington Post*, April 22, 2002, available at www.washingtonpost.com/wp-dyn/content/article/2006/08/10/AR2006081000763 .html (accessed October 13, 2014). World Bank data for per capita GDP.

[12] U.S. estimates based on GPI (Genuine Progress Indicator) prepared by the policy institute Redefining Progress and available at rprogress.org/sustainability_indicators/ genuine_progress_indicator.htm (accessed September 3, 2014).

[13] Data from Jonathon W. Moses, "EMIG 1.2: A Global Time Series of Annual Emigration Flows," *International Migration* (online publication, 2012).

[14] Data from Moses, "EMIG 1.2."

[15] Data from the UN High Commissioner for Refugee at www.unhcr.org/53a155bc6.html (accessed June 20, 2014).

[16] Remittance data from UN Conference on Trade and Development: unctadstat.unctad.org/ (accessed May 29, 2014).

[17] Data from the World Bank.

[18] This paragraph draws from Rhacel Salazar Parreñas, *Servants of Globalization: Women, Migration, and Domestic Work* (Stanford, CA: Stanford University Press, 2001). The Reyes quote comes from p. 89 and "stupid" from p. 151. Both are based on interviews done in 1995–1996.

[19] Data from the World Bank website: data.worldbank.org/ (accessed October 26, 2014).

[20] Patrick Manning, *Migration in World History*, 2nd ed. (New York: Routledge, 2013), 175.

[21] Data from *Far Eastern Economic Review*, December 13, 1998, and January 7, 1999; Hirst and Thompson, *Globalization in Question*, 2nd ed. (Cambridge, UK: Polity, 1999), 137.

[22] Quoted in Edmund L. Andrews, "Greenspan Concedes Error on Regulation," *New York Times* (online ed.), October 23, 2008.

[23] Quotes from Nicholas D. Kristof, "Asians Worry That U.S. Aid Is a New Colonialism," *New York Times* (online ed.), February 17, 1998.

[24] Mazlish, *The New Global History*, 36.

[25] The data in this section unless otherwise noted come from Branko Milanovic, "Global Income Inequality in Numbers: in History and Now," *Global Policy* 4 (May 2013): 198–208; and UN Secretariat, Department of Economic and Social Affairs, *Inequality Matters: Report of the World Social Situation 2013* (New York: United Nations, 2013), particularly Chapters 1 and 2.

[26] Data from Angus Maddison, "Historical Statistics of the World Economy: 1–2008 AD," available at www.ggdc.net/maddison/Historical_Statistics/horizontal-file_02-2010 .xls (accessed October 11, 2014).

[27] Data on GDP per capita and life expectancy from World Bank, *Africa Development Indicators 2012/2013* (Washington, DC: The World Bank, 2013), 11, 86. Population data from Population Reference Bureau, "2014 World Population Data Sheet," available at www.prb.org (accessed June 26, 2014).

[28] UN findings reported in Somini Sengupta, "800 Million People Still Malnourished, U.N. Says," *New York Times* (online ed.), September 16, 2014.

[29] J. R. McNeill, *Something New under the Sun: An Environmental History of the Twentieth-Century World* (New York: Norton, 2000), 3 (quote), 360–361 (data).

[30] Lorraine Elliott, *The Global Politics of the Environment*, 2nd ed. (New York: New York University Press, 2004), 46.

[31] David Archer, *The Long Thaw: How Humans Are Changing the Next 100,000 Years of Earth's Climate* (Princeton, NJ: Princeton University Press, 2009), 1.

[32] International polling done by the Pew Research Global Attitudes Project, released December 2, 2009, and available at www.pewglobal.org/2009/12/02/global-warming-seen-as-a-major-problem-around-the-world-less-concern-in-the-us-china-and-russia/ (accessed August 8, 2013).

[33] Quote from Philip H. Gordon and Sophie Meunier, *The French Challenge: Adapting to Globalization* (Washington, DC: Brookings Institution Press, 2001), 89.

[34] This quote from the UN Charter comes from www.un.org/en/documents/charter/ chapter1.shtml (accessed July 25, 2014).

[35] AP, "Castro Denounces Lenders at Meeting of Poor Nations," *New York Times*, April 13, 2000, A12.

[36] Historical data from the Organisation for Co-operation and Development available at www.compareyourcountry.org/chart?cr=20001&cr1=oecd&lg=en&project=oda&page=1# (accessed June 26, 2013).

[37] Data for 1988 from the Global Policy Forum website at www.globalpolicy.org/images/pdfs/images/pdfs/Size_of_UN_PK_force_by_year_-_2011_.pdf and at www.globalpolicy.org/images/pdfs/Z/pk_tables/expend.pdf (budget) and from UN website at www.un.org/en/peacekeeping/documents/operationslist.pdf (all accessed November 6, 2014). Data for 2014 from the UN website: www.un.org/en/peacekeeping/resources/statistics/factsheet.shtml (accessed October 19, 2014).

[38] NGO data from David Clark MacKenzie, *A World Beyond Borders: An Introduction to the History of International Organizations* (Toronto: University of Toronto Press, 2010), 113, 117, 121, 328.

[39] Data from UN High Commissioner for Refugees for long-term trends at www.unhcr.org/statistics/Ref_1960_2013.zip) and for Syria at data.unhcr.org/syrianrefugees/syria.php (both accessed December 10, 2014). Quote from Julie Mertus et al., eds., *The Suitcase: Refugee Voices from Bosnia and Croatia*, trans. Jelica Todosijevic et al. (Berkeley: University of California Press, 1997), 153.

[40] Data on percentage infected from the WHO HIV/AIDS data and statistics page, annex 8, at www.who.int/hiv/data/en/ (accessed June 1, 2014). For total deaths reported by WHO in 2014: www.who.int/gho/hiv/en/ (accessed October 12, 2014).

[41] George Soros interview from 1997 reproduced in Anthony Giddens and Christopher Pierson, *Conversations with Anthony Giddens: Making Sense of Modernity* (Stanford, CA: Stanford University Press, 1998), 225–226; Joseph Stiglitz, "What I Learned at the World Economic Crisis," *The New Republic*, April 17, 2000, available at www.globalpolicy.org/component/content/article/209-bwi-wto/42760-what-i-learned-at-the-world-economic-crisis.html (accessed September 24, 2014); Amartya Sen, "How to Judge Globalism," *The American Prospect* (Winter 2002) at prospect.org/article/how-judge-globalism (accessed November 2, 2013).

[42] "The Siena Declaration," September 1998, printed as an advertisement in the *New York Times*, November 24, 1998, A7, and also available at www.twnside.org.sg/title/siena-cn.htm (accessed July 25, 2014).

[43] Interview by Miguel Bocangera for the University of Washington's WTO History Project (apparently done shortly after the 1999 Seattle WTO meeting), available at depts.washington.edu/wtohist/Interviews/Krill.htm (accessed March 30, 2003).

[44] Quotes from the Universal Declaration of Human Rights ("barbarous acts"), adopted by the UN General Assembly in December 1948, available at www.un.org/rights/50/decla.htm (accessed October 6, 2014); and from a preparatory memo, March 27, 1947, in Paul Gordon Lauren, *The Evolution of International Human Rights: Visions Seen*, 3rd ed. (Philadelphia: University of Pennsylvania Press, 2011), 210 ("ideas and principles").

[45] Quote from Kirkpatrick Sale, *The Green Revolution: The American Environmental Movement, 1962–1992* (New York: Hill and Wang, 1993), 83.

[46] Quote from Norman Myers, *Ultimate Security: The Environmental Basis of Political Stability* (New York: Norton, 1993), 25.

[47] *Selected Speeches of Indira Gandhi*, vol. 2 (New Delhi: Ministry of Information and Broadcasting, 1975), 448; and data on CO_2 production in early 1990s from William K. Stevens, "Climate Talks Enter Harder Phase of Cutting Back Emissions," *New York Times*, April 11, 1995, B7.

[48] Quotes from Sale, *The Green Revolution*, 77 (green vegetables); and from *Public Papers of the Presidents of the United States: William J. Clinton, 1997* (Washington, DC: U.S. Government Printing Office, 1998), 2: 994 (whistle blowing).

[49] Data from Population Reference Bureau and the World Bank.

CHAPTER 11   A REGIONALLY CONFIGURED WORLD

[1] David S. Mason, *The End of the American Century* (Lanham, MD: Rowman and Little-field, 2009), 215.

[2] Henry R. Luce, "The American Century," *Life* 10 (February 17, 1941): 61–65.

[3] These findings come from Gallup surveys available at www.gallup.com/poll/149399/ Congressional-Job-Approval.aspx and at www.gallup.com/poll/149543/Americans-Say-Federal-Gov-Wastes-Half-Every-Dollar.aspx (both accessed August 4, 2014).

[4] Quoted in Susan A. Aaronson, *Trade and the American Dream: A Social History of Postwar Trade Policy* (Lexington: University Press of Kentucky, 1996), 147.

[5] Organisation for Economic Co-operation and Development surveys on comparative education levels reported in Kevin Carey, "Americans Think We Have the World's Best Colleges. We Don't." *New York Times* (online edition), June 28, 2014; and Vaclav Smil, *Made in the USA: The Rise and Retreat of American Manufacturing* (Cambridge, MA: MIT Press, 2013), 112.

[6] Inequality data from Population Reference Bureau, "2013 World Population Data Sheet," which is available at www.prb.org and which like other inequality reports builds on the research of Emmanuel Saez and Thomas Piketty.

[7] Luce, "The American Century,", 65; and Russell Sage findings on family net worth reported in Anna Bernasek, "The Typical Household, Now Worth a Third Less," *New York Times* (online ed.), July 26, 2014.

[8] Data on social spending from OECD and International Monetary Fund (the latter summarized at graphics8.nytimes.com/images/2011/02/19/opinion/19blowcht/19blowcht-popup-v5.gif).

[9] The most noticed of these claims came from Samuel Huntington, "The Clash of Civilizations?" *Foreign Affairs* (1993); Thomas Friedman, *The Lexus and the Olive Tree* (1999); and Francis Fukuyama, "The End of History," *National Interest* (1989).

[10] Dick Cheney, *Defense Strategy for the 1990s: The Regional Defense Strategy* ([Washington, DC: U.S. Department of Defense,] January 1993), 27.

[11] Data on military spending and nuclear inventory from Stockholm International Peace Research Institute website at www.sipri.org/research/armaments/milex/recent-trends and www.sipri.org/media/pressreleases/2014/nuclear_May_2014 (accessed August 11, 2014).

[12] *Public Papers of the Presidents of the United States* [hereafter PPP]: *George Bush, 1991* (Washington, DC: U.S. Government Printing Office, 1992), 1: 197.

[13] William Kristol and Robert Kagan, "Toward a Neo-Reaganite Foreign Policy," *Foreign Affairs* 75 (July-August 1996): 20, 23.

[14] George W. Bush, address at the U.S. Military Academy, June 1, 2002, in *PPP: George W. Bush* (Washington, DC: U.S. Government Printing Office, 2004), 1: 919.

[15] Quoted in Peter Baker, *Days of Fire: Bush and Cheney in the White House* (New York: Doubleday, 2013), 247.

[16] UN findings on dire situation in Iraq reported in Somini Sengupta, "800 Million People Still Malnourished, U.N. Says," *New York Times* (online ed.), September 16, 2014; Bush aide in summer 2002 on creating own reality, quoted in Lloyd Gardner, *The Long Road to Baghdad: A History of U.S. Foreign Policy from the 1970s to the Present* (New York: New Press, 2008), 105; and polling data from Andrew Kohut, "What Foreign Policy Agenda?" *New York Times* (online ed.), March 13, 2008.

[17] These findings from surveys in 2008 conducted by the Pew Research Center, available at www.pewglobal.org/category/publications/2008/ (accessed July 28, 2014); and from Pew Reseach Center survey, released June 23, 2005, in particular pp. 19–21, 23, 30, and available at www.pewglobal.org/files/pdf/247.pdf (accessed July 13, 2014).

[18] Obama, address at the U.S. Military Academy, December 1, 2009, in *PPP: Barack Obama, 2009* (Washington, DC: U.S. Government Printing Office, 2010), 2: 1749.

[19] Quoted in Greg Grandin, "The Instruction of Great Catastrophe: Truth Commission, National History, and State Formation in Argentina, Chile, and Guatemala," *American Historical Review* 110 (February 2005): 60.

[20] Immigration data from Jeffrey S. Passel, D'Vera Cohn, and Ana Gonzalez-Barrera, "Net Migration from Mexico Falls to Zero—and Perhaps Less," Pew Research Center, April 23, 2012, at www.pewhispanic.org/2012/04/23/net-migration-from-mexico-falls-to-zero-and-perhaps-less/ (accessed January 28, 2015).

[21] Statement at the UN General Assembly, September 23, 2009, available at www.un.org/ga/64/generaldebate/pdf/BR_en.pdf (accessed October 11, 2013).

[22] Trade data for 2012 from World Trade Organization. Public sector employment for Egypt for 2008 from International Labour Organization.

[23] Pew Research Center database, available at www.pewglobal.org/database/indicator/1/group/6/response/Unfavorable/ (accessed July 17, 2014); Pew Research Center survey, released July 14, 2014, and available at http://www.pewglobal.org/2014/07/14/chapter-1-the-american-brand/ (accessed March 1, 2015); and Beverley Milton-Edwards, *Islamic Fundamentalism Since 1945*, 2nd ed. (London: Routledge, 2014), 158.

[24] Pew Research Center survey, released January 21, 2011, and available at www.pewresearch.org/?p=1874/egypt-protests-democracy-islam-influence-politics-islamic-extremism?src=prc-latest&proj=peoplepress (accessed March 1, 2015) .

[25] Bin Laden, declaration of February 23, 1998, in *Messages to the World: The Statements of Osama bin Laden*, ed. Bruce Lawrence and trans. James Howarth (London: Verso, 2005), 61; and his post-9-11 comment in Gilles Kepel, *The War for Muslim Minds: Islam and the West*, trans. Pacale Ghazaleh (Cambridge, MA: Harvard University Press, 2004), 125–126.

[26] Gilles Kepel, "Islamists versus the State in Egypt and Algeria," *Daedalus* 124 (Summer 1995): 121.

[27] Quote from Ray Takeyh, "Iran's Emerging National Compact," *World Policy Journal* 19 (Fall 2002): 45–46.

[28] Two reports from March and July 2010 by the London-based International Council on Security and Development available at www.icosgroup.net/2010/conflict/afghans-interviewed/ and www.icosgroup.net/2010/report/afghanistan-relationship-gap/ (both accessed July 17, 2014).

[29] Anthony Shadid, "Waiting to Fight Another Day," *Washington Post National Weekly Edition*, December 6–12, 2004, p. 16.

[30] The data here come from the master of national accounting, Angus Maddison: "Shares of the Rich and the Rest in the World Economy: Income Divergence between Nations, 1820–2030," *Asian Economic Policy Review* 3 (June 2008): 8–9.

[31] Data from Maddison, "Shares of the Rich and the Rest in the World Economy," 8–9.

[32] Quoted in Edward Wong, "China Turns Up the Rhetoric Against the West," *New York Times* (online ed.), November 11, 2014.

[33] Poem from Peter H. Gries, *China's New Nationalism: Pride, Politics, and Diplomacy* (Berkeley: University of California Press, 2004), 106.

[34] World Bank comparative data on povery cited in *The Economist* 319 (May 4, 1991), p. 8 of "Survey of India"; population and per capita GDP data from Angus Maddison, *Contours of the World Economy, 1–2030 AD* (Oxford, UK: Oxford University Press, 2007), 176, 336; and population projections from Population Reference Bureau, "2014 World Population Data Sheet" (available at www.prb.org), p. 2.

[35] Quoted phrase from James Mann, *About Face: A History of America's Curious Relationship with China, from Nixon to Clinton* (New York: Alfred A. Knopf, 1999), 223.

[36] Clinton remarks at the Nitze School of Advanced International Studies, Washington, DC, March 8, 2000, in *PPP: William J. Clinton, 2000–2001* (Washington, DC: U.S. Government Printing Office, 2001), 1: 407.

[37] David W. Ellwood, *The Shock of America: Europe and the Challenge of the Century* (Oxford, UK: Oxford University Press, 2012), 513.

[38] European Commission, *How Europeans See Themselves: Looking through the Mirror with Public Opinion Surveys* (Luxembourg: Office for Official Publications of the European Communities, 2001), 13, 50–51.

[39] Pew Research Center, survey results released May 13, 2013 (on economy), available at www.pewglobal.org/2013/05/13/the-new-sick-man-of-europe-the-european-union/ (accessed September 21, 2014); and Eurobarometer report on "Public Opinion in the European Union," released July 2013 based on spring surveys, data from pp. 9–10 (on trust and view of EU), available at ec.europa.eu/public_opinion/archives/eb/eb79/eb79_first_en.pdf (accessed September 21, 2014).

[40] Benard Stasi, report to the French president, December 11, 2003, in Robert O'Brien, *The Stasi Report: The Report of the Committee of Reflection on the Application of the Principle of Secularity in the Republic* (Buffalo, NY: Hein & Co., 2005), 21.

[41] Gale Stokes, *The Walls Came Tumbling Down: The Collapse of Communism in Eastern Europe* (New York: Oxford University Press, 1993), 233.

[42] Maddison, *Contours of the World Economy*, 342.

[43] Quote from Fiona Hill and Clifford G. Gaddy, *Mr. Putin: Operative in the Kremlin* (Washington, DC: Brookings Institution Press, 2013), 36.

[44] Pew Research Center, "A Year After Iraq War Mistrust of America in Europe Ever Higher, Muslim Anger Persists" (released March 16, 2004), pp. 8–9, available at www.people-press.org/2004/03/16/a-year-after-iraq-war/ (accessed October 24, 2014).

[45] Ulrich Beck and Anthony Giddens, "Open Letter on the Future of Europe," June 2005, reproduced in Giddens, *Europe in the Global Age* (Cambridge, UK: Polity Press, 2007), 233.

[46] Data from Organisation for Economic Co-operation and Development: www.oecd.org/els/soc/OECD2014-Social-Expenditure-Update-Nov2014-Figures-Data.xlsx (accessed December 6, 2014). The EU core refers to what the OECD designates as the EU 21: the pre-2004 members together with the Czech Republic, the Slovak Republic, Poland, and Hungary.

[47] Edward W. Said, "The Clash of Ignorance," *The Nation* 273 (October 22, 2001): 12.

FINAL REFLECTIONS ON THE POST-1945 WORLD

[1] Litany from the 1886 edition of *The Book of Common Prayer*.

CREDITS

Hanan Ashrawi. Poem from Hanan Ashrawi, *This Side of Peace*, p. 89. Copyright © 1995 by Hanan Mikhail-Ashrawi. Reprinted with the permission of Simon & Schuster.

"En Guatemala", CANCIÓN DE GESTA, Fundacion Pablo Neruda, 2015. English translation copyright © 1976 by Miguel Algarín. Reprinted by permission of HarperCollins Publishers, Inc.

Lyrics to "Born in the U.S.A" (4 lines) by Bruce Springsteen. Copyright © 1984 Bruce Springsteen. All rights reserved. Reprinted by permission.

INDEX

Pages in italics followed by a letter refer to: *f* figures, including charts and graphs; *i* illustrations, including photographs; *m* maps; and *t* tables.

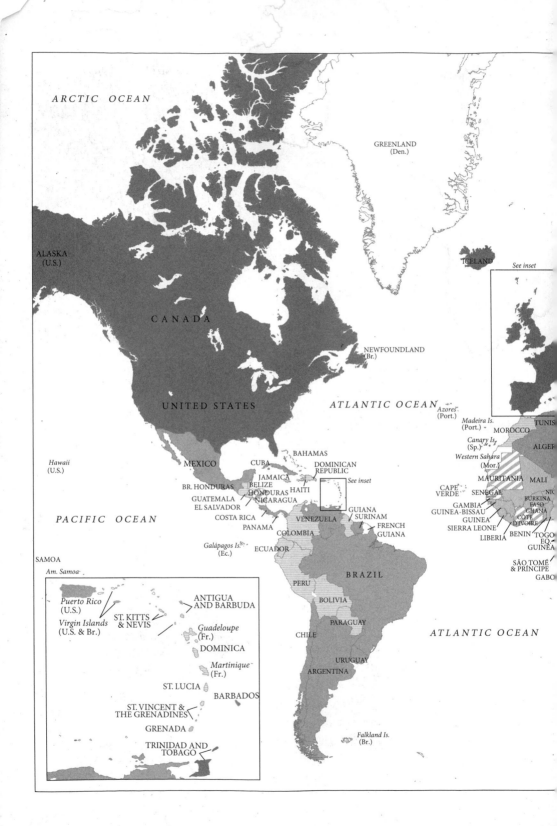

ARCTIC OCEAN

GREENLAND
(Den.)

ALASKA
(U.S.)

CANADA

ICELAND

See inset

NEWFOUNDLAND
(Br.)

ATLANTIC OCEAN

UNITED STATES

Azores
(Port.)

Madeira Is.
(Port.)

TUNIS

MOROCCO

Hawaii
(U.S.)

MEXICO

CUBA

BAHAMAS

DOMINICAN
REPUBLIC

See inset

Canary Is.
(Sp.)

Western Sahara
(Mor.)

ALGER

JAMAICA

BR. HONDURAS
BELIZE
GUATEMALA
EL SALVADOR
HONDURAS
NICARAGUA

HAITI

CAPE
VERDE

MAURITANIA

MALI

NIC

SENEGAL

PACIFIC OCEAN

COSTA RICA
PANAMA

VENEZUELA

GUIANA
SURINAM

FRENCH
GUIANA

GAMBIA
GUINEA-BISSAU
GUINEA

BURKINA
FASO
GHANA
CÔTE
D'IVOIRE

SAMOA

Am. Samoa

Puerto Rico
(U.S.)

Virgin Islands
(U.S. & Br.)

ST. KITTS
& NEVIS

Galápagos Is.
(Ec.)

COLOMBIA

ECUADOR

PERU

ANTIGUA
AND BARBUDA

Guadeloupe
(Fr.)

DOMINICA

Martinique
(Fr.)

BRAZIL

SIERRA LEONE

LIBERIA

BENIN

TOGO
EQ.
GUINEA

SÃO TOMÉ
& PRÍNCIPE

GABO

BOLIVIA

PARAGUAY

CHILE

ATLANTIC OCEAN

ST. LUCIA

BARBADOS

ST. VINCENT &
THE GRENADINES

GRENADA

URUGUAY

ARGENTINA

TRINIDAD AND
TOBAGO

Falkland Is.
(Br.)